I'VE JUST POSTED ABOUT IT! CONSIDER THE SOURCE, ASK QUESTIONS – SPEAK UP!

ARTHUR TARIAN IV
@ARTHURTARIAN

My critics R lackeys of status quo. They'll live under my boot heel soon. Nothing stops my rise 2 power!
#ArthurTarian4world domination #losetherepublic

85   1

CRAP, NOT AGAIN!

FEWER PEOPLE ARE CONVINCED BY ARTHUR'S HYPE. OUR VOICES MAKE A DIFFERENCE.

EVALUATION!

...IS THE FINAL KEY TO KEEPING THE REPUBLIC!

WE'VE GOT THIS, ROX. WE'VE JUST GOT TO KEEP OUR SKILLS UP.

DESCRIPTION! ANALYSIS! EVALUATION!

BUMP!

THE POWER IS YOURS!

YAY!!!

KEEP THE REPUBLIC

DESCRIPTION

ANALYSIS

POWER!

EVALUATION

GET A CLUE

SAGE
Premium
Video

BOOST COMPREHENSION. BOLSTER ANALYSIS.

- SAGE Premium Video **EXCLUSIVELY CURATED FOR THIS TEXT**
- **BRIDGES BOOK CONTENT** with application and critical thinking
- Includes short, auto-graded quizzes that **DIRECTLY FEED TO YOUR LMS GRADEBOOK**
- Premium content is **ADA COMPLIANT WITH TRANSCRIPTS**
- Comprehensive media guide to help you **QUICKLY SELECT MEANINGFUL VIDEO** tied to your course objectives

SAGE Outcomes:
MEASURE RESULTS, TRACK SUCCESS

FOR STUDENTS, understanding the objectives for each chapter and the goals for the course is essential for getting the grade you deserve!

FOR INSTRUCTORS, being able to track your students' progress allows you to more easily pinpoint areas of improvement and report on success.

This title was crafted around specific chapter objectives and course outcomes, vetted by experts, and adapted from renowned syllabi. Tracking student progress can be challenging. Promoting and achieving success should never be. We are here for you.

COURSE **OUTCOMES** FOR AMERICAN GOVERNMENT:

ARTICULATE the foundations of American government, including its history, critical concepts, and important documents and achievements.

EXAMINE the main institutions of American government, including their roles and interrelationships.

DESCRIBE the roles and relative importance of major entities and influences in American political life.

ANALYZE the development and impact of important governmental policies.

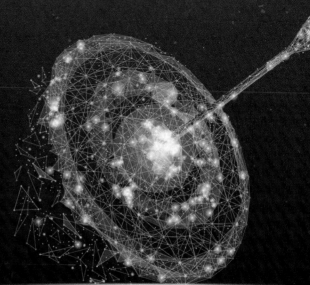

Want to see how these outcomes tie in with this book's chapter-level objectives?
Visit us at edge.sagepub.com/harbourbrief8e for complete outcome-to-objective mapping

We dedicate this book with love to our parents,
Patti Barbour and John Barbour and
Doris and Gerry Wright,
To our kids, Andrea and Monica,
To our grandkids, Liam, Elena, Paloma, and Asher,
And to each other.

Keeping the
REPUBLIC

8th BRIEF Edition

Sara Miller McCune founded SAGE Publishing in 1965 to support the dissemination of usable knowledge and educate a global community. SAGE publishes more than 1000 journals and over 800 new books each year, spanning a wide range of subject areas. Our growing selection of library products includes archives, data, case studies and video. SAGE remains majority owned by our founder and after her lifetime will become owned by a charitable trust that secures the company's continued independence.

Los Angeles | London | New Delhi | Singapore | Washington DC | Melbourne

Keeping the
REPUBLIC

Power and Citizenship in
AMERICAN POLITICS

8th BRIEF Edition

Christine Barbour

Indiana University

Gerald C. Wright

Indiana University

FOR INFORMATION:

CQ Press

An Imprint of SAGE Publications, Inc.

2455 Teller Road

Thousand Oaks, California 91320

E-mail: order@sagepub.com

SAGE Publications Ltd.

1 Oliver's Yard

55 City Road

London, EC1Y 1SP

United Kingdom

SAGE Publications India Pvt. Ltd.

B 1/I 1 Mohan Cooperative Industrial Area

Mathura Road, New Delhi 110 044

India

SAGE Publications Asia-Pacific Pte Ltd

18 Cross Street #10-10/11/12

China Square Central

Singapore 048423

Printed in Canada

ISBN 978-1-5443-1621-5

Executive Publisher: Monica Eckman

Content Development Editors: Anna Villarruel, Sarah Calabi

Editorial Assistant: Sam Rosenberg

Production Editors: Kelly DeRosa, Tori Mirsadjadi

Copy Editor: Amy Marks

Typesetter: C&M Digitals (P) Ltd.

Proofreader: Liann Lech

Indexer: Joan Shapiro

Cover Designer: Gail Buschman

Marketing Manager: Erica DeLuca

This book is printed on acid-free paper.

19 20 21 22 23 10 9 8 7 6 5 4 3 2 1

ABOUT THE AUTHORS

CHRISTINE BARBOUR

Christine Barbour teaches in the Political Science Department and the Hutton Honors College at Indiana University, where she has become increasingly interested in how teachers of large classes can maximize what their students learn. She is working with online course designers to create an online version of her Intro to American Politics class. At Indiana, Professor Barbour has been a Lilly Fellow, working on a project to increase student retention in large introductory courses, and a member of the Freshman Learning Project, a university-wide effort to improve the first-year undergraduate experience. She has served on the *New York Times* College Advisory Board, working with other educators to develop ways to integrate newspaper reading into the undergraduate curriculum. She has won several teaching honors, but the two awarded by her students mean the most to her: the Indiana University Student Alumni Association Award for Outstanding Faculty and the Indiana University Chapter of the Society of Professional Journalists Brown Derby Award. When not teaching or writing textbooks, Professor Barbour enjoys playing with her dogs, traveling with her coauthor, and writing about food. She is the food editor for *Bloom Magazine* of Bloomington and is a coauthor of *Indiana Cooks!* (2005) and *Home Grown Indiana* (2008). She also makes jewelry from precious metals and rough gemstones. If she ever retires, she will open a jewelry shop in a renovated Airstream on the beach in Apalachicola, Florida, where she plans to write a book about the local politics, development, and the fishing industry.

GERALD C. WRIGHT

Gerald C. Wright has taught political science at Indiana University since 1981, and he is currently the chair of the Political Science Department. An accomplished scholar of American politics, and the 2010 winner of the State Politics and Policy Association's Career Achievement Award, his books include *Statehouse Democracy: Public Opinion and Policy in the American States* (1993), coauthored with Robert S. Erikson and John P. McIver. He has published more than fifty articles on elections, public opinion, and state politics. Professor Wright has long studied the relationship among citizens, their preferences, and public policy.

He is currently conducting research funded by grants from the National Science Foundation and the Russell Sage Foundation on the factors that influence the equality of policy representation in the states and in Congress. He is also writing a book about representation in U.S. legislatures. He has been a consultant for Project Vote Smart in the past several elections. Professor Wright is a member of Indiana University's Freshman Learning Project, a university-wide effort to improve the first-year undergraduate experience by focusing on how today's college students learn and how teachers can adapt their pedagogical methods to best teach them. In his nonworking hours, Professor Wright also likes to spend time with his dogs, travel, eat good food, fish, and play golf.

BRIEF CONTENTS

CONTENTS

PREFACE

THIS eighth brief edition of *Keeping the Republic* is designed for those who want a concise, streamlined, inexpensive, and engaging version of its longer, more comprehensive parent. Brief books do not have to be dull! While we have condensed the longer text's account of the American political system, we have taken great pains to preserve the accessibility and enthusiasm of that book. Our goal was to meet the needs of those looking for a shorter text to use with various supplemental readings, as well as those who want broad coverage in a price-sensitive package.

We have also stayed true to our original goal in writing the text: to share the excitement of discovering humankind's capacity to find innovative solutions to those problems that arise from our efforts to live together on a planet too small, with resources too scarce, and with saintliness in too short a supply. In this book we honor the human capacity to manage our collective lives with peace and even, at times, dignity. And, in particular, we celebrate the American political system and the founders' extraordinary contribution to the possibilities of human governance.

This book covers essential topics with clear explanations, but it is also a thematic book, intended to guide students through a wealth of material and to help them make sense of the content both academically and personally. To that end we develop two themes that run throughout every chapter: an analytic theme to assist students in organizing the details and connecting them to the larger ideas and concepts of American politics, and an evaluative theme to help them find personal meaning in the American political system and develop standards for making judgments about how well the system works. Taken together, these themes provide students a framework on which to hang the myriad complexities of American politics.

The analytic theme we chose is a classic in political science: politics is a struggle over limited power and resources, as gripping as a sporting event in its final minutes, but much more vital. The rules guiding that struggle influence who will win and who will lose, so that often the struggles with the most at stake are over the rule making itself. In short, and in the words of a famous political scientist, *politics is about who gets what, and how they get it*. To illustrate this theme, we begin and end every chapter with a feature called **What's at Stake . . . ?** that poses a question about what people want from politics—what they are struggling to get and how the rules affect who gets it.

Our citizenship theme has three dimensions. First, in our **Profiles in Citizenship** feature, present in every chapter, we introduce students to important figures in American politics and ask the subjects why they are involved in public service or some aspect of political life. Based on personal interviews with these people, the profiles model republic-keeping behavior for students, helping them to see what is expected of them as members of a democratic polity. We feel unabashedly that a primary goal of teaching introductory politics is not only to create good scholars but also to create good citizens. Second, at the end of nearly every chapter, the feature **The Citizens and . . .** provides a critical view of what citizens can or cannot do in American politics, evaluating how democratic various aspects of the American system actually are and what possibilities exist for change. Third, the **Don't Be Fooled by . . .** feature assists students to critically examine the various kinds of political information they are bombarded with—from information in textbooks like this one, to information from social networks, to information from their congressional representative or political party.

The book's themes are further illustrated through two unique features that will enhance students' visual literacy and critical thinking skills. Each chapter includes a rich, poster-worthy display called **The Big Picture** that focuses on a key element in the book, complementing the text with a rich visual that grabs students' attention and engages them in understanding *big processes* like how cases get to the Supreme Court, *big concepts* such as when the law can treat people differently, and *big data*, including who has immigrated to the United States and how they have assimilated. In addition, an innovative feature called **Snapshot of America**, reimagined from the Who Are We feature of past editions, describes through graphs, charts, and maps just who we Americans are and where we come from, what we believe, how educated we are, and how much money we make. This recurring feature aims at exploding stereotypes, and **Behind the Numbers** questions lead students to think critically about the political consequences of America's demographic profile. These visual features are the result of a partnership with award-winning designer, educator, and artist Mike Wirth, who has lent his expert hand in information design and data visualization to craft these unique, informative, and memorable graphics.

We have long believed that teaching is a two-way street, and we welcome comments, criticisms, or just a pleasant chat about politics or pedagogy. You can email us directly at barbour@indiana.edu and wright1@indiana.edu.

WHAT'S NEW IN THE EIGHTH BRIEF EDITION

These are strange days in American politics. We have tried to deal with that strangeness bluntly, objectively and clearly. We are in a "moment." Whether that moment becomes the "new normal" or remains a historical blip, we have no way of knowing. Writing about it in real time, we take it as it comes. We are political scientists, not magicians, and thus have a hard bias toward the scientific, the empirical, the observable. Distinguishing between truth and falsity is central to what we do. We can make projections and predictions but our crystal ball has been particularly hazy lately and we make no pretense of knowing the future.

The 2016 election only exacerbated divisions that have been building for decades, the product of economic displacement, demographic change and a widening gap between those with college educations and those without. Some days it really does feel like there are two Americas, and the challenge of writing a textbook for both of them has been heavy at times. We have worked hard to explain the nature of our ideological divisions as objectively as possible, and I suspect we have ruffled a few feathers, including our own. That's as it should be. No one likes to be described as a statistic or a faceless member of a demographic group or have opinions ascribed to them that they may not even knowingly hold, or may actively reject. It's a good thing if this book inspires debate, disagreement, and discovery.

Ideological polarization is not the only characteristic of American politics that has been a challenge to deal with in this edition. We have a president who likes the limelight and, love him or hate him (it's hard to be indifferent), he delights in shattering the norms that underlie the rules of American politics. Indeed, that is his appeal to many Americans who would like to see the system turned upside down. That means we have had to be more careful about focusing on those norms and explaining the roles they play in supporting the Constitution, so that we can fully understand the consequences as we decide whether they matter.

Finally, as we say later in this book, if we have a bias it is unquestionably toward diversity, toward the whole crazy salad of Americans. We can't write effectively for our students unless they can see themselves mirrored in the pages. This book has to belong to them, and so we have deplored the movement to return to an America where women, people of color, immigrants, members of the LGBTQ community, and other minority groups are marginalized. In the last two years some Americans have felt more free to voice disparaging or degrading remarks about members of all those groups. We reject that view.

Writing the eighth brief edition also gave us an opportunity to revitalize the book's theme to reflect the influences of modern technology on power and citizenship, in particular the ways that citizenship is mediated by third parties. To do that, we looked at the ways that controlling the political narrative has translated into political power and how that power has shifted with the advent of new and social media. This coverage is integrated throughout each chapter and is especially notable in the *Citizens and . . .* sections and the *Don't Be Fooled by . . .* boxes' focus on digital media.

Reviews for this edition helped guide some key changes that we hope will make the text even more useful to you and your students. We have sought to streamline both the main narrative and its features to provide a more focused reading experience. New *What's at Stake . . . ?* vignettes examine such topics as the activism of the students of Marjorie Stoneman Douglas High School, the rise of the alt right and the Make America Great Again movement, the appointment of Brett Kavanaugh to the Supreme Court amidst discord in Congress, what happens when outsiders challenge party establishment, the consequences of overturning executive action on climate change, and Donald Trump's presidency. One new *Profiles in Citizenship* interview appears in this edition — we had the opportunity to interview Senator Tammy Duckworth before the 2018 midterms.

DIGITAL RESOURCES

We know how important good resources can be in the teaching of American government. Our goal has been to create resources that not only support but also enhance the text's themes and features. *SAGE edge* offers a robust online environment featuring an impressive array of tools and resources for review, study, and further exploration, keeping both instructors and students on the cutting edge of teaching and learning. SAGE edge content is open access and available on demand. Learning and teaching has never been easier! We gratefully acknowledge Graphic World and Alicia Fisher of California State University, Fullerton for developing the digital resources for this site.

SAGE COURSE OUTCOMES: MEASURE RESULTS, TRACK SUCCESS

The journey to retaining and applying course content differs for every student. To successfully navigate this journey, course goals should remain clear, consistent, and constructive. For instructors, the ability to track and measure individual progress is vital to ensuring student success.

SAGE | CQ Press is invested in mapping measurable course outcomes to chapter-level learning objectives for all introductory textbook offerings through **SAGE course outcomes**. Each title is crafted with specific course outcomes in mind, vetted by leading advisors in the field, and adapted from renowned syllabi from across the country.

Students Benefit

- **A clear path for learners:** Understanding the objectives for each chapter and how those objectives are tied to the goals of the course is essential for getting the grade students want.
- **Meaningful context for skills**: Course outcomes emphasize the skills learned in the course and highlight how they can be applied in the real world after graduation.
- **More targeted instruction:** Students receive better, more targeted feedback when instructors can track and measure individual progress based on course-specific expectations.

Instructors Benefit

- **Effective measuring mechanism:** Being able to track student progress allows you to more easily pinpoint specific areas of improvement, increases course efficacy, allows you to report out on success, and aligns student learning with course and institutional goals.
- **Personalized instruction and feedback:** Promoting student success through targeted and individualized instruction improves retention and increases the likelihood of achieving course mastery.
- **Standardized benchmarking:** Formative and summative assessment is more effective and actionable when assessing student progress against standard course outcome benchmarks.

Course Outcomes for American Government:

- ✓ ARTICULATE the foundations of American government, including its history, critical concepts, and important documents and achievements.
- ✓ EXPLAIN the main institutions of American government, including their roles and interrelationships.
- ✓ DESCRIBE the roles and relative importance of major entities and influences in American political life.
- ✓ ANALYZE the development and impact of important governmental policies.

INSTRUCTOR RESOURCES

⑤SAGE coursepacks

SAGE Coursepacks and SAGE edge online resources are included FREE with this text. For a brief demo, contact your sales representative today.

SAGE COURSEPACKS FOR INSTRUCTORS make it easy to import our quality content into your school's learning management system (LMS)*. Intuitive and simple to use, it allows you to

Say NO to . . .

- required access codes
- learning a new system

Say YES to . . .

- using only the content you want and need
- high-quality assessment and multimedia exercises

For use in: Blackboard, Canvas, Brightspace by Desire2Learn (D2L), and Moodle

Don't use an LMS platform? No problem, you can still access many of the online resources for your text via SAGE edge.

With SAGE coursepacks, you get:

- Quality textbook content delivered **directly into your LMS**;
- An **intuitive, simple format** that makes it easy to integrate the material into your course with minimal effort;
- **Assessment tools** that foster review, practice, and critical thinking, including:

  o Diagnostic chapter **pretests and posttests** that identify opportunities for improvement, track student progress, and ensure mastery of key learning objectives
  o **Test banks** built on Bloom's Taxonomy and SAGE Course Outcomes that provide a diverse range of test items with ExamView test generation
  o **Activity and quiz options** that allow you to choose only the assignments and tests you want
  o **Instructions** on how to use and integrate the comprehensive assessments and resources provided

- **Assignable SAGE Premium video** (available via the interactive eBook version, linked through SAGE Coursepacks) that is tied to learning objectives, created and curated exclusively for this text, featuring:

  o **Corresponding multimedia assessment options** that automatically feed to your gradebook
  o **SAGE original** *Topics in American Government* that recap the fundamentals of American politics
  o *American Government News Clips* that bring current events into the book, connecting brief, 2- to 4-minute news clips with core chapter content
  o A comprehensive, downloadable, easy-to-use *Media Guide in the Coursepack* for **every video resource**, listing the chapter to which the video content is tied, matching learning objective(s), a helpful description of the video content, and assessment questions

- **Assignable data exercises** that build students' data literacy skills with interactive data visualization tools from **SAGE Stats** and **U.S. Political Stats**, offering a dynamic way to analyze real-world data and think critically of the narrative behind the numbers;
- **Chapter-specific discussion questions** that help launch engaging classroom interaction while reinforcing important content;
- Exclusive, influential **SAGE journal and reference content**, built into course materials and assessment tools, that ties influential research and scholarship to chapter concepts;

- Editable, chapter-specific **PowerPoint® slides** that offer flexibility when creating multimedia lectures so you don't have to start from scratch;
- **Integrated links to the interactive eBook** that make it easy for your students to maximize their study time with this "anywhere, anytime" mobile-friendly version of the text. It also offers access to more digital tools and resources, including SAGE Premium Video;
- **All tables and figures** from the textbook.

SAGE EDGE FOR STUDENTS

for CQ Press

http://edge.sagepub.com/barbourbrief8e

SAGE edge for students enhances learning, it's easy for students to use, and offers:

- An open-access site that makes it easy for students to maximize their study time, anytime, anywhere;
- **eFlashcards** that strengthen understanding of key terms and concepts;
- **Practice quizzes** that allow students to practice and assess how much they've learned and where they need to focus their attention;
- **Video resources** that bring concepts to life, are tied to learning objectives, and curated exclusively for this text;
- **Exclusive access to influential SAGE journal and reference content** that ties important research and scholarship to chapter concepts to strengthen learning.

ACKNOWLEDGMENTS

Africans say that it takes a village to raise a child—it is certainly true that it takes one to write a textbook! We could not have done it without a community of family, friends, colleagues, students, reviewers, and editors who supported us, nagged us, maddened us, and kept us on our toes. Not only is this a better book because of their help and support, but it would not have been a book at all without them.

In addition to all the folks we gratefully acknowledge in the full edition of this text, some made a particular contribution to this brief edition. We would like to thank the reviewers who have given us their feedback on the past and current brief editions of our book:

Jean Abshire, Indiana University Southeast

Jordon Barkalow, Bridgewater State University

Vicky Cannon Bollenbacher, Aims Community College

Janet Box-Steffensmeier, Ohio State University

Robert Bradley, Illinois State University

Pam Brunfelt, Vermilion Community College

Betty Chan, American River College

Matthew T. Christensen, Boise State University

David B. Cohen, University of Akron

Victoria Cordova, Sam Houston State University

Timothy Dale, University of Wisconsin–Green Bay

Robert L. Dion, University of Evansville

Heather K. Evans, Sam Houston State University

Richard Flanagan, College of Staten Island, the City University of New York

Nicole R. Foster-Shoaf, Lincoln University

Shane Gleason, Idaho State University–Pocatello

Christi Gramling, Charleston Southern University

Paul Hain, Texas A&M University–Corpus Christi

Charles A. Hantz, Danville Area Community College

Paul L. Hathaway, Jacksonville State University

Cyrus Hayat, IUPU–Indianapolis

Richard Holtzman, Bryant University

Glen D. Hunt, Austin Community College–Northridge

Alana Jeydel, American River College

Joseph Jozwiak, Texas A&M University–Corpus Christi

Ellen Key, Stony Brook University

Robert Klotz, University of Southern Maine

Jamie Lennahan, Germanna Community College–Fredericksburg

Paul Lermack, Bradley University

Allyson M. Lowe, Carlow University

Karen McCurdy, Georgia Southern University

Tom McInnis, University of Central Arkansas

Bryan S. McQuide, University of Idaho

Linda Medcalf, South Puget Sound Community College

Jeff Millstone, Austin Community College–Rio Grande

Cas Mudde, University of Georgia

Gregg Murray, Texas Tech University

Jason C. Myers, California State University Stanislaus

Angela C. Narasimhan, Keuka College

Richard Pacelle, Georgia Southern University

Sarah Poggione, Ohio University

Suzy Prucka, University of Maryland, Baltimore County

Gerald Reed, Middle Tennessee State University

Denise Richardson, Laney College

Thomas A. Schmeling, Rhode Island College

Angela Ugran, Cuyahoga Community College, East Campus

Stacy G. Ulbig, Sam Houston State University

Tim Vercellotti, Western New England College

Ulf Zimmermann, Kennesaw State University

There are several people in particular without whom this edition would never have seen the light of day. Pat Haney, the provider of the nuts and bolts of the foreign policy section, has been a cheerful, tireless collaborator, a good friend and colleague for twenty years now, and we are so grateful to him. Chuck McCutcheon, a huge help and a delight to work with, lent his expertise to the social and economic policy sections.

Finally, it is our great privilege to acknowledge and thank all the people at CQ Press who believed in this book and made this edition possible. In this day and age of huge publishing conglomerates, it has been such a pleasure to work with a small, committed team dedicated to top-quality work.

Christine Barbour
Gerald C. Wright

TO THE STUDENT

SUGGESTIONS ON HOW TO READ THIS TEXTBOOK

1. As they say in Chicago about voting, do it **early and often**. If you open the book for the first time the night before the exam, you will not learn much from it and it won't help your grade. Start reading the chapters in conjunction with the lectures, and you'll get so much more out of class.

2. Pay attention to the **chapter headings** and **In Your Own Words** goals. They tell you what we think is important, what our basic argument is, and how all the material fits together. Often, chapter subheadings list elements of an argument that may show up on a quiz. Be alert to these clues.

3. **Read actively**. Constantly ask yourself: Why is this important? How do these different facts fit together? What are the broad arguments here? How does this material relate to class lectures? How does it relate to the broad themes of the class? When you stop asking these questions, you are merely moving your eyes over the page, and that is a waste of time.

4. **Highlight or take notes**. Some people prefer highlighting because it's quicker than taking notes, but others think that writing down the most important points helps in recalling them later. Whichever method you choose (and you can do both), be sure you're doing it properly.

   - **Highlighting**. An entirely highlighted page will not give you any clues about what is important. Read each paragraph and ask yourself: What is the basic idea of this paragraph? Highlight that. Avoid highlighting all the examples and illustrations. You should be able to recall them on your own when you see the main idea. Beware of highlighting too little. If whole pages go by with no marking, you are probably not highlighting enough.
   - **Outlining**. Again, the key is to write down enough, but not too much. Go for key ideas, terms, and arguments.

5. **Note all key terms**, and be sure you understand the definition and significance.

6. Do not skip **tables and figures**. These things are there for a purpose, because they convey crucial information or illustrate a point in the text. After you read a chart or graph or *Big Picture* infographic, make a note in the margin about what it means.

7. **Do not skip the boxes**. They are not filler! The *Don't Be Fooled by . . .* boxes provide advice on becoming a critical consumer of the many varieties of political information that come your way. Each *Profile in Citizenship* box highlights the achievements of a political actor pertinent to that chapter's focus. They model citizen participation and can serve as a beacon for your own political power long after you've completed your American government course. And the *Snapshot of America* boxes help you understand who Americans are and how they line up on all sorts of dimensions.

8. Make use of the book's web site at **http://edge.sage pub.com/barbourbrief8e**. There you will find chapter summaries, flashcards, and practice quizzes that will help you prepare for exams.

1

Power and Citizenship in American Politics

In Your Own Words

After you've read this chapter, you will be able to

1.1 Describe the role that politics plays in determining how power and resources, including control of information, are distributed in a society.

1.2 Compare how power is distributed between citizens and government in different economic and political systems.

1.3 Describe the enduring tension in the United States between self-interested human nature and public-spirited government and the way that has been shaped in a mediated world.

1.4 Analyze the role of immigration and citizenship in American politics.

1.5 Describe values that most Americans share, and the political debates that drive partisan divisions in American politics.

1.6 Understand the essential reasons for approaching politics from a perspective of critical thinking, analysis, and evaluation.

1.7 Describe the role and responsibilities of citizens in American politics.

What's at Stake . . . in Hashtag Activism?

The last thing they wanted to do was become famous. Not this way, not now. But when seventeen of their classmates and teachers were murdered on February 14, 2018, by a disturbed former student, the students of Marjory Stoneman Douglas High School in Parkland, Florida, decided to make some noise.

They had seen this movie before. There had been mass shootings. Ever since they were little they had practiced what to do if someone showed up with a gun in their classrooms. There was even an armed guard on their campus. And still, it happened again. So they knew the ritual that would follow.

Every time this nation experiences a mass shooting, a grimly familiar routine follows. First there is unrelenting press coverage—of the dead, of the bereaved, of the shooter. Then those who lost loved ones make impassioned calls for more gun control and those who oppose gun control make equally impassioned declarations that we should not politicize tragedy, that it is too soon to talk about it. There are funerals. The president (usually) makes a speech. Then the press moves on to the next big news and only the grieving are left to testify before Congress, create foundations in the names of their loved ones, and implore people not to forget. Lather, rinse, repeat.

But the MSD students knew the drill and were media savvy enough to figure out how to hack it. They were ready. Some, in the drama club, comfortable on stage; some, school journalists, eloquent and at ease with words; others, bright, articulate, privileged to attend a school with an embarrassment of extracurricular activities that had prepared them for their futures. Smart enough to know that their moment in the spotlight would be brief, they were determined to make it count.

The shooting was on a Wednesday. Cameron Kasky was so angry he took to Facebook, first to announce that he and his brother were safe and then to vent. "I just want people to understand what happened and understand that doing nothing will lead to nothing. Why is that so hard to grasp?" His social media posts caught the eye of CNN, which asked him to write an op-ed piece on Thursday, which led to television appearances. It became apparent to Kasky that his words were helping to shape the story of what had happened and what it meant. "People are listening and people care," Kasky wrote. "They're reporting the right things."[1]

To capitalize on that fickle national attention before it turned away, Kasky and several of his friends met that night to plan a social media campaign. By midnight they had a hashtag, #NeverAgain, social media accounts, and a message for politicians: legislate better background checks on gun buyers, or we will vote you out.

MSD student Jaclyn Corin took to her own social media accounts to express her grief and anger at the loss of her friends. She, a girl who had never been political, also began to strategize. With the help of Florida Democratic congresswoman Debbie Wasserman Schultz, she planned a bus trip for one hundred students to Tallahassee to lobby state lawmakers.

By Friday, Corin and Kasky had joined forces, and on Saturday they added David Hogg, a student journalist who had conducted interviews while they were under fire; Sarah Chadwick, already famous for her angry, grief-filled tweets; and Emma González, whose speech at a local rally went viral. On Sunday they hit the morning talk shows to proclaim that the Never Again movement was planning the first March for Our Lives in Washington, D.C., on March 24.

Two weeks later (forever in the typical media cycle), the kids were still making news. Boycotts were organized to put pressure on companies doing business with the National Rifle Association (NRA), which blocked background checks. A National School Walkout was planned for the one-month anniversary of the shooting. Thousands of students across the nation participated. Famous people donated large sums to help fund the March 24 March for Our Lives. As Dahlia Lithwick wrote in *Slate*, "These teens have—by most objective measures—used social media to change the conversation around guns and gun control in America."[2]

The March for Our Lives, when it happened, defied expectations. Huge crowds assembled not just in Washington but in eight hundred places around the world. The only adults who appeared on the D.C. stage were entertainers. The Parkland kids, knowing they had created a unique platform, had invited other kids whose lives had been touched by gun violence. Yolanda King, the nine-year-old granddaughter of Martin Luther King, confidently stood before tens of thousands to lead the crowd in a call and response:

> Spread the word.
>
> Have you heard?
>
> All across the nation.
>
> We
>
> Are going to be
>
> A great generation.

The event highlight was not words, eloquent as many of them were, but silence—four minutes and twenty-six seconds of uneasy, suspenseful silence as Emma González stood like a sculpture, tears tracking down her face, so that the crowd would experience the duration of the shooting that ended seventeen of her friends' and teachers' lives.

Just like the 2017 and 2018 Women's Marches, which brought out millions of pink-hatted women marching for human rights around the world; like Black Lives Matter, founded in 2013 to protest the unwarranted deaths of black men at the hands of police; like Occupy Wall Street, a 2011 movement to protest the unequal distribution of wealth in the United States; and like the It Gets Better Project, which works to convince LGBTQ youths that life does get better after the high school years, #NeverAgain was fueled and spread by social media.

Of course some older people know their way around the Internet, but #NeverAgain was the first mass movement planned and executed by digital natives, people who have never *not* known the world of digital media, for whom navigating digital terrain is second nature. It's not clear what the generation—what Yolanda King called "a great generation"—will be called by history. Gen Z, maybe? iGen? Generational divides are blurry, and few social scientists agree where the dividing lines fall. But the post-millennial generation—those born since the mid-1990s or thereabouts—has an amazing political skill set to use if, like the Parkland students, they choose to do so. They have the ability, as Lithwick said, to "change the conversation," or create a powerful political narrative that they can disseminate and that helps level the playing field with powerful opponents like the NRA.

No movement can create change or defeat an opponent if it is only hashtag activism. Eventually, you have to put your vote where your # is. What is especially remarkable about the Never Again movement is that it emphasizes not just marching but voting. March for Our Life rallies throughout the summer gave them the chance to hone the narrative, register people to vote and activate other students. Youth participation in the 2018 midterms soared.[3] Some writers are calling for the vote to be extended to those who are sixteen years old. Political scientist Jonathan Bernstein says that is a good idea because voting is "the training wheels of political participation."[4] By the time they are eighteen, kids are distracted by the drama of their lives and they tend not to want to be bothered.

In fact, since the military draft ended in 1973, young people have been notoriously uninvolved in politics, often seeing it as irrelevant to their lives and the things they really care about. Knowing that they pay little attention and tend not to vote in large numbers, politicians feel free to ignore their concerns, reinforcing their cynicism and apathy. Young people have turned out in larger numbers since the 2008 election of Barack Obama, however, and the Never Again movement promises to energize even more.

The American founders weren't crazy about the idea of mass movements, political demonstrations, or even political parties, but they did value political engagement, and they knew that democracies needed care and attention in order to survive. In 1787, when Benjamin Franklin was asked by a woman what he and other founders of the Constitution had created, he replied, "A republic, madam, if you can keep it." Today, many commentators worry that we are not "keeping the republic" and that, as new generations who find politics a turn-off become disaffected adults, the system will start to unravel. As one writer says, "a nation that hates politics will not long thrive as a democracy."[5]

Yet protesters like Cameron Kasky, Emma González, David Hogg, and Yolanda King sound as committed to democracy as Benjamin Franklin could have wished, even though their efforts are not focused solely on voting or traditional methods of political engagement. Is a nation of these young activists a nation in trouble, or can movements begun via technology Franklin could not have imagined help to keep the republic? What, exactly, is at stake in *hashtag activism*—what one writer called a "netroots outcry" to follow an online call to political action? We return to this question after we learn more about the meaning of politics and the difference it makes in our lives.

HAVE you got grand ambitions for your life? Do you want to found an Internet start-up and sell it for millions, be the investment banker that funds the project, achieve a powerful position in business, gain influence in high places, and spend money to make things happen? Perhaps you'd like to make a difference in the world, heal the sick, fight for peace, feed the poor. Maybe you want to travel the world, learning languages and immersing yourself in new cultures and working abroad. Or maybe all you want from life is a good education; a well-paying job; a healthy family; a comfortable home; and a safe, prosperous, contented existence. Think politics has nothing to do with any of those things? Think again.

The things that make those goals attainable—a strong national defense, good relations with other countries, student loans, economic prosperity, favorable mortgage rates, secure streets and neighborhoods, cheap and efficient public transportation, affordable health care and family leave protections—are all influenced by or are the products of politics.

Yet if you listen to the news, politics may seem like one long campaign commercial: eternal bickering and finger-pointing by public servants who seem more interested in winning an argument against their ideological opponents than actually solving our collective problems. Far more often than not, political actors with the big bucks seem to have more influence over the process than those of us with normal bank accounts. Politics, which we would like to think of as a noble activity, can take on all the worst characteristics of the business world, where we expect people to take advantage of each other and pursue their own private interests. Can this really be the heritage of Thomas Jefferson and Abraham Lincoln? Can this be the "world's greatest democracy" at work?

In this book we explore that question, getting to the heart of what politics is and how it relates to other concepts such as power, government, rules, economics, and citizenship. We propose that politics can best be understood as the struggle over who gets power and resources in society, and the fight to control the narrative that defines each contestant. Politics produces winners and losers, and much of the reason it can look so ugly is that people fight desperately not to be losers, and to create and perpetuate narratives that celebrate their wins and put the best face possible on their losses. It can get pretty confusing for the average observer.

Contrary to the way they appear in the media, and maybe even in our own minds, the people who are doing that desperate fighting are not some special breed—more corrupt or self-interested or greedy than the rest of us. They are us. Whether they are officials in Washington or mayors of small towns, corporate CEOs or representatives of labor unions, local cops or soldiers in the Middle East, churchgoers or atheists, doctors or lawyers, shopkeepers or consumers, professors or students, they are the people that in a democracy we call citizens.

As we will see, it is the beauty of a democracy that *all* the people, including the everyday people like us, get to fight for what they want. Not everyone can win, of course, and many never come close. There is no denying that some people bring resources to the process that give them an edge, and that the rules give advantages to some groups of people over others. But as the *What's at Stake . . . ?* shows, what makes living today so different from previous eras is that we all have some access to the multiple channels of information through which battles over political narratives take place. The people who pay attention, who learn how the rules work and how to use those communication channels effectively, can begin to increase their chances of getting what they want, whether it is restrictions on ownership of assault weapons, a lower personal tax bill, greater pollution controls, a more aggressive foreign policy, safer streets, a better-educated population, or more public parks. If they become very skilled citizens, they can even begin to change the rules so that people like them have more control of the rules and narratives and a greater chance to end up winners in the high-stakes game we call politics.

In this chapter we introduce you to this fascinating world of politics, focusing on the meaning of politics itself, the varieties of *political* systems and the roles they endorse for the individuals who live under them, the American founders' ideas about democracy and citizenship, the ideas that hold us together as a nation, the ideas that define our political conflicts, and the themes of power and citizenship that will serve as our framework for understanding American politics.

WHAT IS POLITICS?

A peaceful means for determining who gets power and influence in society

Over two thousand years ago, the Greek philosopher Aristotle said that we are political animals, and political animals we seem destined to remain. The truth is that politics is a fundamental and complex human activity. In some ways it is our capacity to be political—to cooperate, bargain, and compromise—that helps distinguish us from all the other animals out there. While it certainly has its baser moments (impeachments, indictments, and intelligence abuses come to mind), politics also allows us to reach more exalted heights than we could ever achieve alone—from dedicating a new public library or building a national highway system, to stabilizing a crashing economy, to curing deadly diseases or exploring the stars.

To explore politics—in all its glory as well as its disgrace—we need to begin with a clear understanding of the word. One of the most famous definitions, put forth by the late, well-known political scientist Harold Lasswell, is still one of the best, and we use it to frame our discussion throughout this book. Lasswell defined **politics** as "who gets what, when, and how."[6] Politics is a way of determining, without recourse to violence, who gets the power and resources in society, and how they get them. **Power** is the ability to get other people to do what you want them to do. The resources in question here might be government jobs, tax revenues, laws that help you get your way, or public policies that work to your advantage.

A major political resource that helps people to gain and maintain power is the ability to control the **media**, not just the press and television but the multiple channels created by companies like Google, Facebook, and Apple through which people get information about politics and that may actually affect the information we get. These days we live in a world of so many complex information networks that sorting out and keeping track of what is happening around us is a task in itself. Anyone who can influence the stories that are told has a big advantage.

Politics provides a process through which we try to arrange our collective lives in some kind of **social order** so that we can live without crashing into each other at every turn, provide ourselves with goods and services we could not obtain alone, and maximize the values and behaviors we think are important. But politics is also about getting our own way. The way we choose may be a noble goal for society or it may be pure self-interest, but the struggle we engage in is a political struggle. Because politics is about power and other scarce resources, there will always be winners and losers. If we could always get our own way, politics would disappear. It is because we cannot always get what we want that politics exists.

Our capacity to be political gives us tools with which to settle disputes about the social order and to allocate scarce resources. The tools of politics are compromise and cooperation;

politics who gets what, when, and how; a process for determining how power and resources are distributed in a society without recourse to violence

power the ability to get other people to do what you want

media the channels—including television, radio, newspapers, and the Internet—through which information is sent and received

social order the way we organize and live our collective lives

discussion and debate; deal making, bargaining, storytelling, even, sometimes, bribery and deceit. We use those tools to agree on the principles that should guide our handling of power and other scarce resources and to live our collective lives according to those principles. Because there are many competing narratives about how to manage power—who should have it, how it should be used, how it should be transferred—agreement on those principles can break down. The tools of politics do not include violence. When people drop bombs, blow themselves up, or fly airplanes into buildings, they have tried to impose their ideas about the social order through nonpolitical means. That may be because the channels of politics have failed, because they cannot agree on basic principles, because they don't share a common understanding of and trust over what counts as negotiation and so cannot craft compromises, because they are unwilling to compromise, or because they don't really care about deal making at all—they just want to impose their will or make a point. The threat of violence may be a political tool used as leverage to get a deal, but when violence is employed, politics has broken down. Indeed, the human history of warfare attests to the fragility of political life.

It is easy to imagine what a world without politics would be like. There would be no resolution or compromise between conflicting interests, because those are political activities. There would be no agreements struck, bargains made, or alliances formed. Unless there were enough of every valued resource to go around, or unless the world were big enough that we could live our lives without coming into contact with other human beings, life would be constant conflict—what the philosopher Thomas Hobbes called in the seventeenth century a "war of all against all." Individuals, unable to cooperate with one another (because cooperation is essentially political), would have no option but to resort to brute force to settle disputes and allocate resources. Politics is essential to our living a civilized life.

POLITICS AND GOVERNMENT

Although the words *politics* and *government* are sometimes used interchangeably, they really refer to different things. Politics is a process or an activity through which power and resources are gained and lost. **Government**, by contrast, is a system or organization for exercising authority over a body of people.

American *politics* is what happens in the halls of Congress, on the campaign trail, at Washington cocktail parties, and in neighborhood association meetings. It is the making of promises, deals, and laws. American *government* is the Constitution and the institutions set up by the Constitution for the exercise of authority by the American people, over the American people.

Authority is power that citizens view as **legitimate**, or "right"—power to which we have implicitly consented. Think of it this way: as children, we probably did as our parents told us or submitted to their punishment if we didn't, because we recognized their authority over us. As we became adults, we started to claim that they had less authority over us, that we could do what we wanted. We no longer saw their power as wholly legitimate or appropriate. Governments exercise authority because people recognize them as legitimate, even if they often do not like doing what they are told (paying taxes, for instance). When governments cease to be regarded as legitimate, the result may be revolution or civil war, unless the state is powerful enough to suppress all opposition.

government a system or organization for exercising authority over a body of people

authority power that is recognized as legitimate, or right

legitimate accepted as "right" or proper

RULES AND INSTITUTIONS

Government is shaped by the process of politics, but it in turn provides the rules and institutions that shape the way politics continues to operate. The rules and institutions of government have a profound effect on how power is distributed and who wins and who loses in the political arena. Life is different in other countries not only because people speak different languages and eat different foods but also because their governments establish rules that cause life to be lived in different ways.

Rules can be thought of as the *how* in the definition "who gets what, . . . and how." They are directives that determine how resources are allocated and how collective action takes place—that is, they determine how we try to get the things we want. We can do it violently, or we can do it politically, according to the rules. Those rules can provide for a single dictator, for a king, for rule by God's representative on Earth or by the rich, for rule by a majority of the people, or for any other arrangement. The point of rules is to provide us with a framework for solving—without violence—the problems generated by our collective lives.

Because the rules we choose can influence which people will get what they want most often, understanding the rules is crucial to understanding politics. Consider for a moment the impact a change of rules would have on the outcome of the sport of basketball, for instance. What if the average height of the players could be no more than 5 feet 10 inches? What if the baskets were lowered? What if foul shots counted for two points rather than one? Basketball would be a very different game, and the teams recruited would look quite unlike the teams for which we now cheer. So it is with governments and politics: change the people who are allowed to vote or the length of time a person can serve in office, and the political process and the potential winners and losers change drastically.

Rules can be official—laws that are passed, signed, and entered into the books; amendments that are ratified; decisions made by bureaucrats; or judgments handed down by the courts. Less visible but no less important are **norms**, the tacitly understood rules about acceptable political behavior, ways of doing things, boundaries between the branches, and traditional practices that grease the wheels of politics and keep them running smoothly. Because norms are understood but not explicitly written down, we often don't even recognize them until they are broken.

Let's take a silly example close to home. Say it's Thanksgiving dinner time and your brother decides he wants the mashed potatoes on the other side of the table. Instead of asking to have them passed, imagine that he climbs up on the table and walks across the top of it with his big, dirty feet, retrieves the potatoes, clomps back across the table, jumps down, takes his seat, and serves himself some potatoes. Everyone is aghast, right? What he has just done just isn't done. But when you challenge him, he says, "What, there's a rule against doing that? I got what I wanted, didn't I?" And you have to admit there isn't and he did. But the reason there is no broken rule is because nobody ever thought one would be necessary. You never imagined that someone would walk across the table because everyone knows there is a norm against doing that, and until your brother broke that norm, no one ever bothered to articulate it. And "getting what you want" is not generally held to be an adequate justification for bad behavior.

Just because norms are not written down doesn't mean they are not essential for the survival of a government or the process of politics. In some cases they are far more

rules directives that specify how resources will be distributed or what procedures govern collective activity

norms informal, unwritten expectations that guide behavior and support formal rule systems; often most noticeable when broken

essential than written laws. A family of people who routinely stomp across the table to get the food they want would not long want to share meals; eating alone would be far more comfortable.

We can think of **institutions** as the *where* of the political struggle, though Lasswell didn't include a "where" component in his definition. They are the organizations where government power is exercised. In the United States, our rules provide for the institutions of a representative democracy—that is, rule by the elected representatives of the people, and for a federal political system. Our Constitution lays the foundation for the institutions of Congress, the presidency, the courts, and the bureaucracy as a stage on which the drama of politics plays itself out. Other systems might call for different institutions, perhaps an all-powerful parliament, or a monarch, or even a committee of rulers.

These complicated systems of rules and institutions do not appear out of thin air. They are carefully designed by the founders of different systems to create the kinds of society they think will be stable and prosperous, but also where people like themselves are likely to be winners. Remember that not only the rules but also the institutions we choose influence which people most easily and most often get their own way.

POWER, NARRATIVES, AND MEDIA

From the start of human existence, an essential function of communication has been recording events, giving meaning to them and creating a story, or narrative, about how they fit into the past and stretch into the future. It is human nature to tell stories, to capture our experiential knowledge and beliefs and weave them together in ways that give larger meaning to our lives. Native peoples of many lands do it with their legends; the Greeks and Romans did it with their myths; the Jews, Christians, Muslims, and other major religious groups do it with their holy texts; and the Grimms did it with their fairytales. Human beings tell stories. It's what we do, and it gives us our history and a way of passing that history down to new generations.

A major part of politics is about competing to have your narrative accepted as the authoritative account. Control of political information has always been a crucial resource when it comes to making and upholding a claim that one should be able to tell other people how to live their lives, but it used to be a power reserved for a few. Creation and dissemination of **political narratives**—the stories that people believe about who has power, who wants power, who deserves power, and what someone has done to get and maintain power—were the prerogative of authoritative sources like priests, kings, and their agents.

Through much of our common history, the storytellers of those narratives were given special status. They were wise men or women, shamans, prophets, oracles, priests, and rabbis. And they were frequently in the service of chiefs, kings, emperors, and other people of enormous power. It's no accident that the storytellers frequently told narratives that bolstered the status quo and kept the power structure in place. The storytellers and the power holders had a monopoly on control for so much of human history because books were in scarce supply and few people could read in any case or had the leisure to amass facts to challenge the prevailing narratives. The **gatekeepers** of information—those who determined what news got reported and how—were very few.

institutions organizations in which government power is exercised

political narrative a persuasive story about the nature of power, who should have it, and how it should be used

gatekeepers journalists and the media elite who determine which news stories are covered and which are not

Before the seventeenth-century era known as the Enlightenment, there may have been competing narratives about who had claims to power, but they were not that hard to figure out. People's allegiance to power was based on tribal loyalties, religious faith, or conquest. Governments were legitimate through the authority of God or the sword, and that was that. Because most people then were illiterate, that narrative was *mediated*, that is, passed to people through channels that could shape and influence it. Information flowed mostly through medieval clergy and monarchs, *the very people who had a vested interest in getting people to believe it.*

Even when those theories of legitimacy changed, information was still easily controlled because literacy rates were low and horses and wind determined the speed of communication until the advent of steam engines and radios. Early newspapers were read aloud, shared, and reshared, and a good deal of the news of the day was delivered from the pulpit. As we will see when we discuss the American founding, there were lively debates about whether independence was a good idea and what kind of political system should replace the colonial power structure, but by the time information reached citizens, it had been largely processed and filtered by those higher up the power ladder. Even the American rebels were elite and powerful men who could control their own narratives. Remember the importance of this when we read the story behind the Declaration of Independence in Chapter 2.

These days, we take for granted the ease with which we can communicate ideas to others all over the globe. Just a hundred years ago, radio was state of the art and television had yet to be invented. Today many of us carry access to a world of information and instant communication in our pockets.

When we talk about the channels through which information flows, and the ways that the channel itself might alter or control the narrative, we are referring to media. Just like a medium is a person through whom some people try to communicate with those who have died, media (the plural of medium) are channels of communication, as mentioned earlier. The integrity of the medium is critical. A scam artist might make money off the desire of grieving people to contact a lost loved one by making up the information she passes on. The monarch and clergy who channeled the narrative of the Holy Roman Empire were motivated by their wish to hold on to power. Think about water running through a pipe. Maybe the pipe is made of lead, or is rusty, or has leaks. Depending on the integrity of the pipe, the water we get will be toxic or colored or limited. *In the same way, the narratives and information we get can be altered by the way they are mediated, by the channels, or the media through which we receive them.*

As we will see, in today's digital world, there are so many channels of information that it is all the more important that people check the integrity of the media they use in order to understand the narratives those media may be pushing.

POLITICS AND ECONOMICS

Whereas politics is concerned with the distribution of power and resources and the control of information in society, economics is concerned specifically with the production and distribution of society's wealth—material goods like bread, toothpaste, and housing, and services like medical care, education, and entertainment. Because both politics and economics focus on the distribution of society's resources, political and economic questions often get confused in contemporary life. Questions about how to pay for government, about government's role in the economy, and about whether government or the private sector should provide certain services have political and economic dimensions. Because there are no clear-cut distinctions here, it can be difficult to keep these terms straight. We can begin by examining different economic systems, shown in Figure 1.1.

The processes of politics and economics can be engaged in procedurally or substantively. In procedural political and economic systems, the legitimacy of the outcome is based on the legitimacy of the process that produced it. In substantive political and economic systems, the legitimacy of the outcome depends on how widely accepted is the narrative the government tells about who should have what. The outcome is based on the decision of a powerful person or people, not a process that people believe is impartial. In procedural systems, the means (process) justify the ends; in substantive systems, the ends justify the means.

CAPITALISM Capitalism is a procedural economic system based on the working of the *market*—the process of supply and demand. In a pure capitalist economy, all the means that

economics production and distribution of a society's material resources and services

capitalist economy an economic system in which the market determines production, distribution, and price decisions, and property is privately owned

FIGURE 1.1

A Comparison of Economic Systems

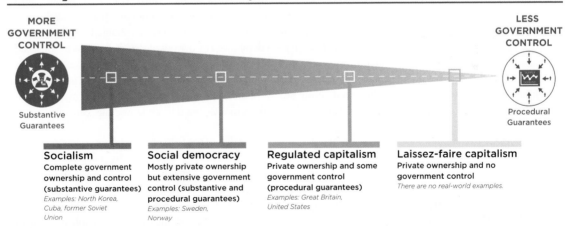

MORE GOVERNMENT CONTROL

LESS GOVERNMENT CONTROL

Substantive Guarantees

Procedural Guarantees

Socialism
Complete government ownership and control (substantive guarantees)
Examples: North Korea, Cuba, former Soviet Union

Social democracy
Mostly private ownership but extensive government control (substantive and procedural guarantees)
Examples: Sweden, Norway

Regulated capitalism
Private ownership and some government control (procedural guarantees)
Examples: Great Britain, United States

Laissez-faire capitalism
Private ownership and no government control
There are no real-world examples.

Economic systems are defined largely by the degree to which government owns the means by which material resources are produced (for example, factories and industry) and controls economic decision making. On a scale ranging from socialism—complete government ownership and control of the economy (on the left)—to laissez-faire capitalism—complete individual ownership and control of the economy (on the right)—social democracies would be located in the center. These hybrid systems are characterized by mostly private ownership of the means of production but considerable government control over economic decisions.

President for Life

In March 2018, China's legislature, the National People's Congress, voted to change the country's constitution to eliminate the existing ten-year presidential term limit. This step toward authoritarianism sets up President Xi Jinping as a potential president for life.

are used to produce material resources (industry, business, and land, for instance) are privately owned, and decisions about production and distribution are left to individuals operating through the free-market process. Capitalist economies rely on the market—the process of supply and demand—to decide how much of a given item to produce or how much to charge for it. In capitalist countries, people do not believe that the government is capable of making such judgments; they want to keep these decisions out of the hands of government and in the hands of individuals, who they believe know best about what they want. The most extreme philosophy that corresponds with this belief is called *laissez-faire capitalism*, from a French term that, loosely translated, means "let people do as they wish." The government has no economic role at all in such a system. However, no economic system today maintains a purely unregulated form of capitalism, with the government completely uninvolved.

Like most other countries today, the United States has a system of **regulated capitalism**. It maintains a capitalist economy, and individual freedom from government interference remains the norm, but it allows government to step in and regulate the economy to guarantee individual rights and to provide **procedural guarantees** that the rules will work smoothly and fairly. Although in theory the market ought to provide everything that people need and want, and should regulate itself as well, sometimes it fails.

The notion that the market, an impartial process, has "failed" is a somewhat substantive one—it is the decision of a government that the outcome is not acceptable and should be replaced or altered to fit a substantive vision of what the outcome should be. When markets have ups and downs—periods of growth followed by periods of slowdown or recession—individuals and businesses look to government for economic security. If the market fails to produce some goods and services, like schools or highways, individuals expect the government to step in to produce them (using taxpayer funds). It is not *very* substantive—the market process still largely makes all the distributional decisions—but it is not laissez faire capitalism, either.

SOCIALISM In a **socialist economy** like that of the former Soviet Union, economic decisions are made not by individuals through the market but rather by politicians, based on their judgment of what society needs. In these systems the state often owns the factories, land, and other resources necessary to produce wealth. Rather than trusting the market process to determine the proper distribution of material resources among individuals, politicians decide what the distribution ought to be—according to some principle like equality, need, or political reward—and then create economic policy to bring about that outcome. In other words, they emphasize not procedural guarantees of fair rules and process, but rather **substantive guarantees** of what they believe to be fair outcomes.

The societies that have tried to put these theories into practice have ended up with very repressive political systems, even though Karl Marx, the most famous of the theorists associated with socialism, hoped that eventually humankind would evolve to a point where each

regulated capitalism a market system in which the government intervenes to protect rights and make procedural guarantees

procedural guarantees government assurance that the rules will work smoothly and treat everyone fairly, with no promise of particular outcomes

socialist economy an economic system in which the state determines production, distribution, and price decisions, and property is government owned

substantive guarantees government assurance of particular outcomes or results

individual had control over his or her own life—a radical form of democracy. Since the social-ist economies of the former Soviet Union and Eastern Europe have fallen apart, socialism has been left with few supporters, although some nations, such as China, North Korea, and Cuba, still claim allegiance to it. Even China, however, introduced market-based reforms in the 1970s and in 2015 ranked as the world's second largest economy, after the United States.

SOCIAL DEMOCRACY Some countries in Western Europe, especially the Scandinavian nations of Norway, Denmark, and Sweden, have developed hybrid economic systems. As noted in Figure 1.1, these systems represent something of a middle ground between socialist and capitalist systems. Primarily capitalist, in that they trust the market process and they believe most property can be privately held, proponents of social democracy nonetheless argue that the equitable outcomes often promoted by socialism are attractive and can be brought about by democratic reform rather than revolution. Believing that the economy does not have to be owned by the state for its effects to be controlled by the state, social democratic countries attempt to strike a difficult balance between providing substantive guarantees of fair outcomes and procedural guarantees of fair rules.

Since World War II, the citizens of many Western European nations have elected social democrats to office, where they have enacted policies to bring about more equality—for instance, the elimination of poverty and unemployment, better housing, and adequate health care for all. Even where social democratic governments are voted out of office, such programs have proved so popular that it is often difficult for new leaders to alter them. Socialism and social democracy do not generally find much support in the United States, although Bernie Sanders's campaign for the Democratic nomination in 2016 gained a surprising amount of traction, and many of his proposals found their way into the Democratic Party platform.

In Your Own Words Describe the role that politics plays in determining how power and resources, including control of information, are distributed in a society.

POLITICAL SYSTEMS AND THE CONCEPT OF CITIZENSHIP

Competing ideas about power and the social order, different models of governing

Just as there are different kinds of economic systems on the substantive-to-procedural scale, there are many sorts of political systems, based on competing ideas about who should have power and what the social order should be—that is, how much substantive regulation there should be over individual decision making. For our purposes, we can divide political systems into two types: those in which the government has the substantive power to impose a particular social order, deciding how individuals ought to behave, and those pro-cedural systems in which individuals exercise personal power over most of their own behavior and ultimately over government as well. These two types of systems are different not just in a theoretical sense. The differences have very real implications for the people who live in them; the notion of citizenship (or the lack of it) is tied closely to the kind of political system a nation has.

social democracy a hybrid system combining a capitalist economy and a government that supports equality

authoritarian governments systems in which the state holds all power over the social order

totalitarian a system in which absolute power is exercised over every aspect of life

authoritarian capitalism a system in which the state allows people economic freedom but maintains stringent social regulations to limit noneconomic behavior

FIGURE 1.2

A Comparison of Political Systems

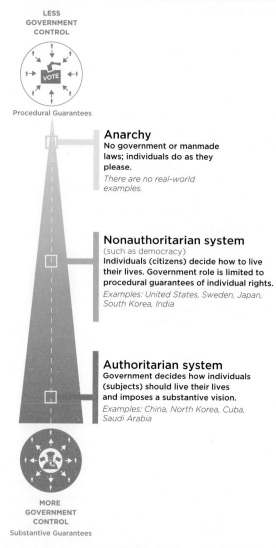

LESS GOVERNMENT CONTROL

Procedural Guarantees

Anarchy
No government or manmade laws; individuals do as they please.
There are no real-world examples.

Nonauthoritarian system
(such as democracy)
Individuals (citizens) decide how to live their lives. Government role is limited to procedural guarantees of individual rights.
Examples: United States, Sweden, Japan, South Korea, India

Authoritarian system
Government decides how individuals (subjects) should live their lives and imposes a substantive vision.
Examples: China, North Korea, Cuba, Saudi Arabia

MORE GOVERNMENT CONTROL

Substantive Guarantees

Political systems are defined by the extent to which individual citizens or governments decide what the social order should look like—that is, how people should live their collective, noneconomic lives. Except for anarchies, every system allots a role to government to regulate individual behavior—for example, to prohibit murder, rape, and theft. But beyond such basic regulation, they differ radically on who gets to determine how individuals live their lives, and whether government's role is simply to provide procedural guarantees that protect individuals' rights to make their own decisions or to provide a much more substantive view of how individuals should behave.

Figure 1.2 compares these systems, ranging from the more substantive authoritarian governments that potentially have total power over their subjects to more procedural nonauthoritarian governments that permit citizens to limit the state's power by claiming rights that the government must protect. Figure 1.3 shows what happens when we overlie our economic and political figures, giving us a model of most of the world's political/economic systems. Note that when we say *model*, we are talking about abstractions from reality used as a tool to help us understand. We don't pretend that all the details of the world are captured in a single two-dimensional figure, but we can get a better idea of the similarities and differences by looking at them this way.

AUTHORITARIAN SYSTEMS

Authoritarian governments give ultimate power to the state rather than to the people to decide how they ought to live their lives. By *authoritarian governments*, we usually mean those in which the people cannot effectively claim rights against the state; where the state chooses to exercise its power, the people have no choice but to submit to its will. Authoritarian governments can take various forms: sovereignty can be vested in an individual (dictatorship or monarchy), in God (theocracy), in the state itself (fascism), or in a ruling class (oligarchy).

When a system combines an authoritarian government with a socialist economy, we say that the system is **totalitarian**. That is, as in the earlier example of the former Soviet Union, it may exercise its power over every part of society—economic, social, political, and moral—leaving little or no private realm for individuals.

An authoritarian state may also limit its own power. In such cases, it may deny individuals rights in those spheres where it chooses to act, but it may leave large areas of society, such as a capitalist economy, free from government interference. Singapore is an example of this type of **authoritarian capitalism**; people have considerable economic freedom, but stringent social regulations limit their noneconomic behavior.

Often authoritarian governments pay lip service to the people, but when push comes to shove, as it usually does in such states, the people have no effective power against the government. Again, government does not just provide guarantees of fair processes for individuals; it guarantees a substantive vision of what life will be like—what individuals will believe, how they will act, what they will choose.

DEMOCRACY AND NONAUTHORITARIAN SYSTEMS

In nonauthoritarian systems, ultimate power rests with the individuals to make decisions concerning their lives. The most extreme form of nonauthoritarianism is called **anarchy**. Anarchists would do away with government and laws altogether. People advocate anarchy because they value the freedom to do whatever they want more than they value the order and security that governments provide by forbidding or regulating certain kinds of behavior. Few people are true anarchists, however. Anarchy may sound attractive in theory, but the inherent difficulties of the position make it hard to practice. For instance, how could you even organize a revolution to get rid of government without some rules about who is to do what and how decisions are to be made?

A less extreme form of nonauthoritarian government, and one much more familiar to us, is **democracy** (from the Greek *demos*, meaning "people"). In democracies, government is not external to the people, as it is in authoritarian systems; in a fundamental sense, government is the people. Recognizing that collective life usually calls for some restrictions on what individuals may do (laws forbidding murder, for instance, or theft), democracies nevertheless try to maximize freedom for the individuals who live under them. Although they generally make decisions through some sort of majority rule, democracies still provide procedural guarantees to preserve individual rights—usually protections of due process (guarantee of a fair trial, right to a lawyer, and so on) and minority rights. This means that if individuals living in a democracy feel their rights have been violated, they have the right to ask government to remedy the situation.

Democracies are based on the principle of **popular sovereignty**; that is, there is no power higher than the people and, in the United States, the document establishing their authority, the Constitution. The central idea here is that no government is considered legitimate unless the governed consent to it, and people are not truly free unless they live under a law of their own making. Democratic narratives vary, however, in how much active control they give to individuals:

- Theorists of **elite democracy** propose that democracy is merely a system of choosing among competing leaders; for the average citizen, input ends after the leader is chosen.[7] In this view, elections are merely symbolic—to perpetuate the illusion that citizens have consented to their government.
- Advocates of **pluralist democracy** argue that what is important is not so much individual participation but rather membership in groups that participate in government decision making on their members' behalf.[8] As a way of trying to influence a system that gives them a limited voice, citizens join groups of people with whom they share an interest, such as labor unions, professional associations, and environmental or business groups.
- Supporters of **participatory democracy** claim that individuals have the right to control *all* the circumstances of their lives, and direct democratic participation should take place not only in government but in industry, education, and community affairs as well.[9] For advocates of this view, democracy is more than a way to make decisions: it is a way of life, an end in itself.

anarchy the absence of government and laws

democracy a government that vests power in the people

popular sovereignty the concept that the citizens are the ultimate source of political power

elite democracy a theory of democracy that limits the citizens' role to choosing among competing leaders

pluralist democracy a theory of democracy that holds that citizen membership in groups is the key to political power

participatory democracy a theory of democracy that holds that citizens should actively and directly control all aspects of their lives

These theories about how democracy should (or does) work locate the focus of power in elites, groups, and individuals, respectively. Real-world examples of democracy probably include elements of more than one of these theories; they are not mutually exclusive.

The people of many Western countries have found the idea of democracy persuasive enough to found their governments on it. In recent years, especially since the mid-1980s, democracy has been spreading rapidly through the rest of the world as the preferred form of government. No longer the primary province of industrialized Western nations, attempts at democratic governance now extend into Asia, Latin America, Africa, Eastern Europe, and the republics of the former Soviet Union. There are many varieties of democracy other than our own. Some democracies make the legislature (the representatives of the people) the most important authority, some retain a monarch with limited powers, and some hold referenda at the national level to get direct feedback on how the people want the government to act on specific issues.

Most democratic forms of government, because of their commitment to procedural values, practice a capitalist form of economics. Fledgling democracies may rely on a high degree of government economic regulation, but **advanced industrial democracies** combine a considerable amount of personal freedom with a free-market (though still usually regulated) economy. It is rare to find a country that is truly committed to individual political freedom that also tries to regulate the economy heavily. The economist Karl Marx believed that radical democracy would coexist with communally owned property in a form of **communist democracy**, but such a system has never existed, and most real-world systems fall somewhere along the horizontal continuum shown in Figure 1.3.

THE ROLE OF THE PEOPLE

What is important about the political and economic systems we have been sorting out here is that they have a direct impact on the lives of the people who live in them. So far we have given a good deal of attention to the latter parts of Lasswell's definition of politics. But easily as important as the *what* and the *how* in Lasswell's formulation is the *who*. Underlying the different political theories we have looked at are fundamental differences in the powers and opportunities possessed by everyday people.

In authoritarian systems, the people are **subjects** of their government. They possess no rights that protect them from that government; they must do whatever the government says or face the consequences, without any other recourse. They have obligations to the state but no rights or privileges to offset those obligations. They may be winners or losers in government decisions, but they have very little control over which it may be.

Everyday people in democratic systems have a potentially powerful role to play. They are more than mere subjects; they are **citizens**, or members of a political community with rights as well as obligations. Democratic theory says that power is drawn from the people—that the people are sovereign, that they must consent to be governed, and that their government must respond to their will. In practical terms, this may not seem to mean much, since not consenting doesn't necessarily give us the right to disobey government. It does give us the option of leaving, however, and seeking a more congenial set of rules elsewhere. Subjects of authoritarian governments rarely have this freedom.

Theoretically, democracies are ruled by "the people," but different democracies have at times been very selective about whom they count as citizens. Beginning with our days as colonists, Americans have excluded many groups of people from citizenship: people of the "wrong" religion, income bracket, race, ethnic group, lifestyle, and gender have all been

advanced industrial democracy a system in which a democratic government allows citizens a considerable amount of personal freedom and maintains a free-market (though still usually regulated) economy

communist democracy a utopian system in which property is communally owned and all decisions are made democratically

subjects individuals who are obliged to submit to a government authority against which they have no rights

citizens members of a political community having both rights and responsibilities

FIGURE 1.3
Political and Economic Systems

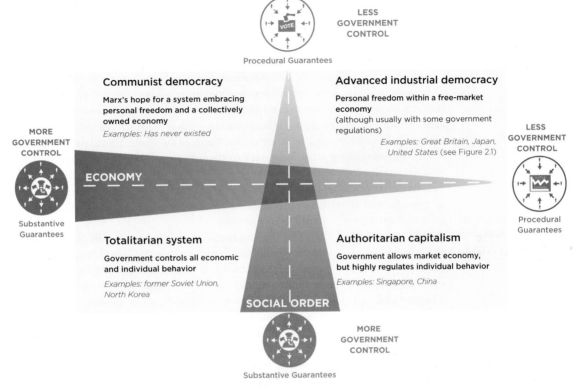

LESS GOVERNMENT CONTROL

Procedural Guarantees

MORE GOVERNMENT CONTROL

Substantive Guarantees

LESS GOVERNMENT CONTROL

Procedural Guarantees

MORE GOVERNMENT CONTROL

Substantive Guarantees

Communist democracy

Marx's hope for a system embracing personal freedom and a collectively owned economy

Examples: Has never existed

Advanced industrial democracy

Personal freedom within a free-market economy
(although usually with some government regulations)

Examples: Great Britain, Japan, United States (see Figure 2.1)

ECONOMY

Totalitarian system

Government controls all economic and individual behavior

Examples: former Soviet Union, North Korea

Authoritarian capitalism

Government allows market economy, but highly regulates individual behavior

Examples: Singapore, China

SOCIAL ORDER

Political systems work in conjunction with economic systems, but government control over the economy does not necessarily translate into tight control over the social order. We have identified four possible combinations of these systems, signified by the labeled points in each quadrant. These points are approximate, however, and some nations cannot be classified so easily. Sweden is an advanced industrial democracy by most measures, for instance, but because of its commitment to substantive economic values, it would be located much closer to the vertical axis.

excluded from enjoying the full rights of colonial or U.S. citizenship at different times. In fact, American history is the story of those various groups fighting to be included as citizens. Just because a system is called a democracy is no guarantee that all or even most of its residents possess the status of citizen.

In democratic systems, the rules of government can provide for all sorts of different roles for those they designate as citizens. At a minimum, citizens possess certain rights, or powers to act, that government cannot limit. Just what these rights are varies in different democracies, but they usually include freedoms of speech and the press, the right to assemble, and certain legal protections guaranteeing fair treatment in the criminal justice system. Almost all of these rights are designed to allow citizens to criticize their government openly without threat of retribution by that government—in essence to retain some of that power over the narrative that we discussed earlier. Citizens can usually vote in periodic and free elections. They may be able to run for office, subject to certain conditions, like age or residence. They can support candidates for office, organize political groups or parties, attend meetings, write letters to officials or the press, march in protest or support of various causes, even speak out on street corners. As we noted earlier, increasingly, citizens can vocalize their views and disseminate them electronically, through social networks, blogs, and self-published work.

Citizens of democracies also possess obligations or responsibilities to the public realm. They have the obligation to obey the law, for instance, once they have consented to the government (even if that consent amounts only to not leaving). They may also have the obligation to pay taxes, serve in the military, or sit on juries. Some theorists argue that truly virtuous citizens should put community interests ahead of personal interests. A less extreme version of this view holds that while citizens may go about their own business and pursue their own interests, they must continue to pay attention to their government, following the news to keep a critical eye on their elected officials. Participating in its decisions is the price of maintaining their own liberty and, by extension, the liberty of the whole. Should citizens abdicate this role by tuning out of public life, the safeguards of democracy can disappear, to be replaced with the trappings of authoritarian government. There is nothing automatic about democracy. If left unattended by nonvigilant citizens, the freedoms of democracy can be lost to an all-powerful state, and citizens can become transformed into subjects of the government they failed to keep in check.

> **Do subjects enjoy any advantages that citizens don't have?**

This Western notion of citizenship as conferring both rights and responsibilities first became popular in the 1700s, as Europeans emerged from the Middle Ages and began to reject notions that rulers were put on Earth by God to be obeyed unconditionally. Two British philosophers, Thomas Hobbes and John Locke, led the new way of thinking about subjecthood and citizenship. Governments are born not because God ordains them, but because life without government is "solitary, poor, nasty, brutish, and short" in Hobbes's words, and "inconvenient" in Locke's. The foundation of government is reason, not faith, and reason leads people to consent to being governed because they are better off that way.

People have freedom and rights before government exists, declared Locke. When they decide they are better off with government than without it, they enter into a social contract, giving up some of those rights in exchange for the protection of the rest of their rights by a government established by the majority. If that government fails to protect their rights, it has broken the contract, and the people are free to form a new government or not, as they please. But the key element here is that for authority to be legitimate, citizens must consent to it. Note, however, that nowhere did Locke suggest that all people ought to participate in politics, or that people are necessarily equal. In fact, he was concerned mostly with the preservation of private property, suggesting that only property owners would have cause to be bothered with government because only they have something concrete to lose. Still, the political narratives of classical liberalism that emerged from the Enlightenment emphasized individual rights and non authoritarianism.

Meanwhile, as philosophers in Europe were beginning to explore the idea of individual rights and democratic governance, there had long been democratic stirrings on the founders' home continent. The Iroquois Confederacy was an alliance of five (and eventually six) East Coast Native American nations whose constitution, the "Great Law of Peace," impressed such American leaders as Benjamin Franklin with its suggestions of federalism, separation of powers, checks and balances, and consensus-building. Although historians are not sure that these ideas had any direct influence on the founders' thinking about American governance, they were clearly part of the stew of ideas that the founders could dip into, and some scholars make the case that their influence was significant.[10]

social contract the notion that society is based on an agreement between government and the governed, in which people agree to give up some rights in exchange for the protection of others

classical liberalism a political ideology dating from the seventeenth century emphasizing individual rights over the power of the state

DEMOCRACY IN AMERICA

*Limited participation to limit the
impact of a volatile, self-interested citizenry*

For our purposes, the most important thing about these ideas about politics is that they were prevalent at the same time the American founders were thinking about how to build a new government. Locke particularly influenced the writings of James Madison, a major author of our Constitution. The founders wanted to base their new government on popular consent, but they did not want to go too far. Madison, as we will see, was particularly worried about a system that was too democratic.

THE DANGERS OF DEMOCRACY

Enthusiastic popular participation under the government established by the Articles of Confederation—the document that tied the colonies together before the Constitution was drafted—almost ended the new government before it began. Like Locke, Madison thought government had a duty to protect property, and if people who didn't have property could get involved in politics, they might not care about protecting the property of others. Worse, they might form "factions," groups pursuing their own self-interests rather than the public interest, and even try to get some of that property for themselves. So Madison rejected notions of "pure democracy," in which all citizens would have direct power to control government, and opted instead for what he called a "republic."

republic a government in which decisions are made through representatives of the people

A **republic**, according to Madison, differs from a democracy mainly in that it employs representation and can work in a large state. Most theorists agree that democracy is impossible in practice if there are a lot of citizens and all have to be heard from. But we do not march to Washington or phone our legislator every time we want to register a political preference. Instead, we choose representatives—members of the House of Representatives, senators, and the president—to represent our views for us. Madison thought this would be a safer system than direct participation (all of us crowding into town halls or the Capitol) because public passions would be cooled off by the process. You might be furious about health care costs when you vote for your senator, but he or she will represent your views with less anger. The founders hoped the representatives would be older, wealthier, and wiser than the average American and that they would be better able to make cool and rational decisions.

Citizens Stepping Up
Americans may be individualists, but that doesn't mean they don't pitch in to help others in need—at least some of the time. When Hurricane Maria struck Puerto Rico in 2017, chef José Andrés jumped into action via his organization World Central Kitchen to provide meals to people across the islands who had lost power, or even their homes.

Eric Rojas/World Central Kitchen

THE EVOLUTION OF AMERICAN CITIZENSHIP

Unlike the founders, certainly, but even unlike most of the people currently running this country (who are, let's face it, kind of old), people born in this century are almost all **digital natives**. They have been born in an era in which not only are most people hooked up to electronic media, but they also live their lives partly in cyberspace as well as in "real space." For many of us, the lives we live are almost entirely mediated—that is, most of our relationships, our education, our news, our travel, our sustenance, our purchases, our daily activities, our job seeking, and our very sense of ourselves are influenced by, experienced through, or shared via electronic media.

Essentially we are conducting our lives through channels that, like that water pipe we talked about earlier, may be made of lead, may be rusty, or may be full of holes. When we search online, certain links are offered first according to the calculations made by the search engine we use. When we shop online, we are urged to buy certain products that an algorithm thinks we will like or that people like us have purchased. When we travel, certain flights and hotels are flagged, and when we use social media, certain posts appear while others don't. Most of us don't check very hard to ensure that the information on which we base our choices isn't emerging from the cyberequivalent of lead pipes.

A mediated world has all kinds of implications for everyday living and loving and working. The implications we care about here are the political implications for our roles as citizens—the ones to do with how we exercise and are impacted by power. We will be turning to these implications again and again throughout this book.

Even though Americans today still largely adhere to the basic governing narrative the founders promoted, the country is now light years removed from the founding era, when communication was limited by illiteracy and the scarcity of channels through which it could pass. Consider the timeline in Figure 1.4. It follows the development of the media through which we get information, receive narratives, and send out our own information (see also *Snapshot of America: How Do We Engage Politically Online*). Being a citizen in a mediated world is just flat out different from being one in the world in which James Madison wrote the Constitution. It's the genius of the Constitution that it has been able to navigate the transition successfully, so far. The mediated world we live in gives us myriad new ways to keep the republic and some pretty high-tech ways to lose it. That puts a huge burden on us as **mediated citizens**, and also opens up a world of opportunity.

Among the things we disagree on in this country is what it means to be a citizen. James Madison obviously had ideas about this. As mentioned earlier, he hoped people would be so filled with what he called republican virtue that they would readily sacrifice their self-interest to advance the public interest. As we will see in Chapter 2, this **public-interested citizenship** proved not to be the rule, much to Madison's disappointment. Instead, early Americans demonstrated **self-interested citizenship**, trying to use the system to get the most they could for themselves. This was a dilemma for Madison because he was designing a constitution that depended on the nature of the

digital native an individual born after the advent of digital technology who is proficient in and dependent on its use

mediated citizens those for whom most personal and commercial relationships; access to information about the world and recreational or professional activities; and communication with others passes through third-party channels, which may or may not modify or censor that information

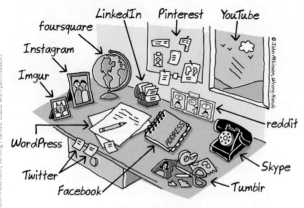

vintage social networking

foursquare
Instagram
Imgur
LinkedIn
Pinterest
YouTube
WordPress
Twitter
Facebook
reddit
Skype
Tumblr

© John Atkinson, Wrong Hands • wronghands1.com

FIGURE 1.4
Media Timeline

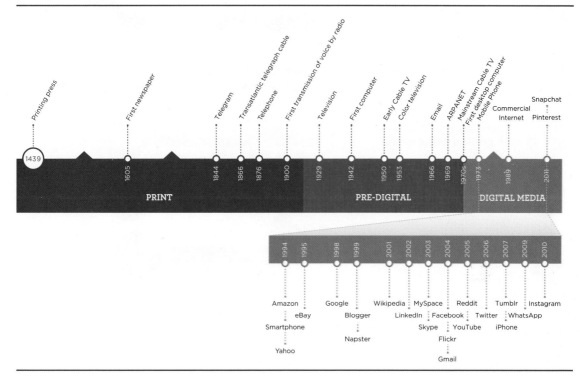

people being governed. He believed he had solved that dilemma by creating a political system that would check our self-interested nature and produce laws that would support the public interest.

Still, the Constitution has not put that conflict to rest. Today there are plenty of people who put country first—who enlist in the armed services, sometimes giving their lives for their nation, or who go into law enforcement or teaching or other lower paying careers because they want to serve. There are people who cheerfully pay their taxes because it's a privilege to live in a free democracy where you can climb the ladder of opportunity. Especially in moments of national trouble—after the terrorist attacks on the World Trade Center and the Pentagon in September 2001, for instance—Americans willingly help their fellow citizens.

At the same time, the day-to-day business of life turns most people inward. Many people care about self and family and friends, but most don't have the energy or inclination to get beyond that. John Kennedy challenged his "fellow Americans" in 1961 to "ask not what your country can do for you—ask what you can do for your country," but only a rare few have the time or motivation to take up that challenge.

public-interested citizenship a view of citizenship focused on action to realize the common good

self-interested citizenship a view of citizenship focused on action to realize an individual citizen's interests

Snapshot of America: *How Do We Engage Politically Online?*

"Like" or promote material related to politics or social issues that others have posted — **38%** 45%

Use a social networking site to encourage people to vote — **35%**

Post one's own comments on political/social issues — **34%**

Repost content related to political/social issues that was originally posted by someone else — **33%**

Encourage other people to take action on a political/social issue — **31%**

Post links to political stories or articles for others to read — **28%**

Follow elected officials and candidates for office — **20%**

Impacts of Online Political Engagement

25% **16%** 0.09%

Became more active in a political issue after discussing/reading about it online

Changed views about a political issue after discussing/reading about it online

Became less involved in a political issue after encountering it online

Behind the Numbers

Social media enable citizens to engage with their government, the news media, and each other much more efficiently than in previous decades. But widespread and easy access to political information comes to us with few quality checks. Did you engage politically during the 2016 presidential election in any of the ways listed above? In what ways might social media affect political outcomes?

Source: Pew Research Center: Internet, Science & Tech, "Politics Fact Sheet," www.pewinternet.org/fact-sheets/politics-fact-sheet/ (accessed March 15, 2016).

Unlike the citizens Madison and his colleagues designed a constitution for, mediated citizens experience the world through multiple channels of information and interaction. That doesn't change whether citizens are self-interested or public-interested, but it does give them more opportunities and raise more potential hazards for being both.

Many older Americans who are not digital natives nonetheless experience political life through television or through web surfing and commenting, usually anonymously and often rudely. This is not always a positive addition to our civil discourse, but they are trying to adapt. You may have grandparents who fit this description. They probably want to know why you are not on Facebook.

But younger, more media-savvy digital natives—the Marjory Stoneman Douglas students we discussed in *What's at Stake . . . ?*, millennials, Gen Xers, even some tech-savvy Baby Boomers—not only have access to traditional media if they choose but also are accustomed to interacting, conducting friendships and family relationships, and generally attending to the details of their lives through electronic channels. Their digital selves exist in networks of friends and acquaintances who take for granted that they can communicate in seconds. They certainly get their news digitally and increasingly organize, register to vote, enlist in campaigns, and call each other to action that way.

In fact, as we saw earlier, **hashtag activism**, the forming of social movements through viral calls to act politically—whether to march, to boycott, to contact politicians, or to vote—has become common enough that organizers warn that action has to go beyond cyberspace to reach the real world or it will have limited

> *When, if ever, should individuals be asked to sacrifice their own good for that of their country?*

impact. #BlackLivesMatter, #ItGetsBetter, and #NeverAgain are just three very different, very viral, very successful ways of using all the channels available to us to call attention to a problem and propose solutions.

Although living an intensely mediated life has the potential to broaden our horizons and expose us to multiple views and cultures, it does not automatically produce public-interested citizens. People can easily remain self-interested in this digital world. We can customize our social media to give us only news and information that confirm what we already think. We can live in an **information bubble** where everything we see and hear reinforces our narratives (see *Don't Be Fooled by . . . Your Own Information Bubble*). That makes us more or less sitting ducks for whatever media narrative is directed our way, whether from inside an online media source or from a foreign power that weaponizes social media to influence an election, as the Russians did in 2016. Without opening ourselves up to multiple information and action channels, we can live an unexamined mediated life.

But mediated citizenship also creates enormous opportunities that the founders never dreamed of. Truth to tell, Madison wouldn't have been all that thrilled about the multiple ways to be political that the mediated citizen possesses. He thought citizens should be seen on election day, but not heard most of the time, precisely because he thought we would push our own interests and destabilize the system. He was reassured by the fact that it would take days for an express letter trying to create a dissenting political organization to reach Georgia from Maine. Our mediated world has blown that reassuring prospect to smithereens.

Mediated citizens are not only the receivers and distributors of narratives from powerful people, like the TV-watching couch potato or headphone-wearing student with her eyes fixed on Insta. We can be the creators and disseminators of our own narratives, something that would have terrified the old monarchs comfortably ensconced in their narrative. Even the founders would have been extremely nervous about what the masses might get up to.

As mediated citizens, we have unprecedented access to power, but we are also targets of the use of unprecedented power—attempts to shape our views and control our experiences. That means it is up to us to pay critical attention to what is happening in the world around us.

hashtag activism a form of political engagement that occurs by organizing individuals online around a particular issue

information bubble a closed cycle, sometimes self-created, in which all the information we get reinforces the information we already have, solidifying our beliefs without reference to outside reality checks

Your Own Information Bubble

Technologies that enable citizens to connect with one another, to engage in lively debate, and to organize for common purposes hold great promise for democracy. The power to communicate on a massive scale was once held only by governments and those with access to print or broadcast media outlets, but today it is in the hands of anyone who has access to a cell phone. As every superhero learns quickly, along with great power comes great responsibility. There is no guarantee that what you learn through social media is true, and if you are sharing information that isn't reality based, you are helping to perpetuate a false narrative.

In addition, your social media feeds and even your browser are working against you, ensuring that the news that comes your way is tailored to your interests and preconceptions, creating what one observer calls a *filter bubble*.[11] Whether your news feed is custom made or crowd-sourced, always look before you "like" since social media algorithms can channel information to you that reinforces the narrative you get about "who gets what, and how" in today's political world.

WHAT TO WATCH OUT FOR

- **Don't create your own echo chamber.** Social networking sites and other tools make it easy to create your own custom news channel, ensuring that you see stories from sources you like, about subjects that interest you. Important stories can easily slip past you, and your understanding of political matters will suffer. But if you follow only the political sources you like, that will get you in trouble, too. So open yourself up to alternative sources of news and opinions that you might find offensive or wrong. If what's showing up in your news feed does not challenge your ideas and beliefs from time to time, consider whether you've been censoring news that you don't like. Make sure you're getting all sides of the story, not just the one that you want to hear.[12]

- **Don't trust your browser.** It's not just your self-selected social media feeds that are shaping your information diet: every link you click and word you search is fed into complex algorithms that tailor your results into a custom feed of "things you might like." Just as Amazon knows what items to suggest on your personal Amazon front page based on your browsing and purchase history, your Google results are similarly parsed and packaged for your viewing pleasure. Two people searching on a particular topic may get very different results.[13] Search around—don't just click on the first links offered to you.

- **Separate truth from truthiness.** Some of the most compelling (and viral) political material on the Internet comes from people who are intent on selling you on their narrative. Their arguments may be valid, and their evidence may be strong— but bear in mind that an opinion piece is different from a statement of fact. Take care to seek out news sources that strive for objectivity and don't have an ax to grind (such as the Associated Press or the *news* pages of the *New York Times,* the *Wall Street Journal,* or Politico) alongside those that offer analysis and argument.

In Your Own Words   Describe the enduring tension in the United States between self-interested human nature and public-spirited government and the way that has been shaped in a mediated world.

WHO IS A CITIZEN AND WHO IS NOT?

Native-born and naturalized citizens

Citizenship is not just a normative concept—that is, a prescription for how governments ought to treat residents and how those residents ought to act. It is also a very precise legal status. A fundamental element of democracy is not only the careful specification of the rights granted and the obligations incurred in citizenship but also an equally careful legal description of just who is a citizen and how that status can be acquired by noncitizens.

If you are born in any of the fifty states, in the District of Columbia, or in most of America's overseas territories, such as Puerto Rico or Guam, you are an American citizen, whether your parents are Americans or not and whether they are here legally or not. This rule follows the principle of international law called *jus soli,* which means literally "the right of the soil." The exceptions to this rule in the United States are children born to foreign diplomats serving in the United States and children born on foreign ships in U.S. waters. These children would not be considered U.S. citizens. According to another legal principle, *jus sanguinis* ("the right by blood"), if you are born outside the United States to American parents, you are also an American citizen (or you can become one if you are adopted by American parents). Interestingly, if you are born in the United States but one of your parents holds citizenship in another country, you may be able to hold dual citizenship, depending on that country's laws. Most countries, including the United States, require that a child with dual citizenship declare allegiance to one country on turning age eighteen. It is worth noting that requirements for U.S. citizenship, particularly as they affect people born outside the country, have changed frequently over time.

So far, citizenship seems relatively straightforward. But as we know, the United States since before its birth has been attractive to **immigrants**, people who are citizens or subjects of another country who come here to live and work. Today there are strict limitations on the numbers of immigrants who may legally enter the country. There are also strict rules governing the criteria for entry. If immigrants come here legally on permanent resident visas—that is, if they follow the rules and regulations of the U.S. Citizenship and Immigration Services (USCIS)—they may be eligible to apply for citizenship through a process called **naturalization**.

However, many people who come to the United States do not come as legal permanent residents. The USCIS refers to these people as nonimmigrants. Some arrive seeking asylum, or protection. These are political refugees, who are allowed into the United States if they face or are threatened with persecution because of their race, religion, nationality, membership in a particular social group, or political opinions. Not everyone who feels threatened is given legal **refugee** status, however. The USCIS requires that the fear of persecution be "well founded," and it is itself the final judge of a well-founded fear. Claiming refugee status can be an intensely political act, as evidenced by President Trump's attempt to blame Democrats for the 2018 border crisis caused by his own administration's policy of separating children from their parents in an effort to deter refugees.[14] Refugees may become legal permanent residents after they have lived here continuously for one year (although there are annual limits on the number who may do so), at which time they can begin accumulating the in-residence time required to become a citizen, if they wish to.

Other people who may come to the United States legally but without official permanent resident status include visitors, foreign government officials, students, international representatives, temporary workers, members of foreign media, and exchange visitors. These people are expected to return to their home countries and not take up permanent residence in the United States.

immigrants citizens or subjects of one country who move to another country to live or work

naturalization the legal process of acquiring citizenship for someone who has not acquired it by birth

refugees individuals who flee an area or a country because of persecution on the basis of race, nationality, religion, group membership, or political opinion

PROFILES IN CITIZENSHIP:
Jose Antonio Vargas

Gerry Salva-Cruz

Born in the Philippines, Jose Antonio Vargas was sent by his mother to the United States at age twelve to live with his grandparents, both naturalized U.S. citizens. Until he went to get his driver's license, Vargas had no idea that the papers that had gotten him into the country were fake, paid for by his family in the hopes of giving him a better life.

And his life was great, except for the weight of the secret he carried, forced into a virtual closet and afraid to let anyone except for a few trusted confidants close enough to know him. Even when he became a successful journalist and part of a Pulitzer Prize–winning team at the *Washington Post*, his anxiety about having his secret revealed was so debilitating that in 2011 he decided to come out of the shadows in a long and moving essay in the *New York Times Sunday Magazine*. (The *Post* was afraid to publish the essay because of possible legal repercussions for having hired him.)

So far, Vargas is still here, for the most part left to himself by immigration authorities, and he has made himself a voice for the voice-less, founding the nonprofit Define American and working as an immigration-rights activist and a filmmaker. He has become an entrepreneur because, as an undocumented worker, he can employ others but cannot be hired himself.

On living in the shadows

"I was risking my sanity, I think. And I think I was risking my sense of self. It was almost as if I had to create a different person that had to lie to all of my friends. You know I was the kind of person who, if you had known me six years ago, I just never talked about my family, there were no photos of them anywhere in my house. I never talked about where I was from because, if you talk about where you're from, then it's gonna come up. Well, how'd you get here?"

On the meaning of citizenship

"I just hope that young people in this country do not take their citizenship for granted. And I hope that they realize what was paid for it—literally and figuratively, what paved the way for them to be free. And that freedom isn't comfortable ... [T]here's this quote from Toni Morrison and I didn't realize she got it from [James] Baldwin. The quote was, 'Your crown has been bought and paid for. Your ancestors already gave it up for you. It's already done. Now you can love yourself. It's possible.'"

On keeping the republic

"To me, this country has always been an experiment. It was and it is still an experiment...I think this question of how we define 'American' is at the very core of this republic and how we keep it. Is it laws? Is it papers?"

Source: Vargas spoke with Christine Barbour and Gerald C. Wright on May 13, 2016.

Undocumented immigrants have arrived here by avoiding the USCIS regulations, usually because they would not qualify for one reason or another. Many come as children who, like Jose Antonio Vargas, the subject of this chapter's *Profiles in Citizenship* feature, may not even know they do not have the proper papers. After Congress repeatedly failed to pass the DREAM Act, which would have given permanent legal status to thousands of young adults who were brought to the United States illegally as children, President Obama created the Deferred Action for Childhood Arrivals (DACA) program, which allowed them to stay in the country and go to school or work. The Trump administration is locked in a court battle to end the program, leaving these young adults mostly in political limbo. Congress has so far been unwilling to find a solution for fear of angering constituents, even though a large majority of Americans support allowing the "dreamers" to stay in the country.

American laws have become increasingly harsh with respect to undocumented immigrants. Even so, people continue to come, although the numbers have declined in recent years. Many undocumented immigrants act like citizens, obeying laws, paying taxes, and sending their children to school. Nonetheless, some areas of the country, particularly those near the Mexican-American border, like Texas, California, and Arizona, often have serious problems brought on by those who skirt the immigration laws. Even with border controls to regulate the number of new arrivals, communities can find themselves swamped with new residents, often poor and unskilled, looking for a better life. Because their children must be educated and they themselves may be entitled to receive social services, they can pose a significant financial burden on those communities without necessarily increasing the available funds. Although many undocumented immigrants pay taxes, many also work off the books, meaning they do not contribute to the tax base. Furthermore, most income taxes are federal, and federal money is distributed back to states and localities to fund social services based on the population count in the census. Since undocumented immigrants are understandably reluctant to come forward to be counted, their communities are typically underfunded in that respect as well.

Even people without legal permanent resident status have rights and responsibilities in the United States, just as U.S. citizens do when they travel to other countries. Immigrants enjoy some rights, primarily legal protections. Not only are they entitled to due process in the courts, but the U.S. Supreme Court has ruled that it is illegal to discriminate against immigrants in the United States.[15] Nevertheless, their rights are limited. They cannot, for instance, vote in our national elections (although some localities, in the hopes of integrating immigrants into their communities, allow them to vote in local elections[16]) or decide to live here permanently without permission (which may or may not be granted). In addition, immigrants, even legal ones, are subject to the decisions of the USCIS, which is empowered by Congress to exercise authority in immigration matters.

In Your Own Words Analyze the role of immigration and citizenship in American politics.

WHAT DO AMERICAN CITIZENS BELIEVE?

A common culture based on shared values

Making a single nation out of a diverse group of people is no easy feat. It is possible only because, despite all our differences, Americans share some fundamental attitudes and beliefs about how the world works and how it should work. These ideas, our political culture, pull us together and, indeed, provide a framework in which we can also disagree politically over who gets what without resorting to violence and civil war.

AMERICAN POLITICAL CULTURE: IDEAS THAT UNITE US

Political culture refers to the general political orientation or disposition of a nation—the shared values and beliefs about the nature of the political world that give us a common language in which to discuss and debate political ideas. Values are ideals or principles that most people agree are important, even though they may disagree on exactly how the value—such as "equality" or "freedom"—ought to be defined. Note that statements about values and beliefs are not descriptive of

political culture the broad pattern of ideas, beliefs, and values that a population holds about citizens and government

values central ideas, principles, or standards that most people agree are important

Free Speech, Even When It's Ugly

Americans don't agree on much, but they do cherish their right to disagree: most citizens have little tolerance for censorship and expect the government to protect even the most offensive speech. Here, a police officer flanks a marcher at a Ku Klux Klan rally in South Carolina in 2015.

how the world actually is but rather are prescriptive, or **normative**, statements about how the value-holders believe the world ought to be. Our culture consists of deep-seated, collectively held ideas about how life should be lived. Normative statements aren't true or false but depend for their worth on the arguments made to back them up. Often we take our own culture (that is, our common beliefs about how the world should work) so much for granted that we aren't even aware of it. For that reason, it is often easier to see our own political culture by contrasting it to another.

Political culture is handed down from generation to generation, through families, schools, communities, literature, churches and synagogues, and so on, helping to provide stability for the nation by ensuring that a majority of citizens are well grounded in and committed to the basic values that sustain it. We talk about the process through which values are transferred in Chapter 10, "Public Opinion."

Although political culture is shared, some individuals certainly find themselves at odds with it. When we say, "Americans think . . . ," we mean that most Americans hold those views, not that there is unanimous agreement on them. To the extent that we are increasingly politically polarized—that is, to the extent that our political differences get farther apart—the political culture itself may begin to break down and we may lose the common language that enables us to settle those differences through conventional political means. The 2016 election campaign showed us just how fragile the cultural ties that bind us can be when our differences are stoked and the legitimacy of our system is challenged.

In American political culture, our expectations of government focus on rules and processes rather than on results. For example, we think government should guarantee a fair playing field but not guarantee equal outcomes for all the players. In addition, we believe that individuals are responsible for their own welfare and that what is good for them is good for society as a whole. Our insistence on fair rules is the same emphasis on *procedural guarantees* we saw in our earlier discussion of capitalism, whereas the belief in the primacy of the individual citizen is called **individualism**. American culture is not wholly procedural and individualistic—indeed, differences on these matters constitute some of the major partisan divisions in American politics—but it tends to be more so than is the case in most other nations.

When we say that American political culture is procedural, we mean that Americans generally think government should guarantee fair processes—such as a free market to distribute goods, majority rule to make decisions, and due process to determine guilt and innocence—rather than specific outcomes. By contrast, people in the social democratic countries of Sweden, Norway, and Denmark typically believe that government should actively seek to realize the values of equality—perhaps to guarantee a certain quality of life for all citizens or to increase equality of income. American politics does set some substantive goals for public policy, but Americans are generally more comfortable ensuring that things are done in a fair and proper way, and trusting that the outcomes will be good ones because the rules are fair. Although the American government gets involved in social programs and welfare, and took a big step in a substantive direction with passage of the Patient Protection and Affordable Care Act, it aims more at helping

normative a term used to describe beliefs or values about how things should be or what people ought to do rather than what actually is

individualism the belief that what is good for society is based on what is good for individuals

individuals get on their feet so that they can participate in the market (fair procedures) rather than at cleaning up slums or eliminating poverty (substantive goals). The individualistic nature of American political culture means that individuals, not government or society, are seen as responsible for their own well-being. This notion contrasts

Should it be possible to lose one's citizenship under any circumstances?

with a collectivist social democratic point of view, which holds that what is good for society may not be the same as what is in the interest of individuals. Thus our politics revolves around the belief that individuals are usually the best judges of what is good for themselves; we assume that what is good for society will automatically follow. American government rarely asks citizens to make major economic sacrifices for the public good, although individuals often do so privately and voluntarily. Where Americans are asked to make economic sacrifices, like paying taxes, they are unpopular and more modest than in most other countries. A collective interest that supersedes individual interests is generally invoked in the United States only in times of war or national crisis. This echoes the two American notions of self-interested and collectivist citizenship we discussed earlier. Collectivist citizenship is rarer in the United States precisely because we're such an individualistic culture.

We can see our American procedural and individualistic perspective when we examine the different meanings of three core American values: democracy, freedom, and equality.

DEMOCRACY Democracy in America, as we have seen, means representative democracy, based on consent and majority rule. Basically, American democracy is a procedure for making political decisions, for choosing political leaders, and for selecting policies for the nation. It is seen as a fundamentally just or fair way of making decisions because every individual who cares to participate is heard in the process, and all interests are considered. We don't reject a democratically made decision because it is not fair; it is fair precisely because it is democratically made. Democracy is valued primarily not for the way it makes citizens feel, or the effects it has on them, but for the decisions it produces. Americans see democracy as the appropriate procedure for making public decisions—that is, decisions about government—but generally not for decisions in the private realm. Rarely do employees have a binding vote on company policy, for example, as they do in some Scandinavian countries.

FREEDOM Americans also put a very high premium on the value of freedom, defined as freedom for the individual from restraint by the state. This view of freedom is procedural in the sense that it holds that no unfair restrictions should be put in the way of your pursuit of what you want, but it does not guarantee you any help in achieving those things. For instance, when Americans say, "We are all free to get a job," we mean that no discriminatory laws or other legal barriers are stopping us from applying for any particular position. A substantive view of freedom would ensure us the training to get a job so that our freedom meant a positive opportunity, not just the absence of restraint. Americans' extraordinary commitment can be seen nowhere so clearly as in the Bill of Rights, the first ten amendments to the U.S. Constitution, which guarantees our basic civil liberties, the areas where government cannot interfere with individual action. (See Chapter 4, "Fundamental American Liberties," for a complete discussion of our civil liberties.) Finally, our proceduralism is echoed in the value we attach to economic freedom, the freedom to participate in the marketplace, to acquire money and property, and to do with those resources pretty much as we please. Americans believe that government should protect our property, not take it away or regulate our use of it too heavily. Our commitment to individualism is apparent here, too. Even if society as a whole would be better off if we paid down the federal debt (the amount our government owes from spending more than it brings in), our individualistic view of economic freedom means that Americans have one of the lowest tax rates in the industrialized world. This reflects our national tendency in normal times to emphasize the rights of citizenship over its obligations.

EQUALITY A third central value in American political culture is equality. For Americans, equality is valued not because we want individuals to be the same but because we want them to be treated the same. Equality in America means government should guarantee equality of treatment, of access, and of opportunity, not equality of result. People should have equal access to run the race, but we don't expect them all to finish in the same place. Thus we believe in political equality (one person, one vote) and equality before the law—that the law shouldn't make unreasonable distinctions among people the basis for treating them differently, and that all people should have equal access to the legal system. One problem the courts have faced is deciding what counts as a reasonable distinction. Can the law justifiably discriminate between—that is, treat differently—men and women, minorities and white Protestants, rich and poor, young and old? When the rules treat people differently, even if the goal is to make them more equal in the long run, many Americans get very upset. Witness the controversy surrounding affirmative action policies in this country. The point of such policies is to allow special opportunities to members of groups that have been discriminated against in the past, in order to remedy the long-term effects of that discrimination. For many Americans, such policies violate our commitment to procedural solutions. They wonder how treating people unequally can be fair.

AMERICAN IDEOLOGIES: IDEAS THAT DIVIDE US

Most Americans are united in their commitment to proceduralism and individualism at some level, and to the key values of democracy, freedom, and equality. This shared political culture gives us a common political language, a way to talk about politics that keeps us united even though we may use that common language to tell different narratives about who we are, what's important to us, or what direction we feel the country should move in.

The sets of beliefs and opinions about politics, the economy, and society that help people make sense of their world, and that can divide them into opposing camps, are called ideologies. Again, like the values and beliefs that underlie our culture, our ideologies are based on normative prescriptions. Remember that one of the reasons we can disagree so passionately on political issues is that normative statements about the world are not true or false, good or bad—instead, they depend for their force on the arguments we make to defend them. We cannot even pretend to live in a Norman Rockwell world where we learn our values face to face at our parents' dinner table. In a mediated age there are more and more arguments from more and more channels that are harder and harder to sort out. While it might seem clear as a bell to us that our values are right and true, to a person who disagrees with our prescriptions, we are as wrong as they think we are. And so we debate and argue. In fact, anyone who pays attention to American politics knows that we disagree about many specific political ideas and issues, and that our differences have gotten more passionate and polarized (that is, farther apart) in recent years.

But because we share that political culture, the range of debate in the United States is relatively narrow. We have no successful communist or socialist parties here, for instance. The ideologies on which those parties are founded seem unappealing to most Americans because they violate the norms of procedural and individualistic culture. The two main ideological camps in the United States are the liberals (associated, since the 1930s, with the Democratic Party) and the conservatives (associated with the Republicans), with many Americans falling somewhere in between. But because we are all part of American political culture, we are still

ideologies sets of beliefs about politics and society that help people make sense of their world

procedural and individualistic, and we still believe in democracy, freedom, and equality, even if we are also liberals or conservatives. Even though Bernie Sanders, a self-identified democratic socialist, ran for president in 2016, he did it as a Democrat (a party he had joined only briefly, to run), and he lost the nomination to Hillary Clinton.

There are lots of different ways of characterizing American ideologies. It is conventional to say that conservatives promote a political narrative based on traditional social values, distrust of government action except in matters of national security, resistance to change, and the maintenance of a prescribed social order. Liberals, in contrast, are understood to tell a narrative based on the potential of progress and change, trust in government, innovations as answers to social problems, and the expansion of individual rights and expression. For a more nuanced understanding of ideology in America, however, we can focus on the two main ideological dimensions of economics and social order issues.

Traditionally we have understood ideology to be centered on differences in economic views, much like those located on our economic continuum (see Figure 1.1). Based on these economic ideological dimensions, we often say that the liberals who take a more positive view of government action and advocate a large role for government in regulating the economy are on the far left, and those conservatives, more suspicious of government, who think government control should be minimal are on the far right. Because we lack any widespread radical socialist traditions in the United States, both American liberals and conservatives are found on the right side of the broader economic continuum.

In the 1980s and 1990s, another ideological dimension became prominent in the United States. Perhaps because, as some researchers have argued, most people are able to meet their basic economic needs, many Americans began to focus less on economic questions and more on issues of morality and quality of life. The new ideological dimension, which is analogous to the social order dimension we discussed earlier, divides people on the question of how much control government should have over the moral and social order—whether government's role should be limited to protecting individual rights and providing procedural guarantees of equality and due process, or whether the government should be involved in making more substantive judgments about how people should live their lives.

Few people in the United States want to go so far as to allow government to make all moral and political decisions for its subjects, but there are some who hold that it is the government's job to create and protect a preferred social order, although visions of what that preferred order should be may differ. Clearly this social order ideological dimension does not dovetail neatly with the more traditional liberal and conservative orientations toward government action. Figure 1.5 shows some of the ideological positions that are yielded by these two dimensions, though note that this figure shows a detail of the broader political spectrum that we saw in Figure 1.3 and is focused on the narrower spectrum commonly found in an advanced industrial democracy.

Economic liberals hold views that fall into the upper-left quadrant of the figure because they are willing to allow government to make substantive decisions about the economy, and they tend to embrace procedural individualistic positions on the social order dimension. Some economic policies they favor are job training and housing subsidies for the poor, taxation to support social programs, and affirmative action to ensure that *opportunities* for economic success (but not necessarily outcomes) are truly equal. As far as government regulation of individuals' private lives goes, however, these liberals favor a hands-off stance, preferring

> *Do ideological differences strengthen or weaken a political culture?*

conservatives people who generally favor limited government and are cautious about change

liberals people who generally favor government action and view change as progress

economic liberals those who favor an expanded government role in the economy but a limited role in the social order

individuals to have maximum freedom over their noneconomic affairs. They are willing to let government regulate such behaviors as murder, rape, and theft, but they believe that social order issues such as reproductive choices, marijuana usage, gay rights, and assisted suicide are not matters for government regulation. They value diversity, expanding rights for people who have historically been left out of the power structure in the American social order—women, minorities, gays, and immigrants. Their love for their country is tempered by the view that the government should be held to the same strict procedural standard to which individuals are held—laws must be followed, checks and balances adhered to in order to limit government power, and individual rights protected, even when the individuals are citizens of another country.

Economic conservatives, in the upper-right quadrant of the figure, share their liberal counterparts' reluctance to allow government interference in people's private lives, but they combine this with a conviction that government should limit involvement in the economy as well. These economic conservatives prefer government to limit its role in economic decision making to regulation of the market (like changing interest rates and cutting taxes to end recessions), elimination of "unfair" trade practices such as monopolies, and provision of some public goods such as highways and national defense. When it comes to immigration, they favor more open policies, since immigrants often work more cheaply and help keep the labor market competitive for business. The most extreme holders of economic conservative views are called **libertarians**, people who believe that only minimal government action in any sphere is acceptable. Consequently, economic conservatives also hold the government accountable for sticking to the constitutional checks and balances that limit its own power.

Social liberals, in the lower-left quadrant of the figure, tend to favor a substantive government role in achieving a more equal distribution of material resources (such as welfare programs and health care for the poor) but carry that substantive perspective into the social order as well. Although they continue to want the freedom to make individual moral choices that economic liberals want, they are happy to see some government action to create a more diverse and more equal power structure (including the way different groups are treated in the media and popular culture) and to regulate individual behavior to enhance health and safety (promoting environmental protections, motorcycle helmets, gun control, food labeling, restrictions on how food is produced, and the like). The most extreme adherents of social liberalism are sometimes called **communitarians** for their strong commitment to a community based on radical equality of all people. Because American political culture is procedural both economically and socially, not a lot of Americans are strong adherents of an ideology that calls for a substantive government role in both dimensions. Many economic liberals, however, pick up some of the policy prescriptions of social liberals, like environmentalism and gun control, but do not embrace their more extreme forms of communitarianism.

Social conservatives occupy the lower-right quadrant in our ideological scheme. These people share economic conservatives' views on limited government involvement in the economy but with less force and commitment and perhaps for different reasons. (In fact, many social conservatives, as members of the working class, were once liberals under Franklin Roosevelt's New Deal in the 1930s.) They may very well support government social programs like Social Security or Medicaid for those they consider deserving. Their primary concern is with their vision of the moral tone of life, including an emphasis on fundamentalist values of a variety of religions (demonstrated, for instance, by

economic conservatives those who favor a strictly procedural government role in the economy and the social order

libertarians those who favor a minimal government role in any sphere

social liberals those who favor greater control of the economy and the social order to bring about greater equality and to regulate the effects of progress

communitarians those who favor a strong, substantive government role in the economy and the social order in order to realize their vision of a community of equals

social conservatives those who endorse limited government control of the economy but considerable government intervention to realize a traditional social order; based on religious values and hierarchy rather than equality

FIGURE 1.5

Ideological Beliefs in the United States

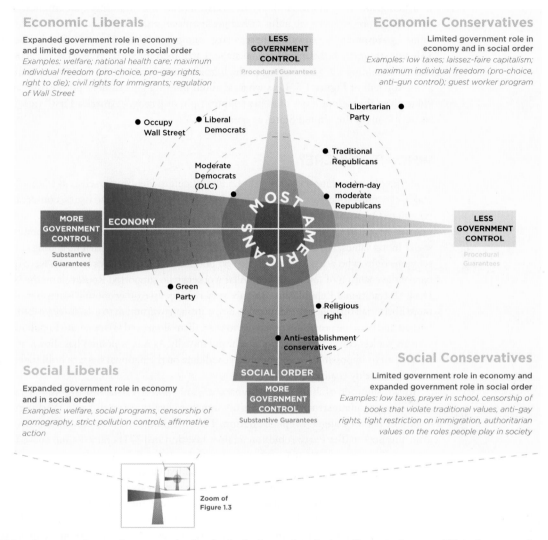

Economic Liberals

Expanded government role in economy and limited government role in social order
Examples: welfare; national health care; maximum individual freedom (pro-choice, pro-gay rights, right to die); civil rights for immigrants; regulation of Wall Street

Economic Conservatives

Limited government role in economy and in social order
Examples: low taxes; laissez-faire capitalism; maximum individual freedom (pro-choice, anti-gun control); guest worker program

LESS GOVERNMENT CONTROL
Procedural Guarantees

• Libertarian Party

• Occupy Wall Street   • Liberal Democrats

• Traditional Republicans

Moderate Democrats (DLC)

Modern-day moderate Republicans

MOST AMERICANS

MORE GOVERNMENT CONTROL
ECONOMY
Substantive Guarantees

LESS GOVERNMENT CONTROL
Procedural Guarantees

• Green Party

• Religious right

• Anti-establishment conservatives

Social Conservatives

Limited government role in economy and expanded government role in social order
Examples: low taxes, prayer in school, censorship of books that violate traditional values, anti-gay rights, tight restriction on immigration, authoritarian values on the roles people play in society

Social Liberals

Expanded government role in economy and in social order
Examples: welfare, social programs, censorship of pornography, strict pollution controls, affirmative action

SOCIAL ORDER
MORE GOVERNMENT CONTROL
Substantive Guarantees

Zoom of Figure 1.3

Although committed generally to a procedural and individualistic political culture (this entire figure would fit in the upper-right quadrant of Figure 1.3), Americans still find plenty of room for political disagreement. This figure outlines the two main dimensions of that conflict: beliefs about government's role in the economy and beliefs about government's role in establishing a preferred social order. Those ideological beliefs on the right side of the figure are conservative beliefs, and those on the left side are more liberal. The axes in these figures are continuums and do not represent all-or-nothing positions; most Americans fall somewhere in between.

government control of reproductive choices, opposition to gay rights, and promotion of public prayer and the display of religious icons). They endorse traditional family roles, and a rejection of change or diversity that they see as destructive to the preferred social order. Immigration is threatening because it brings into the system people who are different and threatens to dilute the majority that keeps the social order in place. Social conservatives seek to protect people's moral character rather than their physical or economic well-being, and they embrace an authoritarian notion of community that emphasizes a hierarchical order (everyone in his or her proper place) rather than equality for all. Since limited government is not valued here, a large and powerful state is appreciated as being a sign of strength on the international stage. Patriotism for social conservatives is not a matter of holding the government to the highest procedural standards, as it is for those at the top half of Figure 1.5. Less worried about limiting government power over individual lives, they adopt more of a "my country right or wrong," "America First" view that sees criticism of the United States as unpatriotic.

WHO FITS WHERE?

Many people, indeed most of us, might find it difficult to identify ourselves as simply "liberal" or "conservative," because we consider ourselves liberal on some issues, conservative on others. Others of us have more pronounced views. The framework in Figure 1.5 allows us to see how major groups in society might line up if we distinguish between economic and social-moral values. We can see, for instance, the real spatial distances that lie among (1) the religious right, who are very conservative on political and moral issues but who were once part of the coalition of southern blue-collar workers who supported Roosevelt on the New Deal; (2) traditional Republicans, who are very conservative on economic issues but often more libertarian on political and moral issues, wanting government to guarantee procedural fairness and keep the peace, but otherwise to leave them alone; and (3) moderate Republicans, who are far less conservative economically and morally. As recent politics has shown, it can be difficult or impossible for a Republican candidate on the national stage to hold together such an unwieldy coalition.

In the summer of 2009, with the nation in economic crisis and the new African American president struggling to pass his signature health care reform in Washington, a wave of populist anger swept the nation. The so-called Tea Party movement (named after the Boston Tea Party rebellion against taxation in 1773) crafted a narrative that was pro-American, anticorporation, and antigovernment (except for programs like Social Security and Medicare, which benefit the Tea Partiers, who tended to be older Americans). Mostly it was angry, fed by emotional appeals of conservative talk show hosts and others, whose narratives took political debate out of the range of logic and analysis and into the world of emotional drama and angry invective. A *New York Times* poll found that Americans who identified as Tea Party supporters were more likely to be Republican, white, married, male, and over forty-five, and to hold views that were more conservative than Republicans generally.[17] In fact, they succeeded in shaking up the Republican Party from 2010 onward, as they supported primary challenges to officeholders who did not share their antigovernment ideology, culminating in the rejection of the party establishment in 2016. The election that year signaled a moment of reckoning for a party that had been teetering on the edge of crisis for more than a decade. As establishment candidates like former Florida governor Jeb Bush and Ohio governor John Kasich fell in the primaries, so too did Tea Party favorites like Florida senator Marco Rubio and Texas senator Ted Cruz. The split in the party left an opening for the very unconventional candidacy of Donald Trump, which—much to the dismay of party leaders like Speaker of the House Paul Ryan and Senate majority leader Mitch McConnell—proved to be more about Trump's personality and the anger of his followers than it did about the Republican Party, although in the end most party members fell in line to vote for him.

The escalating anger of social conservatives who felt inadequately represented by the Republican Party's mainstream came to a peak in the anti-establishment fury displayed in 2016. During that primary season, both Donald Trump and Texas senator Ted Cruz competed to address the anger that drove that group. They felt used and betrayed, especially by a party that had promised and failed to defeat Barack Obama, a president they viewed as illegitimate, partly because of Trump's challenge to the president's birth certificate. The rage of social conservatives seemed to be one of **authoritarian populism**, a mix of populist anger against the economic elite who profited at their expense; nativist anger at the perception that whites seemed to be falling behind while government was reaching out to help people of color; and partisan anger that, since the days of Richard Nixon, economic conservative Republicans had been promising them socially conservative accomplishments without delivering.

Indeed, social scientists trying to understand the surprising phenomenon of the Trump vote found that one particular characteristic predicted it: a commitment to "authoritarian values."[18] These social scientists have found that some social conservatives, when they feel that the proper order and power hierarchy are threatened, either physically or existentially, are attracted to authoritarian narratives that seek to secure the old order by excluding the perceived danger. In the words of one scholar who studies this, the response is, "In case of moral threat, lock down the borders, kick out those who are different, and punish those who are morally deviant."[19] Those who score higher on the authoritarianism scale hold the kind of ideas one would expect from social conservatives seeking to keep faith with a familiar and traditional order—antigay sentiment, anti-immigration views, even white supremacy and overt racism. Interestingly, authoritarianism has been found most recently to correspond to narratives that reject the idea of political correctness, a reaction to the sense that expressing fear and anger about perceived threats is not socially acceptable.[20]

Although there have been major splits in the Democratic coalition in the past, their current divisions are minor, even after an election season when a self-avowed democratic socialist who was not even a party member challenged a more moderate liberal. The Democrats have to satisfy the party's *economic liberals*, who are very procedural on most political and moral issues (barring affirmative action) but relatively (for Americans) substantive on economic concerns; the *social liberals*, substantive on both economic and social issues; and the more middle-of-the-road Democratic groups that are fairly procedural on political and moral issues but not very substantive on economic matters at all. In the late 1960s, the party almost shattered under the weight of anti–Vietnam War sentiment, and in 1972 it moved sharply left, putting it out of the American mainstream. It was President Bill Clinton, as a founder of the now-defunct Democratic Leadership Council (DLC), who in the 1990s helped move his party closer to the mainstream from a position that, as we can see in Figure 1.5, is clearly out of alignment with the position taken by most Americans. Whereas Al Gore, himself a DLC-er, faced a threat from the more extreme segments on the left in 2000, in the 2004 and 2008 presidential races, dislike of George W. Bush united Democrats across their party's ideological spectrum, and recent

authoritarian populism a radical right-wing movement that appeals to popular discontent but whose underlying values are not democratic

Democratic contenders for the presidency have not had to deal with serious interparty conflict. Hillary Clinton's loss of the presidency in 2016 has caused the party to do some soul-searching about where it goes post-Obama.

WHERE DO YOU FIT?

One of the notable aspects of American ideology is that it often shows generational effects. Although we have to be careful when we say that a given generation begins definitively in a certain year (there is much overlap and evolution between generations), it can be helpful to look for patterns in where people stand in order to understand political trends. We know, for instance, that older white Americans tend to be more ideologically conservative, and because they are reliable voters, they get a lot of media attention. But with researchers gathering public opinion data on younger voters, and with those voters promising to turn out on issues they care about, it's a good idea to look at where millennials and post-millennials fall in Figure 1.5.

Keep in mind that all we can do is talk about generalities here—obviously there will be many, many exceptions to the rule, and you may very well be one of them. But as a group, younger voters, especially the *youngest* voters, tend to be economically and socially liberal—that is, they fall in the left-hand side of Figure 1.5. If you want to test yourself, take the quiz at edge.sagepub.com/barbour8e/American-ideology-quiz to see where you fall before you look at the positions of your peers.

FIGURE 1.6

Political Ideology, by Generation

% with political values that are . . .

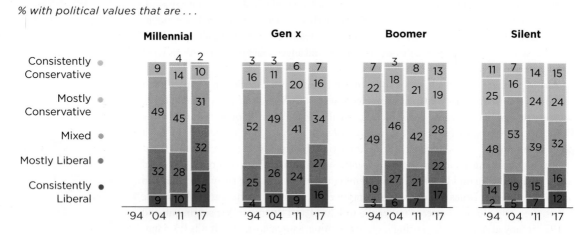

Source: Pew Research Center, "The Generation Gap in American Politics," March 1, 2018, http://www.people-press.org/2018/03/01/the-generation-gap-in-american-politics/.

In Your Own Words Describe values that most Americans share, and the political debates that drive partisan divisions in American politics.

HOW TO USE THE THEMES
AND FEATURES IN THIS BOOK

Our primary goal in this book is to get you thinking critically about American politics—to introduce you to the twin tasks of analysis and evaluation with the aid of the themes of power and citizenship. Lasswell's definition of politics gives us a framework of **analysis** for this book; that is, it outlines how we will break down politics into its component parts in order to understand it. Lasswell's definition provides a strong analytic framework because it focuses our attention on questions we can ask to figure out what is going on in politics.

Accordingly, in this book, we analyze American politics in terms of three sets of questions:

- Who are the parties involved? What resources, powers, and rights do they bring to the struggle?
- What do they have at stake? What do they stand to win or lose? Is it power, influence, position, policy, or values?
- How do the rules shape the outcome? Where do the rules come from? What strategies or tactics do the political actors employ to use the rules to get what they want?

If you know who is involved in a political situation, what is at stake, and how (under what rules) the conflict over resources will eventually be resolved, you will have a pretty good grasp of what is going on, and you will probably be able to figure out new situations, even when your days of taking an American government course are far behind you. To get you in the habit of asking those questions, we have designed some features in this text explicitly to reinforce them.

As you found at the start of your reading, each chapter opens with a *What's at Stake . . . ?* feature that analyzes a political situation in terms of what various groups of citizens stand to win or lose. Each chapter ends with a *Let's Revisit: What's at Stake . . . ?* feature, where we return to the issues raised in the introduction, once you have the substantive material of the chapter under your belt. We reinforce the task of analysis with a *Don't Be Fooled by . . .* feature appearing in some chapters that discusses ways you can improve your **critical thinking** skills by analyzing (that is, taking apart) different kinds of sources of information about politics. The trick to learning how to think critically is to do it. It helps to have a model to follow, however, and we provide one in *The Big Picture* on pages 38–39. *The Big Picture* infographics relate the book's themes to the big concepts, big processes, and big data that will help you make sense of American politics. *Snapshots of America* provide you with a lot more data to help you understand who the American people are, and they include *Behind the Numbers* boxes to help you dig into the question of what challenges our diversity poses for the task of governance.

As political scientists, however, not only do we want to understand how the system works, but we also want to assess *how well* it works. A second task of critical thinking is **evaluation**, or seeing how well something measures up according to a standard or principle. We could choose any number of standards by which to evaluate American politics, but the most relevant, for most of us, is the principle of democracy and the role of citizens.

We can draw on the two traditions of self-interested and public-interested citizenship we have discussed to evaluate the powers, opportunities, and challenges presented to American citizens by the system of government under which they live. In addition to the two competing threads of citizenship in America, we can also look at the kinds of action that citizens engage in and whether they take advantage of the options available to them. The United States has

analysis understanding how something works by breaking it down into its component parts

critical thinking analysis and evaluation of ideas and arguments based on reason and evidence

evaluation assessing how well something works or performs according to a particular standard or yardstick

THE BIG PICTURE:
How to Think Critically

Follow the CLUES
to Critical Thinking

START
Your Comfort Zone

CONSIDER THE SOURCE

ASK YOURSELF

- Where does this information come from?
- Who is the author?
- Who is he or she talking to?
- How do the source and the audience shape the author's perspective?

LAY OUT THE ARGUMENT

ASK YOURSELF

- What argument is the author asking you to accept?
- If you accept the argument, what values are you also buying?
- Does the argument hold together logically?

UNCOVER THE EVIDENCE

ASK YOURSELF

- Did the author do research to back up the conclusions?
- Is there any evidence or data that is not provided that should be there?
- If there is no evidence provided, does there need to be?

*I read it on the Internet.
It must be true.*

*My parents always
watch this TV
station. Of course
it's reliable.*

OCEAN OF EXCUSES

*Arguments sound
like conflict.
I hate conflict.*

*Values are private.
It's rude to pry.*

*Logic gives
me hives!*

*Data means numbers.
Numbers freak me out.*

BRIDGE to ENLIGHTENMENT

*What, do I look like some
kind of detective?*

Who cares? What do I need to know for the test?

SEA OF CONFUSION

There is no way to know what conclusions are right.

Ouch! Thinking is hard work. Wake me up when it's over.

How would I know?

These ideas make me really uncomfortable. They don't click with anything I think I know. Time for a beer!

I don't like this person's values. Why should I care about his or her conclusions?

WISDOM HAPPINESS
SUCCESS BIG BUCKS
GOAL

ASK YOURSELF

- What difference does this argument make to your understanding of the political world?
- How does it affect who gets what and how they get it?
- Was getting this information valuable to you or did it waste your time?

SORT OUT THE POLITICAL SIGNIFICANCE

ASK YOURSELF

- What's the punch line here?
- Did the author convince you that he or she is correct?
- Does accepting the conclusion to this argument require you to change any of your ideas about the world?

EVALUATE THE CONCLUSIONS

elements of the elite, pluralist, and participatory ideals of democracy we discussed earlier, and one way to evaluate citizenship in America is to look at what opportunities for participation exist and whether citizens take advantage of them.

To evaluate how democratic the United States is, we include in each chapter a section called *Citizenship and . . .* , which looks at the changing concept and practice of citizenship in this country with respect to the chapter's subject matter. That feature looks at citizenship from many angles, considering the following types of questions: What role do "the people" have in American politics? How has that role expanded or diminished over time? What kinds of political participation do the rules of American politics (formal and informal) allow, encourage, or require citizens to take? What kinds of political participation are discouraged, limited, or forbidden? Do citizens take advantage of the opportunities for political action that the rules provide them? How do they react to the rules that limit their participation? How do citizens in different times exercise their rights and responsibilities? What do citizens need to do to keep the republic? and How democratic is the United States?

To put all this in perspective, many chapters include another feature that gives you a more concrete idea of what citizen participation might mean on a personal level. *Profiles in Citizenship* introduce you to individuals who have committed a good part of their lives to public service, focusing on what citizenship means to those people and on what they think all citizens can do to keep the republic.

Each of these features is designed to help you to think critically about American politics, either by analyzing power in terms of who gets what, and how, or by evaluating citizenship to determine how well we are following Benjamin Franklin's mandate to keep the republic.

In Your Own Words   Understand the essential reasons for approaching politics from a perspective of critical thinking, analysis, and evaluation.

CITIZENSHIP AND POLITICS

The gap between the democratic narrative and the practice of American politics

One of the core values of American political culture is democracy, an ideal that unites citizens—both those who are born here as well as more newly minted naturalized citizens—in the activity of self-governance. In terms of the right to vote, we have grown more democratic in the past two hundred years. Many more people can participate now—women, African Americans, and eighteen-year-olds. Although it has been subject to some authoritarian battering lately, as have other democracies around the world, our national narrative, one shared by most Americans no matter what our ideological positions, is that we are a strong and active democracy, if not the premier democracy in the world.

> Does it matter to the success of a democracy if relatively few people take an active political role (by paying attention, voting, exchanging political views, and the like)?

The prevailing narrative is that the American notion of democracy doesn't ask much of us except that we pay attention to the news of the day and come together periodically and vote to elect our public officials. But most of us don't even do that. The news we get, as we have seen, is highly mediated by people who are trying to influence our views, American turnout rates (the percentages of people who go to the polls and vote on election days) are abysmally low compared to those of other Western industrialized democracies, and surveys show that many Americans are apathetic toward politics. Even in 2008, a year of unusually high turnout, only about 60 percent of eligible voters cast a vote although, remarkably, that number was almost duplicated in the midterms of 2018.

How does American democracy work with such low rates of participation or interest on the part of the citizenry? One theory, based on the elite notion of democracy described in Chapter 1, claims that it doesn't really matter whether people participate in politics because all important decisions are made by elites—leaders in business, politics, education, the military, and the media. Drawing on the pluralist theory of democracy, another explanation claims that Americans don't need to participate individually because their views are represented in government sufficiently through their membership in various groups. For instance, a citizen may make her views heard through membership in an environmental group, a professional association or labor union, a parent-teacher organization, a veterans' group, a church, or a political party.

By contrast, some educators and social scientists argue that falling levels of involvement, interest, and trust in politics signal a true civic crisis in American politics. They see a swing from the collectivist citizens of republican virtue to the self-interested, individualistic citizens of Madisonian theory so severe that the fabric of American political life is threatened. For instance, Benjamin Barber, discussing the tendency of Americans to take their freedoms for granted and to assume that since they were born free they will naturally remain free, says that citizenship is the "price of liberty."[21] For all the importance of presidents and senators and justices in the American political system, it is the people, the citizens, who are entrusted with "keeping the republic."

The question of how democratic the United States is may seem to be largely an academic one—that is, one that has little or no relevance to your personal life—but it is really a question of who has the power, who is likely to be a winner in the political process. Looked at this way, the question has quite a lot to do with your life, especially as government starts to make more demands on you, and you on it. Are you likely to be a winner or a loser? Are you going to get what you want from the political system? How much power do people like you have to get their way in government?

In Your Own Words   Describe the role and responsibilities of citizens in American politics.

Let's Revisit: What's at Stake . . . ?

We began this chapter by looking at the power of hashtag activism in response to the phenomenal effort of the Parkland students to change the prevailing narrative about guns, increase the involvement of young people in politics, and bring about political change. We asked whether Benjamin Franklin would consider such movements as fulfilling his admonishment to keep the republic. Since then, we have covered a lot of ground, arguing that politics is fundamental to human life and, in fact, makes life easier for us by giving us a nonviolent way to resolve disputes. We pointed out that politics is a method by which power and resources get distributed in society: politics is who gets what and how they get it. Citizens who are aware and involved stand a much better chance of getting what they want from the system than do those who check out or turn away. One clear consequence when young people disregard politics, then, is that they are far less likely to get what they want from the political system. This is exactly what happens.

But the hashtag activists we met in this chapter have been instrumental in changing the narrative of contemporary American politics. As Occupy protester Matt Brandi says:

The objective of Occupy was to change the direction of the national dialogue and debate.... By appearing in strong numbers and generating media interest (both new/social and commercial/mass), Occupy was able to influence the national dialogue. We protested about inequality and exploitation, the corruption of our government by wealth and influence; and while we did not make "demands," people began to talk about inequality, exploitation, and the corruption of democracy. The very way people talked and thought about these issues changed.

What Matt is suggesting was at stake for the Occupy protesters was, in the language of political scientists, agenda setting. A problem not defined as a problem, or not on the national agenda, cannot be solved by public action. It worked for the Occupy protestors who saw income inequality become a major issue between President Obama and his 2012 Republican challenger, Mitt Romney

It was that effort to change the narrative, and to put real political effort behind it, that encouraged the kids in the March for Our Lives project to spend the summer registering young people and getting them fired up to vote for changes in the gun laws. Although the gun laws remain stubbornly the same, the narrative has begun to change. Young people voted in huge numbers for a midterm election and the policy change is likely to follow the change in narrative.

In the same way, the It Gets Better Project helped change the narrative on both bullying and gay rights. In the years since the movement began in 2011, as more and more "mainstream" people have posted videos promising LGBT youth that it does indeed get better, the world in fact *has* gotten better. Certainly, the It Gets Better Project was not solely responsible for these changes, but in significant ways it helped change the narrative that made the changes possible.

And the debates over systemic racism and intersectionality in the 2016 election, at least on the Democratic side, make clear that Black Lives Matter had changed the narrative on race, too. President Obama had been cautious about making race a centerpiece of his administration, but his presidency and the BLM movement freed Hillary Clinton, as candidate, to address it in a more comprehensive way.

These movements highlight the value of grassroots action, and the power of stepping outside the system to put pressure on the status quo to respond to unmet and even previously unvoiced needs. It might not have been what Benjamin Franklin had in mind, but occupying the republic may very well be another means of keeping it.

for CQ Press

Want a better grade?

Get the tools you need to sharpen your study skills. **SAGE edge** offers practice quizzes, eFlashcards, video, and multimedia at **edge.sagepub.com/barbourbrief8e.**

Review

What Is Politics?

Politics (6) is the struggle for **power** (6) and resources in society—who gets what, and how they get it—including control of information via the **media** (6). We can use the tools of politics to allocate scarce resources and to establish our favored vision of the **social order** (6).

Government (7) is an organization set up to exercise **authority** (7)—power that citizens view as **legitimate** (7), or "right"—over a body of people. It is shaped by politics and helps provide the **rules** (8), **norms** (8), and **institutions** (9) that in turn continue to shape the political process. Control of political information—that is, defining the **political narrative** (9) or acting as a **gatekeeper** (10)—is also a crucial form of power.

Politics is different from **economics** (11), which is a system for distributing society's wealth. Economic systems vary in how much control government has over how that distribution takes place, ranging from a **capitalist economy** (12) (or **regulated capitalism** [12], like that of the United States), where the free market reigns but government may provide **procedural guarantees** (12) that the rules are fair, to a **socialist economy** (12), where government makes **substantive guarantees** (12) of what it holds to be fair distributions of material resources. **Social democracy** (13), a market economy that aims to fulfill substantive goals, is in the middle.

Political Systems and the Concept of Citizenship

Economic systems vary according to how much control government has over the economy; political systems vary in how much control government has over individuals' lives and the social order. They range from **totalitarian governments** (14), where an **authoritarian government** (14) might make substantive decisions about how lives are to be lived and the social order arranged, to **anarchy** (15), where there is no control over those things at all. Short of anarchy is **democracy** (15), based on **popular sovereignty** (15), where individuals have considerable individual freedom and the social order provides fair processes rather than specified outcomes. Various economic-political systems include **authoritarian capitalism** (14) and **advanced** industrial democracy (16), as well as **communist democracy** (16), a theoretical possibility with no real-world examples.

An authoritarian government might be a monarchy, a theocracy, a fascist government, or an oligarchy. People who live in such systems are **subjects** (16), unable to claim rights against the government. Theories of democracy—**elite democracy** (15), **pluralist democracy** (15), and **participatory democracy** (15)—vary in how much power they believe individuals do or should have, but all individuals who live under democratic systems are **citizens** (16) because they have fundamental rights that government must protect. The idea that government exists to protect the rights of citizens originated with the idea of a **social contract** (18) between rulers and ruled. The idea that people have individual rights over the power of the state is a hallmark of **classical liberalism** (18).

Democracy in America

The American government is a representative democracy called a **republic** (19). Two visions of citizenship exist in the United States: **self-interested citizenship** (20) holds that individual participation in government should be limited, and that "too much" democracy may be dangerous; **public-interested citizenship** (20) puts its faith in the citizen's ability to act virtuously for the common good. Modern communication and **hashtag activism** (23) have enabled citizens, especially **digital natives** (20), to engage more efficiently with their government and each other, creating new venues for civic engagement and challenging traditional control of the political narrative. However, today's **mediated citizens** (20) rely on self-tailored media streams that can back us into **information bubbles** (23).

Who Is a Citizen and Who Is Not?

Immigrants (25) are citizens or subjects of another country who come to the United States to live and work. Legal immigrants may be eligible to apply for citizenship through the process of **naturalization** (25). Some people arrive here as **refugees** (25) seeking asylum, or protection from persecution, subject to permission from the U.S. Citizenship and Immigration Services.

What Do American Citizens Believe?

Americans share a **political culture** (27)—common **values** (27) and beliefs, or **normative** (28) ideas about how life should be lived, that draw them together. The U.S. political culture emphasizes procedural guarantees and **individualism** (28), the idea that individuals know what is best for themselves. The core values of American culture are democracy, freedom, and equality, all defined through a procedural, individualistic lens.

Within the context of our shared political culture, Americans have divergent beliefs and opinions, called **ideologies** (30), about political and economic affairs. Generally these ideologies are referred to as **conservative** (31) and **liberal** (31), but we can be more specific. Depending on their views about the role of government in the economy and in establishing the social order, most Americans can be defined as one of the following: **economic liberals** (31); **economic conservatives** (32), including **libertarians** (32); **social liberals** (32), including **communitarians** (32); or **social conservatives** (32). Others may support **authoritarian populism** (35), a movement whose underlying values are not democratic. In a two-party political system like ours, it can be hard for either party to maintain the support of a majority when ideologies are so diverse.

How to Use the Themes and Features in This Book

The goal of this book is to teach **critical thinking** (37) about American politics using the tools of **analysis** (37) and **evaluation** (37). We will analyze how American politics works through the framework of our definition of politics—who gets power and resources, and how they get them. We will evaluate how well American politics works by focusing on the opportunities and challenges of citizenship.

2

The Politics of the American Founding

In Your Own Words

After you've read this chapter, you will be able to

2.1 Outline the events and political motivations that led to the colonies' split from England.

2.2 Explain the competing narratives under the Articles of Confederation.

2.3 Identify the competing narratives, goals, and compromises that shaped the Constitution.

2.4 Explain the system of separation of powers and checks and balances.

2.5 Summarize the debate over ratification of the Constitution.

2.6 Evaluate the narratives told about the founding of the United States.

What's at Stake ... in Challenging the Legitimacy of the Government?

Declaring war on the U.S. government is a risky business. Governments depend for their authority on people believing their power is legitimate—when that legitimacy is challenged, so is their authority. Still, the United States is a democracy that guarantees free speech and the right to assemble peacefully, so handling rebellion can be tricky.

That was why the federal government reacted cautiously when Ammon Bundy, leader of a militia group called Citizens for Constitutional Freedom and the son of antigovernment activist Cliven Bundy, responded to what he said was a divine instruction to take over the Malheur National Wildlife Refuge in eastern Oregon on January 2, 2016. Bundy said he was acting to support two ranchers who had been arrested for arson on federal land, though the ranchers disavowed the group. Specifically, Bundy demanded that the wildlife refuge land be given back to the state.

The federal government, which owned the land but was wary of causing a bloody showdown, waited. As various militias came to join the effort, police were able to apprehend Bundy and several of the other leaders traveling in a convoy. Although one person was shot and killed, most surrendered and the siege ended on February 28.[1]

The Malheur National Wildlife Refuge occupation reflected a movement that has gained traction in recent years: declaring that the federal government is abusing the power of the Constitution, and that that power must be returned to the people via the action of private citizens. Timothy McVeigh's 1995 attack on the federal building in Oklahoma City, which killed 168 people, including 19 children, was the bloodiest incident in the antigovernment movement, but the broadest and strongest expression is the Tea Party movement, some of whose members have become part of the federal government themselves.

The birth of the Tea Party in 2010 might have been 1773 all over again. Antitax and antigovernment, the protesters were angry, and if they didn't go as far as to empty shiploads of tea into Boston Harbor, they made their displeasure known in other ways. Though their ire was directed at government in general, the Tea Party had found specific targets. In particular, they opposed the George W. Bush administration's bailouts of big financial institutions through the Troubled Asset Relief Program (TARP) in 2008 and other measures taken in response to the economic crisis that began that year, including mortgage assistance for people facing foreclosure, the stimulus bill, and the health reform act, all passed by Congress in 2009 and 2010 with the strong backing of President Barack Obama.

The Tea Party movement was a decentralized mix of many groups—mostly simply frustrated Republicans (the major party that most Tea Partiers identify with or lean toward). Ted Cruz from Texas and Marco Rubio from Florida won seats in the U.S. Senate with Tea Party support and went on to run for the presidency in 2016. Tea Party members elected to Congress caused many headaches for Speaker of the House John Boehner, leading to his resignation in 2015.

But other members of the rebellious faction chose less establishment paths. David Barstow of the *New York Times* wrote in early 2010 that a "significant undercurrent within the Tea Party movement" was less like a part of the Republican Party than it was like "the Patriot movement, a brand of politics historically associated with libertarians, militia groups, anti-immigration advocates and those who argue for the abolition of the Federal Reserve." He quoted a Tea Party leader so worried about the impending tyranny threatening her country that she could imagine being called to violence in its defense: "I don't see us being the ones to start it, but I would give up my life for my country.... Peaceful means are the best way of going about it. But sometimes you are not given a choice."[2]

Like the extreme Tea Partier quoted above, McVeigh and his associates, the Bundys, and other militia group members are everyday men and women who say they are the ideological heirs of the American Revolution. They liken themselves to the colonial Sons of Liberty, who rejected the authority of the British government and took it upon themselves to enforce the laws they thought were just. The Sons of Liberty instigated the Boston Massacre and the Boston Tea Party, historical events that we celebrate as patriotic but that would be considered treason or terrorism if they took place today—and were considered as such by the British back when they occurred.

Today's so-called Patriot groups claim that the federal government has become as tyrannical as the British government ever was, that it deprives citizens of their liberty and over-regulates their everyday lives. They reject federal laws that do everything from limiting the weapons that individual citizens can own, to imposing taxes on income, to requiring the registration of motor vehicles, to creating the Federal Reserve Bank, to reforming the health care system. The groups base their claim to legitimate existence on the Constitution's Second Amendment, which reads, "A well regulated Militia, being necessary to the security of a free State, the right of the people to keep and bear Arms, shall not be infringed." Members of state militias, and other groups like them, take this amendment literally and absolutely. The web site teaparty.org, though not representative of all Tea Party groups, says "gun ownership is sacred."[3]

Some militias go even further. They may blend their quests for individual liberty with white supremacy or anti-Semitism and see conspiracies aimed at reducing the power of white citizens in the government's actions. In August 2012, with the November election in the offing, a Texas judge, Tom Head, actually called for a tax increase so that police could be prepared for what he anticipated would happen if President Obama were reelected. He said, "He's going to try to hand over the sovereignty of the United States to the UN, and what is going to happen when that happens? . . . I'm thinking the worst. Civil unrest, civil disobedience, civil war maybe."[4]

Although there are some indications that militia membership had declined after the Oklahoma City bombing, it surged after Obama's first election, as did arguments that the federal government (or at least the president) was not legitimate.[5] Donald Trump's loud support for the birther movement, which argued that Obama was not qualified by birth for the presidency, presaged Trump's presidential campaign, which seemed to capitalize on the same anger the Tea Party had thrived on. A number of writers, as we will see in Chapter 5, have argued that some of this increased anger is a panicky reaction of a shrinking white majority to demographic change and the presence of a black man in the White House.[6] In any case it helped propel Donald Trump there in 2016.

The federal government has reacted strongly to limit the threat presented by state militias and others who believe that its authority is not legitimate. Congress passed an antiterrorism bill signed by President Bill Clinton in 1996 that would make it easier for federal agencies to monitor the activities of such groups, and these powers were broadened after September 11, 2001. In June 2014, in reaction to the surging numbers of radicalized people within the country, then–attorney general Eric Holder announced that he would revive the domestic terrorism task force that had been formed after the Oklahoma City bombings but had not met since the attacks of 9/11 turned the nation's attention to terrorism overseas.

How should the federal government respond to these challenges to its legitimacy? Are these groups, as they claim, the embodiment of revolutionary patriotism? Do they support the Constitution, or sabotage it? And where do we draw the line between a Tea Party member who wants to sound off against elected officials and policies she doesn't like, and one who advocates resorting to violence to protect his particular reading of the Constitution? Think about these questions as you read this chapter on the founding of the United States. At the end of this chapter we revisit the question of what's at stake for American politics in a revolutionary challenge to government authority.

SCHOOL children in the United States have had the story of the American founding pounded into their heads. From the moment they start coloring grateful Pilgrims and cutting out construction paper turkeys in grade school, the founding is a recurring focus of their education, and with good reason. Democratic societies, as we saw in Chapter 1, rely on the consent of their citizens to maintain lawful behavior and public order. A commitment to the rules and goals of the American system requires that we feel good about that system. What better way to stir up good feelings and patriotism than by recounting thrilling stories of bravery and derring-do on the part of selfless heroes dedicated to the cause of American liberty? We celebrate the Fourth of July with fireworks and parades, displaying publicly our commitment to American values and our belief that our country is special, in the same way that other nations celebrate their origins all over the world. Bastille Day (July 14) in France, May 17 in Norway, October 1 in China, and July 6 in Malawi all are days on which people rally together to celebrate their common past and their hopes for the future.

Of course, people feel real pride in their countries, and many nations, not only our own, do have amazing stories to tell about their earliest days. But since this is a textbook on politics, not patriotism, we need to look beyond the pride and the amazing stories. As political scientists, we must separate myth from reality. For us, the founding of the United States is central not because it inspires warm feelings of patriotism but because it can teach us about American politics—the struggles for power that forged the political system that continues to shape our collective struggles today.

The history of the American founding has been told from many points of view. You are probably most familiar with this narrative: the early colonists escaped from Europe to avoid religious persecution. Having arrived on the shores of the New World, they built communities that allowed them to practice their religions in peace and to govern themselves as free people. When the tyrannical British king made unreasonable demands on the colonists, they had no choice but to protect their liberty by going to war and by establishing a new government of their own.

Sound historical evidence suggests that the story is more complicated, and more interesting, than that. A closer look shows that early Americans were complex beings with economic and political agendas as well as religious and philosophical motives. After much struggle among themselves, the majority of Americans decided that those agendas could be carried out better and more profitably if they broke their ties with England.[7] Just because a controversial event like the founding is recounted by historians or political scientists one or two hundred years after it happened does not guarantee that there is common agreement on what actually took place. People write history not from a position of absolute truth but from particular points of view. When we read a historical narrative, as critical thinkers we need to ask the same probing questions we ask about contemporary political narratives: Who is telling the story? What point of view is being represented? What values and priorities lie behind it? If I accept this interpretation, what else will I have to accept? (See *Don't Be Fooled by . . . Your Textbook*.)

In this chapter we talk a lot about history—the history of the American founding and the creation of the Constitution. Like all authors, we have a particular point of view that affects how we tell the story. True to the basic theme of this book, we are interested in power and citizenship. We want to understand American government in terms of who the winners and losers are likely to be. It makes sense for us to begin by looking at the founding to see who the winners and losers were then. We are also interested in how rules and institutions make it more likely that some people will win and others lose. Certainly an examination of the early debates about rules and institutions will help us understand that. Because we are interested in winners and losers, the *who* of politics, we are interested in understanding how people come to be defined as players in the system in the first place. It was during the founding that many of the initial decisions were made about who "We, the people" would actually be. Finally, we are interested in the product of all this debate—the Constitution of the United States, the ultimate rule book for who gets what in American politics. Consequently, our discussion of American political history focuses on these issues. Specifically in this chapter we explore the colonial break with England and the Revolution, the initial attempt at American government—the Articles of Confederation, the Constitutional Convention, the Constitution itself, and the ratification of the Constitution.

THE SPLIT FROM ENGLAND

*Making the transition from
British subjects to American citizens*

America was a political and military battlefield long before the Revolution. Not only did nature confront the colonists with brutal winters, harsh droughts, disease, and other unanticipated disasters, but the New World was also already inhabited before the British settlers arrived, both by Native Americans and by Spanish and French colonists. These political actors in North America during the seventeenth and early eighteenth centuries had, perhaps, more at stake than they knew. All were trying to lay claim to the same geographical territory; none could have foreseen that that territory would one day become the strongest power in the world. Whoever won the battle for North America would put their stamp on the globe in a major way.

By the late 1700s the eastern colonies of North America were heavily English. For many reasons, life in England had limited opportunities for freedom, for economic gain, and for political power. English settlers arrived in America seeking, first and foremost, new opportunities. But those opportunities were not available to all. "We, the people" had been defined in various ways throughout the 1600s and 1700s, but never had it meant anything like "everybody" or even "every white male." Religious and property qualifications for the vote, and the exclusion of women and blacks from political life, meant that the colonial leaders did not feel that simply living in a place, obeying the laws, or even paying taxes carried with it the right to participate in government. Following the rigid British social hierarchy, they wanted the "right kind" of people to participate—people who could be depended on to make the kind of rules that would ensure their status and maintain the established order. The danger of expanding the vote, of course, was that the new majority might have wanted something very different from what the old majority wanted.

Those colonists who had political power in the second half of the eighteenth century gradually began to question their relationship with England. For much of the history of colonial America, England had left the colonies pretty much alone, and they had learned to live with the colonial governance that Britain exercised. Of course, they were obliged, as colonies, to make England their primary trading partner. Even goods they exported to other European countries had to pass through England, where taxes were collected on them. However, smuggling and corrupt colonial officials had made those obligations less than burdensome. It is important to remember that the colonies received many benefits by virtue of their status: they were settled by corporations and companies funded with British money, such as the Massachusetts Bay Company; they were protected by the British army and navy; and they had a secure market for their agricultural products.

Whether the British government was actually being oppressive in the years before 1776 is open to interpretation. Certainly the colonists thought so. Britain was deeply in debt, having won the **French and Indian War**, which effectively forced the French out of North America and the Spanish to vacate Florida and retreat west of the Mississippi. The war, fought to defend the British colonies and colonists in America, turned into a major and expensive conflict across the Atlantic as well. Britain, having done its protective duty as a colonial power and having taxed British citizens at home heavily to finance the war, turned to its colonies to help pay for their defense. It chose to do that by levying taxes on the colonies and by attempting to enforce more strictly the trade laws that would increase British profits from American resources.

The series of acts passed by the British infuriated the colonists. The Sugar Act of 1764, which imposed customs taxes, or duties, on sugar, was seen as unfair and unduly burdensome in a depressed postwar economy, and the Stamp Act of 1765 incited protests and demonstrations throughout the colonies. Similar to a tax in effect in Great Britain for nearly a century, it required that a tax be paid, in scarce British currency, on every piece of printed matter in the colonies, including newspapers, legal documents, and even playing cards. The colonists claimed that the law was an infringement on their liberty and a violation of their right not to be taxed without their consent. Continued protests and political changes in England resulted in the repeal of the Stamp Act in 1766. The Townshend Acts of 1767, taxing goods imported from England, such as paper, glass, and tea, and the Tea Act of 1773 were seen by the colonists as intolerable violations of their rights. To show their displeasure, they hurled 342 chests of tea into Boston Harbor in the famous Boston Tea Party. Britain responded by passing the Coercive Acts of 1774, designed to punish the citizens of Massachusetts. In the process, Parliament sowed the seeds that would blossom into revolution in just a few years.

REVOLUTION

From the moment the unpopularly taxed tea plunged into Boston Harbor, it became apparent that Americans were not going to settle down and behave like proper and orthodox colonists. Britain was surprised by the colonial reaction, and it could not ignore it. Even before the

French and Indian War a war fought between France and England, and allied Indians, from 1754 to 1763; resulted in France's expulsion from the New World

Your Textbook

Consider these two narratives describing the same familiar event: Christopher Columbus's arrival in the Americas.[1]

From a 1947 textbook:

At last the rulers of Spain gave Columbus three small ships, and he sailed away to the west across the Atlantic Ocean. His sailors became frightened. They were sure the ships would come to the edge of the world and just fall off into space. The sailors were ready to throw their captain into the ocean and turn around and go back. Then, at last they all saw the land ahead. They saw low green shores with tall palm trees swaying in the wind. Columbus had found the New World. This happened on October 12, 1492. It was a great day for Christopher Columbus—and for the whole world as well.

And from a 1991 text:

When Columbus stepped ashore on Guanahani Island in October 1492, he planted the Spanish flag in the sand and claimed the land as a possession of Ferdinand and Isabella. He did so despite the obvious fact that the island already belonged to someone else—the "Indians" who gathered on the beach to gaze with wonder at the strangers who had suddenly arrived in three great, white-winged canoes. He gave no thought to the rights of the local inhabitants. Nearly every later explorer—French, English, Dutch and all the others as well as the Spanish—thoughtlessly dismissed the people they encountered. What we like to think of as the discovery of America was actually the invasion and conquest of America.

Which one of these passages is "true"? The first was the conventional textbook wisdom through the 1960s in America. The latter reflects a growing criticism that traditional American history has been told from the perspective of history's "winners," largely white males of European background. Together they show that history varies depending on who is doing the telling, when, and to whom. What this means to you is that the critical vigilance we urge you to apply to all information should be applied to your textbooks as well. And, yes, that means this textbook, too. In an age of mediated citizenship, you really have your work cut out for you.

There is some truth to the idea that history is written by the winners, but it is also true that the winners change over time. If history was once securely in the hands of white European males, it is now the battleground of a cultural war between those who believe the old way of telling history was accurate and those who believe it left out the considerable achievements of women and minorities and masked some of the less admirable episodes of our past.[2]

Bias is not reserved for history books; this textbook itself has a point of view. In these pages we have an interest in highlighting power and citizenship, in focusing on the impact of the rules in American politics, and in multiculturalism. We do not think that the outstanding political accomplishments of the traditional heroes of American history warrant ignoring the contributions of people who have not historically been powerful.

The fact that all textbooks have some sort of bias means you must be as careful in what you accept from textbook authors as you are in what you accept from any other source.

Boston Tea Party, mobs in many towns were demonstrating and rioting against British control. Calling themselves the Sons of Liberty, and under the guidance of the eccentric and unsteady Sam Adams, cousin of future president John Adams, they routinely caused extensive damage. In early 1770 they provoked the Boston Massacre, an attack by British soldiers that left six civilians dead and further inflamed popular sentiments.

By the time of the December 1773 Boston Tea Party, also incited by the Sons of Liberty, passions were at a fever pitch. The American patriots called a meeting in Philadelphia in September 1774. Known as the First Continental Congress, the meeting declared the Coercive Acts void, announced a plan to stop trade with England, and called for a second meeting in May 1775. Before they could meet again, in the early spring of 1775, the king's army went marching to arrest Sam Adams and another patriot, John Hancock, and to discover the hiding place of the colonists' weapons. Roused by the silversmith Paul Revere, Americans in Lexington and Concord fired the first shots of rebellion at the British, and the Revolution was truly under way. The narrative about where the locus of power should be spread quickly, even given the limited communication channels of the day. The mobs were not fed by social media or connected electronically—the story was passed by word of mouth and, therefore, could be controlled relatively easily because each person could not disseminate ideas widely. The people who stood to gain the most financially from independence—the propertied and economic elite, the attendees at the Continental Congress—were translating a philosophical explanation for the masses to act on. Because many colonists could not read, they got their news at the tavern or at the Sunday pulpit, where it was colored by the interests of the teller, and then passed it on. The vast majority of citizens were passive recipients of the narrative.

THE DECLARATION OF INDEPENDENCE

In 1776, at the direction of a committee of the Continental Congress, thirty-four-year-old Thomas Jefferson sat down to write a declaration of independence from England. His training as a lawyer at the College of William and Mary and his service as a representative in the Virginia House of Burgesses helped prepare him for his task, but he had an impressive intellect in any case. President John F. Kennedy once announced to a group of Nobel Prize winners he was entertaining that they were "the most extraordinary collection of talents that has ever gathered at the White House, with the possible exception of when Thomas Jefferson dined alone."[8] A testimony to Jefferson's capabilities is the strategically brilliant document that he produced.

The Declaration of Independence is first and foremost a political document. Having decided to make the break from England, the American founders had to convince themselves, their fellow colonists, and the rest of the world that they were doing the right thing. Jefferson did not have to hunt far for a good reason for his revolution. John Locke, whom we discussed in Chapter 1, had handed him one on a silver platter. Remember that Locke said that government is based on a contract between the rulers and the ruled. The ruled agree to obey the laws as long as the rulers protect their basic rights to life, liberty, and property. If the rulers fail to do that, they break the contract, and the ruled are free to set up another government. This is exactly what the second paragraph of the Declaration of Independence says, except that Jefferson changed "property" to "the pursuit of happiness," perhaps to garner the support of those Americans who didn't own enough property to worry about. The rest of the Declaration focuses on documenting the ways in which the colonists believed that England, and particularly George III, had violated their rights and broken the social contract.

> Are there any circumstances in which it would be justifiable for groups in the United States to rebel against the federal government today?

"... THAT ALL MEN ARE CREATED EQUAL"

The Declaration of Independence begins with a statement of the equality of all men. Since so much of this document relies heavily on Locke, and since clearly the colonists did *not* mean that all men are created equal, it is worth turning to Locke for some help in seeing exactly what they did mean. In his most famous work, *A Second Treatise of Government*, Locke wrote,

> Though I have said above that all men are by nature equal, I cannot be supposed to understand all sorts of equality. Age or virtue may give men a just precedency. Excellency of parts and merit may place others above the common level. Birth may subject some, and alliance or benefits others, to pay an observance to those whom nature, gratitude, or other respects may have made it due.[9]

Men are equal in a natural sense, said Locke, but society quickly establishes many dimensions on which they may be unequal. A particularly sticky point for Locke's ideas on equality was his treatment of slavery. Although he hemmed and hawed about it, ultimately he failed to condemn it. Here, too, our founders would have agreed with him.

Declaration of Independence the political document that dissolved the colonial ties between the United States and Britain

AFRICAN AMERICANS AND THE REVOLUTION The Revolution was a mixed blessing for American slaves. On the one hand, many slaves won their freedom during the war. Slavery was outlawed north of Maryland, and many slaves in the Upper South were also freed. The British offered freedom in exchange for service in the British army, although the conditions they provided were not always a great improvement over enslavement. The abolitionist, or antislavery, movement gathered steam in some northern cities, expressing moral and constitutional objections to the institution of slavery. Whereas before the Revolution only about 5 percent of American blacks were free, the proportion grew tremendously with the coming of war.[10]

In the aftermath of war, African Americans did not find their lot greatly improved, despite the ringing rhetoric of equality that fed the Revolution. The economic profitability of slave labor still existed in the South, and slaves continued to be imported from Africa in large numbers. The explanatory myth, that all men were created equal but that blacks weren't quite men and thus could be treated unequally, spread throughout the new country, making even free blacks unwelcome in many communities. By 1786 New Jersey prohibited free blacks from entering the state, and within twenty years northern states started passing laws specifically denying free blacks the right to vote.[11] No wonder the well-known black abolitionist Frederick Douglass said, in 1852, "This Fourth of July is yours, not mine. You may rejoice, I must mourn."

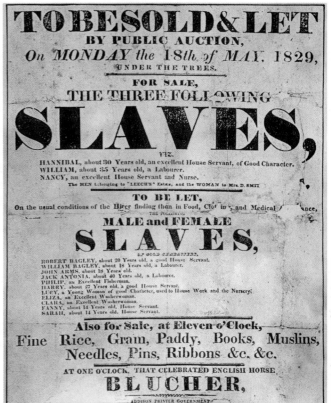

Human Trade

Slaves were used to meet the needs of the South's burgeoning economy in tobacco and cotton, which required plentiful, cheap labor. They were shipped from Africa and sold to farmers alongside rice, books, and other goods. In the eighteenth century, approximately 275 slaves were shipped to the American colonies. Many did not survive the harsh conditions of the passage.

NATIVE AMERICANS AND THE REVOLUTION Native Americans were another group the founders did not consider to be prospective citizens. Not only were they already considered members of their own sovereign nations, but their communal property holding, their nonmonarchical political systems, and their divisions of labor between women working in the fields and men hunting for game were not compatible with European political notions. Pushed farther and farther west by land-hungry colonists, the Indians were actively hostile to the American cause in the Revolution. Knowing this, the British hoped to gain their allegiance in the war. Fortunately for the revolutionary effort, the colonists, having asked in vain for the Indians to stay out of what they called a "family quarrel," were able to suppress early on the Indians' attempts to get revenge for their treatment at the hands of the settlers.[12] There was certainly no suggestion that the claim of equality at the beginning of the Declaration of

Independence might include the peoples who had lived on the continent for centuries before the white man arrived.

WOMEN AND THE REVOLUTION Neither was there any question that "all men" might somehow be a generic term for human beings that would include women. The Revolution proved to be a step backward for women politically: it was after the war that states began specifically to prohibit women, even those with property, from voting.[13] That doesn't mean, however, that women did not get involved in the war effort. Within the constraints of society, they contributed what they could to the American cause. They boycotted tea and other British imports, sewed flags, made bandages and clothing, nursed and housed soldiers, and collected money to support the Continental Army. Under the name Daughters of Liberty, women in many towns met publicly to discuss the events of the day, spinning and weaving to make the colonies less dependent on imported cotton and woolen goods from England, and drinking herbal tea instead of tea that was taxed by the British. Some women moved beyond such mild patriotic activities to outright political behavior, writing pamphlets urging independence, spying on enemy troops, carrying messages, and even, in isolated instances, fighting on the battlefields.[14]

Men's understanding of women's place in early American politics was nicely put by Thomas Jefferson, writing from Europe to a woman in America in 1788:

> But our good ladies, I trust, have been too wise to wrinkle their foreheads with politics. They are contented to soothe & calm the minds of their husbands returning ruffled from political debate. They have the good sense to value domestic happiness above all others. There is no part of the earth where so much of this is enjoyed as in America.[15]

Women's role with respect to politics at the time was plain. They may be wise and prudent, but their proper sphere was the domestic, not the political, world. They were seen as almost "too good" for politics, representing peace and serenity, moral happiness rather than political dissension, the values of the home over the values of the state. This narrative provided a flattering reason for keeping women in "their place" while allowing men to reign in the world of politics.

In Your Own Words Outline the events and political motivations that led to the colonies' split from England.

THE ARTICLES OF CONFEDERATION

Political and economic
instability under the nation's first constitution

constitution the rules that establish a government

Articles of Confederation the first constitution of the United States (1777), creating an association of states with weak central government

In 1777 the Continental Congress met to try to come up with a **constitution**, or a framework that established the rules for the new government. The **Articles of Confederation**, our first constitution, created the kind of government the founders, fresh from their colonial experience, preferred. The rules set up by the Articles of Confederation show that the states jealously guarded their power. Having just won their independence from one large national power, the last thing they wanted to do was create another. They were also extremely wary of one another, and much of the debate over the Articles of Confederation reflected wide concern that the rules not give any states preferential treatment. (See the Appendix for the text of the Articles of Confederation.)

The Articles established a "firm league of friendship" among the thirteen American states, but they did not empower a central government to act effectively on behalf of those states. The Articles were ultimately replaced because, without a strong central government, they were unable to provide the economic and political stability that the founders wanted. Even so, under this set of rules, some people were better off and some problems, namely the resolution of boundary disputes and the political organization of new territories, were handled extremely well.

THE PROVISIONS OF THE ARTICLES

The government set up by the Articles was called a **confederation** because it established a system in which each state retained almost all the power to do what it wanted. In other words, in a confederation, each state is sovereign and the central government has the job of running only the collective business of the states. It has no independent source of power and resources for its operations. Another characteristic of a confederation is that because it is founded on state sovereignty (authority), it says nothing about individuals. It creates neither rights nor obligations for individual citizens, leaving such matters to be handled by state constitutions.

Under the Articles of Confederation, Congress had many formal powers, including the power to establish and direct the armed forces, to decide matters of war and peace, to coin money, and to enter into treaties. However, its powers were quite limited. For example, although Congress controlled the armed forces, it had no power to draft soldiers or to tax citizens to pay for its military needs. Its inability to tax put Congress—and the central government as a whole—at the mercy of the states. The government could ask for money, but it was up to the states to contribute or not as they chose. Furthermore, Congress lacked the ability to regulate commerce between states, as well as between states and foreign powers. It could not establish a common and stable monetary system. In essence, the Articles allowed the states to be thirteen independent units, printing their own currencies, setting their own tariffs, and establishing their own laws with regard to financial and political matters. In every critical case—national security, national economic prosperity, and the general welfare—the U.S. government had to rely on the voluntary good will and cooperation of the state governments. That meant that the success of the new nation depended on what went on in state legislatures around the country.

SOME WINNERS, SOME LOSERS

The era of American history following the Revolution was dubbed "this critical period" by John Quincy Adams, nephew of patriot Sam Adams, son of John Adams, and himself a future president of the country. During this time, while the states were under the weak union of the Articles, the future of the United States was very much up in the air. The lack of an effective central government meant that the country had difficulty conducting business with other countries and enforcing harmonious trade relations and treaties. Domestic politics was equally difficult. Economic conditions following the war were poor. Many people had debts they could not pay. State taxes were high, and the economy was depressed, offering farmers few opportunities to sell their produce, for example, and hindering those with commercial interests from conducting business as they had before the war.

The radical poverty of some Americans seemed particularly unjust to those hardest hit, especially in light of the rhetoric of the Revolution about equality for all.[16] This is a difficulty of having a narrative controlled from on high—if it doesn't match up with the reality on the ground, new narratives can develop. Having used "equality" as a rallying cry during the war, the founders were afterward faced with a population that wanted to take equality seriously and

confederation a government in which independent states unite for common purpose but retain their own sovereignty

eliminate the differences that existed between men.[17] One of the places the American passion for equality manifested itself was in some of the state legislatures, where laws were passed to ease the burden of debtors and farmers. Often the focus of the laws was property, but rather than preserving property, per the Lockean narrative, it frequently was designed to confiscate or redistribute property instead. The "have nots" in society, and the people acting on their behalf, were using the law to redress what they saw as injustices in early American life.

To relieve postwar suffering, they printed paper money, seized property, and suspended "the ordinary means for the recovery of debts."[18] In other words, in those states, people with debts and mortgages could legally escape or postpone paying the money they owed. With so much economic insecurity, naturally those who owned property would not continue to invest and lend money. The Articles of Confederation, in their effort to preserve power for the states, had provided for no checks or limitations on state legislatures. In fact, such actions would have been seen under the Articles as infringing on the sovereignty of the states. What you had was a clash between two visions of what America was to be about.

The political elite in the new country started to grumble about **popular tyranny**. In a monarchy, one feared the unrestrained power of the king, but perhaps in a republican government, one had to fear the unrestrained power of the people. The final straw was **Shays's Rebellion**. Massachusetts was a state whose legislature, dominated by wealthy and secure citizens, had not taken measures to aid the debt-ridden population. Beginning in the summer of 1786, mobs of musket-wielding farmers from western Massachusetts began marching on the Massachusetts courts and disrupting the trials of debtors in an attempt to prevent their land from being foreclosed (taken by those to whom the farmers owed money). The farmers demanded action by a state legislature they saw as biased toward the interests of the rich. Their actions against the state culminated in the January 1787 attack on the Springfield, Massachusetts, federal armory, which housed more than 450 tons of military supplies. Led by a former captain in the Continental Army, Daniel Shays, the mob, now an army of more than 1,500 farmers, stormed the armory. They were turned back, but only after a violent clash with the state militia, raised to counter the uprisings. Such mob action frightened and embarrassed the leaders of the United States, who of course also were the wealthier members of society. The rebellion seemed to foreshadow the failure of their grand experiment in self-governance and certainly challenged their story of what it was about. In the minds of the nation's leaders, it underscored the importance of discovering what James Madison would call "a republican remedy for those diseases most incident to republican government."[19] In other words, they had to find a way to contain and limit the will of the people in a government that was to be based on that will. If the rules of government were not producing the "right" winners and losers, the rules would have to be changed before the elite lost control of their narrative and the power to change the rules.

In Your Own Words   Explain the competing narratives under the Articles of Confederation.

THE CONSTITUTIONAL CONVENTION
Division and compromise over state power and representation

State delegates were assigned the task of trying to fix the Articles of Confederation, but it was clear that many of the fifty-five men who gathered in May 1787 were not interested in saving the existing framework at all. Many of the delegates represented the elite of American society—wealthy lawyers, speculators, merchants, planters, and investors—and thus they were among those most injured under the Articles. Members of the delegations met through a sweltering Philadelphia summer to reconstruct the foundations of American government (see *Snapshot of America: Who Were the Founders?*). As the delegates had hoped, the debates at the **Constitutional Convention** produced a very different system of rules than that

popular tyranny the unrestrained power of the people

Shays's Rebellion a grassroots uprising (1787) by armed Massachusetts farmers protesting foreclosures

Constitutional Convention the assembly of fifty-five delegates in the summer of 1787 to recast the Articles of Confederation; the result was the U.S. Constitution

established by the Articles of Confederation. Many of them were compromises to resolve conflicting interests brought by delegates to the convention.

HOW STRONG A CENTRAL GOVERNMENT?

Put yourself in the founders' shoes. Imagine that you get to construct a new government from scratch. You can create all the rules and arrange all the institutions just to your liking. The only hitch is that you have other delegates to work with. Delegate A, for instance, is a merchant with a lot of property. He has big plans for a strong government that can ensure secure conditions for conducting business and can adequately protect property. Delegate B, however, is a planter. In Delegate B's experience, big government is dangerous. Big government is removed from the people, and it is easy for corruption to take root when people can't keep a close eye on what their officials are doing. People like Delegate B think that they will do better if power is decentralized (broken up and localized) and there is no strong central government. In fact, Delegate B would prefer a government like that provided by the Articles of Confederation. How do you reconcile these two very different agendas?

The solution adopted under the Articles of Confederation basically favored Delegate B's position. The new Constitution, given the profiles of the delegates in attendance, was moving strongly in favor of Delegate A's position. Naturally, the agreement of all those who followed Delegate B would be important in ratifying, or getting approval for, the final Constitution, so their concerns could not be ignored. The compromise chosen by the founders at the Constitutional Convention is called federalism. Unlike a confederation, in which the states retain the ultimate power over the whole, federalism gives the central government its own source of power, in this case the Constitution of the people of the United States. But unlike a unitary system, which we discuss in Chapter 3, federalism also gives independent power to the states.

Compared to how they fared under the Articles of Confederation, the advocates of states' rights were losers under the new Constitution, but they were better off than they might have been. The states could have had *all* their power stripped away. The economic elite, people like Delegate A, were clear winners under the new rules. This proved to be one of the central issues during the ratification debates. Those who sided with the federalism alternative, who mostly resembled Delegate A, came to be known as Federalists. The people like Delegate B, who continued to hold on to the strong-state, weak-central-government option, were called Anti-Federalists. We return to them shortly.

LARGE STATES, SMALL STATES

Once the convention delegates agreed that federalism would provide the framework of the new government, they had to decide how to allot power among the states. Should all states count the same in decision making, or should the large states have more power than the small ones? The rules chosen here would have a crucial impact on the politics of the country. If small states and large states had equal amounts of power in national government, residents of large states such as Virginia, Massachusetts, and New York would actually have less voice in the government than residents of small states like New Jersey and Rhode Island.

Picture two groups of people trying to make a joint decision, each group with one vote to cast. If the first group has fifty people in it and the second has only ten, the individuals in the second group are likely to have more influence on how their single vote is cast than the

federalism a political system in which power is divided between the central and regional units

Federalists supporters of the Constitution who favored a strong central government

Anti-Federalists advocates of states' rights who opposed the Constitution

Snapshot of America: *Who Were the Founders?*

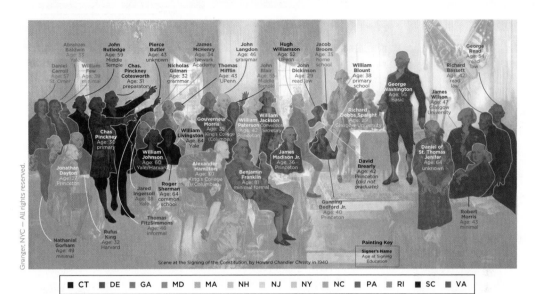

Scene at the Signing of the Constitution, by Howard Chandler Christy in 1940

Painting Key
Signer's Name
Age at Signing
Education

■ CT ■ DE ■ GA ■ MD ■ MA ■ NH NJ NY ■ NC ■ PA RI ■ SC ■ VA

Occupations of the Founders

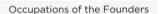

Lawyer | Merchant/Businessman | Planter/Farmer | Doctor | Politician | Educator | Printer

Religions of the Founders

20 Episcopalian
12 Presbyterian
7 Congregationalist
3 Quaker
2 Methodist
2 Roman Catholic
2 Anglican

1 Lutheran
1 Christian Reformed
1 Dutch Reformed
1 Calvinist
1 Deist
1 Unknown

Ratification by State

New Hampshire - June 21, 1788
New York - July 26, 1788
Massachusetts - Feb. 7, 1788 (including Maine)
Connecticut - Jan. 9, 1788
Rhode Island - May 29, 1790
Pennsylvania - Dec. 12, 1787
New Jersey - Dec. 18, 1787
Delaware - Dec. 7, 1787
Maryland - Apr. 28, 1788
Virginia - June 26, 1788
North Carolina - Nov. 21, 1789
South Carolina - May 23, 1788
Georgia - Jan. 2, 1788

How Many Signed and How Many Didn't?

39   **16**

Walked out and didn't sign
Oliver Ellsworth (CT)
James McClurg (VA)
George Wythe (VA)
Alexander Martin (NC)
William R. Davie (NC)
Robert Yates (NY)
John Lansing Jr. (NY)
William Houstoun (GA)
William Pierce (GA)
Caleb Strong (MA)
John F. Mercer (MD)
Luther Martin (MD)
William Houston (NJ)

Abstained from signing
Elbridge Gerry (MA)
George Mason (VA)
Edmund J. Randolph (VA)

Behind the Numbers

The founders were clearly an elite group of men. They attended the top schools and most were successful and wealthy. In general, how does one's economic and social status affect one's political views? Are your views shaped by your own circumstances? Can a government created by "an assembly of demigods" work for the rest of us mortals?

THE BIG PICTURE:
How We Got to the Constitution From the Articles of Confederation

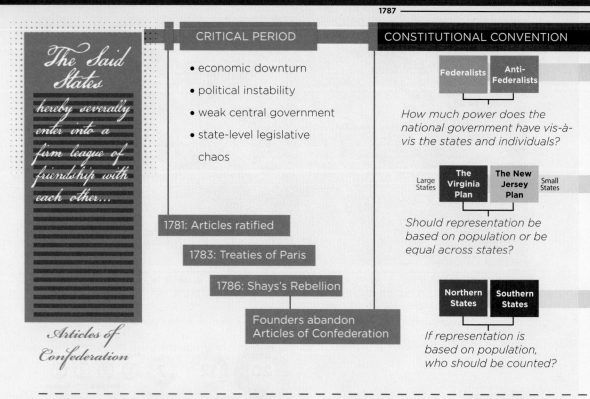

1787

CRITICAL PERIOD

- economic downturn
- political instability
- weak central government
- state-level legislative chaos

The Said States hereby severally enter into a firm league of friendship with each other...

Articles of Confederation

1781: Articles ratified

1783: Treaties of Paris

1786: Shays's Rebellion

Founders abandon Articles of Confederation

CONSTITUTIONAL CONVENTION

Federalists | Anti-Federalists

How much power does the national government have vis-à-vis the states and individuals?

Large States | The Virginia Plan | The New Jersey Plan | Small States

Should representation be based on population or be equal across states?

Northern States | Southern States

If representation is based on population, who should be counted?

Articles of Confederation

- State sovereignty
- State law is supreme
- Unicameral legislature; equal votes for all states
- Two-thirds vote to pass important laws
- No congressional power to levy taxes, regulate commerce
- No executive branch; laws executed by congressional committee
- No national judiciary
- All states required to pass amendments

The Virginia Plan

- Popular sovereignty
- National law is supreme
- Bicameral legislature; representation in both houses based on population
- Majority vote to pass laws
- Congressional power to regulate commerce and tax
- No restriction on strong single executive
- National judiciary
- Popular ratification of amendments

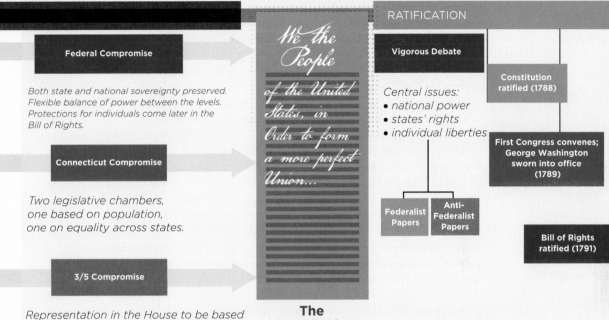

Federal Compromise

Both state and national sovereignty preserved. Flexible balance of power between the levels. Protections for individuals come later in the Bill of Rights.

Connecticut Compromise

Two legislative chambers, one based on population, one on equality across states.

3/5 Compromise

Representation in the House to be based on population, counting all "free Persons" and "three fifths of all other Persons."

We the People of the United States, in Order to form a more perfect Union...

The Constitution

RATIFICATION

Vigorous Debate

Central issues:
- *national power*
- *states' rights*
- *individual liberties*

Federalist Papers

Anti-Federalist Papers

Constitution ratified (1788)

First Congress convenes; George Washington sworn into office (1789)

Bill of Rights ratified (1791)

The New Jersey Plan	The Constitution
State sovereignty	People are sovereign
State law is supreme	National law is supreme
Unicameral legislature; one vote per state	Bicameral legislature; equal votes in Senate; representation by population in House
Extraordinary majority to pass laws	Simple majority to pass laws in Congress; presidential veto
Congressional power to regulate commerce and tax	Congressional power to regulate commerce and tax
Multiple executive	Strong executive
No national judiciary	Federal court system
All states required to pass amendments	Amendment process is complex

individuals in the first group. If, however, the first group has five votes to cast and the second only one, the individuals are equally represented, but the second group is effectively reduced in importance when compared to the first. This was the dilemma faced by the representatives of the large and small states at the Constitutional Convention. Each wanted to make sure that the final rules would give the advantage to states like his own.

Two plans were offered by convention delegates to resolve this issue. The first, the Virginia Plan, was the creation of James Madison. Fearing that his youth and inexperience would hinder the plan's acceptance, he asked fellow Virginian Edmund Randolph to present it to the convention. The Virginia Plan represented the preference of the large, more populous states. This plan proposed a strong national government run by two legislative houses. One house would be elected directly by the people, one indirectly by a combination of the state legislatures and the popularly elected national house. The numbers of representatives would be determined by the taxes paid by the residents of the state, which would reflect the free population in the state. In other words, large states would have more representatives in both houses of the legislature, and national law and policy would be weighted heavily in their favor. Just three large states—Virginia, Massachusetts, and Pennsylvania—would be able to form a majority and carry national legislation their way. The Virginia Plan also called for a single executive, to see that the laws were carried out, and a national judiciary, both appointed by the legislature, and it gave the national government the power to override state laws.

A different plan, presented by William Paterson of New Jersey, was designed by the smaller states to better protect their interests. The New Jersey Plan amounted to a reinforcement, not a replacement, of the Articles of Confederation. It provided for a multiperson executive, so that no one person could possess too much power, and for congressional acts to be the "supreme law of the land." Most significantly, however, the Congress would be much like the one that had existed under the Articles. In its one house, each state would have only one vote. The delegates would be chosen by the state legislatures. Congressional power was stronger than under the Articles, but the national government was still dependent on the states for some of its funding. The large states disliked this plan because the small states together could block what the large states wanted, even though the large states had more people and contributed more revenue.

The prospects for a new government could have foundered on this issue. The stuffy heat of the closed Convention Hall shortened the tempers of the weary delegates, and frustration made compromise difficult. Each side had too much to lose by yielding to the other's plan. The solution finally arrived at was politics at its best and shows the triumph of the compromise narrative. The Great Compromise kept much of the framework of the Virginia Plan. It proposed a strong federal structure headed by a central government with sufficient power to tax its citizens, regulate commerce, conduct foreign affairs, organize the military, and exercise other central powers. It called for a single executive and a national judicial system. The compromise that allowed the small states to live with it involved the composition of the legislature. Like the Virginia Plan, it provided for two houses. The House of Representatives would be based on state population, giving the large states the extra clout they felt they deserved, but in the Senate each state would have two votes. This would give the small states much more power in the Senate than in the House of Representatives. Members of the House of Representatives would be elected directly by the people, members of the Senate by the state legislatures. Thus the government would be directly binding on the people as well as on the states. A key to the compromise was that most legislation would need the approval of both houses, so that neither large states nor small states could hold the entire government hostage

Virginia Plan a proposal at the Constitutional Convention that congressional representation be based on population, thus favoring the large states

New Jersey Plan a proposal at the Constitutional Convention that congressional representation be equal, thus favoring the small states

Great Compromise the constitutional solution to congressional representation: equal votes in the Senate, votes by population in the House

to their wishes. The small states were sufficiently happy with this plan that most of them voted to ratify the Constitution quickly and easily. See this chapter's *The Big Picture* for a visual illustration of how the Founders got from the Articles of Confederation to the Constitution.

NORTH AND SOUTH

The compromise reconciling the large and small states was not the only one the delegates crafted. The northern and southern states, which is to say the non-slave-owning and the slave-owning states, were at odds over how population was to be determined for purposes of representation in the lower house of Congress. The southern states wanted to count slaves as part of their population when determining how many representatives they got, even though they had no intention of letting the slaves vote. Including slaves would give them more representatives and thus more power in the House of Representatives. For exactly that reason, the northern states said that if slaves could not vote, they should not be counted. The bizarre compromise, also a triumph of politics if not humanity, is known as the **Three-fifths Compromise**. It was based on a formula developed by the Confederation Congress in 1763 to allocate tax assessments among the states. According to this compromise, for representation purposes, each slave would count as three-fifths of a person—that is, every five slaves would count as three people. Interestingly, the actual language in the Constitution is a good deal cagier than this. It says that representatives and taxes shall be determined according to population, figured "by adding to the whole Number of free Persons, including those bound to Service for a Term of Years, and excluding Indians not taxed, three fifths of all other Persons."

The issue of slavery was divisive enough for the early Americans that the most politically safe approach was not to mention it explicitly at all and thus to avoid having to endorse or condemn it. Implicitly, of course, the silence had the effect of letting slavery continue. Article I, Section 9, of the Constitution, in similarly vague language, allows that

> The Migration or Importation of such Persons as any of the States now existing shall think proper to admit, shall not be prohibited by Congress prior to the Year one thousand eight hundred and eight, but a Tax or duty may be imposed on such Importation, not exceeding ten dollars for each Person.

Even more damning, Article IV, Section 2, obliquely provides for the return of runaway slaves:

> No Person held to Service or Labour in one State under the Laws thereof, escaping into another, shall, in Consequence of any Law or Regulation therein, be discharged from such Service or Labour, but shall be delivered up on Claim of the Party to whom such Service or Labour may be due.

The word *slavery* did not appear in the Constitution until it was expressly outlawed in the Thirteenth Amendment, passed in December 1865, nearly eighty years after the writing of the Constitution.

In Your Own Words Identify the competing narratives, goals, and compromises that shaped the Constitution.

Three-fifths Compromise the formula for counting five slaves as three people for purposes of representation, which reconciled northern and southern factions at the Constitutional Convention

THE CONSTITUTION

Three branches—legislative, executive, and judicial—separate and checked

The document produced as a result of these compromises was a political innovation. All governments must have the power to do three things: (1) legislate, or make the laws; (2) administer, or execute the laws; and (3) adjudicate, or interpret the laws. Because of their fear of concentrated power, however, the founders did not give all the power to one institution, but rather provided for separate branches of government to handle it, and then ensured that each branch would have the ability to check the others. In this section we review briefly the U.S. Constitution and the principles that support it. While we are focused on the rules as written in the Constitution, we also need to be aware of the importance of the commitment to play by those rules. In Chapter 1 we discussed the power of norms—the unspoken understandings about how to behave that underlie the rules of law. One hugely important norm, the one that makes the rules meaningful, is the commitment not to cheat by breaking, bending, or skirting the rules, and the obligation to report anyone who does break them. Another important norm is to accept the results of the rules, even if it means you lose. If we tolerate the breaking of norms, then the bad behavior become "normal" and the rules become meaningless. What makes rules work is the norm that most of us agree to follow them and penalize anyone who doesn't.

> **How would American politics be different today if we had retained the Articles of Confederation instead of adopting the Constitution?**

THE LEGISLATIVE BRANCH

Legislative power is lawmaking power. The body of government that makes laws is called the **legislature**. The U.S. Congress is a **bicameral legislature**, meaning that there are two chambers—the House of Representatives and the Senate. Article I, by far the lengthiest article of the Constitution, sets out the framework of the legislative branch of government. Since the founders expected the legislature to be the most important part of the new government, they spent the most time specifying its composition, the qualifications for membership, its powers, and its limitations. The best-known part of Article I is the famous Section 8, which spells out the specific powers of Congress. This list is followed by the provision that Congress can do anything "necessary and proper" to carry out its duties. The Supreme Court has interpreted this clause so broadly that there are few effective restrictions on what Congress can do.

THE RULES The House of Representatives, where representation is based on population, was intended to be truly representative of all the people—the "voice of the common man," as it were. To be elected to the House, a candidate need be only twenty-five years old and a citizen for seven years. Since House terms last two years, members run for reelection often and can be ousted fairly easily, according to public whim. The founders intended this office to be accessible to and easily influenced by citizens, and to reflect frequent changes in public opinion.

The Senate is another matter. Candidates have to be at least thirty years old and citizens for nine years—older, wiser, and, the founders hoped, more stable than the representatives in the House. Because senatorial terms last for six years, senators are not so easily swayed by

legislature the body of government that makes laws

bicameral legislature a legislature with two chambers

changes in public sentiment. In addition, senators were originally elected by members of the state legislatures, not directly by the people. (This was changed by constitutional amendment in 1913.) Election by state legislators, themselves a "refinement" of the general public, would ensure that senators were a higher caliber of citizen: older and wiser but also more in tune with "the commercial and monied interest," as Massachusetts delegate Elbridge Gerry put it at the Constitutional Convention.[20] The Senate would thus be a more aristocratic body—that is, it would look more like the British House of Lords, where members are admitted on the basis of their birth or achievement, not by election.

THE NORMS   The Constitution created two bodies that have to agree on a law in the exact same form for it to pass. But it does not also spell out the norms—the assumptions underlying those procedures. For instance, the founders assumed that legislating meant compromise. If they hadn't wanted to force compromise, a unicameral legislature (a one-chambered legislature) would have been an easier way to go. They rejected that. Given that the authors of the Constitution themselves had to compromise with those who preferred the Articles of Confederation, we can infer that *compromise* is an important democratic norm. The founders also set up the Senate to be the older and more stable chamber. That means the founders expected more from senators, that they behave with more *dignity* than the more unruly House. Senators were expected to act like the adults in the room. Finally, the members of Congress were to be elected, so they intended that the results of fair elections would be recognized by all parties. This implies the norm of *good sportsmanship*, another way of saying that one occasionally has to be a good loser. When one side loses, it doesn't take its marbles and go home. It doesn't call the other side a cheater or say the win is illegitimate (unless it is). Instead, it accepts the loss knowing it will have another chance, another day.

THE EXECUTIVE BRANCH

The **executive** is the part of government that "executes" the laws, or sees that they are carried out. Although technically executives serve in an administrative role, many end up with some decision-making or legislative power as well. National executives are the leaders of their countries, and they participate, with varying amounts of power, in making laws and policies. That role can range from the U.S. president—who, though not a part of the legislature itself, can propose, encourage, and veto legislation—to European prime ministers, who are part of the legislature and may have, as in the British case, the power to dissolve the entire legislature and call a new election.

The fact that the Articles of Confederation provided for no executive power at all was a testimony to the founders' conviction that such a power threatened their liberty. The chaos that resulted under the Articles, however, made it clear to founders like Alexander Hamilton that a stronger government was called for, not only a stronger legislature but a stronger executive as well. The constitutional debates reveal that many of the founders were haunted by the idea that they might inadvertently reestablish the same tyrannical power over themselves that they had only recently escaped with the Revolution.

THE RULES   The solution finally chosen by the founders is a complicated one, but it satisfied all the concerns raised at the convention. The president, a single executive, would serve an unlimited number of four-year terms. (A constitutional amendment in 1951 limited the president to two elected terms.) But the president would be chosen neither by Congress nor

executive the branch of government responsible for putting laws into effect

directly by the people. Instead, the Constitution provides for the president's selection by an intermediary body called the Electoral College. Citizens vote not for the presidential candidates but for a slate of electors, who in turn cast their votes for the candidates about six weeks after the general election. The founders believed that this procedure would ensure a president elected by well-informed delegates who, having no other lawmaking power, could not be bribed or otherwise influenced by candidates. We say more about how this works in Chapter 12, on elections.

Article II of the Constitution establishes the executive branch. The four sections of that article make the following provisions:

- Section 1 sets out the four-year term and the manner of election (that is, the details of the Electoral College). It also provides for the qualifications for office: that the president must be a natural-born citizen of the United States, at least thirty-five years old, and a resident of the United States for at least fourteen years. The vice president serves if the president cannot, and Congress can make laws about succession if the vice president is incapacitated.
- Section 2 establishes the powers of the chief executive. The president is commander-in-chief of the armed forces and of the state militias when they are serving the nation, and he has the power to grant pardons for offenses against the United States. With the advice and consent of two-thirds of the Senate, the president can make treaties, and with a simple majority vote of the Senate, the president can appoint ambassadors, ministers, consuls, Supreme Court justices, and other U.S. officials whose appointments are not otherwise provided for.
- Section 3 says that the president will periodically tell Congress how the country is doing (the State of the Union address given every January) and will propose to them those measures that he thinks appropriate and necessary. Under extraordinary circumstances, the president can call Congress into session or, if the two houses of Congress cannot agree on when to end their sessions, can adjourn them. The president also receives ambassadors and public officials, executes the laws, and commissions all military officers of the United States.
- Section 4 specifies that the president, vice president, and other civil officers of the United States (such as Supreme Court justices) can be impeached, tried, and convicted for "Treason, Bribery, or other high Crimes and Misdemeanors."

THE NORMS The founders knew what kind of man they wanted to hold the presidency; George Washington was right in front of them, a model executive. But they left that description unspoken. Implied by the rules is the norm of *independence*—a separate executive and legislature make it difficult to ram through legislation and the Constitution strictly guards against any allegiance to another country (hence the requirement of natural-born citizenship and the complicated emoluments clause, which forbids the president from taking expensive gifts from another country). They also wanted the president to demonstrate *dignity*. The office combines the jobs of head of government (the political role) and head of state (the symbolic role). Truth to tell, they never imagined a government as large and complex as ours is today, so the head-of-government role didn't loom as large. But the head-of-state role, representing the country as a whole, was key. So the founders implied the norm of *unity*, of representing the entire country. Finally, it is clear from the impeachment powers of Congress and from limits such as the emoluments clause that the founders had created a limited executive who

Electoral College an intermediary body that elects the president

could be removed from office by Congress for "Treason, Bribery, or other high Crimes and Misdemeanors." So another executive norm is that the president is bound by *the rule of law*.

THE JUDICIAL BRANCH

Judicial power is the power to interpret the laws and to judge whether they have been broken. Naturally, by establishing how a given law is to be understood, the courts (the agents of judicial power) end up making law as well. Our constitutional provisions for the establishment of the judiciary are brief and vague; much of the American federal judiciary under the Supreme Court is left to Congress to arrange. But the founders left plenty of clues as to how they felt about judicial power in their debates and their writings, particularly in *The Federalist Papers*, a series of newspaper editorials written to encourage people to support and vote for the new Constitution.

For instance, the practice of judicial review is introduced through the back door, first mentioned by Hamilton in *Federalist* No. 78 and then institutionalized by the Supreme Court itself with Chief Justice John Marshall's 1803 ruling in *Marbury v. Madison*, a dispute over presidential appointments. Judicial review allows the Supreme Court to rule that an act of Congress or the executive branch (or of a state or local government) is unconstitutional—that is, that it runs afoul of constitutional principles. This review process is not an automatic part of lawmaking; the Court does not examine every law that Congress passes or every executive order to be sure that it does not violate the Constitution. Rather, if an individual or a group challenges a law as unjust or unconstitutional, and if it is appealed all the way to the Supreme Court, the justices may decide to rule on it.

THE RULES This remarkable grant of the power to nullify legislation to what Hamilton called the "least dangerous" branch is not in the Constitution. In *Federalist* No. 78, however, Hamilton argued that it was consistent with the Constitution. In response to critics who objected that such a practice would place the unelected Court in a superior position to the elected representatives of the people, Hamilton wrote that, on the contrary, it raised the people, as authors of the Constitution, over the government as a whole. Thus judicial review enhanced democracy rather than diminished it.

In 1803 Marshall agreed. As the nation's highest law, the Constitution sets the limits on what is acceptable legislation. As the interpreter of the Constitution, the Supreme Court must determine when laws fall outside those limits. It is interesting to note that this gigantic grant of power to the Court was made by the Court itself and remains unchallenged by the other branches. It is ironic that this sort of empire building, which the founders hoped to avoid, appears in the branch that they took the least care to safeguard. We return to *Marbury v. Madison* and judicial review in Chapter 9, on the court system.

Article III of the Constitution is very short. It says that the judicial power of the United States is to be "vested in one Supreme Court, and in such inferior courts as the Congress may from time to time ordain and establish," and that judges serve as long as they demonstrate "good behavior." It also explains that the Supreme Court has original jurisdiction in some types of cases and appellate jurisdiction in others. That is, in some cases the Supreme Court is the only court that can rule. Much more often, however, inferior courts try cases, but their rulings can be appealed to the Supreme Court. Article III provides for jury trials in all criminal cases except impeachment, and it defines the practice of and punishment for acts of treason. Because the Constitution is relatively silent on the role of the courts in America, that role has been left to Congress and, in some cases, the courts themselves to define.

judicial power the power to interpret laws and judge whether a law has been broken

judicial review the power of the courts to rule on the constitutionality of laws

THE NORMS It's a little more difficult to make inferences about the judiciary because the founders didn't spell out the details in the Constitution. They wanted a judiciary to have *independence* from political and public influence, hence the grant of lifetime tenure. And it's pretty clear that the Federalists, at least, wanted it to be *powerful*. Hamilton's argument in *Federalist No. 78* laid the groundwork for John Marshall's decision in *Marbury v. Madison* granting the Court the power of judicial review. They also wanted the federal judiciary to be supreme, something they spelled out gently because it was still a sore spot with Anti-Federalists, but that was reinforced with subsequent rulings. But they also wanted the Court to be perceived as above politics, and one way to achieve that illusion was for the court to remain *nonpartisan* in its rulings. Rulings would undoubtedly have political impact but not show blatant support for the agenda of one party over another.

SEPARATION OF POWERS AND CHECKS AND BALANCES

Separation of powers means that legislative, executive, and judicial powers are not exercised by the same person or group of people, lest they abuse the considerable amount of power they hold. We are indebted to the French Enlightenment philosopher the Baron de Montesquieu for explaining this notion. In his massive book *The Spirit of the Laws*, Montesquieu wrote that liberty could be threatened only if the same group that enacted tyrannical laws also executed them. He said, "There would be an end of everything, were the same man or the same body, whether of nobles or of the people, to exercise those three powers, that of enacting laws, that of executing the public resolutions, and of trying the causes of individuals."[21] Putting all political power into one set of hands is like putting all our eggs in one basket. If the person or body of people entrusted with all the power becomes corrupt or dictatorial, the whole system will go bad. If, however, power is divided so that each branch is in separate hands, one may go bad while leaving the other two intact.

The principle of separation of powers gives each of the branches authority over its own domain. A complementary principle, checks and balances, allows each of the branches to police the others, checking any abuses and balancing the powers of government. The purpose of this additional authority is to ensure that no branch can exercise power tyrannically. In America's case, the president can veto an act of Congress; Congress can override a veto; the Supreme Court can declare a law of Congress unconstitutional; Congress can, with the help of the states, amend the Constitution itself; and so on. Figure 2.1 illustrates these relationships.

THE RULES As we saw, the Constitution establishes separation of powers with articles setting up a different institution for each branch of government. Checks and balances are provided by clauses within these articles:

- Article I sets up a bicameral legislature. Because both houses must agree on all legislation, they can check each other. Article I also describes the presidential veto, with which the president can check Congress, and the override provision, by which two-thirds of Congress can check the president. Congress can also check abuses of the executive or judicial branch with impeachment.
- Article II empowers the president to execute the laws and to share some legislative function by "recommending laws." The president has some checks on the judiciary through the power to appoint judges, but this appointment power is checked by the requirement

separation of powers the institutional arrangement that assigns judicial, executive, and legislative powers to different persons or groups, thereby limiting the powers of each

checks and balances the principle that allows each branch of government to exercise some form of control over the others

FIGURE 2.1

Separation of Powers and Checks and Balances

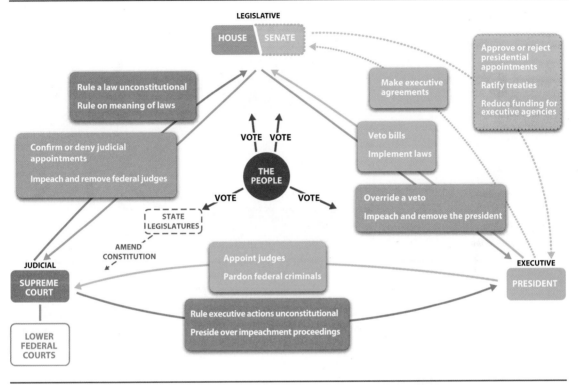

that a majority of the Senate must confirm the president's choices. The president can also check the judiciary by granting pardons. The president is commander-in-chief of the armed forces, but the ability to exercise this authority is checked by the Article I provision that only Congress can declare war.

- Article III creates the Supreme Court. The Court's ruling in the case of *Marbury v. Madison* fills in some of the gaps in this vague article by establishing judicial review, a true check on the legislative and executive branches. Congress can countercheck judicial review by amending the Constitution (with the help of the states).

The Constitution wisely ensures that no branch of the government can act independently of the others, yet none is wholly dependent on the others, either. This results in a structure of separation of powers and checks and balances that is distinctively American.

THE NORMS What the Constitution doesn't say about checks and balances is that the branches have to make it work for it to work. Congress has to hold the president to account through oversight and by withholding consent to unqualified appointments. The president has to veto bills he thinks are wrongheaded or that the country cannot afford in some way. The Courts have to truly be independent—judges must be loyal not to the person who appointed them but to the country and the Constitution. The founders expected checks and

FIGURE 2.2

Amending the Constitution

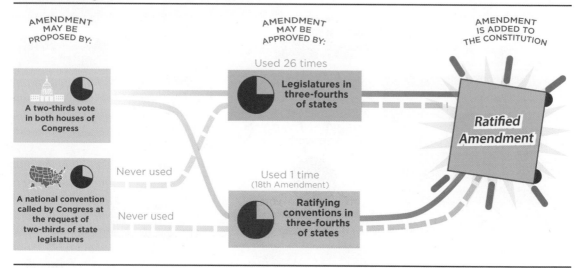

AMENDMENT MAY BE PROPOSED BY:

A two-thirds vote in both houses of Congress

A national convention called by Congress at the request of two-thirds of state legislatures

AMENDMENT MAY BE APPROVED BY:

Used 26 times

Legislatures in three-fourths of states

Never used

Never used

Used 1 time (18th Amendment)

Ratifying conventions in three-fourths of states

AMENDMENT IS ADDED TO THE CONSTITUTION

Ratified Amendment

balances to hold even if a single party held Congress and the White House; they would have chosen a parliamentary system if they wanted the Congress to rubberstamp executive action or the Courts to take partisan sides.

AMENDABILITY

If a constitution is a rule book, then its capacity to be changed over time is critical to its remaining a viable political document. A rigid constitution runs the risk of ceasing to seem legitimate to citizens who have no prospect of changing the rules according to shifting political realities and visions of the public good. A constitution that is too easily revised, on the other hand, can be seen as no more than a political tool in the hands of the strongest interests in society. A final feature of the U.S. Constitution that deserves mention in this chapter is its amendability—the founders' provision for a method of amendment, or change, that allows the Constitution to grow and adapt to new circumstances. In fact, they provided for two methods: the formal amendment process outlined in the Constitution, and an informal process that results from the vagueness of the document and the evolution of the role of the courts (see Figure 2.2).

In the 200-plus years of the U.S. Constitution's existence, more than 10,000 constitutional amendments have been introduced, but the Constitution has been amended only twenty-seven times. By contrast, in the course of interpreting the Constitution, the Supreme Court has, for example, extended many of the Bill of Rights protections to state citizens via the Fourteenth Amendment, permitted the national government to regulate business, prohibited child labor, and extended equal protection of the laws to women (see the next section for more on the Bill of Rights). In some cases, amendments previously introduced to accomplish these goals (such as the Child Labor Amendment and the Equal

amendability the provision for the Constitution to be changed, so as to adapt to new circumstances

Rights Amendment) were not ratified, and in other cases the Court has simply decided to interpret the Constitution in a new way. Judicial interpretation is at times quite controversial. Many scholars and politicians believe that the literal word of the founders should be adhered to, whereas others claim that the founders could not have anticipated all the opportunities and pitfalls of modern life and that the Constitution should be considered a flexible, or "living," document. We return to this controversy when we look more closely at the courts in Chapter 9.

The Constitution is silent on the subject of judicial interpretation, but in part because it is silent, especially in Article III, the courts have been able to create their own role. In contrast, Article V spells out in detail the rather confusing procedures for officially amending the Constitution. These procedures are federal—that is, they require the involvement and approval of the states as well as the national government. The procedures boil down to this: amendments may be proposed either by a two-thirds vote of the House and the Senate or when two-thirds of the states request it by a constitutional convention; they must be approved either by the legislatures of three-fourths of the states or by conventions of three-fourths of the states. Two interesting qualifications are contained in Article V: no amendment affecting slavery could be made before 1808, and no amendment can deprive a state of its equal vote in the Senate without that state's consent. We can easily imagine the North-South and large state–small state conflicts that produced those compromises.

The constitutional convention method of amendment, where change is initiated by the states, has never actually been used, although states have frequently tried to initiate such a movement. In fact, an effort to create a balanced budget amendment in this way is currently in the works. Twenty-seven of the necessary thirty-four states (all Republican-led) have passed resolutions calling on Congress to hold a constitutional convention to pass a balanced budget amendment. Several other efforts are right behind it that would try to put in extra protections for religious freedom (and perhaps defining citizenship as beginning at conception) or limitations on government action. Opponents argue that once a convention is convened, it might be hard to contain the urge to make multiple changes to the Constitution, although three-quarter of the states would still need to approve the amendments.[22]

In Your Own Words   Explain the system of separation of powers and checks and balances.

RATIFICATION
Selling the Constitution to Americans

For the Constitution to become the law of the land, it had to undergo **ratification**, that is, it had to be voted on and approved by state conventions in at least nine states. As it happens, the Constitution was eventually ratified by all thirteen states, but not until some major political battles had been fought.

FEDERALISTS VERSUS ANTI-FEDERALISTS

So strongly partisan were the supporters and opponents of the Constitution that, if the battle were taking place today, Twitter feeds would be on fire and we would probably

ratification the process through which a proposal is formally approved and adopted by vote

find the two sides sniping at each other on cable TV programs like *The Sean Hannity Show* and *Hardball With Chris Matthews*, and Samantha Bee would be busy mocking both groups. It was a fierce, lively battle to control the narrative of what the new republic would be like, but instead of producing viral videos with the lifespan of a fruit fly and high television ratings, it yielded some of the finest writings for and against the American system. Those in favor of ratification called themselves Federalists. The Federalists, like Delegate A in our earlier hypothetical constitution-building scenario, were mostly men with a considerable economic stake in the new nation. Having fared poorly under the Articles, they were certain that if America were to grow as an economic and world power, it needed to be the kind of country people with property would want to invest in. Security and order were key values, as was popular control. The Federalists thought people like themselves should be in charge of the government, although some of them did not object to an expanded suffrage if government had enough built-in protections. Mostly they were convinced that a good government could be designed if the underlying principles of human behavior were known. If people were ambitious and tended toward corruption, then government should make use of those characteristics to produce good outcomes.

The Anti-Federalists told a different story. They rejected the notion that ambition and corruption were inevitable parts of human nature. If government could be kept small and local, the stakes not too large and tempting, and popular scrutiny truly vigilant, then Americans could live happy and contented lives without getting involved in the seamier side of politics. America did not need sprawling urban centers of commerce and trade; nor did it need to be a world power. If it did not stray from its rural roots and values, it could per- manently avoid the creeping corruption that the Anti-Federalists believed threatened the American polity. The reason the Anti-Federalists found the Articles of Confederation more attractive than the Constitution was that the Articles did not call for a strong central gov- ernment that, distant from the voters' eyes, could become a hotbed of political intrigue. Instead, the Articles vested power in the state governments, which could be more easily watched and controlled.

Writing under various aliases as well as their own names, the Federalists and Anti- Federalists fired arguments back and forth in pamphlets and newspaper editorials aimed at persuading undecided Americans to come out for or against the Constitution. Because the channels of communication were limited, the competing ideas were concentrated into two streams. The Federalists were far more aggressive and organized in their "media blitz," hitting New York newspapers with a series of eloquent editorials, known collectively as *The Federalist Papers*, published under the pen name Publius but really written by Alexander Hamilton, James Madison, and John Jay. These essays were bound and distributed in other states where the ratification struggle was close. *The Federalist Papers* is one of the main texts on early American politics today. In response, the Anti-Federalists published essays under names such as Cato, Brutus, and the Federal Farmer.[23]

THE FEDERALIST PAPERS Eighty-five essays were written by Publius. In a contemporary introduction to the essays, compiled as a book, one scholar calls them, along with the Declaration of Independence and the Constitution, part of "the sacred writings of American political history."[24] Putting them on a par with holy things is probably a mistake. Far from being divinely inspired, *The Federalist Papers* are quintessentially the work of human beings. They are clever, well thought out, and logical, but they are also tricky and

The Federalist Papers a series of essays written in support of the Constitution to build support for its ratification

persuasive examples of the "hard sell." Their archaic language makes *The Federalist Papers* generally difficult reading for contemporary students. However, the arguments in support of the Constitution are laid out so beautifully that it is worthwhile to take the trouble to read them. It would be a good idea to turn to them now and read them carefully.

In *Federalist* No. 10, Madison tries to convince Americans that a large country is no more likely to succumb to the effects of special interests than is a small one (preferred by the Anti-Federalists). He explains that the greatest danger to a republic comes from factions, what we might call interest groups. **Factions** are groups of people motivated by a common interest, but one different from the interest of the country as a whole. Farmers, for instance, have an interest in keeping food prices high, even though that would make most Americans worse off. Businesspeople prefer high import duties on foreign goods, even though they make both foreign and domestic goods more expensive for the rest of us. Factions are not a particular problem when they constitute a minority of the population because they are offset by majority rule. They do become problematic, however, when they are a majority. Factions usually have economic roots, the most basic being a difference between the "haves" and "have nots" in society. One of the majority factions that worried Madison was the mass of propertyless people whose behavior was so threatening to property holders under the Articles of Confederation.

To control the *causes* of factions would be to infringe on individual liberty. But Madison believed that the *effects* of factions are easily managed in a large republic. First of all, representation will dilute the effects of factions, and it is in this essay that Madison makes his famous distinction between "pure democracy" and a "republic." In addition, if the territory is sufficiently large, factions will be neutralized because there will be so many of them that no one is likely to become a majority. Furthermore, it will be difficult for people who share common interests to find one another if some live in South Carolina, for instance, and others live in Maine. (Clearly, Madison never anticipated social media or even the telegraph.) We discuss Madison's argument about factions again when we take up the topic of interest groups in Chapter 11. In the meantime, notice how Madison relies on mechanical elements of politics (size and representation) to remedy a flaw in human nature (the tendency to form divisive factions). This is typical of the Federalists' approach to government and reflects the importance of institutions as well as rules in bringing about desired outcomes in politics.

We see the same emphasis on mechanical solutions to political problems in *Federalist* No. 51. Here Madison argues that the institutions proposed in the Constitution will lead neither to corruption nor to tyranny. The solution is the principles of checks and balances and separation of powers we have already discussed. Again building his case on a potential defect of human character, he says, "Ambition must be made to counteract ambition."[25] If men tend to be ambitious, give two ambitious men the job of watching over each other, and neither will let the other have an advantage.

Federalist No. 84, written by Hamilton, is interesting politically because the Constitution was ratified in spite of it, not because of it. In this essay, Hamilton argues that a **Bill of Rights**—a listing of the protections against government infringement of individual rights guaranteed to citizens by government itself—is not necessary in a constitution. The original draft of the Constitution contained no Bill of Rights. Some state constitutions had them, and so the Federalists argued that a federal Bill of Rights would be redundant. Moreover, the limited government set up by the federal Constitution didn't have the power to infringe on individual rights anyway, and many of the rights that would be included in a Bill of

factions groups of citizens united by some common passion or interest and opposed to the rights of other citizens or to the interests of the whole community

Bill of Rights a summary of citizen rights guaranteed and protected by a government; added to the Constitution as its first ten amendments in order to achieve ratification

Rights were already in the body of the text. To the Anti-Federalists, already afraid of the invasive power of the national government, this omission was more appalling than any other aspect of the Constitution.

In *Federalist* No. 84, Hamilton explains the Federalist position, that a Bill of Rights was unnecessary. Then he makes the unusual argument that a Bill of Rights would actually be dangerous. As it stands, he says, the national government doesn't have the power to interfere with citizens' lives in many ways, and any interference at all would be suspect. But if the Constitution were prefaced with a list of things government could *not* do to individuals, government would assume it had the power to do anything that wasn't expressly forbidden. Therefore government, instead of being unlikely to trespass on citizens' rights, would be more likely to do so with a Bill of Rights than without. This argument was so unpersuasive to Americans at the time that the Federalists were forced to give in to Anti-Federalist pressure during the ratification process. The price of ratification exacted by several states was the Bill of Rights, really a "Bill of Limits" on the federal government, added to the Constitution as the first ten amendments.

> **Would we have more freedoms today, or fewer, without the Bill of Rights?**

THE FINAL VOTE

The small states, gratified by the compromise that gave them equal representation in the Senate and believing they would be better off as part of a strong nation, ratified the Constitution quickly. The vote was unanimous in Delaware, New Jersey, and Georgia. In Connecticut (128–40) and Pennsylvania (46–23), the votes, though not unanimous, were strongly in favor of the Constitution. This may have helped to tip the balance for Massachusetts, voting much more closely to ratify (187–168). Maryland (63–11) and South Carolina (149–73) voted in favor of ratification in the spring of 1788, leaving only one more state to supply the requisite nine to make the Constitution law.

The battles in the remaining states were much fiercer. When the Virginia convention met in June 1788, the Federalists felt that it could provide the decisive vote and threw much of their effort into securing passage. Madison and his Federalist colleagues debated with Anti-Federalist advocates such as George Mason and Patrick Henry, promising as they had in Massachusetts to support a Bill of Rights. Virginia ratified the Constitution by the narrow margin of 89 to 79, preceded by a few days by New Hampshire, voting 57 to 47. Establishment of the Constitution as the law of the land was ensured with the approval of ten states. New York also narrowly passed the Constitution (30–27), but North Carolina defeated it (193–75), and Rhode Island, which had

not sent delegates to the Constitutional Convention, refused to call a state convention to put it to a vote. Later both North Carolina and Rhode Island voted to ratify and join the Union, in November 1789 and May 1790, respectively.[26]

Again we can see how important rules are in determining outcomes. The Articles of Confederation had required the approval of all the states. Had the Constitutional Convention chosen a similar rule of unanimity, the Constitution may very well have been defeated. Recognizing that unanimous approval was not probable, however, the Federalists decided to require ratification by only nine of the thirteen states, making adoption of the Constitution far more likely.

In Your Own Words Summarize the debate over ratification of the Constitution.

CITIZENSHIP AND THE FOUNDING
New rights bring obligations

As we said at the beginning of this chapter, there are different narratives to be told about the American founding. We did not want to fall into the oversimplification trap, portraying the founding as a headlong rush to liberty on the part of an oppressed people. Politics is always a good deal more complicated than that, and this is a book about politics. We also wanted to avoid telling a story that errs on the other end of one-sidedness, depicting the American founding as an elite-driven period of history in which the political, economic, and religious leaders decided they were better off without English rule, inspired the masses to revolt, and then created a Constitution that established rules that benefited people like themselves.

Neither of these stories is entirely untrue, but they obscure a very important point. There was not just one "elite" group at work during the founding period. Although political and economic leaders might have acted together over the matter of the break from England (even then, important elites remained loyal to Britain), once the business of independence was settled, it was clear that competing elite groups existed. These groups included leaders of big states and leaders of small states, leaders of northern states and leaders of southern states, merchant elites and agricultural elites, and elites who found their security in a strong national government and those who found it in decentralized power. The power struggle between all those adversaries resulted in the compromises that form the framework of our government today.

Because the debates about the Constitution took place in a pre-digital age, they were vociferous, reasoned, angry, manipulative, and stubborn—but the players were limited. Imagine, if you can, what the arguments over constitutional winners and losers would have looked like in a hypermediated age like ours. Perhaps all of the norms that support the Constitution were easier to respect and observe when there were not multiple channels calling for them to be bent or broken to serve the ends of different players.

In Your Own Words Evaluate the narratives told about the founding of the United States.

Let's Revisit: What's at Stake . . . ?

Having read the history of revolutionary America, what would you say is at stake in the modern militia movement? The existence of state militias and similar groups poses a troubling dilemma for the federal government; and groups whose members are mostly benign, like the Tea Partiers, are even trickier for the government to deal with. Bill Clinton, who was president when Timothy McVeigh bombed the federal building in Oklahoma City, warned at the time of the fifteenth anniversary of those attacks that "there can be real consequences when what you say animates people who do things you would never do." Angry rhetoric and narratives that justify that anger can result in violence that those who goad the anger might not necessarily endorse. The violence at Trump rallies in 2016 was a case in point, and there are those out there, like McVeigh and the Bundys, who "were profoundly alienated, disconnected people who bought into this militant antigovernment line."[27]

The dilemma is that, on the one hand, the purpose of government is to protect our rights, and the Constitution surely guarantees Americans freedom of speech and assembly. On the other hand, government must hold the monopoly on the legitimate use of force in society or it will fall, just as the British government fell to the American colonies. If groups are allowed to amass weapons and forcibly resist or even attack U.S. law enforcers, then they constitute "mini-governments," or competing centers of authority, and life for citizens becomes chaotic and dangerous.

The American system was designed to be relatively responsive to the wishes of the American public. Citizens can get involved; they can vote, run for office, change the laws, and amend the Constitution. By permitting these legitimate ways of affecting American politics, the founders hoped to prevent the rise of groups, like the Bundys, that would promote and act toward violence. The founders intended to create a society characterized by political stability, not by revolution, which is why Jefferson's Declaration of Independence is so careful to point out that revolutions should occur only when there is no alternative course of action.

Some militia members reject the idea of working through the system; they say, as did McVeigh, that they consider themselves at war with the federal government. We call disregard for the law at the individual level "crime," at the group level "terrorism" or "insurrection," and at the majority level "revolution." It is the job of any government worth its salt to prevent all three kinds of activities. Thus it is not the existence or the beliefs of the militia groups that government seeks to control but rather their activities.

What's at stake in challenges to the legitimacy of government are the very issues of government authority and the rights of individual citizens. It is difficult to draw the line between the protection of individual rights and the exercise of government authority. In a democracy, we want to respect the rights of all citizens, but this respect can be thwarted when a small number of individuals reject the rules of the game agreed on by the vast majority.

Review

The Split From England

The battle for America involved a number of groups, including Native Americans, and Spanish, French, and British colonists. By the time the British won the **French and Indian War** (51) to secure the colonists' defense, the colonists, already chafing under British rule, felt secure enough to sever the ties that bound them to the mother country, starting the Revolution and then in 1776 issuing the **Declaration of Independence** (54). Although that document proclaimed the equality of "all men," the American founders clearly did not include African Americans, Native Americans, or women in that category.

The Articles of Confederation

Charged with creating a **constitution** (56), the founders drew up the **Articles of Confederation** (56), establishing a **confederation** (57) of sovereign states. The new government wasn't strong enough to provide political stability in the face of popular discontent, however. Worried about **popular tyranny** (59), which they saw threatened in actions like **Shays's Rebellion** (59), the political elite called for a new constitution.

The Constitutional Convention

At the **Constitutional Convention** (59) in 1787, the founders rejected a confederal system in favor of **federalism** (60), giving the central government and the states each some power of their own. Those who endorsed this political innovation were known as the **Federalists** (60), and those who opposed it, the **Anti-Federalists** (60). Federalists supported a strong central government in which representation was determined by population—a plan, called the **Virginia Plan** (64), favored by the large states. The Anti-Federalists, suspicious of centralized power, favored the **New Jersey Plan** (64), which limited power and gave each state equal congressional representation regardless of its size. These issues were resolved in the **Great Compromise** (64), which created a bicameral legislature, basing representation on population in one house and on equality in the other. The other major conflict among the founders, over how slaves were to be counted for purposes of representation, was resolved by the **Three-fifths Compromise** (65).

The Constitution

The new Constitution was based on **separation of powers** (70) and **checks and balances** (70), keeping the **legislature** (66), the **executive** (67), and the judiciary distinct but allowing each some power over the others. The independence of the branches and the checks between them were enhanced by such institutions as the **bicameral legislature** (66), the **Electoral College** (68), **judicial power** (69), and the practice of **judicial review** (69), though the latter are not mentioned explicitly in the Constitution. The founders provided for **amendability** (72), should circumstances require that the Constitution be changed in the future.

Ratification

The Federalists and the Anti-Federalists waged a battle over **ratification** (73) of the new Constitution, with the former setting out their case in a series of newspaper editorials known today as *The Federalist Papers* (74). In the most famous of these essays, James Madison argued that the new republic would be well able to handle the danger of **factions** (75), and in another, Alexander Hamilton argued that it would be dangerous to add a **Bill of Rights** (75) to the document. Hamilton ultimately lost the argument, and the Bill of Rights was the price the Anti- Federalists demanded for their agreement to ratify the Constitution.

3
Federalism

In Your Own Words

After you've read this chapter, you will be able to

3.1 Identify the ways in which federalism divides power between national and state governments.

3.2 Demonstrate how the flexibility built into the Constitution has allowed it to change with the times.

3.3 Describe the ways in which the national government can influence the states.

3.4 Discuss whether federalism fosters or limits citizen participation in government.

What's at Stake . . . When a State Takes Marijuana Laws Into Its Own Hands?

If you are reading this in Alaska, California, Colorado, Maine, Massachusetts, Nevada, Oregon, Vermont, Washington, or the District of Columbia, or in one of the twenty-nine plus states that has legalized some form of marijuana for medical use, be careful—very careful—how you exercise your rights. Due to the crazy patchwork nature of America's marijuana laws, what is legal in your home state might get you jail or prison time and a hefty fine if you take it on the road. You can thank the founding fathers' invention of federalism for this, although it's doubtful this is what they had in mind when they designed it.

Of course, everyone knows that smoking marijuana is against the law in the United States. Among other things, the U.S. Federal Controlled Substances Act says so. Under that law, passed in 1970, marijuana is a "schedule I drug," equivalent, in legal terms, to heroin and LSD. But most people also know that, although the U.S. government considers marijuana a drug for which there is "no currently accepted medical use," most of the states beg to differ, and nine say, "Who cares? It's just plain fun" (although Vermont and D.C. won't let you buy it).

So if you live in a state with legal medical marijuana and you have a prescription, or if you stop in at the local pot shop in one of the seven that allow commercial sales, you are good, right?

Well, sort of. Maybe. It depends.

Consider the case of B. J. Patel, a thirty-one-year-old man from Arizona who was traveling through Idaho and was stopped for failing to signal by a police officer using license plate recognition software to target out-of-state drivers. The officer saw the medical marijuana card in his wallet, asked where the pot was, and, when shown by Patel, promptly arrested him. No matter how law-abiding Patel had been when he bought the pot, he was breaking the law in Idaho.

Idaho law provides for imprisonment and a $1,000 fine for under three ounces of pot and up to five years in prison and a $10,000 fine for more than three ounces. "Come on vacation, leave on probation," says a Coeur d'Alene, Idaho lawyer.[1]

Or consider the case of the five brothers in Colorado who sold an oil made from a strain of marijuana that doesn't even get you high. The plant is rich in a substance, CBD, that is used to treat seizures. It's legal in Colorado, of course, but there is a global demand for the oil, and the brothers want to expand to meet that demand.[2] The fly in their ointment is

Vince Chandler/The Denver Post/Getty Images

Weedy Territory

Laws regarding marijuana have changed in several states (including Colorado, where this image was taken), but cannabis consumption remains illegal in many other states, and marijuana use is still a federal offense. The resulting patchwork of state laws and changing federal enforcement from one administration to the next make for a confusing pot market.

that, even though the oil is not an intoxicant, it is made from marijuana and marijuana is illegal under federal law. So the brothers got their product classified as "industrial hemp," which is okay by Colorado, but not necessarily by the United States, although it will be if Senate majority leader Mitch McConnell manages to get the Hemp Farming Act of 2018 passed.[3]

Generally, federal law trumps state law when there is a conflict. The Obama administration, however, followed a policy under which the federal government wouldn't prosecute for marijuana use in the states where it was legal, as long as the sale of marijuana was regulated.[4] Try to sell that marijuana, however, or any product made from it, across state lines and the feds would seize it and possibly put the seller in jail. That policy stayed in place until January 2018, when the Trump administration's attorney general, Jeff Sessions, rescinded it. Colorado senator Cory Gardner took the issue straight to Trump, who assured him Colorado's pot smokers were safe from federal action. Trump has stood by that position, although his Department of Justice, led by Sessions, has not. Now that he has fired Sessions that may change, although Sessions had White House allies determined to enforce the federal law. [5]

Finally, consider the case of a Minnesota mom who was arrested in 2014 for giving her fifteen-year-old son marijuana oil on a doctor's advice to relieve chronic pain and muscle spasms from a brain injury. The pot was purchased legally in Colorado but administered in Minnesota, which had passed a law allowing medical marijuana. The catch? It didn't come into effect until July 2015. Said Bob Capecchi, who works for the Marijuana Policy Project in Washington, D.C., "Stunned was my initial reaction. I can't think of an instance where an individual has been brought up on charges like this simply because the effective date hasn't come around yet for the law that has already been passed. Let's not forget, there is a medical marijuana law that has been endorsed by the legislature and by the Governor."[6]

Why is there so much legal turmoil surrounding the use of marijuana, something that a majority of Americans now think should be legal?[7] Why can an activity that is legal in one state get you fined and thrown in jail in another? Why can the federal government forbid an activity but turn a blind eye to it unless you carry it across state lines? How do the laws get so complicated and tangled that you can get yourself arrested in one state for an activity that is legal in the state where you engaged in it, even if it is soon to be legal in the place where you are arrested? What is at stake when states decide to pass their own laws legalizing marijuana? We will return to this question at the end of the chapter, when we have a better grasp of the complex relationships generated by American federalism.

THE Federalists and the Anti-Federalists fought intensely over the balance between national and state powers in our federal system. Debates over the Articles of Confederation and the Constitution show that the founders were well aware that the rules dividing power between the states and the federal government were crucial to determining who would be the winners and the losers in the new country. Where decisions are made—in Washington, D.C., or in the state capitals—would make a big difference in "who gets what, and how." Today the same battles are being fought between defenders of state and national powers. The balance of power has swung back and forth several times since the founders came to their own hard-won compromise, but over the past quarter-century there has been a movement, led largely by Republicans, to give more power and responsibility back to the state governments, a process known as devolution.

More recently, however, as Republicans became more accustomed to holding the reins of power in Washington with their various congressional majorities and their hold on the presidency from 2000 to 2008, their zeal for returning responsibilities to the states became less urgent, slowing the devolutionary trend. Calls for increased national security in the days after September 11, 2001, have also helped reverse the transfer of power to the states. As the state-federal relationship changes, so too do the arenas in which citizens and their leaders make the decisions that become government policy. Fundamental shifts usually mean changes in the probable winners and losers of American politics.

In this chapter we examine the remarkable power-sharing arrangement that is federalism, exploring its challenges, both historical and contemporary. We look at the definition of federalism and the alternatives the founders rejected when they made this compromise, how the balance of power in American federalism has shifted over time, and the structure of federalism today and the ways the national government tries to secure state cooperation.

WHAT IS FEDERALISM?

Balancing power between
national and state governments

Federalism is a political system in which authority is divided between different levels of government (the national and state levels, in America's case). Each level has some power independent of the other levels so that no level is entirely dependent on another for its existence. In the United States, federalism was a significant compromise between those who wanted stronger state governments and those who preferred a stronger national government.

The effects of federalism are all around us. We pay income taxes to the national government, which parcels out the money to the states, under certain conditions, to be spent on programs such as welfare, highways, and education. In most states, local schools are funded by local property taxes and run by local school boards (local governments are created under the authority of the state), and state universities are supported by state taxes and influenced by the state legislature. Even so, both state and local governments are subject to national legislation, such as the requirement that schools be open to students of all races, and both can be affected by national decisions about funding various programs. Sometimes the lines of responsibility can be extremely unclear. Witness the simultaneous presence, in many areas, of city police, county police, state police, and, at the national level, the Federal Bureau of Investigation (FBI), all coordinated, for some purposes, by the national Department of Homeland Security.

Even when a given responsibility lies at the state level, the national government frequently finds a way to enforce its will. For instance, it is up to the states to decide on the minimum drinking age for their citizens. In the 1970s, many states required people to be only eighteen or nineteen before they could legally buy alcohol; today all the states have a uniform

devolution the transfer of powers and responsibilities from the federal government to the states

federalism a political system in which power is divided between the central and regional units

drinking age of twenty-one. The change came about because interest groups persuaded officials in the federal—that is, national—government that the higher age would lead to fewer alcohol-related highway accidents and greater public safety. The federal government couldn't pass a law setting a nationwide drinking age of twenty-one, but it could control the flow of highway money to the states. By withholding 5 percent of federal highway funds, which every state wants and needs, until a state raised the drinking age to twenty-one, Congress prevailed. This is an example of how the relations between levels of government work when neither level can directly force the other to do what it wants.

WHAT DOES THE CONSTITUTION SAY?

No single section of the Constitution deals with federalism. Instead, the provisions dividing power between the states and the national government appear throughout the Constitution. As a state matter, local government is not mentioned in the Constitution at all. Most of the Constitution is concerned with establishing the powers of the national government. Since Congress is the main lawmaking arm of the national government, many of the powers of the national government are the powers of Congress. The strongest statement of national power is a list of the **enumerated powers of Congress** (Article I, Section 8). This list is followed by a clause that gives Congress the power to make all laws that are "necessary and proper" to carry out its powers. The **necessary and proper clause** has been used to justify giving Congress many powers never mentioned in the Constitution. National power is also based on the **supremacy clause** of Article VI, which says that the Constitution and laws made in accordance with it are "the supreme law of the land." This means that when national and state laws conflict, the national laws will be followed. The Constitution also sets limitations on the national government. Article I, Section 9, lists specific powers not granted to Congress, and the Bill of Rights (the first ten amendments to the Constitution) limits the power of the national government over individuals.

The Constitution says considerably less about the powers granted to the states. The Tenth Amendment says that all powers not given to the national government are reserved to the states, although the necessary and proper clause makes it difficult to see which powers are withheld from the national government. The states are given the power to approve the Constitution itself and any amendments to it. The Constitution also limits state powers. Article I, Section 10, denies the states certain powers, mostly the kinds that they possessed under the Articles of Confederation. The Fourteenth Amendment limits the power of the states over individual liberties, essentially a Bill of Rights that protects individuals from state action, since the first ten amendments apply only to the national government.

What these constitutional provisions mean is that the line between the national government and the state governments is not clearly drawn. We can see from Figure 3.1 that the Constitution designates specific powers as national, state, or concurrent. **Concurrent powers** are those that both levels of government may exercise. But the federal relationship is a good deal more complex than this chart would lead us to believe. The Supreme Court has become crucial to establishing the exact limits of provisions such as the necessary and proper clause, the supremacy clause, the Tenth Amendment, and the Fourteenth Amendment. This interpretation has changed over time, especially as historical demands have forced the Court to think about federalism in new ways.

enumerated powers of Congress congressional powers specifically named in the Constitution (Article I, Section 8)

necessary and proper clause constitutional authorization for Congress to make any law required to carry out its powers

supremacy clause constitutional declaration (Article VI) that the Constitution and laws made under its provisions are the supreme law of the land

concurrent powers powers that are shared by the federal and state governments

FIGURE 3.1

The Constitutional Division of Powers Between the National Government and the States

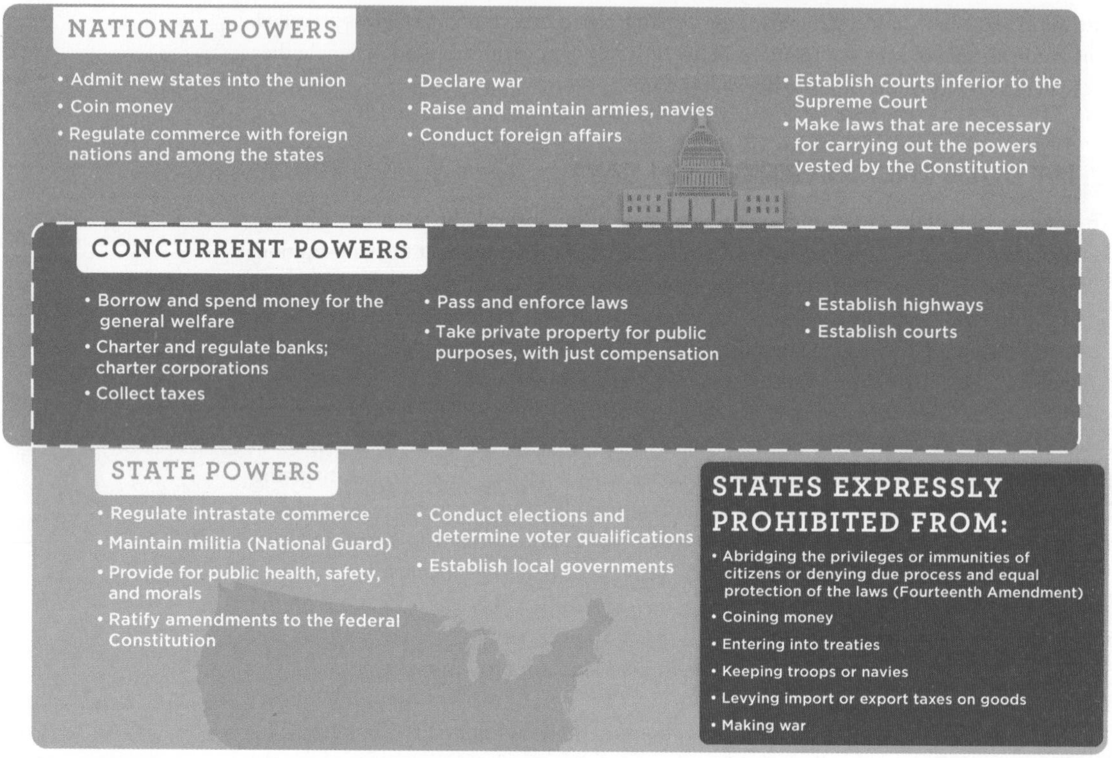

NATIONAL POWERS

- Admit new states into the union
- Coin money
- Regulate commerce with foreign nations and among the states
- Declare war
- Raise and maintain armies, navies
- Conduct foreign affairs
- Establish courts inferior to the Supreme Court
- Make laws that are necessary for carrying out the powers vested by the Constitution

CONCURRENT POWERS

- Borrow and spend money for the general welfare
- Charter and regulate banks; charter corporations
- Collect taxes
- Pass and enforce laws
- Take private property for public purposes, with just compensation
- Establish highways
- Establish courts

STATE POWERS

- Regulate intrastate commerce
- Maintain militia (National Guard)
- Provide for public health, safety, and morals
- Ratify amendments to the federal Constitution
- Conduct elections and determine voter qualifications
- Establish local governments

STATES EXPRESSLY PROHIBITED FROM:

- Abridging the privileges or immunities of citizens or denying due process and equal protection of the laws (Fourteenth Amendment)
- Coining money
- Entering into treaties
- Keeping troops or navies
- Levying import or export taxes on goods
- Making war

TWO VIEWS OF FEDERALISM

dual federalism the federal system under which the national and state governments are responsible for separate policy areas

cooperative federalism the federal system under which the national and state governments share responsibilities for most domestic policy areas

Political scientists have also changed the way they think about federalism. For many years the prevailing theory was known as dual federalism, basically arguing that the relationship between the two levels of government was like a layer cake. That is, the national and state governments were to be understood as two self-contained layers, each essentially separate from the other and carrying out its functions independently. In its own area of power, each level was supreme. Dual federalism reflects the formal distribution of powers in the Constitution, and perhaps it was an accurate portrayal of the judicial interpretation of the federal system for our first hundred years or so.

But this theory was criticized for not describing realistically the way the federal relationship was evolving in the twentieth century. It certainly did not take into account the changes brought about by the New Deal. The layer cake image was replaced by a new bakery metaphor. According to the new theory of cooperative federalism, rather than being two distinct layers, the national and state levels were swirled together like the chocolate and vanilla batter in a marble cake.[8] National and state powers were interdependent, and each level required the cooperation of the other to get things done. In fact, federalism came to be seen by political scientists as a partnership, but one in which the dominant partner was, more often than not, the national government.

Who should have primary responsibility in case of emergencies or natural disasters: the local, state, or national government?

POSSIBLE ALTERNATIVES TO FEDERALISM

The federal system was not the only alternative available to our founders for organizing the relationship between the central government and the states. In fact, as we know, it wasn't even their first choice as a framework for government. The Articles of Confederation, which preceded the Constitution, handled the relationship quite differently. We can look at federalism as a compromise system that borrows some attributes from a unitary system and some from a confederal system. Had the founders chosen either of these alternatives, American government would look very different today.

UNITARY SYSTEMS In unitary systems, the central government ultimately has all the power. Local units (states or counties) may have some power at some time, but basically they are dependent on the central unit, which can alter or even abolish them. Many contemporary countries have unitary systems, among them Britain, France, Japan, Denmark, Norway, Sweden, Hungary, and the Philippines.

Politics in Britain, for example, works very differently from politics in the United States, partly due to the different rules that organize central and local governments. Most important decisions are made in London, from foreign policy to housing policy—even the details of what ought to be included in the school curriculum. Even local taxes are determined centrally. When Margaret Thatcher, then the British prime minister, believed that some municipal units in London were not supportive of her government's policies, she simply dissolved the administrative units. Similarly, in 1972, when the legislature in Northern Ireland (a part of the United Kingdom) could not resolve its religious conflicts, the central government suspended the local lawmaking body and ruled Northern Ireland from London. These actions are tantamount to a Republican president's dissolving a Democratic state that disagreed with his policies, or the national government's deciding during the days of segregation to suspend the state legislature in Alabama and run the state from Washington. Such an arrangement has been impossible in the United States except during the chaotic state of emergency following the Civil War. What is commonplace under a unitary system is unimaginable under our federal rules.

CONFEDERAL SYSTEMS Confederal systems provide an equally sharp contrast to federal systems, even though the names sound quite similar. In confederal systems, the local units hold all the power, and the central government is dependent on them for its existence. The local units remain sovereign, and the central government has only as much power as they allow it to have. Examples of confederal systems include America under the Articles of Confederation and associations such as the United Nations and the European Union, twenty-eight European nations that have joined economic and political forces. The European Union has been experiencing problems much like ours after the Revolutionary War, debating whether it ought to move in a more federal direction. Most of the nations involved, jealously guarding their sovereignty, say no.

unitary systems governments in which all power is centralized

confederal systems governments in which local units hold all the power

WHAT DIFFERENCE DOES FEDERALISM MAKE?

That our founders settled on federalism, rather than a unitary or a confederal system, makes a great deal of difference to American politics. Federalism gave the founders a national government that could take effective action, restore economic stability, and regulate disputes among the states, while allowing the states considerable autonomy. Still, federalism forces the states to continually negotiate their relationships not only with the national government but also with each other. Even though they have the ability to act independently in many respects, they have to be able to cooperate effectively and, frequently, to compete with each other. States are always looking to use their resources in creative ways to win scarce federal benefits, to lure business and economic development opportunities, and to encourage people to relocate within their borders.

Federalism gives both the national government and the states a good measure of flexibility when it comes to experimentation with public policy. If all laws and policies need not be uniform across the country, then different states may try different solutions to common problems and share the results of their experiments, making states what a Supreme Court justice once referred to as the "laboratories of democracy."[9] For instance, the popularity and success of the health care policy passed in Massachusetts under Gov. Mitt Romney in 2006 became the model for President Obama's Affordable Care Act four years later.

In addition, the flexibility that federalism provides can also be helpful when Congress cannot or will not act. As recent polarization in the nation's capital has essentially paralyzed legislative action for most purposes, it leaves a power vacuum that enterprising states can take advantage of. For example, as Congress has gridlocked over the development of fossil fuel resources, the states have leapt into the breach with their own energy policies, many times reflecting the political proclivities of the dominant party in the states. For example, Republican-controlled Pennsylvania has encouraged fracking (the process of pumping water and chemicals into deposits to free gas and oil bound up in rock formations) while neighboring New York, and to a lesser extent Ohio, which share the giant Marcellus Shale deposit, have taken a much more environmentally cautious approach to the development of shale deposits.[10]

However, it is not only units of government but also individuals who stand to benefit from power sharing between nation and states. Federalism means there is real power at levels of government that are close to the citizens. Citizens can thus have access to officials and processes of government that they could not have if there were just one distant, effective unit. Federalism allows government to preserve local standards and to respond to local needs—that is, to solve problems at the levels where they occur. Examples include local traffic laws, community school policies, and city and county housing codes.

Federalism is not a perfect system, however, and it has some disadvantages. Where policies are made and enforced locally, all economies of scale are lost. Many functions are also repeated across the country as states administer national programs locally. Different penalties for the same crime can make it difficult to gauge the consequences of one's behavior across states, as we saw in the *What's at Stake . . . ?* in this chapter. Most problematic is the fact that federalism permits, even encourages, local prejudices to find their way into law. Until the national government took enforcement of civil rights legislation into its own hands in the 1960s, federalism allowed southern states to practice segregation. Before the passage of the Nineteenth Amendment, women could vote in some states but not others. Similarly, before the Supreme Court ruling in 2015 that made marriage equality the law of the land, LGBTQ Americans did not have the same rights in all localities of the United States—although they could marry in states like Massachusetts, Iowa, Vermont, New Hampshire, Connecticut, and the District of Columbia, they did not even have the right to join in civil unions in many other states. To the degree that states have more rather than less power, the uniform enforcement of civil rights cannot be guaranteed.

Overall, federalism has proved to be a flexible and effective compromise for American government. The United States is not the only nation with a federal system, although other countries may distribute power among their various units differently from the way we do. Germany, Canada, Mexico, Australia, and Switzerland are all examples of federal systems.

In Your Own Words Identify the ways in which federalism divides power between national and state governments.

AMERICAN FEDERALISM OVER TIME
Constitutional ambiguity and the role of the Supreme Court

Although the Constitution provides for both national powers and state powers (as well as some shared powers), the balance between the two has changed considerably since it was written. Because of the founders' disagreement over how power should be distributed in the new country, the final wording about national and state powers was intentionally kept vague, which probably helped the Constitution get ratified. Because it wasn't clear how much power the different levels held, it has been possible ever since for both ardent Federalists and states' rights advocates to find support for their positions in the document.

That very vagueness has opened the door for the Supreme Court to interpret the Constitution's meaning. Those interpretations have varied along with the people sitting on the Court and with historical circumstances. As the context of American life has been transformed through events such as the end of slavery and the Civil War, the process of industrialization and the growth of big business, the economic collapse of the Great Depression in the 1930s and the relative prosperity of the late 1990s, the terror attacks of September 11, 2001, and the recession that began in 2008, the demands made on the different levels of government have shifted, too. When we talk about federalism in the United States, we are talking about specific constitutional rules and provisions, but we are also talking about a fairly continuous evolution of how those rules are understood. Consequently, the norms underlying federalism provide less of a fixed standard against which we can measure actual behavior; the norm is that although the federal government is supreme, the relationship is characterized by *flexibility*.

Two trends are apparent when we examine American federalism throughout our history. One is that American government in general is growing in size, at both the state and national levels. We make many more demands of government than did, say, the citizens of George Washington's time, or Abraham Lincoln's, and the apparatus to satisfy those demands has grown accordingly. But within that overall growth, a second trend has been the gradual but uneven strengthening of the national government at the expense of the states.

The increase in the size of government shouldn't surprise us. One indisputable truth about the United States is that, over the years, it has gotten bigger, more industrialized, more urban, and more technical. As the country has grown, so have our expectations of what the government will do for us. We want to be protected from the fluctuations of the market, from natural disasters, from unfair business practices, and from unsafe foods and drugs. We want government to protect our "rights," but our concept of those rights has expanded beyond the first ten amendments to include things like economic security in old age, a minimum standard of living for all citizens, a safe interstate highway system, and crime-free neighborhoods. These new demands and expectations create larger government at all levels, but particularly at the national level, where the resources and will to accomplish such broad policy goals are more likely to exist.

The national government has grown so large, so quickly, that the proper balance of power between the national and state governments is a central and controversial political issue today, and one that has traditionally divided the liberals and conservatives we spoke of in Chapter 1. Liberals believe a strong central government can solve society's problems, especially economically, and conservatives believe that "big government" causes more problems than it solves. People in the latter category, like the Anti-Federalists at the founding, would prefer to see power and the distribution of government services located at the state or local level, closer to the people being governed. From 2000 to 2006, and again after 2016, however, with Republicans holding the reins of power in both the legislative and the executive branches, the conservative distaste for big government waned somewhat, as they were the ones dictating the actions of that government. President George W. Bush's No Child Left Behind Act, for instance, took away many of the prerogatives of local school districts to decide whether to engage in regular testing of students, and yet the law enjoyed the support of many conservatives. Also, as we have noted, many conservatives have begun to argue for an expanded national role in regulating morals, if not the economy, and the need to address national security issues after September 11 stepped up conservative calls for bigger government solutions in that arena as well. Some Republicans themselves have noted that, once they come to Washington, conservatives could be "as bad as liberals" about enforcing the national will on states.[11] After President Barack Obama was elected and the Democrats passed the stimulus bill and health care reform, however, Republicans quickly returned to their traditional views and decried the return of "big government." Both Democrats and Republicans are more willing to entertain the possibility of national government action when they are the ones controlling the national government.

The growth of the national government's power over the states can be traced by looking at four moments in our national history: the early judicial decisions of Chief Justice John Marshall (1801–1835), the Civil War, the New Deal, and the civil rights movement and the expanded use of the Fourteenth Amendment from the 1950s through the 1970s. Since the late 1970s, we have seen increasing opposition to the growth of what is called "big government" on the part of citizens and officials alike, but most of the efforts to cut it back in size and to restore power to the states have been unsuccessful.

JOHN MARSHALL: STRENGTHENING THE CONSTITUTIONAL POWERS OF THE NATIONAL GOVERNMENT

McCulloch v. Maryland the Supreme Court ruling (1819) confirming the supremacy of national over state government

John Marshall, the third chief justice of the United States, was a man committed to the Federalist narrative about strong national power. His rulings did much to strengthen the power of the national government both during his lifetime and after. The 1819 case of *McCulloch v. Maryland* set the tone. In resolving this dispute about whether Congress had the power to charter a bank and whether the state of Maryland had the power to tax that bank, Marshall had plenty of scope for exercising his preference for a strong national government. Congress did have the power, he ruled, even though the Constitution didn't spell it out, because Congress was empowered to do whatever was necessary and proper to fulfill its constitutional obligations. Marshall did not interpret the word *necessary* to mean "absolutely essential," but rather he took a looser view, holding that Congress had the power to do whatever was "appropriate" to execute its powers. If that meant chartering a bank, then the necessary and proper clause could be stretched to include chartering a bank. Furthermore, Maryland could not tax the federal bank because "the power to tax involves the power to destroy."[12] If Maryland could tax the federal bank, that would imply it had the power to destroy it, making Maryland supreme over the national government and violating the Constitution's supremacy clause, which makes the national government supreme.

Marshall continued this theme in *Gibbons v. Ogden* in 1824.[13] In deciding that New York did not have the right to create a steamboat monopoly on the Hudson River, Marshall focused on the part of Article I, Section 8, that allows Congress to regulate commerce "among the several states." He interpreted *commerce* very broadly to include almost any kind of business, creating a justification for a national government that could freely regulate business and that was dominant over the states.

Gibbons v. Ogden did not immediately establish national authority over business. Business interests were far too strong to meekly accept government authority, and subsequent Court decisions recognized that strength and a prevailing public philosophy of laissez-faire. The national government's power in general was limited by cases such as *Cooley v. Board of Wardens of Port of Philadelphia* (1851),[14] which gave the states greater power to regulate commerce if local interests outweigh national interests, and *Dred Scott v. Sanford* (1857),[15] which held that Congress did not have the power to outlaw slavery in the territories.

THE CIVIL WAR: NATIONAL DOMINATION OF THE STATES

The Civil War represented a giant step in the direction of a stronger national government. The war itself was fought for a variety of reasons. Besides the issue of slavery and the conflicting economic and cultural interests of the North and the South, the war was fought to resolve the question of national versus state supremacy. When the national government, dominated by the northern states, passed legislation that would have furthered northern interests, the southern states tried to invoke the doctrine of nullification. Nullification was the idea that states could render national laws null if they disagreed with them, but the national government never recognized this doctrine. The southern states also seceded, or withdrew from the United States, as a way of rejecting national authority, but the victory of the Union in the ensuing war showed decisively that states did not retain their sovereignty under the Constitution.

> What would the U.S. government be like today if states had the power of nullification?

THE NEW DEAL: NATIONAL POWER OVER BUSINESS

The Civil War did not settle the question of the proper balance of power between national government and business interests. In the years following the war, the courts struck down both state and national laws regulating business. In 1895 *Pollock v. Farmer's Loan and Trust Co.* held

Gibbons v. Ogden the Supreme Court ruling (1824) establishing national authority over interstate business

nullification the declaration by a state that a federal law is void within its borders

Redefining American Government

This highly partisan contemporary cartoon shows President Franklin Roosevelt cheerfully steering the American ship of state toward economic recovery, despite detractors in big business. New Deal policies redefined the scope of both national and state powers.

that the federal income tax was unconstitutional (until it was legalized by the Sixteenth Amendment to the Constitution in 1913).[16] *Lochner v. New York* (1905) said that states could not regulate working hours for bakers.[17] This ruling was used as the basis for rejecting state and national regulation of business until the middle of the New Deal in the 1930s. *Hammer v. Dagenhart* (1918) said that national laws prohibiting child labor were outside Congress' power to regulate commerce and therefore were unconstitutional.[18]

Throughout the early years of Franklin Roosevelt's New Deal, designed amid the devastation of the Great Depression of the 1930s to recapture economic stability through economic regulations, the Supreme Court maintained its antiregulation stance. But the president berated the Court for striking down his programs, and public opinion backed the New Deal and Roosevelt himself against the interests of big business. Eventually the Court had a change of heart. Once established as constitutional, New Deal policies redefined the purpose of American government and thus the scope of national and state powers. The relationship between nation and state became more cooperative as the government became employer, provider, and insurer of millions of Americans in times of hardship. Our Social Security system was born during the New Deal, as were many other national programs designed to get America back to work and back on its feet. A sharper contrast to the laissez-faire policies of the early 1900s can hardly be imagined.

CIVIL RIGHTS: NATIONAL PROTECTION AGAINST STATE ABUSE

The national government picked up a host of new roles as American society became more complex, including that of guarantor of individual rights against state abuse.

The Fourteenth Amendment to the Constitution was passed after the Civil War to make sure southern states extended all the protections of the Constitution to the newly freed slaves. In the 1950s and 1960s the Supreme Court used it to strike down state laws that maintained segregated, or separate, facilities for whites and African Americans, from railway cars to classrooms. By the 1970s the Court's interpretation of the Fourteenth Amendment had expanded, allowing it to declare unconstitutional many state laws that it said deprived state citizens of their rights as U.S. citizens. For instance, the Court ruled that states had to guarantee those accused of state crimes the same protections that the Bill of Rights guaranteed those accused of federal crimes. As we will see in more detail in Chapter 4, the Fourteenth Amendment has come to be a means for severely limiting the states' powers over their own citizens, sometimes very much against their will.

The trend toward increased national power has not killed the narrative that states should have more power. In the 1970s and 1980s Presidents Richard Nixon and Ronald Reagan tried hard to return some responsibilities to the states, mainly by giving them more control over how they spent federal money. In the next section, we look at recent efforts to alter the balance of federal power in favor of the states.

In Your Own Words   Demonstrate how the flexibility built into the Constitution has allowed it to change with the times.

FEDERALISM TODAY
A continuing struggle

Clearly, federalism is a continually renegotiated compromise between advocates of strong national government on the one hand and advocates of state power on the other. Making the job of compromise more complex, however, is that, as we have suggested, federalism is not a purely ideological issue; it also reflects pragmatic politics. If a party dominates the federal government for a long time, its members become accustomed to looking to that government to accomplish their aims. Those whose party persists in the minority on the federal level tend to look to the states.[19] In short, most of the time people will fight to have decisions made in the arena (national or state) where they are most likely to prevail, or where the opposition will have the greatest difficulty achieving its policy goals.

THE POLITICS OF CONTEMPORARY FEDERALISM

Although the Supreme Court, since the days of *Marbury v. Madison*, had endorsed an extension of the range of the national government, the conservative Supreme Court under Chief Justice William Rehnquist passed down a set of decisions beginning in 1991 that signaled a rejection of congressional encroachment on the prerogatives of the states—a power shift that was dubbed "devolution." However, that movement came to an abrupt stop in 2002 following the attacks of September 11, 2001. The Court continues to have a conservative majority under Chief Justice John Roberts, and that is unlikely to change as long as Donald Trump is president.[20]

Whether or not the Supreme Court's decisions give the federal government greater latitude in exercising its powers, the states are still responsible for the policies that most affect our lives. For instance, the states retain primary responsibility for everything from education to regulation of funeral parlors, from licensing physicians to building roads and telling us how fast we can drive on them. Most questions of contemporary federalism involve the national government trying to influence how the states and localities go about providing the goods and services and regulating the behaviors that have traditionally been within their jurisdictions.

Why should the national government care so much about what the states do? There are several reasons. First, from a Congress member's perspective, it is easier to solve many social and economic problems at the national level, especially when those problems, like race discrimination or air pollution, affect the populations of multiple states. In some instances, national problem solving involves redistributing resources from one state or region to another, which individual states, on their own, would be unwilling or unable to do. Second, members of Congress profit electorally by passing laws and regulations that bring resources like highway funds; welfare benefits; urban renewal money; and assistance to farmers,

PROFILES IN CITIZENSHIP:
Susana Martinez

Being governor isn't on everyone's list of childhood aspirations, but it had been on Susana Martinez's since she was about fourteen. "I enjoyed watching the news where we would watch senators and congressmen debate each other and argue their points. That I really enjoyed; who would make the better point, and why." But being a senator didn't appeal. She says, "I knew that as one of a hundred, how much change can you bring when you have to convince so many more? I thought the best place to cause the greatest change was being a governor, so that became my goal." She became a lawyer, and then a prosecutor, and then district attorney. She served two terms as governor of New Mexico from 2011 to 2018. When you talk to her about it, it is clear she enjoyed every minute.

On patriotism:

"I would define patriotism as love of one's country and being loyal to it. I also believe it is important to acknowledge our history and God's providence. I think believing in something and having faith is very important. When I was a prosecutor, I remember before I went into the courtroom and after studying all the information—I believed in the case I was prosecuting and in the facts I had collected, and in the end, everything just gelled. Sure there were moments when things weren't always perfect, maybe a piece of information just didn't fit as neatly as we would like or something was said by someone that changed things slightly, but I would assemble all the available information and evidence, and have confidence in what we were pursuing."

On keeping the republic:

"I think to keep the republic, people must stay informed, particularly youth. With the world of technology, it can play both ways as there is an abundance of information, but also a dearth of attention. On my iPhone and iPad, I can access every piece of news I could ever want. From what's happening in the Middle East in *The New York Times* to developments in Congress in *The Washington Post* to our local newspapers, it's all at my fingertips. But at the same time, all that access to information, including movies and other things can take away from—for instance—watching the six o'clock news, which is very important to stay informed. Consuming information is not enough, in that discussion is required, whether you agree with someone's viewpoint or not. A cup of coffee at Starbucks, where the kids hang out, can go a long way to receiving a diversity of opinion. In the end, if we are discussing important issues, we can have more control over determining our own future and crafting our destinies as individuals, as a community and as a nation."

Source: Susana Martinez spoke with Christine Barbour and Gerald C. Wright on September 23, 2014.

ranchers, miners, and educators to their states. Doing well by constituents gets incumbents reelected.[21] Third, sometimes members of Congress prefer to adopt national legislation to preempt what states may be doing or planning to do. In some cases they might object to state laws, as Congress did when it passed civil rights legislation against the strong preferences of the southern states. In other cases they might enact legislation to prevent states from making fifty different regulatory laws for the same product. If Congress makes a set of nationally binding regulations, businesses or corporations—generally large contributors to politicians—do not have to incur the expense of altering their products or services to meet different state standards.

To deliver on their promises, national politicians must have the cooperation of the states. Although some policies, such as Social Security, can be administered easily at the national level, others, such as changing educational policy or altering the drinking age, remain under state authority and cannot be legislated in Washington. This creates one of federal policymakers' biggest challenges: how to get the states to do what federal officials have decided they should do.

HOW THE NATIONAL GOVERNMENT TRIES TO INFLUENCE THE STATES

Congress makes two key decisions when it attempts to influence what the states are doing. The first concerns the character of the rules and regulations that are issued: Will they be broad enough to allow the states flexibility, or narrow and specific enough to guarantee that policy is executed as Washington wishes? The other is about whether the cost of the new programs will be paid for by the national government and, if so, how much of the cost the government will cover. The combination of these two decisions yields the four general congressional strategies for influencing the states that you can see laid out in a grid in this chapter's *The Big Picture*.

- **Option One (No National Government Influence).** In the period of dual federalism, the federal government left most domestic policy decisions to the states. When it chooses to leave a state's authority unchallenged, it provides no instructions (either broad or specific) and no funding (second column, second row in *The Big Picture*). When there is no national government influence, states can act as they wish in the given policy area.
- **Option Two (Categorical Grants).** Sometimes Congress decides that the nation's interests depend on all the states taking actions to solve a particular problem—perhaps the provision of early childhood education or food security for the disadvantaged. The most popular tool Congress has devised for this purpose is the categorical grant (first column, first row in *The Big Picture*), which provides detailed instructions, regulations, and compliance requirements for the states (and sometimes for local governments as well) in specific policy areas. If a state complies with the requirements, federal money is released for those specified purposes. If a state doesn't comply with the detailed provisions of the categorical grant, it doesn't get the money. In many cases the states also have to provide some funding themselves.

The states, like most governments, never have enough money to meet all their citizens' demands, so categorical grants can look very attractive, at least on the surface. The grants can be refused, but that rarely happens. In fact, state and local governments have become so dependent on federal grants that these subsidies now make up more than a quarter of all state and local spending.[22] State politicians, however, chafe under the requirements and all the paperwork that the federal government imposes with categorical grants. States and localities also frequently argue that federal regulations prevent them from doing a good job. They want the money, but they also want more flexibility. Most members of Congress, by contrast, like to use categorical grants—they receive credit for sponsoring specific grant programs, which in turn helps establish them as national policy leaders, building their reputations with their constituents for bringing "home" federal money.

categorical grant federal funds provided for a specific purpose and restricted by detailed instructions, regulations, and compliance standards

- **Option Three (Block Grants).** State politicians understandably want the maximum amount of freedom possible. They want to control their own destinies, not just carry out political deals made in Washington, and they want to please the coalitions of interests and voters that put them in power in the states. Their preferred policy tool, the block grant (first column, second row in *The Big Picture*), combines broad (rather than detailed) program requirements and regulations with funding from the federal treasury. Block grants give the states considerable freedom in using the funds in broad policy areas. State officials find support here from conservative politicians at the national level who, despite the electoral advantages to be gained from them, have long balked at the detailed, Washington-centered nature of categorical grants.

  Congress has generally resisted the block grant approach for both policy and political reasons. In policy terms, many members of Congress fear that the states will pursue their own agendas instead of what Congress intends. One member characterized the idea of putting federal money into block grants as "pouring money down a rat hole"[23] because it is impossible to control how the states deal with particular problems under block grants. Congress also has political objections to block grants. When federal funds are not attached to specific programs, members of Congress can no longer take credit for the programs. From their standpoint, it does not make political sense to take the heat for taxing people's income, only to return those funds to the states as block grants, leaving governors and mayors to get the credit for how the money is spent. In addition, interest groups contribute millions of dollars to congressional campaigns when members of Congress have control over program specifics. If Congress allows the states to assume that control, interest groups have less incentive to make congressional campaign contributions. As a result, the tendency in Congress has been to place more conditions on block grants with each annual appropriation.[24] Categorical grants remain the predominant form of federal aid, amounting to about 80 percent of all aid to state and local governments.

- **Option Four (Unfunded Mandates).** The politics of federalism yields one more strategy. When the federal government issues an unfunded mandate, it imposes specific policy requirements on the states but does not provide a way to pay for those activities. Rather, Congress forces states to comply by either threatening criminal or civil penalties or promising to cut off other, often unrelated, federal funds if the states do not follow its directions.

  Unfunded mandates are more attractive to members of Congress in periods of ballooning national deficits, when the national government has no money to spend.[25] In large part due to complaints from the states, Congress passed the Unfunded Mandate Act of 1995, which promised to reimburse the states for expensive unfunded mandates or to pass a separate law acknowledging the cost of an unfunded mandate. This act has limited congressional efforts to pass "good laws" that cost the U.S. Treasury nothing. However, because Congress can define what the states see as an unfunded mandate in several different ways—classifying a directive as a simple "clarification of legislative intent," for example—Congress has continued to push some policy costs onto the states.[26] Fears of large unfunded mandates played a role in the debates leading up to health care reform. In 2008 a version of the reform that expanded Medicaid for low-income people prompted instant criticism from governors because significant portions of Medicaid (varying from about 25 to 50 percent) are paid for from the state treasuries.[27]

block grants federal funds provided for a broad purpose and unrestricted by detailed requirements and regulations

unfunded mandate a federal order mandating that states operate and pay for a program created at the national level

Congress later backed down and provided assistance to the states to fund the new policy, but that did not stop the states from challenging the act in court.

The current status of federalism is a contradictory mix of narratives about returning power to the states and new national initiatives (and program requirements) in the areas of health, education, and the environment (see *Don't Be Fooled by . . . Political Rhetoric*). Although many actors in the states and even the national government say they want the states to have more power, or simply that they want all levels of government to do *less*, the imperatives of effective policy solutions and congressional and presidential electoral calculations combine to create strong pressures for national solutions to our complex problems.

Advocates for the national government and supporters of the states are engaged in a constant struggle for power, as they have been since the days of the Articles of Confederation. The power of the federal government is enhanced through the mechanisms of cooperative federalism, which gives the federal government an increasing role in domestic policy. As the federal government has used the restrictive rules of categorical grants and the economic threats that provide the muscle of unfunded mandates, critics have claimed that cooperative federalism has been transformed into "coercive federalism," in which the states are pressured to adopt national solutions to their local problems with minimal state input.

It is worth remembering, however, that members of Congress who pass the laws are elected in the states and have their primary loyalties to their local constituencies, not to any national audience. Their states have traditionally been only too happy to accept federal funds to meet the needs of their residents (and voters) for everything from education to highways to welfare and health care for the poor. However, they also chafe under the rules and regulations that typically come with federal dollars. Especially since 2009, the powerful antigovernment rhetoric emerging from the Republican Party and its Tea Party wing strongly opposes the growth of the federal government. All of this opposition can override even the electoral incentives that members of Congress have for supporting policies that bring federal money to their states. For example, roughly one-third of the states have still not accepted federal funds to expand Medicaid to provide health care coverage to low-income citizens under the Affordable Care Act.

This tension is currently playing out in the aftermath of the slower growth that followed the country's longest and worst economic recession since the Great Depression. The states were particularly hard hit as revenues from sales, income, and property taxes dropped dramatically. Federal stimulus funds helped the states deal with about 40 percent of their budget shortfalls, but many conservative governors and legislatures rejected the funds, seeing them as encroachments by a power-hungry federal government rather than as necessary short-term help in hard times.[28] In any case, those funds began drying up in 2010, leaving the states with

"In Two Words, Yes And No"

THE BIG PICTURE:
How the National Government Influences the States

Public demands, policy complexities, and electoral politics all put pressures on the national government to expand its powers beyond those enumerated in the Constitution. To get the states to do its will, Congress has to decide if it is willing to pay for what it wants and how much it trusts the states to comply voluntarily.

FEDERAL GRANTS

STRICT AND SPECIFIC REQUIREMENTS

Categorical Grants (federal funding with strings attached)

Look what we did!

Good for congressional credit-taking

We'll obey.

Ensures state compliance and policy uniformity

State Program

Heavy regulatory burden (red tape)

National policy requirements may not be appropriate for local conditions

---

NO RULES OR BROAD GRANTS OF POWER WITHIN PROGRAMS

Block Grants (federal funding without strings attached)

State Program

Greater state flexibility

State politicians love money without strings

Hey! We helped.

Greater program innovation; undermines congressional credit-taking

STATE GRANT

Grants become highly vulnerable to federal budget cuts

NATIONAL POLICY
a
STATE POLICY *b*
STATE POLICY *c*

Leads to policy diversity and inequality, meeting state rather than national goals

---

Categorical Grants *in real life*:
The Environmental Protection Agency makes categorical grants to states specifically to fund state partnerships in enforcing the Clean Water Act, the Clean Air Act, and the Safe Drinking Water Act. States have no flexibility in how to spend the funds they receive from EPA.

Block Grants *in real life*:
Since 1974, Housing and Urban Development has offered Community Development Block Grants to local government units of the states to provide affordable housing, to deliver services to the disadvantaged, and to draw businesses and jobs to poorer urban areas. Communities have a great deal of flexibility in how they use the funds to meet these needs.

NO FEDERAL GRANTS

Unfunded Mandate (strict and specific requirements)

Very cheap for the federal government

Easy way for members of Congress to garner favor

States complain about unfairness and burdensome regulations

Undermines state cooperation

No Federal Influence (no rules or broad grants of power within programs)

States have autonomy and pay for their own programs

Results in high diversity of policies, including inequality; promotes state competition and its outcomes

Calls for congressional and presidential restraint in exercising their powers

Unfunded Mandates *in real life*:
The No Child Left Behind Act of 2001 required that public schools administer state-wide standardized tests to students. If schools did not show yearly improvement on the tests, they had to take steps at their own expense to raise the quality of the education they provided.

No Federal Influence *in real life*:
Martin Luther King Jr. Day was established as a federal holiday (most federal employees get a paid day off) in 1968. But that was not binding on the states and a number resisted. It took until 2000 for all the states to recognize it, and some states used other names for a time, like Civil Rights Day (New Hampshire) or Lee-Jackson-King Day (Virginia).

Political Rhetoric

You are a hot commodity. Every day, politicians, pundits, advertisers, bloggers, and politically minded folks in your social networks are vying for your attention, your support, your votes, and possibly your dollars, and they employ an entire arsenal of weapons—eloquent words, seductive arguments, tempting promises—designed to get you to buy their political narrative.

As a critical consumer of information, it's important that you understand what you're up against. Learning to identify logical fallacies (forms of faulty reasoning) and to understand different types of persuasive appeals not only can make you a better consumer of political information but also can help you to articulate your own arguments in a way that is both persuasive and ethical.

WHAT TO WATCH OUT FOR

- **The post hoc fallacy.** From the Latin *post hoc ergo propter hoc* (meaning "after this, therefore because of this"), the post hoc fallacy occurs when one draws a cause-and-effect relationship between two events simply because one follows the other. You might observe, for example, that students who take notes on laptops do well on exams. But if you assert that the digital note-taking causes better grades, then you're falling victim to the post hoc fallacy.

- **Appeals to tradition.** Historical evidence is important, but using tradition as a litmus test for what is right or wrong is not always sound. When a pundit points to the way things have always been, it's your job to carefully evaluate whether or not the way things have always been is the way things ought to be. Such appeals are particularly effective in persuading people who are nervous about change, which is one reason

they come up so frequently in political narratives relating to things like marriage and family.

- **Emotional appeals.** One surefire way to get lots of attention fast is to go for the heart: stirring up anger, fear, disgust, or empathy gets a quick reaction. It's impossible to ignore your emotions when something is upsetting, but it pays to take a moment to evaluate whether you are being persuaded by evidence, or just by your own emotions.

- **The "straw man" fallacy.** One way to make an argument appear stronger is to show that competing ideas are weaker. That can be fine when evaluating the strengths and weaknesses of two viable options. However, pundits often pit their argument not against actual alternatives, but instead against a simplified, weaker counterargument (or "straw man") that can easily be knocked down. When someone presents a weak or even ludicrous counterargument, check to see whether the counterargument is even real. Unfortunately, when a straw man argument is also an emotional appeal, it can take on a narrative life of its own. Consider, for example, hysteria over government "death panels" during the fight over the Patient Protection and Affordable Care Act.

- **The slippery slope.** You've heard this one a million times, on both sides of such contentious issues as gun control and freedom of speech: If you limit or allow one thing, that will eventually lead us down a "slippery slope" to anarchy, tyranny, or some other unthinkable outcome. It's often possible that one will lead to another, but when someone presents such connections as inevitable, without any proof, you should take their arguments with the proverbial grain of salt.

- **The false dilemma.** Beware any argument that implies that limited options are available, especially when it comes to policy. Just because the narrative implies there are no compromises or alternatives doesn't mean that's true.

- **Bandwagoning.** The United States may be a democracy governed by, for, and of the people—but facts remain facts whether they are widely held or not. If a writer or commentator is using the popularity of a statement as proof of its validity, you should immediately take a second look. Opinions and beliefs are not credible evidence, even if they are widely agreed upon.

- **Anecdotal evidence and hasty generalizations.** Anecdotes liven up speeches and can lend support to arguments—but they're of limited use when making a point, and they should never be used as evidence of a trend. One story does not carry as much weight as real statistics that come from systematic research.

- **Red herrings.** Take care to sort out and ignore irrelevant or unrelated information, which can be insinuated into arguments purely for the sake of distracting you from the matter at hand.

- **Cherry-picking evidence.** Deciding what evidence to use—and what to leave out—is a crucial step in developing any argument. In the process, it may be tempting to select only the evidence that supports one's own opinion and to ignore evidence that contradicts it. This tendency, which social scientists call confirmation bias, often occurs unconsciously, so it is especially important to be vigilant in weeding it out of any arguments you encounter—including your own.

continuing insufficient funds and forcing them to lay off workers to make up the difference.[29] The recovery of the states continued to lag behind that of the general economy, with the result that many citizens still faced substantially decreased services from the states in the areas of education, health, and public security.[30]

But oddly, as we suggested earlier, as the national policymaking machinery can grind to a halt under divided government, an opportunity has opened up for states to take more action on their own. For several years a conservative Republican-controlled Congress resisted virtually every initiative put forth by the Obama administration, and similarly, President Obama was not shy about using the veto when Congress sent him bills that did not fit with his agenda. National inaction has left a policy vacuum that is being filled with state policy initiatives. Even though President Trump does not face divided government, the Republican caucus itself is split, causing inactivity at the national level that can be countered at the state level.

Three-fifths of the states are under unified control—both houses of the state legislature are controlled by the same party as the governor. This has given them the ability to move where gridlocked Washington cannot; and unlike Washington action that moves policy in the same direction nationwide, the states go their own, separate ways. Take immigration policy, for example. Some Republican-led states, such as Alabama and Arizona, have passed restrictive immigration legislation. Other states, where the Democrats are in control, have passed legislation to make life easier for undocumented workers and their families.

Gridlock between the president and Congress has also elevated the role of interexecutive negotiations in making changes in the major areas of education and health care. Republican governors have negotiated "waivers" with the federal bureaucracy (individualized changes in specific laws) to achieve politically workable solutions to problems in Medicaid and other federally mandated programs. The trend of hyperpartisanship and polarization that has led to gridlock at the national level has taken Congress out of the game as a significant actor in many policy areas, while executives (state and federal) make deals and the states take the initiative to implement policy that fits with their voters' (very different) preferences.[31]

In Your Own Words Describe the ways in which the national government can influence the states.

CITIZENSHIP AND FEDERALISM

Enhanced opportunities for participation and power at the state and local levels

State and local governments are closer to their citizens than is the federal government. Whereas the federal government may seem to take the form of an elite democracy, run by people far removed from everyday citizens, state and local governments allow far more opportunities for participatory governance if citizens choose to get involved. Citizens may vote for initiatives and referenda, run for local office, sit on school boards and other advisory boards, or even take part in citizen judicial boards and community-run probation programs.[32] They can also use social media to organize marches and demonstrations and make their voices heard far more clearly at the local level than at the national level.

But there is another way that citizens can shape state and local policies as surely as when they vote at the polls, and that is by voting with their feet. In a kind of political pressure that the federal government almost never has to confront, citizens can move from a state or locality they don't like to one that suits them better. Consider this: few Americans ever think seriously about changing countries. Other nations may be nice to visit, but most of us, for better or worse, will continue to live under the U.S. government. At the same time, far fewer of us will live in the same state or city throughout our lives. We may move for jobs, for climate, or for a better quality of life. When we relocate, we can often choose where we want to go. Businesses also move—for better facilities, better tax rates, a better labor force, and so on—and they are also in a position to choose where they want to go. This mobility of people and businesses creates incentives for competition and cooperation among states and localities that influence how they operate in important ways. Although we do not conventionally consider the decision to move to be a political act, it affects policy just as much as more traditional forms of citizen participation.

In Your Own Words Discuss whether federalism fosters or limits citizen participation in government.

Let's Revisit: What's at Stake . . . ?

As we have seen in this chapter, the issue of what powers go to the federal government and what powers are reserved to the states has been a hotly contested one since the founding, and one that has no clean, crisp, right answer. As the country and the composition of the Supreme Court have changed, so too have interpretations of states' rights and federal power. All of that means the issue of medical marijuana use, which currently is legal in more than half the country, and recreational marijuana, which is legal in nine states plus the District of Columbia, is an excellent example of the messiness that can characterize federal issues in the United States, where national law dictates that any kind of marijuana is illegal.

The states and the national government both have a stake in protecting their turf against the other when it comes to marijuana laws. One of the chief virtues of federalism is that it gives the states the flexibility to experiment and to respond to their citizens' demands for policy change. Policies are frequently incubated in the states before they are ready for launching on the national stage, or before the national stage is ready to receive them. The trouble when it comes to legalizing marijuana—medical or recreational—is that there is already a binding federal policy in place. The federal government under the George W. Bush administration claimed that its law trumped state laws because of the commerce clause, the part of Article I, Section 8, of the Constitution that gives Congress the power to regulate commerce among the states. The Supreme Court backed that view in 2005, voting six to three in *Gonzales v. Raich*, a case concerning a California medical marijuana law.[31] Defenders of the laws responded that growing, selling, or smoking marijuana for personal medical use within a single state has nothing to do with interstate commerce. Fourteen states passed laws decriminalizing the use of marijuana for medical purposes by prescription, and slowly, federal law swung in their direction. In May 2009 the Supreme Court refused to hear a case challenging the California law, essentially handing a victory to medical marijuana proponents, and that October, the Justice Department, then under the Barack Obama administration, signaled that, as long as use was consistent with state laws, marijuana use by those holding a prescription for it would not be prosecuted.[32] Reading these cues, more states followed suit, only to see the Trump administration rescind the Obama policy, although the policy's current status remains unclear.

State law can conflict, of course, not just with national law but with the laws of other states, and here it is the states that have a stake in enforcing their own marijuana laws— either because their citizens deeply disagree with the laws of other states or because there is profit to be had in prosecuting people from other states who violate the law. As the Idaho example in *What's at Stake . . . ?* suggested, states with different laws and policies can provide treacherous terrain for their citizens, and nice cash cows for the states collecting fines for violations of their laws. The flip side of federalism's ability to permit experimentation and innovation is that on some issues you can end up with fifty different policies regulating the same behavior. As the Idaho example indicates, citizens from one state can be caught flat-footed when visiting another if they don't take care to learn the laws of their destination.

It is not just states that have a stake in setting their own laws on things like marijuana policy; businesses also have a stake in what states do and in resolving the legal confusion that can result from federalism. As is evident in the experience of the brothers who grow nonintoxicating marijuana for medical purposes, but who faced barriers to transporting the medicinal oil across state lines, businesses can face expensive and exasperating delays and roadblocks when they have to accommodate fifty separate state laws. Throw the federal law into the mix as well, and federalism can be an entrepreneur's nightmare.

Finally, citizens have a stake in how the states manage their policies on marijuana. For some supporters of the medical marijuana laws, what is at stake is the ability of ill patients to receive the most effective treatment possible. But they are allied with those who want to put limits on national power, some of whom might not approve of medical marijuana on its own merits. In his dissent in *Gonzales v. Raich*, Justice Clarence Thomas said, "No evidence from the founding suggests that 'commerce' included the mere possession of a good or some purely personal activity that did not involve trade or exchange for value. In the early days of the Republic, it would have been unthinkable that Congress could prohibit the local cultivation, possession, and consumption of marijuana." If the national government can regulate this, it can regulate anything.[33]

Opponents of the medical marijuana laws say that as long as the Court has ruled that the state laws violate the commerce clause, the national law should be enforced. Further, some argue that it does touch the issue of interstate commerce because the provision and purchase of medical marijuana "affects the marijuana market generally," and they worry that if the federal government cannot regulate this, then perhaps the government will be hampered in other areas, like child pornography, as well.[34]

That there is no clear constitutional resolution of such issues; that it is possible for the Court to produce conflicting rulings on this policy; and that the Bush, Obama, and Trump administrations would take such variable stances on it explains both how our federal system has found the flexibility to survive so long and so well, and why the debates over where power resides can be so bitterly fought.

for CQ Press

Want a better grade?

Get the tools you need to sharpen your study skills. **SAGE edge** offers practice quizzes, eFlashcards, video, and multimedia at **edge.sagepub.com/barbourbrief8e**.

Review

What Is Federalism?

Although the founders of the U.S. Constitution could have created a **unitary system** (87) or **confederal system** (87), they instead established a government based on **federalism** (84), in which some powers are held by the national government and some by the states; others, called **concurrent powers** (85), are held by both. Political scientists once held to a theory called **dual federalism** (86) that considered the powers of the two levels to be separate and distinct but now understand their powers to be interrelated, a view known as **cooperative federalism** (86). The Constitution gives a decisive amount of power to the national government via the **enumerated powers of**

Congress (85), which concludes with the **necessary and proper clause** (85) and the **supremacy clause** (85).

Federalism reflects a continually changing compromise between advocates of a strong national government and advocates of strong state governments. The balance of power adopted between central and subnational governments directly affects the national government's ability to act on large policy problems and the subnational units' flexibility in responding to local preferences. Although power was concentrated at the national level for much of the twentieth century, we are currently in a phase known as **devolution** (84)—shifting power from the national level to the states.

American Federalism Over Time

The growth of national power through much of our history can be traced to the early decisions of Chief Justice John Marshall, notably *McCulloch v. Maryland* (90) and *Gibbons v. Ogden* (91); the constitutional consequences of the Civil War, during which the southern states sought to declare federal laws void within their borders, an unconstitutional process called **nullification** (91); the establishment of national supremacy in economics with the New Deal; and the new national responsibilities in protecting citizens' rights that have been associated with the civil rights movement.

Federalism Today

Where states retain power, Congress can use authority and money to encourage state cooperation with its agenda in four ways: it can exercise no influence, letting states have their way; or it can issue **categorical grants** (95), giving states money in exchange for following specific instructions; **block grants** (96), giving states money in exchange for following broad mandates; or **unfunded mandates** (96), giving states no money but expecting compliance with national laws.

4

Fundamental American Liberties

In Your Own Words

After you've read this chapter, you will be able to

4.1 Define rights and liberties and their role in a democratic society.

4.2 Explain how the Bill of Rights relates to the federal government and to the states.

4.3 Describe how the First Amendment protects both church and state, as well as individuals' religious freedom.

4.4 Explain the value of freedom of expression and how its protections have been tested.

4.5 Give examples of different interpretations of the Second Amendment's meaning.

4.6 Describe the protections afforded criminal defendants under the Constitution.

4.7 Discuss the extent of an individual's right to privacy.

4.8 Compare the idea of civil rights with civil obligations.

What's at Stake . . . in Regulating the Internet?

Net neutrality. It's the kind of free expression issue the founders never dreamed of.

Even the founders of the Internet had no idea what they were starting. The early days of the Internet were the wild, wild West—the frontier of information technology. People communicated freely, individuals wrote their own rules, and freewheeling entrepreneurs could take off on exciting adventures, make their fortunes, and create empires. (Hello, Jeff Bezos and Mark Zuckerberg, we are looking at you!) There was no lawman in town, mostly because there were no laws.

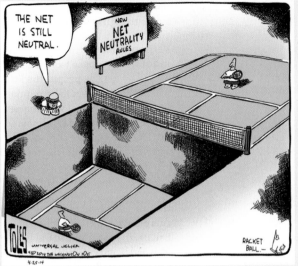

In those formative years of anything-goes-online life, it was hard to imagine that one day we would be asked to pay for access to news sites, have to pay sales tax on purchases made online, or be limited by profit-minded Internet providers in where we could go and how fast we could get there. The world was our electronic oyster.

That was then.

Today the Internet isn't just a quirky place where academics or gamers or other nerdy types hang out. It is a virtual public square that an increasing number of us visit daily, hourly, or constantly, a line of communication on which most of us depend to mediate our social ties, our business lives, our creative work, our faith, and our entertainment. Of course we expect to pay for an Internet provider, but having our online access limited beyond that—to pay different amounts to access sites depending on whether the sites have economic or political clout—seems at once outrageous and fundamentally unfair, as if we were being asked to pay for access to the air we breathe or the ground we walk on.

And that is the issue at the heart of **net neutrality**: the idea that Internet providers should provide the same access to all sites, regardless of content or source. Providers should not favor or promote some sites over others, or offer them at a premium speed, and no sites should be discriminated against by a provider's tax or penalty. In other words, the government should regulate Internet providers so that they provide users equal access to all sites.

Many groups, from the libertarian right to the progressive left, have been in favor of net neutrality. Then-candidate Barack Obama endorsed the idea in 2007, and under his administration the Federal Communications Commission (FCC) adopted a net neutrality policy in 2010.

Obama claimed that net neutrality was necessary for "lowering the cost of a new idea, igniting new political movements, and bringing communities closer together."[1] Other supporters said it was about freedom of expression (one Democratic commissioner said

net neutrality the idea that Internet providers should provide access to all websites without preference or prejudice

that the rule was "no more a plan to regulate the Internet 'than the First Amendment is a plan to regulate free speech'").[2]

Verizon Communications challenged the FCC ruling in court, where it was overturned in 2014. In response to a citizens' petition on the White House's "We the People" site, signed by 105,572 people, the FCC classified Internet providers as "common carriers," which allowed them to be regulated as public utilities under the 1934 Communications Law designed to deal with the new media of radio and television. During a required public comment period, almost four million Americans chimed in on the subject, an FCC record. On February 26, 2015, the FCC voted in favor of the principle that all Internet traffic should be treated the same.[3]

Not surprisingly, the vote was immediately controversial. In April 2016 the House of Representatives passed a bill along party lines that banned the FCC from reviewing the rates that Internet service providers charge, an effort to blunt the effect of the FCC rule change. Although it had no chance of becoming law (even if it got through the Senate, the president would have vetoed it), it was seen as a victory by Republicans who had been trying to strike down net neutrality.[4] A Republican commissioner on the FCC who voted against the new rule said that it would lead to a "monumental shift" toward "government control of the Internet." He argued that rates would go up, service would slow as more users accessed the system for free, and it would open the doors to "billions of dollars in new taxes."[5] A Republican House member who voted for the congressional legislation said, "The last thing we want to throw on there is the cold water of Washington bureaucracy, after the fact regulation, that will stifle competition and innovation."[6]

And then, when Donald Trump became president in 2017, he appointed Republicans to the FCC who overturned the Obama-era policy, allowing Internet service providers to charge what they wanted. Within months, Democratic-backed legislation to overturn the FCC regulations had passed in the Senate with some Republican support. It had no hope of passing in the House, however, and President Trump would have almost certainly vetoed it anyway. Democrats hoped to leverage their position, popular with the public, into electoral advantage in November 2018.[7]

Polls showed that 83 percent of the public favored the Obama-era net neutrality, including a large majority of Republicans.[8] Given our constitutional guarantees of free speech and free press in this country, not to mention the right of the people to assemble, which is the kind of engagement that could easily be promoted, or stifled, on the Internet, it's hard to see where the force of the objections comes from. Why the controversy about a principle that on its face just makes the Internet a more fair and open channel of communication? We'll take a closer look at this issue after we explore the political battles Americans have fought to secure all of their freedoms.

"**GIVE** me liberty," declared patriot Patrick Henry at the start of the Revolutionary War, "or give me death." "Live Free or Die," proudly proclaims the message on the New Hampshire license plate. Americans have always put a lot of stock in their freedom. Certain that they live in the least restrictive country in the world, Americans celebrate their freedoms and are proud of the Constitution, the laws, and the traditions that preserve them.

And yet, living collectively under a government means that we aren't free to do whatever we want. Limits on our freedoms allow us to live peacefully with others, minimizing the conflict that would result if we all did exactly what we pleased. John Locke said that liberty does not equal license; that is, the freedom to do some things doesn't mean the freedom to do everything. Deciding what rights we give up to join civilized society, and what rights we retain, is one of the great challenges of democratic government.

What are these things called "rights" or "liberties," so precious that some Americans are willing to lay down their lives to preserve them? On the one hand, the answer is very simple. *Rights* and *liberties* are synonyms; they mean freedoms or privileges to which one has a claim. In that respect, we use the words more or less interchangeably. But when prefaced by the word *civil*, both *rights* and *liberties* take on a more specific meaning, and they no longer mean quite the same thing.

Our **civil liberties** are individual freedoms that place limitations on the power of government. In general, civil liberties protect our right to think and act without government interference. Some of these rights are spelled out in the Constitution, particularly in the Bill of Rights. These include the rights to express ourselves and to choose our own religious beliefs. Others, like the right to privacy, rest on the shakier ground of judicial decision making. Although government is prevented from limiting these freedoms per se, they are often limited anyway, even if only by another person's rights. Government does play a role in resolving the conflicts between individuals' rights.

While civil liberties refer to restrictions on government action, **civil rights** refer to the extension of government action to secure citizenship rights for all members of society. When we speak of civil rights, we most often mean that the government must treat all citizens equally, apply laws fairly, and not discriminate unjustly against certain groups of people. Most of the rights we consider civil rights are guaranteed by the Thirteenth, Fourteenth, Fifteenth, Nineteenth, and Twenty-sixth Amendments. These amendments lay out fundamental rights of citizenship, most notably the right to vote, but also the right to equal treatment before the law and the right to due process of the law. They forbid government from making laws that treat people differently on the basis of race, and they ensure that the right to vote cannot be denied on the basis of race or gender.

Not all people live under governments whose rules guarantee them fundamental liberties. In fact, we argued earlier that one way of distinguishing between authoritarian and nonauthoritarian governments is that nonauthoritarian governments, including democracies, give citizens the power to challenge government if they believe it has denied them their basic rights. In fact, democracies depend on the existence of rights in at least two ways. First, civil liberties provide rules that keep government limited, so that it cannot become too powerful. Second, civil rights help define who "we, the people" are in a democracy, and they give those people the power necessary to put some controls on their governments.

We will take two chapters to explore in depth the issues of civil liberties and civil rights. In this chapter we begin with a general discussion of the meaning of rights or liberties in a democracy and then focus on the traditional civil liberties that provide a check on the power of government. In Chapter 5 we focus on civil rights and the continuing struggle of some groups of Americans—like women, African Americans, and other minorities—to be fully counted and empowered in American politics.

As an introduction to the basic civil liberties guaranteed to Americans, in this chapter you will learn about the meaning of rights in a democratic society, the Bill of Rights as part of the federal Constitution and its relationship to the states, and several specific rights that it

civil liberties individual freedoms guaranteed to the people primarily by the Bill of Rights

civil rights citizenship rights guaranteed to the people (primarily in the Thirteenth, Fourteenth, Fifteenth, Nineteenth, and Twenty-sixth Amendments) and protected by the government

details—freedom of religion, speech, and the press; the right to bear arms; the rights of people accused of crimes; and the right to privacy.

RIGHTS IN A DEMOCRACY

Limiting government to empower people

The freedoms we consider indispensable to the working of a democracy are part of the everyday language of politics in America. We take many of them for granted: we speak confidently of our freedoms of speech, of the press, and of religion, and of our rights to bear arms, to a fair trial, and to privacy. There is nothing inevitable about these freedoms, however.

In fact, there is nothing inevitable about the idea of rights at all. Until the writing of such Enlightenment figures as John Locke, it was rare for individuals to talk about claiming rights against government. The prevailing narrative was that governments had all the power, their given subjects only such privileges as government was willing to bestow. Locke argued that the rights to life, liberty, and the pursuit of property were conferred on individuals by nature, and that one of the primary purposes of government was to preserve the natural rights of its citizens.

This notion of natural rights and limited government was central to the founders of the American system. Practically speaking, of course, any government can make its citizens do anything it wishes, regardless of their rights, as long as it is in charge of the military and the police. But in nonauthoritarian governments, the public is usually outraged at the invasion of individual rights. Unless the government is willing to dispense with its reputation as a democracy, it must respond in some way to pacify public opinion. Public opinion and the narrative of natural rights can be a powerful guardian of citizens' liberties in a democracy.

Just as rights limit government, they also empower its citizens. A person who can successfully claim that he or she has rights that government must respect is a citizen of that government. A person who is under the authority of a government but cannot claim rights is merely a subject, bound by the laws but without any power to challenge or change them. This does not mean, as we will see, that a citizen can always have things his or her own way. Nor does it mean that noncitizens have no rights in a democracy. It does mean, however, that citizens have special protections and powers that allow them to stand up to government and plead their cases when they believe an injustice is being done.

However, because rights represent power, they are, like all other forms of power, subject to conflict and controversy. Often for one person to get his or her own way, someone else must lose out. People clash over rights in two ways. First, individuals' rights conflict with each other; for instance, one person's right to share a prayer with classmates at the start of the school day conflicts with another student's right not to be subjected to a religious practice against his or her will. Second, individuals' rights can conflict with society's needs and the demands of collective living; for instance, an individual's right to decide whether or not to wear a motorcycle helmet conflicts with society's need to protect its citizens. Since the terror attacks of September 11, 2001, this latter conflict between individual rights and social needs has been thrown into sharp relief, as measures to protect the population have increased the government's ability to do such things as screen airline passengers, intercept email and conduct roving wiretaps, and gain access to library records and bookstore purchases—all at the expense of individual freedom. The balancing of public safety with individuals' rights is complex. We could ensure our safety from most threats, perhaps, if we were willing to give up all of our freedom, but the ultimate problem, of course, is that without our civil liberties, we have no protection from government itself.

Although conflicts over rights sometimes lead to violence, usually they are resolved in the United States through politics—through the process of arguing, bargaining, and compromising over who gets what, and how. All this wrangling takes place within the institutions of American politics, primarily in Congress and the courts, but also in the White House, at the state and local levels, and throughout our daily lives.

In Your Own Words Define rights and liberties and their role in a democratic society.

THE BILL OF RIGHTS AND THE STATES
Keeping Congress and the states in check

The Bill of Rights looms large in any discussion of American civil liberties, but the document that today seems so inseparable from American citizenship had a stormy birth. Controversy raged over whether a bill of rights was necessary in the first place, deepening the split between Federalists and Anti-Federalists during the founding. And the controversy did not end once it was firmly established as the first ten amendments to the Constitution. Over a century passed before the Supreme Court agreed that at least some of the restrictions imposed on the national government by the Bill of Rights should be applied to the states as well.

WHY IS A BILL OF RIGHTS VALUABLE?

Recall from Chapter 2 that we came very close to not having any Bill of Rights in the Constitution at all. The Federalists had argued that the Constitution itself was a bill of rights, that individual rights were already protected by many of the state constitutions, and that to list the powers that the national government did *not* have was dangerous, as it implied that it *did* have every other power (see *The Big Picture: What the Bill of Rights Means to You*).

To some extent they were correct in calling the Constitution a bill of rights in itself. Protection of some very specific rights is contained in the text of the document. The national government may not suspend writs of **habeas corpus**, which means that it cannot fail to bring prisoners, at their request, before a judge and inform the court why they are being held and what evidence exists against them. This provision protects people from being imprisoned solely for political reasons. Both the national and the state governments are forbidden to pass **bills of attainder**, which are laws that single out a person or group as guilty and impose punishment without trial. Neither can they pass **ex post facto laws**, which are laws that make an action a crime after the fact, even though it was legal when carried out. States may not impair or negate the obligation of contracts; here the founders obviously had in mind the failings of the Articles of Confederation. And the citizens of each state are entitled to "the privileges and immunities of the several states," which prevents any state from discriminating against citizens of other states. This provision protects a nonresident's right to travel freely, conduct business,

habeas corpus the right of an accused person to be brought before a judge and informed of the charges and evidence against him or her

bills of attainder laws under which specific persons or groups are detained and sentenced without trial

ex post facto laws laws that criminalize an action after it occurs

THE BIG PICTURE:
What the Bill of Rights Means to You

Americans like to think that the founders were so concerned with our personal freedoms that they created a bedrock of liberty for us to stand on. But, of course, the Bill of Rights is a political document, and the founders weren't motivated so much by concern for us as by fear of a powerful national government that might use the coercive power of the state for its own ends. Notice that not one of our liberties—even the right to life—is absolute.

GOVERNMENT
CONGRESS
RELIGION FREE
SPEECH REDRESS
LAW
ASSEMBLE
PROHIBITING **PRESS**

1ST FREEDOMS OF PRESS, RELIGION, ASSEMBLY & PETITION

YOU CAN go to a church of your own choosing, observe your religious traditions, express your opinions, publish them as you wish, get together with like-minded people, and convey your collective sentiment to the government.

BUT YOU CAN'T...

practice religion in conflict with the law or in the public sphere with public support, taunt people to pick fights with them, threaten national security, or maliciously ruin a reputation.

FREE
MILITIA
PEOPLE REGULATED
INFRINGED
ARMS **STATE**
SECURITY
NECESSARY

2ND RIGHT TO BEAR ARMS

YOU CAN own a gun, just in case the government should find itself in need of a well-trained militia.

BUT YOU CAN'T...

own a gun without background checks or registration (in some places). Can't just shoot at random, either. Murder and mayhem are still against the law.

PEACE
PRESCRIBED
SOLDIER
LAW **HOUSE**
INFRINGED
QUARTERED
CONSENT **OWNER**

3RD QUARTERING OF SOLDIERS

YOU CAN be free from the government forcing you to let soldiers stay in your house without permission.

BUT YOU CAN'T...

get off so easily if your relatives overstay their welcome. ☺

OATH
SECURE
SEARCHES CAUSE
ARMS **WARRANTS**
VIOLATED
PEOPLE
UNREASONABLE

4TH ARRESTS AND SEARCHES

YOU CAN be protected from unreasonable searches and seizures by the police.

BUT YOU CAN'T...

be protected from all searches. Generally, police need a warrant to search your stuff, including using your cell phone to track your movements. But be darned careful what you carry in your car or say on or text from your phone.

FREE
PROPERTY
PROCESS INFAMOUS
LIFE **CRIMINAL**
INFRINGED
JEOPARDY
LIBERTY **PUBLIC**

5TH RIGHTS OF PERSONS ACCUSED OF CRIMES

YOU CAN be safe from arrest, imprisonment, self-incrimination, having your stuff confiscated, and being put to death without due process of law.

BUT YOU CAN'T...

take back a confession given before you were read your Miranda rights. The cat's out of the bag and the confession usually counts.

Turn to the appendix, p. A-16, for the full text of the Constitution's first ten amendments.

GOVERNMENT
WITNESSES
IMPARTIAL PROCESS
CRIMINAL
SPEEDY LAW
ACCUSATION
CONFRONTED DEFENSE

6TH RIGHTS OF PERSONS ON TRIAL FOR CRIMES

YOU CAN expect a speedy trial, to be told what you are accused of, and to have a lawyer to help you sort it all out.

BUT YOU CAN'T...

assume a "speedy trial" won't take years, or that your overworked public defense lawyer won't be something less than crackerjack.

RE-EXAMINED
COMMON
SUITS COURT
LAW TRIAL
ASSEMBLE
STATES JURY

7TH JURY TRIALS IN CIVIL CASES

YOU CAN have a trial by jury.

BUT YOU CAN'T...

avoid jury duty forever. It's an obligation implied by the right to a jury trial.

PUNISHMENT
EXCESSIVE
UNUSUAL FINES
CRUEL INFRINGED
INFLICTED
SECURITY BAIL

8TH AVOID CRUEL AND UNUSUAL PUNISHMENT

YOU CAN hope you never have to ponder what "cruel" and "unusual" mean. Even SCOTUS isn't entirely sure.

BUT YOU CAN'T...

avoid punishments if you've earned them. So don't push your luck.

ENUMERATION
RIGHTS
OTHERS RETAINED
DENY CERTAIN
DISPARAGE
CONSTITUTION
PEOPLE

9TH RIGHTS KEPT BY THE PEOPLE

YOU CAN have more rights than just the ones listed here (this is what Hamilton was talking about in *Federalist* 78).

BUT YOU CAN'T...

rely on that completely. Some Supreme Court justices think you have only the rights listed here and no more.

STATES
CONSTITUTION
PEOPLE PROHIBITED
UNITED
RESERVED
SECURITY POWERS

10TH POWERS KEPT BY THE STATES OR THE PEOPLE

YOU CAN, if you're a state, get all powers not needed by Congress to carry out its duties (see Article 1, Section 8).

BUT YOU CAN'T...

avoid being subject to 50 sets of state laws, which means that joint you packed in Colorado could get you arrested when you're back in Indiana.

and have access to state courts while visiting another state.[9] Of course, nonresidents are discriminated against when they have to pay a higher nonresident tuition to attend a state college or university, but the Supreme Court has ruled that this type of "discrimination" is not a violation of the privileges and immunities clause.

Some Federalists, however, including James Madison, came to agree with such Anti-Federalists as Thomas Jefferson, who wrote, "A bill of rights is what the people are entitled to against every government on earth."[10] Even though, as the Federalists argued, the national government was limited in principle by popular sovereignty (the concept that ultimate authority rests with the people), it could not hurt to limit it in practice as well. A specific list of the rights held by the people would give the judiciary a more effective check on the other branches.

APPLYING THE BILL OF RIGHTS TO THE STATES

Most of the limitations on government action in the Bill of Rights are directed toward Congress. "Congress shall make no law . . . ," begins the First Amendment. Until about the turn of the twentieth century, the Supreme Court clearly stipulated that the Bill of Rights applied only to the national government and not to the states.[11]

Not until the passage of the Fourteenth Amendment in 1868 did the Supreme Court have a tool to require that states protect their citizens' basic liberties. That post–Civil War amendment was designed specifically to force southern states to extend the rights of citizenship to African Americans, but its wording left it open to other interpretations. The amendment says, in part,

> No state shall make or enforce any law which shall abridge the privileges and immunities of citizens of the United States; nor shall any state deprive any person of life, liberty, or property, without due process of the law; nor deny to any person within its jurisdiction the equal protection of the laws.

In 1897 the Supreme Court tentatively began the process of selective nationalization, or **incorporation**, of most (but not all) of the protections of the Bill of Rights into the states' Fourteenth Amendment obligations to guarantee their citizens due process of the law.[12] But it was not until the case of *Gitlow v. New York* (1925) that the Court reversed almost a century of ruling by assuming that some rights are so fundamental that they deserve protection by the states as well as the federal government.[13] This was a clear shift of power from the states to the national government to determine what rights states had to protect, a shift that came as it so often does at the hands of the Supreme Court. But it did not at first mean that all rights necessarily qualified for incorporation; the Court had to consider each right on a case-by-case basis to see how fundamental it was. Over the years, almost all the rights in the first ten amendments have been incorporated (see Table 4.1).

incorporation the Supreme Court action making the protections of the Bill of Rights applicable to the states

Keep in mind that since incorporation is a matter of interpretation rather than an absolute constitutional principle, it is a judicial creation. Like all other judicial creations, the process of incorporation is subject to reversal if the justices change their minds or if the composition of the Court changes, and it is possible that such a reversal may currently be under way as today's more conservative Court narrows its understanding of the rights that states must protect.

TABLE 4.1

Applying the Bill of Rights to the States

AMENDMENT	ADDRESSES	CASE	YEAR
Fifth	Just compensation	*Chicago, Burlington & Quincy v. Chicago*	1897
First	Freedom of speech Freedom of the press	*Gilbert v. Minnesota* *Gitlow v. New York* *Fiske v. Kansas* *Near v. Minnesota*	1920 1925 1927 1931
Sixth	Counsel in capital cases	*Powell v. Alabama*	1932
First	Religious freedom (generally) Freedom of assembly Free exercise Religious establishment	*Hamilton v. Regents of California* *DeJonge v. Oregon* *Cantwell v. Connecticut* *Everson v. Board of Education*	1934 1937 1940 1947
Sixth	Public trial	*In re Oliver*	1948
Fourth	Unreasonable search and seizure Exclusionary rule	*Wolf v. Colorado* *Mapp v. Ohio*	1949 1961
Eighth	Cruel and unusual punishment	*Robinson v. California*	1962
Sixth	Counsel in felony cases	*Gideon v. Wainwright*	1963
Fifth	Self-incrimination	*Malloy v. Hogan*	1964
Sixth	Impartial jury Speedy trial Jury trial in serious crimes	*Parker v. Gladden* *Klopfer v. North Carolina* *Duncan v. Louisiana*	1966 1967 1968
Fifth	Double jeopardy	*Benton v. Maryland*	1969
Second	Right to bear arms	*McDonald v. Chicago*	2010

In Your Own Words Explain how the Bill of Rights relates to the federal government and to the states.

FREEDOM OF RELIGION

*Limiting Congress to protect both
church and state, and the individual's right to believe*

The First Amendment reads, "Congress shall make no law respecting an establishment of religion, or prohibiting the free exercise thereof; or abridging the freedom of speech, or of the press; or the right of the people peaceably to assemble, and to petition the government for a redress of grievances." These are the "democratic freedoms," the liberties that the founders believed to be so necessary to ensuring a free and unfettered people that they crammed them all into the very first of the amendments. For all that, none of these liberties has escaped controversy, and none has been interpreted by the Supreme Court to be absolute or unlimited.

WHY IS RELIGIOUS FREEDOM VALUABLE?

The briefest look around the world tells us what happens when politics and religion are allowed to mix. When it comes to conflicts over religion, over our fundamental beliefs about the world and the way life should be lived, the stakes are enormous. Passions run deep, and compromise is difficult. In the United States, where a majority of people are religious, religious battles tend to take place in the courts, under the guidelines set out by the First Amendment.

Although not all the founders endorsed religious freedom for everyone, some of them, notably Thomas Jefferson and James Madison, cherished the notion of a universal freedom of conscience—the right of all individuals to believe as they pleased. Jefferson wrote that the First Amendment built "a wall of separation between church and State."[14] The founders based their view of religious freedom on two main arguments. First, history has shown, from the Holy Roman Empire to the Church of England, that when church and state are linked, all individual freedoms are in jeopardy. After all, if government is merely the arm of God, what power of government cannot be justified? Furthermore, religion can divide society into the factions that Madison saw as the primary threat to republican government and individual liberty. A second argument for practicing religious freedom is based on the effect that politics can have on religious concerns. Early champions of a separation between politics and religion worried that the spiritual purity and sanctity of religion would be ruined if it was mixed with the worldly realm of politics, with its emphasis on power and influence.[15]

THE ESTABLISHMENT CLAUSE

The beginning of the First Amendment, forbidding Congress to make laws that would establish an official religion, is known as the **establishment clause**. Americans have fought over the meaning of the establishment clause almost since its inception. Although founders like Jefferson and Madison were clear on their position that church and state should be separate realms, other early Americans were not.

A similar division continues today between the **separationists**, who believe that a "wall" should exist between church and state, and the nonpreferentialists, or **accommodationists**, who contend that the state should not be separate from religion but rather should accommodate it, without showing a preference for one religion over another. Accommodationists argue that the First Amendment should not prevent government aid to religious groups, prayer in school or in public ceremonies, public aid to parochial schools, the posting of religious documents such as the Ten Commandments in public places, or the teaching of the Bible's story of creation along with evolution in public schools. Adherents of this position claim that a rigid interpretation of separation of church and state amounts to intolerance of their religious rights or, in the words of Supreme Court Justice Anthony Kennedy, to "unjustified hostility to religion."[16] Presidents Ronald Reagan, George H. W. Bush, and George W. Bush, and many other Republicans, have shared this view, as have many powerful interest groups such as the Christian Coalition.

establishment clause the First Amendment guarantee that the government will not create and support an official state church

separationists supporters of a "wall of separation" between church and state

accommodationists supporters of government nonpreferential accommodation of religion

A lot is clearly at stake in the battle between the separationists and the accommodationists. On one side of the dispute is the separationists' image of a society in which the rights of all citizens, including minorities, receive equal protection under the law. In this society, religions abound, but they remain private, not matters for public action or support. Very different is the view of the accommodationists, which emphasizes the sharing of community values, determined by the majority and built into the fabric of society and political life.

Today U.S. practice stands somewhere between these two views. Sessions of Congress open with prayers, for instance, but a schoolchild's day does not. Although religion is not kept completely out of our public lives, the Court has generally leaned toward a separationist stance.[17]

As the more conservative appointments of Republican presidents Richard Nixon and Reagan began to shape the Court, the Court's rulings moved in a more accommodationist direction. In *Lemon v. Kurtzman* (1971), the Court added to the old test a third provision that a law not foster "an excessive government entanglement with religion."[18] Under the new *Lemon* **test**, the justices had to decide how much entanglement there was between politics and religion, leaving much to their own discretion.

As the current rule in deciding establishment cases, the *Lemon* test is not used consistently, primarily because the justices have not settled among themselves the underlying issue of whether religion and politics should be separate, or whether state support of religion is permissible.[19] The justices still lean in a separationist direction, but their rulings occasionally nod at accommodationism. Meanwhile, many states have taken matters into their own hands by blurring the line, allowing students to give "inspirational" messages at school events, for instance, or allowing schools to offer Bible classes or to teach evolution as a controversy rather than settled science.[20] These practices and laws are the new battlefield over religious establishment, and the Court will no doubt be called on to weigh in before long.

THE FREE EXERCISE CLAUSE

Another fundamental question about religious freedom that divides the public and justices alike is what to do when religious beliefs and practices conflict with state goals. The second part of the First Amendment grant of religious freedom guarantees that Congress shall make no law prohibiting the free exercise of religion. The **free exercise clause**, as it is called, has generated as much controversy as the establishment clause. When is the state justified in regulating religion? Although Americans have an absolute right to believe whatever they want, their freedom to act is subject to government regulation (see *Snapshot of America: What Do We Believe?*).[21] The state's **police power** allows it to regulate behavior in order to protect its citizens and to provide social order and security. These two valued goods of religious freedom and social order are bound to conflict, and the Court has had an uneasy time trying to draw the line between them. Although it waffled a bit before doing so, the Court has said that schoolchildren cannot be required to salute the American flag if it violates their religious principles to do so (as it does for Jehovah's Witnesses).[22]

The Court has gone back and forth on other religious freedom issues as it has struggled to define what actions the state might legitimately seek to regulate. For a while the Court held that any incidental burden placed on religious freedom must be justified by a **compelling state interest**, that is, the state must show that it is absolutely necessary for some fundamental state purpose that religious freedom be limited.[23] How the Court determines what is and what is not a compelling state interest is examined in Chapter 5.

Lemon **test** the three-pronged rule used by the courts to determine whether the establishment clause is violated

free exercise clause the First Amendment guarantee that citizens may freely engage in the religious activities of their choice

police power the ability of the government to protect its citizens and maintain social order

compelling state interest a fundamental state purpose, which must be shown before the law can limit some freedoms or treat some groups of people differently

Snapshot of America: *What Do We Believe?*

Our Religious Identities

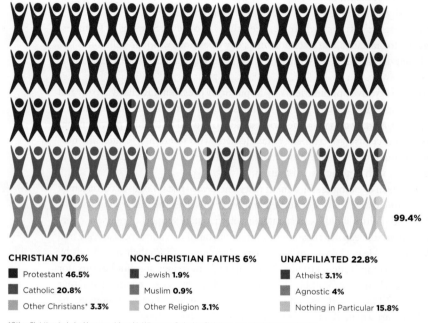

99.4%

CHRISTIAN 70.6%

■ Protestant **46.5%**

■ Catholic **20.8%**

▪ Other Christians* **3.3%**

NON-CHRISTIAN FAITHS 6%

▪ Jewish **1.9%**

▪ Muslim **0.9%**

▪ Other Religion **3.1%**

UNAFFILIATED 22.8%

■ Atheist **3.1%**

▪ Agnostic **4%**

▪ Nothing in Particular **15.8%**

Other Christians includes Mormons, Jehovah's Witnesses, Orthodox Christians, and other Christian religions

How Religious Are We?

26% SOMEWHAT IMPORTANT **53%** VERY IMPORTANT

79% of Americans say that religion is important in their lives.

65% of Americans of all faiths feel that many religions can lead to eternal life.

88% of unaffiliated Americans indicated that they were not looking for a faith that would be right for them.

Behind the Numbers

America has always been a religious nation, and as this infographic shows, it is also an overwhelmingly Christian nation. Americans of Jewish, Muslim, Hindu, and Buddhist faiths, in total, make up less than 10 percent of the population even in diverse cities like New York. Meanwhile, the number of non-religious Americans—those who are not affiliated with any religion—is growing, especially among the youngest Americans. Does the First Amendment provide adequate protection for people of faith? How does it affect those who do not adhere to a specific faith?

Source: Pew Research Center, "America's Changing Religious Landscape," May 12, 2015, www.pewforum .org/2015/05/12/americas-changing-religious-landscape/.

The Court rejected this compelling state interest test, however, in *Employment Division, Department of Human Resources v. Smith* (1990), when it held that if the infringement on religion is not intentional but is rather the by-product of a general law prohibiting socially harmful conduct, applied equally to all religions, then it is not unconstitutional.[24] The Court found that the compelling state interest test, while necessary for cases dealing with matters of race and free speech, was inappropriate for religious freedom issues. Under the *Smith* ruling, a number of religious practices have been declared illegal by state laws on the grounds that the laws do not unfairly burden any particular religion.

Religious groups consider the *Smith* ruling a major blow to religious freedom because it places the burden of proof on the individual or church to show that its religious practices should not be punished, rather than on the state to show that the interference with religious practice is absolutely necessary. In response to the *Smith* decision, Congress in 1993 passed the Religious Freedom Restoration Act (RFRA). This act, supported by a coalition of ninety religious groups, restored the compelling state interest test for state action limiting religious practice and required that when the state did restrict religious practice, it be carried out in the least burdensome way. However, in the 1997 case of *City of Boerne v. Flores*, the Court held that the RFRA was an unconstitutional exercise of congressional power.[25] Congress amended the act in 2003 to apply only to the federal government, and in 2006 the Supreme Court affirmed the amended federal RFRA when it ruled that the act protected a New Mexico church's use of tea containing an illegal substance for sacramental purposes, reinstating the compelling state interest test.[26]

Supporters of greater freedom for religious institutions were heartened greatly in 2012, when the Supreme Court issued a unanimous ruling in *Hosanna-Tabor Evangelical Lutheran Church and School v. Equal Employment Opportunity Commission*, which the *New York Times* called perhaps "its most significant religious liberty decision in two decades."[27] In *Hosanna-Tabor*, the Court held that the hiring practices of religious groups could not be regulated by federal employment law (in this case, law that prohibited discrimination against an employee with a disability), because that would essentially give government the right to tell such groups whom they could hire. Still, the sweeping decision has not stopped critics of the Court's earlier *Boerne* ruling from arguing that to protect religious freedom, the Constitution should be amended to make RFRA the law of the land.[28]

Concern over religious freedom among church members grew after the full implementation of the Patient Protection and Affordable Care Act (ACA) in 2014. The Obama administration interpreted the ACA requirements as meaning that employer-based health insurance should provide birth control coverage, but in 2012 the Supreme Court ruled, in *Burwell v. Hobby Lobby*, that corporations that are not publicly traded (so-called closely held corporations) did not have to provide such coverage if it violated the owners' religious beliefs. This case not only upheld the right of employers not to provide contraception coverage if it conflicted with the employer's religious beliefs but also affirmed that right for some kinds of corporations as well as for individuals.

Meanwhile, when the federal law appeared to be in jeopardy, many states passed their own RFRAs to protect religious practices at the state level, and they have been used to protect a variety of controversial practices on religious grounds, including the denial of services and rights to those in the LGBTQ community. Such laws proliferated again in 2015 and 2016 in the wake of the Supreme Court's ruling that constitutionalized marriage equality. States such as Indiana, Mississippi, and North Carolina suffered serious blowback from companies that considered the intent of such laws to be discriminatory and chose to take their business elsewhere. (We will read more about this in Chapter 5.)

In Your Own Words Describe how the First Amendment protects both church and state, as well as individuals' religious freedom.

FREEDOM OF EXPRESSION

Checking government by protecting speech and the press

Among the most cherished of American values is the right to free speech. The First Amendment reads that "Congress shall make no law . . . abridging the freedoms of speech, or of the press" and, at least theoretically, most Americans agree.[29] When it comes to actually practicing free speech, however, our national record is less impressive. In fact, time and again, Congress has made laws abridging freedom of expression, often with the enthusiastic support of much of the American public. As a nation we have never had a great deal of difficulty restricting speech we don't like, admire, or respect. The challenge of the First Amendment is to protect the speech we despise.

WHY IS FREEDOM OF EXPRESSION VALUABLE?

It is easier to appreciate what is at stake in the battles over when and what kind of speech should be protected if we think about just why we value free speech so much in the first place. Freedom of speech can help to empower citizens and limit government in four ways:

- Free speech is important because citizens are responsible for participating in their government's decisions and they need information provided by an independent, free press to protect them from government manipulation. Mediated citizenship gives us many more channels through which to access information, but that means many more channels to monitor for truth and reliability. In an age in which the president of the United States feels free to label unflattering or critical news coverage "fake news," the imperative to maintain a free press is more critical than ever.
- Free speech can limit government corruption. By being free to voice criticism of government, to investigate its actions, and to debate its decisions, both citizens and journalists are able to exercise an additional check on government that supplements our valued principle of checks and balances.
- Denying free speech sets a dangerous precedent. Censorship in a democracy usually allows the voice of the majority to prevail. One of the reasons to support minority rights as well as majority rule, however, is that we never know when we may fall into the minority on an issue.
- Free speech ensures the vigorous protection of the truth. According to the nineteenth-century English philosopher John Stuart Mill, by allowing the expression of all speech, we discover truths we had previously believed to be false and we develop strong defenses against known falsehoods like racist and sexist ideas.

freedom of expression the right of the people to free speech

free press a press that is able to report fully on government's activities

If free speech is so valuable, why is it so controversial? Like freedom of religion, free speech requires tolerance of ideas and beliefs other than our own, even ideas and beliefs that we find personally repugnant. Those who are convinced that their views are absolutely and eternally true often see no real reason to practice toleration. Many people believe that, in a democracy, the majority should determine the prevailing views and the minority, having lost the vote, so to speak, should shut up. In addition, conflicting ideas about what constitutes the public interest can lead reasonable people to disagree about whether speech ought to be protected or restricted.[30]

SPEECH THAT CRITICIZES THE GOVERNMENT

Sedition, speech that criticizes the government to incite rebellion, has long been a target of restrictive legislation, and most of the founders were quite content that it should be so. Of course, all of the founders had engaged daily in the practice of criticizing their government when they were inciting their countrymen to revolution against England, so they were well aware of the potential consequences of seditious activity. Now that the shoe was on the other foot and they were the government, many were far less willing to encourage dissent. Especially during wartime, it was felt, criticism of the government undermined authority and destroyed patriotism.

Early in our history it was easy enough for those in government to control the information that they felt threatened their power. It didn't take long for American "revolutionaries" to pass the Alien and Sedition Acts of 1798, which outlawed "any false, scandalous writing against the government of the United States." Throughout the 1800s and into the next century, all levels of government, with the support and encouragement of public opinion, squashed the views of radical political groups, labor activists, religious sects, and other minorities. By the end of World War I, thirty-two of forty-eight states had laws against sedition, which essentially prohibited the advocacy of the use of violence or force to bring about industrial or political change. In 1917 the U.S. Congress passed the Espionage Act, which made it a crime to "willfully obstruct the recruiting or enlistment service of the United States," and a 1918 amendment to the act spelled out what that meant. It became a crime to engage in "any disloyal . . . scurrilous, or abusive language about the form of government of the United States, . . . or any language intended to bring the form of government of the United States . . . into contempt, scorn, contumely, or disrepute."[31] Such sweeping prohibitions made it possible to arrest people on the flimsiest of pretexts.

Those arrested and imprisoned under the new sedition laws looked to the Supreme Court to protect their freedom to criticize the government, but they were doomed to disappointment. The Court did not dispute the idea that speech criticizing the government could be punished. The question it dealt with was just how bad the speech had to be before it could be prohibited. The history of freedom of speech cases is a history of the Court devising tests for itself to determine whether certain speech should be protected or could be legitimately outlawed.

In two cases upholding the Espionage Act, *Schenck v. United States* (1919) and *Abrams v. United States* (1919), Justice Oliver Wendell Holmes began to articulate what he called the clear and present danger test.[32] This test, as Holmes conceived it, focused on the circumstances under which language was used. If there were no immediately threatening circumstances, the language in question would be protected, and Congress could not regulate it. But Holmes's views did not represent the Court's majority opinion, and the clear and present danger test was slow to catch on.

With the tensions that led to World War II, Congress again began to fear the power of foreign ideas, especially communism. The Smith Act of 1940 made it illegal to advocate for

sedition speech that criticizes the government to promote rebellion

clear and present danger test the rule used by the courts that allows language to be regulated only if it presents an immediate and urgent danger

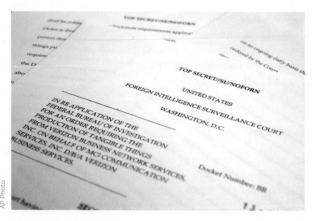

Security or Liberty?

The United States Foreign Intelligence Surveillance Court was created in the 1970s to authorize warrants from agencies like the FBI or the National Security Agency to investigate suspected foreign spies inside the United States. In 2013 it was revealed that the court had authorized the collection of metadata on millions of Americans' phone records, raising a question of what, exactly, is protected by the Fourth Amendment's prohibition of unreasonable searches and seizures.

the violent overthrow of the government or to belong to an organization that did so. The McCarran Act of 1950 required members of the Communist Party to register with the U.S. attorney general. At the same time, Sen. Joseph McCarthy was conducting investigations of American citizens to search out communists, and the House Un-American Activities Committee was doing the same thing. The suspicion or accusation of being involved in communism was enough to stain a person's reputation irreparably, even if there was no evidence to back up the claim. Many careers and lives were ruined in the process.

The clear and present danger test did not protect them. The Supreme Court upheld convictions under the Smith and McCarran Acts even though by Holmes's formulation there was no danger of imminent harm. The Court had used the clear and present danger test intermittently in the years since 1919 but usually not as Justices Holmes and Louis D. Brandeis intended, to limit speech only in the rarest and most dire circumstances. Instead, the clear and present danger test had come to be seen as a kind of balancing act in which the interests of society in prohibiting the speech were weighed against the value of free speech. The emphasis on an obvious and immediate danger was lost.

The Court's record as a supporter of sedition laws ended with the personnel changes that brought Earl Warren to the position of chief justice. In 1969 the Court overturned the conviction of Charles Brandenburg, a Ku Klux Klan leader who had been arrested under Ohio's criminal syndicalism law. In this case the Court ruled that abstract teaching of violence is not the same as incitement to violence. In other words, political speech could be restricted only if it was aimed at producing or was likely to produce "imminent lawless action." Mere advocacy of specific illegal acts was protected unless it led to immediate illegal activity. In a concurring opinion, Justice William O. Douglas pointed out that it was time to get rid of the clear and present danger test because it was so subject to misuse and manipulation. Speech, except when linked with action, he said, should be immune from prosecution.[33] The **imminent lawless action test** continues to be the standard for regulating political speech today.

SYMBOLIC SPEECH

The question of what to do when speech is linked to action remained. Many forms of expression go beyond mere speech or writing. No one disputes that government has the right to regulate actions and behavior if it believes it has sufficient cause, but what happens when that behavior is also expression? Is burning a draft card, wearing an armband to protest a war, or torching the American flag an action or an expression? The Supreme Court, generally speaking, has been more willing to allow regulation of symbolic speech than of speech alone, especially if such regulation is not a direct attempt to curtail the speech.

imminent lawless action test the rule used by the courts that restricts speech only if it is aimed at producing or is likely to produce imminent lawless action

One of the most divisive issues of symbolic speech that has confronted the Supreme Court, and indeed the American public, concerns that ultimate symbol of our country, the American flag. There is probably no more effective way of showing one's dissatisfaction with the United States or its policies than by burning the Stars and Stripes. Emotions ride high on this issue. In 1969 the Court split five to four when it overturned the conviction of a person who had broken a New York law making it illegal to deface or show disrespect for the flag (he had burned it).[34] Twenty years later, with a more conservative Court in place, the issue was raised again. Again the Court divided five to four, voting to protect the burning of the flag as symbolic expression.[35] Because the patriotic feelings of so many Americans were fired up by this ruling, Congress passed the federal Flag Protection Act in 1989, making it a crime to desecrate the flag. In *United States v. Eichmann*, the Court declared the federal law unconstitutional for the same reasons it had overturned the state laws earlier: all were aimed specifically at "suppressing expression."[36] The only way to get around a Supreme Court ruling of unconstitutionality is to amend the Constitution. Efforts to pass an amendment have failed in the House and Senate, meaning that despite the strong feeling of the majority to the contrary, flag burning is still considered protected speech in the United States.

The Court has recently proved willing to restrict symbolic speech, however, if it finds that the speech goes beyond expression of a view. In a 2003 ruling the Court held that cross burning, a favored practice of the Ku Klux Klan and other segregationists that it had previously held to be protected speech, was not protected under the First Amendment if it was intended as a threat of violence.[37] The Court noted that cross burning would still be protected as symbolic speech in certain cases, such as at a political rally.

FREEDOM OF ASSEMBLY

Closely related to symbolic speech is an additional First Amendment guarantee, **freedom of assembly**, or "the right of the people peaceably to assemble, and to petition the government for a redress of grievances." The courts have interpreted this provision to mean not only that people can meet and express their views collectively, but also that their very association is protected as a form of political expression. So, for instance, they have ruled that associations like the NAACP (National Association for the Advancement of Colored People) cannot be required to make their membership lists public[38] (although groups deemed to have unlawful purposes do not have such protection) and that teachers do not have to reveal the associations to which they belong.[39] In addition, the Court has basically upheld people's right to associate with whom they please, although it held that public[40] and, in some circumstances, private groups cannot discriminate on the basis of race or sex.[41]

OBSCENITY AND PORNOGRAPHY

Of all the forms of expression, obscenity has probably presented the Court with its biggest headaches. In attempting to define it in 1964, Justice Potter Stewart could only conclude, "I know it when I see it."[42] The Court has used a variety of tests for determining whether material is obscene, but until the early 1970s, only the most hard-core pornography was regulated.

Coming into office in 1969, however, President Nixon made it one of his administration's goals to control pornography in America. Once the Court began to reflect the ideological change that came with Nixon's appointees, rulings became more restrictive. In 1973 the Court developed the *Miller* test, which returned more control over the definition of obscenity to state legislatures and local standards. Under the *Miller* test, the Court asks "whether the work

freedom of assembly the right of the people to gather peacefully and to petition government

***Miller* test** the rule used by the courts in which the definition of obscenity must be based on local standards

Parody News Sites

The First Amendment is an essential tool for keeping the republic. Americans who wish to speak truth to power are protected—whether they do it in a pamphlet, online, in a song, or on a stage. But what happens when they employ made-up facts or exaggerations as a vehicle to speak truth to power? That is: when a story is fabricated around what seems like a grain of truth, stretched to its absurd limits to make a political point? That's the nature of satire, a form of writing, art, or drama that uses irony, exaggeration, and humor to shed light on specific—and often political—issues.

It can be tricky telling stories that seem like they *could be* true, because it can be remarkably easy to fool people into thinking *they are* true. Consider the web site *Daily Currant*, which during the Obama administration posted fake news stories with no punchlines or discernible humor to be found. It presented completely false headlines (for example, "Obama Nominates Abortion Doctor to Replace Scalia on the Supreme Court" or "Donald Trump: 'I Have the Greatest Toenails in the History of Mankind'") that at some level seem reasonable to at least some readers. Although most folks get the joke, at least a few will invariably click, like, or share, believing the story to be true.[1]

If you've been fooled by a *Daily Currant* piece, don't feel bad: it's also happened to reporters at the *New York Times* and the *Washington Post*.[2] In a warning to his own staff, one editor described the *Currant*'s stories as "semi-believable political wish-fulfillment articles distinguished by a commitment to a complete absence of what most people would recognize as 'jokes.'"[3]

WHAT TO WATCH OUT FOR

It's not always easy to tell the difference between real news and fake news, but there are a few steps you can take to critically assess whether something is real or satire. Whether or not you actually find it funny is wholly up to you.

- **Notice the presentation.** Fake news sites take great pains to look and sound like authentic journalism while "reporting" stories that are completely untrue. Site names like *Daily Currant*, *National Report*, *Empire News*, and *World News Daily Report* sound like legitimate news sources, and their format and style mimic hard news. Even the well-known satire site *The Onion*, despite its silly name and often hilarious headlines, still gets mistaken for real news often enough that, by 2015, Facebook was considering adding a "satire" tag to *Onion* stories shared on the site.[4] Remember that if something looks like news and sounds like news . . . it still might not be news. Googling the site's name will usually tell you if it's true.

- **Know your satire sources.** Most people know satire when they see it, and stories from traditional comedy sites (like *Saturday Night Live*'s "Weekend Update" or *The Daily Show*) are hard to mistake as real news. But as a consumer of news from Internet sources, it's up to you to know which "news" sites are real and which are satire. Further muddying the waters are blogs connected to more traditional news publications, such as *The New Yorker*'s "Borowitz Report," which, other than the inclusion of the word "humor" in the site's URL, is not always recognizable as satire.

- **Follow the links.** Is what you are reading original reporting, or is it a story about a story from another web site or news source? If the source of a story is a link to another story—check the original source.

- **Don't make laughter your guide.** Remember that satire doesn't have to be funny to be fake: some news satire sites are, for the most part, completely devoid of anything you might call a "joke," depending on shock value or sheer unlikeliness for their appeal.

- **Beware news reports that seem to skewer someone you already don't like.** When individuals come across something that seems to support their preferred narrative, they tend to want to believe it. In 2013, for example, a *Daily Currant* report that liberal economist Paul Krugman had filed for bankruptcy was quickly picked up by conservative blogs, and another *Daily Currant* story that Sarah Palin had joined *Al Jazeera* was reposted to liberal ones.[5] If something you read seems to "prove" you were right all along about celebrity X or politician Y, consider whether you are perhaps too eager to believe.

1. *Daily Currant*, March 22, 2016.
2. David Weigel, "'I Want to Believe': Why Does the Media Keep Running Fake Stories From a Joke-Free Satire Site?" *Slate*, March 11, 2013, www.slate.com/articles/news_and_politics/politics/2013/03/daily_currant_satire_the_fake_news_website_keeps_fooling_journalists.html.
3. Max Read, "Breitbart Fooled by Joke News Site After Blasting Writer for Being Fooled by Same Joke News Site," *Gawker*, March 11, 2013, gawker.com/5989887/breitbartcom-fooled-by-joke-news-site-after-blasting-writer-for-being-fooled-by-same-joke-news-site.
4. Alex Goldman, "Facebook Attempts to Teach Its Users to Recognize Satire—With a 'Satire' Tag," *On the Media*, August 18, 2014, www.onthemedia.org/story/facebook-attempts-teach-its-users-recognize-satire-satire-tag/.
5. Ibid.

depicts or describes, in a patently offensive way, sexual conduct specifically defined by state law" and "whether the work, taken as a whole, lacks serious literary, artistic, political or scientific value" (called the SLAPS test).[43] These provisions have also been open to interpretation, and the Court has tried to refine them over time. The emphasis on local standards has meant that pornographers can look for those places with the most lenient definitions of obscenity in which to produce and market their work, and the Court has let this practice go on.

Still, the question of whether obscenity should be protected speech raises some fundamental issues, chief among them defining what is obscene. Justice John Marshall Harlan was quite right when he wrote that "one man's vulgarity is another man's lyric,"[44] raising the inescapable possibility of majorities enforcing decisions on minorities. People offended by what they consider to be obscenity might advocate banning adult bookstores, nude dancing at bars, and naked women on magazine covers at the supermarket. Many feminists argue that pornography represents aggression toward women and should be banned primarily because it perpetuates stereotypes and breeds violence. And some people carry the notion of obscenity further, arguing that selling violent video games to minors is obscene. (The Court has ruled it is not.[45])

FIGHTING WORDS AND OFFENSIVE SPEECH

Among the categories of speech the Court has ruled may be regulated is one called **fighting words**, words whose express purpose is to create a disturbance and incite violence in the person who hears the speech.[46] However, the Court rarely upholds legislation designed to limit fighting words unless the law is written very carefully. Consequently, it has held that threatening and provocative language is protected unless it is likely to "produce a clear and present danger of serious substantive evil that rises far above public inconvenience, annoyance, or

fighting words speech intended to incite violence

unrest."[47] It has also ruled that offensive language, though not protected by the First Amendment, may occasionally contain a political message, in which case constitutional protection applies.[48]

These rulings have taken on modern-day significance in the wake of the political correctness movement that swept the country in the late 1980s and 1990s, especially on college campuses. Political correctness refers to an ideology, held primarily by some liberals, including some civil rights activists and feminists, that language shapes society in critical ways and, therefore, that racist, sexist, homophobic, or any other language that demeans any group of individuals should be silenced to minimize its social effects. An outgrowth of the political correctness movement is the adoption of speech codes on college campuses, banning speech that might be offensive to women or ethnic and other minorities. Critics of speech codes, and of political correctness in general, argue that such practices unfairly repress free speech, which should flourish on, of all places, college campuses. In 1989 and 1991, federal district court judges agreed, finding speech codes on two campuses, the University of Michigan and the University of Wisconsin, in violation of students' First Amendment rights.[49] Neither school appealed. The Supreme Court spoke on a related issue in 1992 when it struck down a Minnesota "hate crime law" that prohibited activities that "arouse anger, alarm or resentment in others on the basis of race, color, creed, religion or gender." The Court held that it is unconstitutional to outlaw such broad categories of speech based on its content.[50]

> **How much free speech do we need on our college campuses?**

FREEDOM OF THE PRESS

The First Amendment covers not only freedom of speech but also freedom of the press. Many of the controversial issues we have already covered apply to both of these areas, but some problems are confronted exclusively, or primarily, by the press: the issue of prior restraint, libel restrictions, and the conflict between a free press and a fair trial.

PRIOR RESTRAINT Prior restraint, a restriction on the press before its message is actually published, was the primary target of the founders when they drew up the First Amendment. The Supreme Court has shared the founders' concern that prior restraint is a particularly dangerous form of censorship and has almost never permitted it. Two classic judgments illustrate their view. In *Near v. Minnesota*, the Court held that a Minnesota law infringed on a newspaper publisher's freedom of the press. Although an extreme emergency, such as war, might justify previous restraint on the press, wrote Justice Charles Evans Hughes, the purpose of the First Amendment is to limit it to those rare circumstances.[51] Similarly and more recently, in *New York Times Company v. United States*, the Court prevented the Nixon administration from stopping the publication by the *New York Times* and the *Washington Post* of the *Pentagon Papers*, a "top-secret" document about U.S. involvement in Vietnam. The Court held that "security" is too vague a concept to be allowed to excuse the violation of the First Amendment. To grant such power to the president, it ruled, would be to run the risk of destroying the liberty that the government is trying to secure.[52]

LIBEL Freedom of the press also collides with the issue of libel, the written defamation of character (verbal defamation is called slander). Obviously, it is crucial to the watchdog and information-providing roles of the press that journalists be able to speak freely about the character and actions of those in public service. At the same time, because careers and reputations are ruined easily by rumors and innuendoes, journalists ought to be required to "speak"

political correctness the idea that language shapes behavior and therefore should be regulated to control its social effects

prior restraint censorship of or punishment for the expression of ideas before the ideas are printed or spoken

libel the written defamation of character

Bill Maher

Bill Maher is a big fan of the First Amendment. That's because he says what few of us dare to say, what most of us dare not even think. The gasp of laughter that follows the comedian's one-liners is not just shocked amusement; it's shocked recognition that, uncomfortable, unflattering, and unpalatable as his observations are, they're often right on target. Maher has made a career out of mocking the emperor's anatomy, while most of us are still oohing and aahing over the splendor of his new clothes. Usually the First Amendment saves his bacon.

And sometimes it doesn't. On September 17, 2001, he went on his ABC comedy show, *Politically Incorrect*, and said, about the suicide bombing of the World Trade Center: "We have been the cowards, lobbing cruise missiles from miles away. That's cowardly. Staying in the airplane when it hits the building—say what you want about it, it's not cowardly." Advertisers balked, and Maher's show was canceled.

He's back now, with a cable show called *Real Time with Bill Maher*, where he continues to speak his mind. Still, there are limits. He says: "I can't get up there every week and just rail about the environment and global warming and whatever is going on that I think is most important. But I push it as far as I can."

On patriotism

"Well, it means being loyal to your country above other countries. And I am . . . . [But] it has to be put in context and also it has to be put side by side with a greater humanity . . . . Americans who say, 'This is the greatest country in the world,' without having any clue what goes on in any other countries, are just pulling it out of nowhere. There are many things that I'm proud of in this country. I'm proud of how my parents and other people stopped fascism and communism. I'm certainly proud of what we started in 1776. It was a new dawn of freedom and liberty in the world. But I'm not proud of slavery. I'm not proud of the genocide of the Indians. I'm not proud of much of what goes on today. So I still believe in the promise of America, but most of America looks at itself through rose-colored glasses. And that's not healthy."

On keeping the republic

"Take it upon [yourself] to learn the basics . . . . [K]ids need . . . to learn history. Because kids say to me all the time when I say something from history: 'How should I know about that? I wasn't born.' Oh, really? So nothing happened before you were born? . . . Kids need to learn history so they can put themselves in the proper place, which is of great insignificance . . . . The problem with kids today is not too little self-esteem, it's too much. And history, I think, learning a big picture, is very important in that."

Source: Bill Maher spoke with Christine Barbour and Gerald C. Wright on May 9, 2005.

responsibly. The Supreme Court addressed this issue in *New York Times v. Sullivan*, in which it ruled that public officials, as opposed to private individuals, when suing for libel, must show that a publication acted with "actual malice," which means not that the paper had an evil intent but that it acted with "knowledge that [what it printed] was false or with reckless disregard for whether it was false or not."[53] Shortly thereafter, the Court extended the ruling to include public figures other than officials, including entertainment or sports celebrities, as well as people whose actions put them in a public position—such as a candidate running for office, or an author promoting her book.

The Court's rulings attempt to give the press some leeway in its actions. Without *Sullivan*, investigative journalism would never have been able to uncover the role of the United States in Vietnam, for instance, or the Watergate cover-up. Freedom of the press, and thus the public's interest in keeping a critical eye on government, are clearly the winners here. The Court's view is that when individuals put themselves in the public domain, the public's interest in the truth outweighs the protection of their privacy.

THE RIGHT TO A FAIR TRIAL Freedom of the press also confronts head-on another Bill of Rights guarantee, the right to a fair trial. Media coverage of a crime can make it very difficult to find an "impartial jury," as required by the Sixth Amendment. On the other side of this conflict, however, is the "public's right to know." The Sixth Amendment promises a "speedy and public trial," and many journalists interpret this provision to mean that the proceedings ought to be open. On the whole the Court has ruled in favor of media access to most stages of legal proceedings and courts have been extremely reluctant to uphold gag orders, which would impose prior restraint on the press during those proceedings.[54]

CENSORSHIP ON THE INTERNET

Lawmakers do not always know how to deal with new outlets for expression as they become available. Modern technology has presented the judiciary with a host of free speech issues the founders never anticipated. The latest to make it to the courts is the question of censorship on the Internet. Some web sites contain explicit sexual material, obscene language, and other content that many people find objectionable. Because children often find their way onto the Internet on their own, parents and groups of other concerned citizens have clamored for regulation of this medium. Congress obliged in 1996 with the Communications Decency Act, which made it illegal to knowingly send or display indecent material over the Internet. In 1997 the Supreme Court ruled that such provisions constituted a violation of free speech, and that communication over the Internet, which it called a modern "town crier," is subject to the same protections as nonelectronic expression.[55] When Congress tried again with a more narrowly tailored bill, the Child Online Protection Act, the Court struck it down, too.[56]

The Court has not always ruled on the side of a completely unregulated Internet. While not restricting the creation of content, the Supreme Court in 2003 upheld the Children's Internet Protection Act, which required public libraries that received federal funds to use filtering software to block material that is deemed harmful to minors, such as pornography.[57] However, these filters can create some problems. Many companies and institutions use them to screen offensive incoming email, but such filters often have unwanted consequences, blocking even legitimate messages and publications.[58] The Internet can also have the effect of freeing people from censorship, however. As many people who have worked on their high school newspapers know, the Court has ruled that student publications are subject to censorship by school officials if the restrictions serve an educational purpose. The Internet, however, offers students an alternative medium of publication that the courts say is not subject to censorship.[59]

The increasing use of the Internet not just as a source of information but also as a mechanism for people to download books, music, movies, and other forms of entertainment has set up another clash of rights. This conflict is between authors and creators of content, who claim a copyright to their works, and the public, who want to access those works, frequently without paying full fare for their use. Two bills, one in the House (the Stop Online Piracy Act, or SOPA) and one in the Senate (the Protect IP Act, or PIPA), attempted to address this issue in 2012 by requiring Internet providers to monitor their users and block access to international sites that share files. Companies like Google, Yahoo, Bing, Facebook, Twitter, and Tumblr, which depend on open Internet access, opposed the legislation, claiming it would require them to censor their users' practices and stifle free speech and innovation. Many of them went dark or threatened to do so in protest of the bills, and leaders in both houses postponed votes, effectively killing the proposed legislation in its current form.[60] The issue of the protection of intellectual property rights on the Internet remains unresolved.

The question of whether the Internet needs to be regulated to ensure protection of people's personal data privacy has become an important one in Congress, especially since we have learned that users of some sites, such as Facebook, have been manipulated into giving up their own data as well as information about everyone in their address books to firms like the now-defunct Cambridge Analytica. Unfortunately, congressional hearings revealed that members of Congress know next to nothing about how social media works, making it likely that we will leave the wolves in charge of the digital henhouse.

In Your Own Words Explain the value of freedom of expression and how its protections have been tested.

THE RIGHT TO BEAR ARMS

Providing for militias to secure the state or securing an individual right?

The Second Amendment to the Constitution reads, "A well-regulated militia, being necessary to the security of a free state, the right of the people to keep and bear arms, shall not be infringed." This amendment has been the subject of some of the fiercest debates in American politics. Originally it was a seemingly straightforward effort by opponents of the Constitution to keep the federal government in check by limiting the power of standing, or permanent, armies. Over time it has become a rallying point for those who want to engage in sporting activities involving guns, those who believe that firearms are necessary for self-defense, those who oppose contemporary American policy and want to use revolution to return to what they think were the goals of the founders, and those who simply don't believe that it is government's business to make decisions about who can own guns.

WHY IS THE RIGHT TO BEAR ARMS VALUABLE?

During the earliest days of American independence, the chief source of national stability was the state militia system—armies of able-bodied men who could be counted on to assemble, with their own guns, to defend their country from external and internal threats, whether from the British, Native Americans, or local insurrection. Local militias were seen as far less dangerous to the fledgling republic than a standing army under national leadership. Such an army could seize control and create a military dictatorship, depriving citizens of their hard-won rights.

The restructuring of the U.S. military, and the growing evidence that under civilian control it did not pose a threat to the liberties of American citizens, caused many people to view the Second Amendment as obsolete. Although the militia system that gave rise to the amendment is now defunct, supporters of rights for gun owners, such as the National Rifle Association (NRA), argue that the amendment is as relevant as ever. They offer at least four reasons the right to bear arms should be unregulated. First, they argue that hunting and other leisure activities involving guns do not hurt anybody (except, of course, the hunted) and are an important part of American culture. Second, gun rights advocates claim that possession of guns is necessary for self-defense. Their third argument is that citizens should have the right to arm themselves to protect their families and property from a potentially tyrannical government. Finally, advocates of unregulated gun ownership say that it is not government's business to regulate gun use.

Opponents of these views, such as Handgun Control, Inc., and the Coalition to Stop Gun Violence, counter with several arguments of their own. First, they say that none of the claims of gun rights advocates has anything to do with the Second Amendment, which refers only to the use and ownership of guns by state militia members. Their second argument is that countries with stricter gun control laws have less violence and fewer gun deaths. Third, they argue that none of the rights of Americans, even such fundamental ones as freedom of speech and the press, is absolute. Finally, they point to the irony in claiming the protection of the Constitution to own weapons that could be used to overthrow the government based on that Constitution.[61]

LEGISLATION AND JUDICIAL DECISIONS

Although various kinds of gun control legislation have been passed at the state and local levels, powerful interest groups like the NRA have kept it to a minimum at the federal level. The 1990s, however, saw the passage of three federal bills that affect the right to bear arms: the 1993 Brady Bill, requiring background checks on potential handgun purchasers; the 1994 Crime Bill, barring semiautomatic assault weapons; and a 1995 bill making it illegal to carry a gun near a school. The 1995 law and the interim provisions of the Brady Bill, which imposed a five-day waiting period for all gun sales, with local background checks until a national background check system could be established, were struck down by the Supreme Court on the grounds that they were unconstitutional infringements of the national government into the realm of state power.[62] In September 2004, Congress let the ban on semiautomatic weapons expire. While some Democrats in Congress promised to reintroduce the ban, action proved impossible because the powerful NRA has framed the conversation around guns in terms of rights. The narrative they have persuaded most Americans to believe is that the Second Amendment unequivocally guarantees all Americans the right to own guns (when even a cursory reading disputes that) and that any limitation on that right is an assault on the Constitution and the beginning of the slippery slope to the end of American liberty. *Business Insider* says the NRA is "a juggernaut of influence in Washington" because it is simultaneously "a lobbying firm, a campaign operation, a popular social club, a generous benefactor and an industry group."[63] By *industry group*, the author means that the NRA not only represents gun owners but that much of its financial and political clout comes from gun manufacturers who stand to make considerable money when people feel their guns or lives are threatened. In part, its strength also comes from its members, not because they are a majority of Americans, but because they are an intense minority, passionately unwilling to tolerate any compromise in the protection of what they believe is an essential right.

That has made the NRA one of the most powerful forces in the United States. From one gun massacre to the next—whether at a movie theater, at a shopping mall, or, increasingly, inside a school—rhetoric favoring gun regulation has bloomed and then . . . nothing happens. The NRA and its spokespeople argue that the issue is mental health, not guns, and that more guns, not fewer, are necessary to stop gun violence.

Between the Sandy Hook shootings in 2012 and the Marjory Stoneman Douglas shootings in 2018, more than four hundred additional people were killed in more than two hundred school shootings.[64] The Parkland, Florida, deaths added seventeen to that total. As we saw in *What's at Stake . . . ?* in Chapter 1, the students from Parkland created a much more effective counternarrative in response to the NRA: "Why is your right to a gun more important than my right to life?" By the numbers of voluntary surrenders of AR-15s following the shootings at MSD, it was clear that this was a narrative that resonated even among some assault weapon enthusiasts. Unfortunately, it did not resonate quickly enough to save lives. Narratives take time to change and the NRA has lots of money and power behind it. In 2018, many Democratic members were elected to Congress who do not owe the NRA but they cannot pass legislation by themselves. Mass shootings (defined as four or more deaths, not counting the shooter's) have been occurring almost weekly since Parkland. In fact, the 2018 midterm election on Nov. 6 was bookended by a massacre killing eleven people at worship in a Pittsburgh synagogue on October 27 and a shooting at a bar in Thousand Oaks, California, that killed twelve on November 7.

Until 2008 the Supreme Court had ruled on only a handful of cases that had an impact on gun rights and the Second Amendment, mostly interpreting the Second Amendment as intending to arm state militias, and letting state gun-related legislation stand.[65] In 2008, however, the Supreme Court heard arguments for the first time since 1939 on whether the Constitution guarantees an individual the right to bear arms. In a five-to-four decision, the Court held that it did, striking down a Washington, D.C., law that banned handgun possession in the home. While the Court held that the D.C. law violated an individual's right to own a gun for self-protection, the majority was careful to say that the right to own guns is not unlimited. For instance, it does not encompass military-grade weapons, and it does not extend to felons and the mentally ill.[66] In 2010 the Court took the ruling a step further, holding that not only could the federal government not violate an individual's right to bear arms, as it had in the D.C. case, but neither could a state government.[67] Writing for the Court in a five-to-four decision, Justice Samuel Alito said, "It is clear that the Framers . . . counted the right to keep and bear arms among those fundamental rights necessary to our system of ordered liberty."[68] Further cases will determine exactly what the parameters of this interpretation are—which state laws violate the right and which do not—but gun rights advocates are hoping to see it applied broadly, as evidenced by the Virginia law, passed just days after the Supreme Court ruling, that allows bar patrons to carry concealed weapons as long as they are not drinking.[69]

In Your Own Words   Give examples of different interpretations of the Second Amendment's meaning.

THE RIGHTS OF CRIMINAL DEFENDANTS

Protecting the accused from an arbitrary government

Half of the amendments in the Bill of Rights and several clauses in the Constitution itself are devoted to protecting the rights of people who are suspected or accused of committing crimes. The Fourth through Eighth Amendments protect people against unreasonable searches and seizures, self-incrimination, and cruel and unusual punishment, and they guarantee people accused of a crime the right to legal advice, the right to a speedy and public trial, and various other procedural protections.

WHY ARE THE RIGHTS OF CRIMINAL DEFENDANTS VALUABLE?

A primary reason for protecting the rights of the accused is to limit government power. One way governments can stop criticism of their actions is by eliminating the opposition, imprisoning them, or worse. The guarantees in the Bill of Rights provide checks on government's ability to prosecute its enemies.

Another reason for guaranteeing rights to those accused of crimes is the strong tradition in American culture, coming from our English roots, that a person is innocent until proven guilty. An innocent person, naturally, still has the full protection of the Constitution, and even a guilty person is protected to some degree, for instance, against cruel and unusual punishment. All Americans are entitled to what the Fifth and Fourteenth Amendments call **due process of the law**, which means that laws must be reasonable and fair, and that those accused of breaking the law—and who stand to lose life, liberty, or property as a consequence—have the right to appear before their judges to hear the charges and evidence against them, to have legal counsel, and to present any contradictory evidence in their defense. Due process means essentially that those accused of a crime have a right to a fair trial.

During the 1960s and 1970s the Supreme Court expanded the protection of the rights of the accused and incorporated them so that the states had to protect them as well. Yet the more conservative 1980s and 1990s witnessed a considerable backlash against a legal system perceived as having gone soft on crime—overly concerned with the rights of criminals at the expense of safe streets, neighborhoods, and cities, and deaf to the claims of victims of violent crimes. We want to protect the innocent, but when the seemingly guilty go free because of a technicality, the public is often incensed. The Supreme Court has had the heavy responsibility of drawing the line between the rights of defendants and the rights of society.

PROTECTION AGAINST UNREASONABLE SEARCHES AND SEIZURES

The Fourth Amendment guards against "unreasonable searches and seizures" and requires "probable cause" to obtain a warrant. The founders were particularly sensitive on this question because the king of England had had the right to order the homes of his subjects searched without cause, looking for any evidence of criminal activity. For the most part this amendment has been interpreted by the Court to mean that a person's home is private and cannot be invaded by police without a warrant, obtainable only if they have very good reason to think that criminal evidence lies within.

WHAT'S REASONABLE? Under the Fourth Amendment, there are a few exceptions to the rule that searches require warrants. Automobiles present a special case, for example, since by their nature they are likely to be gone by the time an officer appears with a warrant. Cars can be searched without warrants if the officer has probable cause to think a law has been broken, and the Court has gradually widened the scope of the search so that it can include luggage or closed containers in the car.

Modern innovations like wiretapping and electronic surveillance presented more difficult problems for the Court because, of course, they are not mentioned in the Constitution.

due process of the law the guarantee that laws will be fair and reasonable and that citizens suspected of breaking the law will be treated fairly

A "search" was understood legally to require some physical trespass, and a "seizure" involved taking some tangible object. Not until the case of *Katz v. United States* (1967) did the Court require for the first time that a warrant be obtained before phones could be tapped,[70] although the 2001 Patriot Act makes it a good deal easier to get a warrant. In 2012 the Court ruled that a search warrant was needed in order to put a GPS tracking device on a suspect's car.[71]

Physical searches of cell phones have also presented a modern conundrum for the courts, as cell phones have been considered to be part of the content of one's pockets, which the Supreme Court had determined could be legally searched. But in 2014, writing for a unanimous Court, Chief Justice John Roberts acknowledged that "[t]he average smartphone user has installed 33 apps which together can form a revealing montage of the user's life." Thus, our phones are "mini-computers" that contain the same kind of information about us that our houses have traditionally contained, and just as our houses cannot be searched without a warrant, now neither can our cell phones (at least most of the time). It bears repeating, however, that warrants are not that hard to come by, so people storing information they prefer to keep private on their cell phones or computers should in general be cautious.[72]

Analog Searches Only

Although police can examine personal items in certain circumstances, the Supreme Court in 2014 ruled that the digital information stored on one's cell phone is protected by the Fourth Amendment. If the police want to look at your data, they must get a search warrant first.

Yet another modern area in which the Court has had to determine the legality of searches is mandatory random testing for drug or alcohol use, usually by urine or blood tests. These are arguably a very unreasonable kind of search, but the Court has tended to allow them where the violation of privacy is outweighed by a good purpose—for instance, discovering the cause of a train accident,[73] preventing drug use in schools,[74] or preserving public safety by requiring drug tests of train conductors and airline pilots.

Finally, in 2012 the Court held, five to four, that the Fourth Amendment is not violated by the requirement that someone arrested for a minor infraction and not suspected of concealing a weapon or drugs could nonetheless be subjected to an invasive strip search. In *Florence v. Board of Chosen Freeholders of County of Burlington*, the majority ruled that the plaintiff could be subjected to a strip search despite the fact that he had been arrested for something that he had not in fact done and that would not have been a crime in any case. The key issue for the Court was that the defendant was going to be held in the general jail population, and correctional officers are rightly concerned with jail security, which outweighs an individual's privacy rights.[75]

THE EXCLUSIONARY RULE By far the most controversial part of the Fourth Amendment rulings has been the exclusionary rule. In a 1914 case, *Weeks v. United States*, the Court confronted the question of what to do with evidence that had been obtained illegally. It decided that such evidence should be excluded from use in the defendant's trial.[76]

This **exclusionary rule**, as it came to be known, meant that even though the police might have concrete evidence of criminal activity, if obtained unlawfully, the evidence could not be used to gain a conviction of the culprit.

The exclusionary rule has been controversial from the start. In some countries, including England, illegally obtained evidence can be used at trial, but the defendant is allowed to sue the police in a civil suit or to bring criminal charges against them. The object is clearly to deter misbehavior on the part of the police, while not allowing guilty people to go free. But the exclusionary rule, while it does serve as a deterrent to police, helps criminals avoid punishment. The Court itself has occasionally seemed uneasy about the rule.[77] Not until the 1961 case of *Mapp v. Ohio* was the exclusionary rule finally incorporated into state as well as federal practice.[78] But extending the reach of the exclusionary rule did not end the controversy. Although the Warren Court continued to uphold it, the Burger and Rehnquist Courts cut back on the protections it offered. In 1974 they ruled that the exclusionary rule was to be a deterrent to abuse by the police, not a constitutional right of the accused.[79] The Court subsequently ruled that illegally seized evidence could be used in civil trials[80] and came to carve out what it called a *good faith exception*, whereby evidence is admitted to a criminal trial, even if obtained illegally, if the police are relying on a warrant that appears to be valid at the time or on a law that appears to be constitutional (though either may turn out to be defective),[81] or on a warrant that is obtained in error. In 2009 the Roberts Court ruled that to trigger the exclusionary rule, the police conduct must be deliberate.[82] The Court's more conservative turn on this issue has not silenced the debate, however. Some observers are appalled at the reduction in the protection of individual rights, whereas others do not believe that the Court has gone far enough in protecting society against criminals.

PROTECTION AGAINST SELF-INCRIMINATION

No less controversial than the rulings on illegally seized evidence are the Court's decisions on unconstitutionally obtained confessions. The Fifth Amendment provides for a number of protections for individuals, among them that no person "shall be compelled in any criminal case to be a witness against himself." The Supreme Court has expanded the scope of the protection against self-incrimination from criminal trials, as the amendment dictates, to grand jury proceedings, legislative investigations, and even police interrogations. It is this last extension that has proved most controversial.

In 1966 the Warren Court ruled, in *Miranda v. Arizona*, that police had to inform suspects of their rights to remain silent and to have a lawyer present during questioning to prevent them from incriminating themselves. The *Miranda* rights are familiar to viewers of police dramas: "You have the right to remain silent. Anything you say can and will be used against you. . . ." If a lawyer could show that a defendant had not been "read" his or her rights, information gained in the police interrogation would not be admissible in court. Like the exclusionary rule, the *Miranda* ruling could and did result in criminals going free even though the evidence existed to convict them.

Reacting to public and political accusations that the Warren Court was soft on crime, Congress passed the Crime Control and Safe Streets Act of 1968, which allowed confessions to be used in federal courts not according to the *Miranda* ruling, but according to the "totality of the circumstances" surrounding the confession. In 2000, despite the fact that some justices

exclusionary rule the rule created by the Supreme Court that evidence seized illegally may not be used to obtain a conviction

had been highly critical of the *Miranda* ruling over the years, the Court upheld the 1966 decision, stating that it had become an established part of the culture, and held the 1968 Crime Control Act to be unconstitutional.[83]

RIGHT TO COUNSEL

Closely related to the *Miranda* decision, which upholds the right to a lawyer during police questioning, is the Sixth Amendment declaration that the accused shall "have the assistance of counsel for his defense." The founders' intentions are fairly clear from the Crimes Act of 1790, which required courts to provide counsel for poor defendants only in capital cases—that is, those punishable by death. Defendants in other trials had a right to counsel, but the government had no obligation to provide it. The Supreme Court's decisions were in line with that act until 1938, when, in *Johnson v. Zerbst*, it extended the government's obligation to provide counsel to impoverished defendants in all criminal proceedings in federal courts.[84] Only federal crimes carried that obligation until 1963. Then, in one of the most dramatic tales of courtroom appeals (so exciting that it was made into both a book and a movie called *Gideon's Trumpet*), a poor man named Clarence Earl Gideon was convicted of breaking and entering a pool hall and stealing money from the vending machine. Gideon asked the judge for a lawyer, but the judge told him that the state of Florida was not obligated to give him one. He tried to defend the case himself but lost to the far more skilled and knowledgeable prosecutor. Serving five years in prison for a crime he swore he did not commit, he filed a handwritten appeal with the Supreme Court. In a landmark decision, *Gideon v. Wainwright*, the Court incorporated the Sixth Amendment right to counsel.[85]

The *Gideon* decision was a tremendous financial and administrative burden for the states, which had to retry or release many prisoners. Conservatives believed that *Gideon* went far beyond the founders' intentions. Both the Burger and Rehnquist Courts succeeded in rolling back some of the protections won by *Gideon*, ruling, for instance, that the right to a court-appointed attorney does not extend beyond the filing of one round of appeals, even if the convicted indigent person is on death row.[86]

PROTECTION AGAINST
CRUEL AND UNUSUAL PUNISHMENT

The Eighth Amendment, which says, in part, that "cruel and unusual punishments" shall not be inflicted, has generated some major political controversies. Like some of the earlier amendments, this guarantee reflects a concern of English law, which sought to protect British subjects from torture and inhumane treatment by the king. It is easy to see why it would be controversial, however. What is "cruel," and what is "unusual"? Despite intense lobbying on the part of impassioned interest groups, however, the Court has not ruled that the death penalty itself is cruel or unusual (except in the case of intellectually disabled individuals, juveniles, and crimes against an individual that do not result in the victim's death),[87] and most states have death penalty laws.

The strongest attack on the death penalty began in the 1970s, when the NAACP Legal Defense Fund joined with the American Civil Liberties Union and the American Bar Association to argue that the death penalty was disproportionately given to African Americans, especially those convicted of rape. They argued that this was a violation of the Eighth Amendment and of the Fourteenth Amendment guarantee of equal protection of the law. Part of the problem was that state laws differed about what constituted grounds for imposing the death penalty, and juries had no uniform standards to rely on. Consequently, unequal patterns of application of the penalty developed.

In *Furman v. Georgia* (1972) and two related cases, the Court ruled that Georgia's and Texas's capital punishment laws were unconstitutional, but the justices were so far from agreement that they all filed separate opinions, totaling 231 pages.[88] Thirty-five states passed new laws trying to meet the Court's objections and to clarify the standards for capital punishment. By 1976 six hundred inmates waited on death row for the Court to approve the new laws. That year the Court ruled in several cases that the death penalty was not unconstitutional, although it struck down laws requiring the death penalty for certain crimes.[89] The Court remained divided over the issue. In 1977 Gary Gilmore became the first person executed after a ten-year break.

In 1987 *McCleskey v. Kemp* raised the race issue again, but by then the Court was growing more conservative. It held, five to four, that statistics showing that blacks who murder whites received the death penalty more frequently than whites who murder blacks did not prove a racial bias in the law or in how it was being applied.[90] The Rehnquist Court continued to knock down procedural barriers to imposing the death penalty. In 2006 the Roberts Court held that death-row inmates could challenge state lethal injection procedures in lower courts on cruel and unusual punishment grounds. Several of those courts came to different conclusions. In 2008, in *Baze v. Rees*,[91] the Supreme Court upheld Kentucky's lethal injection practice, and other states, waiting for a sign from the Court, went ahead with their own practices.

Public support for capital punishment appears to be softening in recent years, not because of opposition in principle but because of fears that the system might be putting innocent people on death row. This feeling grew as DNA testing cleared some death-row residents, and careful investigation showed that others, too, were innocent. After thirteen death-row convicts in his state were exonerated between 1977 and 2000, Illinois governor George Ryan, a moderate Republican who supported the death penalty in principle, called for a statewide halt to executions. "I cannot support a system, which, in its administration, has proven so fraught with error," Ryan explained, "and has come so close to the ultimate nightmare, the state's taking of an innocent life."[92] Following his lead, then–Maryland governor Parris Glendening issued a moratorium in 2002, but that action was quickly reversed by the new governor, Robert Ehrlich, in January 2003. In 2007 the New Jersey legislature banned the death penalty in the state—the first state to do so since the Supreme Court declared capital punishment constitutional in 1976.[93] Despite misgivings, the American public continues to favor capital punishment. In 2016 a Pew poll found 49 percent of the public supporting the death penalty, with 42 percent opposed, even though majorities of both supporters and opponents thought it meant that sometimes an innocent person would be put to death.[94]

In Your Own Words Describe the protections afforded criminal defendants under the Constitution.

THE RIGHT TO PRIVACY
The personal meets the political

One of the most controversial rights in America is not even mentioned in the Constitution or the Bill of Rights: the right to privacy. This right is at the heart of one of the deepest divisions in American politics, the split over abortion rights and contraceptive use, and is fundamental to two other controversial areas of civil liberties: gay rights and the right to die.

WHY IS THE RIGHT TO PRIVACY VALUABLE?

Although the right to privacy is not spelled out in the Bill of Rights, it goes hand in hand with the founders' insistence on limited government. Their goal was to keep government from getting too powerful and interfering with the lives and affairs of individual citizens. They certainly implied a right to privacy, and perhaps even assumed such a right, but they did not make it explicit.

The right to privacy, to be left alone to do what we want, is so desirable that it scarcely needs a defense. The problem, of course, is that a right to privacy without any limits is anarchy, the absence of government altogether. Clearly government has an interest in preventing some kinds of individual behavior—murder, theft, and rape, for example. But what about other, more subtle behaviors that do not directly affect public safety but arguably have serious consequences for the public good—such as prostitution, drug use, and gambling? Should these behaviors fall under the right to privacy, or should the state be able to regulate them?

REPRODUCTIVE RIGHTS

Throughout the 1940s, people had tried to challenge state laws that made it a crime to use birth control, or even to give out information about how to prevent pregnancies. The Supreme Court routinely refused to hear these cases until the 1965 case of *Griswold v. Connecticut* challenged a Connecticut law making it illegal to use contraceptive devices or to distribute information about them. The Court held that, although the right to privacy is not explicit in the Constitution, a number of other rights, notably those in Amendments One, Three, Four, Five, and Nine, create a "zone of privacy" in which lie marriage and the decision to use contraception. It said that the specific guarantees in the Bill of Rights have "penumbras," or outlying shadowy areas, in which can be found a right to privacy. The Fourteenth Amendment applies that right to the states, and so Connecticut's law was unconstitutional.[95]

Because of the Court's insistence that reproductive matters are not the concern of the government, abortion rights advocates saw an opportunity to use the *Griswold* ruling to strike down state laws prohibiting or limiting abortion. The Court had tried to avoid ruling on the abortion issue, but by 1973 it had become hard to escape. In *Roe v. Wade*, the justices held that the right to privacy did indeed encompass the right to abortion. It tried to balance a woman's right to privacy in reproductive matters with the state's interest in protecting human life, however, by treating the three trimesters of pregnancy differently. In the first three months of pregnancy, it held, there can be no compelling state interest that offsets a woman's privacy rights. In the second three months, the state can regulate access to abortions if it does so reasonably. In the last trimester, the state's interest becomes far more compelling, and a state can limit or even prohibit abortions as long as the mother's life is not in danger.[96] The *Roe* decision launched the United States into an intense and divisive battle over abortion. States continued to try to limit abortions by requiring the consent of husbands or parents, by outlawing clinic advertising, by imposing waiting periods, and by erecting other roadblocks. The Court struck down most of these efforts, at least until 1977, when it allowed some state limitations. But the battle was not confined to statehouses. Congress, having failed to pass a constitutional amendment banning abortions, passed over thirty laws restricting access to abortions in various ways. For instance, it limited federal funding for abortions through Medicaid, a move the Supreme Court upheld in 1980.[97] Presidents got into the fray as well. President Reagan and the first President Bush were staunch opponents of *Roe* and worked hard to get it overturned. Reagan appointed only anti-abortion judges to federal courts, and his administration was active in pushing litigation that would challenge *Roe*.

The balance on the Supreme Court was crucial. *Roe* had been decided by a seven-to-two vote, but many in the majority were facing retirement. When Burger retired, Reagan elevated William Rehnquist, one of the two dissenters, to chief justice, and appointed conservative Antonin Scalia in his place. Reagan's appointees did finally turn the Court in a more conservative direction, but even they were not willing to completely overturn *Roe*, though it has been limited in some respects, including a 2007 decision by the Roberts Court that upheld a ban on partial-birth abortion.[98] In any case, the debate over reproductive rights in this country is certainly not over. Indeed, all the vitriolic debate that surrounded the 2014 *Hobby Lobby* case shows that even the idea that contraception use is entirely a matter of private conscience is not wholly settled.[99] And the Court's decision in that case that corporations, too, may have a private conscience muddies the water considerably for the privacy rights of individuals.

Rejection of the notion that there is a constitutional right to privacy has long been a rallying point for the Christian Right, which has become a powerful part of the Republican Party. And although some Democrats also oppose abortion rights, abortion has become largely a partisan issue. Since 1980 the Republicans have included a commitment to a constitutional amendment banning abortion in their presidential party platform. Unable to effect change at a national level, many have directed their efforts to the states. One strategy, pursued by right-to-life groups in Colorado, Mississippi, Oklahoma, and others, is the attempt to pass personhood amendments that would define life as beginning from the moment of conception, creating a legal person possessing citizenship rights. Such amendments would have the effect of making not just abortion illegal, but also, opponents fear, some forms of birth control and the disposal of fertilized eggs after in vitro fertilization processes.[100] A number of state legislatures have focused on making abortions harder to obtain, or more emotionally difficult for women (for instance, by requiring them to view an ultrasound of the fetus).[101] In 2016 the Supreme Court struck down a Texas law that reduced the number of abortion providers in the state, because it placed an undue burden on the right to an abortion, making it likely that other state restrictions will fall as well.[102] With a topic as contentious as that of reproductive rights, the outcome may depend heavily on the Supreme Court's composition with new justice Brett Kavanaugh a potential fifth vote against abortion.

GAY RIGHTS

The *Griswold* and *Roe* rulings have opened up a variety of difficult issues for the Supreme Court. If there is a right to privacy, what might be included under it? On the whole, the Court has been very restrictive in expanding such a right beyond the reproductive rights of the original cases. Most controversial was its ruling in *Bowers v. Hardwick* (1986).[103]

Michael Hardwick was arrested under a Georgia law outlawing heterosexual and homosexual sodomy. Hardwick challenged the law (although he wasn't prosecuted under it), claiming that it violated his right to privacy. The Court disagreed. Looking at the case from the perspective of whether there was a constitutional right to engage in sodomy, rather than from the dissenting view that what took place between consenting adults was none of its business, the Court held, five to four, that the state of Georgia had a legitimate interest in regulating such behavior. Justice Lewis Powell, who provided the fifth vote for the majority, said after his retirement that he regretted his vote in the *Bowers* decision, but by then, of course, it was too late. Several states have also been critical of the Court's ruling. The Georgia Supreme Court struck down Georgia's sodomy law in 1998 on privacy grounds, but in a case involving heterosexual rather than homosexual activity. Not until 2003, in *Lawrence v. Texas*, did the Court, in a six-to-three decision, finally overturn *Bowers* on privacy grounds.[104] Interestingly, despite its longtime reluctance to overturn *Bowers*, the Court in 1996 used the equal protection clause of the Fourteenth Amendment to strike down a Colorado law that would have made it difficult for gays to use the Colorado courts to fight discrimination and it has used that logic in subsequent cases, as we will see in the next chapter.[105] Thus the Court can pursue several constitutional avenues to expand the rights of gay Americans, should it want to do so.

THE RIGHT TO DIE

A final right-to-privacy issue that has stirred up controversy for the Court is the so-called right to die. In 1990 the Court upheld the state of Missouri's refusal to allow the parents of a woman who had been in a vegetative state and on life-support systems for seven years to withdraw her life support, because they said the daughter's wishes were not clear. But the Court held that when an individual's wishes were made clear

AP Photo/Carl Costas

On Her Own Terms

Twenty-nine-year-old Brittany Maynard shocked the country when she publicly announced her decision to end her life. "I do not want to die," she later wrote. "But I am dying. And I want to die on my own terms." Maynard, stricken with terminal brain cancer, moved from California to Oregon to take advantage of that state's right-to-die laws. After she died in 2014, her mother, seen here, and other family members successfully campaigned for a right-to-die law in California.

in advance, either in person or via a living will, that person's right to terminate medical treatment was protected under the Fourteenth Amendment's due process clause.[106]

The question of a person's right to suspend treatment is different from another legal issue—whether individuals have the right to have assistance ending their lives when they are terminally ill and in severe pain. Oregon provided the first test of this policy. In 1997 it passed a referendum allowing doctors under certain circumstances to provide lethal doses of medication to enable terminally ill patients to end their lives. In late 2001, then–U.S. attorney general John Ashcroft effectively blocked the law by announcing that doctors who participated in assisted suicides would lose their licenses to prescribe federally regulated medications, an essential part of medical practice. In 2004 a federal appellate court ruled that Ashcroft overstepped his authority under federal law, and in early 2006 the Supreme Court upheld the Oregon law. In 2015 California passed a law making it the fifth state, after Oregon, Washington, Vermont, and Montana, to allow physician-assisted suicide in the United States, although it has faced some legal turmoil.[107]

In Your Own Words   Discuss the extent of an individual's right to privacy.

CITIZENSHIP AND CIVIL LIBERTIES
Individual rights yield a collective benefit

In the United States, we are accustomed to thinking about citizenship as a status that confers on us certain rights. A political system based on obligation without rights is an authoritarian dictatorship, but rights without obligation leads to a state of nature—anarchy—with no government at all. Plainly, the status of a citizen in a democracy requires both rights and duties in order to "keep the republic."

The Constitution itself suggests the basics. Obligations are very much the flip side of rights; for every right guaranteed, there is a corresponding duty to use it, sometimes in an explicit law and often in an unwritten norm. For instance, the provisions for elected office and the right to vote imply a duty to vote. It's not a law but a norm that democracies depend on for survival. Congress is authorized to collect taxes, duties, and excises, including an income tax; citizens are obligated to pay those taxes. That, of course, is a law. Congress can raise and support armies, provide and maintain a navy, provide for and govern militias; correspondingly, Americans have a duty to serve in the military. That is merely a norm in peacetime, and one that carries more force in wartime, although not enough to have kept us from having a military draft in five military conflicts. The Constitution defines treason as waging war against the states or aiding or abetting their enemies; citizens have an obligation not to betray their country or state. Again, it's a norm and, depending on how egregious the treason, a law as well. Amendments Five and Six guarantee grand juries and jury trials to those accused of crimes; it is citizens who must serve on those juries. Though people successfully evade it, there is a heavy presumption that they will serve.

But Americans are notoriously lax in fulfilling some of these obligations. We turn out to vote in low numbers; we like to avoid paying taxes; and the draft, like jury duty, is an obligation many Americans have actively sought to escape. It might be worthwhile considering what the political consequences are for a democratic republic when the emphasis on preserving civil liberties is not balanced by a corresponding commitment to fulfilling political obligations.

In Your Own Words Compare the idea of civil rights with civil obligations.

Let's Revisit: What's at Stake . . . ?

We opened this chapter with a look at the political controversy surrounding the Trump administration's reversal of the FCC's decision to enforce net neutrality—the idea that no Internet provider could provide "fast-lane" service or special access to advertisers or privileged businesses or charge more for access to others. That this was a political hot potato was clear from the fact, first, that there was never sufficient support in Congress to get it passed and, second, that it had to be done by administrative fiat at the urging of a public petition and President Obama, who had campaigned on it. The flood of public comments following the FCC rule change, Trump's flip on it and the congressional disarray only makes it more apparent that this was a high-stakes issue.

But why? What is at stake in net neutrality? For one thing, as we can guess after reading this chapter, regulation itself, no matter what the subject, is controversial in American politics. Democrats tend to see the government as a benign creature tasked to look out for the welfare of its citizens and increase their freedoms, and Republicans think it is an incompetent monster whose job it is to limit civil liberties, burden business, and slow down the economy. That alone is enough to explain why net neutrality gets people's political juices going.

There is also the fact, however, that lots of money is to be made on the Internet—and while access is free and open, one of the main channels of revenue is closed off to

Internet providers. Those providers—Comcast, Viacom, AT&T, and other mega-corporations (as we will see in Chapter 13)—own much of the media in this country and media owners have traditionally acted as gatekeepers, deciding what counts as news, what information about the world we should get. Give them the power to charge companies or otherwise exact costs for faster access, and they'd be foolish not to take the maximum advantage of it. For example, with multiple companies vying to be the top distributor of on-demand movies, the ones that can guarantee faster download times would command a premium. Whether it enhances innovation as its supporters claim, a net neutrality–free world certainly enhances the profitability of Internet providers, powerful actors in the lobbying universe with considerable sway over legislators.

Against the Internet providers' financial stake is the less tangible but equally valuable stake that consumers of the Internet have to a right to the free flow of information—a key goal of the founders in creating the Bill of Rights. One of the repeated themes of this book is that access to information and the ability to control or contribute to the narrative about who has and should have power is power itself. The free and open Internet has been a potent force, for good and for bad, in opening up the possibility of narrative control to all of us. Net neutrality preserves that and its loss endangers the democratization of power over the political narrative.

for CQ Press

Want a better grade?

Get the tools you need to sharpen your study skills. **SAGE edge** offers practice quizzes, eFlashcards, video, and multimedia at **edge.sagepub.com/barbourbrief8e.**

Review

Rights in a Democracy

Civil liberties (109) and **civil rights** (109) define the powers that we as citizens have in a democratic polity. Our civil liberties are individual freedoms that place limitations on the power of government. The idea that we should have equal access to all the ideas shared on the Internet is at the heart of **net neutrality** (107).

The Bill of Rights and the States

Most of our rights are spelled out in the text of the Constitution—for instance, that government may not suspend **habeas corpus** (111) or pass **bills of attainder** (111) or **ex post facto laws** (111)—or in its first ten amendments, the Bill of Rights. But some rights have developed over the years through judicial decision making. The rights in the Bill of Rights limit only the national government's action, but through a process of **incorporation** (114) the Supreme Court has made some of them applicable to the states.

Freedom of Religion

According to the **establishment clause** (116) and **free exercise clause** (117) of the First Amendment, citizens of the United States have the right not to be coerced to practice a religion in which they do not believe, as well as the right not to be prevented from practicing the religion they espouse. Because these rights can conflict, **separationists** (116) and **accommodationists** (116) have fought over the meaning of religious freedom since the founding. The courts have played a significant role in navigating the stormy waters of religious expression since then, applying the ***Lemon* test** (117) to determine whether government is entangled with religion, and using the **compelling state interest** (117) test to see if laws affecting religion go beyond the legitimate use of the government's **police power** (117).

Freedom of Expression

Freedom of expression (120), also provided for in the First Amendment, is often considered the hallmark of our democratic government. Freedom of expression, a **free press** (120), and **freedom of assembly** (123) help limit corruption, protect minorities, and promote a vigorous defense of the truth. Again, it has been left to the courts to balance freedom of expression with social and moral order, for instance, by applying the **clear and present danger test** (121) and the **imminent lawless action test** (122) to see if **sedition** (121) laws restrict speech unconstitutionally, and by applying the ***Miller* test** (123) to determine what is obscene. The Court has allowed the regulation of some speech, such as **fighting words** (125), although it has been reluctant to follow codes of **political correctness** (126), to allow **prior restraint** (126), or to ease the laws of **libel** (126).

The Right to Bear Arms

The right to bear arms, supported by the Second Amendment, has also been hotly debated. Most often the debate over gun laws is carried out in state legislatures.

The Rights of Criminal Defendants

The founders believed that to limit government power, people needed to retain **due process of the law** (132) throughout the process of being accused, tried, and punished for criminal activities. Thus they devoted some of the text of the Constitution as well as the Bill of Rights to a variety of procedural protections, including the right to a speedy and public trial, protection from unreasonable search and seizure—including the judge-made **exclusionary rule** (134)—and the right to legal advice.

The Right to Privacy

Though the right to privacy is not mentioned in either the Constitution or the Bill of Rights—and did not even enter the American legal system until the late 1800s—it has become a fiercely debated right on a number of levels, including reproductive rights, gay rights, and the right to die.

5

The Struggle for Equal Rights

In Your Own Words

After you've read this chapter, you will be able to

5.1 Outline the criteria used by the courts to determine if and when the law can treat people differently.

5.2 Summarize key events and outcomes in the struggle for equality of African Americans.

5.3 Explain the different paths to equality taken by other racial and ethnic groups.

5.4 Describe how women have fought for equality and the changing role of women in American politics.

5.5 Recognize examples of other groups that face discrimination.

5.6 Explain how pluralism helped realize the promise of civil rights.

What's at Stake . . . When a Racial Majority Becomes a Minority?

Even before Donald Trump's unexpected win in the presidential election, it was apparent that 2016 was a time for coming out of the shadows. At an American Renaissance conference in Tennessee that year, the excitement was palpable. "We're on the winning side for the first time in my experience," said Richard Spencer, the chair of the National Policy Institute, a white nationalist organization. "Even if Trump loses, he's already shown that immigration and economic nationalism and the whole concept of 'America first' works electorally," said Peter Brimelow, the founder of an anti-immigration and white nationalist web site.[1]

More overtly racist espousers of the same views claim a so-called "alt-right" ideology, an alternative, extremist version of the far right that opposes immigration, multiculturalism, and the classical democratic values that undergird the American political system. Journalist Rosie Gray calls it "white supremacy perfectly tailored for our times: 4chan-esque racist rhetoric combined with a tinge of Silicon Valley–flavored philosophizing, all riding on the coattails of the Trump boom."[2]

The Trump boom. Even though the Donald Trump campaign refused to comment for the above-cited articles on the white supremacist movement, members of that movement were convinced he was their guy. After President Barack Obama was elected, Trump was the most prominent member of the birther movement, claiming that Obama's presidency was illegitimate if he wouldn't produce his birth certificate. His remarks on immigrants being rapists, on Jews being focused on making money, on Muslims being dangerous, on various women being fat pigs, or dogs, or disgusting animals (or, if he likes them, "hot") have encouraged their bigotry. His slowness to reject an endorsement from noted Ku Klux Klan member David Duke (who later tweeted on Trump's victory: "GOD BLESS DONALD TRUMP! It's time to do the right thing, it's time to TAKE AMERICA BACK!!!#MAGA #AmericaFirst #LockHerUp #GodBlessAmerica")[3]; his referring to U.S. senator Elizabeth Warren, who claims Native American ancestry, as "Pocahontas"; his dispute with a Gold Star family about their Muslim son's sacrifice; his conviction that "the big problem this country has is being politically correct"[4]; and his claim that his fame makes sexual assault welcome by women, has, intentionally or not, ignited and given hope to a dark side of American politics. If this sounds harsh, political scientists have found that the Trump campaign made deliberate appeals to voters' sense of racial and gender grievance.[5]

Many of the people to whom Trump appealed felt liberated by his campaign. Before 2016, the white supremacist movement had existed largely out of sight of most people, lurking in the obscurity of their own, secretive information channels like Breitbart News (whose publisher, Steve Bannon, signed on as Trump campaign CEO and later served in the White House), or in other social media where it often made its presence virulently felt in the comments sections. They gathered physically in out-of-the-way places precisely because they knew their ideas were out of line with mainstream America. One of the things that enraged them was that the expression of their views of misogyny, white supremacy, or anti-Semitism was considered politically incorrect and they felt that mainstream society was censoring their views.

But Trump's popularity changed things. "The success of the Trump campaign just proves that our views resonate with millions," Rachel Pendergraft, organizer of a white supremacist group, told reporters for the progressive journal *Mother Jones*. "They may not be ready for the Ku Klux Klan yet, but as anti-white hatred escalates, they will."[6] The Klan was among the white supremacists marching in an August 2017 Unite the Right rally in Charlottesville, Virginia, where clashes with counterprotesters left thirty people injured and a man affiliated with the white supremacists drove his car into a crowd, killing a woman. Trump refused to condemn the white supremacists, saying there was bigotry on both sides and, later, that there were "very fine people on both sides."[7]

The anger that Trump tapped into is due at least in part to rapid changes across America. The country is becoming ever more diverse, and the groups the white nationalists disdain are slowly becoming the majority, even as they themselves become a smaller and smaller percentage of the American population. Perhaps therein lies the rub. Although the avowed white nationalists were fired up at the prospect of a Trump presidency, they were only a small minority of Trump's supporters.

The majority of his most committed base is the much larger group of white Americans, largely rural males without college educations, who would never think of themselves as racists, who recognize the white privilege they have been born with only in its absence as they compete for a dwindling share of an American Dream they were told was their birthright, and who in fact believe they themselves are the target of racist behavior. Even before he became the widely accepted candidate of a Republican Party that didn't quite know what to do with him, Trump was speaking to the concerns of a gradually shrinking white population who felt that their jobs were being given to immigrants who worked too cheaply; who felt that "Black Lives Matter" meant their lives didn't; who believed that a Christian black president in the White House was a Muslim Kenyan, unqualified by birth for the office; who saw policies like the despised "Obamacare" as just another handout of "free stuff" to African Americans at their expense; and who felt that they were struggling to survive in a system that was rigged by the establishment against them and yet offered them no help.

As one observer noted, Trump's very language was keyed to evoke a nostalgia for an America long gone—his frequent use of the words *again* ("Make America Great Again") and *back* (bringing back jobs, law and order, and American power) were speaking to people for whom America is no longer as great as it was. These words appeared on hats, on T-shirts, and as the basis of chants at rallies where they were filmed and shown incessantly on cable TV. Democratic pollster Cornell Belcher says, "It's almost a cultural nostalgia, for when white male culture [was] most dominant.... When women, African American and Hispanic voters hear that...they get the joke that going back to the past [would be] great for some but at the expense of others."[8]

The frustration and despair of the white, blue-collar, working class is not an imaginary malady, or mere sour grapes that they are no longer on top. Writes one researcher, "The highest costs of being poor in the U.S. are...in the form of unhappiness, stress, and lack of hope." And it is lower-class, rural whites who feel the relative deprivation the most as the rich get impossibly richer, blacks and Hispanics improve their economic position, and they seem to be stuck or falling even if their incomes are actually above the average.[9] A 2015 study showed that mortality rates for *almost* all groups in the

United States were dropping; the exception was for non-college-educated middle-aged whites. They were less healthy and dying younger, and of causes such as suicide, drug overdose, and alcoholism.[10]

Studies by political scientists disagreed on whether you could predict these early Trump supporters by their attitudes toward authoritarianism (an ideology based on the belief that there is a proper hierarchical order in society that a strong leader should enforce)[11] or populism (distrust of elites and experts and advocacy of strong nationalist values).[12] Either way, it boiled down to the idea that some American people were more authentically American and therefore more privileged than others; that is, it boiled down to race. Wrote one political scientist, Trump's core of support in the primaries was among "Republicans who held unfavorable views of African Americans, Muslims, immigrants, and minority groups in general. Perceptions that whites are treated unfairly in the United States and that the country's growing diversity is a bad thing were also significantly associated with Trump in the primaries."[13]

Race has been a permanent thread in the fabric of American politics and perhaps it always will be. But today it confronts some undeniable facts. The fact is that the racial landscape is changing in irreversible ways. The fact is that whites are a diminishing racial group in the United States, as people of color are growing in numbers. The fact is that nearly eleven million undocumented immigrants live and work in the United States, with no easy or affordable way to repatriate them. The fact is that Muslim Americans are deeply integrated into communities throughout the country. The fact is that a black man was elected to and served two terms in the White House and left with a significant majority approving of the job he had done, although the elected Republican government promptly began to dismantle his legacy.

The American landscape is changing in some nonracial ways as well that are relevant to the grievances to which Trump's candidacy spoke. Although the United States did not elect its first woman president in 2016, Hillary Clinton got more popular votes than did Donald Trump. Young people seem to have more open minds not just about race but also about social issues like marriage equality, transgender rights, and legalization of pot. The economy has changed in permanent ways that mean some traditional working-class jobs are gone forever and the government has failed to provide funding and training for alternative sources of employment. We live in a world where global terror threats can be monitored but probably never eliminated. And we live in a mediated world where third parties have powerful motivations to drive their own narratives and more ways than ever to circulate them.

Authoritarianism, populism, and racism are often reactions to perceived threats to a group's security, well-being, and prosperity. Are these facts of modern life—all indicators that the way we live is shifting in significant ways—sufficient threats to bring out the racial animus that seemed to buoy Trump and elate white nationalists? What exactly is at stake when a demographic group that is accustomed to being automatically in power starts to lose its majority status? We take a close look at race, ethnicity, and gender equality in this chapter, and return to this important question after examining what is at stake in civil rights politics in general.

WHEN you consider where we started, the progress toward equality in the United States can look pretty impressive. Nowhere is the change more vivid than in the case of racial equality. In the early 1950s, it was illegal for most blacks and whites to go to the same schools in the American South or to use the same public facilities, like swimming pools and drinking fountains. Today, for most of us, the segregated South is a distant memory. On August 28, 2008, forty-five years from the day that civil rights leader Martin Luther King Jr. declared that he had a dream that one day a child would be judged on the content of his character rather than the color of his skin, the nation watched as Barack Hussein Obama, born of a white mother from Kansas and a black father from Kenya, accepted the Democratic Party's nomination to the presidency of the United States, an office he would go on to win twice. Such moments, caught in the media spotlight, illuminate a stark contrast between now and then.

But in some ways, the changes highlighted at such moments are only superficial. Though black cabinet members are not uncommon—George W. Bush had two African American secretaries of state, Obama appointed the first two black attorneys general, and Trump has an African American secretary of housing and urban development—there have been remarkably few blacks in national elected office. *USA Today* pointed out in 2002 that "if the US Senate and the National Governors Association were private clubs, their membership rosters would be a scandal. They're virtually lily white,"[14] and not much has changed since then. Out of a total of 1,974 U.S. senators since the founding, only ten have been African Americans. Ironically, Obama's election to the presidency in 2008 removed the only black senator serving at the time.

For the first time in our history, there are three African American senators serving simultaneously: Cory Booker, D-N.J., and Tim Scott, R-S.C., both elected in 2014; and Kamala Harris, D-Calif, elected in 2016.

Even though legal discrimination ended more than half a century ago and there are positive signs of improvement in the lives of African Americans, including a newfound optimism about the future,[15] inequality still pervades the American system and continues to be reflected in economic and social statistics. On average, blacks are less educated and much poorer than whites, they experience higher crime rates, they are more likely to be incarcerated and killed in altercations with the police, they live disproportionately in poverty-stricken areas, they score lower on standardized tests, and they rank at the bottom of most social measurements. Life expectancy is lower for African American men and women than for their white counterparts (although recent studies have shown the gap closing), and a greater percentage of African American children live in single-parent homes than do white or Hispanic children. The statistics illustrate what we suggested in Chapter 4—that rights equal power, and long-term deprivation of rights results in powerlessness. Unfortunately, the granting of formal **civil rights**, which we defined in Chapter 4 as the citizenship rights guaranteed by the Thirteenth, Fourteenth, Fifteenth, Nineteenth, and Twenty-sixth Amendments, may not bring about speedy changes in social and economic status.

African Americans are not the only group that shows the effects of having been deprived of its civil rights. Native Americans, Hispanics, and Asian Americans have all faced or face unequal treatment in the legal system, the job market, and the schools. Women, making up over half the population of the United States, have long struggled to gain economic parity with men. People in America are also denied rights, and thus power, on the basis of their sexual orientation, their age, their physical abilities, and their citizenship status. People who belong to multiple groups face the complex issues of **intersectionality**—the overlapping discrimination and oppression that results when you are black, female, and poor, for instance. A country once praised by French observer Alexis de Tocqueville as a place of extraordinary equality, the United States

civil rights citizenship rights guaranteed to the people (primarily in the Thirteenth, Fourteenth, Fifteenth, Nineteenth, and Twenty-sixth Amendments) and protected by the government

intersectionality the interdependent discrimination and oppression that result when an individual is a member of more than one oppressed or minority group

today is haunted by traditions of unequal treatment and intolerance that it cannot entirely shake. And, as we noted in *What's at Stake . . . ?*, the growing attention to the various groups that have been denied rights is seen by some white people as diminishing their own rights.

In this chapter we look at the struggles of these groups to gain equal rights and the power to enforce those rights. The struggles are different because the groups themselves, and the political avenues open to them, vary in important ways. To understand how groups can use different political strategies to change the rules and win power, in this chapter you will learn more about the meaning of political inequality; the struggle of African Americans to claim rights denied to them because of race; the struggle of Native Americans, Hispanics, and Asian Americans to claim rights denied to them because of race or ethnicity; women's battle for rights denied to them on the basis of gender; and the fight by other groups in society to claim rights denied to them on a variety of bases.

THE MEANING OF POLITICAL INEQUALITY

When is different treatment okay?

Despite the deeply held American expectation that the law should treat all people equally, laws by nature must treat some people differently from others. Not only are laws designed in the first place to discriminate between those who abide by society's rules and those who don't,[16] but the laws can also legally treat criminals differently once they are convicted. For instance, in all but two states, Maine and Vermont, felons are denied the right to vote for some length of time, and in ten states, felons forfeit voting rights permanently.[17] But when particular groups are treated differently because of some characteristic like race, religion, gender, sexual orientation, age, or wealth, we say that the law discriminates against them, that they are denied equal protection of the laws. Throughout our history, legislatures, both state and national, have passed laws treating groups differently based on characteristics such as these. Sometimes those laws have seemed just and reasonable, but often they have not. Deciding which characteristics may fairly be the basis for unequal treatment is the job of all three branches of our government, but especially of our court system.

> **What would a legal system that treated all people exactly the same look like?**

WHEN CAN THE LAW TREAT PEOPLE DIFFERENTLY?

The Supreme Court has expended considerable energy and ink on this problem, and its answers have changed over time as various groups have waged the battle for equal rights against a backdrop of ever-changing American values, public opinion, and politics. Before we look at the struggles those groups have endured in their pursuit of equal treatment by the law, we should understand the Court's current formula for determining what sorts of discrimination need what sorts of legal remedy.

The Court has divided the laws that treat people differently into three tiers (see this chapter's *The Big Picture*):

suspect classification
a classification, such as race, for which any discriminatory law must be justified by a compelling state interest

- The top tier refers to classifications of people that are so rarely constitutional that they are immediately "suspect." Suspect classifications require the government to have a compelling state interest for treating people differently. Race is a **suspect classification**. To determine whether a law making a suspect classification is constitutional, the Court subjects it to a heightened standard of review called **strict scrutiny**. Strict scrutiny means that the Court looks very carefully at the law and the government interest involved. (The catch, as we will see, is that while laws that discriminate *against* a suspect class are examined carefully, so are laws that discriminate in their favor.) As we saw in Chapter 4, laws that deprived people of some fundamental religious rights were once required to pass the compelling state interest test; at that time, religion was viewed by the Court as a suspect category.

- Classifications that the Court views as less potentially dangerous to fundamental rights fall into the middle tier. These "quasi-suspect" classifications may or may not be legitimate grounds for treating people differently. Such classifications are subject not to strict scrutiny but to an **intermediate standard of review**. That is, the Court looks to see if the law requiring different treatment of people bears a substantial relationship to an important state interest. An "important interest test" is not as hard to meet as a "compelling interest test." Laws that treat women differently from men fall into this category.

- Finally, the least-scrutinized tier of classifications is that of "nonsuspect" classifications; these are subject to the **minimum rationality test**. The Court asks whether the government had a rational basis for making a law that treats a given class of people differently. Laws that discriminate on the basis of age, such as a curfew for young people, or on the basis of economic level, such as a higher tax rate for those in a certain income bracket, need not stem from compelling or important government interests. The government must merely have had a rational basis for making the law, which is fairly easy for a legislature to show.

The significance of the three tiers of classification and the three review standards is that all groups that feel discriminated against want the Court to view them as a suspect class so that they will be treated as a protected group. Civil rights laws might cover them anyway, and the Fourteenth Amendment, which guarantees equal protection of the laws, might also formally protect them. However, once a group is designated as a suspect class, the Supreme Court is unlikely to permit *any* laws to treat them differently. Thus gaining suspect status is crucial in the struggle for equal rights.

After over one hundred years of decisions that effectively allowed people to be treated differently because of their race, the Court finally agreed in the 1950s that race is a suspect class. Women's groups, however, have failed to convince the Court, or to amend the Constitution, to make gender a suspect classification. The intermediate standard of review was devised by the Court to express its view that it is a little more dangerous to classify people by gender than by age or wealth, but not as dangerous as classifying them by race or religion. Some groups in America—those in the LGBTQ community, for instance—have not even managed to get the Court to consider them in the quasi-suspect category. Although the lower courts have flirted with changing that status, the Supreme Court didn't specify a standard of review when it struck down the Defense of Marriage Act in 2013. Some states and localities have passed legislation to prevent discrimination on the basis of sexual orientation, but gays can still be treated differently by law as long as the state can demonstrate a rational basis for the law.

These standards of review make a real difference in American politics—they are part of the rules of politics that determine society's winners and losers. Americans who are treated unequally by the law consequently have less power to use the democratic system to get what they need and want (like legislation to protect and further their interests), to secure the resources available through the system (like education and other government benefits), and to gain new resources (like jobs and material goods). People who cannot claim their political rights have little, if any, standing in a democratic society.

strict scrutiny a heightened standard of review used by the Supreme Court to assess the constitutionality of laws that limit some freedoms or that make a suspect classification

intermediate standard of review a standard of review used by the Supreme Court to evaluate laws that make a quasi-suspect classification

minimum rationality test a standard of review used by the Supreme Court to evaluate laws that make a nonsuspect classification

THE BIG PICTURE:
When the Law Can Treat People Differently

The Supreme Court has expended considerable energy and ink on this problem, and its answers have changed over time as various groups have waged the battle for equal rights against a backdrop of ever-changing American values, public opinion, and politics. Before we look at the struggles those groups have endured in their pursuit of equal treatment by the law, we should understand the Court's current formula for determining what sorts of discrimination need what sorts of legal remedy.

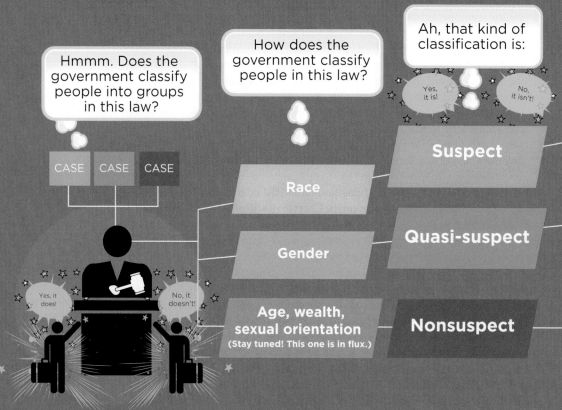

Hmmm. Does the government classify people into groups in this law?

CASE   CASE   CASE

Yes, it does!   No, it doesn't!

How does the government classify people in this law?

Ah, that kind of classification is:

Yes, it is!   No, it isn't!

Race

Gender

Age, wealth, sexual orientation
(Stay tuned! This one is in flux.)

Suspect

Quasi-suspect

Nonsuspect

EXAMPLE OF CLASSIFICATION UPHELD	**SUSPECT** Government had a compelling state interest (national security) in relocating Japanese Americans from the West Coast during World War II. *Korematsu v. United States* (1944)
CLASSIFICATION STRUCK DOWN	State government had no compelling reason to segregate schools to achieve state purpose of educating children. *Brown v. Board of Education* (1954)

So, what standard should I use?

That means I have to ask:

If the answer is yes, the government will...

No, you must use a higher standard!

No, you must use a lower standard!

There is a compelling interest.

There is NO compelling interest.

Strict scrutiny standard of review

Is there a compelling state interest in this classification?

CITIZEN   GOVERNMENT

most likely lose, and the law will be struck down.

Intermediate standard of review

Is there an important state purpose for this classification?

CITIZEN   GOVERNMENT

often lose, and the law will be struck down.

Minimum rationality standard of review

Is there a rational basis for this classification?

CITIZEN   GOVERNMENT

probably prevail, and the law will be upheld.

QUASI-SUSPECT
Court upheld federal law requiring males but not females to register for military service (the draft). *Rostker v. Goldberg* (1981)

Court struck down an Alabama law requiring husbands but not wives to pay alimony after divorce. *Orr v. Orr* (1979)

NONSUSPECT
Court found a Missouri law requiring public officials to retire at age seventy to have a rational basis. *Gregory v. Ashcroft* (1991)

Court struck down an amendment to the Colorado constitution that banned legislation to protect people's rights on the basis of their sexual orientation because it had no rational relation to a legitimate state goal. *Romer v. Evans* (1996)

DIFFERENT KINDS OF EQUALITY

The notion of equality is controversial in the United States. The disputes arise in part because we often think that equal must mean "identical" or "the same." Thus equality can seem threatening to the American value system, which prizes people's freedom to be different, to be unique individuals. We can better understand the controversies over the attempts to create political equality in this country if we return briefly to a distinction we made in Chapter 1 between substantive and procedural equality.

In American political culture, we prefer to rely on government to guarantee fair treatment and equal opportunity (a *procedural* view), rather than to manipulate fair and equal outcomes (a *substantive* view). We want government to treat everyone the same, and we want people to be free to be different, but we do not want government to treat people differently in order to make them equal at the end. This distinction poses a problem for the civil rights movement in America, the effort to achieve equal treatment by the laws for all Americans. When the laws are changed, which is a procedural solution, substantive action may still be necessary to ensure equal treatment in the future.

In Your Own Words   Outline the criteria used by the courts to determine if and when the law can treat people differently.

RIGHTS DENIED ON THE BASIS OF RACE: AFRICAN AMERICANS
The battle to end the legacy of slavery and racism, fought mainly in the courts

We cannot separate the history of our race relations from the history of the United States. Americans have struggled for centuries to come to terms with the fact that citizens of African nations were kidnapped, packed into sailing vessels, exported to America, and sold, often at great profit, into a life that destroyed their families, their spirit, and their human dignity. The narratives of white supremacy and black inferiority, told to numb the sensibilities of European Americans to the horror of their own behavior, have been almost as damaging as slavery itself and have lived on in the American psyche—and in political institutions—much longer than the practice they justified. As we saw in *What's at Stake . . . ?*, these narratives are very much alive today. **Racism**, institutionalized power inequalities in society based on the perception of racial differences, is not a "southern problem" or a "black problem"; it is an American problem, and one that we have not yet managed to eradicate from national culture.

Not only has racism had a decisive influence on American culture, but it also has been central to American politics. From the start, those with power in America have been torn by the issue of race. The framers of the Constitution were so ambivalent that they would not use the word *slavery*, even while that document legalized its existence. Although some early politicians were morally opposed to the institution of slavery, they were, in the end, more reluctant to offend their southern colleagues by taking an antislavery stand. Even the Northwest Ordinance of 1787, which prohibited slavery in the northwestern territories, contained the concession to the South that fugitive slaves could legally be seized and returned to their owners. The accumulated tensions associated with slavery exploded in the American Civil War.

racism institutionalized power inequalities in society based on the perception of racial differences

THE CIVIL WAR AND ITS AFTERMATH: WINNERS AND LOSERS

We can't begin to cover here all the causes of the Civil War, which tore apart the country from April 1861 to May 1865. Suffice it to say that the war was not fought simply over the moral evil of slavery. Slavery was an economic and political issue as well as an ethical one. The southern economy depended on slavery, and when, in an effort to hold the Union together in 1863, President Abraham Lincoln issued the Emancipation Proclamation, he was not simply taking a moral stand; he was trying to use economic pressure to keep the country intact. The proclamation, in fact, did not free all slaves, only those in states rebelling against the Union.[18]

It is hard to find any real "winners" in the American Civil War. Indeed, the war took such a toll on North and South that neither world war in the twentieth century would claim as many American casualties. The North "won" the war, in that the Union was restored, but the costs would continue to be paid for decades afterward. Politically, the northern Republicans, the party of Lincoln, were in the ascendance, controlling both the House and the Senate, but after Lincoln was assassinated in April 1865, their will was often thwarted by President Andrew Johnson, a Democrat from Tennessee who was sympathetic toward the South.

The Thirteenth Amendment, banning slavery, was passed by Congress in January 1865 and ratified in December of that year. This was a huge blow to southern white power. In retaliation, and to ensure that their political and social dominance of southern society would continue, the southern white state governments legislated black codes. Black codes were laws that essentially sought to keep blacks in a subservient economic and political position by legally restricting most of the freedoms (voting, property owning, education) they had gained by becoming citizens.[19]

Congress, led by northern Republicans, tried to check southern obstruction in 1865 by instituting a period of federal control of southern politics called Reconstruction. In an attempt to make the black codes unconstitutional, Congress passed the Fourteenth Amendment, guaranteeing all people born or naturalized in the United States the rights of citizenship and ensuring that no state could take away those rights. Further, no state could deprive any person of life, liberty, or property without due process of the law, or deny any person equal protection of the law. As we saw in Chapter 4, the Supreme Court has made varied use of this amendment, but its original intent was to bring some semblance of civil rights to southern blacks. The Fifteenth Amendment followed in 1870, effectively extending the right to vote to all adult males.

At first Reconstruction worked as the North had hoped. Under northern supervision, southern life began to change. Blacks voted, were elected to some local posts, and cemented Republican dominance with their support. But southern whites responded with violence. Groups like the Ku Klux Klan terrorized blacks in the South. Lynchings, arson, assaults, and beatings made claiming one's rights or associating with Republicans a risky business. Congress fought back vigorously and suppressed the reign of terror for a while, but by 1876, political problems in the North and resurgent white power in the South effectively brought Reconstruction to an end. Shortly after that, southern whites set about the business of stripping blacks of their newfound political power.

Without the intervention of the northern Republicans, disenfranchising blacks turned out to be easy to accomplish. The strategy chosen by the Democrats, who now controlled the southern state governments, was a sly one. Under the Fifteenth Amendment the vote could not be denied on the basis of race, color, or previous condition of servitude, so the Democrats, who now controlled the southern state governments, set out to deny it on legal bases that would have the primary effect of targeting blacks. Poll taxes, which required the payment of a small tax before

black codes a series of laws in the post–Civil War South designed to restrict the rights of former slaves before the passage of the Fourteenth and Fifteenth Amendments

Reconstruction the period following the Civil War during which the federal government took action to rebuild the South

poll taxes taxes levied as a qualification for voting

voters could cast their votes, effectively took the right to vote away from the many blacks who were too poor to pay, and literacy tests, which required potential voters to demonstrate some reading skills, excluded most blacks who, denied an education, could not read. Even African Americans who were literate were often kept from voting because a white registrar administered the test unfairly. To permit illiterate whites to vote, literacy tests were combined with grandfather clauses, which required passage of such tests only by those prospective voters whose grandfathers had not been allowed to vote before 1867. Thus, unlike the black codes, these new laws, called Jim Crow laws, obeyed the letter of the Fifteenth Amendment, never explicitly saying that they were denying blacks the right to vote because of their race, color, or previous condition of servitude. This strategy proved devastatingly effective, and by 1910, registration of black voters had dropped dramatically, and registration of poor, illiterate whites had fallen as well.[20] Southern Democrats were back in power and had eliminated the possibility of competition.

Jim Crow laws were not just about voting but also concerned many other dimensions of southern life. The 1900s launched a half-century of segregation in the South—that is, of separate facilities for blacks and whites for leisure, business, travel, education, and other activities. The Civil Rights Act of 1875 had guaranteed that all people, regardless of race, color, or previous condition of servitude, were to have full and equal accommodation in "inns, public conveyances on land or water, theaters, and other places of public amusement," but the Supreme Court struck down the law, arguing that the Fourteenth Amendment restricted the behavior only of states, not of private individuals.[21] Having survived the legal test of the Constitution, Jim Crow laws continued to divide the southern world in two. But it was not a world of equal halves. The whites-only facilities were invariably superior to those intended for blacks; they were newer, cleaner, and more comfortable. Before long, the laws were challenged by blacks who asked why equal protection of the law shouldn't translate into some real equality in their lives.

In *Plessy v. Ferguson*, in which a Louisiana statute requiring blacks and whites to travel in separate railway cars was challenged, the Court held that enforced separation of the races did not mean that one race was inferior to the other. As long as the facilities provided were equal, states were within their rights to require them to be separate. Rejecting the majority view, Justice John Marshall Harlan wrote in a famous dissent, "Our Constitution is color-blind, and neither knows nor tolerates classes among citizens."[22] It would be over fifty years before a majority on the Court shared his view. In the meantime, everyone immediately embraced the "separate," and forgot the "equal," part of the ruling. Segregated facilities for whites and blacks had received the Supreme Court's seal of approval.

THE LONG BATTLE TO OVERTURN *PLESSY*: THE NAACP AND ITS LEGAL STRATEGY

The years following the *Plessy* decision were bleak ones for African American civil rights. The formal rules of politics giving blacks their rights had been enacted at the national level, but no branch of government at any level was willing to enforce them. The Supreme Court had firmly rejected attempts to give the Fourteenth Amendment more teeth. Congress was not inclined to help once the Republican fervor for reform had worn off. Nor were the southern state governments likely to support black rights.

The National Association for the Advancement of Colored People (NAACP), founded in 1910, aimed to help individual blacks; to raise white society's awareness of the atrocities of contemporary race relations; and most important, to change laws and court rulings that kept blacks from true equality. The NAACP, over time, was able to develop a legal strategy that was finally the undoing of Jim Crow and the segregated South.

literacy tests tests requiring reading or comprehension skills as a qualification for voting

grandfather clauses provisions exempting from voting restrictions the descendants of those able to vote in 1867

Jim Crow laws southern laws designed to circumvent the Thirteenth, Fourteenth, and Fifteenth Amendments and to deny blacks rights on bases other than race

segregation the practice and policy of separating races

National Association for the Advancement of Colored People (NAACP) an interest group founded in 1910 to promote civil rights for African Americans

Beginning with a challenge to segregation in law schools, a form of discrimination that Supreme Court justices would be most likely to see as dangerous, NAACP lawyers made the case that separate could not be equal in education. A series of victories over legal education set the stage for tackling the issue of education more broadly.

The NAACP had four cases pending that concerned the segregation of educational facilities in the South and the Midwest. In 1954 the Court ruled on all of them under the case name *Brown v. Board of Education of Topeka*. In their now-familiar arguments, NAACP lawyers emphasized the intangible aspects of education, including how it made black students feel to be made to go to a separate school. They cited sociological evidence of the low self-esteem of black schoolchildren, and they argued that it resulted from a system that made black children feel inferior by treating them differently.

Under the new leadership of Chief Justice Earl Warren, the Court ruled unanimously in favor of Linda Brown and the other black students. Without explicitly denouncing segregation or overturning *Plessy*, lest the South erupt in violent outrage again, the Warren Court held that separate schools, by their very definition, could never be equal because it was the fact of separation itself that made black children feel unequal. Segregation in education was inherently unconstitutional.[23] The principle of "separate but equal" was not yet dead, but it had suffered serious injury.

The *Brown* decision did not bring instant relief to the southern school system. The Court, in a 1955 follow-up to *Brown*, ruled that school desegregation had to take place "with all deliberate speed."[24] Such an ambiguous direction was asking for school districts to drag their feet. The most public and blatant attempt to avoid compliance took place in Little Rock, Arkansas, in September 1957, when Gov. Orval Faubus posted the National Guard at the local high school to prevent the attendance of nine African American children. Rioting white parents, filmed for the nightly news, showed the rest of the country the faces of southern bigotry. Finally, President Dwight Eisenhower sent one thousand federal troops to guarantee the safe passage of the nine black children through the angry mob of white parents who threatened to lynch them rather than let them enter the school. The *Brown* case and the attempts to enforce it proved to be catalysts for a civil rights movement that would change the whole country.

THE CIVIL RIGHTS MOVEMENT

In the same year that the Court ordered school desegregation to proceed "with all deliberate speed," a woman named Rosa Parks sat down on a bus in Montgomery, Alabama, and started a chain of events that would end with a Court order to stop segregation in all aspects of southern life. When Parks refused to yield her seat to a white passenger, as the law required, she was arrested and sent to jail.

Overnight, local groups in the black community organized a boycott of the Montgomery bus system. A **boycott** seeks to put economic pressure on a business to do something by encouraging people to stop purchasing its goods or services. Montgomery blacks, who formed the base of the bus company's clientele, wanted the bus company to lose so much money that it would force the local government to change the bus laws. Against all expectations, the bus boycott continued for over a year. In the meantime the case wound its way through the legal system, and a little over a year after the boycott began, the Supreme Court affirmed a lower court's judgment that Montgomery's law was unconstitutional.[25] Separate bus accommodations were not equal.

TWO KINDS OF DISCRIMINATION The civil rights movement launched by the Montgomery bus boycott confronted two different types of discrimination. **De jure discrimination**

boycott the refusal to buy certain goods or services as a way to protest policy or force political reform

de jure discrimination discrimination that arises from or is supported by the law

AP Photo/Bill Hudson, File

Defying the Jaws of Injustice

A seventeen-year-old demonstrator in Birmingham, Alabama, is attacked by a police dog after defying a city antiparade ordinance on May 3, 1963. This photograph ran on the cover of the New York Times the next day and drew the attention of President John F. Kennedy. As images and stories of other similar events spread, more people increasingly demanded that the violence end and that blacks be given equal rights and opportunities.

(discrimination by law) is created by laws that treat people differently based on some characteristic like race. This is the sort of discrimination most blacks in the South faced. Especially in rural areas, blacks and whites lived and worked side by side, but by law they used separate facilities. Although the process of changing the laws was excruciatingly painful, once the laws were changed and the new laws were enforced, the result was integration.

The second sort of discrimination, called **de facto discrimination** (discrimination in fact), however, produces a kind of segregation that is much more difficult to eliminate. Segregation in the North was of this type because blacks and whites did not live and work in the same places to begin with. It was not laws that kept them apart, but past discrimination, tradition, custom, economic status, and residential patterns. This kind of segregation is hard to remedy because there are no laws to change; the segregation is woven more complexly into the fabric of society.

We can look at the civil rights movement in America as having two stages. The initial stage involved the battle to change the laws so that blacks and whites would be equally protected by the laws, as the Fourteenth Amendment guarantees. The second stage, and one that is ongoing today, is the fight against the aftereffects of those laws, and of centuries of discrimination, that leave many blacks and whites still living in communities that are worlds apart.

de facto discrimination
discrimination that is the result not of law but rather of tradition and habit

CHANGING THE RULES: FIGHTING DE JURE DISCRIMINATION Rosa Parks and the Montgomery bus boycott launched a new strategy in blacks' fight for equal rights. Although it took the power of a court judgment to move the city officials, blacks themselves had exercised considerable power through peaceful protest and massive resistance to the will of whites. One of the leaders of the boycott was a young Baptist minister named Martin Luther King Jr. A founding member of the Southern Christian Leadership Conference, a group of black clergy committed to expanding civil rights, King became known for his non-violent approach to political protest. This philosophy of peacefully resisting enforcement of laws perceived to be unjust, and marching or "sitting in" to express political views, captured the imagination of supporters of black civil rights in both the South and the North. Black college students, occasionally joined by whites, staged peaceful demonstrations, called sit-ins, to desegregate lunch counters in southern department stores and other facilities. The protest movement was important for the practices it challenged directly—such as segregation in motels and restaurants, on beaches, and in other recreational facilities—but also for the pressure it brought to bear on elected officials and the effect it had on public opinion, particularly in the North, which had been largely unaware of southern problems.

The nonviolent resistance movement, in conjunction with the growing political power of northern blacks, brought about remarkable social and political change in the 1960s. The administration of Democratic president John F. Kennedy, not wanting to alienate the support of southern Democrats, tried at first to limit its active involvement in civil rights work. But the political pressure of black interest groups forced Kennedy to take a more visible stand. The Reverend King was using his tactics of nonviolent protest to great advantage in the spring of 1963. Kennedy responded to the political pressure, so deftly orchestrated by King, by sending to Birmingham federal mediators to negotiate an end to segregation, and then by sending to Congress a massive package of civil rights legislation.

Kennedy did not live to see his proposals become law, but they became the top priority of his successor, Lyndon Johnson. During the Johnson years, the president, bipartisan majorities in Congress (southern Democrats split off to vote against their president and started a slow process of leaving the party altogether), and the Supreme Court were in agreement on civil rights issues, and their joint legacy is impressive. The Kennedy-initiated Civil Rights Act of 1964 reinforced the voting laws, allowed the attorney general to file school desegregation lawsuits, permitted the president to deny federal money to state and local programs that practiced discrimination, prohibited discrimination in public accommodations and in employment, and set up the Equal Employment Opportunity Commission (EEOC) to investigate complaints about job discrimination. Johnson also sent to Congress the Voting Rights Act of 1965, which, when passed, disallowed discriminatory tests like literacy tests and provided for federal examiners to register voters throughout much of the South. The Supreme Court, still the liberal Warren Court that had ruled in *Brown*, backed up this new legislation.[26] In addition, the Twenty-fourth Amendment, outlawing poll taxes in federal elections, was ratified in 1964.

Because of the unusual cooperation among the three branches of government, life in the South—though far from perfect—was radically different for blacks by the end of the 1960s. In 1968, 18 percent of southern black students went to schools with a majority of white students; in 1970 the percentage rose to 39 and in 1972 to 46. The comparable figure for black students in the North was only 28 percent in 1972.[27] Voter registration had also improved dramatically: from 1964 to 1969, black voter registration in the South nearly doubled, from 36 to 65 percent of adult blacks.[28]

CHANGING THE OUTCOMES: FIGHTING DE FACTO DISCRIMINATION

Political and educational advances did not translate into substantial economic gains for blacks. As a group, they remained at the very bottom of the economic hierarchy, and ironically the problem was most severe not in the rural South but in the industrialized North. Many southern blacks who had migrated to the North in search of jobs and a better quality of life found conditions not much different from those they had left behind. Abject poverty, discrimination in employment, and segregated schools and housing led to frustration and inflamed tempers. In the summers of 1966 and 1967, race riots flashed across the northern urban landscape. Impatient with the passive resistance of the nonviolent protest movement in the South, many blacks became more militant in their insistence on social and economic change. The Black Muslims, led by Malcolm X until his assassination in 1965; the Black Panthers; and the Student Nonviolent Coordinating Committee all demanded "black power" and radical change. These activists rejected King's philosophy of working peacefully through existing political institutions to bring about gradual change.

Northern whites who had applauded the desegregation of the South grew increasingly nervous as angry African Americans began to target segregation in the North. The de facto segregation there meant that black inner-city schools and white suburban schools were often as segregated as if the hand of Jim Crow had been at work. In the 1970s the courts and some politicians, believing they had a duty not only to end segregation laws in education but also to integrate all the nation's schools, instituted a policy of busing in some northern cities. Students from majority-white schools would be bused to mostly black schools, and vice versa. The policy was immediately controversial; riots in South Boston in 1974 resembled those in Little Rock seventeen years earlier.

Not all opponents of busing were reacting from racist motives. Busing students from their homes to a distant school strikes many Americans as fundamentally unjust. Parents who move to better neighborhoods so that they can send their children to better schools do not want to see those children bused back to their old schools, and they fear for the safety of their children when they are bused into poverty-stricken areas with high crime rates. Parents of both races want their children to be part of a local community and its activities, which is hard when the children must leave the community for the better part of each day.

The Supreme Court has shared America's ambivalence about busing. Although it endorsed busing as a remedy for segregated schools in 1971,[29] three years later it ruled that busing plans could not merge inner-city and suburban districts unless officials could prove that the district lines had been drawn in a racially discriminatory manner.[30] Since many whites were moving out of the cities, there were fewer white students to bus, and busing did not really succeed in integrating schools in many urban areas. More than sixty years after the *Brown* decision, many schools, especially those in urban areas, remain largely segregated.[31]

The example of busing highlights a problem faced by civil rights workers and policymakers: deciding whether the Fourteenth Amendment guarantee of equal protection simply requires that the states not sanction discrimination or whether it imposes an active obligation on them to integrate blacks and whites. As the northern experience shows, the absence of legal discrimination does not mean equality. In 1965 President Johnson issued an executive order that not only prohibited discrimination in firms doing business with the government but also ordered them to take affirmative action to compensate for past discrimination. In other words, if a firm had no black employees, it wasn't enough not to have a policy against hiring them; the firm now had to actively recruit and hire blacks. The test would not be federal law or company policy, but the actual racial mix of employees.

Johnson's call for affirmative action was taken seriously not only in employment situations but also in university decisions. Patterns of discrimination in employment and higher education showed the results of decades of decisions by white males to hire or admit other white males. Blacks, as well as other minorities and women, were relegated to low-paying, low-status jobs. After Johnson's executive order, the EEOC decided that the percentage of blacks

busing achieving racial balance by transporting students to schools across neighborhood boundaries

affirmative action a policy of creating opportunities for members of certain groups as a substantive remedy for past discrimination

working in firms should reflect the percentage of blacks in the labor force. Many colleges and universities reserved space on their admissions lists for minorities, sometimes accepting minority applicants with grades and test scores lower than those of whites.

We have talked about the tension in American politics between procedural and substantive equality, between equality of treatment and equality of results. That is precisely the tension that arises when Americans are faced with policies of busing and affirmative action, both of which are instances of American policy attempting to bring about substantive equality. The end results seem attractive, but the means to get there—treating people differently—seem inherently unfair in the American value system. The Supreme Court reflected the public's unease with affirmative action policies but did not reject the idea, holding in 1978 that schools can have a legitimate interest in having a diversified student body and that they can take race into account in admissions decisions, just as they can consider geographic location, for instance.[32]

Few of the presidents after Kennedy and Johnson took strong pro–civil rights positions, but none effected a real reversal in policy until Ronald Reagan. Reagan's strong conservatism led him to regret the power that had been taken from the states by the Supreme Court's broad interpretation of the Fourteenth Amendment, and he particularly disliked race-based remedies for discrimination, like busing and affirmative action. The Reagan administration lobbied the Court strenuously to get it to change its rulings on the constitutionality of those policies, but it wasn't until the end of Reagan's second term, when the effect of his conservative appointments to the Court kicked in, that a true change in policy occurred.

In 1989 the Court fulfilled civil rights advocates' most pessimistic expectations. In a series of rulings, it held that the Fourteenth Amendment did not protect workers from racial harassment on the job,[33] that the burden of proof in claims of employment discrimination was on the worker,[34] and that affirmative action was on shaky constitutional ground.[35] The Democratic-led Congress sought to undo some of the Court's late-1980s rulings by passing the Civil Rights Act of 1991, which made it easier for workers to seek redress against employers who discriminate, but the country had turned rightward and the civil rights era was over.

BLACKS IN CONTEMPORARY AMERICAN POLITICS

The Supreme Court's use of strict scrutiny on laws that discriminate on the basis of race has put an end to most de jure discrimination. However, de facto discrimination remains, with all the consequences that stem from the fact that tradition and practice in the United States endorse a fundamental inequality of power. Although groups like Black Lives Matter have called public attention to the fact that young black men are often racially profiled, killed by police without justification, and incarcerated at higher rates than whites, there are other, more subtle ways that we fall short of true racial equality.

Affirmative action, one of the few remedies for de facto discrimination, continues to be a controversial policy in America. Voters in California declared affirmative action illegal in their state in 1996, and voters in Washington did the same in 1998. Michigan voted in 2006 to ban affirmative action in the state's public colleges and government contracting, and in 2008 affirmative action was struck down by voters in Nebraska. In 2010 Arizona passed a constitutional ban on government-sponsored affirmative action programs. Despite the controversy, however, there remains considerable support for affirmative action in the United States. Efforts to end affirmative action have failed in state legislatures in New Jersey, Michigan, Colorado, and almost a dozen other states. Still, as the 2006 success of the so-called Michigan Civil Rights Initiative and the 2008 defeat of affirmative action in Nebraska show, campaigns in the public can succeed where the legislature may balk. The American public remains divided: opinion polls show support for the ideals behind affirmative action but not if it is perceived to be giving minorities preferential treatment.[36]

The federal courts, while still supportive of the spirit of affirmative action, have taken the notion that race is a suspect classification to mean that any laws treating people differently according to race must be given strict scrutiny, even if their intent is to benefit rather than harm the group they single out. So, for instance, in 2003 the Supreme Court threw out the University of Michigan's undergraduate admissions policy because it was tantamount to setting racial quotas,[37] but in another case that year the Court held, five to four, that the law school's holistic approach of taking into account the race of the applicant was constitutional because of the importance of creating a diverse student body.[38] Ten years later, a considerably more conservative Court held that race-based admissions standards had to be given strict scrutiny and, in a separate ruling, upheld a Michigan ban on using race in admissions decisions.[39] Then in 2016 the Court affirmed that the goal of having a diverse student body justified taking race into account in admissions decisions.[40]

One of the consequences of the continued de facto discrimination in the United States is a gap between the income and wealth of whites and blacks. Although there is a large and growing black middle class in many parts of the country, the median household income for African Americans in 2014 was $35,398; for whites, it was $60,256. Though blacks constituted about 14.3 percent of the U.S. population in 2014, they lag behind whites in businesses owned, small business loans received, homeownership, and other indicators of achieving the promises of the American Dream.[41]

Because people of lower income and education levels are less likely to vote, African Americans' economic disadvantage had, until 2008, translated into a political limitation as well, especially in a country with a history of suppressing the black vote. The Voting Rights Act of 1965 put protections in place, but in 2013, in a five-to-four decision, the Supreme Court threw out a part of the law that it claims requires updating: the clause that requires nine southern states to "pre-clear" with the Department of Justice any changes they make to their voting laws to be sure they are race neutral. The ruling left the door open for new congressional legislation to qualify states for pre-clearance, but so far, although Democrats have pushed for such legislation, Republican stalling tactics have held it off.[42] It remains to be seen how Democrats will fare in future years in the face of more restrictive voting rules. In the meantime, the courts have continued to push back at what they see as more egregious attempts to limit voting rights. In 2017, for instance, the Supreme Court let stand a 2016 federal appeals court decision that struck down a North Carolina voter ID law that was unconstitutional because it targeted African American voters with almost "surgical precision."[43] In 2018 the Supreme Court refrained from taking a clear stand against gerrymandering.

African Americans have had difficulty overcoming barriers not just on the voting side of the democratic equation. In terms of elected officials, progress has been mixed. By 2001 there were slightly more than nine thousand black elected officials in the United States, in posts ranging from local education and law enforcement jobs to the U.S. Congress. But the number of African Americans is much higher at local levels of government, where the constituents who elect them are more likely to be African American themselves. As the constituencies grow larger and more diverse, the task of black candidates gets tougher. In 2016 there were well over five hundred black mayors but no African American governors.[44] This seems likely to continue in 2018, with two African American gubernatorial candidates facing razor thin deficits in their races as of this writing. In the 116th Congress, elected in 2018, more than 50 of 435 members of the House of Representatives were black, and there were three black senators.

In 2008 the nation elected its first African American president. Barack Obama served two terms and left office a popular president. It's tempting to think that that signals the end of racial discrimination in politics, and it is true that when Obama was on the ballot, African American voter turnout was way up. Due in large part to President Obama's effective voter mobilization effort, African American turnout in 2012 was a robust 13 percent of the electorate, but it was only 12 percent of a smaller electorate in 2016. Obama's administration promised to usher in a much more relaxed attitude toward race, but he faced unprecedented obstruction from Congress and a significant percentage of Americans who believed he was not born in the United States and thus was never qualified to be president. As we saw in *What's at Stake . . . ?*, his election may have served to ratchet up the anxiety of whites who felt their status was threatened, making them ripe targets for the high-strung, racially tinged rhetoric of right-wing entertainer-commentators and ultimately resulting in the election of Donald Trump.

It's an open question whether Obama's presidency will have had an overall effect on the numbers of African Americans in U.S. politics, especially if black turnout in elections remains below the levels in 2008 and 2012. In the wake of Obama's election, African Americans appeared to be more optimistic about black progress. A majority (53 percent) said life will be better for blacks in the future (compared to 44 percent who said so in 2007), and 54 percent of blacks said Obama's election had improved race relations. But by 2013, only 32 percent said that a lot of progress had been made toward Martin Luther King's dream of racial equality.[45] By 2015 the Black Lives Matter movement had formed to protest the killings of young black men by police in the wake of teenage Trayvon Martin's murder by a vigilante in Florida and the killing of Michael Brown in Ferguson, Missouri. By the time police shootings of two more black men in suspicious circumstances received extensive media coverage in the summer of 2016, racial tensions were running high and reflected in the presidential campaign. Even Obama had begun to speak out more on race. Racial tensions were further inflamed in the wake of Trump's election, causing one commentator to call it a "whitelash" to Obama's presidency.[46]

In Your Own Words Summarize key events and outcomes in the struggle for equality of African Americans.

RIGHTS DENIED ON THE BASIS OF OTHER RACIAL AND ETHNIC IDENTITIES

Different paths to equality for
Native Americans, Hispanics, and Asian Americans

African Americans are by no means the only Americans whose civil rights have been denied on racial or ethnic grounds. Native Americans, Hispanic Americans, and Asian Americans have all faced their own particular kind of discrimination. For historical and cultural reasons, these groups have had different political resources available to them, and thus their struggles have taken shape in different ways.

NATIVE AMERICANS

Native Americans of various tribes shared the so-called New World for centuries before it was "discovered" by Europeans. The relationship between the original inhabitants of this continent and the European colonists and their governments was difficult, marked by the new arrivals' clear intent to settle and develop the Native Americans' ancestral lands, and complicated by the Europeans' failure to understand the Indians' cultural, spiritual, and political heritage. The lingering effects of these centuries-old conflicts continue to color the political, social, and economic experience of Native Americans today.

The precise status of Native American tribes in American politics and in constitutional law is complicated. The tribes always saw themselves as sovereign independent nations, making treaties, waging war, and otherwise dealing with the early Americans from a position of strength and equality. But that sovereignty has not consistently been recognized by the U.S. government, and many of the treaties that the government made with Indian tribes were broken as the tribes were forced off their native lands. The commerce clause of the Constitution (Article I, Section 8) gives Congress the power to regulate trade "with foreign nations, among the several states, and with the Indian tribes," but it also has been interpreted as giving Congress guardianship over Indian affairs. The creation of the Bureau of Indian Affairs in 1824 as part of the Department of War (moved to the Department of the Interior in 1849) institutionalized that guardian role.

Modern congressional policy toward the Native Americans has varied from trying to assimilate them into the broader, European-based culture to encouraging them to develop economic independence and self-government. The combination of these two strategies—stripping them of their native lands and cultural identity, and reducing their federal funding to encourage more independence—has resulted in tremendous social and economic dislocation in the Indian communities. Poverty, joblessness, and alcoholism have built communities of despair and frustration for many Native Americans. Their situation has been aggravated as Congress has denied them many of the rights promised in their treaties in order to exploit the natural resources so abundant in the western lands they have been forced onto, or as they have been forced to sell rights to those resources in order to survive.

The political environment in which Native Americans found themselves in the mid-twentieth century was very different from the one faced by African Americans. Essentially, Native American tribes find themselves in a relationship with the national government that mimics elements of federalism—what some scholars have called "fry-bread federalism."[47] Although that relationship has evolved over time, the gist of it is that American Indians are citizens of tribes as well as citizens of the United States, with rights coming from each. It was not clear what strategy the Native Americans should follow in trying to get their U.S. rights recognized. Denied them were not simply formal rights, or their enforcement, but the fulfillment of old promises and the preservation of a culture that did not easily coexist with modern American economic and political beliefs and practices. State politics did not provide any remedies, not merely because of local prejudice, but because Indian reservations are separate legal entities under the federal government. Because Congress itself was largely responsible for denying the rights of Native Americans, it was not a likely source of support for their expansion. Nor were the courts anxious to extend rights to Native Americans.

Like many other groups shut out from access to political institutions, Native Americans took their political fate into their own hands. Focusing on working outside the system to change public opinion and to persuade Congress to alter public policy, the Indians formed interest groups like the National Congress of American Indians (NCAI), founded in 1944, and the American Indian Movement (AIM), founded in 1968, to fight for their cause. For all the militant activism of the 1960s and 1970s, Native Americans have made no giant strides in redressing the centuries of dominance by white people. They remain at the bottom of the income scale in America, earning less than African Americans on average, and their living conditions are often poor. In 2016, 26.2 percent of American Indians lived in poverty, compared to only 14.0 percent of the total U.S. population.[48] And in 2016 only 79.9 percent of adult Native Americans (aged twenty-five years or older) held a high school diploma, compared to 87.5 percent of the overall adult population.[49] Consider, for example, the individuals on the Pine Ridge Indian Reservation in South Dakota. Some 70 percent are unemployed, fewer than 10 percent have graduated from high school, and life expectancy is somewhere in the high forties, much lower than the national average, which approaches eighty years.[50]

Since the 1980s, however, an ironic twist of legal interpretation has enabled some Native Americans to parlay their status as semisovereign nations into a foundation for economic prosperity. Close to thirty states now allow Indian gambling casinos, which in 2016 brought in more than $31 billion, more than Native Americans received in federal aid.[51] In 2016, Native American gaming revenue represented 44.5 percent of all casino gambling revenue nationwide,[52] although many tribes and individuals have no share in it. Casino gambling is controversial on several counts. Native Americans themselves are of two minds about it— some see gambling as their economic salvation and others, as spiritually ruinous. The revenue created by the casinos has allowed Indian tribes to become major donors to political campaigns in states such as California, which has increased their political clout though leaving them open to criticism for making big money donations while many reservations remain poverty stricken. Many other Americans object for economic reasons. Opponents like President Donald Trump, a casino owner, claim that Congress is giving special privileges to Native Americans that may threaten their own business interests. Regardless of the moral and economic questions unleashed by the casino boom, for many Native Americans it is a way to recoup at least some of the resources lost in the past.

Politically, there has been some improvement as well. Although recent Supreme Court cases have failed to support religious freedom for Native Americans, some lower court orders have supported their rights. In 1996 President Bill Clinton issued an executive order that requires federal agencies to protect and provide access to sacred religious sites of American Indians, which has been a major point of contention in Indian-federal relations. Until the Supreme Court ruled in 1996 that electoral districts could not be drawn to enhance the power of particular racial groups, Native Americans had been gaining strength at the polls, to better defend their local interests.

Still, the number of American Indian state representatives has increased slightly in the past few years.[53] Two American Indians, Tom Cole and Markwayne Mullin, both Republicans from Oklahoma, are currently serving in the House of Representatives and Sharice Davids, a Democrat from Kansas, became the first American Indian woman elected to the House in 2018. Democratic senator Elizabeth Warren of Massachusetts also claims American Indian ancestry.

HISPANIC AMERICANS

Hispanic Americans, often also called Latinos, are a diverse group with yet another story of discrimination in the United States. Among the reasons the Hispanic experience is different from that of other groups we discuss are the diversity within the Hispanic population; the language barrier that many face; and the political reaction to immigration, particularly illegal immigration, from Mexico into the United States.

Hispanics are the largest minority group in the United States today, making up over 16 percent of the population. Their numbers have more than tripled in recent years, from

14.6 million in 1980 to 57.5 million in 2016.[54] Between 2000 and 2010, the Hispanic population grew at a rate that is four times the U.S. average.[55] This population growth is strikingly diverse; Hispanics' roots may be in Mexico, Puerto Rico, Cuba, Central and South America, as well as other Spanish-speaking parts of the world. These groups have settled in different parts of the country as well. Mexican Americans are located largely in California, Texas, Arizona, and New Mexico. Puerto Ricans live primarily in New York, New Jersey, and other northern cities. Cubans tend to be clustered in South Florida.

These groups differ in more than place of origin and settlement. Cubans are much more likely to have been political refugees, escaping the communist government of Fidel Castro, whereas those from other countries tend to be economic refugees looking for a better life. Because educated, professional Cubans are the ones who fled, they have largely regained their higher socioeconomic status in this country. For instance, almost 26 percent of Cuban Americans are college educated, a percentage matching that found in the U.S. population as a whole, but only 9 percent of Mexican Americans and 16 percent of Puerto Ricans are college graduates.[56] Consequently, Cuban Americans also hold more professional and managerial jobs, and their standard of living, on average, is much higher. Although their numbers suggest that if they acted together they would wield considerable clout, their diversity has led to fragmentation and powerlessness. However, college attendance among Hispanics has increased sharply in recent years, so some of those differences may even out in time.[57]

Language has also presented a special challenge to Hispanics. The United States today ranks sixth in the world in the number of people who consider Spanish a first language, with an active and important Spanish-language media of radio, television, and press. This preponderance of Spanish speakers is probably due less to a refusal on the part of Hispanics to learn English than to the fact that new immigrants are continually arriving.[58] Nonetheless, especially in areas with large Hispanic populations, white Anglos feel threatened by what they see as the encroachment of Spanish, and many communities have launched **English-only movements** to make English the official language, precluding foreign languages from appearing on ballots and official documents.

A final concern that makes the Hispanic struggle for civil rights unique in America is the reaction against immigration, particularly illegal immigration from Mexico. A backlash against illegal immigration has some serious consequences for Hispanic American citizens, who may be indistinguishable in appearance, name, and language from recent immigrants. All of this makes acceptance into American society more difficult for Hispanics; encourages segregation; and makes the subtle denial of equal rights in employment, housing, and education, for instance, easier to carry out. The contentious nature of the immigration debate means the narratives driving the debate are mediating people's opinions on the people involved.

Though Hispanics face formidable barriers to assimilation, their political position is improving. Like African Americans, they have had some success in organizing and calling public attention to their circumstances. Cesar Chavez, as leader of the United Farm Workers in the 1960s, drew national attention to the conditions under which farm workers labored. Following the principles of the civil rights movement, he highlighted concerns of social justice in his call for a nationwide boycott of grapes and lettuce picked by nonunion labor, and in the process he became a symbol of the Hispanic struggle for equal rights. More recently groups like the National Council of La Raza, the Mexican American Legal Defense and Education Fund (MALDEF), and the League of United Latin American Citizens (LULAC) continue to lobby for immigration reform, for Latino civil engagement, and for the end of discrimination against Hispanic Americans.

English-only movements efforts to make English the official language of the United States

There were thirty-one Hispanic representatives in the 115th Congress and four Hispanic senators. There are two Hispanic governors (Brian Sandoval of Nevada and Susana Martinez of New Mexico). In 2004 President Bush appointed Alberto Gonzales to be the first Hispanic attorney general, and in 2009 President Obama appointed Sonia Sotomayor to be the first Hispanic justice on the U.S. Supreme Court.

The voter turnout rate for Hispanics has traditionally been low because they are disproportionately poor and poor people are less likely to vote, but this situation is changing. Where the socioeconomic status of Hispanics is high and where their numbers are concentrated, as in South Florida, their political clout is considerable. Presidential candidates, mindful of Florida's twenty-nine electoral votes, regularly make pilgrimages to South Florida to denounce Cuba's communist policies, a position popular among the Cuban American voters there. Grassroots political organization has also paid off for Hispanic communities. In Texas, for instance, local groups called Communities Organized for Public Service (COPS) have brought politicians to Hispanic neighborhoods so that poor citizens can meet their representatives and voice their concerns. Citizens who feel they are being listened to are more likely to vote, and COPS was able to organize voter registration drives that boosted Hispanic participation. Similarly, the Southwest Voter Registration Project has led over one thousand voter registration drives in several states, including California, Texas, and New Mexico. Such movements have increased registration of Hispanic voters by more than 50 percent. Nationally, Hispanics made up only 7 percent of all registered voters in 2008. Fifty percent of all Latinos voted that year, compared to only 45 percent in 2000.[59] Turnout has been creeping up in general elections; it was about 9.2 percent in 2016, about the same as 2012.[60] Issues like immigration have helped to politicize Hispanic Americans, and as the Republican base has become solidly against immigration reform, Hispanics have increasingly voted Democratic.

Because of the increase in the number of potential Hispanic voters, and because of the prominence of the Hispanic population in battleground states such as Florida, New Mexico, Colorado, and Nevada, and even in places such as Iowa, where one might not expect a significant Hispanic population, candidates generally court Hispanic voters, as Barack Obama and Mitt Romney did in 2012. Although at one time there was bipartisan consensus on immigration reform, in recent years it has become a partisan issue, with Democrats proposing more generous immigration policies, and Republicans seeking to tighten them. Republicans made it a point to defeat the DREAM (Development, Relief, and Education for Alien Minors) Act, different versions of which would have provided a path to permanent residency and even citizenship for the children of illegal immigrants who came to this country as minors, but who have completed high school here and maintained a good moral character. In the summer of 2012, Obama announced a version of his own DREAM Act when his administration decided to defer the deportation of young people who had been brought to the country illegally but who were in school or in the armed forces. Ultimately, the 2012 Latino vote broke for Obama, 71 to 27 percent. In the immediate aftermath of the election, Republicans held a "postmortem" to see where their voter outreach efforts needed to be beefed up. The initial consensus was that they needed to join Democrats behind immigration reform or they would lose the Latino vote for a generation or more. Such a plan proved too much for the Tea Party faction of the party, however, and the efforts of more moderate party members came to nothing. Donald Trump made opposition to immigration the original plank of his campaign, and Hillary Clinton won the Latino vote handily. Despite the presence of an immigration opponent on the ballot, however, Hispanic turnout wasn't up enough to cost Trump the election.

ASIAN AMERICANS

Asian Americans share some of the experiences of Hispanics, facing cultural prejudice as well as racism and absorbing some of the public backlash against immigration. Yet the history of Asian American immigration, the explosive events of World War II, and the impressive educational and economic success of many Asian Americans mean that the Asian experience is also in many ways unique.

Like Hispanics, the Asian American population is diverse. There are Americans with roots in China, Japan, Korea, the Philippines, India, Vietnam, Laos, and Cambodia, to name just a few. Today Asian Americans live in every region of the United States. As of 2015, Asians were the fastest growing racial or ethnic group in the country, with 60 percent of their growth coming from international migration.[61] Los Angeles had the largest Asian population of any U.S. county. The more recent immigrants are spread unevenly throughout the country, with increasing numbers in the South.

Asians have faced discrimination in the United States since their arrival. The fact that they are identifiable by their appearance has made assimilation into the larger European American population difficult. While most immigrants dream of becoming citizens in their new country, and eventually gaining political influence through the right to vote, that option was not open to Asians. The Naturalization Act of 1790 provided for only white immigrants to become naturalized citizens, and with few exceptions—for Filipino soldiers in the U.S. Army during World War II, for example—the act was in force until 1952. Exclusionary immigration reflected this country's long-standing hostility toward Asians, but anti-Asian sentiment was especially evident in the white American reaction to Japanese Americans during World War II. In 1942 the U.S. government rounded up Japanese Americans, forced them to abandon or sell their property, and put them in detention camps for purposes of "national security." The government was worried about security threats posed by people with Japanese sympathies, but two-thirds of the 120,000 people incarcerated were American citizens. Perhaps the greatest insult was the Supreme Court's approval of curfews and detention camps for Japanese Americans.[62] Although the government later reversed its policy and, in 1988, paid $1.25 billion in reparations to survivors of the ordeal, Japanese American internment is an ugly scar on America's civil rights record.

One unusual feature of the Asian American experience is their overall academic success and corresponding economic prosperity. High school and college graduation rates are higher among Asian Americans than among other ethnic groups and are at least as high as, and in some places higher than, those of whites. In 2017, 22.2 percent of incoming freshmen at Harvard were Asian, as were 22.5 percent at Stanford, 56.2 percent at MIT, and 42.4 percent at the University of California, Berkeley.[63] Although all Asian groups have not been equally successful (groups that have immigrated primarily as refugees—like the Vietnamese—have higher rates of poverty than do others), median household income in 2014 was $74,297 for Asian and Pacific Islanders, compared with $60,256 for whites, $42,491 for Hispanics, and $35,398 for blacks.[64] A number of factors probably account for this success. Forced out of wage labor in the West in the 1880s by resentful white workers, Asian immigrants developed entrepreneurial skills, and many came to own their own businesses and restaurants. A cultural emphasis on hard work and high achievement lent itself particularly well to success in the American education system and culture of equality of opportunity. Furthermore, many Asian immigrants were highly skilled and professional workers in their own countries and passed on the values of their achievements to their children.

According to our conventional understanding of what makes people vote in the United States, participation among Asian Americans ought to be quite high. Voter turnout usually rises along with education and income levels, yet Asian American voter registration and turnout rates have been among the lowest in the nation. Particularly in states with a sizable number of Asian Americans such as California, their political representation and influence do not reflect their numbers. Political observers account for this lack of participation in several ways. Until after World War II, as we saw, immigration laws restricted the citizenship rights of Asian Americans. In addition, the political systems that many Asian immigrants left behind did not have traditions of democratic political participation. Finally, many Asian Americans came to the United States for economic reasons and have focused their attentions on building economic security rather than on learning to navigate an unfamiliar political system.[65]

Some evidence indicates, however, that this trend of nonparticipation is changing. Researchers have found that where Asian Americans do register, they tend to vote at rates higher than those of other groups.[66] In 2018 there was one Asian American governor (David Ige of Hawaii). The 116th Congress saw eleven Asian American members of the House of Representatives and two Asian American senators (Mazie Hirono of Hawaii and Tammy Duckworth of Illinois). Asian American turnout has generally lagged behind its numbers in the population, but early turnout was up in 2016, and the vote went overwhelmingly to Hillary Clinton.

One reason for the increasing participation of Asian Americans, in addition to the voter registration drives, is that many Asian Americans are finding themselves more and more affected by public policies. Welfare reform that strips many elderly legal immigrants of their benefits, changes in immigration laws, and affirmative action are among the issues driving Asian Americans to the polls. However, even continued efforts to register this group are unlikely to bring about electoral results as dramatic as those that we are starting to see for Hispanics, because Asian Americans tend to split their votes more or less equally between Democrats and Republicans.[67] Interestingly, a survey of Asian Americans found that nearly 40 percent claim no partisan affiliation.[68]

In Your Own Words Explain the different paths to equality taken by other racial and ethnic groups.

RIGHTS DENIED ON THE BASIS OF GENDER

Fighting the early battles for equality at the state level

Of all the battles fought for equal rights in the American political system, the women's struggle has been perhaps the most peculiar. While certainly denied most imaginable civil and economic rights, women were not outside the system in the same way that racial and ethnic groups have been. Most women lived with their husbands or fathers, and many shared their view that men, not women, should have power in the political world. Women's realm, after all, was considered to be the home, and the prevailing narrative was that women were too good, too pure, too chaste, to deal with the sordid world outside. A New Jersey senator argued in the late 1800s, for instance, that women should not be allowed to vote because they have "a higher and holier mission. . . . Their mission is at home."[69] Today there are still some women as well as men who agree with the gist of this sentiment. That means that the struggle for women's rights not only has failed to win the support of all women but also has been actively opposed by some, as well as by many men whose power, standing, and worldview it has threatened.

The legal and economic position of women in the early nineteenth century, though not exactly "slavery," in some ways was not much different. According to English common law, on which our system was based, when a woman married, she merged her legal identity with her husband's, which is to say in practical terms, she no longer had one. Once married, she could not be a party to a contract, bring a lawsuit, own or inherit property, earn wages for any service, gain custody of her children in case of divorce, or initiate divorce from an abusive husband. If her husband was not a U.S. citizen, she lost her own citizenship. Neither married nor unmarried women could vote. In exchange for the legal identity his wife gave up, a husband was expected to provide security for her, and if he died without a will, she was entitled to one-third of his estate. If he made a will and left her out of it, however, she had no legal recourse to protect herself and her children.[70]

THE STRUGGLE FOR SUFFRAGE

Although individual women may have rebelled at this state of affairs, the women's movement itself is commonly dated from an 1848 convention on women's rights held in Seneca Falls, New York. At the convention, propositions that were enthusiastically and unanimously approved included calls for the right to own property, to have access to higher education, and to receive custody of children after divorce. The only resolution not to receive unanimous support, even among the supporters of women's rights at the convention, was one calling for women's right to vote.

The women's movement picked up steam after Seneca Falls, but it had yet to settle on a political strategy. The courts were closed to women, since they had no independent legal identity. For a long time, women's rights advocates worked closely with the antislavery movement, assuming that when blacks received their rights, they and the Republican Party would rally to the women's cause. Not only did that fail to happen, but the passage of the Fourteenth Amendment marked the first time the word *male* appeared in the Constitution, causing a bitter split between the two movements.

Regularly, from 1878 to 1896 and again after 1913, a federal women's suffrage amendment called the Susan B. Anthony Amendment, named after an early advocate of women's rights, was introduced into Congress but failed to pass. Other women's rights advocates focused efforts at the state level, taking on the more practical task of changing state electoral laws. It was this state strategy that would finally create the conditions under which the Nineteenth Amendment would be passed and ratified in 1920.

The state strategy was a smart one for women. Unlike the situation blacks faced after the war, the national government was not behind their cause. It was possible for women to have an impact on state governments, however, even those where discrimination was a problem. Different states have different cultures and traditions, and the Constitution allows them to decide who may legally vote. Women were able to target states that were sympathetic to them, and then gradually gain enough political clout that their demands were listened to on the national level.

Women were able to vote beginning in 1869 in the Territory of Wyoming, and when Wyoming was admitted to the Union in 1890, it was the first state to give women the vote. Wyoming's experience did not prove contagious, however. From 1870 to 1910, women waged

480 suffrage campaigns in thirty-three states, caused seventeen referenda to be held in eleven states, and won in only two of them—Colorado (1893) and Idaho (1896). In 1910 women began to refine their state strategy and were soon able to win two more referenda, in Washington (1910) and California (1911). By 1912, with the addition of Arizona, Kansas, Oregon, and Illinois, women could vote in states that controlled 74 of the 483 Electoral College votes that decided the presidency.

In 1914 an impatient, militant offshoot of the women's movement began to work at the national level again, picketing the White House and targeting the presidential party, contributing to the defeat of twenty-three of forty-three Democratic candidates in the western states where women could vote. The appearance of political power gave momentum to the state efforts. In 1917 North Dakota gave women presidential suffrage. Ohio, Indiana, Rhode Island, Nebraska, and Michigan soon followed suit. Arkansas and New York joined the list later that year. A major women's rights group issued a statement to Congress that if it would not pass the Susan B. Anthony Amendment, its members would work to defeat every legislator who opposed it. The amendment passed in the House but not the Senate, and the group targeted four senators. Two were defeated, and two held on to their seats by a narrow margin. Nine more states gave women the right to vote in presidential elections.

In 1919 the Susan B. Anthony Amendment was reintroduced into Congress with the support of President Woodrow Wilson and passed by the necessary two-thirds majority in both houses. When, in August 1920, Tennessee became the thirty-sixth state to ratify the Nineteenth Amendment, women finally had the vote nationwide. Unlike the situation faced by African Americans after the passage of the Fifteenth Amendment, the legal victory ended the women's suffrage battle. Although many women were not inclined to use their newly won right, enforcement of women's suffrage was not as difficult as enforcement of black suffrage. But right to the end, opposition to women's suffrage had been petty and virulent, and the victory was only narrowly won.

The debate over women's suffrage, like the fight over black civil rights, was bitter because so much was at stake. If women were to acquire political rights, opponents feared, an entire way of life would end. In many ways, of course, they were right. The opposition to women's suffrage came from a number of different directions. In the South, white men rejected it for fear that women would encourage enforcement of the Civil War amendments, giving political power to blacks. And if women could vote, then of course black women could vote, further weakening the white male position. In the West, and especially the Midwest, brewing interests fought suffrage, believing that women would force temperance on the nation. Liquor interests fought the

Going to the Dance
With the Nineteenth Amendment headed toward final ratification in 1919, women began to sense the first signs of real political power.

women's campaign vigorously, stuffing ballot boxes and pouring huge sums of money into antisuffrage efforts. In the East, women's opponents were industrial and business interests, who were concerned that voting women would pass enlightened labor legislation and would organize for higher wages and better working conditions. Antisuffrage women's groups, usually representing upper-class women, claimed that women's duties at home were more than enough for them to handle and that suffrage was unnecessary because men represented and watched out for women's interests.[71] For well-to-do women, the status quo was comfortable, and changing expectations about women's roles could only threaten that security.

Everything these opponents feared eventually came to pass, though not necessarily as a result of women voting. Although women's rights advocates were clear winners in the suffrage fight, it took a long time for all the benefits of victory to materialize. As the battle over the Equal Rights Amendment would show, attitudes toward women were changing at a glacial pace.

THE EQUAL RIGHTS AMENDMENT

The Nineteenth Amendment gave women the right to vote, but it did not ensure the constitutional protection against discrimination that the Fourteenth Amendment had provided for African Americans. It was unconstitutional to treat people differently on account of race but not on account of gender. Following ratification of the Nineteenth Amendment in 1920, some women's groups turned their attention to the passage of an **Equal Rights Amendment (ERA)**, which would ban discrimination on the basis of gender and guarantee women equal protection under the law. Objections to the proposed amendment again came from many different directions. Traditionalists, both men and women, opposed changing the status quo and giving more power to the federal government. But even some supporters of women's rights feared that requiring laws to treat men and women the same would actually make women worse off

Is it possible to have too much equality?

by nullifying legislation that sought to protect women. Many social reformers, for instance, had worked for laws that limited working hours or established minimum wages for women, and these laws would now be in jeopardy. Opponents also feared that the ERA would strike down laws preventing women from being drafted and sent into combat. Many laws in American society treated men and women differently, and few would survive under the ERA.

In the early 1970s, several pieces of legislation expanded women's rights. Among these was Title IX of the Education Amendments, which in 1972 banned gender discrimination in schools receiving federal funds. This meant, among other things, that schools had to provide girls with an equal opportunity and equal support to play sports. The ERA was, however, less successful.

The House of Representatives finally passed the ERA in 1970, but the Senate spent the next two years refining the language of the amendment. Finally, on March 22, 1972, the Senate passed the amendment, and the process of getting the approval of three-quarters of the state legislatures began. By early 1973, thirty states had ratified the amendment, but over the next four years, only five more states voted for ratification, bringing the total to thirty-five states, three short of the necessary thirty-eight. Despite the extension of the ratification deadline from 1979 to 1982, the amendment died unratified (although Illinois recently ratified the amendment in a largely symbolic gesture).

The ERA failed to pass for several reasons. First, although most people supported the idea of women's rights in the abstract, they weren't sure what the consequences of such an

Equal Rights Amendment (ERA) a constitutional amendment passed by Congress but never ratified that would have banned discrimination on the basis of gender

amendment would be, and they feared the possibility of radical social change. Second, the ERA came to be identified in the public's mind with the 1973 Supreme Court ruling in *Roe v. Wade*, ensuring women's abortion rights in the first trimester of a pregnancy—a ruling that, as we saw in Chapter 4, remains controversial today.[72] Finally, the Supreme Court had been striking down some (though not all) laws that treated women differently from men, using the equal protection clause of the Fourteenth Amendment. According to some opponents, this made the ERA unnecessary.[73]

GENDER DISCRIMINATION TODAY

Despite the failure of the ERA, most of the legal barriers to women's equality in this country have been eliminated. But because the ERA did not pass and there is no constitutional amendment specifically guaranteeing equal protection of the law regardless of gender, the Supreme Court has not been willing to treat gender as a suspect classification, although it has come close at times. Laws that treat men and women differently are subject only to the intermediate standard of review, not the strict scrutiny test. Examples of laws that have failed that test, and thus have been struck down by the Court, include portions of the Social Security Act that give benefits to widows but not to widowers, and laws that require husbands but not wives to be liable for alimony payments.[74] Some laws that do treat men and women differently—for instance, statutory rape laws and laws requiring that only males be drafted—have been upheld by the Court.

Having achieved political if not legal equality, women still face some striking discrimination in the workplace. They earn only seventy-seven cents for every dollar earned by men, and the National Committee on Pay Equity, a nonprofit group in Washington, D.C., calculates that the pay gap may cost some women almost half a million dollars over their work lives.[75] Women's ability to seek remedies for this discrimination has been limited by law. In 2007 the U.S. Supreme Court ruled in a five-to-four decision that a female worker's right to sue for discrimination was constrained by the statutes of limitations in existing civil rights law.[76] On January 29, 2009, the first bill signed into law by President Obama was the Lilly Ledbetter Act, extending the time frame so that workers could still sue even if the wage discrimination against them revealed itself over time. A companion piece to this legislation, the Paycheck Fairness Act, would prohibit discrimination and retaliation against workers who bring discrimination claims. It passed in the House in 2009 but stalled in the Senate. It remains a controversial proposal, with Democrats claiming women should have increased legal protection in the workplace, and Republicans arguing that women make less money than men for reasons other than discrimination (like the decision to leave the labor market to have children), and that market forces ought to prevail without regulation. In 2017 the Trump administration halted an Obama policy that would have required companies with more than one hundred employees to disclose salaries by gender and race so that people would know whether they were making less than their colleagues.[77] In the meantime, some states, such as New Jersey, have passed strong equal pay acts of their own, and in 2018 the U.S. Court of Appeals for the Ninth Circuit held that employers could not ask about a woman's pay history in setting current salary, preventing a history of unequal pay from being perpetuated.[78]

In addition to earning lower wages, women are tremendously underrepresented at the upper levels of corporate management and academic administration, as well as in other positions of power. Some people argue that the reason women earn less than men and wield less power is that many women leave and enter the job market several times or put their careers on hold to have children. Such interruptions prevent them from accruing the kind of seniority that pays dividends for men. The so-called mommy track has been blamed for much of the disparity between men's and women's positions in the world. Others argue that there is an enduring difference in the hiring and salary patterns of women that has nothing to do with childbearing or that reflects male inflexibility when it comes to integrating motherhood and corporate responsibility. These critics claim that there is a "glass ceiling" in the corporate world, invisible to the eye but impenetrable, which prevents women from realizing their full potential. The Civil Rights Act of 1991 created the Glass Ceiling Commission to study this phenomenon, and among the commission's conclusions was the observation that business is depriving itself of a large pool of talent by denying leadership positions to women.

Some analysts have argued that the glass ceiling is a phenomenon that affects relatively few women. Most women today are less preoccupied with moving up the corporate ladder than with making a decent living, or getting off what one observer has called the "sticky floor" of low-paying jobs.[79] Although the wage gap between men and women with advanced education is narrowing, women still tend to be excluded from the more lucrative blue-collar positions in manufacturing, construction, communication, and transportation.[80]

Getting hired, maintaining equal pay, and earning promotions are not the only challenges women face on the job. They are often subject to unwelcome sexual advances, comments, or jokes that make their jobs unpleasant, offensive, and unusually stressful. Now technically illegal, **sexual harassment** is often difficult to define and document, and women have traditionally faced retribution from employers and fellow workers for calling attention to such practices. The much-publicized cases of sexual harassment in the military show that progress toward gender equality in the armed forces still has a long way to go.

Sexual harassment in the civilian world came to the national stage with an explosion during the 2016 campaign, where in one surreal moment candidate Donald Trump—accused of sexual assault by several women and on the basis of his own tape-recorded words—invited to the presidential debate women who had accused President Bill Clinton of sexual assault in an effort to intimidate Hillary Clinton, the first serious woman candidate for president. Women's reaction to Trump's election resulted in the Women's Marches held across the country the day after his inauguration—numbers of marchers in Washington alone far exceeded the number who had attended the ceremonies the day before. The March was reprised in 2018, and the gathering anger of women at what they saw as a disrespectful culture designed to peel away their rights resulted in record numbers of women on the ballots (and winning) at all levels in 2018.

The #MeToo movement in 2017–2018 showed that the problem is pervasive not just in politics but in the entertainment, news, culinary, and many other fields. The male power advantage persists, however. In 2018, Dr. Christine Blasey Ford, a California psychologist, testified during the confirmation hearings on Judge Brett Kavanaugh for the Supreme Court that he had attempted to rape her in high school. Her story was persuasive enough to call for a serious investigation, but received only a cursory one (neither she nor Kavanaugh were even questioned). Kavanaugh called her a liar and the Republicans closed ranks to ensure his confirmation along near party lines.

sexual harassment
unwelcome sexual speech or behavior that creates a hostile work environment

WOMEN IN CONTEMPORARY POLITICS

Women still face discrimination not only in the boardroom but in politics as well. Although more women today hold elected office than at any other time in history, women remain the most underrepresented group in Congress and the state legislatures. However, the representation of women in government is clearly better than it was. A January 2014 poll even showed that 77 percent of those surveyed think that the United States would have a woman president within the next ten years.[81] Americans, of course, have still failed to elect a female president, despite Hillary Clinton's winning of the popular vote in 2016. It was her concession speech in 2008, when she lost the primary to Barack Obama, that most clearly put her candidacies into context:

> Now, on a personal note—when I was asked what it means to be a woman running for president, I always gave the same answer: that I was proud to be running as a woman but I was running because I thought I'd be the best president. But I am a woman, and like millions of women, I know there are still barriers and biases out there, often unconscious.
>
> I want to build an America that respects and embraces the potential of every last one of us.
>
> I ran as a daughter who benefited from opportunities my mother never dreamed of. I ran as a mother who worries about my daughter's future and a mother who wants to lead all children to brighter tomorrows. To build that future I see, we must make sure that women and men alike understand the struggles of their grandmothers and mothers, and that women enjoy equal opportunities, equal pay, and equal respect. Let us resolve and work toward achieving some very simple propositions: There are no acceptable limits and there are no acceptable prejudices in the twenty-first century.
>
> You can be so proud that, from now on, it will be unremarkable for a woman to win primary state victories, unremarkable to have a woman in a close race to be our nominee, unremarkable to think that a woman can be the president of the United States. And that is truly remarkable.[82]

Nancy Pelosi became the first female Speaker of the House in 2007 (and again in 2019), and three of the last four U.S. secretaries of state have been women. In fact, in 2010, the second and fourth officials in the line of succession to the president of the United States were women (the Speaker of the House follows the vice president, and the secretary of state comes after the president pro tem of the Senate). In 1971, women comprised only 2 percent of Congress members and less than 5 percent of state legislators. By 2014, 18.5 percent of Congress members and 24.2 percent of state legislators were female, both all-time highs. In the 115th Congress, 82 of 435 members of the House of Representatives were female and there were twenty-one female senators. In 2018, Tammy Duckworth, D-Ill., became the first U.S. senator to give birth while in office, forcing the once all-male Senate to deal with the issue of accommodating a nursing mother. In 2014, women held 22.6 percent of all statewide executive offices including five governorships, eleven lieutenant governorships,[83] and 249, or 18.4 percent, of the cities with populations of more than 30,000 had female mayors.[84] In 2014 the state of New Hampshire had elected an all-female congressional delegation (two members of the House and two senators) as well as a female governor.

Nonetheless, the underrepresentation of women throughout government may have real policy consequences when we look at the variety of decisions that get made—about issues ranging from women in the marketplace to women's health—often without a significant female voice. In the last few years alone we have seen political battles over whether all women should be provided with services that help protect them against domestic violence, whether they should be able to sue easily for discrimination in the workplace, whether they should be guaranteed equal pay for equal work, whether they should have access to all forms of birth control, whether they are entitled to have that birth control covered by their health insurance policies, whether they should have to undergo an invasive form of ultrasound in order to have a legal abortion, and other similar issues. The Democrats' victory in the House in 2018, however, may keep these issues of the table. Some research suggests that states that have a stronger female presence in the government may enact more "women-friendly" policies, although other political factors matter as well.[85]

In Your Own Words   Describe how women have fought for equality and the changing role of women in American politics.

RIGHTS DENIED ON OTHER BASES

Challenging other classifications in the courts

Race, ethnicity, and gender, of course, are not the only grounds on which the laws treat people differently in the United States. Three other classifications that provide interesting insights into the politics of rights in America are sexual orientation, age, and disability.

SEXUAL ORIENTATION

Gays and lesbians have faced two kinds of legal discrimination in this country. On the one hand, overt discrimination simply prohibits some behaviors: until 2011, gays could not serve openly in the military, for instance, and in some states they cannot adopt children or teach in public schools. But a more subtle kind of discrimination doesn't forbid their actions or behavior; it simply fails to recognize them legally. Thus until 2015, when the Supreme Court ruled that marriage equality is the law of the land in *Obergefell v. Hodges*, many states made it impossible for gays to marry or claim the rights that married people share, such as collecting their partner's Social Security, being covered by a partner's insurance plan, being each other's next of kin, or having a family. Being gay, unlike being black or female or Asian, is something that can be hidden from public view, and until the 1970s many gays escaped overt discrimination by denying or concealing who they were, but that too is a serious deprivation of civil rights.[86]

The legal status of gays in America was spelled out in the case of *Bowers v. Hardwick*, discussed in Chapter 4.[87] Here the Supreme Court argued that there was no constitutionally protected right to engage in homosexual behavior, nor any reason why the states could not regulate or outlaw it. The Court did not require that a law that treated people differently on the basis of sexual orientation fulfill either a compelling or an important state purpose; it merely had to be a reasonable use of state power. The *Bowers* judgment remained more or less intact until 1996, when a bitterly split Court struck down an amendment to the Colorado constitution that would have prevented gays from suing for discrimination in housing and employment. The Court ruled that gays could not be singled out and denied the fundamental protection of the law—that "a state cannot deem a class of persons a stranger to its laws." Although the majority on the Court did not rule that sexual orientation was a suspect classification, it did hint at greater protection than the minimum rationality test would warrant.[88] For the first time, it treated gay rights as a civil rights issue.

Dan Savage

Savage, a journalist and the author of the advice column and podcast *Savage Love* at the Seattle indie paper *The Stranger*, came of age as an activist in the AIDS awareness group ACT-UP. He says, "I've always felt that one of the jobs from people like me, who still considers himself an activist, is not to guilt, and not to harangue, and not to 'where were you' when you weren't at the meeting; it's to identify the doable thing that people who can't be active 24/7 can do, and say, 'Here's this doable thing. Do it.'"

So when, in 2010, he read about the lonely suicide of a kid named Billy Lucas was bullied because kids said he was gay. It filled him with rage and determination to do the one doable thing. He and his husband, Terry Miller, taped a simple message: "It Gets Better." It told of the bullying they faced as kids and the lives they live today, the promise that the intolerance of others would one day fade, if they could just look forward. He and Terri posted their video on YouTube and spread the word: "Here's a doable thing. You can sit in front of your computer for ten minutes and you can talk."

In time, people added their own stories—one doable thing at a time—until today there are more than fifty thousand videos on itgetsbetter.org. Billy Lucas had become a catalyst for the saving of so many others.

And in the process, it accelerated the normalization of being LGBT as a simple part of being human. The nature of single doable acts is that they don't work alone. It is Savage's genius to take advantage of that and to use social media in pursuit of social change. Here's some of what he had to say.

On patriotism

"We're an idea, and we're a document, and we're a promise . . . I do believe that the United States is the last best hope on Earth, as Lincoln said…because the United States, in its founding documents, in its founding idea, was an idea about creating a more perfect union…That's what fills me with kind of patriotic fervor. It's the political process and the idea that America is an unfinished thing that is imperfect and will never be perfect, but that we can keep working on making more perfect."

On keeping the republic

"You're either going to be the person who can identify the doable thing, which I think is the most effective kind of activism, or be a person who is willing to jump in when asked to do the doable thing. Those are your options. Pick one or pick the other. Don't be that person who does nothing: doesn't pitch in, doesn't help, can't be bothered to do the doable thing, and then sit there and complain about the state of the world…"

Source: Dan Savage spoke with Christine Barbour and Gerald C. Wright on September 9, 2016.

A number of cases followed *Bowers*, most of them reinforcing the message that sexual orientation was provided no protections by the law. By 2003, however, public opinion on gay rights, as well as the Court's opinion on the subject, were changing. First, in *Lawrence v. Texas*, the Supreme Court overturned the *Bowers* decision, ruling that state sodomy laws were a violation of the right to privacy.[89] Even though many states had already repealed their sodomy laws, or failed to enforce them, the *Lawrence* decision was substantively and symbolically a break with previous judicial opinion that allowed the states to regulate the sexual behavior of gays and lesbians. Also in 2003, the Massachusetts Supreme Judicial Court ruled, in an extremely controversial four-to-three decision, that marriage was a civil right and that the state's law banning

Equal Access to the Wedding Aisle

When Rep. Barney Frank wed his longtime partner James Brady in the summer of 2012, their marriage was not recognized in many states. The Supreme Court struck down the Defense of Marriage Act in 2015, ensuring marriage equality for all Americans.

homosexual marriage violated the equal protection and due process clauses in the Massachusetts constitution.[90] The Massachusetts court ruling sent shockwaves throughout the country as the nation's first legal gay marriages were performed in Massachusetts.

Almost immediately after the ruling, social conservatives began urging an amendment to the Constitution defining marriage as a union between a man and a woman. However, because Congress had already passed a Defense of Marriage Act (DOMA) in 1996 asserting that states need not recognize gay marriages performed in other states, the amendment failed to garner much immediate congressional support.

In 2013 the Supreme Court struck down DOMA as well, followed by *Obergefell* two years later to the day. Conservatives were furious with what they saw as an activist Court, but marriage equality was legal across all the states. Although the Court did not clearly say that sexual orientation was a suspect class, some members hinted that their thinking might be going in that direction. Opponents of gay rights did find solace in the 2018 *Masterpiece Cakeshop* decision that backed a baker who refused to bake a wedding cake for a gay couple for religious reasons, but the seven-to-two opinion was based on narrow grounds, which means it was decided on a technical issue that does not necessarily apply to other similar cases.[91]

The courts were not the only political avenue open to gays in their struggle for equal rights. Gays have also been effective in parlaying their relatively small numbers into a force to be reckoned with electorally. It is difficult to gain an accurate idea of the size of the gay population in the United States,[92] although some estimates say between 4 and 5 percent of the electorate self-identifies as gay, lesbian, or bisexual.[93] Gays wield political power not just as individuals, however. They began to organize politically in 1969, after riots following police harassment at a gay bar in New York City, the Stonewall Inn. Today many interest groups are organized around issues of concern to the gay community. Although in the past gays have primarily supported the Democratic Party, a growing number identify themselves as independent, and a group of conservative gays calling themselves the Log Cabin Republicans has become active on the political right. Openly gay members of Congress have been elected from both sides of the partisan divide, and in 2016 the Senate confirmed Eric Fanning as the first openly gay Secretary of the Army.

One area in which gay voters have had some impact is the issue of gays in the military. In 1992, acting on a campaign promise made to gays, President Bill Clinton decided to end the ban on gays in the military with an executive order, much as President Harry Truman had ordered the racial integration of the armed forces in 1948. Clinton, however, badly miscalculated the public reaction to his move. The Christian Right and other conservative and military groups were outraged. In the ensuing storm, Clinton backed off his support for ending the ban and settled instead for a "don't ask, don't tell" (DADT) policy. Members of the armed forces did not need to disclose their sexual orientation, but if they revealed it, or the military otherwise found out, they could still be disciplined or discharged. In 2008 Barack Obama campaigned on the repeal of DADT, and in 2010 his administration signaled its intention to examine and repeal the policy banning gays in the military.[94] Although down to the wire, a lame-duck session of Congress finally broke a Republican filibuster led by Sen. John McCain and voted to repeal the policy in December 2010. It finally ended in September 2011.

Another issue of active concern to gays is workplace discrimination. The Employment Non-Discrimination Act would make it illegal to discriminate on the basis of sexual orientation in hiring, firing, pay, and promotion decisions. Despite repeated efforts to pass the bill (since 1994 it has been introduced in every Congress except one), it has so far failed to get through both houses. As it became clear that the 113th Congress would once again refuse to act, President Obama announced in 2014 that he was preparing an executive order that would make it illegal for federal contractors and subcontractors to discriminate against LGBTQ employees.

The issue of gay rights has come to the forefront of the American political agenda not only because of gays' increasing political power but also because of the fierce opposition of social conservatives. Their determination to banish what they see as an unnatural and sinful lifestyle—and their conviction that protection of the basic rights of homosexuals means that they will be given "special privileges"—has focused tremendous public attention on issues that most of the public would rather had remained private. The spread of AIDS and the political efforts of gay groups to fight for increased resources to battle the disease also heightened public awareness of gay issues. Public opinion has remained mixed on the subject for some time, but, driven by more accepting values among young people, it has changed more rapidly on the issue of the acceptance of gay rights than on practically any issue. For instance, in 2001, 57 percent of Americans opposed gay marriage; but in 2016, 55 percent approved of it.[95]

AGE

In 1976 the Supreme Court ruled that age is not a suspect classification.[96] That means that if governments have rational reasons for doing so, they may pass laws that treat younger or older people differently from the rest of the population, and courts do not have to use strict scrutiny when reviewing those laws. Young people are often not granted the full array of rights of adult citizens, being subject to curfews or locker searches at school; nor are they subject to the laws of adult justice if they commit a crime. Some observers have argued that children should have expanded rights to protect them in dealings with their parents.

Can we end de facto discrimination without imposing substantive solutions?

Older people face discrimination most often in the area of employment. Compulsory retirement at a certain age regardless of an individual's capabilities or health may be said to violate basic civil rights. The Court has generally upheld mandatory retirement requirements.[97] Congress, however, has sought to prevent age discrimination with the Age Discrimination in Employment Act of 1967, outlawing discrimination against people up to seventy years of age in employment or in the provision of benefits, unless age can be shown to be relevant to the job in question. In 1978 the act was amended to prohibit mandatory retirement before age seventy, and in 1986 all mandatory retirement policies were banned except in special occupations.

Unlike younger people, who can't vote until they are eighteen and don't vote in great numbers after that, older people defend their interests very effectively. Voter participation rates rise with age, and older Americans are also extremely well organized politically. AARP (formerly the American Association of Retired Persons), a powerful interest group with over thirty million members, has been active in pressuring government to preserve policies that benefit elderly people. In the debates in the mid-1990s about cutting government services, AARP was very much present, and in the face of the organization's advice and voting power, programs like Social Security and Medicare (providing health care for older Americans) remained virtually untouched.

DISABILITY

People with physical and mental disabilities have also organized politically to fight for their civil rights. Advocates for the disabled include people with disabilities themselves, people who work in the social services catering to the disabled, and veterans' groups. Even though laws do not prevent disabled people from voting, staying in hotels, or using public phones, circumstances often do. Inaccessible buildings, public transportation, and other facilities can pose barriers as insurmountable as the law, as can public attitudes toward and discomfort around disabled people.

The 1990 Americans with Disabilities Act (ADA), modeled on the civil rights legislation that empowers racial and gender groups, protects the rights of the more than forty-four million mentally and physically disabled people in this country. Disabilities covered under the act need not be as dramatic or obvious as confinement to a wheelchair or blindness. Among the individuals covered are people with AIDS, those recovering from drug and alcohol addiction, and those with heart disease or diabetes. The act provides detailed guidelines for access to buildings, mass transit, public facilities, and communication systems. It also guarantees protection from bias in employment. The EEOC is authorized to handle cases of job discrimination because of disabilities, as well as race and gender. The act was controversial because many of the required changes in physical accommodations, such as ramps and elevators, are extremely expensive to install. Advocates for the disabled respond that these expenses will be offset by increased business from disabled people and by the added productivity and skills that the disabled bring to the workplace. The reach of the act was limited in 2001, when the Supreme Court ruled that state employees could not sue their states for damages under the ADA because of the seldom discussed, but extremely important, Eleventh Amendment, which limits lawsuits that can be filed against the states.[98] The Court's five-to-four decision was criticized by disability rights advocates as severely limiting the ADA.

In Your Own Words   Recognize examples of other groups that face discrimination.

CITIZENSHIP AND CIVIL RIGHTS TODAY

The power of group action

The stories of America's civil rights struggles are the stories of citizen action. Of the three models of democratic participation that we discussed in Chapter 1—elite, pluralist, and participatory—the pluralist model best describes the actions citizens have taken to gain protection of their civil rights from government. Pluralism emphasizes the ways that citizens can increase their individual power by organizing into groups. The civil rights movements in the United States have been group movements. Groups succeeded in gaining rights where individual action and pleas for government action were unavailing. They are also more likely to control the channels of information in which narratives are built and disseminated. To the extent that groups in America have been unable to organize effectively to advance their interests, their civil rights progress has been correspondingly slowed.

In Your Own Words Explain how pluralism helped realize the promise of civil rights.

Let's Revisit: What's at Stake . . . ?

We began this chapter with a look at the white supremacy and xenophobia (fear of strangers) that were given new life by Donald Trump's candidacy for the presidency. We saw that he generated huge enthusiasm among avowed white supremacist groups but also possessed a strong appeal to much larger groups of everyday white voters who felt that they were losing some vague but real racial privilege and economic status. We asked what was at stake when a majority group in society faces minority status.

As we now know, rights are power, and racism and sexism have never been too far below the surface of American politics. The difference is that today, with sites like Breitbart or other alt-right media channels, it is easier to find people who agree with you and to build a collective sense of grievance. When you have an economic system based on slavery or when you deny half the population any legal rights, you have to develop a moral narrative that allows you to live with what you are doing and still believe that you are a good person. The idea that Africans are uncivilized savages, or lazy and stupid; that immigrants are rapists or criminals or imbeciles for not speaking English; that women are delicate and incapable and need the sheltering protection of men; or that gays and lesbians live godless lives are all narratives that have been told and retold in the tapestry of American history. These narratives allow the people perpetuating them to maintain a narrative about themselves—that they are deserving, superior, and righteous in keeping the other groups in their place. That is power.

But as we have seen, the facts and the narratives of American power have changed and continue to change dramatically. Where once even such civil rights giants as Abraham Lincoln and Lyndon Johnson held views at odds with racial equality, even as they recognized racial injustice, it is now viewed as racially insensitive at best—or racist at worst—to express the views that regularly came out of these men's mouths. For some white people, particularly white men, privilege was once seen as so natural that they didn't even know it was privilege. It can then be deeply unnerving and confusing for them to hear other people weave narratives in which not only are they no longer the heroes, but all too frequently they are the villains, especially when they can't tell what it is they are supposed to have done wrong.

It is easy to laugh at a figure like the buffoonish, blue-collar worker Archie Bunker, the antihero of the groundbreaking 1970s sitcom *All in the Family*, who railed at a world in which diverse groups were claiming rights, each of which meant that he lost a little bit of power that he considered his. But it must be jarring to actually *be* Archie Bunker, almost fifty years later, confronting not just the claims for equal treatment that drove him crazy but also the loss of the majority status that made his own claims to power legitimate in his eyes in the first place.

For people like Archie Bunker, race is for other groups; the majority group doesn't have to think of itself as a race because it is the dominant group. If whites are just one group among many, then they begin to experience race in a way they have not had to do before. They might indeed wonder why people are talking about reparations for past discrimination against other groups when it feels to them like they are being discriminated against today. And it might be hard to understand why people are getting excited about the election of presidents who don't look like them, precisely *because* they don't look like them. And it might indeed be infuriating to find that they have no language with which to talk about what is happening to them because, when they complain about what they perceive as their unjust treatment, they are told they are "politically incorrect," insensitive, and racist. Right-wing radio host Rush Limbaugh has made a career of stirring up just such resentment, and it is now a potent political force.

Many European countries have thriving right-wing political parties that base their appeal on nationalism and on keeping the "other" out. We have had such movements in our past, and we have one now, culminating in Donald Trump's election to the presidency in 2016, tellingly won by the Electoral College even as he was outnumbered in the popular vote. The demographic trends that are reconstituting the American population and reducing whites to minority status can only be anxiety-producing for them, especially when they feel economically marginalized and threatened by external events. The rhetoric of a candidate like Donald Trump, inflaming but also validating the unease and concern they have already experienced, must have been a breath of fresh air to the people feeling downtrodden. To white supremacists, it was as if the power they seek was finally in sight. To Trump supporters who were not white supremacists, but who were nonetheless a beleaguered and bewildered group hemorrhaging numbers and power, it must have felt as if someone, finally, was listening.

As difficult and even lopsided as it might seem, given the racial atrocities of our American history, acknowledging that feeling of white disorientation and grievance might be necessary for us to fully understand the stakes in civil rights politics today and the challenges it will have to meet in the future. Nativist movements in other countries have successfully played off such emotions where the culture has not found a way to respond.

SAGE edge™
for CQ Press

Want a better grade?

Get the tools you need to sharpen your study skills. **SAGE edge** offers practice quizzes, eFlashcards, video, and multimedia at **edge.sagepub.com/barbourbrief8e.**

Review

The Meaning of Political Inequality

Throughout U.S. history, various groups, because of some characteristic beyond their control, have been denied their **civil rights** (147) and have fought for equal treatment under the law. All laws treat people differently on some basis, and the Supreme Court has come up with a formula to determine when that discrimination is constitutional. When a law treats people differently according to race or religion, the Court rules that it is making a **suspect classification** (148), which is subject to **strict scrutiny** (149) to see if the state has a compelling purpose to pass the law. If not, the law is struck down. Laws that discriminate according to gender are subject to an easier standard called an **intermediate standard of review** (149); those that discriminate according to age, wealth, or sexual orientation are subject to the easiest standard for the state to meet, the **minimum rationality test** (149). Individuals who are of more than one oppressed or minority group may experience issues of **intersectionality** (147) as they deal with multiple forms of discrimination.

Rights Denied on the Basis of Race: African Americans

African Americans have experienced two kinds of **segregation** (154): that created by **de jure discrimination** (155), laws that treat people differently; and that created by **de facto discrimination** (156), which occurs when societal tradition and habit lead to social segregation. De jure discrimination, now illegal, included the passage of **black codes** (153) prior to the Civil War and then, after **Reconstruction** (153), **poll taxes** (153), **literacy tests** (154), **grandfather clauses** (154), and other **Jim Crow laws** (154) designed to return the South to the pre–Civil War days. By forming interest groups such as the **National Association for the Advancement of Colored People (NAACP)** (154) and developing strategies of nonviolent resistance such as sit-ins and **boycotts** (155), African Americans eventually defeated de jure discrimination. De facto discrimination persists in America, signified by the education and wage gap between African Americans and whites. Programs like **busing** (158) and **affirmative action** (158), which could remedy such discrimination, remain controversial. Although African Americans have made great strides in the past several decades, **racism** (152) is a persistent problem, and much inequality remains.

Rights Denied on the Basis of Other Racial and Ethnic Identities

Native Americans, Hispanic Americans, and Asian Americans have also fought to gain economic and social equality. Congressional control over their lands has led Native Americans to assert economic power through the development of casinos. Using boycotts and voter education drives, Hispanics have worked to stem the success of **English-only movements** (164) and anti-immigration efforts. Despite their smaller numbers, Asian Americans also aim for equal political clout, but it is through a cultural emphasis on scholarly achievement that they have gained considerable economic power.

Rights Denied on the Basis of Gender

Women's rights movements represented challenges to power, to a traditional way of life, and to economic profit. Early activists found success through state politics because they were restricted from using the courts and Congress, and they were finally able to earn women the right to vote in 1920. After repeated efforts to pass the **Equal Rights**

Amendment (ERA) (170) failed, current efforts focus on the courts to give women greater protection under the law, especially, in recent years, through lawsuits regarding **sexual harassment** (172) experienced by women.

Rights Denied on Other Bases

Gays, youth, the elderly, and the disabled enjoy the most fundamental civil rights, but they still face de jure and de facto discrimination. Although moral concerns motivate laws against gays, social order and cost-efficiency concerns mark the restrictions against youth, the elderly, and disabled Americans.

6

Congress

In Your Own Words

After you've read this chapter, you will be able to

6.1 Describe the tensions between local representation and national lawmaking.

6.2 Explain how checks and balances work between the Congress and the executive and judicial branches.

6.3 Identify the ways that politics influences how congressional districts are defined and who runs for Congress.

6.4 Summarize the central role that the parties play in Congress.

6.5 Describe the process of congressional policymaking.

6.6 Discuss the relationship between the people and Congress.

What's at Stake . . . in the Senate's Obligation to Give Advice and Consent to the President?

Within hours of the February 13, 2016, announcement that Supreme Court justice Antonin Scalia had died unexpectedly, even before the proper condolences to the family had been voiced, politics set in.

Of course, politics always surrounds the appointment of a new Supreme Court justice, as the Brett Kavanaugh hearings demonstrated so dramatically in 2018. The Constitution sets it up that way, giving the president the power to nominate a new justice "with the Advice and Consent of the Senate." "Advice and Consent" is purposely vague—it's intended to put a legislative check on presidents while keeping primary control in their hands.

This new Supreme Court vacancy was more political than many. Scalia, after all, had been the larger-than-life, gregarious and outspoken justice who defined the conservative end of the Court, which often broke five-to-four on significant cultural and political issues. If President Barack Obama replaced him with someone closer to the president's own more progressive values, as he could be expected to do (see Chapter 9), then the balance of the Court would swing the other way. And besides, Republicans had been making it a point of pride to thwart Obama wherever they could. Blocking his opportunity to leave a lasting legacy on the Court was an opportunity too good to be missed.

And it wasn't. With the stakes so high, the gloves came off quickly and completely. Senate majority leader Mitch McConnell, in his first public announcement in the hour after the announcement of Scalia's death, concluded his expression of sorrow to the Scalia family with this opening gambit: "The American people should have a voice in the selection of their next Supreme Court Justice. Therefore, this vacancy should not be filled until we have a new president."[1] What he meant, he later explained, is not that the Senate would refuse to confirm the president's as-yet-unnamed nominee, but that they would not even hold hearings or a vote on his candidate for the Court.

Of course, 2016 was an election year, which brings out crazy politics in the best of times and, arguably, nothing about 2016 was the best. But Supreme Court justices have been nominated and even confirmed in election years many times before. The Constitution does not give the president the power to make nominations to the Court only through the first three years of a term but through all four. And so in time, President Obama gave his own speech, in which he implicitly responded to McConnell:

> I plan to fulfill my constitutional responsibilities to nominate a successor in due time. There will be plenty of time for me to do so, and for the Senate to fulfill its responsibility to give that person a fair hearing and a timely vote. These are responsibilities that I take seriously, as should everyone. They're bigger than any one party.
>
> They are about our democracy. They're about the institution to which Justice Scalia dedicated his professional life, and making sure it continues to function as the beacon of justice that our Founders envisioned.

Thus began a battle of narratives over how to understand the meaning of "advice and consent": a proxy for what was clearly a power struggle to decide the future of the Court. After considering various candidates, conducting interviews, and talking to advisors in the White House, Obama nominated Merrick Garland, a well-liked and respected judge on the D.C. Circuit Court whose rulings tended to be somewhat left of center but hardly the liberal counterpart of Scalia. The nomination angered progressives who wanted to see Obama nominate a liberal firebrand, but it was meant to appease conservatives, many of whom had spoken favorably of Garland, and convince them to give the nominee a hearing.[2]

The strategy didn't work. Two warring narratives took over the communication networks—according to the Republican narrative, presidents in their last year in office should not impose their choices on the people about to vote for their replacement, which meant the job of advising and giving consent meant ignoring the nomination entirely. Although some senators agreed to chat with Judge Garland, only two Republicans thought he should be given the usual hearings. The Democratic narrative said that presidents were elected for four-year, not three-year terms, and that the Senate was within its rights to deny Garland confirmation, but that "advice and consent" meant they had to give him a hearing.

By early summer, polls showed that most of the American people were buying the Democratic version of the story, though that did not move McConnell, who risked infuriating the Republican base if he went back on his decision. But Republicans in close races for the Senate began to see their polls tighten, putting pressure on McConnell, who wanted to keep the Senate majority in his party's hands. By June, the nomination was in a standoff that lasted through the fall.

Why was what is usually a routine, if consequential, part of Senate business so fraught with drama in 2016? Why did the Republicans go to such lengths to construct and stick to a narrative that most people did not buy? What exactly is at stake in the constitutional obligation of Congress to give advice and consent to the president? We will be better able to answer these questions after examining the precarious relationship between Congress and the White House and this chapter's *CLUES to Critical Thinking*.

THE U.S. Congress is the world's longest-running and most powerful democratic legislature. If politics is all about who gets what, and how, then Congress is arguably also the center of American national politics. Not only does it often decide exactly who gets what, but Congress also has the power to alter many of the rules (or the how) that determine who wins and who loses in American political life and the narratives that define the conflicts. Social media has enhanced dramatically the way representatives can reach out to constituents—to convey messages, exchange opinions, inform them of actions taken in Congress, solicit funds. In a mediated political world, the power of the representative's narrative is strengthened but so is the power of constituents to break out of that narrative and represent their own views.

The Capitol building in Washington, D.C., home to both the House of Representatives and the Senate, has become as much a symbol of America's democracy as are the Stars and

Stripes or the White House. We might expect Americans to express considerable pride in their national legislature, with its long tradition of serving democratic government. But if we did, we would be wrong.

Congress is generally distrusted, seen by the American public as incompetent, corrupt, torn by partisanship, and at the beck and call of special interests.[3] Yet despite their contempt for the institution of Congress as a whole, Americans typically like their representatives and senators and generally reelect them often enough that critics have long been calling for term limits to get new people into office. How can we understand this bizarre paradox?[4]

There are two main reasons for America's love-hate relationship with Congress. The first is that the behaviors that help a member of Congress keep his or her job—creating satisfied constituents and supporting party positions—don't always make the institution more popular. On the one hand, voters want their representatives in Washington to take care of their local or state interests and to ensure that their home districts get a fair share of national resources. Parties want their members to be loyal to the party itself and not to "go rogue"—voting with the other party, for instance, or being seen as independent. On the other hand, citizens also want Congress to take care of the nation's business, and to look like a mature, deliberative, and collegial body, a goal not necessarily furthered by individual legislators' efforts to keep their jobs.

The second reason for citizens' love-hate relationship with Congress is that the rules that determine how Congress works were designed by the founders to produce slow, careful lawmaking based on compromise that can often seem motionless to an impatient public. When citizens are looking to Congress to produce policies that they favor or to distribute national resources, the built-in slowness can look like intentional foot-dragging and partisan bickering. That it is instead part of the constitutional safeguard of checks and balances is a civics lesson most Americans have long forgotten.

Keeping in mind these two dynamics—our legislators' struggle to keep their jobs while meeting national expectations and our own frustration with Congress' institutionalized slowness—will take us a long way toward understanding our mixed feelings about our national legislature. In this chapter we focus on who—including citizens, other politicians, and members of Congress themselves—gets the results they want from Congress, and how the rules of legislative politics help or hinder them. You will learn about the clash between representation and lawmaking, the powers and responsibilities of Congress, congressional membership and elections, the organization of Congress, and the rules of congressional operation.

UNDERSTANDING CONGRESS

The essential tensions among
representation, lawmaking, and partisanship

representation the efforts of elected officials to look out for the interests of those who elect them

national lawmaking the creation of policy to address the problems and needs of the entire nation

We have traditionally counted on our elected representatives in both the House and the Senate to perform two major roles: representation and lawmaking. By **representation**, we mean that those we elect should represent, or look out for, our local interests and carry out our will. Representatives know far more about what we want in a mediated age and might have to respond to constituents who are informed and passionate. At the same time, we expect our legislators to address the country's social and economic problems by **national lawmaking**—passing laws that serve the interest of the entire nation.

Because the roles of representation and lawmaking often conflict (what is good for us and our local community may not serve the national good), scholars have long noted that members of Congress would usually favor their roles as representatives since they get reelected by pleasing voters in their districts. Thus national problems go unaddressed while local problems get attention, resources, and solutions.

The tension between representation and lawmaking, however, is complicated further by the fact that members of Congress have to be responsive not only to their constituents and the nation, but also to their party. Since the early days of the republic, partisanship—the loyalty to a party that helps shape how members see the world, how they define problems, and how they determine appropriate solutions—has been an important part of how members of Congress identify and organize themselves. They have juggled a commitment to the party with the simultaneous need to represent voters and to solve national problems, usually creating some kind of balance among the three.

REPRESENTATION

Representation means working on behalf of one's constituency, the folks back home in the district who voted for the member, as well as those who did not. To help us understand this complex job, political scientists often speak about four types of representation.[5] Most members of Congress try to excel at all four functions so that constituents will rate them highly and reelect them:

- Policy representation refers to congressional work for laws that advance the economic and social interests of the constituency. For example, House members and senators from petroleum-producing states can be safely predicted to vote in ways favorable to the profitability of the oil companies, members from the Plains states try to protect subsidies for wheat farmers, and so on.
- Voters have also come to expect a certain amount of allocative representation, in which the congressperson gets projects and grants for the district. Such perks, traditionally called pork barrel benefits but now known as *earmarks*, are paid for by all the taxpayers but enjoyed by just a few. Congress members who are good at getting pork barrel projects for their districts (for example, highway construction or the establishment of a research institution) are said to "bring home the bacon."
- Senators and representatives also represent their states or districts by taking care of the individual problems of constituents, especially problems that involve the federal bureaucracy. This kind of representation is called casework, or constituency service, and it covers things such as finding out why a constituent's Social Security check has not shown up, sending a flag that has flown over the nation's capital to a high school in the district, or helping with immigration and naturalization problems.
- Another kind of representation is called symbolic representation. In this elusive but important function, the member of Congress tries to represent many of the positive values Americans associate with public life and government. Thus members are glad to serve as commencement speakers at high school graduations or to attend town meetings to explain what is happening in Washington. Symbolic representation can be in person or virtual— communication around patriotic and regional messages is easy and inexpensive online.

NATIONAL LAWMAKING

But representation is not the only business of our senators and representatives. A considerable part of their jobs involves working with one another in Washington to define and solve the

---

partisanship loyalty to a party that helps shape how members see the world, define problems, and identify appropriate solutions

constituency the voters in a state or district

policy representation congressional work to advance the issues and ideological preferences of constituents

allocative representation congressional work to secure projects, services, and funds for the represented district

pork barrel public works projects and grants for specific districts paid for by general revenues

casework legislative work on behalf of individual constituents to solve their problems with government agencies and programs

symbolic representation efforts of members of Congress to stand for American ideals or identify with common constituency values

nation's problems. We expect Congress to create laws that serve the common good. One scholar calls this view of effective lawmaking "collective responsibility."[6] By this he means that Congress should be responsible for the effectiveness of its laws in solving national problems. A variety of factors go into a representative's calculation of how to vote on matters of national interest. He or she might be guided by conscience or ideology, by what opinion polls say the local constituents want, or by party position. And these considerations may very well be at odds with the four kinds of representation just described, frequently making it difficult, if not impossible, for members to fulfill their collective responsibility.

PARTISANSHIP

As we noted earlier in the chapter, complicating the already difficult balance between representation and lawmaking is a commitment to party that we call partisanship. Party affiliations have always been an important part of the identities of members of Congress, but in recent years they have come to trump other considerations in what political scientists refer to as hyperpartisanship, or the raising of party above all other commitments. This hyperpartisanship is worsened by increased party polarization, which means that the issue positions and ideological stances of Democrats and Republicans have been growing apart and each party has become more internally homogeneous. As a result, bipartisanship (working with members of the opposite party) is increasingly rare, especially when the very act of cooperating with the other side can be seen as a betrayal of one's own. The information bubbles we live in and through which we get our news can exacerbate this by demonizing our opponents without providing any other perspectives.

Hyperpartisanship was last at play to this extent in the early 1900s (we discuss partisan eras in more detail in Chapter 11), but since the mid-1990s partisanship has again become a fierce divider of the American public. In fact, a recent study found that the American public is more divided by party than by race, class, gender, or age,[7] and members of Congress have not been so polarized by party since the Civil War.[8] In practical terms this polarization has real implications for how laws get made in Congress. Voters sort themselves into parties with greater internal ideological purity (that is, dissent is frowned on), and tend to live nearer to those with whom they share values. Add to that the fact that the districts from which members are elected are increasingly drawn by state legislatures (also in the grips of hyperpartisanship) so that they are safe for Democrats or safe for Republicans, with fewer members of the other party. The people running for Congress have little incentive to appeal to more moderate voters, as they used to do. If the hyperpartisan representative wants to keep his or her job and not face a primary election challenge from a candidate viewed by the party as more ideologically pure, he or she has to pick party over what's best for the district or the nation.[9] The results can slow government to a crawl or even bring it to the brink of disaster.

Two influential political scientists, one at the Brookings Institution (a liberal think tank) and one at the American Enterprise Institute (a conservative think tank) but both with solid reputations as impartial scholars, wrote a book in 2012 in which they argued that the problem of hyperpartisanship in the first part of this century has not affected both parties equally. They point out that the Republicans, at least so far, are more prone to internal purity tests and using obstruction to get their way. Their argument is not that there is anything wrong with the substance of what Republicans want or with their policies or with conservative ideology. Rather, the problem is that the recent Republican strategy of putting party first, not tolerating internal dissent, and refusing to compromise has ground American government to a halt.[10] They say,

hyperpartisanship
a commitment to party so strong that it can transcend other commitments

party polarization
greater ideological (liberal versus conservative) differences between the parties and increased ideological consensus within the parties

"We have been studying Washington politics and Congress for more than 40 years, and never have we seen them this dysfunctional. In our past writings, we have criticized both parties when we believed it was warranted. Today, however, we have no choice but to acknowledge that the core of the problem lies with the Republican Party."[11]

The consequence, they say, is that American government is in trouble: "Today, thanks to the GOP, compromise has gone out the window in Washington."[12] In fact, instead of following the legislative norm dictated by the procedural orientation that we discussed in Chapter 1 as a part of American political culture—that the process of a free election legitimates the results—the GOP took a more substantive stance—that if the procedures of the government didn't endorse their plan, they would simply block them and hope that the failure of the system would frustrate the public sufficiently that people would vote Republicans into power.

In 2012, voters finally delivered a rebuke to the Republican effort to stalemate government—reelecting President Obama, increasing the Democratic majority in the Senate, and even adding Democrats to the House. Obama believed that his reelection would cool the fervor of Republican opposition efforts, but instead, Tea Party Republicans in Congress, calling themselves the Freedom Caucus, only stiffened their resolve to block the president.[13] Their efforts culminated in a government shutdown in October 2013, another norm broken, when House Republicans refused to pass a continuing budget resolution (which would allow the government to continue operating) unless it defunded the Patient Protection and Affordable Care Act, also known as "Obamacare." The Senate Democrats would not agree to this killing of the administration's signature legislation. After sixteen days and an estimated $10 billion lost to the U.S. economy, the House Republicans agreed to a Senate bill, gaining only a token concession of trivial legislative importance.[14] That defeat didn't cool the fever either, and in September 2015, tired of trying to keep his unruly members on the same page, Speaker of the House John Boehner resigned the speakership and left Congress entirely. After his party scrambled to find someone to take on the job, former vice-presidential candidate Paul Ryan reluctantly took the office, but he did not have much better luck marshalling his troops.

As we saw in *What's at Stake . . . ?*, in February 2016, Senate majority leader Mitch McConnell showed the same hyperpartisanship at work in the Senate, an institution that used to consider itself collegial and bipartisan when he refused to hold hearings on Merrick Garland, President Obama's nominee to replace Antonin Scalia on the Supreme Court. Denying a president hearings on his choice to fill a Supreme Court seat in the hopes that a future election would bring a Republican president who would nominate someone more pleasing to Republicans was another stunning breakage of a legislative norm.

As we will see in Chapter 11 (and as we mentioned in Chapter 1), a power struggle within the Republican Party has reduced its ability to compromise with Democrats and to get anything done that doesn't have majority Republican support. When the president is of the same party as a majority of Congress, that party can and should be able to ease the passage of the president's agenda; but conflict in the party resulted more often in bringing politics to a grinding halt. The same forces frustrated voters to such an extent that they eliminated the Republican majority in the House in the 2018 midterms.

For very committed, very conservative Republicans who fundamentally disagree with liberal goals and policies, it may seem like a perfectly reasonable strategy to refuse to compromise with Democrats in an effort to hold out for what they want. In fact, there is an influential movement by some conservative organizations, including, for example, the Tea Party, the Club for Growth, and Americans for Tax Reform, and individuals like Sheldon

DUTY CALLS

MITCH McCONNELL

SENATE MAJORITY LEADER

Constitutional Responsibility

Decline   Accept

Adelson (who pitched in $30 million to help the Republican Party hold the House in 2018), the Koch brothers, or the Mercer family, to punish and replace Republican members who vote the "wrong way" on issues they care about or do not heed the party line.[15] Since they truly believe that what they want for the nation is in its best interest, that is the narrative they tell: that the nation faces a crisis that can be fixed only by not going further into debt or by repealing Obamacare, which requires closing the government in order to pressure the president to give in; that raising the debt ceiling amounts to giving the president a blank check (it does not); that failing to give the president's nominee to the Supreme Court a hearing is "letting the people's voice be heard"; that supporting the current leadership in Israel is our chief foreign policy obligation; and that repealing environmental protections is removing burdens that hamper economic growth. In each case the Democrats have a competing narrative about what is happening, but for the most part the contention just confuses voters, causing them to blame all establishment politicians for not getting anything done. Sometimes deliberately confusing voters with conflicting media reports can be an effective strategy for getting them to just tune out.

As a consequence, representatives and senators, especially Republicans, have been focused more on representing their party—and especially the most ideologically extreme members of their party—than they are on the compromise and bipartisan activity that enables Congress to make laws that respond to policy needs at the local and particularly the national levels. Sometimes this causes more moderate Republicans to try to satisfy their Tea Party critics, but it leads others to leave public service altogether. Republican senator Olympia Snowe of Maine retired in 2012, decrying the end of bipartisanship in the institution she had served since 1995. Later that same year, Ohio Republican representative Steve LaTourette, who had already won his primary and was almost certainly going to be reelected, decided to leave the House, saying, "I have reached the conclusion that the atmosphere today, and the reality that exists in the House of Representatives, no longer encourages the finding of common ground."[16] In 2018, multiple Republicans decided not to run for reelection. One of the first to make the decision, probably because he had decided he would face a primary from the right and have trouble hanging on to his job, Sen. Jeff Flake of Arizona announced his retirement with an eloquent condemnation of the breaking of essential political norms:

> In this century, a new phrase has entered the language to describe the accommodation of a new and undesirable order, that phrase being the new normal. That we must never adjust to the present coarseness of our national dialogue with the tone set at the top. We must never regard as normal the regular and casual undermining of our democratic norms and ideals. We must never meekly accept the daily sundering of our country. The personal attacks, the threats against principles, freedoms, and institutions, and the flagrant disregard for truth and decency, the reckless provocations, most often for the pettiest and most personal reasons, reasons having nothing whatsoever to do with the fortunes of the people that we have been elected to serve.[17]

CONGRESSIONAL POWERS AND RESPONSIBILITIES

Expansive powers held in check by the Constitution

The Constitution gives the U.S. Congress enormous powers, although it is safe to say that the founders could not have imagined the scope of contemporary congressional power since they never anticipated the growth of the federal government to today's size. As we will see, they were less concerned with the conflict between local and national interests we have been discussing than they were with the representation of short-term popular opinion versus long-term national interests. The basic powers of Congress are laid out in Article I, Section 8, of the Constitution (see Chapter 2 and the Appendix). They include the powers to tax, to pay debts, to regulate interstate commerce, and to provide for the common defense and welfare of the United States, among many other things.

DIFFERENCES BETWEEN THE HOUSE AND THE SENATE

The term *Congress* refers to the institution that is formally made up of the U.S. House of Representatives and the U.S. Senate. Congresses are numbered so that we can talk about them over time in a coherent way. Each Congress covers a two-year election cycle. The 116th Congress was elected in November 2018, and its term runs from January 2019 through the end of 2020. The **bicameral** (two-house) **legislature** is laid out in the Constitution. As we discussed in earlier chapters, the founders wanted two chambers so that they could serve as a restraint on each other, strengthening the principle of checks and balances. The framers' hope was that the smaller, more elite Senate would "cool the passions" of the people represented in the House. Accordingly, although the two houses are equal in their overall power—both can initiate legislation (although tax bills must originate in the House), and both must pass every bill in identical form before it can be signed by the president to become law—there are also some key differences, particularly in the extra responsibilities assigned to the Senate. In addition, the two chambers operate differently, and they have distinct histories and norms of conduct (that is, informal rules and expectations of behavior).[18] Some of the major differences are outlined in Table 6.1.

The single biggest factor determining the differences between the House and the Senate is size. With 100 members, the Senate is less formal; the 435-person House needs more rules and hierarchy in order to function efficiently. The Constitution also provides for differences in terms: two years for the House, six for the Senate (on a staggered basis—all senators do not come up for reelection at the same time). In the modern context, this means that House members (also referred to as congresspersons or members of Congress, a term that sometimes applies to senators as well) never stop campaigning. Senators, in contrast, can suspend their preoccupation with the next campaign for the first four or five years of their terms and thus, at least in theory, have more time to spend on the affairs of the nation. The minimum age of the candidates is different as well: members of the House must be at least twenty-five years old, senators thirty. This again reflects the founders' expectation that the Senate would be

bicameral legislature
a legislature with two chambers

older, wiser, and better able to deal with national lawmaking. This distinction was reinforced in the constitutional provision that senators be elected not directly by the people, as were members of the House, but by state legislatures. Although this provision was changed by constitutional amendment in 1913, its presence in the original Constitution reflects the convictions of its authors that the Senate was a special chamber, one step removed from the people.

Budget bills are initiated in the House of Representatives. In practice this is not particularly significant since the Senate has to pass budget bills as well, and differences are usually negotiated between the two houses most. The budget process has gotten quite complicated, as demonstrated by congressional struggles to deal with the deficit, which called for reductions in spending at the same time that constituencies and interest groups were pleading for expensive new programs. The budget process illustrates once again the constant tension for

TABLE 6.1

Differences Between the House and the Senate

DIFFERENCES	HOUSE	SENATE
Constitutional		
Term length	2 years	6 years
Minimum age	25	30
Citizenship required	7 years	9 years
Residency	In state	In state
Apportionment	Changes with population	Fixed; entire state
Impeachment	Impeaches official	Tries the impeached official
Treaty-making power	No authority	2/3 approval
Presidential appointments	No authority	Majority approval
Organizational		
Size	435 members	100 members
Number of standing committees	20	16
Total committee assignments per member	Approx. 6	Approx. 11
Rules Committee	Yes	No
Limits on floor debate	Yes	No (filibuster possible)
Electoral, 2018		
Average Incumbent raised	$1,814,000	$15,357,000
Average Challenger raised	$904,000	$4,963,000
Most expensive campaign (candidate expenditures)	$20,629,000	$93,853,000
Incumbency advantage	93% (93.1% is 56-year average)	86% (81.4% is 56-year average)

Sources: Roger H. Davidson, Walter J. Oleszek and Frances E. Lee, *Congress and its Members,* 13th ed. (Washington, D.C. CQ Press, 2008), 44, 187; Federal Election Commission data compiled by the Center for Responsive Politics, 2018, https://www.opensecrets.org/overview/index.php.

members of Congress between being responsive to local or particular interests, supporting the party leadership, and at the same time trying to make laws in the interest of the nation as a whole.

Other differences between the House and the Senate include the division of power on impeachment of public figures such as presidents and Supreme Court justices. The House impeaches, or charges the official with "Treason, Bribery, or other high Crimes and Misdemeanors," and the Senate tries the official. Both Andrew Johnson and Bill Clinton were impeached by the House, but in both cases the Senate failed to find the president guilty of the charges brought by the House. In addition, only the Senate is given the responsibility for confirming appointments to the executive and judicial branches, and for sharing the treaty-making power with the president.

CONGRESSIONAL CHECKS AND BALANCES

The founders were concerned generally about the abuse of power, but since they were most anxious to avoid executive tyranny, they granted Congress the bulk of the lawmaking power. The Constitution gives Congress the power to regulate commerce; the exclusive power to raise and to spend money for the national government; the power to provide for economic infrastructure (roads, postal service, money, patents); and significant powers in foreign policy, including the power to declare war, to ratify treaties, and to raise and support the armed forces. But the Constitution also limits congressional powers through the protection of individual rights and by the watchful eyes of the other two branches of government, with which Congress shares power.

Our system of checks and balances means that, to exercise its powers, each branch has to have the cooperation of the others. Thus Congress has the responsibility for passing bills, but the bills do not become law unless (1) the president signs them or, more passively, refrains from vetoing them, or (2) both houses of Congress are able to muster a full two-thirds majority to override a presidential veto. The president cannot vote on legislation or even introduce bills, but the Constitution gives the chief executive a powerful policy formulation role in calling for the president's annual State of the Union address and in inviting the president to recommend to Congress "such measures as he shall judge necessary and expedient."

One of the most important checks on the executive that the Constitution gives to Congress is **congressional oversight** of the executive to ensure that the president and bureaucracy are carrying out the laws as Congress intended. This is usually done through hearings and selective investigations of executive actions and is essential for Congress to be certain its will is being carried out. When Congress and the White House are controlled by opposite parties, however, oversight can become a political weapon in the hands of Congress, with Congress keeping the executive continually on the defensive by requiring it to defend itself against accusations that are frequently made to hamstring that branch. Consequently, the number of congressional investigations of executive behavior increases sharply when the president faces a House of Representatives controlled by the opposition party.[19]

Unlike most of its predecessors, the Obama administration proved to be remarkably scandal-free. Though the GOP had tried hard to find a target to tarnish the administration,[20] investigations into Solyndra, *Fast and Furious*, and the death of four Americans in Benghazi, Libya, yielded nothing of note before the 2012 election.[21]

Nevertheless, the Republican majority in Congress set out with a new series of investigations of the administration, including the creation in 2014 of a seven-person Select Committee

congressional oversight efforts by Congress, especially through committees, to monitor agency rule making, enforcement, and implementation of congressional policies

on Benghazi with the goal, in the words of then-Speaker John Boehner, of "getting to the truth" about whether the Obama administration misled the public about the deadly attack in Libya. Two years and $7 million later the committee found no wrong-doing on Secretary of State Hillary Clinton's part.[22]

Just as a Congress can be hard on an administration of the opposite party, it can go easy on its own. The Republican House oversight of Russian intervention into the 2016 election was unable to get to the bottom of Russia's role because President Trump viewed their charge as implying that his election was illegitimate. Although the House Intelligence Committee conceded that Russia had interfered, committee chair Devin Nunes, R-Calif., refused to investigate whether Trump colluded, much to the frustration of his Democratic counterpart, ranking member Adam Schiff, D-Calif. The Senate Intelligence Committee conducted more thorough and bipartisan oversight, though they, too, diverged on how deeply to investigate Trump's role.

Oversight also comes into play when Congress delegates authority to regulatory agencies in the executive branch. Often the agencies do what they are supposed to do, which can make the job of keeping an eye on them boring and unrewarding. If Congress does not keep watch, however, the agencies can develop unhealthy relationships with those they are supposed to be regulating. This was the case with the Securities and Exchange Commission, which failed to protect us from the risky investment practices that resulted in the economic meltdown in late 2008. Similarly, the Minerals Management Service's failure to adequately police offshore drilling procedures contributed to the ecological disaster in the Gulf of Mexico following the 2010 explosion of BP's *Deepwater Horizon* drilling platform. The Marine Mammal Protection Act and the National Environmental Policy Act were routinely violated by regulators seeking bonuses for encouraging offshore oil drilling.[23] Since these relationships develop far from public scrutiny, we rely on Congress to ensure, through oversight, that agencies do the job they were set up to do, though there is a strong temptation for members to slight congressional responsibility here in favor of splashier and more electorally rewarding activities.

Another congressional check on the executive is the constitutional requirement that major presidential appointments, for instance, to cabinet posts, ambassadorships, and the federal courts, must be made with the **advice and consent** of the Senate. More than a norm, this is an actual constitutional duty. Historically, most presidential appointments have proceeded without incident, but as we saw in *What's at Stake . . . ?*, appointments have become increasingly political in recent administrations. Senators sometimes use their confirmation powers to do more than advise on and consent to the appointment at hand. They frequently tie up appointments, either because they oppose the nominee on account of his or her ideology or because they wish to extract promises and commitments from the president. In today's highly polarized Congress, senators of the opposing party are quick to object to many of the president's appointees. The result is that many appointments languish and high offices in the federal government go unfilled for months or even years.

As *What's at Stake . . . ?* and the events following Justice Anthony Kennedy's retirement in 2018 have made painfully clear, the constitutional duty to provide advice and consent can become political theater with serious consequences. The Senate loses the important norm of cooperation with the president on judicial appointments, setting a dangerous precedent for future appointments under divided government. And clearly, presidents can find the Senate's ability to block their appointments incredibly frustrating, as it gums up the works of the executive and judicial branches, preventing agencies and courts from taking care of their business. Sometimes stymied presidents have taken advantage of a constitutional provision that allows

advice and consent
the constitutional obligation that the Senate approve certain executive appointments

them to make temporary appointments without Senate approval if a vacancy occurs when the Senate is not in session. These so-called "recess appointments" were designed to let presidents fill vacancies in an era when it might take the Senate long weeks to convene, but modern-day presidents sometimes use them to get around Senate opposition. Senators determined to deny a president the opportunity to make a recess appointment have taken to keeping Congress in session on a technicality, even when they are not in Washington. President Obama, facing such obstruction, argued that Congress was really in recess when its members were not present and made several appointments, some of which were challenged in court. In 2014 the Supreme Court voided recess appointments that Obama made while the Senate was technically in session, calling it an overreach of his authority because it is up to Congress to decide when it is or isn't in session.[24]

A final built-in source of institutional conflict between Congress and the president is the difference in constituencies. Presidents look at each policy in terms of a national constituency and their own policy program, whereas members of Congress necessarily take a narrower view. For example, the president may decide that clean air should be a national priority, whereas for some members of Congress a clean air bill might mean closing factories in their districts. Increasingly, within an era of hyperpartisanship, opposition members can get their bases excited just by opposing the president's agenda, whatever it may be.

Checks and balances, of course, require the cooperation of Congress not only with the executive branch but also with the judiciary. The constitutional relationship between the federal courts and Congress is simple in principle: Congress makes the laws, and the courts interpret them. The Supreme Court also has the lofty job of deciding whether laws and procedures are consistent with the Constitution, although this power of judicial review is not mentioned in the Constitution.

We think of the judiciary as independent of the other branches, but this self-sufficiency is only a matter of degree. Congress, for example, is charged with setting up the lower federal courts and determining the salaries for judges, with the interesting constitutional provision that a judge's salary cannot be cut. Congress also has considerable powers in establishing some issues of jurisdiction—that is, deciding which courts hear which cases (Article III, Section 2)—and in limiting the courts' discretion to rule or impose the sentences judges think best. And, as we just indicated, in accepting and rejecting presidential Supreme Court and federal court nominees, the Senate influences the long-term operation of the courts.[25]

In Your Own Words Explain how checks and balances work between the Congress and the executive and judicial branches.

CONGRESSIONAL ELECTIONS

*Political calculations to define
districts and determine who will run*

If we want to understand how Congress works, the place to begin is with the election of its members. With House terms of two years and Senate terms of six years, getting elected occupies a great deal of a representative's time. In fact, one professor argues that most aspects of Congress are designed to aid the reelection goals of its members.[26] Furthermore, the way in which the districts they run in are drawn goes a long way to determining how successful they will be.

THE POLITICS OF DEFINING CONGRESSIONAL DISTRICTS

The Constitution provides that each state will have two senators, which is easy to determine, and that seats in the House of Representatives will be allocated on the basis of population, which is less so because state populations fluctuate over time. Reapportionment is the process in which the 435 House seats are reallocated among the states after each ten-year census yields a new population count. States whose populations grow gain seats, which are taken from those whose populations decline or remain steady. The winners are mostly in the rapidly growing Sun Belt states of the South and Southwest; the losers are largely in the Northeast and Midwest.

Not only must the 435 delegates be apportioned among the fifty states, but, in a process called redistricting, districts within the states have to be redrawn to keep them relatively equal in population. In 1964 the Supreme Court decided that for the U.S. House of Representatives as well as for state legislatures, Americans should be represented under the principle of "one person, one vote" and that the districts therefore must have equal populations.[27] The average population of a house district in the year 2010 was 710,767.[28] Redistricting, which is carried out by the state legislatures (or by commissions they empower), can turn into a bitter political battle because how the district lines are drawn will have a lot to do with who gets elected.

> *Why is geography a better basis for congressional representation than, say, race, religion, gender, occupation, or socioeconomic group?*

Gerrymandering is the process of drawing district lines to benefit one group or another, and it can result in some extremely strange shapes by the time the state politicians are through. Gerrymandering usually is one of three kinds. Pro-incumbent gerrymandering takes place when a state legislature is so closely divided that members can't agree to give an advantage to one party or the other, so they agree to create districts that reinforce the current power structure by favoring the people who already hold the seats.[29] A second kind of gerrymandering is partisan gerrymandering. Generally, the goal of the party controlling the redistricting process in a particular state legislature is to draw districts to maximize the number of House seats their party can win. As a result of partisan gerrymandering, it is easily possible for a party to win a substantial majority of seats in the legislature while losing the popular vote. For instance, the Republican success in the 2010 elections gave the party control of the redistricting process in a majority of states. Artful districting in North Carolina resulted in Republicans winning nine of the state's thirteen congressional districts, even though Democrats took 51 percent of the two-party vote. Similar results occurred in Arizona, Michigan, Pennsylvania, and Wisconsin. All contributed to the odd outcome of the Republicans' holding a majority in Congress (234 to 201 seats) while Democrats received 1.4 million more votes for the House.[30] One analyst says that, because of the way House districts were drawn in 2010, Democrats would have to win 55 percent of the vote to regain the majority until the next census sets off a new round of redistricting.[31] While some states, like Ohio, have taken on themselves the serious job of drawing equitable partisan districts, the Supreme Court has tended to side-step issues of partisan gerrymandering, and in 2018 it did so again, twice, returning questions of parties drawing districts for partisan advantage back to the states.[32]

Finally, racial gerrymandering occurs when district lines are drawn to favor or disadvantage an ethnic or racial group. For many years, states in the Deep South drew district lines to ensure that black voters would not constitute a majority that could elect an African American to Congress. The 1965 Voting Rights Act, as we have seen, was intended to ease the way for African Americans to exercise their voting rights. For a time, states with discriminatory backgrounds were subject to federal supervision to ensure they did not intend their voting laws to discriminate. Since the 1982

reapportionment a reallocation of congressional seats among the states every ten years, following the census

redistricting the process of dividing states into legislative districts

gerrymandering redistricting to benefit a particular group

partisan gerrymandering redistricting controlled by the majority party in a state's legislature, to increase the number of districts that party can expect to carry

racial gerrymandering redistricting to enhance or reduce the chances that a racial or ethnic group will elect members to the legislature

FIGURE 6.1

Gerrymanders and Earmuffs

Illinois Fourth Congressional District

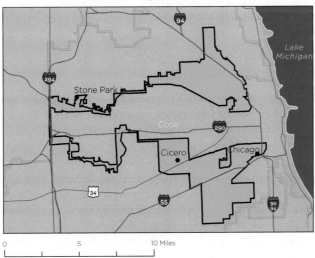

Back in 1812, district lines in the state of Massachusetts were drawn to concentrate Federalist support in a few key districts. A contemporary cartoon likened one particularly convoluted district to a long-necked monster, nicknamed the "Gerry-mander" after Massachusetts governor Elbridge Gerry. Redistricting after the 2010 Census proved that the gerrymander is alive and well, as evidenced by the new map of the Illinois Fourth Congressional District, nicknamed the "earmuffs" district, which joins two predominantly Latino areas in Chicago.

Source: "Congressional District 4," NationalAtlas.gov; Library of Congress.

Voting Rights Act, the drawing of such lines has been used to maximize the likelihood that African Americans will be elected to Congress. Both Republicans and minority (African American and Latino) political activists have backed the formation of majority-minority districts, in which African Americans or Hispanics constitute majorities. This has the effect of concentrating enough minority citizens to elect one of their own, and at the same time, it takes these (usually Democratic) voters out of the pool of voters in other districts—a process aptly termed *bleaching*—thus making it easier for nonminority districts to be won by Republicans.[33] When sufficient numbers of minority voters are not concentrated in a geographic area, majority-minority districts take bizarre shapes. One of many examples is the Fourth Congressional District in Illinois, which joined two Hispanic communities (see Figure 6.1). The district has been named "earmuffs."[34]

Racial gerrymandering, however, remains highly controversial. While politicians and racial and ethnic group leaders continue to jockey for the best district boundaries for their own interests, the courts struggle to find a "fair" set of rules for drawing district lines. In 2013 the Court struck down part of the 1965 Voting Rights Act and directed Congress to update it, which never happened. In 2018 the Court looked at a Texas map that a lower court had found to be intentionally discriminatory. In a five-to-four decision the Court ruled that Texas Republicans had not intentionally drawn their districts to disadvantage minorities and they let most of the map stand. The upshot is that the remaining protections make it very difficult to prove such intentionality in the future, essentially gutting parts of the 1965 Voting Rights Act.[35] Making laws that deal explicitly with race is tricky in any case. Since, as we discussed in Chapter 5, race is a suspect classification, a law that uses race to treat citizens differently is subject to strict scrutiny, and the law must fulfill a compelling state purpose, whether it penalizes them or benefits them.[36] In recent cases the Supreme Court declared that race cannot be the predominant factor in drawing congressional districts. It can be taken into account, but so must other factors, such as neighborhood and community preservation.

DECIDING TO RUN

The formal qualifications for Congress are not difficult to meet. In addition to the age and citizenship requirements listed in Table 6.1, the Constitution requires that you live in the state you want to represent, although state laws vary on how long or when you have to have lived there. Custom also dictates that if you are running for the House, you live in the district you want to represent. There are no educational requirements for Congress.

Constitutionally the qualifications for Congress are looser than those for many other jobs you may apply for when you graduate. Nevertheless, most members of Congress have gone to college, three-quarters have graduate degrees, nearly half are lawyers, many are businesspeople, and quite a few are millionaires. By most estimations, Congress comprises an educational, occupational, and economic elite. Congress is also an overwhelmingly white male institution. White males make up 40 percent of the U.S. population, but they account for more than 80 percent of the members of the U.S. Congress. Congress is, however, more representative today than it has been through most of our history, though its progress is slow (see *Snapshot of America: Who Represents Us in Congress?*).

Like most prospective members of Congress, if you decide to run you are probably motivated by a desire to serve the public. These days, if you are contemplating a run for Congress you are also increasingly likely to be motivated by your ideology—that is, you are probably a conservative Republican or a liberal Democrat who wants to run from a sense of personal conviction and commitment to enact policy that represents your particular strongly held values. But your wish to run for Congress may also be enhanced by the fact that it is a very attractive job in its own right. First, there is all the fun of being in Washington, living a life that is undeniably exciting and powerful. The salary, $174,000 in 2014, puts representatives and senators among the top wage earners in the nation, and the "perks" of office are rather nice as well. These include generous travel allowances, ample staff, franking privileges (the ability to send mailings to constituents free of charge), free parking at Reagan National Airport, health and life insurance, and substantial pensions.[37] Offsetting these enviable aspects of serving in Congress are the facts that the work is awfully hard, it is expensive to keep up two homes (one in D.C. and one in the home district), and the job security is nonexistent.

To have an outside chance of winning, nonincumbent candidates for Congress need political and financial assets. The key political asset for a potential candidate is experience, such as working for other candidates, serving as a precinct chair, or holding an office in the local party organization. Even more helpful is experience in elective office. Political amateurs without such experience are considered "low-quality" candidates for Congress because, except under unusual circumstances, they almost never win—unless they happen to be famous sports stars, television personalities, or wealthy businesspeople who have personal resources that can help them beat the odds.[38]

"High-quality" candidates with the requisite political assets need to be careful not to squander them. They do not want to use up favors and political credibility in a losing effort, especially if they have to give up something valuable, like money or an office they currently hold, in order to run. Strategic politicians act rationally and carefully in deciding whether a race is worth running by asking four key questions:

1. *Is this a district or state I can win?* Liberals do not do well in conservative parts of the South, African Americans have great difficulty getting elected in predominantly white districts, Republicans have a hard time in areas that are mostly Democratic, and so forth.
2. *Who is my opponent likely to be?* Whether an opponent is vulnerable is governed largely by the incumbency advantage, which refers to the edge in visibility, experience, organization, and fundraising ability possessed by the people who already hold the job. It can make them hard to defeat (see the box "The 116th Congress"). The best bet from a challenger's perspective is an open seat, but these are likely to draw more than one high-quality candidate.
3. *Can I get the funds necessary to run a winning campaign?* Modern political campaigns are expensive. Winning nonincumbents over the past decade have spent on average more than four times as much as nonincumbents who did not win, and even then the winning nonincumbents could not keep up with the spending of incumbents.[39] Incumbents have access to a lot more funds than do nonincumbents.
4. *What kind of year is this?* Some years are good for Democrats, some for Republicans. These tides are a result of such things as presidential popularity, the state of the economy, and military engagements abroad. If it is a presidential election year, enthusiasm for a popular presidential candidate might sweep fellow party members to victory in what is known as the coattail effect, but this has been less significant in recent elections.

The strength of coattails might be declining, but there is no arguing with the phenomenon of the midterm loss. This is the striking regularity with which the presidential party loses seats in Congress in the midterm elections, also called "off-year" elections—those congressional elections that fall in between presidential election years. The 1994 election that brought Republicans to power in Congress for the first time in forty years was a striking example of the midterm loss.[40] In general, the presidential party losses depend on the president's standing with the public and the state of the economy; an unpopular president and a sour economy make the loss worse, but it generally happens regardless. In recent years only 1998 and 2002 broke the midterm loss pattern, and both of those were unusual circumstances.

In 2010 a sputtering economic recovery, high unemployment, and President Obama's correspondingly low approval ratings cost the Democrats the majority in the House. The GOP gain of sixty-three House seats was the largest for that party in six decades, eclipsing the historic 1994 victory and easily wiping out the Democrats' gains in the previous two election cycles. The Democrats were especially vulnerable because they had won in a large number of Republican districts in 2006 and again in 2008. With fewer seats at stake in the Senate, the Democrats lost only six seats, keeping majority control in that chamber, but not by much. In 2014 the Democrats again lost seats in the House but this time lost control of the Senate as well, giving the coveted leadership spot to Senator Mitch McConnell from Kentucky. In 2018 the tables were turned. The economy was roaring, but the president remained extremely unpopular. While the Republicans didn't have a lot of exposure in the Senate, they were highly exposed at the House level, making them vulnerable to Democratic takeovers. While Trump did his best to rally his supporters—effectively putting himself on the ballot by saying Democrats would impeach him—Democrats were enthused and motivated. People of color and young people, not always reliable midterm voters, turned out, and an enormous gender

incumbency advantage the electoral edge afforded to those already in office

coattail effect the added votes received by congressional candidates of a winning presidential party

midterm loss the tendency for the presidential party to lose congressional seats in off-year elections

Snapshot of America: *Who Represents Us in Congress?*

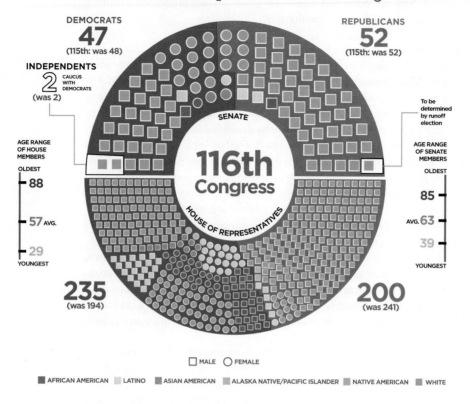

DEMOCRATS
47
(115th: was 48)

INDEPENDENTS
2 CAUCUS WITH DEMOCRATS
(was 2)

REPUBLICANS
52
(115th: was 52)

To be determined by runoff election

SENATE

116th Congress

HOUSE OF REPRESENTATIVES

AGE RANGE OF HOUSE MEMBERS
OLDEST
88
57 AVG.
29
YOUNGEST

AGE RANGE OF SENATE MEMBERS
OLDEST
85
AVG. **63**
39
YOUNGEST

235
(was 194)

200
(was 241)

☐ MALE   ◯ FEMALE

■ AFRICAN AMERICAN   ■ LATINO   ■ ASIAN AMERICAN   ■ ALASKA NATIVE/PACIFIC ISLANDER   ■ NATIVE AMERICAN   ■ WHITE

NUMBER OF CONGRESSIONAL MEMBERS BY RACE AND GENDER SINCE 1900

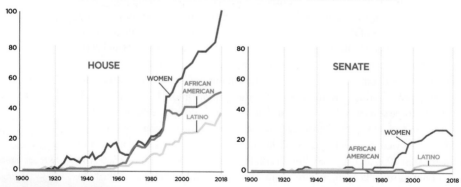

HOUSE
WOMEN
AFRICAN AMERICAN
LATINO

SENATE
WOMEN
AFRICAN AMERICAN
LATINO

Behind the Numbers

Congress has been dominated by white males—and it still is, but less so than in the past (bottom line charts). What difference does it make if more minorities and women are elected to Congress? Does it matter which party they serve?

Source: CQ Weekly Guide to the New Congress, November 12, 2018.

Note: Includes likely winners of races not settled at press time.

The 116th Congress

Midterm elections rarely prove to be winners for the president's party, and 2018 proved the rule. We've talked elsewhere about the "blue wave" that put Democrats into governors offices, state legislatures, and other state leadership positions.

As far as Congress goes, the blue wave was limited by the fact that the Republican Senate had limited exposure—that is, they were not defending many seats. They may have even gained a few when the dust settles.

But the story in the House is different. Republican exposure was high and Democrats took the unusual (for them) step of fielding candidates in almost every district, no matter how remote their chances were. Often a party will leave a seat uncontested if they don't think they will win but the Democratic enthusiasm, especially among women, to take on President Trump gave them good candidates to take advantage of retirements, scandals, or luck.

The new Congress coming in will have more or less the same Senate, controlled by Mitch McConnell whose primary goal has been to get Trump's list of judges approved, something he can do easily without the threat of a filibuster.

But the House is new—demographically diverse and led by a Speaker who has a history of holding her caucus together better than either of her two predecessors. While the House can't pass laws without the Senate it is likely, if patterns hold, there will be little cooperation between the two chambers.

The legislative agenda in the House is headed by health care, the issue Democratic voters said most concerned them. Because Obamacare has become an albatross around the necks of Republicans it is possible that some compromise could succeed in taking the issue off the table. Additional states voted for Medicaid expansion in the midterms which means that Obamacare is not likely going anywhere; it's just a matter of whether the Trump administration can paralyze it by allowing low cost, high deductible plans that can charge a premium for pre-existing conditions.

Immigration is another issue the Democrats really want to move on but while there are clearly Republicans who would like to join them in a compromise solution, President Trump has made blocking immigrants and refugees a key part of his agenda and Republicans are not likely to challenge his base unless his popularity ratings sink further.

What the Democrats can do, however, is to engage in congressional oversight. When Speaker Pelosi came into office in 2007 she had the Bush administration's Iraq War in her sights and she is likely to be focused on investigating the Trump administration. How that will interact with Robert Mueller's investigation into Russian interference with the 2016 election isn't clear and there will undoubtedly be overlap as some Democrats are itching to get their hands on Trump's tax returns to see why he has refused to release them as previous presidents have done.

Source: Guide to the New Congress, CQ Roll Call, November 12, 2018.

gap sent women suburban voters to the Democratic side while men tended to vote Republican. In the end, the Republicans held the Senate and may have picked up a few seats pending the results of recounts, but the Democrats took almost 40 House seats, their biggest gain since Watergate.

In Your Own Words Identify the ways that politics influences how congressional districts are defined and who runs for Congress.

CONGRESSIONAL ORGANIZATION

The key role of political parties and congressional committees

In spite of the imperatives of reelection and the demands of constituency service, the primary business of Congress is making laws. Lawmaking is influenced a great deal by the organization of Congress—that is, the rules of the institution that determine where the power is and who can exercise it.

THE CENTRAL ROLE OF PARTY

Political parties are central to how Congress functions for several reasons. First, Congress is organized along party lines. In each chamber, the party with the most members—the majority party—decides the rules for each chamber and gets the top leadership posts, such as the Speaker of the House, the majority leader in the Senate, and the chairs of all the committees and subcommittees.

Party is also important in Congress because it is the mechanism for members' advancement. Because all positions are determined by the parties, members have to advance within their party to achieve positions of power in the House or the Senate, whether as a committee chair or in the party leadership.

Finally, party control of Congress matters because the parties stand for very different things. Across a wide range of issues, Democrats embrace more liberal policies, whereas Republicans advocate more conservative ones. Upon winning office, these candidates vote very differently from each other. Thus, although Americans like to downplay the importance of parties in their own lives, political parties are fundamental to the operation of Congress and, hence, to what the national government does.

Parties have become much more significant in Congress in recent years due to the process of party polarization, described earlier in the chapter. Recall that this refers to the growing ideological differences between the two parties, the greater ideological agreement within the parties, and the lack of members falling in between. In today's era of hyperpartisanship, almost all the Democrats in Congress are pretty liberal, and to an even greater extent the vast majority of congressional Republicans are very conservative. This makes it harder for the parties to work together because the two parties' members are committed to such divergent positions across the whole range of issues with which Congress must deal.

We also noted that hyperpartisanship has become such a force in congressional voting that members will often vote against their own ideological preferences just to vote against the other side. While the Democrats held a majority (before the 2010 election), President Obama was successful in getting his priorities enacted by the House of Representatives, but solid Republican opposition to anything he favored was enough to block his policy initiatives after the midterm. It was also nearly impossible for him to get his policies passed in the Senate, even when the Democrats held a majority, because the Republicans used the filibuster to block him when they could (see "How a Bill Becomes a Law—Some of the Time," later in this chapter).

THE LEADERSHIP

majority party the party with the most seats in a house of Congress

The majority and minority parties in each house elect their own leaders, who are, in turn, the leaders of Congress. Strong, centralized leadership allows Congress to be more efficient in enacting party or presidential programs, but it gives less independence to members to take care of their own constituencies or to pursue their own policy preferences.[41] Although the nature of leadership in the House of Representatives has varied over time, the current era had been one of considerable centralization of power until recently, when Republican factions began to challenge the leadership. Because the Senate is a smaller chamber and thus easier to manage, its power is more decentralized.

The Constitution provides for the election of some specific congressional officers, but Congress itself determines how much power the leaders of each chamber will have. The main leadership offices in the House of Representatives are the Speaker of the House, the majority leader, the minority leader, and the whips. The real political choice about who the party leader should be occurs within the party groupings in each chamber. The **Speaker of the House** is elected by the majority party and, as the person who presides over floor deliberations, is the most powerful House member. The House majority leader, second in command, is given wide-ranging responsibilities to assist the Speaker.

The leadership organization in the Senate is similar but not as elaborate. The presiding officer of the Senate is the vice president of the United States, who can cast a tie-breaking vote when necessary but otherwise does not vote. When the vice president is not present, which is almost always the case, the president pro tempore of the Senate officially presides, although the role is almost always performed by a junior senator. Because of the Senate's much freer rules for deliberation on the floor, the presiding officer has less power than in the House, where debate is generally tightly controlled. The locus of real leadership in the Senate are the majority leader and the minority leader. Each is advised by party committees on both policy and personnel matters, such as committee appointments.

In both chambers, Democratic and Republican leaders are assisted by party whips. (The term *whip* comes from an old English hunting expression; the "whipper in" was charged with keeping the dogs together in pursuit of the fox.) Elected by party members, whips find out how people intend to vote so that on important party bills the leaders can adjust the legislation, negotiate acceptable amendments, or employ favors (or, occasionally, threats) to line up support. Whips work to persuade party members to support the party on key bills, and they are active in making sure supportive members are available to vote when needed.

Leaders can exercise only the powers that their party members give them. From the members' standpoint, the advantage of a strong leader is that he or she can move legislation along, get the party program passed, do favors for members, and improve the party's standing. The disadvantage is that a strong party leader can pursue national party (or presidential) goals at the expense of members' pet projects and constituency interests, and he or she can withhold favors.

The power of the Speaker of the House has changed dramatically over time. At the turn of the century, the strong "boss rule" of Speaker Joe Cannon greatly centralized power in the House. Members rebelled at this and moved to the **seniority system**, which vested great power in committee chairs instead of the Speaker. Power followed seniority, or length of service on a committee, so that once a person assumed the chair of a committee, business was run very much at his or her pleasure.[42] The seniority system itself was reformed in the 1970s by a movement that weakened the grip of chairs and gave some power back to the committees and subcommittees, but especially to the Speaker and the party caucuses.[43]

Speaker of the House the leader of the majority party who serves as the presiding officer of the House of Representatives

seniority system the accumulation of power and authority in conjunction with the length of time spent in office

U.S. Senate Photographic Studio;
Renee Bouchard

PROFILES IN CITIZENSHIP:
Tammy Duckworth

For Senator Tammy Duckworth, her steel and titanium legs are a sign of strength, her wheel chair is a badge of honor. She doesn't look at November 12 as a day of self-pity. On that day in 2018, coincidently when Veteran's Day was observed, she tweeted:

"Today is my Alive Day, the anniversary of the day I almost died but didn't. On this day 14 years ago, an RPG tore through the cockpit of the helicopter I was flying over Iraq, taking my legs and partial use of my right arm with it. I was quite literally in pieces, but my buddies risked their lives and refused to leave me behind. Every day I think about what they did for me and what I can do to repay them. Making sure I don't let them down is what drives me to do everything I can for our Veterans and troops."

As the highest ranking amputee at Walter Reed Hospital, Duckworth was already taking a leadership position among her fellow wounded warriors. Senator Dick Durbin from Illinois came to visit and invited her to one of President George W. Bush's State of the Union addresses. He talked her into running for Congress and although she lost her first campaign, she was invited to run the Illinois Department of Veterans Affairs and later the U.S. Department of Veterans Affairs. Today she's in the Senate where she makes a significant impact as a strong advocate for her fellow veterans.

One of the main issues she is focused on is the creation of a national community service program that she hopes will get to the floor for a vote soon. Her bill is an invitation for Americans of all backgrounds to serve in a variety of non-mandatory capacities. Every person would get a letter in the mail detailing the opportunities available to them when they turn 18. Under current law, serving in the Armed Forces gets you four years of college, but Duckworth is keen to show young people that there are multiple ways to show ones commitment to the country, from Teach for America to AmeriCorps, to opportunities not yet invented – from the national to the local level. Unless you opt out, a letter would continue to arrive every two years until you are thirty, to see if your life has changed in a way that makes service feasible and attractive.

On the importance of service

"I don't know that young people know that they can serve. I feel like there is a disconnect between military families who know about serving and they serve and the same ones serve over and over again, and poor families know about service often times because it's the only way out."

On keeping the republic

"Vote. Really. Vote. Because not voting is just ceding your voice to someone who may not truly represent you."

Source: Tammy Duckworth spoke with Christine Barbour and Gerald C. Wright on September 27, 2018.

The Speaker's powers were enhanced further with the Republican congressional victories in the 1994 election, when Rep. Newt Gingrich, R-Ga., became Speaker. Gingrich quickly became the most powerful Speaker in the modern era. His House Republican colleagues were willing to give him new powers because his leadership enabled them to take control of the House and to enact the well-publicized conservative agenda that they called the "Contract With America."[44] Gingrich continued as the powerful Republican congressional spokesperson and leader until he resigned in the wake of the almost unprecedented reversal of the 1998 midterm loss, to be replaced by Dennis Hastert, a Republican from Illinois.

When the Democrats won control of the House in 2006, Nancy Pelosi was elected Speaker, the first woman to hold that position. In response to those who wondered if Pelosi could wield power as effectively as her male counterparts, Pelosi herself stated, "Anybody who's ever dealt with me knows not to mess with me."[45] Pelosi's role in passing Obama's health care reform bill was crucial, and she was effective at maintaining the support and discipline of her Democratic majority in the House, holding on to her leadership position in the party even after the Republicans regained the majority in 2010.[46] Although Republicans tried to make her an issue in the 2018 election, few of the red-state Democrats who repudiated her won. Although she has acknowledged the need for younger leadership, and has called herself a "transitional Speaker," there is little doubt she will lead the Democrats for another term in office starting in 2019.

John Boehner's lot as Speaker was more difficult in many ways. His leadership skills were challenged by the effort of holding together a diverse caucus, divided between traditional Republicans and the newly elected Tea Partiers who came to Congress determined not to compromise in accomplishing their ambitious agenda. Indeed, Speaker Boehner was so battered during the fractious 113th and 114th Congresses that there were continued calls for his resignation from both liberals and conservatives, and he finally resigned in 2015.[47] Paul Ryan replaced him reluctantly, knowing that the caucus would be hard to lead, and immediately found himself dealing with some of the same challenges Boehner faced, even though his own conservative credentials had been impeccable. He himself announced his retirement three years later.

The leaders of the Senate have never had as much formal authority as those in the House, and that remains true today. The traditions of the Senate, with its much smaller size, allow each senator to speak or to offer amendments when he or she wants. The highly individualistic Senate would not accept the kind of control that some Speakers wield in the House. But though the Senate majority leader cannot control senators, he or she can influence the scheduling of legislation, a factor that can be crucial to a bill's success. The majority leader may even pull a bill from consideration, a convenient exercise of authority when defeat would embarrass the leadership.

The current majority leader, Mitch McConnell of Kentucky, replaced Democrat Harry Reid, a highly effective manager in the biggest legislative victories of Obama's first years as president, shepherding the health care bill through the Senate and also helping to get major legislation passed in the lame-duck session after the 2010 election.[48] McConnell, who had hoped to win the majority leader's seat for several elections in a row, only to see his chances slip away, has used his time in office to push through as much of his party's agenda as he can. His determination to block as much of Obama's policies as possible, his prevention of hearings on Merrick Garland, his refusal to get behind a bipartisan warning that our electoral system was under attack by Russia, and his breaking of norms on procedure were accomplished with very little dissension from his party. Despite the ideological unruliness of the party, McConnell has kept his eyes on the prize of holding power very effectively.

The Treatment

As Senate majority leader and later as president, Lyndon Johnson was legendary for his ability to cajole, charm, bully, and—by any and all means necessary—persuade others to see things his way. Here, the six-foot, four-inch tall Johnson makes a point or two, towering over colleagues while invading their personal space.

THE COMMITTEE SYSTEM

Meeting as full bodies, the House and the Senate would not be able to consider and deliberate on all of the 10,000 bills and 100,000 nominations they receive every two years.[49] Hence, the work is broken up and handled by smaller groups called committees.

The Constitution says nothing about congressional committees; they are completely creatures of the chambers of Congress they serve. The committee system has developed to meet the needs of a growing nation as well as the evolving goals of members of Congress. Initially, congressional committees formed to consider specific issues and pieces of legislation; after they made their recommendations to the full body, they dispersed. As the nation grew, and with it the number of bills to be considered, this ad hoc system became unwieldy and Congress formed a system of more permanent committees. Longer service on a committee permitted members to develop expertise and specialization in a particular policy area, and thus bills could be considered more efficiently. Committees also provide members with a principal source of institutional power and the primary position from which they can influence national policy.

WHAT COMMITTEES DO It is at the committee and, even more, the subcommittee stages that the nitty-gritty details of legislation are worked out. Committees and subcommittees do the hard work of considering alternatives and drafting legislation. Committees are the primary information gatherers for Congress. Through hearings, staff reports, and investigations, members gather information on policy alternatives and discover who will support different policy options. Thus committees act as the eyes, ears, and workhorses of Congress in considering, drafting, and redrafting proposed legislation.

Committees do more, however, than write laws. Committees also undertake the congressional oversight discussed earlier in the chapter. That is, they check to see that executive agencies are carrying out the laws as Congress intended them to. Committee members gather information about agencies from the media, constituents, interest groups, staff, and special investigations. A lot of what is learned in oversight is reflected in changes to the laws that give agencies their power and operating funds.

Members and the general public all agree strongly on the importance of congressional oversight; it is part of the "continuous watchfulness" that Congress mandated for itself in the Legislative Reorganization Act of 1946 and reiterated in its Legislative Reorganization Act of 1970. Nevertheless, oversight tends to be slighted in the congressional process. The reasons are not hard to find. Oversight takes a lot of time, and the rewards to individual members are less certain than from other activities like fundraising or grabbing a headline in the district with a new pork project. Consequently, oversight most often takes the form of "fire-alarm" oversight, in which some scandal or upsurge of public interest directs congressional attention to a problem in the bureaucracy rather than careful and systematic reviews of agencies' implementation of congressional policies.[50] Like so much of our lives in a mediated world, congressional attention is herd-like—following the loudest noises and the narratives that catch the eye of their constituents.

TYPES OF COMMITTEES Congress has four types of committees: standing, select, joint, and conference. The vast majority of work is done by the **standing committees**. These are permanent committees, created by statute, that carry over from one session of Congress to the next. They review most pieces of legislation that are introduced to Congress. So powerful are the standing committees that they scrutinize, hold hearings on, amend, and, frequently, kill legislation before the full Congress ever gets the chance to discuss it.

The standing committees deal with issues in specific policy areas, such as agriculture, foreign relations, or justice. Each committee is typically divided into several subcommittees that focus on detailed areas of policy. There are 20 standing committees and 104 subcommittees in the House. The Senate has 16 standing committees and 72 subcommittees. Not surprisingly, committees are larger in the House, with membership rising to more than seventy on some committees, compared to thirty or fewer on the Senate committees. The size of the committees and the ratio of majority- to minority-party members on each are determined at the start of each Congress by the majority leadership in the House and by negotiations between the majority and minority leaders in the Senate. Standing committee membership is relatively stable as seniority on the committee is a major factor in gaining subcommittee or committee chairs; the chairs wield considerable power and are coveted positions.

The policy areas represented by the standing committees of the two houses roughly parallel each other, but the **House Rules Committee** exists only in the House of Representatives. (There is a Senate Rules and Administration Committee, but it does not have equivalent powers.) The House Rules Committee provides a "rule" for each bill that specifies when it will be debated, how long debate can last, how it can be amended, and so on. Because the House is so large, debate would quickly become chaotic without the organization and structure provided by the Rules Committee. Such structure is not neutral in its effects on legislation, however. Since the committees are controlled by the majority party in the House, and especially by the Speaker, the rule that structures a given debate will reflect the priorities of the majority party.

standing committees permanent committees responsible for legislation in particular policy areas

House Rules Committee the committee that determines how and when debate on a bill will take place

When a problem before Congress does not fall under the jurisdiction of a standing committee, a **select committee** may be appointed. These committees are usually temporary and do not recommend legislation, per se. They are used to gather information on specific issues, like the Select Committee on Homeland Security did after the September 11 terror attacks, or to conduct an investigation, as did the Select Bipartisan Committee to Investigate the Preparation for and Response to Hurricane Katrina.

Joint committees are made up of members of both houses of Congress. Although each house generally considers bills independently (making for a lot of duplication of effort and staff), in some areas they have coordinated activities to expedite consideration of legislation. The joint committees in the 115th Congress were on printing, economics, taxation, and the library and will probably be similar in the 116th.

Before a bill can become law, it must be passed by both houses of Congress in exactly the same form. But because the legislative process in each house often subjects bills to different pressures, they may be very different by the time they are debated and passed. **Conference committees** are temporary committees made up of members of both houses of Congress commissioned to resolve these differences, after which the bills go back to each house for a final vote. Members of the conference committees are appointed by the presiding officer of each chamber, who usually taps the senior members, especially the chair, of the committees that considered the bill. Most often the conferees are members of those committees.

In the past, conference committees have tended to be small (five to ten members). In recent years, however, as Congress has tried to work within severe budget restrictions and across the divide of increased party polarization, it has taken to passing huge "megabills" that collect many proposals into one. Conference committees have expanded in turn, sometimes ballooning into gigantic affairs with many "subconferences."[51] This has given rise to a relatively new process of "omnibus" legislation in which the committees play a less central role and congressional leadership is much more involved, even at early stages. We discuss these changes later when we talk about policymaking.

COMMITTEE ASSIGNMENTS Getting on the right standing committee is vital for all members of Congress because so much of what members want to accomplish is realized through their work on these committees. Members who like to focus on national lawmaking might try to get assigned to committees like Commerce or Foreign Affairs, which have broad jurisdictions and often deal with weighty, high-profile concerns. The House Ways and Means Committee and the Senate Finance Committee, because they deal with taxation—a topic of interest to nearly everyone—are highly prized committee assignments, as are the Senate Appropriations, Armed Services, and Foreign Relations Committees.[52]

Decisions on who gets on what committee vary by party and chamber. Occasionally the parties have used committee assignments to reward those who support party positions, but in general both the Democrats and the Republicans accommodate their members when they can, since the goal of both parties is to support their ranks and help them be successful.

COMMITTEE CHAIRS For much of the twentieth century, congressional power rested with the committee chairs of Congress; their power was unquestioned under the seniority system. Today, seniority remains important, but chairs serve at the pleasure of their party

select committee
a committee appointed to deal with an issue or a problem not suited to a standing committee

joint committees
combined House-Senate committees formed to coordinate activities and expedite legislation in a certain area

conference committees temporary committees formed to reconcile differences in House and Senate versions of a bill

caucuses and the party leadership. The committees, under this system, are expected to reflect more faithfully the preferences of the average party member rather than just those of the committee chair or current members.[53]

CONGRESSIONAL RESOURCES

For Congress to guide government lawmaking, it needs expertise and information. Members find, however, that alone they are no match for the enormous amount of information generated by the executive branch, on the one hand, or the sheer informational demands of the policy process—economic, social, military, and foreign affairs—on the other. The need for independent, expert information, along with the ever-present reelection imperative, has led to a big growth in what we call the congressional bureaucracy. Congress has over 22,000 employees, paid for by the federal government. This makes it by far the largest staffed legislature in the world.

The vast majority of congressional staff—secretaries, computer personnel, clericals, and professionals—work for individual members or committees. The staff handle mailings; meet visiting constituents; answer mail, phone calls, faxes, and email messages; create and maintain member web sites; and contact the executive agencies on behalf of constituents. They arrange meetings for members in their constituencies, and they set up local media events. House members have an average staff of eighteen per member; the Senate averages twice that, with the sizes of Senate staff varying with state population.

The committees' staffs (about 2,200 in the House and 1,200 in the Senate) do much of the committee work, from honing ideas, suggesting policy options to members, scheduling hearings, and recruiting witnesses, to actually drafting legislation.[54] In most committees, each party also has its own staff. Following the 1994 election, committee staffs were cut by one-third; however, members did not force any cuts in the sizes of their personal staffs.

Reflecting a reluctance dating from Vietnam and Watergate to be dependent on the executive branch for information, Congress also has nonpartisan staff that run research organizations and agencies to facilitate its work, providing expert advice and technical assistance. The Congressional Research Service (CRS), a unit of the Library of Congress, employs over eight hundred people to do research for members of Congress. For example, if Congress is considering a bill to relax air quality standards in factories, it can have the CRS determine what is known about the effects of air quality on worker health. The Government Accountability Office (formerly the General Accounting Office but still known as the GAO), with its 3,200 employees, audits the books of executive departments and conducts policy evaluation and analysis. The Congressional Budget Office (CBO) is Congress' economic adviser, providing members with economic estimates about the budget, the deficit or surplus, and the national debt, and forecasts of how they will be influenced by different tax and spending policies. Congress has a stronger and more independent role in the policy process when it is not completely dependent on the executive branch for information and expertise.

In Your Own Words Summarize the central role that the parties play in Congress.

HOW CONGRESS WORKS

An already complex process,
complicated further by external and internal forces

The policies passed by Congress are a result of both external and internal forces. The external environment includes the problems that are important to citizens at any given time—sometimes the economy, sometimes foreign affairs, at other times national security or the federal deficit or the plight of the homeless, and so forth. The policy preferences of the president loom large in this external environment as well. It is often said, with some exaggeration but a bit of truth, that "the president proposes, the Congress disposes" of important legislation. And as we have frequently noted, the role of parties, always important, has increased dramatically in an age of hyperpartisanship, often overriding other pressing concerns.

THE CONTEXT OF CONGRESSIONAL POLICYMAKING

Congress has a distinct internal institutional environment that shapes the way it carries out its business. Three characteristics of this environment are especially important: the requirement that bills must be passed in identical form in both houses, the fragmentation inherent in policymaking, and the norms of conduct in each house.

First, Congress is bicameral. Almost all congressional policy has to be passed, in identical form, by both houses. This requirement, laid out by the founders in the Constitution, makes the policy process difficult because the two houses serve different constituencies and operate under different decision-making procedures. The House, for example, because of its size and traditions, is much more hierarchically organized. The leadership has a good deal of influence over committees and particularly over how legislation is considered. The Senate is more egalitarian and its debate wide open; the leadership has less control and fewer powers.

Because the houses are different, getting legislation through both is difficult. Interests that oppose a bill and lose in one chamber can often be successful at defeating the bill in the other. The opposition only has to stop a bill in one place to win, but the proponents of a bill have to win in both houses. In Congress, it is much easier to play defense than offense.

The second overriding feature of the institutional environment of Congress as a policymaking institution is its fragmentation. As you read the next section on how a bill becomes a law, think about the piecemeal nature of the policy process in Congress. Legislation is broken into bits, each considered individually in committees. It is very difficult to coordinate a bill with those laws that are already on the books or with what another committee might be doing in a closely related area. Thus Congress does such seemingly nonsensical things as subsidizing both tobacco growers and antismoking campaigns. This fragmentation increases opportunities for constituencies, individual members, and well-organized groups to influence policy on issues they really care about. It also makes it very hard for national policymakers—the president or congressional leaders—to take a large-scale, coordinated approach to major policy problems.

The third institutional influence on Congress is congressional norms. We have discussed repeatedly in this book the importance of norms, or informal rules that establish accepted ways of doing things. As much as anywhere in our government, they are a critical feature of the institutional environment of Congress. These are sometimes called "folkways" and are usually learned quickly by newcomers when they enter Congress. Norms include the idea that members should work hard, develop a specialization, treat other members with the utmost courtesy, reciprocate favors generally, and take pride in their chambers and in Congress. The purpose of congressional norms is to constrain conflict and personal animosity in an arena where disagreements are inevitable, but they also aid in getting business done. Although congressional norms continue to be important, they are less constraining on members today than they were in the 1950s and 1960s.[55] The extent to which the norms of respect and decorum have been stretched in a hyperpartisan Congress was illustrated when Rep. Joe Wilson, R-S.C., yelled out "You lie!" during President Obama's nationally televised health care address before a joint session of Congress in 2009, and we have mentioned other examples in this chapter. Ironically, the norms of collegial deference are even more important in the current era of intense partisan conflict where they struggle to survive.

HOW A BILL BECOMES A LAW—SOME OF THE TIME

When we see something personally that seems unfair in business or in the workplace, or when we hear through social media or groups that we follow that government is doing something we don't like or when disaster strikes and causes much suffering, when workers go on strike and disrupt our lives—whenever a crisis occurs, we demand that government do something to solve the problem that we cannot solve on our own. This means government must have a policy, a set of laws, to deal with the problem. We consider two aspects of congressional policy here: (1) the agenda, or the source of ideas for new policies; and (2) the legislative process, or the steps a bill goes through to become law. Very few proposed policies, as it turns out, actually make it into law, and those that do have a difficult path to follow.

SETTING THE AGENDA Before a law can be passed, it must be among the things that Congress thinks it ought to do. There is no official list of actions that Congress needs to take, but when a bill is proposed that would result in a significant change in policy, it must seem like a reasonable thing for members to turn their attention to—a problem that is possible, appropriate, and timely for them to try to solve with a new policy. That is, it must be on the legislative agenda. Potential new laws can get on Congress' agenda in several ways. First, because public attention is focused so intently on presidential elections and campaigns, new presidents are especially effective at setting the congressional agenda. Their proposals may be efforts to fulfill campaign promises, to pay political debts, to realize ideological commitments, or to deal with a crisis.

A second way an issue gets on the legislative agenda is when it is triggered by a well-publicized event—especially one that monopolizes cable news or our social media feeds—even if the problem it highlights is not a new one at all. For example, the 2010 explosion of BP's oil-drilling platform *Deepwater Horizon* and the subsequent release of millions of barrels of crude oil into the Gulf of Mexico drew the nation's attention to energy policy, the adequacy of regulatory procedures, and the need to protect the environment. What leaders in Washington will actually do in response to such an event is hard to predict, especially in circumstances in which they are unable to do much of anything (the federal government had neither the technical know-how nor the equipment to plug the oil well, for instance). Nonetheless, such events create a public demand that the government "do something!"

A third way an idea gets on the agenda is for some member or members to find it in their own interests, either politically or ideologically, to invest time and political resources in pushing the policy. Many members of Congress want to prove their legislative skills to their constituents, key supporters, the media, and fellow lawmakers. The search for the right issue to

legislative agenda
the slate of proposals and issues that representatives think it worthwhile to consider and act on

How does a bill become a law? Sometimes it seems like our lawmakers are playing some goofy game to which no one really understands the rules. In fact, it is not quite that bad, but the process is far more complicated than the *Schoolhouse Rock* cartoon version of poor, dejected Bill, sitting on Capitol Hill, would have you believe. Take a close look at this version of the lawmaking process, and you will not be surprised that so many bills fail to make it to the president's desk. The founders wanted a slow, incremental lawmaking process in which the brakes could be applied at multiple points, and that is exactly what they got.

+

The code of a bill

H. R. 301 [110]

| House Of | Repre senta tives | # in which bill was received | Congressional Session |

+ **CBO** or the Congressional Budget Office is a nonpartisan office charged with checking and creating budget estimates.

+ **A Lobbyist** is an activist paid by an interest group to promote its position in the legislature. He or she can also work to change public opinion through advertising and other media outlets.

Lobbyist

Represen tative

A State Legislature

The People

Executive Branch

+ All legislation involving appropriations must originate in HOR.

Bill

Like a bill, but less common

Joint Resolution

Con Current Resolution

Not legislation

Simple Resolution

Regards House operations

Introducing Legislation

Committee Assignment

Committee Work

Meetings

Report Includes purpose and justification for bill; explains how it changes existing law; offers a cost estimate for implementation.

could fail to pass

Final Reading & Vote — Vote on final amendments and proposed bill as a whole.

Public Hearings — Collect information and testimony from opponents and supporters.

Markup — Edit and revise to reflect hearings.

could be "tabled"

+ **HOR** has 435 members and 20 standing committees.

Lobbyist

Quorum of one hundred required to open debate. Chair determines length of debate.

Committee of the Whole

Bill read section by section; only germane amendments proposed, and must include a list of "earmarks."

Second Reading

Debate closes.

Committee Rises

Vote on each amendment individually.

House Action

could send back to committee

A simple majority is required to pass a bill.

House Vote

could fail to pass

Debate & Amend

Put on Calendar

CBO must confirm the bill adheres to spending and revenue constraints in most recent budget.

Reconciliation

Budget & Engrossment

HOR can approve as amended

OR

Request a conference

HOUSE OF REPRESENTATIVES

Senator

HOR Act

Bill

Introducing Legislation

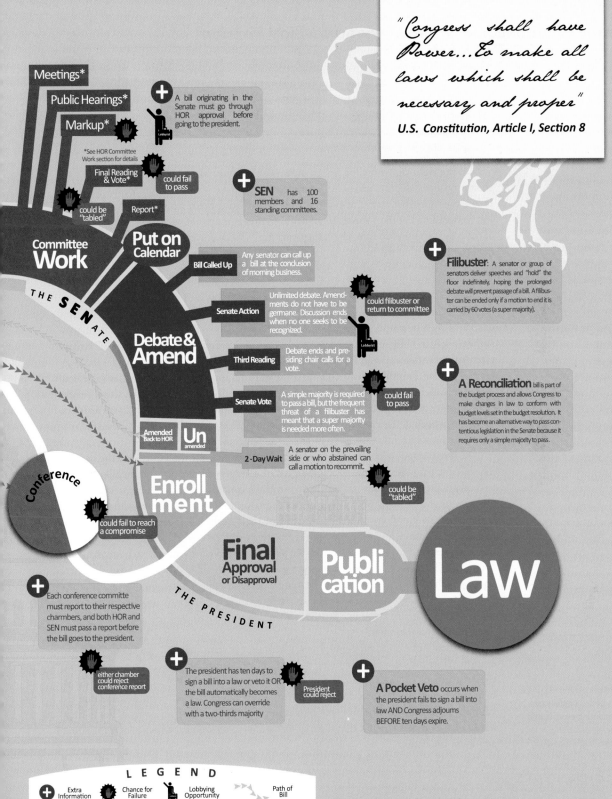

"Congress shall have Power...To make all laws which shall be necessary and proper"

U.S. Constitution, Article I, Section 8

Meetings*

Public Hearings*

Markup*

*See HOR Committee Work section for details

Final Reading & Vote*

could fail to pass

could be "tabled"

Report*

Committee Work

Put on Calendar

THE SENATE

A bill originating in the Senate must go through HOR approval before going to the president.

Lobbyist

SEN has 100 members and 16 standing committees.

Bill Called Up — Any senator can call up a bill at the conclusion of morning business.

Debate & Amend

Senate Action — Unlimited debate. Amendments do not have to be germane. Discussion ends when no one seeks to be recognized.

could filibuster or return to committee

Lobbyist

Third Reading — Debate ends and presiding chair calls for a vote.

Senate Vote — A simple majority is required to pass a bill, but the frequent threat of a filibuster has meant that a super majority is needed more often.

could fail to pass

Amended Back to HOR

Un amended

2 - Day Wait — A senator on the prevailing side or who abstained can call a motion to recommit.

could be "tabled"

Filibuster: A senator or group of senators deliver speeches and "hold" the floor indefinitely, hoping the prolonged debate will prevent passage of a bill. A filibuster can be ended only if a motion to end it is carried by 60 votes (a super majority).

A Reconciliation bill is part of the budget process and allows Congress to make changes in law to conform with budget levels set in the budget resolution. It has become an alternative way to pass contentious legislation in the Senate because it requires only a simple majority to pass.

Conference

could fail to reach a compromise

Enroll ment

Final Approval or Disapproval

Publi cation

THE PRESIDENT

Law

Each conference committee must report to their respective chambers, and both HOR and SEN must pass a report before the bill goes to the president.

either chamber could reject conference report

The president has ten days to sign a bill into a law or veto it OR the bill automatically becomes a law. Congress can override with a two-thirds majority

President could reject

A Pocket Veto occurs when the president fails to sign a bill into law AND Congress adjourns BEFORE ten days expire.

L E G E N D

Extra Information

Chance for Failure

Lobbying Opportunity

Path of Bill

FIGURE 6.2

How a Bill Becomes a Law: Neat and Tidy Version

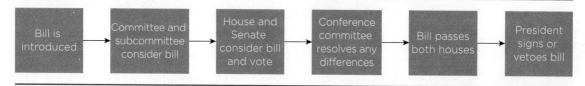

Bill is introduced → Committee and subcommittee consider bill → House and Senate consider bill and vote → Conference committee resolves any differences → Bill passes both houses → President signs or vetoes bill

push at the right time is called **policy entrepreneurship**. Most members of Congress to greater or lesser degrees are policy entrepreneurs. Those with ambition, vision, and luck choose the issues that matter in our lives and that can bring them significant policy influence and recognition, but most successful policy entrepreneurs are not widely recognized outside of the policy communities in which they operate.[56] Policy entrepreneurship by members is important in setting the congressional policy agenda, and it can reap considerable political benefits for those associated with important initiatives.

LEGISLATIVE PROCESS Bills, even those widely recognized as representing the president's legislative program, must be introduced by members of Congress. The formal introduction is done by putting a bill in the "hopper" (a wooden box) in the House, where it goes to the clerk of the House, or by giving it to the presiding officer in the Senate. The bill is then given a number (for example, HR932 in the House or S953 in the Senate) and begins the long journey that *might* result in its becoming law. Figure 6.2 shows the much-simplified, general route for a bill once it is introduced in either the House or the Senate, but the actual details can get messy, and there are many exceptions (see this chapter's *The Big Picture* to get an idea). A bill introduced in the House goes first through the House and then on to the Senate, and vice versa. However, bills may be considered simultaneously in both houses.

The initial stages of committee consideration are similar for the House and the Senate. The bill first has to be referred to committee. This is largely automatic for most bills; they go to the standing committee with jurisdiction over the content of the bill. A bill to change the way agricultural subsidies on cotton are considered would start, for example, with the House Committee on Agriculture. In some cases, a bill might logically fall under more than one committee's jurisdiction, and here the Speaker exercises a good deal of power. He or she can choose the committee that will consider the bill or even refer the same bill to more than one committee. This gives the Speaker important leverage in the House because he or she often knows which committees are likely to be more or less favorable to different bills. Senators do not worry quite as much about where bills are referred because they have much greater opportunity to make changes later in the process than do representatives. We'll see why when we discuss floor consideration.

Bills then move on to subcommittees, where they may, or may not, get serious consideration. Most bills die in committee because the committee members don't care about the issue (it isn't on their agenda) or they actively want to block it. Even if the bill's life is brief, the member who introduced it can still campaign as its champion. In fact, a motivation for the introduction of many bills is not that the member seriously believes they have a chance of passing but that the member wants to be seen back home as taking some action on the issue.

policy entrepreneurship the practice of legislators becoming experts and taking leadership roles in specific policy areas

When a subcommittee decides to consider a bill, it will hold hearings—testimony from experts, interest groups, executive department secretaries and undersecretaries, and even other members of Congress. The subcommittee deliberates and votes the bill back to the full committee. There the committee further considers the bill and makes changes and revisions in a process called *markup*. If the committee votes in favor of the final version of the bill, it goes forward to the floor. Here, however, a crucial difference exists between the House and the Senate.

In the House, bills go from the standing committee to the Rules Committee. This committee, highly responsive to the Speaker of the House, gives each bill a "rule," which includes when and how the bill will be considered. Some bills go out under an "open rule," which means that any amendments can be proposed and added as long as they are germane, or relevant, to the legislation under consideration. More typically, especially for important bills, the House leadership gains more control by imposing restrictive rules that limit the time for debate and restrict the amendments that can be offered. For example, if the leadership knows that there is a lot of sentiment in favor of action on a tax cut, it can control the form of the tax cut by having a restrictive rule that prohibits any amendments to the committee's bill. In this way, even members who would like to vote for a different kind of tax cut face pressure to go along with the bill because they can't amend it; it is either this tax cut or none at all, and they don't want to vote against a tax cut. Thus, for some bills, not only can the House Rules Committee make or break the bill, but it can also influence the bill's final content.

Unlike the House, the Senate generally guarantees all bills an "open rule" by default; thus senators have access to the floor for whatever they want in a way that is denied to representatives. Furthermore, whereas in the House the rule for each bill stipulates how long a member can debate, the Senate's tradition of "unlimited debate" means that a member can talk indefinitely. Senators opposed to a bill can **filibuster** in an effort to tie up the floor of the Senate in nonstop debate to prevent the Senate from voting on a bill.

A filibuster can be stopped only by **cloture**. Cloture, a vote to cut off debate and end a filibuster, requires an extraordinary three-fifths majority, or sixty votes. A dramatic example of a filibuster occurred when southern senators attempted to derail Minnesota senator Hubert Humphrey's efforts to pass the Civil Rights Act of 1964. First, they filibustered Humphrey's attempt to bypass the Judiciary Committee, whose chair, a southern Democrat, opposed the bill. This was known as the "minibuster" and it stopped Senate business for sixteen days.[57] It was considered "mini" because from March 30 to June 30, 1964, these same southern Democrats filibustered the Civil Rights Act and created a twenty-week backlog of legislation.[58] Often these senators resorted to reading the telephone book in order to adhere to the rules of constant debate. The consequence of a filibuster, as this example suggests, is that a minority in the Senate is able to thwart the will of the majority. Even one single senator can halt action on a bill by placing a hold on the legislation, notifying the majority party's leadership that he or she plans to filibuster the bill. That threat alone often keeps the leadership from going forward with the legislation.[59] Recent congressional sessions have seen a striking increase in the use of the filibuster. Rarely used until the 1960s, when southern Democrats unpacked it to derail civil rights legislation, it has become increasingly popular, with Congresses now averaging around forty attempts at cloture. Only about a third of these have been successful in mustering the necessary sixty votes, so a minority has prevailed over the majority most of the time. The use of the filibuster is considered hardball politics; its greater use in the past fifteen to twenty years reflects the growing party polarization we discussed earlier.

filibuster a practice of unlimited debate in the Senate in order to prevent or delay a vote on a bill

cloture a vote to end a Senate filibuster; requires a three-fifths majority, or sixty votes

The filibuster is not in the Constitution and can be gotten around by legislative maneuvering. After months of being lobbied by members of his party, then–Senate majority leader Harry Reid was ready to pull the trigger on the so-called **nuclear option** to bypass the filibuster.[60] The nuclear option Reid crafted was not designed to do away with the filibuster entirely—he didn't have enough Democratic votes for that. The minority would still retain a veto over legislation and Supreme Court nominees. But for appointments to head up the federal bureaucracy or to fill the vacancies on the lower courts that were resulting in judicial bottlenecks, a simple majority would suffice.

Republicans were furious, calling Reid's move a "power grab" and warning Democrats that when they retook the Senate they would do away with the filibuster for everything, legislation and Supreme Court nominees as well, making the Democrats sorry they had ever thought to change the rules. Said Mitch McConnell, soon to be the majority leader again himself, "I say to my friends on the other side of the aisle: you'll regret this. And you may regret it a lot sooner than you think."[61] Indeed, after McConnell refused to hold hearings for President Obama's Supreme Court nominee, Merrick Garland, he didn't have a filibuster-proof majority to get Donald Trump's nominee, Neil Gorsuch, approved, so he extended the nuclear option to Supreme Court nominees as well.

In the highly charged partisan atmosphere of the U.S. Senate today, use of the filibuster and the consequent cloture motions have become business as usual with little prospect for change.[62] Now that the nuclear option has been used, we can probably expect to see an increase in its use, especially for votes the majority party considers crucial to the running of the government.

Because the legislative process is so difficult and allows so many interests to weigh in, the bills that emerge frequently can't get majority support because everyone can find some part to object to, because members anticipate a presidential veto, or because of partisan differences. Since the 1980s, congressional leaders have dealt with the logjam of bills by packaging them together in what is usually called **omnibus legislation**, a large bill that contains so many important elements, including the money necessary to fund the government, that members can't afford to defeat it and the president can't afford to veto it, even if the bill contains elements they dislike. This "unorthodox lawmaking"[63] has become the norm for most of the budget and many other difficult-to-pass bills. The result is that (1) more power has been concentrated in the party leadership, (2) the White House is more involved than was traditionally the case, and (3) the traditional power of standing committees has waned as they are more frequently bypassed or overridden as the leadership moves legislation along. The overly large bills that sometimes result go unread by some members and are criticized by outsiders as an abuse of the legislative process. The public, as we have seen, finds the entire process a turn-off. It is, nevertheless, an important mechanism that Congress has developed to pass needed legislation and to keep the government running.

A BILL BECOMES A LAW A bill must survive a number of challenges to get out of Congress alive. A bill can be killed, or just left to die, in a subcommittee, the full committee, the House Rules Committee, or any of the corresponding committees in the Senate. And, of course, it has to pass votes on the floors of both houses.

There are multiple ways for the House of Representatives to vote, including a simple voice vote ("all in favor say 'aye'"), but most important legislation requires each member to explicitly vote "yea" or "nay" in what are called **roll call votes**. These are a matter of public record and

nuclear option
a controversial Senate maneuver by which a simple majority can decide to allow a majority to bypass the filibuster for certain kinds of votes

omnibus legislation
a large bill that contains so many important elements that members can't afford to defeat it and the president can't afford to veto it, even if the bill contains elements they dislike

roll call votes publicly recorded votes on bills and amendments on the floor of the House or the Senate are monitored by the media, interest groups, and sometimes even constituents. A variety of influences come to bear on the senator or member of Congress as he or she decides how to vote. Studies have long shown that party affiliation is the most important factor in determining roll call voting, but constituency also plays a big role, as does presidential politics. Busy representatives often take cues from other members whom they respect and with whom they generally agree.[64] They also consult with their staff, some of whom may be very knowledgeable about certain legislation. Finally, interest groups have an effect on how a member of Congress votes, but studies suggest that their impact is much less than we usually imagine. Lobbying and campaign contributions buy access to members so that the lobbyists can try to make their case, but they do not actually buy votes.[65] The congressperson or senator who is committed to passing or defeating a particular bill cannot do so alone, however, and he or she looks to find like-minded members for political support. Once a representative or senator knows where he or she stands on a bill, the fate of that bill can be influenced by a variety of methods, many of them effective long before the floor vote takes place. Congressional politics—using the rules to get what one wants— can entail many complex strategies, including controlling the agenda (whether a bill ever reaches the floor), proposing amendments to a bill, influencing its timing, and forming coalitions with other members to pass or block a bill. Knowing how to use the rules makes a huge difference in congressional politics.

Does it matter that Americans dislike Congress so much? Why?

If a bill emerges from the roll call process in both houses relatively intact, it goes to the president, unless the chambers passed different versions. If the bills differ, then the two versions go to a conference committee made up of members of both houses, usually the senior members of the standing committees that reported the bills. If the conferees can reach an agreement on a revision, then the revised bill goes back to each house to be voted up or down; no amendments are permitted at this point. If the bill is rejected, that chamber sends it back to the conference committee for a second try.

Finally, any bill still alive at this point moves to the president's desk. The president has several choices of action. The simplest choice is to sign the bill, in which case it becomes law. If the president doesn't like it, however, he can veto it. In that case, the president sends it back to the originating house of Congress with a short explanation of what he does not like about the bill. Congress can then attempt a **veto override**, which requires a two-thirds vote of both houses. Because the president can usually count on the support of *at least* one-third of *one* of the houses, the veto is a powerful negative tool. It is hard for Congress to accomplish legislative goals that the president opposes. They can, however, bundle policies together so that the bill that arrives on the president's desk contains elements that he would typically want to veto, along with legislation that is very hard to turn down.

The president can also kill a bill with the **pocket veto**, which occurs when Congress sends a bill to the president within ten days of the end of a session and the president does not sign it. The bill fails simply because Congress is not in session to consider a veto override. The president might choose this option when he wants to veto a bill without drawing much public attention to it. Similarly, the president can do nothing, and if Congress remains in session, a bill will automatically become law in ten days, excluding Sundays. This seldom-used option signals presidential dislike for a bill but not enough dislike to use the veto power.

The striking aspect of our legislative process is how many factors have to fall into place for a bill to become law. At every step there are ways to kill bills, and a well-organized group of members in the relatively decentralized Congress has a good chance, in most cases, of

veto override reversal of a presidential veto by a two-thirds vote in both houses of Congress

pocket veto presidential authority to kill a bill submitted within ten days of the end of a legislative session by not signing it

blocking a bill to which these members strongly object. In terms of procedures, Congress is better set up to ensure that bills do not impinge on organized interests than it is to facilitate coherent, well-coordinated attacks on the nation's problems. Once again, we see the tensions among representation, effective lawmaking, and partisanship.

In Your Own Words   Describe the process of congressional policymaking.

CITIZENSHIP AND CONGRESS
Public frustration with a slow-moving institution

Since 1974, periodic Gallup polls have shown that from half to less than a third of the public "approves of the way Congress is handling its job," with levels of approval dipping below 10 percent in 2014, although it recovered slightly afterward. Part of the blame may be attributed to a general decline in respect for societal institutions ranging from government to organized religion to the media.[66] However, the intense partisanship of the contemporary Congress and its repeated legislative crises as the parties are unable to compromise is no doubt a major contributor to our generally low regard for the institution.

At least four factors help to explain why citizens are not always very happy with Congress. First, some candidates encourage a negative image of the institution they want to join—running for Congress by running against it, and declaring their intention to fight against special interests, bureaucrats, and the general incompetence of Washington.[67] We saw this in 2016, evidenced by the fact that Donald Trump, a man with no government experience, captured the Republican nomination and the presidency. Second, in the post-Watergate wave of investigative reporting, media coverage of Congress has gotten more negative, more continuous, and harder to avoid. Third, since the 1970s, the law requires that information about how much campaigns cost and who contributes to them must be made public, casting a shadow of suspicion on the entire process and raising the concern that congressional influence can be bought. Finally, citizens are turned off by what they see as the incessant bickering and partisanship in Congress.[68]

Given the reasons why many Americans are unhappy with Congress, the reforms currently on the agenda are not likely to change their minds. One of the most popular reforms being advocated is term limits. The specific proposals vary, but the intent is to limit the number of terms a member of Congress can serve, usually to somewhere between eight and twelve years. Term limits might work if there were evidence that serving in Congress corrupts good people, but there is no evidence of this at all. It just puts them in the public eye.

Other reforms, however, might make a difference in public support for Congress. Campaign finance reform, for instance, could have a significant impact. Institutional reforms might be able to speed up congressional lawmaking and reduce the need to compromise on details.

Such reforms, however, will probably not fundamentally change how the public feels about Congress. Congress does have the power to act, and when it is unified and sufficiently motivated, it usually does. When Congress reflects a sharply divided society, however, it has a harder time getting things done. It is unable to act *because it is a representative institution*, not because members are inattentive to their districts or in the grip of special interests. Furthermore, Congress has more incentives on a daily basis to be a representative institution than a national lawmaking body. It is important to remember, too, that this is not entirely an accident. It was the founders' intention to create a legislature that would not move hastily or without deliberation. The irony is that the founders' mixed bag of incentives works so well that Congress today often does not move very much at all.

The truth is that democracy is messy. Bickering arises in Congress because members represent many different Americans with varied interests and goals. It has always been this way, and probably always will be. However, it seems worse today because the parties have come to represent warring ideological armies. The rhetoric is coarse, and party activists and outside groups increasingly view bipartisan cooperation as a weakness. It is precisely our bickering, our inefficiency, and the need to compromise—even when it is hard to do—that preserve the freedoms Americans hold dear. It is the nature of our representative government.[69]

We conclude where we began. Congress has the conflicting goals of representing constituents, working together to solve national problems, and operating as members of opposing partisan teams. The practice of congressional politics is fascinating to many close-up observers but looks less appealing to average citizens, watching the nightly news and following political campaigns from afar. It is important to understand that this view of Congress stems as much from the difficulties inherent in the conflicting incentives of the job as from the failings of the people we send to Washington.

In Your Own Words   Discuss the relationship between the people and Congress.

Let's Revisit: What's at Stake...?

We opened this chapter by asking why the constitutional requirement that the Senate provide the president with advice and consent to major appointments had become almost akin to a hostage situation by the middle of 2016. No action was taken on Merrick Garland's nomination, despite the fact that President Obama continued to campaign for him and Hillary Clinton called on the Senate to take action.

But the stakes were high in what amounted to a politically sophisticated game of risk.

For the Republicans, if Justice Scalia's replacement were to be nominated by a Democrat—either President Obama or a future President Clinton—they stood to lose the majority they had held in the Court. For the party base, few things were more important than a justice who could be counted on to vote against reproductive rights and for gun rights and religious freedom. That base put enormous pressure on Senate majority leader Mitch McConnell not to hold hearings, and he could not afford to give in, especially before the election.

In an effort to galvanize that base to hold his own seat and campaign for fellow Republicans up for reelection to the Senate, the late Republican senator John McCain pledged that if voters would just choose Republican candidates, they would block all Supreme Court nominations if Hillary Clinton should win the presidency.[70]

The risk McConnell had to juggle, of course, was that the Republicans would lose their thin Senate majority and that a new majority leader, Democrat Chuck Schumer, would hold hearings on anyone President Hillary Clinton nominated. If the Democrats voted to dispense with the filibuster for Supreme Court nominations—a so-called nuclear option they had employed in the past for other nominations—a far more liberal justice than Merrick Garland might join the Court.

Without knowing the election outcome, Democrats, and particularly President Obama, wanted Garland's nomination confirmed because it would help ensure the continuity of the president's legacy. But Democrats were torn. Progressives thought they might get a far more liberal justice if Hillary Clinton became president, and given that it looked more and more likely that she would, waiting seemed a reasonable bet.

But the likelihood of a Clinton victory and the possibility of a Senate loss had Republicans scrambling to minimize the damage. Sen. Jeff Flake of Arizona, who had staunchly opposed Donald Trump's nomination as president, said he was encouraging his Senate colleagues to go ahead and confirm Garland in the lame-duck session (the remainder of the term before the new congress—and president—were sworn in in January 2017), on the assumption that Garland would be far more acceptable to Republicans that anyone Clinton might nominate. His colleague Senate judiciary chair Chuck Grassley said there would be no lame-duck vote but granted that the Senate would at least have to act on a Clinton nominee. "If that new president happens to be Hillary, we can't just simply stonewall," he said before the election.[71]

In the end, McConnell's risky gambit paid off in a nail-biter of an election outcome. Although Hillary Clinton did indeed win the popular vote, she lost the prize and the Democrats lost the ability to appoint Scalia's replacement. The Senate also lost an important norm of cooperation with the executive branch, making the stakes of future appointments under divided government very high indeed. The absence of norms of bipartisanship and cooperation that John McCain values so highly in the following *CLUES to Critical Thinking* were again apparent when Justice Anthony Kennedy announced his retirement in 2018 (after a good deal of prompting and deal making with the Trump administration about who his replacement would be). Trump nominated Judge Brett Kavanaugh whose hearings seemed to be going well until Dr. Christine Blasey Ford, a Stanford psychologist, came forth with accusations that she had been attacked by Kavanaugh in high school. She believed he had intended to rape her but was too drunk to prevent her escape. Her testimony before Congress was moving and credible—even President Trump said he found it so—but a well-coached Kavanaugh came out swinging, defending his name and essentially calling Blasey Ford a liar. There was no pretense that this was a nonpartisan hearing. A crucial Kavanaugh vote, Republican Senator Jeff Flake, on the brink of retirement, said he would not vote for confirmation until an investigation had been completed. The White House-controlled investigation proved to be a farce (neither Blasey Ford nor Kavanaugh was interviewed) but the Republicans declared themselves satisfied and confirmed Kavanaugh on a near party-line vote.

The Kavanaugh hearings were reminiscent of the 1991 Clarence Thomas hearings in which law professor Anita Hill accused Thomas of sexual harassment when she had worked for him. Again, the accusations were credible enough to be investigated but were not and Thomas was confirmed after what he called a "high tech lynching." In both cases the men portrayed themselves as the victims and the Senate bought their stories and confirmed them. In both cases, like the case of Merrick Garland, partisan politics defined the stakes for advice and consent.

Want a better grade?

Get the tools you need to sharpen your study skills. **SAGE edge** offers practice quizzes, eFlashcards, video, and multimedia at **edge.sagepub.com/barbourbrief8e.**

Review

Understanding Congress

Members of Congress are responsible for both **representation** (186) and **national lawmaking** (186), both of which must take place within the constraints of **partisanship** (187). These two duties are often at odds because what is good for a local **constituency** (187) may not be beneficial for the country as a whole, and partisanship requires that members also consider what is best for their party. In an era of **hyperpartisanship** (188), which can cause increased **party polarization** (188), it can become hard to find common ground on which to craft solutions to national problems.

Representation style takes four forms—**policy representation** (187), **allocative representation** (187) (including the infamous **pork barrel** [187] spending), **casework** (187), and **symbolic representation** (187)—and congresspersons attempt to excel at all four. However, since the legislative process designed by the founders is meant to be very slow, representatives have fewer incentives to concentrate on national lawmaking when reelection interests, and therefore local interests, are more pressing.

Congressional Powers and Responsibilities

The founders created our government with a structure of checks and balances centered around our **bicameral legislature** (191). Not only do the two houses check each other, but Congress can check the other two branches, including the prerogative of **congressional oversight** (193) and the power to give **advice and consent** (194) to the president, which allows Congress to keep tabs on the executive, and the House and the Senate to be checked by either the president or the courts. Congress can be very powerful but must demonstrate unusual strength and consensus to override presidential vetoes and to amend the Constitution.

Congressional Elections

Citizens and representatives interact in congressional elections. Seats are allocated among states through the process of **reapportionment** (196), and the districts are drawn up through **redistricting** (196) to correct for malapportionment. **Gerrymandering** (196)—especially **partisan gerrymandering** (196) and **racial gerrymandering** (196)—makes redistricting a highly political process. Congressional races can be influenced, among other things, by the powerful **incumbency advantage** (199), the presidential **coattail effect** (199), and the phenomenon of the **midterm loss** (199).

Congressional Organization

Congress is organized by the political parties. The **majority party** (202) in each house has considerable power because it selects the leadership positions, including the **Speaker of the House** (203), filled by the party caucuses. The business of Congress—crafting legislation and engaging in oversight—is done in committees where the leadership is determined by party leaders and by the **seniority system** (203). **Standing committees** (207), including the powerful **House Rules Committee** (207), do most of the work, although **select committees** (208), **joint committees** (208), and **conference committees** (208) are key as well.

How Congress Works

Laws get placed on the **legislative agenda** (211) in a variety of ways, often through the efforts of **policy entrepreneurship** (214). They go first to committee before being reported onto the floor, where they are discussed, debated, and subject to a **roll call vote** (216). In the Senate, the **filibuster** (215) can prevent a vote unless **cloture** (215) is obtained or, in rare cases, the **nuclear option** (216) is invoked. Often, the only way consensus can be found is to bundle things everyone likes and dislikes together in **omnibus legislation** (216). When the bill emerges from Congress it goes to the president, who can sign it or veto it (or kill it with the less public **pocket veto** [217]), subject to a **veto override** (217) by both houses.

Olivier Douliery-Pool/Getty Images

7

The Presidency

In Your Own Words

After you've read this chapter, you will be able to

7.1 Explain what the president's job entails.

7.2 Compare the modern presidency with the founders' expectations for a limited executive.

7.3 Identify strategies and tools that presidents employ to overcome the constitutional limitations of the office.

7.4 Describe the organization and functions of the executive office.

7.5 Evaluate the importance of leadership style and image as they relate to presidential power.

7.6 Describe how public opinion affects the relationship between citizens and the president.

What's at Stake . . .
in Donald Trump's Presidency?

President Donald J. Trump. You may love him. You may hate him. But you can't ignore him.

A polarizing political figure who has taken Washington by storm, he is the elephant in the country's classrooms (and textbooks). With students split between supporters and detractors, every discussion is a potential minefield. It would be easy to talk about nothing but Trump. Imagine your political science instructors turned into cable news hosts. It would be hair-on-fire education in an era of hair-on-fire politics; every tweet a crisis that consumes a class. Exciting for you, maybe, but it would leave very little time for more conventional details like how a bill becomes a law. Yet the alternative—dodging the tweets, the scandals, the media distractions, the next big news, and generally ignoring the elephant—would be to risk normalizing a moment in American politics that is, frankly, not normal at all.

So let us take another route, douse our hair with a fire hose and take a giant step back from the adrenalin-fueled politics to look closely at the political, media, and entertainment phenomenon that is Donald Trump. The fact that he is such a huge and divisive figure in American politics today suggests that he has tapped into the American psyche in ways that say a lot about who we are and where we might be going as a country. We would be smart to unpack this presidency and figure out what its stakes are for us going forward.

Consider: With no background in politics, Donald Trump cleared a field of more than a dozen establishment Republican candidates to get the nomination. The consummate entertainer, he left no air for the other candidates, who struggled to get out from under whatever childish but searingly effective nickname he had saddled them with. After a scorched earth campaign against Democrat Hillary Clinton, he won the Electoral College vote but failed to gain a majority of the popular vote by three million. Still, 30 percent of Americans stand by him no matter what. As he once said, he could "stand in the middle of Fifth Avenue and shoot somebody" without losing support. That may be one of the few things he hasn't actually tried.

He came into office not only a reality TV host but a businessman, who learned his craft in the anything-goes world of New York real estate. He takes deals where he finds them and has carefully shielded his financial dealings from public scrutiny. He blows through long-established norms—not revealing his tax returns, hiring his own children, and profiting off government use of his many properties, for instance. His administration has not vetted his appointments carefully and has left many positions unfilled. The turnover in the White House is unprecedented. His preferred management style is chaotic; he likes to pit employees against each other and revels in the competition for his approval. When he upsets a political apple cart by pulling out of a treaty, pardoning a renegade sheriff, threatening to veto a bill his party passed, making a comment that is ambiguous enough that many Americans are certain it is sexist or racist, or just tweeting something unexpected that throws his staff off their stride, he is happy. People say he can be charming in person and that he just really, really wants to be liked. When people don't like him, he becomes angry and is quick to "fight back" or to call bad news "fake."

To supporters, he is a breath of fresh air, a much needed kick in the pants to elites whose power is entrenched and whose interests seem miles away from theirs. They applaud what they hear as an authentic voice willing to bust through the constraints of political correctness, and for whom no sentiment is too outrageous to say out loud. When he claims victimhood, it echoes the victimhood they feel too, from the elites that look down on them, the government that ignores them, and a future that doesn't seem to have a place for them. When Trump rocks the boat and the elite (but especially the liberal elite) start talking about the threat to democracy, they cheer him on. They wanted change, and, boy, is he ever change!

To his detractors, he is a narcissistic attention-hungry scam artist who got lucky in a presidential election he never seriously thought he would win. Without any background in politics or commitment to democratic values, he endangers the system he finds himself leading by breaking rules that are needed for the long-term health of democracy. His detractors may be Democrats or Republicans—what they have in common is a devotion to constitutional norms that many suspect he does not care much about. Whether they like the status quo or not, they want to see it changed by democratic means, not by blowing it up.

It is probably not possible to say definitively which of these groups is right or wrong—they live in different media worlds, make decisions based on different perceptions of reality and, for the most part, think the other is crazy. Americans have not seen a leader like President Trump before. Just what is at stake in such an unusual presidency?[1]

AS the American narrative has it, and indeed as much of the world would agree, the most powerful person on the planet is the president of the United States. He is the elected leader of the nation that has one of the most powerful economies, one of the greatest military forces, and the longest-running representative government the world has ever seen. Media coverage enforces this narrative; the networks and news services all have full-time reporters assigned to the White House. The 24-hour news cycle keeps us posted on what presidents do every day, even if they only went to church or played a round of golf, and the White House helps feed and control the narrative with a web site, Facebook page, Twitter account, and other social media connections. Today, with the president's own direct media presence and all the public reaction to it, the centrality of the presidency to the nation's political narrative is what one scholar calls the presidency's "monopolization of the public space."[2] In a perfect storm of telegenic personality and social media potential, that has never been more true than it has in the Trump years.

Typically, when anything of significance happens, whether it is a school shooting, a foreign terrorist attack, a natural disaster, or a big drop in the stock market, we, and the media, look to the president to solve our problems and to represent the nation in our times of struggle, tragedy, and triumph. The irony is that the U.S. Constitution provides for a relatively weak chief executive, and one whose job encompasses two roles—head of government and head of state—so often at loggerheads that most countries separate them into two distinct jobs handled by different people. The American public's and, indeed, the world's high expectations of the office constitute a major challenge for modern presidents. That, along with the need to cooperate with the other two branches with whom they share power and the extensive executive branch that they oversee, makes the job of being president a prestigious one but one that is difficult to do well.

THE PRESIDENTIAL JOB DESCRIPTION
The founders' notion of a limited executive

Since the legislature was presumed by all to be the real engine of the national political system, the presidency was not a preoccupation of the framers when they met in Philadelphia in 1787. The breakdown of the national government under the Articles of Confederation, however, demonstrated the need for some form of a central executive. Nervous about trusting the general public to choose the executive, the founders provided for an Electoral College, a group of people who would be chosen by the states for the sole purpose of electing the president. The assumption was that this body would be made up of leading citizens who would exercise care and good judgment in casting their ballots and who would not make postelection claims on him. Because of their experience with King George III, the founders also wished to avoid the concentration of power that a strong executive could abuse.

Although the majority's concept of a limited executive is enshrined in the Constitution, many of the arguments we hear today for a stronger executive were foreshadowed by the case that Alexander Hamilton made in *Federalist* No. 70 for a more "energetic" president. We can see much of this tension play out in the fact that the job of the presidency combines two very different roles: the more symbolic head of state and the more energetic head of government.

HEAD OF STATE VS. HEAD OF GOVERNMENT

The founders who pictured a more limited executive probably had in mind something of a figurehead, someone who would sit at the top of the then-very-small executive branch, command the armed forces, and represent the nation. This role is known as the **head of state**—the symbol of the hopes and dreams of a people, responsible for enhancing national unity by representing that which is common and good in the nation. In many countries this is an apolitical role, so the head of state is not seen as a divisive figure—in Great Britain it is the queen. That the founders wanted the presidency to carry the dignity, if not the power, of a monarch is evident in George Washington's wish that the president might bear the title "His High Mightiness, the President of the United States and the Protector of Their Liberties."[3]

Americans were not ready for such a pompous title, but we nevertheless do put presidents, as the embodiment of the nation, on a higher plane than other politicians. Consequently, the American president's job includes a ceremonial role for activities like greeting other heads of state, attending state funerals, tossing out the first baseball of the season, and consoling survivors of national tragedies. The vice president can relieve the president of some of these responsibilities, but there are times when only the president's presence will do.

Our system of checks and balances, however, gives the president real political powers, which are intended to help keep the other branches in check. So presidents also serve as the **head of government**, in which capacity they are supposed to run the government, make law, and function as the head of a political party. These functions will result in some citizens winning more than others, some losing, and some becoming angry—all of which works against the unifying image of the head of state. In Great Britain, as in many other countries, the head-of-government role is given to the prime minister, who not only can be political but, as the official head of a

head of state the apolitical, unifying role of the president as symbolic representative of the whole country

head of government the political role of the president as leader of a political party and chief arbiter of who gets what resources

Head of Government, Head of State

The presidency is one office, but the president plays two roles. When President Obama signed his signature health care reform bill, he was leading on a potentially controversial government policy complete with arm twisting and ample use of the bully pulpit—the quintessential head of government. When President Bush visited Ground Zero after September 11, spoke to first responders via bullhorn, and reached out to console them individually, his goal was to unify us and speak for the nation as head of state.

party in charge, is expected to be. In fact, the prime minister is a much more powerful executive position than the president of the United States, even though the president's political roles have expanded far beyond the founders' intentions since Franklin Roosevelt's New Deal. Nonetheless, the president is expected to execute the laws, to make government work. When things go well, no one thinks much about it. But when things go wrong, the president is held accountable, even for things that are outside his control. Reflecting this idea, President Harry Truman kept a sign on his desk that read "The Buck Stops Here."

We explore the rest of the president's powers in greater detail later in this chapter. What is important for our purposes here is that all these roles place the president in an inherently and unavoidably contradictory position. On the one hand, presidents are the symbol of the nation, representing all the people (head of state); on the other hand, they have to take the lead in politics that are inherently divisive (head of government). Thus the political requirements of presidents' role as head of government necessarily undermine their unifying role as head of state.

The hyperpartisanship that has infected the U.S. Congress in recent years makes it even more difficult for the president to bridge these conflicting roles. The distinction depends on our ability as a nation to insist on respect for the office even when we disagree with the specific views or actions of the person holding it. When politics leads us to move from criticizing the policies of the president to insulting the office, it is more difficult for the president to act as a unifying figure when necessary.

QUALIFICATIONS AND CONDITIONS OF OFFICE

The framers' conception of a limited presidency can be seen in the brief attention the office receives in the Constitution. Article II is short and not very precise. It provides some basic details on the office:

- The president is chosen by the Electoral College to serve four-year terms. The number of terms was unlimited until 1951, when, in reaction to Franklin Roosevelt's unprecedented four terms in office, the Constitution was amended to limit the president to two terms.

- The president must be a natural-born citizen of the United States, at least thirty-five years old, and a resident for at least fourteen years.
- The president is succeeded by the vice president if he dies or is removed from office. The Constitution does not specify who becomes president in the event that the vice president, too, is unable to serve, but in 1947 Congress passed the Presidential Succession Act, which establishes the order of succession after the vice president: Speaker of the House, president pro tempore of the Senate, and the cabinet secretaries in the order in which their offices were established.
- The president can be removed from office by impeachment and conviction by the House of Representatives and the Senate for "Treason, Bribery, or other high Crimes and Misdemeanors." The process of removal involves two steps: First, after an in-depth investigation, the House votes to impeach by a simple majority vote, which charges the president with a crime. Second, the Senate tries the president on the articles of impeachment and can convict by a two-thirds majority vote.

Only two American presidents, Andrew Johnson and Bill Clinton, have been impeached (in 1868 and 1998, respectively), but neither was convicted. The power of impeachment is meant to be a check on the president, but it is most often threatened for partisan purposes. Impeachment resolutions were filed against Ronald Reagan (over the invasion of Grenada and the Iran-contra affair), George H. W. Bush (over Iran-contra), and George W. Bush (for a host of offenses ranging from falsifying evidence justifying the war in Iraq to failing to respond adequately to Hurricane Katrina). Republicans called for President Obama's impeachment for causes ranging from supposedly lacking a birth certificate; to covering up what the administration knew about the terrorist attack on the U.S. diplomatic compound in Benghazi, Libya; to trading Taliban combatants for captive U.S. soldier Bowe Bergdahl; to taking executive actions regarding, among other things, EPA regulations on power plants.[4]

Although some Democrats have called for Trump's impeachment, it is not a popular stance in the party, which would rather let Robert Mueller do his job and, now that they are in the House majority, conduct their own oversight of Trump's actions. There are more ways to provide checks and balances than impeachment, and as the Clinton years taught us, impeachments can be expensive, time consuming, and punishing for the party that conducts them. Few of the impeachment resolutions over the years have made it to the floor for a vote in the House, in part because such actions bring governing virtually to a halt and are not popular with the public.[5]

THE CONSTITUTIONAL POWERS OF THE PRESIDENT

The Constitution uses vague language to discuss some presidential powers and is silent on the range and limits of others. It is precisely this ambiguity that allowed the Constitution to be ratified by both those who wanted a strong executive power and those who did not. In addition, this vagueness has allowed the powers of the president to expand over time without constitutional amendment. We can think of the president's constitutional powers as falling into three areas: executive authority to administer government, and legislative and judicial power to check the other two branches.

impeachment the process used to charge, try, and remove public officials for misconduct while in office

EXECUTIVE POWERS Article II, Section 1, of the Constitution begins, "The executive power shall be vested in a president of the United States of America." However, the document does not explain exactly what "executive power" entails, and scholars and presidents through much of our history have debated the extent of these powers.[6] Section 3 states the president "shall take care that the laws be faithfully executed." Herein lies much of the executive authority; the president is the chief administrator of the nation's laws. This means that the president is the chief executive officer of the country, the person who, more than anyone else, is held responsible for agencies of the national government and the implementation of national policy.

The Constitution also specifies that the president, with the approval of the majority of the Senate, will appoint the heads of departments, who will oversee the work of implementation. These heads, who have come to be known collectively as the cabinet, report to the president. Today presidents are responsible for the appointments of more than four thousand federal employees: cabinet and lower administrative officers, federal judges, military officers, and members of the diplomatic corps. These responsibilities place the president at the top of a vast federal bureaucracy. But the president's control of the federal bureaucracy is limited because, even though presidents can make a large number of appointments, they are not able to fire many of the people they hire.

Other constitutional powers place the president, as commander-in-chief, at the head of the command structure for the entire military establishment. The Constitution gives Congress the power to declare war, but as the commander-in-chief, the president has the practical ability to wage war. These two powers, meant to check each other, instead provide for a battleground on which Congress and the president struggle for the power to control military operations. Congress passed the War Powers Act of 1973 after the controversial Vietnam War, which was waged by Presidents Lyndon Johnson and Richard Nixon but never officially declared by Congress. The act was intended to limit the president's power to send troops abroad without congressional approval. Most presidents have ignored the act, however, when they wished to engage in military action abroad, and since public opinion tends to rally around the president at such times, Congress has declined to challenge popular presidential actions. The War Powers Act remains more powerful on paper than in reality.

Finally, the president's executive powers include the role of chief foreign policy maker. This role is not spelled out in the Constitution, but the foundation for it is laid in the provision that the president negotiates treaties—formal international agreements with other nations— with the approval of two-thirds of the Senate. The president also appoints ambassadors and receives ambassadors of other nations, a power that essentially amounts to determining what nations the United States will recognize.

Although the requirement of Senate approval for treaties is meant to check the president's foreign policy power, much of U.S. foreign policy is made by the president through executive agreements with other heads of state, which avoids the slower and more cumbersome route of treaty-making.[7] Executive agreements are used much more frequently; over 10,000 have been executed since 1970, compared to fewer than 1,000 treaties.[8] This heavy reliance on executive agreements gives the president considerable power and flexibility in foreign policy. However, even though the executive agreement is a useful and much-used tool, Congress may still thwart the president's intentions by refusing to approve the funds needed to put an agreement into action.

LEGISLATIVE POWERS Even though the president is the head of the executive branch of government, the Constitution also gives the president some legislative power to check Congress, directing that the holder of the office "shall from time to time give to the Congress information of the state of the union, and recommend to their consideration such measures

chief administrator the president's executive role as the head of federal agencies and the person responsible for the implementation of national policy

cabinet a presidential advisory group selected by the president, made up of the vice president, the heads of the federal executive departments, and other high officials to whom the president elects to give cabinet status

commander-in-chief the president's role as the top officer of the country's military establishment

chief foreign policy maker the president's executive role as the primary shaper of relations with other nations

treaties formal agreements with other countries; negotiated by the president and requiring approval by two-thirds of the Senate

executive agreement a presidential arrangement with another country that creates foreign policy without the need for Senate approval

as he shall judge necessary and expedient." Although the framers' vision of this activity was quite limited, today the president's **State of the Union address**, delivered before the full Congress every January, is a major statement of the president's policy agenda. In this chapter's *The Big Picture* you can see "wordle" images for key State of the Union addresses from different presidents. Notice how this form of rendering the speech allows you to compare the issues that were important to each administration.

The Constitution gives the president the nominal power to convene Congress and, when there is a dispute about when to disband, to adjourn it as well. Before Congress met regularly, this power, though limited, actually meant something. Today we rarely see it invoked. Some executives, such as British prime ministers who can dissolve Parliament and call new elections, have a much more formidable convening power than that available to the U.S. president.

The principal legislative power given the president by the Constitution is the **presidential veto**. A president who objects to a bill passed by the House and the Senate can veto it, sending it back to Congress with a message indicating the reasons. Congress can override a veto with a two-thirds vote in each house, but because mustering the two-thirds support is quite difficult, the presidential veto is a substantial power. Even the threat of a presidential veto can have a major impact on getting congressional legislation to fall in line with the administration's preferences.[9] As can be seen in the first column of figures in Table 7.1, the number of vetoes has varied a great deal from one president to the next. Most of the time, presidents are successful in having the vetoes sustained. The least successful was President George W. Bush. Although he joined John Quincy Adams and Thomas Jefferson as the only presidents who did not veto a bill during their first terms,[10] following the 2006 midterm elections, Bush vetoed dozens of the new Democratic majority's bills. These were overridden at a record rate that can be explained partially by Bush's falling popularity and by public disenchantment with the war in Iraq so that the Democrats in Congress had little concern about their challenging an unpopular president.

Congress has regularly sought to get around the obstacle of presidential vetoes by packaging a number of items together in a bill. Traditionally, presidents have had to sign a complete bill or reject the whole thing. Thus, for example, Congress regularly adds such things as a building project or a tax break for a state industry to, say, a military appropriations bill that the president wants. Often presidents calculate that it is best to accept such add-ons, even if they think them unjustified or wasteful, in order to get passed what they judge to be important legislation.

Another of the president's key legislative powers comes from the vice president's role as presiding officer of the Senate. Although the vice president rarely actually presides over the Senate, Article I, Section 3, says that the vice president may cast a tie-breaking vote when the 100-member Senate is evenly divided. The fact that the president can count on the vice president to break a tie when the Senate is split over controversial legislation is an often underappreciated legislative power. Vice President Mike Pence broke six ties his first year in office—more than any previous vice president in a single year—and continued at a good clip his second year.

Although the Constitution does not grant the president the power to make law, the power to do so has grown over time and now is generally accepted. Presidents can issue **executive orders**, which are supposed to clarify how laws passed by Congress are to be implemented by specific agencies (not to be confused with the executive agreements they can make with other nations). Some of the most significant presidential actions have come from executive orders, including President Franklin Roosevelt's order to hold Japanese Americans in internment

State of the Union address a speech given annually by the president to a joint session of Congress and to the nation announcing the president's agenda

presidential veto a president's authority to reject a bill passed by Congress; may be overridden only by a two-thirds majority in each house

executive orders clarifications of congressional policy issued by the president and having the full force of law

TABLE 7.1

Presidential Vetoes, Roosevelt to Trump

YEARS	PRESIDENT	TOTAL VETOES	REGULAR VETOES	POCKET VETOES	VETOES OVERRIDDEN	VETO SUCCESS RATE
1933–1945	Franklin Roosevelt	635	372	263	9	97.6%
1945–1953	Harry Truman	250	180	70	12	93.3
1953–1961	Dwight Eisenhower	181	73	108	2	97.3
1961–1963	John F. Kennedy	21	12	9	0	100.0
1963–1969	Lyndon Johnson	30	16	14	0	100.0
1969–1974	Richard Nixon	43	26	17	7	73.1
1974–1977	Gerald Ford	66	48	18	12	75.0
1977–1981	Jimmy Carter	31	13	18	2	84.6
1981–1989	Ronald Reagan	78	39	39	9	76.9
1989–1993	George H. W. Bush	46	29	17*	1	96.6
1993–2001	Bill Clinton	37	36	1	2	96.4
2001–2009	George W. Bush	12	11	1	4	66.7
2009–2017	Barack Obama	12	12	0	1	91.7
2017–2018	Donald J. Trump	0	0	0	0	–

Source: "Summary of Bills Vetoed, 1789–Present," www.senate.gov/reference/Legislation/Vetoes/vetoCounts.htm.

*Although they are counted here, Congress did not recognize two of Bush's pocket vetoes and considered the legislation enacted.

camps during World War II, President Truman's order that black and white military troops be integrated, President Kennedy's and President Johnson's affirmative action programs, and many of the post–September 11 security measures.

Frustrated by the partisan divide in Congress and unable to get much beyond absolute emergency legislation through the Republican-controlled House of Representatives following the 2010 elections, President Obama launched a conscious and explicit program to expand the use of executive orders and other executive authority, under a campaign labeled "We Can't Wait." Obama's executive orders ranged from an order to the Justice Department to stop defending the Defense of Marriage Act, which bars federal recognition of same-sex marriages, to a directive that immigration authorities not focus resources on deporting undocumented workers who were brought to the United States as children, to significant steps to deal with climate change through new rules on greenhouse gas emissions.[11] While this aggressive use of presidential power was a reversal of Obama's stand as a U.S. senator and his presidential

THE BIG PICTURE
How Presidents Talk to the Nation

Visualizing the State of the Union

GEORGE WASHINGTON (1790)

Just after his inauguration, the first American president carefully shepherds the new nation over rocky terrain.

ABRAHAM LINCOLN (1862)

In the second year of the Civil War, the president who hadn't been able to save the Union tries to hold the remnants of his country together.

FRANKLIN D. ROOSEVELT (1944)

The year before he died, the president who saw the country through the Great Depression and into World War II reassures and encourages Americans to hold the course.

JOHN F. KENNEDY (1962)

In the middle of his short time in office, the first president born in the 20th century faces new challenges.

New Technology and New Ways to Talk to the Nation

First presidential public address (1789)

First presidential press conference (1913)

First presidential radio address (1923)

Fireside Chats (1933–44)

First televised presidential speech (1947)

First presidential whistlestop tour (1948)

LYNDON B. JOHNSON (1965)

In the first year of his own term, the president who came to office because of the murder of another seeks to raise the spirits of a nation and secure his legacy.

RONALD REAGAN (1985)

After a landslide reelection, the president who became a conservative icon lays out his agenda for his second term.

GEORGE W. BUSH (2002)

The year after 9/11, the president who had come to office objecting to nation building rallies the country for war.

DONALD TRUMP (2018)

The president's speech was a nod to a possible "new America moment" and focused on jobs, the economy, infrastructure, immigration, trade, and national security.

First televised presidential debate (1960)

First televised State of the Union (1965)

First White House web site (1994)

First presidential Facebook page (2009)

First presidential tweet (2010)

"In order to reduce the deficit, what costs would you cut and what investments would you keep? BO."

First live streamed debate (2012)

behavior his first two years in office, it was, for some experts, what we should expect: "This is what presidents do. . . . It's taken Obama two years to get there, but this has happened throughout history. You can't be in that office with all its enormous responsibilities—when things don't happen, you get blamed for it—and not exercise all the powers that have accrued to it over time."[12]

With some exceptions (notably President Obama), executive orders tend to be released at a higher rate at the beginning of a president's term as the president immediately implements key policies and at the end of the term as the president tries to leave a legacy.[13] Indeed, presidents often release particularly symbolic executive orders on their first days in office. Since executive orders are not Congress-made laws, new presidents can reverse any of their predecessors' orders.[14] Donald Trump has been especially zealous in undoing as many of his predecessor's executive actions as possible.

JUDICIAL POWERS Presidents can have tremendous long-term impact on the judiciary, but in the short run their powers over the courts are meager. Their continuing impact comes from nominating judges to the federal courts, including the Supreme Court. The political philosophies of individual judges influence significantly how they interpret the law, and this is especially important for Supreme Court justices, who are the final arbiters of constitutional meaning. Since judges serve for life, presidential appointments have a long-lasting effect. For instance, today's Supreme Court is considered to be distinctly more conservative than its immediate predecessors, due to the appointments made by Presidents Reagan and Bush in the 1980s and early 1990s. Moreover, President Reagan is credited by many with having ushered in a "judicial revolution." He, together with his successor, George H. W. Bush, appointed 550 of the 837 federal judges, most of them conservatives. Bill Clinton appointed moderates to the courts, angering many Democrats, who felt that his appointees should have been more liberal. President George W. Bush revived the conservative trend that was halted under Clinton.[15] Although President Obama's pick of Sonia Sotomayor for the Supreme Court pleased liberals, his nomination of Elena Kagan caused some observers to worry that his selections would follow Clinton's more moderate record.[16] His final nomination, Judge Merrick Garland, also was a more moderate choice, but this was partly in the hopes of encouraging the Republican-led Senate to give him a hearing, which never happened. In general, Obama's choices for the judiciary were fairly liberal. Many of the appointments he made were blocked by Republicans in the Senate, however, and their refusal to recognize his final Supreme Court nominee with hearings was an unprecedented denial of power to shape the Court.[17] Obama's nominations, however, produced a more diverse federal judiciary: he nominated more women, Asians, and Hispanics than any previous president as well as twelve openly gay federal judges and the first-ever Native American female judge in the country's history.[18] President Trump's picks for the courts, beginning with his selection of Neil Gorsuch for the Supreme Court position that had been Obama's to fill, and his choice of Brett Kavanaugh to replace retiring Justice Kennedy, have been consistently conservative. He has appointed people to the federal bench quickly, and the Senate has as quickly approved them now that there is no filibuster to hold up such votes. As of March 2018, Trump's eighty-seven nominations to the courts have been overwhelmingly white (92 percent) and male (77 percent).[19]

The presidential power to appoint is limited to an extent by the constitutional requirement for Senate approval of federal judges. Traditionally, most nominees have been approved, with occasional exceptions. Sometimes rejection stems from questions about the candidate's competence, but in other instances rejection is based more on style and judicial philosophy. The Democratic-led Senate's rejection of President Reagan's very conservative Supreme Court nominee Robert Bork in 1987 is one of the more controversial cases.[20] Some observers believe that the battle over the Bork nomination signaled the end of deference to presidents and opened up the approval process to endless challenges and partisan bickering.[21] Today the increased party polarization in Congress increases the pressure for the president to put his ideological stamp on the courts. The frequent threat of the filibuster and the use of anonymous holds in the Senate once allowed the party opposing the president to hold up nominations. With both of those tools now gone, it is much easier for a bare majority to have its way in shaping the courts in its partisan image.

A president's choice of judges for the federal district courts can also be limited by the tradition of senatorial courtesy, whereby a senior senator of the president's party or both senators of either party from the state in which the appointees reside have what amounts to a veto power over the president's choice. If presidents should ignore the custom of senatorial courtesy and push a nomination unpopular with one of the home state senators, fellow senators used to refuse to confirm the appointee.[22] In today's era of broken norms, even senatorial courtesy is not a given.

The least controversial way a president can try to influence a court decision is to have the Justice Department invest resources in arguing a case. The third-ranking member of the Justice Department, the solicitor general, is a presidential appointee whose job is to argue cases for the government before the Supreme Court. The solicitor general is thus a bridge between the executive and the judiciary, not only deciding which cases the government will appeal to the Court, but also filing petitions stating the government's (usually the president's) position on cases to which the government is not even a party. The Court takes these petitions, called *amicus curiae* ("friend of the court") briefs, very seriously. The government is successful in its litigation more often than any other litigant, winning over two-thirds of its cases in the past half-century, and often having its arguments cited by the justices themselves in their opinions.[23]

One additional judicial power granted to the president by the Constitution is the pardoning power, which allows a president to exempt a person, convicted or not, from punishment for a crime. This power descends from a traditional power of kings as the court of last resort and thus is a check on the courts. Pardons are usually not controversial, although they have occasionally backfired in dramatic ways when they are seen as partisan moves rather than disinterested checks on the judiciary.[24] For instance, after President Gerald Ford's post-Watergate pardon of Richard Nixon, Ford experienced a tremendous backlash that may have contributed to his 1976 loss to Jimmy Carter. Similarly President Trump's pardons of controversial Arizona sheriff Joe Arpaio, long a Trump supporter and fellow opponent of immigration, who had been convicted for refusing to stop profiling Latinos, and of Scooter Libby, former chief of staff to Vice President Dick Cheney, who had been convicted of leaking the identity of CIA agent Valerie Plame for political reasons, were seen as sending messages to those involved in the Mueller investigation that he could be relied on to pardon those who stayed loyal to him. Unusual for presidents, who have tended to wait until later in their terms, Trump issued eleven pardons or commutations in his first two years of office. None seemed to have an impact on his already low approval ratings.

In Your Own Words   Explain what the president's job entails.

senatorial courtesy the tradition of granting senior senators of the president's party considerable power over federal judicial appointments in their home states

solicitor general the Justice Department officer who argues the government's cases before the Supreme Court

pardoning power a president's authority to release or excuse a person from the legal penalties of a crime

THE EVOLUTION OF
THE AMERICAN PRESIDENCY

From restrained administrator to energetic problem solver

As we saw, the framers designed a much more limited presidency than the one we have today. The constitutional provisions give most of the policymaking powers to Congress, or at least require power sharing and cooperation. For most of our history, this arrangement was not a problem. As leaders of a rural nation with a relatively restrained government apparatus, presidents through the nineteenth century were largely content with a limited authority that rested on the grants of powers provided in the Constitution. But the presidency of Franklin Roosevelt, beginning in 1932, ushered in a new era in presidential politics.

THE TRADITIONAL PRESIDENCY

The presidency that the founders created and outlined in the Constitution is not the presidency of today. In fact, so clearly have the effective rules governing the presidency changed that scholars speak of two different presidential eras—that before the 1930s and that after. Although the constitutional powers of the president have been identical in both eras, the interpretation of how far the president can go beyond those constitutional powers has changed dramatically.

The traditional presidency—the founders' limited vision of the office—survived more or less intact for a little over one hundred years, although several early presidents exceeded the powers granted in the Constitution. George Washington expanded the president's foreign policy powers, for instance; Jefferson entered into an agreement for the Louisiana Purchase; Andrew Jackson developed the role of president as popular leader; and Abraham Lincoln, during the emergency conditions of the Civil War, stepped outside his constitutional role to try to save the Union.

These presidents believed that they had what modern scholars call inherent powers to fulfill their constitutional duty to "take care that the laws be faithfully executed." Some presidents, like Lincoln, claimed that national security required a broader presidential role. Others held that the president, as our sole representative in foreign affairs, needed a stronger hand abroad than at home. Inherent powers are not listed explicitly in the Constitution but are implied by the powers that are granted, and they have been supported, to some extent, by the Supreme Court.[25] Most nineteenth- and early-twentieth-century presidents, conforming to the founders' expectations, took a more retiring role, causing one observer to claim that "twenty of the twenty-five presidents of the nineteenth century were lords of passivity."[26] The job of the presidency was seen as a primarily administrative office, in which presidential will was clearly subordinate to the will of Congress.

traditional presidency the founders' vision of limited executive power

inherent powers presidential powers implied but not stated explicitly in the Constitution

modern presidency the ongoing trend toward a higher degree of executive power since the 1930s

THE MODERN PRESIDENCY

The modern presidency, a time of evolving executive power since the 1930s, is still a work in progress. The rural nature of life in the United States changed rapidly in the century and a half after the founding. Government in the nineteenth century sought bit by bit to respond to the new challenges of its changing people and economy, and as it responded, it grew beyond the bounds of the rudimentary administrative structure supervised by George Washington. With the crisis of the Great Depression and Franklin Roosevelt's New Deal solution, the size of government exploded and popular ideas about government changed radically.

Nothing in their prior experience had prepared Americans for the calamity of the Great Depression. Following the stock market crash of October 1929, the economy went into a tailspin. Unemployment soared to 25 percent, and the gross national product (GNP) plunged from around $100 billion in 1928 to less than $60 billion in 1932.[27] President Herbert Hoover held that the U.S. government had only limited powers and responsibility to deal with what was, he believed, a private economic crisis. There was no widespread presumption, as there is today, that the government was responsible for the state of the economy or for alleviating the suffering of its citizens.

The election of Roosevelt in 1932, and his three reelections, initiated an entirely new level of government activism. For the first time, the national government assumed responsibility for the economic well-being of its citizens on a substantial scale. Relying on the theory mentioned earlier, that foreign affairs are thought to justify greater presidential powers than domestic affairs, Roosevelt portrayed himself as waging war against the Depression and sought from Congress the powers "that would be given to me if we were in fact invaded by a foreign foe."[28] The New Deal programs he put in place tremendously increased the size of the federal establishment and its budget. The number of civilians (nonmilitary personnel) working for the federal government increased by more than 50 percent during Roosevelt's first two terms (1933–1941). The crisis of the Great Depression created the conditions for extraordinary action, and Roosevelt's leadership created new responsibilities and opportunities for the federal government. Congress delegated a vast amount of discretionary power to Roosevelt so that he could implement his New Deal programs.

The legacy of the New Deal is that Americans now look to the president and the government to regulate the economy, solve social problems, and provide political inspiration. No other president has had such a profound impact on how Americans live their lives today.[29] Roosevelt's New Deal was followed by Truman's Fair Deal. Eisenhower's presidency was less activist, but it was followed by Kennedy's New Frontier and Johnson's Great Society. All of these comprehensive policy programs did less than they promised, but they reinforced Americans' belief that it is the government's, and in particular the president's, job to make ambitious promises. That, combined with the ascendance of the United States as a world power, its engagement in the Cold War, and its participation in undeclared wars such as Korea and Vietnam, made the office very powerful indeed—what historian Arthur Schlesinger called, in a 1973 book, "the imperial presidency."[30] The philosophy behind the imperial presidency was summed up neatly by Richard Nixon, ironically several years after he was forced to resign, when he declared, "When the president does it, that means it's not illegal."[31]

© Underwood Archives/Getty Images

The Policies and Persona of the Modern Presidency

The challenges of the Great Depression and World War II were met with a greatly increased role of the national government in American lives, the economy, and the world. Franklin Roosevelt's New Deal policies, and his central leadership role in the war effort, combined with his use of radio to speak directly to the public, transformed the nature of the office. The president became the central figure in American politics, and politics became more central to the lives of Americans.

The modern presidency, bolstered by court rulings that supported the president's inherent powers in foreign affairs, generated something of a backlash in Congress over the belief that neither the Johnson nor the Nixon administration had been sufficiently forthcoming over the Vietnam War. Frustration with that, as well as with Nixon's abuse of his powers during Watergate and his unwillingness to spend budgeted money as Congress had appropriated it, led Congress to pass the War Powers Act (1973), which we discussed earlier; the Foreign Intelligence and Surveillance Act (1978), designed to put a check on the government's ability to spy on people within the United States; and the Independent Counsel Act (1978), which was intended to provide an impartial check on a president's activities but was ultimately left open to abuse.

> *How might presidential behavior change if we once again allowed presidents to serve more than two terms?*

THE BATTLE OVER EXECUTIVE AUTHORITY TODAY

The modern presidency had been so diminished by post-Watergate developments and the Clinton impeachment that when the George W. Bush administration came to power, Bush and his vice president, Dick Cheney, were determined to restore the luster and power of the office. In January 2002 Vice President Cheney remarked that the presidency is "weaker today as an institution because of the unwise compromises that have been made over the last 30 to 35 years," and he highlighted the "erosion of the powers and the ability of the president" of the United States to do his job.[32] Indeed, many of Bush's executive orders were designed to reinstate those powers, as were his administration's claims of executive privilege. In addition, Bush expanded the practice of using signing statements (specifications of the president's interpretation of what a law obligated him to do—an understanding that could not be vetoed or checked by Congress). Typically, presidents used the presidential veto to block legislation they didn't like, whereupon Congress could override the veto if the bill had sufficient support. But unlike his predecessors, Bush had not vetoed a single bill by the time he had been in office for five years. Instead he had issued a huge number of signing statements, over 750, compared to 232 by his father in his four years in the White House, and only 140 issued by Bill Clinton in his eight years. Many of Bush's actions reflected a strong commitment to the theory of the unitary executive, a controversial legal view held by members of the administration that the Constitution requires that all executive power be held only by the president and, therefore, that it cannot be delegated to or wielded by any other branch.[33]

Critics of the Bush administration howled when they realized what was going on, accusing Bush of doing an end-run around Congress and claiming that he was setting up himself, and thus the executive branch, as the ultimate decider of what is constitutional, a function generally thought to belong to the Supreme Court. "There is no question that this administration has been involved in a very carefully thought-out, systematic process of expanding presidential power at the expense of the other branches of government," said one scholar.[34]

The terrorist attacks of September 11, 2001, provided Bush and Cheney with a strong and persuasive rationale for their desire to create a more muscular presidency. Citing concern about future attacks, the Bush administration increased its efforts to make the office more powerful and his extraordinarily high approval ratings in the days following the attacks made Congress reluctant to take him on. The Republicans in Congress were supportive of the administration's efforts, and the Democrats feared being seen as soft on terrorism and so went along with Bush's plans. He was able to initiate the wars in Afghanistan and Iraq for reasons that were later shown to have been largely exaggerated and fabricated, and the Patriot Act passed handily in 2001. Only the

Supreme Court, in the 2004 case *Hamdi v. Rumsfeld* and the 2006 case *Hamdan v. Rumsfeld*, attempted to put on the brakes. As we argue in this chapter, high approval ratings can give a president power beyond that granted by the Constitution, and Bush used that power throughout his first term. Only after Bush's reelection in 2004, with waning approval ratings, was he seen as vulnerable enough for Congress to criticize him seriously. By 2006 his public approval was so low that Democrats easily won back control of both the House and the Senate and began to undertake the job of congressional oversight that had been largely lacking for the previous six years.

Overall, it is not clear whether the Bush-Cheney efforts to bulk up the executive will have lasting effect. Obama wrestled with the same challenges of office as have all presidents in the modern age. A former constitutional law professor, he seemed to be aware of the necessity of maintaining checks and balances, and he showed no signs of embracing the Bush philosophy of the unitary executive. Trump, by contrast, with the opportunity to appoint more judges and justices than most presidents, clearly believes in a strong presidency and will probably appoint judges to back up that power.

Still, as relations between the Obama White House and Congress became impossibly strained, with Congress' determination to pass no element of his agenda, the president turned more and more to executive action to get his agenda accomplished. Although the magazine *Politico* found that most of Obama's actions would take some time to make their impact felt, they included a higher minimum wage for federal workers and antidiscrimination measures in the federal workplace for gays, a new retirement savings plan, new workplace reforms, efforts to halt climate change by boosting fuel efficiency standards and reducing emissions, the creation of a marine sanctuary, assistance repaying student loans, regulation of for-profit colleges, small business assistance, a change in the loophole that allowed those purchasing guns at gun shows to avoid background checks, changes in immigration policy, the institution of net neutrality, and other similar programs that could be accomplished with the executive pen or by encouraging executive agencies to act in a particular way.[35]

As executive actions, few, if any, of these decisions will long survive Obama's presidency. Although Obama's political legacy has been significant and his approval ratings as he ended his term were in the mid-50s, Trump's victory has allowed the Republicans to reverse much of Obama's work, including, in all likelihood, his signature health care plan. All presidents and congresses have at least occasionally adversarial relationships, but Obama may be one of the few presidents whose conflict with Congress survives his administration. Donald Trump, in fact, promised to undo as much of Obama's legacy as he could, as quickly as he could, and Congress has helped out where it could.

THE TRUMP PRESIDENCY

As we noted in *What's at Stake . . . ?*, there are no previous models for the Trump presidency so it is difficult to discuss him in the terms that have applied to previous presidents. We noted that he has pleased his fans and inflamed his critics. Running the executive branch as he ran his business, Donald Trump has chafed at the limits of checks and balances since taking office, pushing against the notion that the president is bound by the rule of law. He views people in the bureaucracy as being there to serve him rather than to serve the Constitution, and he has shown evidence of wanting to use the power of the federal government to punish those he views as his enemies. For instance, he lobbied the U.S. Postal Service to double the rates that would affect clients like Amazon, whose founder, Jeff Bezos, Trump blames for his negative coverage in the *Washington Post*, which Bezos also owns.

Trump has differed from other presidents from the beginning by deciding not to forgive those who didn't vote for him. Most presidents reach out to the other side and, especially when dealing with issues of national concern, speak not as a partisan politician but as a nonpolitical head of state. Trump has largely bypassed that role. When the Trumps held their first state dinner, no Democrats (or journalists) were invited. When tragedies like school shootings have occurred, many families of victims say he has not contacted them. When he does speak out, it is often via tweet, which lacks the gravitas of a traditional presidential statement. But if Trump has ignored the head-of-state role, he hasn't spent a lot of time on the head-of-government role, either. He has blown up deals with Congress rather than trying to broker agreements and bring people on board his side. He has shown little interest in the health of the Republican Party he leads, and when that vacuum has been filled by his vice president, his staff has reacted with suspicion about Pence's motives.[36]

Trump's novel approach to governance is based partly on his personality, partly on his reliance on what has worked for him in business, and partly on his refusal to learn the gritty details of how government works. Because of his lack of political background, he entered office with less of an idea of how to work with the other branches or, indeed, with the rest of the executive branch than have other new presidents. Political scientists have coined the term **weak presidency** to refer to presidents who do not excel at managing their executive offices. The early indications are that Trump joins former president Jimmy Carter in this camp. That term should not be confused with the notion that Trump is necessarily a weak man—he can be very influential with those who seek his favor—but it does mean he isn't a very good manager of the people around him.

In Your Own Words Compare the modern presidency with the founders' expectations for a limited executive.

PRESIDENTIAL POLITICS
The struggle for power in a constitutionally limited office

Presidential responsibilities and the public's expectations of what the president can accomplish have increased greatly since the start of the twentieth century. But, as we have discussed, the Constitution has not been altered to give the president more power, resulting in an **expectations gap** that makes the job inherently challenging. To avoid failure, presidents have to seek power beyond that which is explicitly granted by the Constitution, and even beyond what they can claim as part of their inherent powers. They do that with varying degrees of success.

THE EXPECTATIONS GAP AND THE NEED FOR PERSUASIVE POWER

Even those presidents who have drawn enthusiastically on their inherent powers to protect national security or conduct foreign policy, or who support the theory of the unitary executive, cannot summon the official clout needed to ensure that their legislation gets through Congress, that the Senate approves their appointments, and that other aspects of their campaign promises are fulfilled.

weak presidency a term that refers to presidents who do not excel at managing their executive offices

expectations gap the gap between popular expectations of what modern presidents can and should do, and their constitutional powers to get things done

New presidents quickly face the dilemma of having high visibility and status but limited constitutional authority. Yet people continue to run for and serve as president, and, as we have seen, they deal with the expectations gap by attempting to augment their power with executive orders, executive agreements, claims of executive privilege, signing statements, and the like. All of these give the president some ability to act unilaterally. However, to be successful with larger policy initiatives, presidents seek to develop their primary extraconstitutional power, which is, in one scholar's phrase, the **power to persuade**.[37] To achieve what is expected of them, the argument goes, presidents must persuade others to cooperate with their agendas—most often members of Congress, but also the courts, the media, state and local officials, bureaucrats, foreign leaders, and especially the American public. Other scholars, however, doubt that it is really persuasion alone that allows a president to get things done. They argue that there is not a great deal of evidence that presidents are able to influence important actors, or even the public, to change their policy priorities or preferences, and that presidents' substantial policy successes are primarily due to their ability to see and exploit existing opportunities.[38] These may be political ambitions of members of Congress; latent concerns or yearnings in the public; or changes in public mood or media attention about unexpected events, such as the economic collapse of the 2008 Great Recession or the terrorist attacks of September 11, 2001. Presidents vary in their ability to capitalize on the political context they face as much as in their ability to single-handedly change minds, either in Washington or in the country at large.[39] Whether the power to persuade really works for presidents or not, sometimes it is all they have in their political tool box to get lawmakers to go along with their agendas.

GOING PUBLIC

A central strategy that presidents follow in their efforts to influence people "inside the Beltway" (that is, the Washington insiders) to go along with their agenda is to reach out and appeal to the public directly for support. This strategy of **going public** is based on the expectation that public support will put pressure on other politicians to give presidents what they want.[40] Presidents use their powers as both head of government and head of state to appeal to the public by creating a narrative that will make what they want seem reasonable and necessary.[41] A president's effort to go public can include a trip to an international summit, a town-meeting-style debate on a controversial issue, the president's annual State of the Union address, or other nationally televised speeches.

At the simplest level of the strategy of going public, presidents just take their case to the people. Consequently, presidential public appearances have increased greatly in the era of the modern presidency. Recent presidents have had some sort of public appearance almost every day of the week, year round. Knowing that the White House press corps will almost always get some airtime on network news, presidents want that coverage to be favorable. Shaping news coverage so that it supports the presidential narrative and generates favorable public opinion for the president is now standard operating procedure.[42] President Trump has largely taken his communications strategy into his own hands and runs it via Twitter and well-placed leaks to members of the media. Although this ensures that the media spotlight is always on him, he does not control the actual message as well as he could. The mainstream media are talking about Trump constantly, to be sure, but they are not always saying what he wants them to say.

power to persuade
a president's ability to convince Congress, other political actors, and the public to cooperate with the administration's agenda

going public
a president's strategy of appealing to the public on an issue, expecting that public pressure will be brought to bear on other political actors

Going Public by Tweet

President Trump has largely circumvented the traditional media and used Twitter to speak to his supporters, make announcements, respond to news stories, and fight his political opponents. Occasional efforts by staff to limit the practice have been largely abandoned.

Naturally, only a popular president can use the strategy of going public effectively, so popularity ratings become crucial to how successful a president can be. Since the 1930s the Gallup Organization has been asking people, "Do you approve or disapprove of the way [the current president] is handling his job as president?" The public's rating of the president—that is, the percentage saying they approve of how the president is handling the job—varies from one president to the next and also typically rises and falls within any single presidential term. The president's ratings are a kind of political barometer: the higher they are, the more effective the president is with other political and economic actors; the lower they are, the harder the president finds it to get people to go along. For the modern presidency, the all-important power to persuade is intimately tied to presidential popularity. This is perhaps one of the greatest weaknesses Trump faces. By never reaching out beyond his base, his approval ratings have been remarkably steady but low. His base is with him, but few Americans support him, which helped account for the blue wave of the 2018 midterm election.

Three factors in particular can affect a president's popularity: the cycle effect, the economy, and unifying or divisive current events.[43] The **cycle effect** refers to the tendency for presidents to begin their terms of office with relatively high popularity ratings, which decline as they move through their four-year terms (see Figure 7.1). During the very early months of this cycle, often called the **honeymoon period**, presidents are frequently most effective with Congress. Often, but not always, presidential ratings rise going into their second terms, but this seldom approaches the popularity they had immediately after being elected the first time. The post-honeymoon drop in approval may occur because by then presidents have begun to try to fulfill the handsome promises on which they campaigned. Fulfilling promises requires political action, and as presidents exercise their head-of-government responsibilities, they lose the head-of-state glow they bring with them from the election. Political change seldom favors everyone equally, and when someone wins, someone else usually loses. The cycle effect means that presidents need to present their programs early, while they enjoy popular support. Unfortunately, much opportunity available during the honeymoon period can be squandered because of inexperience, as it was for Bill Clinton. George W. Bush avoided the pitfalls of the early Clinton administration by bringing an experienced staff to the White House with him, but by summer 2001, there were definite signs that Bush's honeymoon, too, was over. Only the surge in support for the president following the September 11 attacks allowed him to break the usual cycle effect in his first term. Similarly, President Obama chose as his first chief of staff veteran White House staffer (from the Clinton administration) and U.S. representative Rahm Emanuel, who helped him to accomplish an unusually ambitious legislative agenda in his first two years before going on to be elected mayor of Chicago. Trump, whose approval ratings have been low and remarkably stable, never really enjoyed a honeymoon period, partly because a majority voted against him and he never reached out to them to include them in a unifying vision for the country.

cycle effect the predictable rise and fall of a president's popularity at different stages of a term in office

honeymoon period the time following an election when a president's popularity is high and congressional relations are likely to be productive

FIGURE 7.1

Average Quarterly Presidential Approval Ratings, From Eisenhower to Trump

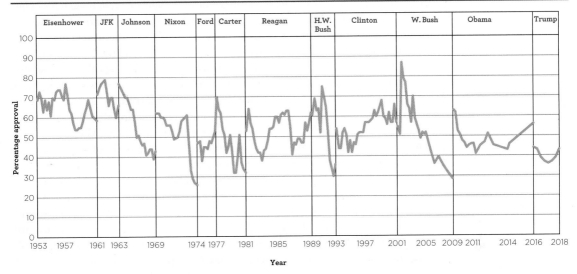

Source: Quarterly data for 1953–2000 provided by Robert S. Erikson; developed for Robert S. Erikson, James A. Stimson, and Michael B. MacKuen, *The Macro Polity* (Cambridge, U.K.: Cambridge University Press, 2002); data for 2001–2018 calculated by authors from the Gallup Organization.

Note: Respondents were asked, "Do you approve or disapprove of the way [the current president] is handling his job as president?"

The second important factor that consistently influences presidential approval is the state of the economy. Since Franklin Roosevelt's administration, the government has taken an active role in regulating the national economy, and every president promises economic prosperity. In practice, presidential power over the economy is quite limited, but we nevertheless hold our presidents accountable for economic performance. George H. W. Bush lost the presidency in large measure because of the prolonged recession in the latter part of his term. Bill Clinton won it with a campaign focused on his plan for economic recovery. Obama came into office during the worst economic recession to hit the nation since the Great Depression of the 1930s. His ratings reflected a traditional honeymoon effect, but they dropped as unemployment rose and continued to decline as the economic recovery was slower than the public hoped.[44] Then they rose right before his reelection in 2012 and again as the economy began to pick up real steam in 2016 as his term came to an end. Although the Obama economy continued to grow in the early Trump years, Trump's approval ratings have been remarkably unaffected by the good health of the economy. Whether that is because Obama continues to get the credit or whether Trump's ratings would be even lower with a worse economy is hard to say. In many ways the rules that help us understand the executive office simply don't apply to Trump since he has refused to follow the traditional model of the office.

Newsworthy current events can also influence presidential approval. Even those over which presidents have no control can be opportunities for them to demonstrate leadership. Besides being tests of a president's leadership, newsworthy events can be both divisive and unifying. Political controversy, almost by definition, is divisive and generally hurts presidential ratings. And, of course, controversy in politics is unavoidable even though the public at large is reluctant to accept this fact of democratic governance.[45] Knowing that their cooperation would only bolster Obama, congressional Republicans decided to make a concerted effort to deny him support whenever they could, ensuring that bills that passed on a party-line vote would be portrayed in the media narrative as controversial and would thus be unpopular. Whereas divisive events hurt presidents, unifying events can help them. Unifying events tend to be those that focus attention on presidents' head-of-state role, making them "look presidential," or that deal with perceived threats to the nation. For instance, President George H. W. Bush's ratings soared during the Gulf War, and his high profile was topped by his son's ratings following the terrorist attacks of 2001. President Obama experienced a small bump in his approval ratings after he announced the killing of Osama bin Laden in the spring of 2011. Thus most modern presidents necessarily play the ratings game, although Trump's refusal to reach out beyond the people who elected him has put a ceiling on how high his ratings are likely to go.[46] The lack of an effective response to the disaster that followed Hurricane Maria's direct hit on Puerto Rico was seen as the federal government's fault, but Trump's approval ratings did not take a hit—possibly because the people who were going to disapprove of his handling of the storm's aftermath already disapproved of his job performance. His handling of the separation of refugee families at border controls may have had a greater impact on his ratings, but Trump has not really tried to backtrack on his actions. In the past, those who chose not to play suffered the consequences: Truman, Johnson, and Ford tended not to heed the polls so closely, and they either had a hard time in office or were not reelected.[47] We will see if that pattern holds true in a deeply divided America.

WORKING WITH CONGRESS

Presidents do not always try to influence Congress by going public. They must often deal directly with Congress itself, and sometimes they combine strategies and deal with the public and Congress at the same time. The Constitution gives the primary lawmaking powers to Congress. Thus, presidents need congressional cooperation to be successful with their policy agendas. This depends in part on whether they have a reputation for being an effective leader among members of Congress and other Washington elites.[48] Such success varies with several factors, including the compatibility of the president's and Congress' goals and the party composition of Congress.

Presidents usually conflict with Congress in defining the nation's problems and their solutions. In addition to the philosophical and partisan differences that may exist between the president and members of Congress, each has different constituencies to please. The president, as the one leader elected by the whole nation, needs to take a wider, more encompassing view of the national interest. Members of Congress have relatively narrow constituencies and tend to represent their particular interests. Thus, in many cases, members of Congress do not want the same things the president does.

What can presidents do to get their legislation through a Congress made up of members whose primary concern is with their individual constituencies? For one thing, presidents have a staff of assistants to work with Congress. The legislative liaison office specializes in determining what members of Congress are most concerned about, what they need, and how legislation can be tailored to get their support. In some cases, members just want their views to be heard; they do not want to be taken for granted. In other cases, the details of the president's program have to be explained adequately. It is electorally useful for members to have this done in person, by the president, complete with photo opportunities for release to the papers back home.

When the president and the majority of Congress are of the same party, the president is more successful at getting programs passed. When presidents face divided government—that is, when the president is of a different party than the majority in one or both houses—they do not do as well.[49] Part of the problem is that in our highly polarized politics today, passage of a bill supported by the president is evaluated not only in terms of its policy impact, but also as giving a victory to the president, which is something the opposition is loath to do. An equally important part of the problem of divided government is that members of different parties stand for different approaches and solutions to the nation's problems. Democratic presidents and members of Congress tend to be more liberal than the average citizen, and Republican presidents and members of Congress tend to be more conservative.

Under divided government, presidents are not likely to succeed at getting their agendas met (see Figure 7.2). Dramatic examples of the impact of divided government can be seen in Bill Clinton's, George W. Bush's, and Barack Obama's administrations. For his first two years in office, Clinton worked with a Democratic majority in both houses, and Congress passed 86 percent of the bills he supported. The next two years the Republicans had a majority in both houses, and Clinton's success rate dropped to 46 percent.[50] Bush enjoyed impressive success, with an average of more than three-quarters of his favored bills enacted into law when he had Republican majorities in Congress. But when Bush had to deal with a Democratic Congress after the 2006 midterm election, his success rate dropped dramatically. With 96.7 percent of his preferred bills making it into law, Obama in 2009 had the most successful year of any president in the fifty-six years that *Congressional Quarterly* had been keeping track. These results are attributable to the large Democratic majorities in the House and the Senate, coupled with the president's ambitious agenda and a tanking economy that required action.[51] The 2010 midterm elections, which replaced the Democratic majority in the House of Representatives with a conservative Republican majority, spelled an end to Obama's high rate of success, dropping from an average of 91 percent under the Democratic majority to just over 55 percent when he had to deal with a Republican House.

Divided government, however, does not doom Washington to inaction. When national needs are pressing or the public mood seems to demand action, the president and opposition majorities have managed to pass important legislation.[52] For example, the government was divided with a Democrat in the White House and Republicans in control of both houses of Congress when major welfare reform was passed with the Personal Responsibility and Work Opportunity Act of 1996. But national needs do not always cause Congress to step up. In 2011 and 2012, Congress was unable to agree on policies to deal with revenue shortfalls and the budget, or even the previously routine extension of the national debt limit to enable it to pay its bills. Congress has managed at best stop-gap temporary measures to stave off impending crises, like a national default on debt payments. Members failed to bridge the ideological divide in October 2013 when House Republicans' insistence on defunding Obamacare resulted in a government shutdown for sixteen days.

legislative liaison
executive personnel who work with members of Congress to secure their support in getting a president's legislation passed

divided government
the situation that exists when political rule is split between two parties, in which one controls the White House and the other controls one or both houses of Congress

FIGURE 7.2

Presidential Success Under Unified and Divided Government, Eisenhower to Trump

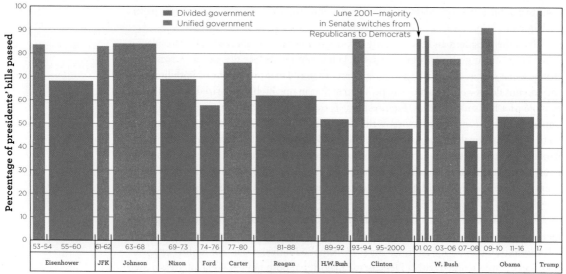

Source: Data from "Presidential Support Background," *CQ Weekly*, January 11, 2010, 117; "Table 6-7: Presidential Victories on Votes in Congress, 1953–2010," in Harold W. Stanley and Richard G. Niemi, eds., *Vital Statistics on American Politics 2011-2012* (Washington, D.C.: CQ Press, 2011), 246–248; Sam Goldfarb, "2011 Vote Studies: Presidential Support," *CQ Weekly*, January 16, 2012, 98–104; "2012 Vote Studies: Presidential Support," *CQ Weekly*, January 21, 2013; Emily Ethridge, "2013 Vote Studies: Presidential Support," *CQ Weekly*, February 3, 2014; Shawn Zeller, CQ Staff, "2014 Vote Studies: Running on Empty," *CQ Weekly*, March 16, 2015, 26; CQ Staff, "2015 Vote Studies: Presidential Support Hits Low for Obama," *CQ Weekly*, February 8, 2016; CQ Staff, "CQ Vote Studies: Next Hit: Presidential Support—Trump Divided, Conquered," *CQ Weekly*, February 12, 2018.

Congress remained so ideologically divided that progress on longer-term solutions was not likely while Obama remained in office, and perhaps after. Even President Trump, with his party leading both houses of the legislature, succeeded in getting a tax cut passed and justices confirmed to the Court only because those were also the goals of Republicans in Congress. Other priorities like his border wall have not fared as well. Although Trump does not face a divided government, his party's own divided priorities and the lack of congruence between his agenda and theirs has led to a mostly stalemated legislative record. Now that Trump does face divided government, he has a choice—either to keep playing to his base or to do what Bill Clinton did and work with the other party to make deals where they could find common ground. It requires a fair amount of consistency and compromise to do that, however, and a willingness to take on one's own base, and Trump has not shown any desire to do that.

In Your Own Words   Identify strategies and tools that presidents employ to overcome the constitutional limitations of the office.

MANAGING THE PRESIDENTIAL ESTABLISHMENT

The challenges of supervising an unwieldy bureaucracy

The modern president is one individual at the top of a large and complex organization called the presidency, which itself heads the even larger executive branch of government. George Washington got by with no staff to speak of and consulted with his small cabinet of just three department heads, but citizens' expectations of government, and consequently the sheer size of the government, have grown considerably since then, and so has the machinery designed to manage that government. We mentioned earlier that a president without the skills to successfully manage this machinery can be seen as weak because running the executive branch is his charge.

Today the executive branch is composed of the cabinet with its fifteen departments, the Executive Office of the President, and the White House staff, amounting altogether to hundreds of agencies and two million civilian employees and almost a million and a half active-duty military employees. Modern presidents require a vast bureaucracy to help them make the complex decisions they face daily, but at the same time the bureaucracy itself presents a major management challenge. The reality of the modern presidency is that presidents are limited in their ability to accomplish what they want by the necessity of dealing with this complex bureaucracy. The executive bureaucracy becomes part of the "how" through which presidents try to get what they want—for the country, their party, or themselves as politicians. But at the same time, it becomes another "who," a player in government that goes after its own goals and whose goals can conflict with those of the president.

THE CABINET

Each department in the executive branch is headed by a presidential appointee; collectively, these appointees form the president's cabinet. Today the cabinet is composed of fifteen posts heading up fifteen departments. The newest cabinet-level department is the Department of Homeland Security, created in 2003. The cabinet is not explicitly set up in the Constitution, though that document does make various references to the executive departments, indicating that the founders were well aware that the president would need special advisers in certain areas. President Washington's cabinet included just secretaries of state, treasury, and war (now called the secretary of defense). The original idea was for the cabinet members to be the president's men overseeing areas for which the president was responsible but that he was unable to supervise personally.

All of that has changed. Today presidents consider the demands of organized interests and political groups and the stature of their administration in putting together the cabinet. The number of departments has grown as various interests (for example, farmers, veterans, workers) have pressed for cabinet-level representation. Appointments to the cabinet in part serve presidential political goals. Thus the cabinet secretaries typically are chosen with an eye to the constituencies most affected by the departments. Presidents may also seek ethnic and gender balance in their cabinet choices. Bill Clinton made good on his promise to appoint a cabinet of exceptional diversity, and George W. Bush and Barack Obama followed suit. In addition, the president tends to choose cabinet members who have independent stature and reputation before their appointments. President Obama borrowed from Abraham Lincoln's notion of building a "team of rivals" when he appointed Hillary Clinton to be his first secretary of state and when he retained Bush's secretary of defense, Robert Gates.

Trump's norm-busting behavior might be most on show in his cabinet choices. Late in making many of his decisions, picking people with no experience, leaving many candidates unvetted, removing people from office after a short time, picking people best known for working in the industries they would be in charge of regulating, and requiring that cabinet secretaries publicly praise him in meetings, Trump has treated the cabinet as a less august and more personal board of directors than have other presidents. The president's sense of legitimacy is typically underscored by having top-quality people working in the administration, but Trump has seemed unconcerned with this. Generally presidents want people who are ideologically similar to them in the policy areas they will be handling.[53] This is not easily achieved (and may not be possible) given the other considerations presidents must weigh, but Trump has been less shy about selecting people who will give him his own way and who show him personal loyalty over other considerations.

The combination of these factors in making cabinet choices—political payoffs to organized interests, and the legitimacy provided by top people in the area—often results in a "team" that may not necessarily be focused on carrying out the president's agenda. There are exceptions to the typically guarded relationship between cabinet members and the president, but the political considerations of their appointment, coupled with their independent outlook, generally mean that cabinet members will provide the president with a wide variety of views and perspectives. They do not usually, as a group, place loyalty to the president's agenda above other considerations in their advice to the president. Consequently, presidents tend to centralize their decision making by relying more on their advisers in the Executive Office of the President for advice they can trust.[54]

EXECUTIVE OFFICE OF THE PRESIDENT

The **Executive Office of the President** (EOP) is a collection of organizations that form the president's own bureaucracy. Instituted by Franklin Roosevelt in 1939, the EOP was designed specifically to serve the president's interests, supply information, and provide expert advice.[55] Among the organizations established in the EOP is the **Office of Management and Budget** (OMB), which helps presidents to exert control over the departments and agencies of the federal bureaucracy by overseeing their budgets. The director of OMB works to ensure that the budget reflects the president's own policy agenda. Potential regulations created by the agencies of the national government must be approved by OMB before going into effect. This gives the president an additional measure of control over what the bureaucracy does.

Because modern presidents are held responsible for the performance of the economy, all presidents attempt to bring about healthy economic conditions. The job of the **Council of Economic Advisers** is to predict for presidents where the economy is going and to suggest ways to achieve economic growth without much inflation.

The **National Security Council** (NSC) gives the president daily updates about events around the world. The NSC's job is to provide the president with information and advice about foreign affairs; however, the council's role has expanded at times into actually carrying out policy—sometimes illegally, as in the Iran-contra affair.[56] When the existing federal bureaucracy is less than fully cooperative with the president's wishes, some presidents have simply bypassed the agencies by running policy from the White House. One strategy that presidents since Nixon have followed is to appoint so-called policy czars who have responsibility for

Executive Office of the President the collection of organizations that help the president with policy and political objectives

Office of Management and Budget the organization within the Executive Office of the President that oversees the budgets of departments and agencies

Council of Economic Advisers the organization within the Executive Office of the President that advises the president on economic matters

National Security Council the organization within the Executive Office of the President that provides foreign policy advice to the president supervising policy across agencies. Obama used this strategy extensively to coordinate policy in such areas as health care, energy, and the economy. He made over forty of these appointments in his first term, to establish firm White House control over the bureaucracy.[57]

WHITE HOUSE STAFF

Closest to the president, both personally and politically, are the members of the White House Office, which is included as a separate unit of the EOP. White House staffers have offices in the White House, and their appointments do not have to be confirmed by the Senate. Just as the public focus on the presidency has grown, so has the size of the president's staff. The White House staff, around 60 members under Roosevelt, grew to the 300–400 range under Eisenhower and in 2013 rested at about 460.[58]

The chief of staff and the other top assistants to presidents have to be their eyes and ears, and they act on the president's behalf every day. The criteria for a good staffer are very different from those for a cabinet selection. First and foremost, the president demands loyalty. This loyalty is developed from men and women who have hitched their careers to the president's. That is why presidents typically bring along old friends and close campaign staff as personal assistants.

Although Donald Trump asked Republican National Committee chair Reince Priebus to be his chief of staff after the 2016 election, Priebus did not last long in a dysfunctional West Wing. He was soon replaced with John Kelly, Trump's initial choice for Secretary of Homeland Security. Kelly, with a military background, did a better job of focusing the president's attention and managing his schedule, but Trump is a person who notoriously does not like to be managed and it is possible that Kelly's days too will turn out to be numbered. If he had his way, Trump would probably prefer not to have any chief of staff at all.

The different backgrounds and perspectives of the White House staff and the cabinet mean that the two groups are often at odds. The cabinet secretaries, dedicated to large departmental missions, want presidential attention for those efforts; the staff want the departments to put the president's immediate political goals ahead of their departmental interests. As a result, the past several decades have seen more and more centralization of important policymaking in the White House, and more decisions have been taken away from the traditional turf of the departments.[59]

THE VICE PRESIDENT

For most of our history, vice presidents have not been important actors in presidential administrations. Because the original Constitution awarded the vice presidency to the second-place presidential candidate, these officials were seen as potential rivals to the president and were excluded from most decisions and any meaningful policy responsibility. That was corrected with the Twelfth Amendment (1804), which provided for electors to select both the president and the vice president. However, custom for most of the period since then has put a premium on balancing the ticket in terms of regional, ideological, or political interests, which has meant that the person in the second spot is typically not close to the president. In fact, the vice president has sometimes been a rival even in modern times, as when John F. Kennedy appointed Lyndon Johnson, the Senate majority leader from Texas, as his vice president in 1960 in an effort to gain support from the southern states.

White House Office the more than four hundred employees within the Executive Office of the President who work most closely and directly with the president

chief of staff the person who oversees the operations of all White House staff and is traditionally expected to control access to the president

Since the Constitution provides only that the vice president acts as president of the Senate, which carries no power unless there is a tie vote, most vice presidents have tried to make small, largely insignificant jobs seem important, often admitting that theirs was not an enviable post. Thomas Marshall, Woodrow Wilson's vice president, observed in his inaugural address that "I believe I'm entitled to make a few remarks because I'm about to enter a four-year period of silence."[60] Roosevelt's first vice president, John Nance Garner,

expressed his disdain for the office even more forcefully, saying that the job "is not worth a pitcher of warm piss."[61]

Ultimately, however, the job of vice president is what the president wants it to be. President Reagan largely ignored George H. W. Bush, for instance, whereas Al Gore, serving under President Bill Clinton, had a central advisory role.[62] Dick Cheney also brought a good deal of Washington experience, upon which President George W. Bush relied heavily; Cheney had a stronger résumé than many presidents bring to office and wielded much more power than previous vice presidents. President Obama's vice president, Joe Biden, also brought the heft of a lengthy résumé from six terms in the U.S. Senate and his longtime service on the Senate Foreign Relations Committee. Obama did not relinquish as much authority to his vice president as Bush did, but Biden proved to be an effective, independent, and valued policy adviser to the president (see *Profiles in Citizenship*). He was an administration spokesperson on a wide range of issues, including his specialty area of foreign relations. Donald Trump picked Indiana governor Mike Pence, ostensibly as a gesture to reassure traditional social conservatives. Pence's role as legislator and governor was also a good counterpoint to Trump's lack of governing experience.

Thus, even though the office of the vice presidency is not a powerful one, vice presidents who establish a relationship of trust with the president can have a significant impact on public policy. The office is important as well, of course, because it is the vice president who assumes the presidency if the president dies, is incapacitated, resigns, or is impeached. Many vice presidents also find the office a good launching pad for a presidential bid. Four of the last ten vice presidents—Lyndon Johnson, Richard Nixon, Gerald Ford, and George H. W. Bush—ended up in the Oval Office, although Al Gore did not enjoy similar success in 2000.

THE FIRST SPOUSE

The office of the first lady is undergoing immense changes that reflect the tremendous flux in Americans' perceptions of the appropriate roles for men and women. Even the term "first lady" seems strangely antiquated in an age when a woman came within a whisper of winning the presidency. The office of the first lady contains controversial elements, partly the result of conflict over the role of women in politics, but also because the intimate relationship between husband and wife gives the presidential spouse, an unelected position, unique insight into and access to the president's mind and decision-making processes. For all the checks and balances in the American system, there is no way to check the influence of the first spouse. It will be interesting to see whether "first gentlemen" become as controversial as their female counterparts.

Since the 1960s and the advent of the women's movement, the role of the first lady has been seen by the public as less an issue of individual personality and quirks, and more a national commentary on how women in general should behave. As a surrogate for our cultural confusion on what role women should play, the office of the first lady has come under uncommon scrutiny, especially when she takes on a more overtly political role, as did Rosalyn Carter, who even attended cabinet meetings at her husband's request. Public objections to her activities and her position as informal presidential adviser showed that the role of the first lady was controversial even in the late 1970s. Hillary Rodham Clinton shook up public expectations of the first lady's role even more. A successful lawyer who essentially earned the family income while her husband, Bill, served four low-paid terms as governor of Arkansas, Hillary was the target of both public acclaim and public hatred.

Writing Their Own Job Description

First Lady Michelle Obama shares a giggle with Secretary of State Hillary Rodham Clinton at an event in 2010. Clinton redefined the role of first lady, and served in a number of political capacities before becoming the first female major-party presidential candidate in 2016. Obama chose a more traditional path, raising public awareness about health and nutrition and reaching out to military families.

Her nontraditional tenure as first lady was capped in 2000, at the end of her husband's second term, by her election as the junior senator from New York, followed by her own nearly successful run for the Democratic nomination for president in 2008, her appointment as Obama's secretary of state, and her win of the popular vote as the Democratic Party's candidate in the 2016 presidential election.

The politically safest strategy for a first lady appears to be to stick with a noncontroversial moral issue and ask people to do what we all agree they ought to do. Lady Bird Johnson beseeched us to support highway beautification; Nancy Reagan suggested, less successfully, that we "just say no" to drugs; and Laura Bush focused on the issues of education, youth, and literacy.

First Lady Michelle Obama said flatly that she did not intend to take on an active policymaking role, with a West Wing office and extensive staff to match. "I can't do everything," she explained. A committed and active mother to two children still at home, she wanted to keep their lives as normal as possible while living in the White House. Insofar as she took on a public role, it was in the noncontroversial style of Reagan and Bush, as an advocate for working parents, and particularly those in the military, who juggle career loads with the demands of raising families, and as a strong supporter of a healthy diet as an antidote to rising childhood obesity rates.[63] Avoiding policy and partisan conflict, Michelle Obama had popularity ratings much higher than the president's.[64]

Melania Trump has been more mysterious than most first ladies. Trump's third wife, she did not move into the White House right away because she did not want to take their son, Barron, out of school in New York. When she did move to Washington, her role has been mostly out of the public spotlight, especially during some embarrassing scandals concerning Trump's extramarital behavior. In spring 2018 she launched an initiative called "Be Best" aimed at reducing Internet bullying.

In Your Own Words Describe the organization and functions of the executive office.

THE PRESIDENTIAL PERSONALITY

Translating leadership style and image into presidential power

Effective management of the executive branch is one feature of a successful presidency, but there are many others. Historians and presidential observers regularly distinguish presidential success and failure, even to the extent of actually rating presidential greatness.[65] Political scientists also assess presidential success, usually in terms of how frequently presidents can get their legislative programs passed by Congress.[66] In addition to the material assets and management skills they bring to the office, the personal resources of a president can also help lead to success or contribute to failure.

Most presidents share some personality characteristics—giant ambition and large egos, for instance—but this does not mean that they are carbon copies of one another. They clearly differ in fundamental ways. A number of scholars have developed classification schemes of presidential personalities. Each of these schemes is based on the expectation that knowing key dimensions of individual presidential personalities will help explain, or even predict, how presidents will behave in certain circumstances. The most famous of these schemes was developed by James David Barber, who classifies presidents on two dimensions: their energy level (passive or active) and their orientation toward life (positive or negative).[67]

Some of our best and most popular presidents have been active-positives. They have had great energy and a very positive orientation toward the job of being president. Franklin Roosevelt, Bill Clinton, and Barack Obama represent this type. Others have had less energy (passives) or have been burdened by the job of being president (negatives). They have acted out their roles, according to Barber, as they thought they should, out of duty or obligation. Ronald Reagan and George W. Bush fit the model of the passive-positive president. They liked being leaders but believed that their job was one of delegating and setting the tone rather than of taking an active policymaking role. Richard Nixon is usually offered as one of the clearest examples of an active-negative president; he had lots of energy but could not enjoy the job of being president. Given what little we've seen of Donald Trump's executive experience, it's difficult to gauge how he will fit into the role.

Assessing individual personalities is a fascinating enterprise, but it is fraught with danger. Few politicians fit neatly into Barber's boxes (or the categories of other personality theorists) in an unambiguous way. Although some scholars find that personality analysis adds greatly to their understanding of the differences between presidencies, others discount it altogether, claiming that it leads one to overlook the ways in which rules and external forces have shaped the modern presidency.[68]

In addition to their personality differences, presidents strive to create their own **presidential style**, an image that symbolically captures who the president is for the American people and for leaders of other nations. These personal differences in how presidents present themselves are real, but they are also carefully cultivated.[69]

For example, Harry Truman was known for his straight, sometimes profane, talk and no-nonsense decision making. In contrast, Dwight Eisenhower developed his "Victorious General" image as a statesman above the fray of petty, day-to-day politics. John F. Kennedy, whose term followed Eisenhower's, evoked a theme of "getting the country moving again" and embodied this with a personal image of youth and energy.

Bill Clinton's style combined the image of the highly intellectual Rhodes scholar with that of a compassionate leader, famous for "feeling America's pain." That carefully managed image could not disguise the fact that Clinton was also a man of large appetites, however, from his jogging breaks to eat at McDonald's to his extramarital affairs. While people approved of

presidential style the image that presidents project that represents how they would like to be perceived at home and abroad

Sexism, the Glass Ceiling, and the 2016 Election

The United States, unlike most Western democracies and even many developing nations, has yet to put a female chief executive into office. Clinton came as close as anyone has, and if not for the Electoral College she would have pulled it off. Her achievement is singular and historic.

Her loss can still teach us some valuable lessons about how women and leadership are perceived in American culture. Our very notions of leadership are gendered.[1] Think about the words we use to describe a leader—*strong, authoritative, active, decisive, ambitious*—and then think about how our cultural narratives apply those words to men and women.

Strong. Just because it's not politically correct any longer to say that women are the "weaker sex," don't imagine that it's not ingrained into the narrative.

Authoritative. When men wield power, we see them as exercising authority. When women do so, the narrative is that they are "bossy." In a culture where bosses have traditionally been men, it is curious that the word "bossy" is saved for women who step into a role seen as belonging to men.

Active. Our leadership narratives all put a premium on taking action. Trump's slogan "Make America Great Again" was an action statement. Clinton, on the other hand, was frequently accused of not having a message. Her slogan, "Stronger Together," presented a cooperative, collaborative vision that focused more on a way of being than on acting. Our notions of leadership are so gendered that unless the message is full of tough action verbs, many of us miss it altogether.

Decisive. There are different ways of making decisions. George W. Bush frequently said, "I am the decider." Trump's convention speech featured

Fighting for Equal Footing
Hillary Clinton, the 2016 Democratic presidential nominee, concedes the election on November 9, 2016.

the words, "I alone can fix it." Hillary Clinton has said that it took years for her to be able to use the word "I" rather than "we" in a political context, and she is famous for writing a book about raising children called It Takes a Village.[2] Researchers have noted that women often use a more collaborative and consultative decision-making style.

Ambitious. The cultural narrative says men are supposed to be ambitious but finds something dubious about women who seek higher goals. Research shows that to be successful, ambitious women have to demonstrate that they can be as assertive and powerful as men, but when they do they are seen as unfeminine and unlikeable.[3]

Consider that a campaign is really a job interview. Clinton clearly won the three presidential debates in 2016. She received 92 percent of newspaper endorsements. Her campaign was well organized, her policy positions clearly articulated. In a way, the story is that of every woman who worked her way to the top through sheer grit, only to lose the plum job to a less qualified man.

Was sexism the only reason? Almost certainly not. But we can't discount it either. While Hillary Clinton won the popular vote by three million, a poll still shows today that almost two-thirds of Republicans don't want to see a woman president in their lifetime.[4] As the old cigarette commercial had it, women have come a long way, baby, but apparently not long enough.

1. Anne M. Koenig et al., "Are Leader Stereotypes Masculine? A Meta-Analysis of Three Research Paradigms," *Psychological Bulletin*, 137 (2011): 616–642, www.uni-klu.ac.at/gender/downloads/FP_Koenig_Eagly_2011.pdf.

2. Emily Crockett, "Why the Word 'I' Causes Hillary Clinton So Much Trouble," *Vox*, April 6, 2016, www.vox.com/2016/4/6/11377220/hillary-clinton-i-pronouns-sexism-trouble.

3. Laurie Rudman et al., "Status Incongruity and Backlash Effects: Defending the Gender Hierarchy Motivates Prejudice Against Female Leaders," *Journal of Experimental Social Psychology*, 48 (2012): 165–179, http://rutgerssocialcognitionlab.weebly.com/uploads/1/3/9/7/13979590/rudman_moss-racusin_phelan__nauts_2012.pdf.

4. Tim Marcin, "Nearly 60 Percent of Republicans Don't Want a Woman President in Their Lifetime, Poll Finds," *Newsweek*, April 26, 2018, www.newsweek.com/nearly-60-percent-republicans-dont-want-woman-president-lifetime-poll-902254.

Clinton's leadership through the end of his presidency, a majority of citizens noted concerns about his honesty and moral character.

George W. Bush came into office with an opposite set of characteristics. Widely perceived as a nonintellectual who joked that C students could grow up to be president, he cultivated the image of the chief executive officer he was: a president interested primarily in results, not academic debates, who was willing to set a course and leave others to get the job done. Despite a reputation for hard drinking and high living in his youth, including a drunk driving arrest, his pledge of abstinence, traditional marriage, and frequent references to Jesus Christ helped to put a moral tone on his presidency that Clinton's had lacked.

Barack Obama brought an even-keeled disposition to the White House. His calm demeanor (symbolized by the unofficial slogan of his first campaign—"No Drama Obama") remained consistent through the economic and environmental crises of the first term of his presidency. As he said of himself, "I don't get too high when things are going well, and I don't get too low when things are going tough." Obama's image incorporated elements of the styles of several of his predecessors, combining Ronald Reagan's optimism, Bill Clinton's braininess, and George W. Bush's faith and commitment to family.[70]

At least one part of his presidential style seemed to be uniquely Obama's own. In his first term, he brought to office a deep commitment to bipartisanship that at least one observer said "had all the markings of an obsessive disorder" given the president's persistence in attempting to find common ground with an opposition party that had made defeating him its chief goal.[71] Many of Obama's own supporters were infuriated by what they viewed as too conciliatory an approach on his part and were heartened to see that, by 2011, Obama was taking a more confrontational stance toward his own campaign and negotiations with congressional Republicans, a stance he seemed likely to bring with him to his second term.

Even after two years, it is difficult to classify Donald Trump—he probably falls more toward a passive-negative. He rarely looks as though he is enjoying being president, his tweets reveal a lot of personal disgruntlement, and his frequent weekends playing golf make it clear that he misses his old life very much. Stymied at getting some of his signature domestic programs through Congress, he has taken a more active foreign policy stance.

As we have seen repeatedly, Donald Trump's presidential style is his own. We have already seen his brash and flamboyant television personality, and his willingness to say whatever comes into his mind, regardless of who might be offended by it. Although his supporters liked what they called his lack of political correctness, commentators kept waiting for Trump to pivot to a more presidential style through his first two years in office. Trump himself said that even his family wanted him to be more toned down but that although he could easily be presidential, he didn't want to because "it would be boring as hell."[72] Time will tell how Trump resolves that issue and whether he listens to his own voice or that of his advisers.

Presidential style is an important but subtle means by which presidents communicate. It can be an opportunity for enhancing public support and thereby the president's ability to deal effectively with Congress and the media. But any style has its limitations, and the same behavioral and attitudinal characteristics of a style that help a president at one juncture can prove a liability later. Furthermore, as Bill Clinton's experience shows, the president does not always have total control over the image the public sees. Political enemies and an investigative press can combine to counter the image the president wants to project. Because public perception is tied so closely to leadership ability, a significant portion of the president's staffers end up concerning themselves with "image management."

In Your Own Words   Evaluate the importance of leadership style and image as they relate to presidential power.

CITIZENSHIP AND THE PRESIDENCY
The critical role of public opinion

Although the Constitution does not say so, the citizens of the United States have the ultimate power over the president. We elect the president, it is true, but our power goes beyond a once-every-four-years vote of approval or disapproval. Modern polling techniques, as we have seen, allow us to conduct a "rolling election," as the media and the politicians themselves track popular approval of the president throughout his term. The presidential strategy of going public is made possible by the fact that all Americans—citizens, the president, and members of Congress—know just where the president stands with the public and how much political capital he has to spend.

The institution of the American presidency, like most of the government designed by the framers, was meant to be insulated from the whims of the public. It is an irony that in contemporary American politics, presidents are more indebted to the citizens for their power than to the Electoral College, Congress, the courts, or any of the political elites the founders trusted to stabilize American government.

In Your Own Words   Describe how public opinion affects the relationship between citizens and the president.

Let's Revisit: What's at Stake . . . ?

We began this chapter with a question that might have seemed a little odd – What is at stake in the unusual presidency of Donald Trump?

Now that we know about the conventional role and powers of the American president, it is probably easier to see why we asked that question. President Trump rejects, in almost every way he can, the established role of the presidency. Presidents have varied at how effective they are at the job, but rarely have they acted without regard for precedent, ignoring the typical expectations the country and the world have for an American president.

To many Americans who feel that the system is rigged or unfair or inaccessible, that is exactly his appeal. An article by a journalist who spent time attending his rallies begins an article this way:

> The instant you attend your first Trump rally you are confronted by an uncomfortable truth: to figure out what's happening you have to acknowledge the love. It may not be pure and selfless. It may be narcissistic and at times even threatening. But love is very much in the air.[72]

People speak of getting positive energy from him, of feeling peaceful among like-minded people who are willing to say what they think without regard for political correctness. They certainly line up to get into these rallies, and it is at these rallies that Trump seems to find his joy. He smiles widely, he embraces the crowd with his arms. He loves rallies, he loves his supporters, and he loves being loved.

This is very reminiscent of the *tribalism* that Laila Lalami describes in the *CLUES to Critical Thinking* article in Chapter 11. To give you a taste of her argument, she says

> The impulse to belong to a clan is deeply human, however, and new tribes continue to form, organized not around ancestry but along fuzzier lines of ideology or demography.... They rule over separate territories, listen to different oracles, uphold distinct values and dismiss contradictory information as unreliable propaganda or "fake news." ... Above all, tribe members protect one another from perceived attacks by outsiders.[73]

By that definition, President Trump sounds less like a textbook American president and more like a tribal leader, which may be why *these* textbook writers, at least, have such difficulty writing about him. There is plenty to say about Trump—he's a fascinating character—but it's a challenge to talk about Trump "the president" when he declines to perform the role in the way we are accustomed to, from highly popular Republican presidents, such as Ronald Reagan, to, more recently, Barack Obama.

One of the main stakes we have discussed throughout this book is the principle that political norms should be respected and observed. Trump isn't concerned with political norms, doesn't always know when he is stepping on them, and often enjoys it when he finds out he is. What do his deviations from these norms mean for the next person to hold this office? Is Trump heralding a new normal or will American democracy return to its less colorful but more stable roots?

Another stake is free speech. Trump's criticism of the mainstream press, including CNN and the *New York Times*, and support for conservative outlets like Fox News indicate that news that flatters Trump is good, news that doesn't is fake. Other presidents might have wanted to give in to this tidy dichotomy—plenty have bent the truth, and some have outright lied—but none has so consistently refused to admit the truth of information that conflicts with his worldview.

The founders put free speech and press in the First Amendment for a reason: being freely able to criticize and debate the actions of politicians is one of the main supports of democratic culture. Trump undermines that right by insulting journalists, barring them from his press room, and sowing doubt about the truth. He isn't bothered or embarrassed by his lies and many of his supporters aren't either. In the article about his rallies we cited earlier, they either believed him or chalked it up to "just joking."

But then, there is the love. The feeling people have of being heard, of belonging. That is something most of us crave and is no less an important stake in politics. Without it, citizens are alienated and angry, and alienated and angry citizens aren't good for democracy either.

The disconcerting part of all of this is that Trump hasn't reached out to include all of us in the love. He has defied the traditional unifying role of head of state. You have to love him first; he won't woo you like most politicians and if you don't love him from the start, he doesn't seem to consider you part of his tribe. If you don't fit his image of an American, he comes to the same conclusion. Almost all of us have lived through presidencies we didn't choose, under heads of government and state we didn't vote for. And yet, it is rare, if not politically suicidal, for those presidents to so openly disregard those from the other tribe. The job of president has historically included rising above the tribal divisions and having a thick enough skin that being hated is just all in a day's work.

That is not Trump's style. You are in the tribe, or you are not. And what is at stake may be American democracy as we have known it.

Want a better grade?

Get the tools you need to sharpen your study skills. **SAGE edge** offers practice quizzes, eFlashcards, video, and multimedia at **edge.sagepub.com/barbourbrief8e.**

Review

The Presidential Job Description

When it comes to their relationship with the American public, presidents must reconcile the conflicting roles of **head of government** (226) and **head of state** (226).

Disagreeing about how much power the executive should have, the founders decided the president could be removed from office only by **impeachment** (228) for "high Crimes and Misdemeanors." They devised rules that both empowered and limited the office, in terms of its ability to check, and be checked by, the other branches. As the executive the president is the **chief administrator** (229), appointing federal employees including members of the **cabinet** (229). The president is the **commander-in-chief** (229) and the **chief foreign policy maker** (229), with the power to execute **treaties** (229) (shared with the Senate) and **executive agreements** (229). The president's legislative powers include the ability to set his agenda through the **State of the Union address** (230), to wield the **presidential veto** (230) over legislation he dislikes, and to issue **executive orders** (230). The president's judicial powers include the power to appoint federal judges—tempered by **senatorial courtesy** (235)—to influence court decisions via the **solicitor general** (235), and to exercise the **pardoning power** (235).

The Evolution of the American Presidency

Until the 1930s the era of the **traditional presidency** (236) described chief executives who mainly lived within the limits of their constitutional powers, although testing the limits of their **inherent powers** (236) in times of crisis. Since the expansion of government in Franklin Roosevelt's New Deal, the **modern presidency** (236) has seen a more complex relationship, in which the public looks to the president to solve its problems, but the president's formal powers remain unchanged. A **weak president** (240) is one who does not excel at managing his executive offices.

Presidential Politics

Under pressure from the public, but with limited constitutional powers to satisfy its demands, the modern president must resort to the **power to persuade** (241), **going public** (241) to convince Americans to pressure their representatives to give the president what he wants. Thus, due to the **cycle effect** (242), the president's best opportunities to get programs passed come during the **honeymoon period** (242), before public and press become disillusioned because of the **expectations gap** (240). Although presidents employ a **legislative liaison** (245) to smooth the way with Congress, getting their way can be difficult, especially if they are part of a **divided government** (245).

Managing the Presidential Establishment

Presidents preside over a vast bureaucracy, including the cabinet, the **Executive Office of the President** (248)—which encompasses the **Office of Management and Budget** (248), the **Council of Economic Advisers** (248), and the **National Security Council** (248)— and the **White House Office** (249), headed up by the president's **chief of staff** (249). The president's closest advisers are generally focused on his interests, but the variety of other staff and agency heads—often with their own agendas and often difficult to control—can make life difficult for the chief executive.

The Presidential Personality

Presidential success is the product of many factors, including political savvy and management skills, but also of the more intangible resource of character. In part, that character is revealed through **presidential style** (253)—the image that presidents project of how they would like to be perceived by the public.

Drew Angerer/Getty Images

8

The Bureaucracy

In Your Own Words

After you've read this chapter, you will be able to

8.1 Explain how the characteristics and features of bureaucracy influence decision making.

8.2 Outline the organization and roles of the federal bureaucracy.

8.3 Describe power struggles between political appointees and professional bureaucrats.

8.4 Outline the relationship between the federal agencies and the three branches of the federal government.

8.5 Analyze the tension between transparency and efficiency in the federal bureaucracy.

What's at Stake . . . in Rolling Back Regulations?

It was a Republican's dream. Not since Reagan had a president come into office and unraveled the regulatory fabric of the U.S. government with such gusto. Although Donald Trump's campaign rhetoric had been populist and anti-establishment, in one way he was following as traditional a playbook as Republicans have—shrinking the bureaucracy and getting rid of regulations, the rules that limited individual or corporate behavior, generally to protect the public good.[1]

Democrats and Republicans had different views of regulation. The narrative repeated in the media read by Democrats emphasizes the public health benefits of required health insurance, the environmental stakes of emissions controls, the financial stability that resulted from the Consumer Financial Protection Bureau, and the open communication of an unrestricted Internet. That narrative—enforced over and over through progressive blogs, liberal commentators, and thousands of tweets—is that government is benign, not always as efficient as it could be, but a force for the improvement of its citizens' lives.

For Republicans, government is not the "good guy." Prone to inefficiencies and unintended consequences, they think it generally favors the collective good over the individual good. Remember, too, that there is a strong strain in American political culture that puts individual profit over public welfare. In conservative eyes, universal health mandates are restrictions on the freedom *not* to be insured, environmental regulation is costly and an administrative burden for businesses, consumer protection just mean limitations on banks and lending, and the Internet is a private utility that can be manipulated like any other commodity. The antiregulation narrative was amplified through conservative media channels until the very science on which the regulations were based came to be seen as false propaganda. Against the best science of the day, Republicans have even claimed there is no human-made climate change needing to be addressed.

The Obama administration—eight years of health care reform, picking up an ailing economy, establishing environmental protections, and the like—infuriated conservatives and provided a strong motive for Republican voters who were not attracted by Trump's ideology of grievance to vote for him anyway.

They were rewarded. After just nine months with Trump in office, one journalist was already writing about what he called the "Trump Effect"—the use of administrative directives to the bureaucracy to rewrite the rules according to which Americans live their lives.[2]

- Opened up the Dakota Access oil pipeline
- Stepped up enforcement of deportations on undocumented immigrants

Fourteen times Trump used the Congressional Review Act, a legislative instrument that had been used only once 16 years before, to fast track the reversal of regulations Obama had passed in his last months. And just as Obama had turned to executive action in the face of a recalcitrant Congress, Trump used executive directives to undo what Obama had done. One way or another, Trump undid more than 800 Obama regulations in his first six months. In just his first year in office he had issued 47 executive orders to get rid of other regulations.

Among the regulations the Trump administration rolled back and the new guidelines he provided were some that face legal challenges—his Muslim travel ban, his reversal of the DACA, his ban on transgendered members of the military—but others have already begun to shape American life. Here are just a dozen:

- Opened up the Dakota Access oil pipeline
- Stepped up enforcement of deportations on undocumented immigrants
- Withdrew from the Paris Climate Agreement
- Rolled back protections for retirement savings
- Allowed   companies that violate labor laws to win federal contracts
- Made it easier to fire federal employees
- Cancelled restrictions on internet providers using private data
- Revised standards for health insurance, allowing lower quality plans back on the market
- Revoked forgiveness programs for student loans taken for fraudulent university programs
- Unveiled plans to roll back anti-pollution and fuel efficiency requirements for automobiles
- Permitted states to re-establish drugs tests for unemployment benefits
- Eased restrictions on for-profit colleges[3]

As you can see, in ways big and small, regulations influence the lives we live—for the better or the worse, depending on your perspective. After we discuss the bureaucracy— the giant regulation-making machine in government, we will return to the question of what is at stake in rolling them back.

KIDS have dramatic aspirations for their futures: they want to be adventurers or sports stars, doctors or lawyers, even president of the United States. Almost no one aspires to be what so many of us become: bureaucrats. But bureaucrats are the people who make national, state, and local government work for us. They are the people who give us our driving tests and renew our licenses, who deliver our mail, who maintain our parks, who order books for our libraries. Bureaucrats send us our Social Security checks, find us jobs through the unemployment office, process our student loans, and ensure we get our military benefits. In fact, bureaucrats defend our country from foreign enemies, chase our crooks at home, and get us aid in times of natural disasters. We know them as individuals. We greet them, make small talk, laugh with them. They may be our neighbors or friends. But civil servants are seldom much admired or esteemed in this country. Indeed, they are often the target of scorn or jokes, and the people who work in the organizations we call bureaucracies are derided as lazy, incompetent, power hungry, and uncaring.

Such a jaded view, like most other negative stereotypes, is based on a few well-publicized bureaucratic snafus and the frustrating experiences we all have at times with the bureaucracy: filling out financial aid forms, going through customs at the airport, signing up for a new health care policy, or waiting for a package being delivered via the U.S. Postal Service (better known as "snail mail"). In addition, the bureaucracy is the source of many of the rules that can help us get what we want from government but that often irritate us with their seeming arbitrariness and rigidity. Though they aren't elected, bureaucrats can have a great deal of power over our lives.

Bureaucracies are essential to running a government. Bureaucracy, in fact, is often the only ground on which citizens and politics meet, the only contact many Americans have with government except for their periodic trips to the voting booth. Bureaucrats are often called "civil servants" because, ultimately, their job is to serve the civil society in which we all live. In this chapter—as we give bureaucracy a closer look—you will learn about the definition of *bureaucracy*; the evolution, organization, and roles of the federal bureaucracy; politics inside the bureaucracy; and the relationship between the federal bureaucracy and the branches of the federal government.

WHAT IS BUREAUCRACY?

A top-down organizational system aiming for competence and fairness

In simplest terms, a **bureaucracy** is any organization that is structured hierarchically: those at the top—with responsibility for the organization's success—give the orders, and those on the bottom follow them. The classic definition comes to us from German sociologist Max Weber. Weber's model of bureaucracy features the following four characteristics:[4]

- *Hierarchy.* A clear chain of command exists in which all employees know who their bosses or supervisors are, as well as for whom they are in turn responsible.
- *Specialization.* The effectiveness of the bureaucracy is accomplished by having tasks divided and handled by expert and experienced full-time professional staffs.
- *Explicit rules.* Bureaucratic jobs are governed by rules rather than by bureaucrats' own feelings or judgments about how the job should be done. Thus bureaucrats are limited in the discretion they have, and one person in a given job is expected to make pretty much the same decisions as another. This leads to standardization and predictability.
- *Merit.* Hiring and promotions are often based on examinations but also on experience or other objective criteria. Politics, in the form of political loyalty, party affiliation, or dating the boss's son or daughter, is not supposed to play a part.

As governments make their bureaucracies look more like Weber's model, we say the closer they are to achieving "neutral competence."[5] **Neutral competence** represents the effort to depoliticize the bureaucracy, or to take politics out of administration, by having the work of government done expertly, according to explicit standards rather than personal preferences or party loyalties. The bureaucracy in this view should not be a political arm of the president or of Congress, but rather it should be neutral, administering the laws of the land in a fair, evenhanded, efficient, and professional way.

BUREAUCRACY AND DEMOCRACY

Much of the world is organized bureaucratically. Large tasks require organization and specialization. The Wright brothers may have been able to construct a rudimentary airplane, but no two people or even small group could put together a Boeing 787 Dreamliner. Similarly, though we idolize individual American heroes, we know that military undertakings like the D-Day invasion of Europe or the war on terrorism take enormous coordination and planning. Less glamorous, but still necessary, are routine tasks like issuing driver's licenses, doing security prechecks to make air travel easier, and stamping a passport.

Obviously, many bureaucracies are public, like those that form part of our government. But the private sector has the same demand for efficient expertise to manage large organizations.

bureaucracy an organization characterized by hierarchical structure, worker specialization, explicit rules, and advancement by merit

neutral competence the principle that bureaucracy should be depoliticized by making it more professional

Corporations and businesses are bureaucracies, as are universities and hospitals. It is not being public or private that distinguishes a bureaucracy; rather, it is the need for a structure of hierarchical, expert decision making. Naturally, in this chapter we focus on public bureaucracies.

The existence of bureaucratic decision making, where hierarchy and specialization count and decisions are often made behind closed doors, may seem like a real puzzle in a country that prides itself on its democratic traditions. Consider, however, that democracy may not be the best way to make every kind of decision. If we want to ensure that many voices are heard, democracy is an appropriate way to make decisions. But those decisions will be made slowly (it takes a long time to poll many people on what they want to do), and although they are likely to be popular, they are not necessarily made by people who know what they are doing. When you're deciding whether to have open-heart surgery, you don't want to poll the American people, or even the hospital employees. Instead, you want an expert, a heart surgeon, who can make the "right" decision, not the popular decision, and make it quickly.

Democracy could not have designed the rocket ships that formed the basis of America's space program, decided the level of toxic emissions allowable from a factory smokestack, or determined the temperature at which beef must be cooked in restaurants to prevent food poisoning. Bureaucratic decision making, by which decisions are made at upper levels of an organization and carried out at lower levels, is essential when we require expertise and dispatch.

Study Now, Pay Later

Applying for a student loan is never fun. But imagine what the experience would be like if student loan awards were made democratically, rather than through the neutral and impartial bureaucracy that is tasked with the job.

ACCOUNTABILITY AND RULES

Bureaucratic decision making does leave open the problem of accountability: Who is in charge, and to whom does that person answer? Where does the buck stop? Unlike private bureaucracies, where the need to turn a profit usually keeps bureaucrats relatively accountable, the lines of accountability are less clear in public bureaucracies. Because the Constitution does not provide specific rules for the operation of the bureaucracy, Congress has filled in a piecemeal framework for the bureaucracy that, generally speaking, ends up promoting the goals of members of Congress and the interests they represent.[6] Presidents, nominally the head of the executive branch of government, also have goals and objectives they would like the bureaucracy to serve. Thus at the very highest level, the public bureaucracy must answer to several bosses who often have conflicting goals.

> **When does bureaucratic decision making become a threat to democracy?**

The problem of accountability exists at a lower level as well. Even if the lines of authority from the bureaucracy to the executive and legislative branches were crystal clear, no president or congressional committee would be interested in supervising the day-to-day details of bureaucratic workings or would have the time to do so. To solve the problem of accountability within the bureaucracy and to prevent the abuse of public power at all levels, we again resort to rules. If the rules of bureaucratic policy are clearly defined and well publicized, it is easier to tell if a given bureaucrat is doing his or her job and not taking advantage of the power that comes with it.

accountability the principle that bureaucratic employees should be answerable for their performance to supervisors, all the way up the chain of command

There can also be negative consequences associated with the bureaucratic reliance on rules. Bureaucrats' jobs can quickly become rule-bound—that is, deviations from the rules become unacceptable, and individuality and creativity are stifled. Sometimes the rules that bind bureaucrats do not seem relevant to the immediate task at hand, and the workers are rewarded for following the rules, not for fulfilling the organization's goals. Furthermore, compliance with rules has to be monitored, and the best way we have developed to guarantee compliance is to generate a paper or electronic record of what has been done—thus the endless forms for which the bureaucracy is so famous.

For the individual citizen applying for a driver's license, a student loan, or food stamps, the process can become a morass of seemingly unnecessary rules, regulations, constraints, forms, and hearings. We call these bureaucratic hurdles **red tape**, after the red tape that seventeenth-century English officials used to bind legal documents. Citizens may feel that they are treated as little more than numbers, that the system is impersonal and alienating. These excessive and anonymous procedures cause citizens to think poorly of the bureaucracy, even while they value many of the services that it provides.

Rules thus generate one of the great trade-offs of bureaucratic life. If we want strict fairness and accountability, we must tie the bureaucrat to a tight set of rules. If we allow the bureaucrat discretion to try to reach goals with a looser set of rules or to waive a rule when doing so seems appropriate, we may gain some efficiency but lose accountability. Given the vast numbers of people who work for the federal government, we have opted for accountability, even while we howl with frustration at the inconvenience of the rules.

In Your Own Words   Explain how the characteristics and features of bureaucracy influence decision making.

THE AMERICAN FEDERAL BUREAUCRACY

A patchwork of agencies and commissions to meet growing public demands

In 2018 nearly three million civilians worked for the federal government, including about half a million U.S. Postal Service employees, and almost a million people were in the military. Only a relative handful, approximately 63,000 employees, work in the legislative branch or the judiciary. The remaining more than two and a half million are in the executive branch, home of the federal bureaucracy. Another five million or so contract and grant workers make the federal workforce larger than its official numbers would indicate.[7] In this section we look at the evolution of the federal bureaucracy, its present-day organization, and its basic functions.

THE SPOILS SYSTEM

red tape the complex procedures and regulations surrounding bureaucratic activity

spoils system the nineteenth-century practice of rewarding political supporters with public office

patronage a system in which successful party candidates reward supporters with jobs or favors

Americans have not always been so concerned with the norm of neutral competence in the bureaucracy. Under a form of bureaucratic organization called the **spoils system**, practiced through most of the nineteenth century, elected executives—the president, governors, and mayors—were given wide latitude to hire their friends, family, and political supporters to work in their administrations (a practice known as **patronage**). They may not have had social media, but the interconnected personal relationships created a similar tightly knit web. The spoils system is often said to have begun with the administration of President Andrew Jackson and gets its name from the adage "To the victor belong the spoils of the enemy." But Jackson was neither the first nor the last politician to see the acquisition of public office as a means of feathering his cronies' nests.

Filling the bureaucracy with political appointees almost guarantees incompetence, because those who get jobs for political reasons are more likely to be politically motivated than genuinely skilled in a specific area. America's disgust with the corruption and inefficiency of the spoils system, as well as our collective distrust of placing too much power in the hands of any one person, led Congress to institute various reforms of the American **civil service**, as it is sometimes called, aimed at achieving a very different sort of organization.

One of the first reforms, and certainly one of the most significant, was the Civil Service Reform Act of 1883. This act, usually referred to as the **Pendleton Act**, created the initial Civil Service Commission, under which federal employees would be hired and promoted on the basis of merit rather than patronage. It prohibited firing employees for failure to contribute to political parties or candidates.

Protection of the civil service from partisan politicians got another boost in 1939 with the passage of the **Hatch Act**, designed to take the pressure off civil servants to work for the election of parties and candidates. They cannot run for federal political office, head up an election campaign, or make contributions or public speeches on behalf of candidates, although they can get involved in election activities that do not focus on just one candidate or party. The Hatch Act was an attempt to neutralize the political effects of the bureaucracy, but in doing so it denies federal employees a number of activities that are open to other citizens.

EVOLUTION OF THE FEDERAL BUREAUCRACY

The central characteristic of the federal bureaucracy is that most of its parts developed independently of the others in a piecemeal and political fashion, rather than emerging from a coherent plan.[8] Federal agencies fall into three categories:[9]

- Some government departments deal with fundamental activities. For example, the Departments of State, War (now Defense), and the Treasury were the first cabinet offices because the activities they handle are essential to the smooth functioning of government. The Department of State exists to handle diplomatic relations with other nations. The Department of Defense supervises the air force, army, navy, marines, and, in time of war, the coast guard. The Department of the Treasury, which oversees the Internal Revenue Service (IRS), performs the key tax collection function, prints the money we use, and oversees the horrendous job of managing the national debt.

- Other government departments developed in response to national problems and to meet the changing needs of the country as it industrialized and evolved into an urban society. For instance, the Department of the Interior was created in 1848 to deal with some of the unforeseen effects of westward expansion. The Interstate Commerce Commission, Federal Reserve System, Federal Trade Commission, and other agencies were created to regulate the burgeoning American marketplace. The Social Security Administration was designed to supplement inadequate and failed old-age pensions during a time of economic hardship. The Office of Economic Opportunity and the Department of Housing and Urban Development were intended to cope with the poverty that continued to exist as America prospered after the New Deal. The

civil service
nonmilitary employees of the government who are appointed through the merit system

Pendleton Act the 1883 civil service reform that required the hiring and promoting of civil servants to be based on merit, not patronage

Hatch Act the 1939 law that limited the political involvement of civil servants in order to protect them from political pressure and keep politics out of the bureaucracy

National Science Foundation and the National Aeronautics and Space Administration (NASA) were crafted to help America respond to the intellectual challenges of the Cold War. Much more recently, the September 11, 2001, terror attacks on the United States led to the establishment of the cabinet-level Department of Homeland Security to coordinate efforts to protect the country. You can imagine new national needs—especially the looming challenges of automation and artificial intelligence in the workplace, for instance—driving new growth of the federal bureaucratic landscape. It is precisely our inability to foresee the consequences of global, economic, and technological changes that lead us to demand that government protect us from them.

- Still other government departments develop in response to different **clientele groups**, which want government to do something for them. These may include interest groups—groups of citizens, businesses, or industry members who are affected by the regulatory action of the government and who organize to try to influence policy. Or they may include unorganized groups, such as poor people, to which the government has decided to respond. Departments in these areas are sensitive to the concerns of specific groups rather than focusing on what is good for the nation as a whole. The U.S. Department of Agriculture (USDA), among the first of these departments, was set up in 1862 to assist U.S. agricultural interests. It began by providing research information to farmers and later arranged subsidies and developed markets for agricultural products. Politicians in today's budget-cutting climate talk about reducing agricultural subsidies, but no one expects the USDA to change its focus of looking out, first and foremost, for the farmer. Similar stories can be told of the Departments of Labor, Commerce, Education, and Veterans Affairs.

ORGANIZATION OF THE FEDERAL BUREAUCRACY

The federal bureaucracy consists of four types of organizations: (1) cabinet-level departments, (2) independent agencies, (3) regulatory agencies, and (4) government corporations. Making the job of understanding the bureaucracy more complicated, some agencies can fit into more than one of those classifications. The difficulty in classifying an agency as one type or another stems partly from Congress' habit of creating hybrids: agencies that act like government corporations, for instance, or cabinet-level departments that regulate. The overall organizational chart of the U.S. government makes this complex bureaucracy look reasonably orderly. To a large extent the impression of order is an illusion.

DEPARTMENTS The federal government currently has fifteen **departments**. *The Big Picture* in this chapter shows how and when these departments were created. The heads of departments are known as secretaries—for example, the secretary of state or the secretary of defense—except for the head of the Department of Justice, who is called the attorney general. These department heads collectively make up the president's cabinet, appointed by the president, with the consent of the Senate, to provide advice on critical areas of government affairs such as foreign relations, agriculture, education, and so on. These areas are not fixed, and presidents may propose different cabinet offices. Although the secretaries are political appointees who usually change when the administration changes (or even more frequently), they sit at the heads of the large, more or less permanent, bureaucracies we call departments. Cabinet heads may not have any more actual power than other agency leaders, but their posts do carry more status and prestige. Donald Trump's cabinet includes the same officials, but the mission of some, for example, the head of the Environmental Protection Agency (EPA), has changed dramatically.

clientele groups
groups of citizens whose interests are affected by an agency or a department and who work to influence its policies

departments one of the major subdivisions of the federal government, represented in the president's cabinet

INDEPENDENT AGENCIES Congress has established a host of agencies outside the cabinet departments. The independent agencies are structured like the cabinet departments, with a single head appointed by the president. Their areas of jurisdiction tend to be narrower than those of the cabinet departments. Congress does not follow a blueprint for how to make an independent agency or a department. Instead, it expands the bureaucracy to fit the case at hand, given the mix of political forces of the moment—that is, given what groups are demanding what action, and with what resources. As a result, the independent agencies vary tremendously in size, from fewer than 320 employees in the Federal Election Commission to over 62,000 for the Social Security Administration.[10] Although agencies are called independent because of their independence from cabinet departments, they vary in their independence from the president. This is not accidental but political. When Congress is not in agreement with the current president, it tends to insulate a new agency from presidential control by making the appointments for fixed terms that do not overlap with the president's, or they remove budgetary oversight from the Office of Management and Budget.[11] Thus some agency heads serve at the president's discretion and can be fired at any time; others serve fixed terms, and the president can appoint a new head or commissioner only when a vacancy occurs. Independent agencies also vary in their freedom from judicial review. Congress has established that some agencies' rulings cannot be challenged in the courts, whereas others' can be.[12]

INDEPENDENT REGULATORY BOARDS AND COMMISSIONS Independent regulatory boards and commissions make regulations for various industries, businesses, and sectors of the economy. Regulations are simply limitations or restrictions on the behavior of an individual or a business; they are bureaucratically determined prescriptions for how business is to take place. This chapter opened with the battle over regulations from an ideological point of view—do they serve the public, or do they not? Regulations usually seek to protect the public from some industrial or economic danger or uncertainty. The Securities and Exchange Commission, for example, regulates the trading of stocks and bonds on the nation's stock markets, while the Food and Drug Administration regulates such things as how drugs must be tested before they can be safely marketed and what information must appear on the labels of processed foods and beverages sold throughout the country. Regulation usually pits the individual's freedom to do what he or she wants, or a business's drive to make a profit, against some vision of what is good for the public. But the parties differ significantly on whether regulations are a good thing or an inhibition of individual freedom and entrepreneurship. How each trade-off is made among freedom, profit, and public safety is a question of ideology and public policy.

The number of agencies of the federal government whose principal job it is to issue and enforce regulations about what citizens and businesses can do, and how they have to do it is something of a moving target.[13] Agencies are cut, redefined, and multiplied with new administrations. Given the scope of the undertaking, it is not surprising that regulation occasionally gets out of hand. If an agency exists to regulate, regulate it probably will, whether or not a clear case can be made for restricting action. The average cheeseburger in America, for instance, is the subject of over 40,000 federal and state regulations, specifying everything from the vitamin content of the flour in the bun, to the age and fat content of the cheese, to the temperature at which it must be cooked, to the speed at which the ketchup must flow to be certified Grade A Fancy.[14] Some of these rules are undoubtedly crucial; we all want to be able to buy a cheeseburger without risking food poisoning and possible death. Others are informative; those of us on restrictive diets need to know what we are eating, and none of us likes to be ripped off by

independent agencies government organizations independent of the departments but with a narrower policy focus

independent regulatory boards and commissions government organizations that regulate various businesses, industries, or economic sectors

regulations limitations or restrictions on the activities of a business or an individual

THE BIG PICTURE:
How the Federal Bureaucracy Grew So Much

The country started out with a minimum of agencies needed to support a nation:
The Departments of State (diplomacy with other nations), War (now Defense, for when diplomacy fails), and Treasury (to collect taxes). As the nation grew, greater industrialization and urbanization inevitably produced new problems, which have resulted in a greater role for government—and new agencies—to regulate and maintain an increasingly complex society.

Number of Employees in Thousands, 2016

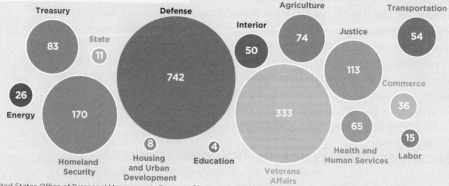

Treasury — 83
State — 11
Defense — 742
Interior — 50
Agriculture — 74
Justice — 113
Transportation — 54
Energy — 26
Homeland Security — 170
Housing and Urban Development — 8
Education — 4
Veterans Affairs — 333
Health and Human Services — 65
Commerce — 36
Labor — 15

Source: United States Office of Personnel Management, Common Characteristics of the Government Fiscal Year 2016, www.opm.gov/policy-data-oversight/data-analysis-documentation/federal-employment-reports/common-characteristics-of-the-government/ccog2016.pdf.

Spending per Capita in Constant 2013 Dollars / Timeline of Department Creation

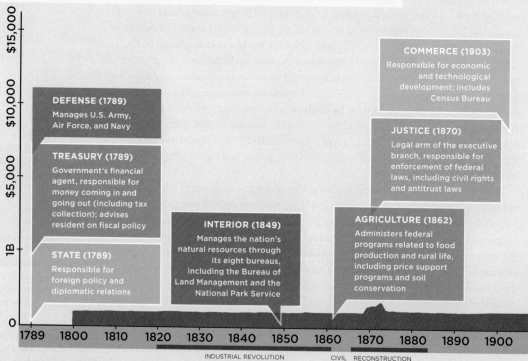

COMMERCE (1903)
Responsible for economic and technological development; includes Census Bureau

JUSTICE (1870)
Legal arm of the executive branch, responsible for enforcement of federal laws, including civil rights and antitrust laws

DEFENSE (1789)
Manages U.S. Army, Air Force, and Navy

TREASURY (1789)
Government's financial agent, responsible for money coming in and going out (including tax collection); advises resident on fiscal policy

INTERIOR (1849)
Manages the nation's natural resources through its eight bureaus, including the Bureau of Land Management and the National Park Service

AGRICULTURE (1862)
Administers federal programs related to food production and rural life, including price support programs and soil conservation

STATE (1789)
Responsible for foreign policy and diplomatic relations

INDUSTRIAL REVOLUTION | CIVIL WAR | RECONSTRUCTION

1789 1800 1810 1820 1830 1840 1850 1860 1870 1880 1890 1900

Sources: Table Ea636-643, Table Aa6-8, hsus.cambridge.org/HSUSWeb/HSUSEntryServlet, and U.S. Bureau of the Census, "Annual Population Estimates," NST-EST2012-01,

Annual Spending in Billions, 2017

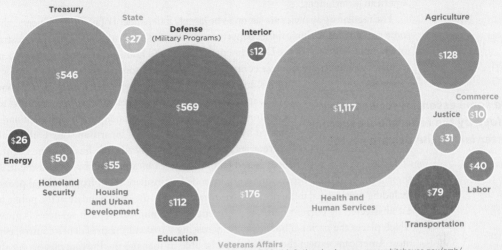

Treasury **$546**
State **$27**
Defense (Military Programs) **$569**
Interior **$12**
Agriculture **$128**
Energy **$26**
Homeland Security **$50**
Housing and Urban Development **$55**
Education **$112**
Veterans Affairs **$176**
Health and Human Services **$1,117**
Commerce **$10**
Justice **$31**
Labor **$40**
Transportation **$79**

Source: Office of Management and Budget, Historical Tables, Table 4.1: Outlays by Agency, www.whitehouse.gov/omb/budget/Historicals.

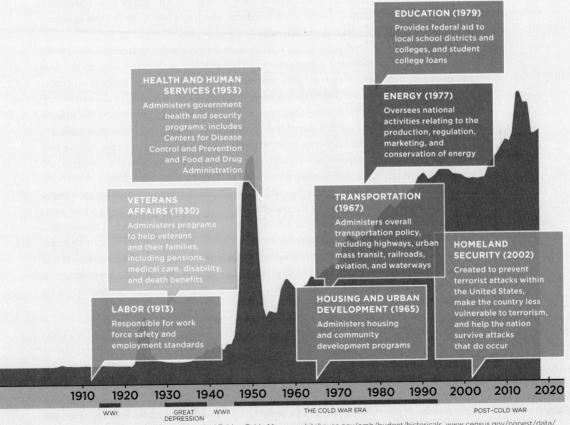

EDUCATION (1979)
Provides federal aid to local school districts and colleges, and student college loans

ENERGY (1977)
Oversees national activities relating to the production, regulation, marketing, and conservation of energy

HEALTH AND HUMAN SERVICES (1953)
Administers government health and security programs; includes Centers for Disease Control and Prevention and Food and Drug Administration

TRANSPORTATION (1967)
Administers overall transportation policy, including highways, urban mass transit, railroads, aviation, and waterways

HOMELAND SECURITY (2002)
Created to prevent terrorist attacks within the United States, make the country less vulnerable to terrorism, and help the nation survive attacks that do occur

VETERANS AFFAIRS (1930)
Administers programs to help veterans and their families, including pensions, medical care, disability, and death benefits

HOUSING AND URBAN DEVELOPMENT (1965)
Administers housing and community development programs

LABOR (1913)
Responsible for work force safety and employment standards

1910 1920 1930 1940 1950 1960 1970 1980 1990 2000 2010 2020

WWI — GREAT DEPRESSION — WWII — THE COLD WAR ERA — POST-COLD WAR

Office of Management and Budget, "Historical Tables: Table 1.1, www.whitehouse.gov/omb/budget/historicals, www.census.gov/popest/data/national/totals/2012/index.html.

getting something other than what we think we are paying for. Others seem merely silly; when we consider that adult federal employees are paid to measure the speed of ketchup, we readily sympathize with those who claim that the regulatory function is getting out of hand in American government.

The regulatory agencies are set up to be largely independent of political influence, though some are bureaus within cabinet departments—the federal Food and Drug Administration, for example, is located in the Department of Health and Human Services. Most independent regulatory agencies are run by a commission of three or more people who serve overlapping terms, and the terms of office, usually between three and fourteen years, are set so that they do not coincide with presidential terms. Commission members are nominated by the president and confirmed by Congress, often with a bipartisan vote. Unlike cabinet secretaries and some agency heads, the heads of the regulatory boards and commissions cannot be fired by the president. All of these aspects of their organization are intended to insulate them from political pressures, including presidential influence, in the expectation that they will regulate in the public interest unaffected by current partisan preferences. The number of such agencies is growing, which places the national bureaucracy increasingly beyond the president's control, even as most Americans expect the president to be able to manage the bureaucracy to get things done.[15] Nonetheless, as we saw in *What's at Stake . . . ?*, a focused agenda by an administration can put pressure on the civil service, especially if it starves them of money or jeopardizes their job security, as the Trump administration has done, which can lead to ineffective agencies, demoralized personnel, and stalled initiatives.[16]

> *Are some essential services now provided by the federal bureaucracy better left to the private sector?*

Congress wants to limit presidential influence on the regulatory agencies because, as we have seen, not all presidential administrations view regulation the same way, and as they approach the job of appointing regulatory officials accordingly, presidents can have an impact on how the agencies operate during their tenures in office. *What's at Stake . . . ?* showed us that, as holders of a conservative ideology that, in general, prefers to see less regulation and to leave control of industry to the market, Republican presidents tend to appoint businesspeople and others sympathetic to the industries being regulated. Democrats, by contrast, believe that regulation by impartial experts can smooth out many of the externalities of an unregulated market and tend to appoint those with a record of regulatory accomplishment and scientific expertise.[17] This difference in approach could be seen in action when President Barack Obama came into office in 2009. Reversing the trend set by President George W. Bush's administration, he reinvigorated the regulatory mission of agencies such as the EPA, the Occupational Safety and Health Administration, and the Securities and Exchange Commission, in what one progressive author called "the quiet revolution."[18] And the "Trump Effect" we saw earlier was to decisively reverse much of that revolution, just as quietly. A good deal of the lawmaking that affects our everyday lives takes place off the public stage and with little accountability unless Congress practices active oversight.

GOVERNMENT CORPORATIONS We do not often think of the government as a business, but public enterprises are, in fact, big business. The U.S. Postal Service, a **government corporation**, is one of the larger businesses in the nation in terms of sales and personnel. The Tennessee Valley Authority and the Bonneville Power Administration of the northwestern states are both in the business of generating electricity and selling it to citizens throughout their regions. If you ride the rails as a passenger, you travel by Amtrak (technically called the

government corporations companies created by Congress to provide to the public a good or service that private enterprise cannot or will not profitably provide

National Railroad Passenger Corporation). All of these businesses are set up to be largely independent of both congressional and presidential influence. This independence is not insignificant. Consider, for example, how angry citizens are when the postal rates go up. Because the Postal Commission is independent, both the president and Congress avoid the political heat for such unpopular decisions. In a twist, however, the rise of online shopping at private companies like Amazon has proved to be a boon to the postal service's survival. Ironically, in an effort to punish Amazon's owner, Jeff Bezos, President Trump has been putting pressure on the postal service to raise the rates it charges companies like Amazon, an effort that will likely hurt the postal service much more than Amazon.[19]

ROLES OF THE FEDERAL BUREAUCRACY

Federal bureaucrats at the broadest level are responsible for helping the president to administer the laws, policies, and regulations of government. Bureaucrats are not confined to administering the laws, however. Although the principle of separation of powers—by which the functions of making, administering, and interpreting the laws are carried out by the executive, legislative, and judicial branches—applies at the highest level of government, it tends to dissolve at the level of the bureaucracy. In practice, the bureaucracy is an all-in-one policymaker. It administers the laws, but it also effectively makes and judges compliance with laws.

BUREAUCRACY AS ADMINISTRATOR We expect the agencies of the federal government to implement the laws passed by Congress and signed by the president. Operating under the ideal of neutral competence, a public bureaucracy serves the political branches of government in a professional, unbiased, and efficient manner. In many cases this is exactly what happens, and with admirable ability and dedication. The rangers in the national parks help visitors enjoy our natural resources, police officers enforce the statutes of criminal law, social workers check for compliance with welfare regulations, and postal workers deliver letters and packages in a timely way. All these bureaucrats are simply carrying out the laws that have been made elsewhere in government.

BUREAUCRACY AS RULE MAKER The picture of the bureaucrat as an impartial administrator removed from political decision making is an incomplete and unrealistic one. The bureaucracy has a great deal of latitude in administering national policy. Because it often lacks the time, the technical expertise, and the political coherence and leverage to write clear and detailed legislation, Congress frequently passes laws that are vague, contradictory, and overly general. To carry out or administer the laws, the bureaucracy must first fill in the gaps. Congress has essentially delegated some of its legislative power to the bureaucracy. Its role here is called bureaucratic discretion. Top bureaucrats must use their own judgment, which under the ideal of neutral competence should remain minimal, in order to carry out the laws of Congress. Congress does not say how many park rangers should be assigned to Yosemite versus Yellowstone, for instance; the National Park Service has to interpret the broad intent of the law and make decisions on this and thousands of other specifics. Bureaucratic discretion is not limited to allocating personnel and other "minor" administrative details. Congress cannot make decisions on specifications for military aircraft, dictate the advice the agricultural extension agents should give to farmers, or determine whether the latest sugar substitute is safe for our soft drinks. The appropriate bureaucracy must fill in all those details.

The procedures of administrative rule making are not completely insulated from the outside world, however. Before they become effective, all new regulations must first be publicized in

bureaucratic discretion bureaucrats' use of their own judgment in interpreting and carrying out the laws of Congress

the *Federal Register*, which is a primary source of information for thousands of interests affected by decisions in Washington. Before adopting the rules, agencies must give outsiders—the public and interest groups—a chance to be heard.

BUREAUCRACY AS JUDGE The third major function of government is adjudication, or the process of interpreting the law in specific cases for potential violations and deciding the appropriate penalties when violations are found. This is what the courts do. However, a great deal of adjudication in America is carried out by the bureaucracy. For example, regulatory agencies not only make many of the rules that govern the conduct of business but also are responsible for seeing that individuals, but more often businesses, comply with their regulations. Tax courts, under the IRS, for instance, handle violations of the tax codes, and their decisions have the full force of law.

WHO ARE THE FEDERAL BUREAUCRATS?

The full civilian workforce of the federal bureaucracy reflects the general workforce fairly accurately. For example, 46.9 percent of the U.S. civilian labor force is female and 42.7 percent of the civil service is female. African Americans make up 11.9 percent of the civilian workforce and 18.3 percent of the civil service.[20] The distributions are similar for other demographic characteristics such as ethnic origin or level of education. This representative picture is disturbed, however, by the fact that not all bureaucratic positions are equal. Policymaking is done primarily at the highest levels, and the upper grades are staffed predominantly by well-educated white males. Women and minorities are distinctly underrepresented in the policymaking (and higher-paying) levels of the bureaucracy.[21]

In Your Own Words Outline the organization and roles of the federal bureaucracy.

POLITICS INSIDE THE BUREAUCRACY

Power struggles between political appointees and professional bureaucrats, constrained by cultural norms

Politicians and bureaucrats alike are wary about the effects of politics on decision making. They act as if fairness and efficiency could always be achieved if only the struggle over competing interests could be set aside through an emphasis on strict rules and hierarchical organization. We know, of course, that the struggle can't be set aside. As a fundamental human activity, politics is always with us, and it is always shaped by the particular rules and institutions in which it is played out. Politics within bureaucracies is a subset of politics generally, but it takes on its own cast according to the context in which it takes place.

BUREAUCRATIC CULTURE

The particular context in which internal bureaucratic politics is shaped is called **bureaucratic culture**—the accepted values and procedures of an organization. Consider any place you may have been employed. When you began your job, the accepted standards of behavior may not have been clear, but over time you figured out who had power, what your role was, which rules

Federal Register the publication containing all federal regulations and notifications of regulatory agency hearings

bureaucratic culture the accepted values and procedures of an organization

could be bent and which had to be followed strictly, and what the goals of the enterprise were. That's all a way of saying that you understood the accepted power narrative in your workplace. Chances are you came to share some of the values of your colleagues, at least with respect to your work. Those things add up to the culture of the workplace. Bureaucratic culture is just a specific instance of workplace culture.

Knowing the four main elements of bureaucratic culture—policy commitment, adoption of bureaucratic behavior, specialization and expertise, and identification with the agency—will take us a long way toward understanding why bureaucrats and bureaucracies behave the way they do. Essentially these elements define what is at stake within a bureaucracy, and what bureaucrats need to do to ensure that they are winners and not losers in the bureaucratic world.

Good bureaucrats develop a commitment to the policy issues they are tasked with. For instance, an

Low Morale
Government employees can come to strongly identify with the agency for which they work, supporting the mission they are tasked with and feeling protective of its legacy and turf. This can lead to low morale if the agency's mission is not a priority for a president, or, worse, if that mission runs counter to the president's own goals. The Trump administration's skepticism around climate change has led to anxiety at NASA and the EPA.

employee of the USDA will eventually come to believe that agricultural issues are among the most important facing the country, even if he or she never thought much about farming before. In the same way, those working at NASA place a priority on investigating outer space, and bureaucrats at the National Institutes of Health believe fervently in health research. They will share a commitment to their policy area not only because their jobs depend on it but also because all the people around them believe in it.

New bureaucrats will soon start to see the logic of behaving bureaucratically; they may even start to sound like bureaucrats. Bureaucratese is the formal and often (to outsiders) amusing way that bureaucrats sometimes speak in their effort to convey information without controversy. Bureaucrats also develop a dependency on the rules because relying on the rules relieves them of the responsibility of relying on their own judgment. They learn that exercising such bureaucratic discretion, as we discussed earlier, can leave them vulnerable if their decisions are not clearly within the rules. They also adjust to the hierarchical organization in which they are dependent on their superiors for work assignments, promotions, budget allotments, and vacation authorizations. Those superiors will have the same relationships with their bosses.

Departments, agencies, and bureaus have specialized areas of responsibility and expertise. There is not a great deal of interagency hopping; most bureaucrats spend their whole professional lives working in the same area, often in the same department. Lawyers in the Justice Department, scientists at the National Science Foundation, physicians at the National Institutes of Health, and even soybean experts at the USDA all have specialized knowledge as the base of their power.

The characteristics of bureaucratic culture discussed so far lead to the fourth: identification with and protection of the agency. As bureaucrats become attached to the policy interests of their agencies, committed to the rules and structures of the bureaucracy, concerned with the fortunes of their superiors, and appreciative of their own and their colleagues' specialized knowledge, they identify their interests with those of their agencies.

They will come to identify with the department, not just because their job depends on it but because they believe in what it does.

This pervasive bureaucratic culture has a number of political consequences. On the plus side, it holds the bureaucracy together, fostering values of commitment and loyalty to what could otherwise be seen as an impersonal and alienating work environment. It means that the people who work in the federal government, for the most part, really believe in what they do.

But bureaucratic culture can lead to negative consequences as well. As former Federal Bureau of Investigation (FBI) agent Coleen Rowley pointed out in testimony before the Senate Judiciary Committee in June 2002, this culture very likely had a role in the failure of our law enforcement and intelligence agencies to foresee and prevent the attacks of September 11, 2001. Rowley's office, in Minneapolis, had known that a possible terrorist, Zacarias Moussaoui, was seeking to take flying lessons. Finding his activities suspicious and worrisome, Minneapolis agents tried to get a warrant to search his computer but were unable to do so. In her testimony, Rowley targeted the FBI's hierarchical culture, with its implicit norm that said field agents did not go over the heads of their superiors, who frequently second-guessed their judgment.[22] Not only did bureaucratic culture keep the FBI from knowing what information it had prior to September 11, but it also kept the FBI and the Central Intelligence Agency (CIA) from communicating with each other about the various pieces of the puzzle they had found. Between them they had much of the information needed to have discovered the plot, but no one connected the dots. Why? The cultures are different. The FBI is primarily a law enforcement agency; agents are rewarded for making arrests. Its antiterrorist activities prior to September 11 were focused on after-the-fact investigations of terrorist attacks (leading to convictions) but not on preventing such attacks against domestic targets.[23]

The CIA, by contrast, is focused on clandestine activity to develop information about non-American groups and nations. It is more secretive and less rule-bound, more focused on plans and intentions than on after-the-fact evidence and convictions. Agents focus on relationships, not individual achievement. One reporter covering the two agencies wrote that though the two agencies need to work with each other, "they have such different approaches to life that they remain worlds apart. In fact, they speak such different languages that they can barely even communicate."[24]

When an agency is charged with making the rules, enforcing them, and even adjudicating them, it is relatively easy to cover up less catastrophic agency blunders. If Congress, the media, or the public had sufficient information and the expertise to interpret it, this would not be as big a problem. However, specialization necessarily concentrates the expertise and information in the hands of the agencies, and this is one of the places where the channels of communication are narrow and restricted and news is limited. Perhaps for this reason, rumors and conspiracy theories about "the deep state" thrive on the Internet. Congress and the media are generalists. They can tell something has gone wrong when terrorists attack the United States seemingly without warning, but they cannot evaluate the hundreds of less obvious problems that may have led to the failure to warn that only an expert would even recognize. And in the absence of facts, imaginations run wild.

Congress has tried to check the temptation for bureaucrats to cover up their mistakes by offering protection to whistleblowers. **Whistleblowers**, like Coleen Rowley in the earlier example, are employees who expose instances or patterns of error, corruption, or waste in their agencies, whose consciences will not permit them to protect their agencies and superiors at the expense of what they believe to be the public good. They are often unpopular with their colleagues, as you might imagine. The Whistleblower Protection Act of 1989 established an

whistleblowers individuals who publicize instances of fraud, corruption, or other wrongdoing in the bureaucracy

independent agency to protect employees from being fired, demoted, or otherwise punished for exposing wrongdoing. The act's intention to protect whistleblowers is one way to counteract the negative tendency of organizational behavior, but it does little to offset the pressure that bureaucrats are under to protect their

When is rocking the bureaucratic boat (blowing the whistle) a good thing, and when is it not?

programs and the agencies from harm, embarrassment, and budget cuts. Because the agency that rules in these cases usually sides with the bureaucracy over the whistleblower, the law hasn't worked quite as its authors intended.[25]

PRESIDENTIAL APPOINTEES AND THE CAREER CIVIL SERVICE

Another aspect of internal bureaucratic politics worth noting is the giant gulf between those at the very top of the department or agency who are appointed by the president and those in the lower ranks who are long-term civil service employees. Of the nearly three million civilian employees in the U.S. civil service, about 3,500 are appointed by the president or the president's immediate subordinates.

The presidential appointees are sometimes considered "birds of passage" by the career service because of the regularity with which they come and go.[26] Though generally quite experienced in the agency's policy area, appointees have their own careers or the president's agenda, rather than the long-established mission of the agency, as their primary objective. The professional civil servants, in contrast, have worked in their agencies for many years and expect to remain there.[27] Chances are they were there before the current president was elected, and they will be there after the president leaves office. They are wholly committed to their agencies.

Minor clashes are frequent, but they can intensify into major rifts when the ideology of a newly elected president varies sharply from the central values of the operating agency. Nevertheless, even though the political appointees have the advantage of higher positions of authority, the career bureaucrats have time working on their side. Not surprisingly, the bureaucrat's best strategy when the political appointee presses for a new but unpopular policy direction is to stall. This is easily achieved by consulting the experts on feasibility, writing reports, drawing up implementation plans, commissioning further study, doing cost-benefit analyses, consulting advisory panels of citizens, and on and on.

Given the difficulty that presidents and their appointees can have in dealing with the entrenched bureaucracy, presidents who want to institute an innovative program are better off starting a new agency than trying to get an old one to adapt to new tasks. In the 1960s, when President John F. Kennedy wanted to start the Peace Corps, a largely volunteer organization that provided assistance to developing countries by working at the grassroots level with the people themselves, he could have added it to any number of existing departments. The problem was that either these existing agencies were unlikely to accept the idea that nonprofessional volunteers could do anything useful, or they were likely to subvert them to their own purposes, such as spying or managing aid. Thus President Kennedy was easily persuaded to have the Peace Corps set up as an independent agency, a frequent occurrence in the change-resistant world of bureaucratic politics.[28]

In Your Own Words Describe power struggles between political appointees and professional bureaucrats.

EXTERNAL BUREAUCRATIC POLITICS

*Turf wars among agencies and
with the three branches of government*

Politics affects relationships not only within bureaucratic agencies but also between those agencies and other institutions. The bureaucracy is not one of the official branches of government, since it falls technically within the executive branch, but it is often called the fourth branch of government because it wields so much power. It can be checked by other agencies, by the executive, by Congress, or even by the public, but it is not wholly under the authority of any of those entities. In this section we examine the political relationships that exist between the bureaucracy and the other main actors in American politics.

INTERAGENCY POLITICS

As we have seen, agencies are fiercely committed to their policy areas, their rules and norms, and their own continued existence. The government consists of a host of agencies, all competing intensely for a limited amount of federal resources and political support. They all want to protect themselves and their programs, and they want to grow, or at least to avoid cuts in personnel and budgets.

To appreciate the agencies' political plight, we need to see their situation *as they see it*. Bureaucrats are a favorite target of the media and elected officials. Their budgets are periodically up for review by congressional committees and the president's budget department. Consequently, agencies are compelled to work for their survival and growth. They have to act positively in an uncertain and changing political environment in order to keep their programs and their jobs.

One way agencies compete to survive is by building groups of supporters. Members of Congress are sensitive to voters' wishes, and because of this, support among the general public as well as interest groups is important for agencies. As a result, agencies try to control some services or products that are crucial to important groups. In most cases, the groups are obvious, as with the clientele groups of, say, the USDA. Department of Agriculture employees work hard for farming interests, not just because they believe in the programs but also because they need strong support from agricultural clientele to survive. Agencies whose work does not earn them a lot of fans, like the IRS, whose mission is tax collection, have few groups to support them. When Congress decided to reform the IRS in 1998, there were no defenders to halt the changes.[29] The survival incentives for bureaucratic agencies do not encourage agencies to work for the broader public interest but rather to cultivate special interests that are likely to be more politically active and powerful.

Even independent regulatory commissions run into this problem. Numerous observers have noted the phenomenon of **agency capture**, whereby commissions tend to become creatures of the very interests they are supposed to regulate. In other words, as the regulatory bureaucrats become more and more immersed in a policy area, they come to share the views of the regulated industries. The larger public's preferences tend to be less well formed and certainly less well expressed because the general public does not hire teams of lawyers, consultants, and lobbyists to represent its interests. The regulated industries have a tremendous amount at stake. Over time, regulatory agencies' actions may become so favorable to regulated industries that in some cases the industries themselves fight deregulation, as did the airlines when Congress and the Civil Aeronautics Board deregulated air travel in the

agency capture
a process whereby regulatory agencies come to be protective of and influenced by the industries they were established to regulate

1980s.[30] Agencies also compete and survive by offering services that no other agency provides. Departments and agencies are set up to deal with the problems of fairly specific areas. They do not want to overlap with other agencies because duplication of services might indicate that one of them is unnecessary, inviting congressional cuts. Thus, in many instances, agencies reach explicit agreements about dividing up the policy turf to avoid competition and duplication. This turf jealousy can undermine good public policy. Take, for example, the

military. For years, the armed services successfully resisted a unified weapons procurement, command, and control system. Each branch wanted to maintain its traditional independence in weapons development, logistics, and communications technologies, costing the taxpayers millions of dollars. Getting the branches to give up control of their turf was politically difficult, although it was accomplished eventually.

THE BUREAUCRACY AND THE PRESIDENT

As we discussed in Chapter 7, one of the president's several jobs is that of chief administrator. In fact, organizational charts of departments and agencies suggest a clear chain of command with the cabinet secretary at the top reporting directly to the president. But in this case, being "the boss" does not mean that the boss always, or even usually, gets his or her way. The long history of the relationship between the president and the bureaucracy is largely one of presidential frustration. President Kennedy voiced this exasperation when he said that dealing with the bureaucracy "is like trying to nail jelly to the wall." The reasons for presidential frustration lie in the fact that, although the president has some authority over the bureaucracy, the bureaucracy's different perspectives and goals often thwart the chief administrator's plans.

Still, presidents can often use the mechanisms of the bureaucracy to accomplish some of their goals, primarily through executive orders, as we saw in Chapter 7, but also through other administrative suggestions, directives, and encouragement. Usually presidents gain their policy objectives by working with Congress, but when that proves too controversial, or, in the case of Barack Obama, simply impossible, presidents can resort to implementing existing laws so as to achieve some of their preferred policies. Thus, Obama was also able to make strides on net neutrality, on climate change policy through the EPA, on immigration reform through directives to agencies in the Department of Homeland Security not to deport Dreamers or their families, and on marriage equality through the Justice Department's determination that the Defense of Marriage Act was not constitutional. In addition, he directed the Justice Department not to use its limited resources to challenge state marijuana laws that ran counter to federal law, and he directed the Bureau of Alcohol, Tobacco, Firearms and Explosives to close the so-called gun show loophole. Likewise, as we saw in *What's at Stake . . . ?*, Trump reversed much of what Obama did by the simple expedient of undoing his directions to the bureaucracy, or cancelling them. His 2018 decision to separate refugee families at the border was clearly his interpretation of a law that had never been used that way before even though he blamed Democrats for it. Such executive action is always subject to court challenge, especially if Congress is hostile, but a friendly bureaucracy, such as the Department of Justice in the refugee case, can help the president make such policy changes by not obstructing them. In addition, presidents have a few specific ways they can shape the bureaucracy.

Presidents have some substantial powers at their disposal for controlling the bureaucracy. The first is the power of appointment. The appointment process begins early in a new administration when the president is working to gain support for the administration's overall program, so the choices are rarely too controversial. This desire for early widespread support means presidents tend to play it safe and to nominate individuals with extensive experience in the policy areas they will oversee. Their backgrounds mean that the president's men and women have divided loyalties. They arrive on the job with some sympathy for the special interests and agencies they are to supervise on the president's behalf as well as with loyalty to the president.

Recent presidents have sought to achieve political control over agencies by expanding the numbers of their appointees at the top levels of agencies, especially those agencies whose missions are not consistent with the administration's policy agenda.[31] President George W. Bush was especially adept at this "politicization" of the bureaucracy. For instance, in his second term, he appointed one of his most trusted personal advisers to head the Department of Justice. Officials in that department then fired existing U.S. attorneys and replaced them with conservatives who would be more sympathetic to Republican policy concerns, which blunted the agency's traditionally aggressive enforcement of civil rights laws.[32]

President Obama's appointees were named with less of an eye to their ideological views than to their scientific expertise. As a Democrat, Obama attempted to reinvigorate the regulatory purpose and effective competence of the agencies in the bureaucracy, but Senate Republicans still refused to approve many of his recommendations because they generally disapprove of the agencies' regulatory mission. Rather than let agencies languish, Obama sought to get his nominations through with the use of recess appointments, a practice authorized by the Constitution that allows the president to make appointments without Senate approval when Congress is not in session. Intended to allow the president to deal with emergency appointments when the Senate cannot meet, presidents of both parties have used the strategy to get around recalcitrant Senates. In Obama's case the Republican House refused to agree to recess in order to thwart an impending Obama recess appointment, keeping both itself and the Senate in nominal session even while taking breaks. When the practice was challenged, the Supreme Court sided unanimously with the Senate, thus invalidating the president's appointment to the agency in question, the National Labor Relations Board, and tipping the balance toward Congress in the ongoing presidential-congressional battle for control of the bureaucracy.[33]

As we mentioned earlier, Trump has taken a somewhat scattershot approach to filling the bureaucratic branch. One hundred days into his administration, 87 percent of his executive branch positions were unstaffed.[34] He has had difficulty finding career bureaucrats who want to be associated with his administration's eccentric approach to governing, and they have experienced high turnover. He fills the positions in which he is interested, leaving others to languish or to be taken under the vice president's wing.

The second major power that presidents have in dealing with the bureaucracy is their key role in the budget process. About fifteen months before a budget request goes to Congress, the agencies send their preferred budget requests to the Office of Management and Budget (a White House agency serving the preferences of the president), which can lower, or raise, departmental budget requests. Thus the president's budget, which is sent to Congress, is a good statement of the president's overall program for the national government, reflecting priorities, new initiatives, and intended cutbacks. The president's political appointees and the civil servants who testify before Congress are expected to defend the president's budget.

And they do defend the president's budget, at least in their prepared statements. However, civil servants have contacts with interest group leaders, congressional staff, the media, and members of Congress themselves. Regardless of what the president wants, the agencies' real preferences are made known to sympathetic members of the key authorizations and appropriations committees. Thus the president's budget is a beginning bargaining point, but Congress can freely add to or cut back presidential requests, and most of the time it does so. The president's budget powers, while not insignificant, are no match for an agency with strong interest group and congressional support. Presidential influence over the bureaucratic budget is generally more effective in terminating an activity that the president opposes than in implementing a program that the agency opposes.[35]

The president also can try to reorganize the bureaucracy, combining some agencies, eliminating others, and generally restructuring the way government responsibilities are handled. Such reorganization efforts have become a passion with some presidents, but they are limited in their efforts by the need for congressional approval.[36] President Trump in 2018 proposed an ambitious restructuring program for the federal bureaucracy. The plan calls for the merging of the departments of Education and Labor into a new Department of Education and the Workforce, reorganizing the Department of Health and Human Services, and creating a new Federal Food Safety Agency. However, since the changes require congressional approval, the Republicans' loss of the House in the 2018 midterms likely means little progress will be made on this front.[37]

The final major power that presidents have over the bureaucracy is an informal one: the prestige of the office itself. The Office of the President impresses just about everyone. For presidents intent on change in an agency, their powers of persuasion and the sheer weight of the office can produce results. Few bureaucrats could stand face to face with the president of the United States and ignore a legal order. But presidents have limited time in office, their political pressures are many, and they need to choose their priorities carefully. The media, for example, will not permit presidents to spend a good part of each day worrying about programs that they think are trivial. A president who does so will be publicly criticized for wasting time on "minor matters." Thus the president and top White House staff have to move on to other things. The temptation for a bureaucracy that does not want to cooperate with a presidential initiative is to wait it out, to take the matter under study, or to be "able" to accomplish only a minor part of the president's agenda. The agency or department can then begin the process of regaining whatever ground it lost. It, after all, will be there long after the president leaves office.

THE BUREAUCRACY AND CONGRESS

Relationships between the bureaucracy and Congress are not any more clear-cut than those between the agencies and the president, but in the long run individual members of Congress, if not the whole institution itself, have more control over what specific bureaucracies do than does the executive branch. This is not due to any particular constitutional grant of power but rather to informal policymaking relationships that have grown up over time and are now all but institutionalized.

Much of the effective power in making policy in Washington is lodged in what political scientists call iron triangles. An **iron triangle** is a tight alliance between congressional committees, interest groups or representatives of regulated industries, and bureaucratic agencies, in which policy comes to be made for the benefit of the shared interests of all three, not for the benefit of the greater public. Politicians are themselves quite aware of the pervasive triangular monopoly of power. Former secretary of Health, Education, and Welfare John Gardner once declared before the Senate Government Operations Committee, "As everyone in this room knows but few people outside of Washington understand, questions of public policy nominally lodged with the Secretary are often decided far beyond the Secretary's reach by a trinity—not exactly a holy trinity—consisting of (1) representatives of an outside lobby, (2) middle-level bureaucrats, and (3) selected members of Congress."[38]

A good example of an iron triangle is the natural resources policy shown in Figure 8.1. In 2010, as oil gushed into the Gulf of Mexico from the ruined oil rig *Deepwater Horizon*,

iron triangle the phenomenon of a clientele group, a congressional committee, and a bureaucratic agency cooperating to make mutually beneficial policy

FIGURE 8.1
The Oil Industry–BOEM Iron Triangle

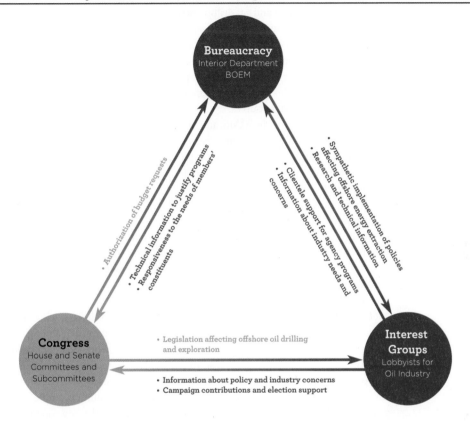

Bureaucracy
Interior Department
BOEM

• Authorization of budget requests

• Technical information to justify programs
• Responsiveness to the needs of members' constituents

• Sympathetic implementation of policies affecting offshore energy extraction
• Research and technical information

• Clientele support for agency programs
• Information about industry needs and concerns

Congress
House and Senate
Committees and
Subcommittees

**Interest
Groups**
Lobbyists for
Oil Industry

• Legislation affecting offshore oil drilling and exploration

• **Information about policy and industry concerns**
• **Campaign contributions and election support**

Iron triangles (involving Congress, the bureaucracy, and special interest groups) exist on nearly every subgovernment level. In this example, you can see how the BOEM (the Bureau of Ocean Energy Management), which depends on the House and the Senate for its budget, influences and is influenced by oil company lobbyists, who in turn influence and are influenced by House and Senate committees and subcommittees. This mutual interdependence represents a monopoly of power.

the Minerals Management Service (MMS), an obscure agency that few citizens had heard of, was blasted into the news. The MMS, which was in charge of issuing leases, collecting royalties, and overseeing the dangerous work of offshore drilling for oil and gas on America's continental shelf, was accused of having cozy and even illegal relationships with the industry it was charged with regulating. Agency employees were said to have accepted meals, gifts, and sporting trips from the oil industry, and some agency staff were accused of having had sex and using drugs with industry employees. How could this happen?

At the agency's top sat people like J. Steven Griles, who had worked as an oil industry lobbyist before joining the government. In middle management, the line between the industry and its regulators in the field was blurred.[39] As one MMS district manager put it, "Obviously we're all oil industry. . . . We're all from the same part of the country. Almost all our inspectors have worked for oil companies out on the [Gulf] platforms. They grew up in the same towns."[40] The industry and agency shared a goal of maximizing oil and gas production with hardly more than a whisper of concern for the effects of what was believed to be an unlikely accident. Not surprisingly, many key congressional leaders of the committees with jurisdiction over oil and gas drilling policies are from states with large petroleum interests. The House Committee on Natural Resources and its subcommittee on Energy and Mineral Resources have several members whose districts have major financial interests in oil and gas production, and most of these members receive substantial contributions from the oil and gas industry. The oil- and gas-producing states of Louisiana, Texas, Oklahoma, Colorado, and New Mexico all have members of Congress who receive major contributions from oil and gas industry sources.[41]

Thus the oil industry, the MMS, and members of Congress with responsibility for overseeing the agency all possessed interests in protecting energy production that reinforced one another in a cozy triangle and disregarded the general public's interests in avoiding environmental catastrophe and receiving the appropriate royalties from oil and gas use. The drug and sex scandals, along with the media's relentless coverage of the *Deepwater Horizon* disaster, focused national attention on the problem and spurred the Obama administration to reorganize the agency, now called the Bureau of Ocean Energy Management (BOEM). However, the forces that created this situation—that is, the intertwined interests among members of Congress who serve on committees that oversee agencies that regulate the industries that affect voters in their districts—are a fundamental part of our political-economic system. As long as citizens and industry are free to "petition Congress for redress of grievances," iron triangles will remain.

The metaphor of the iron triangle has been refined by scholars, who speak instead of **issue networks**.[42] The iron triangle suggests a particular relationship among a fixed interest group and fixed agencies and fixed subcommittees. The network idea suggests that the relationships are more complex than a simple triangle. There are really clusters of interest groups, policy specialists, consultants, and research institutes ("think tanks") that are influential in the policy areas. To continue with the offshore drilling example, environmental groups such as the League of Conservation Voters monitor the environmental records of members of Congress, and outside groups use existing laws to force agencies like the MMS to change their procedures. So, for example, the Center for Biological Diversity sought to sue the Department of the Interior (of which the MMS was part) for failing to get appropriate environmental permits required by the Marine Mammal Protection Act and the Endangered Species Act.[43] Thus "outsiders" can use the courts, and they often lobby sympathetic members of Congress to contest the relationships that develop as iron triangles. Their participation shows that the concept of an iron triangle does not always incorporate all the actors in a particular policy area. That is, although the relationships identified by the iron triangle remain important, the full range of politics is frequently captured better by the concept of issue networks.

Congressional control of the bureaucracy is found more in the impact of congressional committees and subcommittees than in the actions of the institution as a whole. Congress, of course, passes the laws that create the agencies, assigns them their responsibilities, and funds their operations. Furthermore, Congress can, and frequently does, change the laws under which the agencies operate. Thus Congress clearly has the formal power to control the bureaucracy. It also has access to a good deal of information that helps members monitor the bureaucracy. This process is called **congressional oversight**. Members learn about agency behavior through required reports, oversight hearings, and reports by congressional

issue networks
complex systems of relationships among groups that influence policy, including elected leaders, interest groups, specialists, consultants, and research institutes

congressional oversight efforts by Congress, especially through committees, to monitor agency rule making, enforcement, and implementation of congressional policies

agencies such as the former Office of Technology Assessment and the Government Accountability Office, and from constituents and organized interests. But Congress is itself often divided about what it wants to do and is unable to set clear guidelines for agencies. During the first six years of the George W. Bush administration, the Republican majority was more intent on supporting the president than on protecting congressional prerogatives in the policy process. This aided the president's expansion of control of the bureaucracy.[44] Only when a congressional consensus exists on what an agency should be doing is congressional control fully effective.

THE BUREAUCRACY AND THE COURTS

Agencies can be sued by individuals and businesses for not following the law. If a citizen disagrees with an agency ruling on welfare eligibility, or the adequacy of inspections of poultry processing plants, or even a ruling by the IRS, he or she can take up the issue with the courts. In some cases the courts have been important. A highly controversial example involves the timber industry. Environmentalists sued the Department of the Interior and the U.S. Forest Service to prevent logging in some of the old-growth forests of the Pacific Northwest. They sought protection for the spotted owl under the terms of the Endangered Species Act. After a decade-long struggle, logging was greatly restricted in the area in 1992, despite opposition by the economically important timbering interests of the region. However, under the more business-friendly Bush administration, the issue was once again on the agenda and, as the timber industry gained ground, the environmental groups were back in court. In 2009 the Obama administration reversed the Bush administration policy that had doubled the amount of logging allowed.[45] The Trump administration, in turn, has undone regulations that preserved the federal forests.[46]

More often, though, the courts play only a modest role in controlling the bureaucracy. One of the reasons for this limited role is that, since the Administrative Procedures Act of 1946, the courts have tended to defer to the expertise of the bureaucrats when agency decisions are appealed. That is, unless a clear principle of law is violated, the courts usually support administrative rulings.[47] So, for example, while the Supreme Court did restrict some aspects of the George W. Bush administration's policies of unlimited detention of "enemy combatants" held at Guantánamo Bay, it did not go nearly as far as civil liberties advocates wanted.[48]

Another reason is that Congress explicitly puts the decisions of numerous agencies, such as the Department of Veterans Affairs, beyond the reach of the courts. They do this, of course, when members expect they will agree with the decisions of an agency but are uncertain about what the courts might do. Some agencies like the IRS and those dealing with immigration have their own units to resolve disputes. Finally, even without these restrictions, the courts' time is extremely limited. The departments and independent agencies make thousands of important decisions each year; the courts can act on only those decisions about which someone feels sufficiently aggrieved to take the agency to court. Court proceedings can drag on for years, and meanwhile the agencies go about their business making new decisions. In short, the courts can, in specific instances, decide cases that influence how the bureaucracy operates, but such instances are the exception rather than the rule.

In Your Own Words Outline the relationship between the federal agencies and the three branches of the federal government.

Political Cartoons

Political cartoons do more than elicit a laugh or a chuckle. Frequently they avoid humor altogether, going for outrage, indignation, ridicule, or scathing contempt. Often, they are aimed at well-known public figures—easy targets like the president, a major celebrity, or a well-known business leader. But cartoonists also use their pens (and their wits) to shine light on less glamorous and less recognizable aspects of the political ecosystem.

The bureaucracy, for example, is almost by definition an unsexy subject. Stories about federal agencies are a snore, and there is usually precious little that a photograph can say about what they do. But a cartoonist, communicating with both words and pictures and armed with an arsenal of devices—among them exaggeration, irony, sarcasm, symbolism, shock, and humor—can make profound and attention-grabbing statements about topics that otherwise might be ignored. With this barrage of weapons aimed at you, your critical thinking skills are crucial.[1]

WHAT TO WATCH OUT FOR

- **What is the event or issue that inspired the cartoon?** Political cartoonists do not attempt to inform you about current events; they assume that you already know what has happened. Their job is to comment on the news, and so your first step in savvy cartoon readership is to be up on what's happening in the world. In this case, the situation being lampooned is the very nature of bureaucracy itself.

- **Who, or what, is the subject?** Are there any real people in the cartoon? Who are they? Many cartoonists do not confine their art to real people. Some will use a generic person sometimes labeled to represent a group (big business, the U.S. Senate, environmentalists, a political party, or a federal agency). The subject here is an almost-faceless bureaucrat, playing off the idea that bureaucrats are automatons without personal identity.

- **Are there symbols in the cartoon? What do they represent?** Without a key to the symbols that cartoonists use, their art can be incomprehensible. Uncle Sam stands in for the United States and is often used to depict specific federal agencies; donkeys are Democrats, and elephants are Republicans. Often these symbols are combined in unique ways. Again, the lack of a full face for the bureaucrat reduces him to his title, a symbol of bureaucracy run rampant.

- **What is the cartoonist's opinion about the topic of the cartoon?** Do you agree with it or not? Why? The cartoonist here is gently mocking the bureaucracy's typically bureaucratic efforts to make itself less bureaucratic.

---

1. Questions are based on the PoliticalCartoons.com teachers' guide, www.cagle.com/teacher.

Clay Bennett/© the Christian Science Monitor (www.CSMonitor.com). Reprinted with permission.

ASSISTANT TO THE AIDE OF THE DEPUTY VICE CHAIRMAN OF THE COMMITTEE TO REDUCE PENTAGON BUREAUCRACY

CITIZENSHIP AND THE BUREAUCRACY
The tension between transparency and efficiency

To help increase bureaucratic responsiveness and sensitivity to the public, Congress has made citizen participation a central feature of the policymaking of many agencies. The opening up of media channels to increase transparency and engagement has made this easier, although it is still not an open democratic process. (See *Don't Be Fooled by . . . Political Cartoons* for tips on evaluating some media depictions of the bureaucracy.) Much increased transparency has taken the form of citizen advisory councils that, by statute, subject key policy decisions of agencies to outside consideration by members of the public. There are more than 1,200 such committees and councils in the executive branch. The people who serve on these councils are not representative of the general public. Rather, they are typically chosen by the agency and have special credentials or interests relevant to the agency's work.

Other reforms have attempted to make the bureaucracy more accessible to the public. Citizen access has been enhanced by the passage of sunshine laws, which require that meetings of policymakers be open to the public. However, most national security and personnel meetings, as well as many criminal investigation meetings, are exempt. The right to attend a meeting is of little use if one doesn't know that it is being held in the first place. The Administrative Procedure Act requires advance published notice of all hearings, proposed rules, and new regulations so that the public can attend and comment on decisions that might affect them. These announcements appear in the *Federal Register*.

A related point of access is the Freedom of Information Act (FOIA), which was passed in 1966 and has been amended several times since. This act provides citizens with the right to copies of most public records held by federal agencies. Citizens also receive protection under the Privacy Act of 1974, which gives them the right to find out what information government agencies have about them. It also sets up procedures so that erroneous information can be corrected and ensures the confidentiality of Social Security, tax, and related records.

These reforms may provide little practical access for most citizens, however. Few of us have the time, the knowledge, or the energy to plow through the *Federal Register* and to attend meetings regularly. Similarly, while many citizens no doubt feel that they are not getting the full story from government agencies, they have little idea of what it is they don't know. Hence few of us ever use the FOIA.

In Your Own Words Analyze the tension between transparency and efficiency in the federal bureaucracy.

citizen advisory councils citizen groups that consider the policy decisions of an agency; a way to make the bureaucracy responsive to the general public

sunshine laws legislation opening the process of bureaucratic policymaking to the public

Freedom of Information Act (FOIA) the 1966 law that allows citizens to obtain copies of most public records

Privacy Act of 1974 a law that gives citizens access to the government's files on them

Let's Revisit: What's at Stake . . . ?

At the beginning of this chapter we discussed the many regulations, mostly enacted by the Obama administration, that President Trump was intent on rolling back. In many cases he was successful – we mentioned a dozen but there were hundreds. We also said that regulations are controversial, but that they affect our lives (positively or negatively) every day in all kinds of ways.

Now that we know much more about regulations and the regulatory infrastructure that lets us swallow pills, eat dinner, or put our kids to sleep at night with a reasonable assurance that disaster will not befall us, we know that a wholly unregulated life is something most of us probably don't want to accept. Life can be hazardous and often government is the only one in a position to provide protection.

But like so many things in life, this is a line-drawing problem. Everyone wants to regulate murder and poisonous pills and flammable baby pajamas, but not everyone wants to protect the environment or limit the cost of college loans or police the loans made by banks. Just what is at stake in unrolling the regulations that the Obama administration put in place?

Most of the regulations of the Obama years, at least the ones targeted by Trump, were designed to safeguard the environment, protect the health of individuals, manage the economic crisis and keep the less fortunate segments of the population from being taken advantage of by the powerful segments. If you think about what those things have in common, most of them are costly to wealthy people while providing benefits to the less well off.

That means wealthier people have a stake in getting rid of them; there will be huge business savings and increased profits for many industries without government telling them to be socially responsible. Supporters argue that these savings and profits will trickle down and benefit workers and consumers too, though much ink has been spilled debating this point.

Fiscally conscious people have a stake in rolling back regulations because the bureaucracy is often inefficient and wasteful, and many things cost much more than they need to. But the flip side is that regulations can also save money in the long run even if they cost more in the short run. The Clues to Critical Thinking in this chapter makes that point, and we have evidence in the fact that under Obamacare health care costs were coming down for everyone. And saving the environment now is undoubtedly cheaper than trying to colonize space when we've depleted this planet.

Those who worry about the environment or the climate also have huge stakes in the rolling back of Obama regulations because scientists are convinced that the window for protecting the planet is rapidly closing.[49] Eliminating emissions standards and getting out of the Paris Climate Agreement are likely to be incredibly costly in the long run.

The stakes in regulation boil down to two issues – whether you think it is government's job to help protect individuals and the planet from the consequences of our or others' actions, and whether we would rather pay for those consequences, some of which are undeniable, in the short term, or hope for the best in the long term. The current administration's policy is to save now and hope individuals and the future can take care of themselves.

Review

What Is Bureaucracy?

Bureaucracy (264), a form of hierarchical organization that aspires to **neutral competence** (264), is everywhere today, in the private as well as the public sphere. Bureaucratic decision making can be more efficient and expert in many cases than democratic decision making. The central problem of bureaucracy is **accountability** (265). **Red tape** (266), though cumbersome and irritating, also helps increase accountability by providing a paper trail and eliminating the discretion of lower-level bureaucrats to do their jobs in an idiosyncratic way.

The American Federal Bureaucracy

The **Pendleton Act** (267) and the **Hatch Act** (267) have moved the federal bureaucracy from the **patronage**-based (266) **spoils system** (266) of the nineteenth century to a **civil service** (267) based on merit. The U.S. bureaucracy has grown from just three cabinet **departments** (268) at the founding to a gigantic apparatus of fifteen cabinet-level departments and hundreds of **independent agencies** (269), **independent regulatory boards and commissions** (269), and **government corporations** (272). This growth has been in response to the expansion of the nation, the politics of special economic and social **clientele groups** (268), and the emergence of new problems that require solutions and **regulations** (269).

Many observers believe that the bureaucracy should simply administer the laws the political branches have enacted. In reality, the agencies of the bureaucracy make government policy, using **bureaucratic discretion** (273) to interpret the laws of Congress and to make new regulations, which are then published in the *Federal Register* (274), and they play the roles of judge and jury in enforcing those policies.

Politics Inside the Bureaucracy

Bureaucratic culture (274) refers to how agencies operate—their assumptions, values, and habits, including their reliance on a formal and confusing language called bureaucratese. The bureaucratic culture increases employees' belief in the programs they administer, their commitment to the survival and growth of their agencies, and their tendency to rely on rules and procedures rather than goals, but it can also lead to the kinds of mistakes and conflicts of interest sometimes exposed by **whistleblowers** (276).

External Bureaucratic Politics

Agencies work actively for their political survival. They attempt to establish strong support outside the agency, to avoid direct competition with other agencies, and to jealously guard their own policy jurisdictions. Sometimes agencies identify so thoroughly with the industries they are designed to regulate that we speak of **agency capture** (278). Presidential powers are only modestly effective in controlling the bureaucracy. The affected clientele groups working in close cooperation with the agencies and the congressional committees that oversee them form powerful **iron triangles** (282) and **issue networks** (284). Congress exercises control through the process of **congressional oversight** (284).

Drew Angerer/Getty Images

9

The American Legal System and the Courts

In Your Own Words

After you've read this chapter, you will be able to

9.1 Describe the role that law plays in a democratic society.

9.2 Discuss the role of Congress and the Constitution in establishing the judiciary.

9.3 Explain how federalism plays out in the dual court system.

9.4 Outline the institutional rules and political influences that shape the Supreme Court and the decisions it makes.

9.5 Describe the relationship between citizens and the courts in America.

What's at Stake . . . When the Supreme Court Gets Involved in Partisan Politics?

There is a cherished narrative in American politics that says justice is blind and the Supreme Court is an apolitical, impartial dispenser of it. The marble pillars, red velvet drapes, and black robes are all in aid of keeping that narrative going. Don't let any of it fool you.

The Supreme Court is a thoroughly political institution. There is no more classic example of the Supreme Court dabbling in politics than the 2000 presidential election between George W. Bush and Al Gore and the resulting five-to-four decision in *Bush v. Gore*. The case must have set Alexander Hamilton spinning in his grave. In *The Federalist Papers*, the American founder gave life to the narrative when he wrote confidently that the Supreme Court would be the least dangerous branch of government. Having the power of neither the sword nor the purse, it could do little other than judge, and Hamilton blithely assumed that those judgments would remain legal ones, not matters of raw power politics.

More than two hundred years later, however, without military might or budgetary power, the Supreme Court took into its own hands the very political task of deciding who would be the next president of the United States and, what's more, made that decision right down party lines. On a five-to-four vote (five more conservative justices versus four more liberal ones), the Supreme Court overturned the decision of the Florida Supreme Court to allow a recount of votes in the contested Florida election and awarded electoral victory to Bush.

How had it come to this? The presidential vote in Florida was virtually tied, recounts were required by law in some locations, and voting snafus in several other counties had left untold numbers of votes uncounted. Whether those votes should, or even could, be counted or whether voter error and system failure had rendered them invalid was in dispute. Believing that a count of the disputed ballots would give him the few hundred votes he needed for victory, Al Gore wanted the recount. Bush did not. The Florida secretary of state, a Republican appointed by the governor, Bush's brother, ordered the vote counting finished. The Florida Supreme Court, dominated heavily by Democrats, ruled instead that a recount should go forward.

Bush appealed to the U.S. Supreme Court, asking it to overturn the Florida Supreme Court's decision and to stay, or suspend, the recount pending its decision. A divided Court issued the stay. Justice John Paul Stevens took the unusual route of writing a dissent from the stay, arguing that it was unwise to "stop the counting of legal votes." Justice Antonin Scalia wrote in response that the recount would pose "irreparable harm" to Bush by "casting a cloud on what he claims to be the legitimacy of his election."

The split between the justices, so apparent in the order for the stay, reappeared in the final decision, where six separate opinions ended up being written. On a five-to-four vote, the majority claimed that if the recount went forward under the Florida Supreme Court's order with different standards for counting the vote in different counties, it would amount to a denial of equal protection of the laws. The amount of work required to bring about a fair recount could not be accomplished before the December 12 deadline. A three-person subset of the majority added that the Florida court's order was illegal in the first place.

The dissenters argued instead that the December 12 deadline was not fixed and that the recount could have taken place up to the meeting of the Electoral College on December 18, that there was no equal protection issue, that the Supreme Court should defer to the Florida Supreme Court on issues of state law, and that by involving itself in the political case, the Court risked losing public trust. While the winner of the election was in dispute, wrote Stevens, "the loser is perfectly clear. It is the nation's confidence in the judge as an impartial guardian of the rule of law."

Who was right here? The issue was debated by everyone from angry demonstrators outside the Court to learned commentators in scholarly journals, from families at the dinner table to editorial writers in the nation's press. Was Scalia correct that Bush had really already won and that it was up to the Court to save the legitimacy of his claim to power? Or was Stevens right: that by engaging in politics so blatantly, the Court had done itself irremediable damage in the public's eyes? What was really at stake for the Court and for America in the five-to-four decision of *Bush v. Gore*?

IMAGINE a world without laws. You careen down the road in your car, at any speed that takes your fancy. You park where you please and enter a store that sells drugs of all sorts, from Prozac to LSD to vodka and beer. You purchase what you like—no one asks you for proof of your age or for a prescription—and there are no restrictions on what or how much you buy. There are no rules governing the production or usage of currency, either, so you hope that the dealer will accept what you have to offer in trade.

Life is looking pretty good as you head back out to the street, only to find that your car is no longer there. Theft is not illegal, and you curse yourself for forgetting to set the car alarm and for not using your wheel lock. There are no police to call, and even if there were, tracking down your car would be virtually impossible since there are no vehicle registration laws to prove you own it in the first place.

Rather than walk—these streets are quite dangerous, after all—you spot a likely car to get you home. You have to wrestle with the occupant, who manages to clout you over the head before you drive away. It isn't much of a prize, covered with dents and nicks from innumerable clashes with other cars jockeying for position at intersections where there are neither stop signs nor lights and the right of the fastest prevails. Arriving home to enjoy your beer in peace and to gain a respite from the war zone you call your local community, you find that another family has moved in while you were shopping. Groaning with frustration, you think that surely there must be a better way!

And there is. As often as we might rail against restrictions on our freedom, such as not being able to buy beer if we are under twenty-one, or having to wear a motorcycle helmet, or not being able to speed down an empty highway, laws actually do us much more good than harm. British philosophers Thomas Hobbes and John Locke, whom we discussed in Chapter 1, both imagined a "prepolitical" world without laws. Inhabitants of Hobbes's state of nature found life without laws to be dismal or, as he put it, "solitary, poor, nasty, brutish and short." And although residents of Locke's state of nature merely found the lawless life to be "inconvenient," they had to mount a constant defense of their possessions and their lives. One of the reasons both Hobbes and Locke thought people would be willing to leave the state of nature for civil society, and to give up their freedom to do whatever they wanted, was to gain security, order, and predictability in life. Because we tend to focus on the laws that stop us from doing the things we want to do, or that require us to do things we don't want to do, we often forget the full array of laws that make it possible for us to live together in relative peace and to leave behind the brutishness of Hobbes's state of nature and the inconveniences of Locke's.

Laws occupy a central position in any political society, but especially in a democracy, where the distinguishing characteristic is that rule is ultimately by citizen-made law and not by the whim of a tyrant. Laws are the "how" in the formulation of politics as "who gets what, and how"—they dictate how our collective lives are to be organized, what rights we can claim, what principles we should live by, and how we can use the system to get what we want. Laws can also be the "what" in the formulation, as citizens and political actors use the existing rules to create new rules that produce even more favorable outcomes for themselves.

In this chapter you will learn about the notion of law and the role that it plays in a democratic society in general and in the American legal system in particular, the constitutional basis for the American judicial system, the dual system of state and federal courts in the United States, and the Supreme Court and the politics that surround and support it.

LAW AND THE AMERICAN LEGAL SYSTEM
Rules of the game that make collective living possible

Thinking about the law can be confusing. On the one hand, laws are the sorts of rules we have been discussing: limits and restrictions that get in our way, or that make life a little easier. On the other hand, we would like to believe in the narrative, reinforced by our founding, that our legal system is based on rules that represent enduring principles of justice, that create for us a higher level of civilization. The truth is a bit of both. Laws are products of the political process, created by political human beings to help them get valuable resources. Those resources may be civil peace and security, or a particular moral order, or power and influence, or even goods or entitlements. Thus, for security, we have laws that eliminate traffic chaos, enforce contracts, and ban violence. For moral order (and for security as well!), we have laws against murder, incest, and rape. And for political advantage, we have laws like those that give large states greater power in the process of electing a president and those that allow electoral districts to be drawn by the majority party. Laws dealing with more concrete resources are those that, for example, give tax breaks to homeowners or subsidize dairy farmers.

For the purpose of understanding the role of law in democratic political systems, we can focus on five important functions of laws:[1]

- The most obvious function follows directly from Hobbes and Locke: laws provide security (for people and their property) so that we may go about our daily lives in relative harmony.
- Laws provide predictability, allowing us to plan our activities and go about our business without fearing a random judgment that tells us we have broken a law we didn't know existed.
- Because laws are known in advance and identify punishable behaviors, they have a role in conflict resolution: neutral third parties, the **courts**, resolve conflicts according to the law.

courts institutions that sit as neutral third parties to resolve conflicts according to the law

- Laws reflect and enforce conformity to society's values—for instance, that murder is wrong or that parents (or others) should not be allowed to abuse children.
- Laws distribute the benefits and rewards society has to offer and allocate the costs of those good things, whether they are welfare benefits, civil rights protection, or tax breaks.

THE AMERICAN LEGAL TRADITION

The U.S. legal system, and that of all fifty states except Louisiana, is based on common law, which developed in Great Britain and the countries that once formed the British Empire. The **common law tradition** relied on royal judges making decisions based on their own judgment and on previous legal decisions, which were applied uniformly, or *commonly*, across the land. The emphasis was on preserving the decisions that had been made before, what is called relying on **precedent**, or *stare decisis* (Latin for "let the decision stand"). Judges in such a system have far more power in determining what the law is than do judges in civil law systems, and their job is to determine and apply the law as an impartial referee, not to take an active role in discovering the truth.

The legal system in the United States, however, is not a pure common law system. Legislatures do make laws, and attempts have been made to codify, or organize, them into a coherent body of law. American legislators, however, are less concerned with creating such a coherent body of law than with responding to the various needs and demands of their constituents. As a result, American laws have a somewhat haphazard and hodgepodge character. But the common law nature of the legal system is reinforced by the fact that American judges still use their considerable discretion to decide what the laws mean, and they rely heavily on precedent and the principle of *stare decisis*. Thus, when a judge decides a case, he or she will look at the relevant law but will also consult previous rulings on the issue before making a ruling of his or her own.

KINDS OF LAW

Laws are not all of the same type, and distinguishing among them can be difficult. It's not important that we understand all the shades of legal meaning. In fact, it often seems that lawyers speak a language all their own. Nevertheless, most of us will have several encounters with the law in our lifetimes, and it's important that we know what laws regulate what sorts of behavior.

We have used the terms *substantive* and *procedural* elsewhere in this book to refer to political culture, but the words also have precise legal meanings that describe specific kinds of laws. **Substantive laws** are those whose actual content or "substance" defines what we can and cannot legally do. **Procedural laws**, by contrast, establish the procedures used to conduct the law—that is, how the law is used, or applied, and enforced. Thus a substantive law spells out what behaviors are restricted—for instance, driving over a certain speed or killing someone. Procedural laws refer to how legal proceedings are to take place: how evidence will be gathered and used, how defendants will be treated, and what juries can be told during a trial. Because our founders were concerned with limiting the power of government to prevent tyranny, our laws are filled with procedural protections for those who must deal with the legal system—what we call guarantees of **procedural due process**. Given their different purposes, these two types of laws sometimes clash. For instance, someone guilty of breaking a

common law tradition a legal system based on the accumulated rulings of judges over time, applied uniformly—judge-made law

precedent a previous decision or ruling that, in common law tradition, is binding on subsequent decisions

substantive laws laws whose content, or substance, defines what we can or cannot do

procedural laws laws that establish how laws are applied and enforced—how legal proceedings take place

procedural due process procedural laws that protect the rights of individuals who must deal with the legal system

substantive law might be spared punishment if procedural laws meant to protect him or her were violated because the police failed to read the accused his or her rights or searched the accused's home without a warrant. Such situations are complicated by the fact that not all judges interpret procedural guarantees in the same way.

Another important distinction in the American system is between criminal and civil law. Criminal laws prohibit specific behaviors that the government (state, federal, or both) has determined are not conducive to the public peace: behaviors as heinous as murder or as relatively innocuous as stealing an apple. Since these laws refer to crimes against the state, it is the government that prosecutes these cases, rather than the family of the murder victim—or the owner of the apple. The penalty, if the person is found guilty, will be some form of payment to the public, for example, community service, jail time, or even death, depending on the severity of the crime and the provisions of the law. In fact, we speak of criminals having to pay their "debt to society," because in a real sense their actions are seen as harming society.

> **Is justice a matter of enduring principles or the product of a political process?**

Civil laws, by contrast, regulate interactions between individuals. If one person sues another for damaging his or her property, or for causing physical harm, or for failing to fulfill the terms of a contract, it is not a crime against the state that is alleged but rather an injury to a specific individual. A violation of civil law is called a *tort* instead of a crime. The government's purpose here is not to prosecute a harm to society but to provide individuals with a forum in which they can peacefully resolve their differences. Apart from peaceful conflict resolution, government has no stake in the outcome.

Sometimes a person will face both criminal charges and a civil lawsuit for the same action. An example might be a person who drives while drunk and causes an accident that seriously injures a person in another car. The drunk driver would face criminal charges for breaking laws against driving while intoxicated and might be sued by the injured party to receive compensation for medical expenses, missed income, and pain and suffering. Such damages are called *compensatory damages*. The injured person might also sue the bar that served the alcohol to the drunk driver in the first place; this is because people suing for compensation often target the involved party with the deepest pockets—that is, the one with the best ability to pay. A civil suit may also include a fine intended to punish the individual for causing the injury. These damages are called *punitive damages*.

Another kind of law, which we have discussed often in this book so far, is constitutional law. This refers, of course, to the laws in the Constitution. These laws establish the basic powers of and limitations on government institutions and their interrelationships, and they guarantee the basic rights of citizens. In addition, constitutional law refers to the many decisions that have been made by lower court judges in the United States, as well as by the justices on the Supreme Court, in their attempts to decide precisely what the Constitution means and how it should be interpreted. Because of our common law tradition, these decisions, once made, become part of the vast foundation of American constitutional law. All of the civil liberties and civil rights cases we have discussed are part of the constitutional law of this country. As we have seen, constitutional law evolves over time as circumstances change, justices are replaced, cases are overturned, and precedent is reversed.

Most laws in the country are not written in the Constitution, however, but rather are made by Congress and the state legislatures, by the bureaucracy under the authority of Congress, and even by the president. Statutory laws are those laws that legislatures make at either the state or the national level. Statutes reflect the will of the bodies elected to represent the people,

criminal laws laws prohibiting behavior the government has determined to be harmful to society; violation of a criminal law is called a crime

civil laws laws regulating interactions between individuals; violation of a civil law is called a tort

constitutional law law stated in the Constitution or in the body of judicial decisions about the meaning of the Constitution handed down in the courts

statutory laws laws passed by a state or the federal legislature and they can address virtually any behavior. Statutes tell us to wear seatbelts, stay home from work on Memorial Day, and pay taxes. According to the principle of judicial review (discussed in the next section), judges may declare statutes unconstitutional if they conflict with the basic principles of government or the rights of citizens established in the Constitution.

Because legislatures cannot be experts on all matters, they frequently delegate some of their lawmaking power to bureaucratic agencies and departments. When these bureaucratic actors exercise their lawmaking power on behalf of Congress, they are making **administrative laws**. Administrative laws include the thousands of regulations that agencies create concerning how much coloring and other additives can be in the food you buy, how airports will monitor air traffic, what kind of material can be used to make pajamas for children, and what deductions can be taken legally when figuring your income tax. These laws, although made under the authority of elected representatives, are not, in fact, made by people who are directly accountable to the citizens of America. The implications of the undemocratic nature of bureaucratic decision making were discussed in Chapter 8.

More Than One Day in Court

The American justice system not only makes decisions on criminal cases but also allows citizens to seek compensation for injury or damage. In some cases, defendants may face both kinds of trials. In 2018 the actor Bill Cosby was convicted of criminal charges and sentenced to three to ten years in prison for drugging and sexually assaulting a woman, while he was simultaneously embroiled in several civil cases involving similar accusations.

Finally, some laws, called **executive orders**, are made by the president. These, as we explained in Chapter 7, are laws made without any participation by Congress, and they need be binding only during the issuing president's administration. Famous executive orders include President Harry Truman's desegregation of the armed forces in 1948 and President Lyndon Johnson's initiation of affirmative action programs for companies doing business with the federal government in 1967.

In Your Own Words   Describe the role that law plays in a democratic society.

CONSTITUTIONAL PROVISIONS AND THE DEVELOPMENT OF JUDICIAL REVIEW

The role of Congress and the Constitution in establishing the judiciary

Americans may owe a lot of our philosophy of law (called *jurisprudence*) to the British, but the court system we set up to administer that law is uniquely our own. Like every other part of the Constitution, the nature of the judiciary was the subject of hot debate during the nation's founding. Large states were comfortable with a strong court system as part of the strong national government they advocated; small states, cringing at the prospect of national dominance, preferred a weak judiciary. Choosing a typically astute way out of their quandary, the authors of the Constitution postponed it, leaving it to Congress to settle later.

administrative laws laws established by the bureaucracy, on behalf of Congress

executive orders clarifications of congressional policy issued by the president and having the full force of law

'Congress shall make no law'. . . now, I wonder what they meant by that . . .?

Article III, Section 1, of the Constitution says simply this about the establishment of the court system: "The judicial power of the United States, shall be vested in one supreme court, and in such inferior courts as Congress may from time to time ordain and establish." It goes on to say that judges will hold their jobs as long as they demonstrate "good behavior"—that is, they are appointed for life—and that they will be paid regularly and cannot have their pay reduced while they are in office. The Constitution does not spell out the powers of the Supreme Court. It only specifies which cases must come directly to the Supreme Court (cases affecting ambassadors, public ministers and consuls, and states); all other cases come to it only on appeal. It was left to Congress to say how. By dropping the issue of court structure and power into the lap of a future Congress, the writers of the Constitution neatly sidestepped the brewing controversy. It would require an act of Congress, the Judiciary Act of 1789, to begin to fill in the gaps on how the court system would be organized.

THE LEAST DANGEROUS BRANCH

The idea of an independent judiciary headed by a supreme court was a new one to the founders. No other country had one, not even England. Britain's highest court was also its Parliament, or legislature. To those who put their faith in the ideas of separation of powers and checks and balances, an independent judiciary was an ideal way to check the power of the president and the Congress, and an important part of the narrative they were creating about limited power. But to others it represented an unknown threat. To put those fears to rest, Alexander Hamilton penned *Federalist* No. 78, arguing that the judiciary was the least dangerous branch of government. It lacked the teeth of the other branches; it had neither the power of the sword (the executive power) nor the power of the purse (the legislative budget power), and consequently it could exercise "neither force nor will, but merely judgment."[2]

For a while, Hamilton was right. The Court was thought to be such a minor player in the new government that several of George Washington's original appointees to that institution turned him down.[3] Many of those who served on the Court for a time resigned to take other positions thought to be more prestigious. Further indicating the Court's lack of esteem was the fact that when the capital was moved to Washington, D.C., city planners forgot to design a location for it. As a result, the highest court in the land had to meet in the basement office of the clerk of the U.S. Senate.[4]

JOHN MARSHALL AND JUDICIAL REVIEW

judicial review the power of the Supreme Court to rule on the constitutionality of laws

The low prestige of the Supreme Court was not to last for long, however, and its elevation was due almost single-handedly to the work of one man. John Marshall was the third chief justice and an enthusiastic Federalist. During his tenure in office, he found several ways to strengthen the Court's power, the most important of which was having the Court create the power of judicial review—the power that allows the Court to review acts of the other branches of government and to invalidate them if they are found to run counter to the principles in the Constitution.

The Constitution does not give the power of judicial review to the Court, but it doesn't forbid the Court to have that power either, and Hamilton had supported the idea in *Federalist* No. 78. Chief Justice Marshall shrewdly engineered the adoption of the power of judicial review in *Marbury v. Madison* in 1803. This case involved

> **What would American politics look like today if Chief Justice John Marshall hadn't adopted the power of judicial review?**

a series of judicial appointments to federal courts made by President John Adams in the final hours of his administration. Most of those appointments were executed by Adams's secretary of state, but the letter appointing William Marbury to be justice of the peace for the District of Columbia was overlooked and not delivered. (In an interesting twist, John Marshall, who was finishing up his job as Adams's secretary of state, had just been sworn in as chief justice of the United States; he would later hear the case that developed over his own incomplete appointment of Marbury.) These "midnight" (last-minute) appointments irritated the new president, Thomas Jefferson, who wanted to appoint his own candidates, so he had his secretary of state, James Madison, throw out the overlooked Marbury letter, along with several other appointment letters. According to the Judiciary Act of 1789, it was up to the Supreme Court to decide whether Marbury got his appointment, which put Marshall in a fix. If he exercised his power under the act and Jefferson ignored him, the Court's already low prestige would be severely damaged. If he failed to order the appointment, the Court would still look weak.

From a legal point of view, Marshall's solution was breathtaking. Instead of ruling on the question of Marbury's appointment, which was a no-win situation for him, he focused on the part of the act that gave the Court the authority to make the decision. This he found to go beyond what the Constitution had intended. That is, according to the Constitution, Congress didn't have the power to give the Court that authority. So Marshall ruled that although he thought Marbury should get the appointment (he had originally made it, after all), he could not enforce it because the relevant part of the Judiciary Act of 1789 was unconstitutional and therefore void. He justified the Court's power to decide what the Constitution meant by saying "it is emphatically the province of the judicial department to say what the law is."[5] In making this ruling, Marshall chose to lose a small battle in order to win a very large war. By creating the power of judicial review, he vastly expanded the potential influence of the Court and set it on the road to being the powerful institution it is today. While Congress and the president still have some checks on the judiciary through the powers to appoint, to change the number of members and the jurisdiction of the Court, to impeach justices, and to amend the Constitution, the Court now has the ultimate check over the other two branches: the power to declare what they do to be null and void. What is especially striking about the gain of this enormous power is that the Court gave it to itself. What would have been the public reaction if Congress had voted to make itself the final judge of what is constitutional?

Aware of just how substantially their power was increased by the addition of judicial review, justices have tended to use it sparingly. The power was not used from its inception in 1803 until 1857, when the Court struck down the Missouri Compromise.[6] Since then it has been used only about 180 times to strike down acts of Congress, although it has been used much more frequently (more than 1,300 times) to invalidate acts of the state legislatures.[7]

In Your Own Words   Discuss the role of Congress and the Constitution in establishing the judiciary.

Marbury v. Madison
the landmark case that established the U.S. Supreme Court's power of judicial review

FEDERALISM AND THE AMERICAN COURTS

The structure and organization of the dual court system

In response to the Constitution's open invitation to design a federal court system, Congress immediately got busy putting together the Judiciary Act of 1789. The system created by this act was too simple to handle the complex legal needs and the growing number of cases in the new nation, however, and it was gradually crafted by Congress into the very complex network of federal courts we have today. But understanding just the federal court system is not enough. Our federal system of government requires that we have two separate court systems, state and national, and in fact most of the legal actions in this country take place at the state level. Because of the diversity that exists among the state courts, some people argue that in truth we have fifty-one court systems. Since we cannot look into each of the fifty state court systems, we will take the "two-system" perspective and consider the state court system as a whole (see Figure 9.1).

UNDERSTANDING JURISDICTION

A key concept in understanding our dual court system is the issue of jurisdiction, the courts' authority to hear particular cases. Not all courts can hear all cases. In fact, the rules regulating which courts have jurisdiction over which cases are very specific. Most cases in the United States fall under the jurisdiction of state courts. As we will see, cases go to federal courts only if they qualify by virtue of the kind of question raised or the parties involved.

The choice of a court, though dictated in large part by constitutional rule and statutory law (both state and federal), still leaves room for political maneuvering. Four basic characteristics of a case help determine which court has jurisdiction over it: the involvement of the federal government (through treaties or federal statutes) or the Constitution; the parties to the case (if, for instance, states are involved); where the case arose; and how serious an offense it involves.[8] Once a case is in either the state court system or the federal court system, it almost always remains within that system. It is extremely rare for a case to start out in one system and end up in the other. Just about the only time this occurs is when a case in the highest state court is appealed to the U.S. Supreme Court, and this can happen only for cases involving a question of federal law.

Cases come to state and federal courts under either their original jurisdiction or their appellate jurisdiction. A court's original jurisdiction refers to those cases that can come straight to it without being heard by any other court first. The rules and factors just discussed refer to original jurisdiction. Appellate jurisdiction refers to those cases that a court can hear on appeal—that is, when one of the parties to a case believes that some point of law was not applied properly at a lower court and asks a higher court to review it. Almost all the cases heard by the U.S. Supreme Court come to it on appeal. The Court's original jurisdiction is limited to cases that concern ambassadors and public ministers and to cases in which a state is a party—usually amounting to no more than two or three cases a year.

All parties in U.S. lawsuits are entitled to an appeal, although more than 90 percent of losers in federal cases accept their verdicts without appeal. After the first appeal, further appeals are at the discretion of the higher court; that is, the court can choose to hear them or not. The highest court of appeals in the United States is the U.S. Supreme Court, but its appellate jurisdiction is also discretionary. When the Court refuses to hear a case, it may mean, among other things, that the Court regards the case as frivolous or that it agrees with the lower court's judgment. Just because the Court agrees to hear a case, though, does not mean that it is going

jurisdiction a court's authority to hear certain cases

original jurisdiction the authority of a court to hear a case first

appellate jurisdiction the authority of a court to review decisions made by lower courts

appeal a rehearing of a case because the losing party in the original trial argues that a point of law was not applied properly

FIGURE 9.1
The Dual Court System

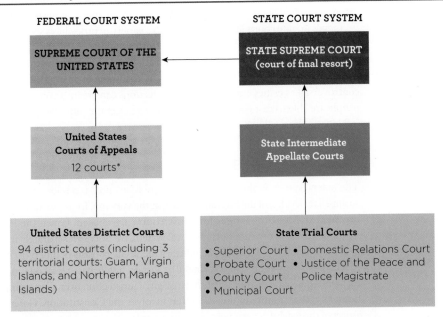

FEDERAL COURT SYSTEM

STATE COURT SYSTEM

SUPREME COURT OF THE UNITED STATES

STATE SUPREME COURT (court of final resort)

United States Courts of Appeals

12 courts*

State Intermediate Appellate Courts

United States District Courts

94 district courts (including 3 territorial courts: Guam, Virgin Islands, and Northern Mariana Islands)

State Trial Courts

- Superior Court
- Probate Court
- County Court
- Municipal Court
- Domestic Relations Court
- Justice of the Peace and Police Magistrate

There are 12 U.S. circuit courts of appeals with general jurisdiction. In addition, the U.S. Court of Appeals for the Federal Circuit handles specialized cases (e.g., patents, international trade).

to overturn the lower court's ruling, although it does so about 70 percent of the time. Sometimes the Court hears a case in order to rule that it agrees with the lower court and to set a precedent that other courts will have to follow.

STATE COURTS

Although each state has its own constitution, and therefore its own set of rules and procedures for structuring and organizing its court system, the state court systems are remarkably similar to each other in appearance and function. State courts generally fall into three tiers, or layers. The lowest, or first, layer is the trial court, including major trial courts and courts where less serious offenses are heard. The names of these courts vary—for example, they may be called county or municipal courts at the minor level and superior or district courts at the major level. Here cases are heard for the first time, under original jurisdiction, and most of them end here as well.

Occasionally, however, a case is appealed to a higher decision-making body. In about three-fourths of the states, intermediate courts of appeals hear cases appealed from the lower trial courts. In terms of geographic organization, subject matter jurisdiction, and number of judges, courts of appeals vary greatly from state to state. The one constant is that these courts all hear appeals directly from the major trial courts and, on very rare occasions, directly from the minor courts as well.

Each of the fifty states has a state supreme court, although again the names vary. Since they are appeals courts, no questions of fact can arise, and there are no juries. Rather, a panel of five to nine *justices*, as supreme court judges are called, meet to discuss the case, make a decision, and issue an opinion. As the name suggests, a state's supreme court is the court of last resort, or the final court of appeals, in the state. All decisions rendered by these courts are final unless a case involves a federal question and can be heard on further appeal in the federal court system.

Judges in state courts are chosen through a variety of procedures specified in the individual state constitutions. The procedures range from appointment by the governor or election by the state legislature to the more democratic method of election by the state population as a whole. Thirty-nine states hold elections for at least some of their judges, but this procedure is controversial as critics argue that judicial elections can create a conflict of interest, that few people are able to cast educated votes in judicial elections, and that the threat of defeat may influence judges' rulings.

FEDERAL COURTS

The federal system is also three-tiered. There is an entry-level tier, called the district courts; an appellate level; and the Supreme Court, at the very top. In this section we discuss the lower two tiers and how the judges for those courts are chosen. Given the importance of the Supreme Court in the American political system, we discuss it separately in the next section.

The lowest level of the federal judiciary hierarchy consists of ninety-four U.S. federal district courts. These courts are distributed so that each state has at least one and the largest states each have four. The district courts have original jurisdiction over all cases involving any question of a federal nature or any issue that involves the Constitution, Congress, or any other aspect of the federal government. Such issues are wide ranging but might include, for example, criminal charges resulting from a violation of the federal anticarjacking statute or a lawsuit against the Environmental Protection Agency.

The district courts hear both criminal and civil cases. In trials at the district level, evidence is presented and witnesses are called to testify and are questioned and cross-examined by the attorneys representing both sides. In criminal cases the government is always represented by a U.S. attorney. U.S. attorneys, one per district, are appointed by the president, with the consent of the Senate. In district courts, juries are responsible for returning the final verdict.

Any case appealed beyond the district court level is slated to appear in one of the U.S. courts of appeals. These courts are arranged in twelve circuits, essentially large superdistricts that encompass several of the district court territories, except for the twelfth, which covers just Washington, D.C. This twelfth circuit court hears all appeals involving government agencies, and so its caseload is quite large even though its territory is small. (A thirteenth federal circuit court hears cases on such specialized issues as patents and copyrights.) Cases are heard in the circuit that includes the district court where the case was heard originally. Therefore, a case that was tried initially in Miami, in the southern district in Florida, would be appealed to the Court of Appeals for the Eleventh Circuit, located in Atlanta, Georgia.

The jurisdiction of the courts of appeals, as their name suggests, is entirely appellate in nature. The sole function of these courts is to hear appeals from the lower federal district courts and to review the legal reasoning behind the decisions reached there. As a result, the proceedings involved in the appeals process differ markedly from those at the district court level. No evidence is presented, no new witnesses called, and no jury impaneled. Instead, the lawyers for both sides present written briefs summarizing their arguments and make oral arguments as well. The legal reasoning used to reach the decision in the district court is scrutinized, but the facts of the case are assumed to be the truth and are not debated.

The decisions in the courts of appeals are made by a rotating panel of three judges who sit to hear the cases. Although many more than three judges are assigned to each federal appeals circuit (for instance, the Court of Appeals for the Ninth Circuit, based in San Francisco, has twenty-two active judges), the judges rotate in order to provide a decision-making body that is as unbiased as possible. In rare cases when a decision is of crucial social importance, all the judges in a circuit will meet together, or *en banc*, to render a decision. Having all the judges present, not just three, gives a decision more legitimacy and sends a message that the decision was made carefully.

The Constitution is silent about the qualifications of judges for the federal courts. It specifies only that they shall be appointed by the president, with the advice and consent of the Senate, and that they shall serve lifetime terms under good behavior. They can be removed from office only if impeached and convicted by the House of Representatives and the Senate, a process that has resulted in only fifteen impeachments and eight convictions in more than two hundred years.

Traditionally, federal judgeships have been awarded on the basis of several criteria, including rewarding political friendship; supporting and cultivating future support, especially of a gender or an ethnic or racial group; and ideology. Throughout most of the country's history, the courts have been demographically uniform—white, male, and predominantly Christian. President Jimmy Carter broke that trend, vowing to use his nominations to increase the diversity in the federal courts. President Bill Clinton renewed that commitment: nearly half of his appointees were women and minorities.[9] President George W. Bush, while not quite emulating Clinton's record, still made a point of nominating a diverse slate of candidates, especially increasing the number of Hispanics on the bench.[10] Barack Obama also made increasing the diversity on the courts a top priority. According to the White House counsel, Obama wanted "the federal courts to look like America."[11] Only 38 percent of Obama's appointments to district courts were white men (as opposed to 67 percent under Bush, 53 percent under Clinton, and 85 percent under Reagan). Nearly half, 43 percent, were women. Twelve were gay. And in 2016 Obama nominated the first Muslim judge to the federal bench.[12] Because the Obama administration cast a wider net, looking for diverse candidates but also for those with less traditional backgrounds (more government lawyers and law professors, for instance, than litigators), it was slower to fill the openings on the bench.[13] Without concerns about diversity, Trump was quick to start filling empty slots with candidates who were primarily white and male.[14]

These days an increasingly important qualification for the job of federal judge is the ideological or policy positions of the appointee. In the 1970s, Richard Nixon ran for president on the idea that the courts were liberal policymaking institutions, soft on crime, and in need of conservative correction. As presidents have taken advantage of the opportunity to shape the courts ideologically, the Senate confirmation process has become more rancorous. But the nomination process has been more important to conservatives than to liberals. Republican presidents Richard Nixon, Ronald Reagan, and George H. W. Bush made a conscious effort to redirect what they saw as the liberal tenor of court appointments in the years since the New Deal, and Democrat Jimmy Carter countered with liberal appointees, but the moderate ideology of most of Democratic president Bill Clinton's appointees meant that the courts did not swing back in a radically liberal direction.[15] By the end of George W. Bush's second term, 56.2 percent of the authorized judicial positions had been filled by Republicans, tilting the federal bench in a solidly conservative direction. Barack Obama, focused on the diversity of his appointees, had come under criticism from liberals for not filling seats quickly enough, and thus for failing to build a liberal judicial legacy, but at the end of his second term the federal bench had a narrow Democratic majority.[16]

How would the federal judiciary be different if judges were elected rather than appointed?

This was despite the fact that the Republicans blocked votes on *all* Obama nominations, even moderate ones that would typically have enjoyed bipartisan support, in order to stall the Obama administration's efforts and to gain leverage for other things they wanted.[17] Ironically, when those nominations eventually came to a vote, they passed with the support of many of the Republicans who had engaged in the filibuster to delay the vote in the first place. These delay tactics scored the party a short-term political victory, and many federal judgeships went unfilled as a consequence. Because of the ensuing backlog of cases in the courts, then–Senate majority leader Harry Reid eventually invoked what is known as the nuclear option, eliminating the filibuster on non–Supreme Court federal nominees.

When Trump came into office, that slim Democratic majority on the courts was quickly undone. The Trump administration, urged on by Senate majority leader Mitch McConnell, has focused on filling the federal bench. McConnell said, "Obviously, this has been my top priority," and, unchecked by the filibuster they had helped to destroy, Republicans have made great strides appointing conservative judges.[18]

The upshot is that, before the removal of the filibuster, the increasing politicization of the confirmation process meant that many of a president's nominees faced a grueling battle in the Senate, and even if they got through the Senate Judiciary Committee hearings, they were lucky to get as far as a vote on the floor. That is still the case if the president is of a different party than the Senate majority, as was Obama. A president with a Senate majority behind him can put a major stamp on the judiciary, however. Even before the recent changes in Senate procedure, including the end of a tradition that let members of the minority put holds on nominations, the Republicans were more effective at shaping the bench. Observers chalk this up to the greater discipline among Republican senators. Said one liberal advocate during George W. Bush's administration, "Republican senators have voted in lock step to confirm every judge that Bush has nominated. The Democrats have often broken ranks."[19] In addition, the Republican base has been more energized about the courts as a political issue because of concern about core issues like preserving gun rights and overturning abortion, affirmative action, and gay-friendly legislation; the Democrats have not had that single-minded focus.

Another, and related, influence on the appointment of federal judges is the principle of senatorial courtesy, which we discussed in Chapter 7. In reality, senators do most of the nominating of district court judges, often aided by applications made by lawyers and state judges. Traditionally, a president who nominated a candidate who failed to meet with the approval of the state's senators was highly unlikely to gain Senate confirmation of that candidate, even if the president was lucky enough to get the Senate Judiciary Committee to hold a hearing on the nomination. In recent years the practice of senatorial courtesy was weakened somewhat by George W. Bush's administration and Senate Republicans who forced confirmation hearings despite the objections of Democratic home-state senators.[20] But once Obama was elected, Senate Republicans sought to restore the policy, sending a letter to the White House promising to block any appointments that didn't meet with the home-state senator's approval, and even a member of Obama's own party put a hold on one of his nominees.[21] Under Trump and McConnell, the Republicans switched gears again, essentially rejecting the norm.[22]

The growing influence of politics in the selection of federal judges does not mean that merit is unimportant. As the nation's largest legal professional association, the American Bar Association (ABA) has had the informal role since 1946 of evaluating the legal qualifications of potential nominees. While poorly rated candidates are occasionally nominated and

senatorial courtesy the tradition of granting senior senators of the president's party considerable power over federal judicial appointments in their home states

confirmed, perhaps because of the pressure of a senator or a president, most federal judges receive the ABA's professional blessing. The ABA's role has become more controversial in recent years, as Republicans are convinced that it has a liberal bias. The Bush administration announced in 2001 that it would no longer seek the ABA's ratings of its nominees, breaking a tradition that went back to Eisenhower. The ABA continued to rate the nominees (and the Bush White House boasted that 99 percent of its nominees had been rated as "qualified" or "well qualified"), but it did so independently.[23] In March 2009 the Obama administration restored the ABA's traditional role in the nomination process, only to find that a number of Obama's potential nominees failed to rank as qualified, perhaps because they were less likely to have the traditional backgrounds as litigators that the litigator-heavy ABA panel may have been looking for.[24] The administration's decision to drop those nominees who were not ranked as qualified was another reason it had a slower nominating process than its predecessors. Trump has ignored the ABA in making his appointments, resulting in a higher percentage of "unqualified" nominees.[25]

In Your Own Words Explain how federalism plays out in the dual court system.

THE SUPREME COURT

A political institution

At the very top of the nation's judicial system reigns the U.S. Supreme Court. The nine justices do not wear the elaborate wigs of their British counterparts in the House of Lords, the highest court of appeals in Britain, but they do don long black robes to hear their cases and sit against a majestic background of red silk, perhaps the closest thing to the pomp and circumstance of royalty that we have in American government. Polls show that even after its role in the contested presidential election of 2000 (see this chapter's *What's at Stake . . . ?*), the Court gets higher ratings from the public than does Congress or the president, and that it doesn't suffer as much from the popular cynicism about government that afflicts the other branches.[26]

The American public seems to believe the narrative that the Supreme Court is indeed above politics, as the founders wished them to believe. If the Court is seen as apolitical, its rulings will have greater force and legitimacy. Such a view, while gratifying to those who want to believe in the purity and wisdom of at least one aspect of their government, is not strictly accurate. The members of the Court themselves are protected by the rule of lifetime tenure from continually having to seek reelection or reappointment, but they are not removed from the political world around them. It is more useful, and closer to reality, to regard the Supreme Court as an intensely political institution. In at least three critical areas—how its members are chosen, how they make decisions, and the effects of the decisions they make—the Court is a decisive allocator of who gets what, when, and how.

HOW MEMBERS OF THE COURT ARE SELECTED

In a perfect world, the country's wisest and most intelligent jurists would be appointed to make the all-important constitutional decisions daily faced by members of the Supreme Court. In a political world, however, the need for wise and intelligent justices has to be balanced against the demands of a system that makes those justices the choice of an elected president, confirmed by elected senators. The need of these elected officials to be responsive to their constituencies means that the nomination process for Supreme Court justices is often a battleground of competing views of the public good. To take a recent and prominent example, as we saw in *What's at Stake . . . ?* in Chapter 6, within hours of the announcement of Justice Antonin Scalia's death in February 2016, Senate majority leader Mitch McConnell had announced that the Senate would not hold hearings on anyone President Obama might nominate. The ostensible reason for his decision was that it was a presidential election year and the people should have a chance to weigh in, yet a number of justices had been confirmed in election years, and in 2018, speaking about Justice Anthony Kennedy's retirement, McConnell said he would move right away to replace him.[27] He followed through, and Brett Kavanaugh was confirmed just months before the midterm elections. McConnell's real reason for refusing to consider Obama's nominee, as we saw earlier, was to try to hold out for the election of a Republican president who would nominate someone as conservative as Scalia had been, a gamble that proved successful. Merit is certainly important, but it is tempered by other considerations resulting from a democratic selection process.

On paper, the process of choosing justices for the Supreme Court is not a great deal different from the selection of other federal judges, though no tradition of senatorial courtesy exists at the high court level. Far too much is at stake in Supreme Court appointments to even consider giving any individual senator veto power. The Constitution, silent on so much concerning the Supreme Court, does not give the president any handy list of criteria for making these critical appointments. But the demands of the president's job suggest that merit, shared ideology, political reward, and demographic representation all play a role in this choice.[28]

MERIT The president will certainly want to appoint the most qualified person and the person with the highest ethical standards who also meets the other prerequisites. Scholars agree that most of the people who have served the Court over the years have been among the best legal minds available, but they also know that sometimes presidents have nominated people whose reputations have proved questionable.[29] The ABA passes judgment on candidates for the Supreme Court, as it does for the lower courts, issuing verdicts of "well qualified," "qualified," "not opposed," and "not qualified." The FBI also checks out each nominee's background. We have already noted that Trump does not consider the ABA ratings important in the nomination process.

POLITICAL IDEOLOGY Although presidents want to appoint well-qualified candidates to the Court, they are constrained by the desire to find candidates who share their views on politics and the law. Political ideology here involves a couple of dimensions. One is the traditional liberal-conservative dimension. Supreme Court justices, like all other human beings, have views on the role of government, the rights of individuals, and the relationship between the two. Presidents want to appoint justices who look at the world the same way they do, although they are occasionally surprised when their nominee's ideological stripes turn out to be different from what they had anticipated. Republican president Dwight Eisenhower called the appointment of Chief Justice Earl Warren, who turned out to be quite liberal in his legal judgments, "the biggest damn fool mistake I ever made."[30] Although there have been notable exceptions, most presidents appoint members of their own parties in an attempt to get ideologically compatible justices. Overall, roughly 90 percent of Supreme Court nominees belong to the nominating president's party.

But ideology has another dimension when it refers to the law. Justices can take the view that the Constitution means exactly what it says it means and that all interpretations of it must be informed by the founders' intentions. This approach, called **strict constructionism**, holds that if the meaning of the Constitution is to be changed, it must be done by amendment, not by judicial interpretation. Judge Robert Bork, a Reagan nominee who failed to be confirmed by the Senate, was a strict constructionist. During his confirmation hearings, when he was asked about the famous reapportionment ruling in *Baker v. Carr*, that the Constitution effectively guarantees every citizen one vote, Bork replied that if the people of the United States wanted their Constitution to guarantee "one man one vote," they were free to amend the document to say so. In Bork's judgment, without that amendment, the principle was simply the result of justices' rewriting the Constitution. When the senators asked him about the right to privacy, another right enforced by the Court but not specified in the Constitution, Bork simply laughed.[31] The opposite position to strict constructionism, what might be called **judicial interpretivism**, holds that the Constitution is a living document, that the founders could not possibly have anticipated all possible future circumstances, and that justices should interpret the Constitution in light of social changes. When the Court ruled, in *Griswold v. Connecticut*, that although there is no right to privacy in the Constitution, the Bill of Rights can be understood to imply such a right, it was engaging in judicial interpretation. Strict constructionists would deny that there is a constitutional right to privacy.

Although interpretivism tends to be a liberal position because of its emphasis on change, and strict constructionism tends to be a conservative position because of its adherence to the status quo, the two ideological scales do not necessarily go hand in hand. For instance, even though the Second Amendment refers to the right to bear arms in the context of militia membership, many conservatives would argue that this needs to be understood to protect the right to bear arms in a modern context, when militias are no longer necessary or practical—not a strict constructionist reading of the Constitution. Liberals, by contrast, tend to rely on a strict reading of the Second Amendment to support their calls for tighter gun controls.

In the George W. Bush administration, another ideological element rose in importance along with the strict constructionist–interpretivist divide. Bush was concerned with finding nominees who not only would interpret the Constitution strictly but also would support a strengthening of executive power. As we saw in Chapter 7, many members of the Bush administration supported the unitary theory of the executive, which claims that the Constitution permits only the president to wield executive power. Under this theory, efforts by Congress to create independent agencies outside of the president's purview are unconstitutional. The administration also objected to efforts by Congress and the courts to limit or interpret executive power in matters of national security. For both of his nominations to the Court, John Roberts and Samuel Alito, Bush chose candidates who were supporters of a strong executive office.

President Obama's Supreme Court nominees reflected his own center-left, interpretivist ideology. His first nomination, Sonia Sotomayor, who joined the Court in September 2009, was more controversial for remarks she had made about her ethnicity and gender than for her judicial views. When Obama nominated former solicitor general Elena Kagan to the Court in 2010, however, her lack of a history of clear judicial rulings left her ideology something of a mystery, and many liberals feared she would end up being a moderate voice on the Court.[32] Likewise, Merrick Garland, whom Obama nominated to replace Justice Scalia, was a more moderate judge who Obama hoped would meet with the approval of Republicans as a replacement for the conservative icon. After they refused to even hold hearings on Garland's nomination, Trump nominated and the Senate confirmed conservative, strict

strict constructionism a judicial approach holding that the Constitution should be read literally, with the framers' intentions uppermost in mind

judicial interpretivism a judicial approach holding that the Constitution is a living document and that judges should interpret it according to changing times and values

constructionist Neil Gorsuch to the Court. Gorsuch's conservatism is of the "plain text" variety—that is, the simple meaning of the words in laws is what matters, not their congressional or historical context. [33] Brett Kavanaugh, Trump's second appointee, is also conservative. He spent time as a political operative as well as a judge and has taken a more partisan stance to the Court, threatening those who were critical of his nomination, telling them "what comes around, comes around."[34]

The trend over the past few decades, since Nixon made a campaign issue of not appointing justices who were "soft on crime," is for Republican presidents to carefully pick conservative nominees, to avoid disappointments of the Eisenhower-Warren variety. Democratic presidents, however, particularly Bill Clinton and Barack Obama, have not seemed to share the urgency to put liberals on the Court; Clinton was not overly liberal himself and Obama was a constitutional scholar who weighted many issues other than ideology. The Trump-McConnell effort to get the maximum number of conservatives on the Court has only solidified the Court's move to the right; scholars have noted that both conservative and liberal justices have grown more conservative over time, shifting the Court in that direction.

REWARD More than half of the people who have been nominated to the Supreme Court have been personally acquainted with the president.[35] Often nominees are friends or political allies of the president or other people the president wishes to reward in an impressive fashion. Harry Truman knew and had worked with all four of the men he appointed to the Court, Franklin Roosevelt appointed people he knew (and who were loyal to his New Deal), John F. Kennedy appointed his longtime friend and associate Byron White, and Lyndon Johnson appointed his good friend Abe Fortas.[36] While several FOBs (Friends of Bill) appeared on Clinton's short lists for his appointments, none was actually appointed. Though George W. Bush tried to appoint his friend and White House counsel Harriet Miers to the Court, she was forced to withdraw her name amid criticism that she wasn't sufficiently qualified. Barack Obama had a longtime working relationship with one of his nominees, Elena Kagan, who had been his first solicitor general.

REPRESENTATION Finally, presidents want to appoint people who represent groups they feel should be included in the political process, or whose support they want to gain. Lyndon Johnson appointed Thurgood Marshall at least in part because he wanted to appoint an African American to the Court. After Marshall retired, President George H. W. Bush appointed Clarence Thomas to fill his seat. Although Bush declared that he was making the appointment because Thomas was the person best qualified for the job, and not because he was black, few believed him. In earlier years, presidents also felt compelled to ensure that there was at least one Catholic and one Jew on the Court. This necessity has lost much of its force today as interest groups seem more concerned with the political than the denominational views of appointees, but Hispanic groups rejoiced when President Obama made Sonia Sotomayor the first Hispanic member of the Court in 2009. The issue of ethnic representation on the Court was put front and center during Sotomayor's confirmation hearings, when she drew fire from Republicans who noted a line in a speech she had given in 2001, where she had argued that "I would hope that a wise Latina woman with the richness of her experiences would more often than not reach a better conclusion than a white male who hasn't lived that life."[37]

The current composition of the Supreme Court, reflected in Table 9.1, does not reflect the population of the United States, although it can certainly be argued that it comes closer than it ever has before. There are six men on the Court and three women. Six Five justices are

TABLE 9.1

Composition of the Supreme Court, as of September 2018

JUSTICE	YEAR BORN	YEAR APPOINTED	POLITICAL PARTY	APPOINTING PRESIDENT	HOME STATE	COLLEGE/ LAW SCHOOL	RELIGION	POSITION WHEN APPOINTED
Clarence Thomas	1948	1991	Rep.	G. H. W. Bush	Georgia	Holy Cross/ Yale	Catholic	U.S. Appeals Court Judge
Ruth Bader Ginsburg	1933	1993	Dem.	B. Clinton	New York	Cornell/ Columbia	Jewish	U.S. Appeals Court Judge
Stephen G. Breyer	1938	1994	Dem.	B. Clinton	California	Stanford, Oxford/ Harvard	Jewish	U.S. Appeals Court Judge
John G. Roberts Jr.	1955	2005	Rep.	G. W. Bush	Maryland	Harvard/ Harvard	Catholic	U.S. Appeals Court Judge
Samuel A. Alito Jr.	1950	2006	Rep.	G. W. Bush	New Jersey	Princeton/ Yale	Catholic	U.S. Appeals Court Judge
Sonia Sotomayor	1954	2009	Ind.	Obama	New York	Princeton/ Yale	Catholic	U.S. Appeals Court Judge
Elena Kagan	1960	2010	Dem.	Obama	New York	Oxford/ Harvard	Jewish	Solicitor General
Neil Gorsuch	1967	2017	Rep.	Trump	Colorado	Columbia/ Harvard	Catholic/ Episcopal*	U.S. Appeals Court Judge
Brett M. Kavanaugh	1965	2018	Rep.	Trump	Maryland	Yale/Yale	Catholic	U.S. Appeals Court Judge

*Gorsuch was raised Catholic but is currently a member of an Episcopal church.

Source: Supreme Court of the United States, "The Justices of the Supreme Court," www.supremecourtus.gov/about/biographies.aspx.

Catholic (though Gorsuch reportedly now belongs to an Episcopal church), and three Jewish; only Judeo-Christian religions have been represented on the Court so far. Five of the justices were appointed by Republicans, four by Democrats. They have attended an elite array of undergraduate institutions and law schools. In 2018 their ages ranged from fifty-three to eighty-five. There have never been any Native Americans or Asian Americans on the Court; only two African Americans, whose terms did not overlap; and one Hispanic. The historically elite, white, male, Christian character of the Court raises interesting questions. We naturally want our highest judges to have excellent legal educations (although John Marshall barely had any). But should the nation's highest court represent demographically the people whose Constitution it guards? Some observers (including Justice Sotomayor) have suggested that women judges may be sensitive to issues that have not been salient to men and may alter behavior in the courtroom; the same may be true of minority judges as well. In a different vein, what message is sent to citizens when the custodians of national justice are composed primarily of a group that is itself fast becoming a minority in America?

CONFIRMATION BY THE SENATE As with the lower courts, the Senate must approve presidential appointments to the Supreme Court. We already mentioned the immediate and inflexible rejection by the Senate majority leader of any hearings for Obama's nominee to replace Scalia. Generally, however, the Senate Judiciary Committee plays the largest role, holding hearings and inviting the nominee, colleagues, and concerned interest groups to testify. Sometimes the hearings, and the subsequent vote in the Senate, are mere formalities, but increasingly, as the appointments have become more ideological and when the Senate majority party is not the party of the president, the hearings have had the potential to become political battlefields. Even when the president's party controls the Senate, the minority party can still influence the choice through the filibuster, although the Senate Republicans in 2005 threatened to halt this tradition.

The Bork hearings are an excellent example of what can happen when interest groups and public opinion get heavily involved in a controversial confirmation battle. These political clashes are so grueling because so much is at stake.

HOW THE COURT MAKES DECISIONS

It is tempting to idealize the way justices make decisions—to believe that the Court's decisions are simply a matter of nine wise and learned people consulting eternal principles of wisdom in order to choose the best way to resolve conflicts. We know by now that what happens is more complicated than that. While the justices decide which cases to hear, make decisions about how those cases should be resolved, and write their opinions, they are subject to the same kinds of political forces that influenced their appointments and confirmations.

CHOOSING WHICH CASES TO HEAR The Supreme Court could not possibly hear the roughly eight thousand petitions it receives each year.[38] Intensive screening is necessary to reduce the number to the more manageable eighty to ninety that the Court finally hears. This screening process, illustrated in this chapter's *The Big Picture*, is a political one; having one's case heard by the Supreme Court is a scarce resource. What rules and which people determine who gets this resource and who doesn't?

Almost all the cases heard by the Court come from its appellate, not its original, jurisdiction, and of these virtually all arrive at the Court in the form of petitions for **writs of certiorari**, in which the losing party in a lower court case explains in writing why the Supreme Court should hear its case. Petitions to the Court are subject to strict length, form, and style requirements and must be accompanied by a $300 filing fee. Those too poor to pay the filing fee are allowed to petition the Court *in forma pauperis*, which exempts them not only from the filing fee but also from the stringent style and form rules. Approximately two-thirds of the 7,000–8,000 case filings each year are in forma pauperis but they are not heard in that proportion.[39] In 2015, twelve of eighty-one cases heard were in forma pauperis. The Court's jurisdiction here is discretionary; it can either grant or deny a writ of certiorari. If it decides to grant certiorari and review the case, then the records of the case will be called up from the lower court where it was last heard. In the 2014 term, seventy-five cases were argued (resulting in sixty-six signed opinions).[40]

Law clerks, usually recent graduates from law school who have served a year as clerk to a judge on a lower court, have tremendous responsibility over certiorari petitions, or "cert pets," as they call them. They must read all the petitions (thirty pages in length plus appendixes) and summarize each in a two- to five-page memo that includes a recommendation to the justices

writ of certiorari a formal request by the U.S. Supreme Court to call up the lower court case it decides to hear on appeal

on whether to hear the case, all with minimal guidance or counsel from their justices.[41] The memos are circulated to the justices' offices, where clerks read them again and make comments on the advisability of hearing the cases. The memos, with the clerks' comments, go on to the justices, who decide which cases they think should be granted cert and which denied. The chief justice circulates a weekly list of the cases he thinks should be discussed, which is known unimaginatively as the "discuss list." Other justices can add to that list the cases they think should be discussed in their Friday afternoon meetings.

Once a case is on the discuss list, it takes a vote of four justices to agree to grant it certiorari. This **Rule of Four** means that it takes fewer people to decide to hear a case than it will eventually take to decide the case itself, and thus it gives some power to a minority on the Court. The denial of certiorari does not necessarily signal that the Court endorses a lower court's ruling. Rather, it simply means that the case was not seen as important or special enough to be heard by the highest court. Justices who believe strongly that a case should not be denied have, increasingly in recent years, engaged in the practice of "dissenting from the denial," in an effort to persuade other justices to go along with them (since dissension at this stage makes the Court look less consensual) and to put their views on record. Fewer than 5 percent of cases appealed to the Supreme Court survive the screening process to be heard by the Court.

One factor that influences whether a case is heard by the Court is whether the United States, under the representation of its lawyer, the **solicitor general**, is party to it. Between 70 and 80 percent of the appeals filed by the federal government are granted cert by the justices, a far greater proportion than for any other group.[42] Researchers speculate that this is because of the stature of the federal government's interests, the justices' trust in the solicitor general's ability to weed out frivolous lawsuits, and the experience the solicitor general brings to the job.[43] Justices are also influenced by **amicus curiae briefs**, or "friend of the court" documents, that are filed in support of about 8 percent of petitions for certiorari by interest groups that want to encourage the Court to grant or deny cert. The amicus briefs do seem to affect the likelihood that the Court will agree to hear a case, and since economic interest groups are more likely to be active here than are other kinds of groups, it is their interests that most often influence the justices to grant cert.[44] As we will see, amicus curiae briefs are also used later in the process.

DECIDING CASES Once a case is on the docket, the parties are notified and they prepare their written briefs and oral arguments for their Supreme Court appearance. Lawyers for each side get only a half-hour to make their cases verbally in front of the Court, and they are often interrupted by justices who seek clarification, criticize points, or offer supportive arguments. The actual decision-making process occurs before and during the Supreme Court conference meeting. Conference debates and discussions take place in private, although justices have often made revealing comments in their letters and memoirs that give insight into the dynamics of conference decision making. A variety of factors affect the justices as they make decisions on the cases they hear. Some of those factors come from within the justices—their attitudes, values, and beliefs—and some are external.

Justices' attitudes toward the Constitution and how literally it is to be taken are clearly important, as we saw earlier in our discussion of strict constructionism and interpretivism. Judges are also influenced by the view they hold of the role of the Court: whether it should be an active lawmaker and policymaker, or should keep its rulings narrow—that is, focused specifically on the most minimal legal issue at hand—and leave lawmaking to the elected

Rule of Four the unwritten requirement that four Supreme Court justices must agree to grant a case certiorari in order for the case to be heard

solicitor general the Justice Department officer who argues the government's cases before the Supreme Court

amicus curiae briefs "friend of the court" documents filed by interested parties to encourage the court to grant or deny certiorari or to urge it to decide a case in a particular way

THE BIG PICTURE:
The Political Path to the Supreme Court

Cases come to the Supreme Court from federal district courts of appeals, state supreme courts, and its original jurisdiction.

1
8
2
3
9
7
10
6
5
4
11

Petitions to the Court for a writ of certiorari
(Approx. 10,000/year)
Reviewed by law clerks, briefs circulated to justices

Oral arguments before the Court

Influence of executive branch (solicitor general)

Precedent

Public opinion

Justices' personal beliefs and attitudes

Supreme Court conference
preliminary vote, opinion assigned

Amicus curiae briefs filed by interest groups

Influence of other justices/ small group dynamics

Opinion writing
Debates about wording, arm twisting, occasional vote-changing

Justice:	Sonia Sotomayor	Ruth Bader Ginsburg	Elena Kagan	Stephen Breyer
Appointed by:	Obama	Clinton	Obama	Clinton
Appointed in:	2009	1993	2009	1994
Ideology*:	-2.151	-1.598	-1.528	-1.133

*Ideological identifications based on Martin-Quinn Scores, which use voting records to rate how liberal or conservative each justice is. Lower numbers are more liberal, higher numbers are more conservative. Shading gradation indicates degrees of liberal ideology (blue) to conservative (red).

The Supreme Court is the final court of appeal in the United States. Don't be fooled by the marble columns and velvet drapes—the Court is a political institution. Power is injected into the process when the justices decide which cases to hear, when they decide cases, and in the impact that those cases have on American lives. This is the political process by which a case gets to the Court.

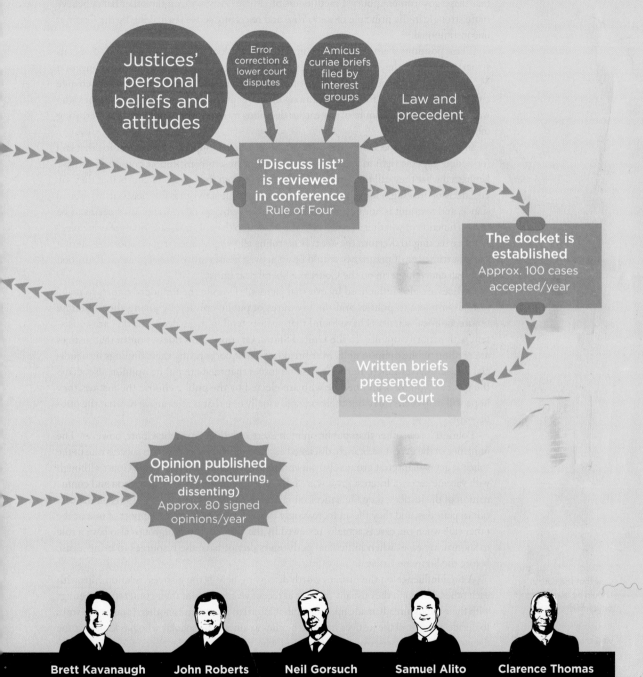

Justices' personal beliefs and attitudes

Error correction & lower court disputes

Amicus curiae briefs filed by interest groups

Law and precedent

"Discuss list" is reviewed in conference
Rule of Four

The docket is established
Approx. 100 cases accepted/year

Written briefs presented to the Court

Opinion published (majority, concurring, dissenting)
Approx. 80 signed opinions/year

Brett Kavanaugh	John Roberts	Neil Gorsuch	Samuel Alito	Clarence Thomas
Trump	GW Bush	Trump	GW Bush	GHW Bush
2018	2005	2017	2005	1991
--**	1.05	1.503	1.677	3.578

** The Martin-Quinn score for Brett Kavanaugh was not available in November 2018.
Source: Administrative office of the United States Courts. Martin-Quinn Scores, http://mqscores.lsa.umich.edu/index.php.

branches of government. Those who adhere to **judicial activism** are quite comfortable with the idea of overturning precedents, exercising judicial review, and otherwise making decisions that shape government policy. Practitioners of **judicial restraint**, on the other hand, believe more strongly in the principle of *stare decisis* and reject any active lawmaking by the Court as unconstitutional.

These positions seem at first to line up with the positions of interpretivism and strict constructionism, and they often do. But exceptions exist, as when liberal justice Thurgood Marshall, who had once used the Constitution in activist and interpretivist ways to change civil rights laws, pleaded for restraint among his newer and more conservative colleagues who were eager to roll back some of the earlier decisions by overturning precedent and creating more conservative law.[45]

In recent years, especially in the wake of a Massachusetts Supreme Court decision that said forbidding gays the right to marry violates the Massachusetts constitution, conservatives have lambasted what they call the activism or "legislating from the bench" of courts that they say take decision making out of the hands of the people. But activism is not necessarily a liberal stance, and restraint is not necessarily conservative. Activism or restraint often seems to be more a function of whether a justice likes the status quo than of any steady point of principle.[46] A justice seeking to overturn the *Roe v. Wade* ruling allowing women to have abortions during the first trimester of pregnancy would be an activist conservative justice; Justice Thurgood Marshall ended his term on the Court as a liberal restraintist.

Justices are also influenced by external factors.[47] Despite the founders' efforts to make justices immune to politics and the pressures of public opinion by giving them lifetime tenure, political scientists have found that justices tend to make decisions that are consistent with majority opinion in the United States. Of course, this doesn't mean that justices are reading public opinion polls over breakfast and incorporating their findings into judicial decisions after lunch. Rather, the same forces that mediate public opinion also shape the justices' opinions, and people who are elected by the public choose the justices they hope will help them carry out their agenda, usually one that is responsive to what the public wants.

Political forces other than public opinion exert an influence on the Court, however. The influence of the executive branch, discussed earlier, contributes to the high success rate of the solicitor general. Interest groups also put enormous pressure on the Supreme Court, although with varying success. Interest groups are influential in the process of nomination and confirmation of the justices, they file amicus curiae briefs to try to shape the decisions on the certiorari petitions, and they file an increasingly large number of briefs in support of one or the other side when the case is actually reviewed by the Court.[48] Interest groups also have a role in sponsoring cases when individual petitioners do not have the resources to bring a case before the Supreme Court.

A final influence on the justices worth discussing here is the justices' relationships with each other. Although they usually (at least in recent years) arrive at their conference meetings with their minds already made up, they cannot afford to ignore one another. It takes five votes to decide a case, and the justices need each other as allies. One scholar who has looked at the disputes among justices over decisions, and who has evaluated the characterization of the Court as "nine scorpions in a bottle," says that the number of disagreements is not noteworthy.[49] On the contrary, what is truly remarkable is how well the justices tend to cooperate, given their close working relationship, the seriousness of their undertaking, and the varied and strong personalities and ideologies that go into the mix.

judicial activism the view that the courts should be lawmaking, policymaking bodies

judicial restraint the view that the courts should reject any active lawmaking functions and stick to judicial interpretations of the past

WRITING OPINIONS   Once a decision is reached, or sometimes as it is being reached, the writing of the opinion is assigned. The **opinion** is the written part of the decision that states the judgment of the majority of the Court; it is the lasting part of the process, read by law students, lawyers, judges, and future justices. As the living legacy of the case, the written opinions are vitally important for how the nation will understand what the decision means. If, for instance, the opinion is written by the least enthusiastic member of the majority, it will be weaker and less authoritative than if it is written by the most passionate member. The same decision can be portrayed in different ways, can be stated broadly or narrowly, with implications for many future cases or for fewer. If the chief justice is in the majority, it is his or her job

opinion the written decision of the court that states the judgment of the majority

to assign the opinion-writing task. Otherwise, the senior member in the majority assigns the opinion. So important is the task that chief justices are known to manipulate their votes, voting with a majority they do not agree with in order to keep the privilege of assigning the opinion to the justice who would write the weakest version of the majority's conclusion.[50] Those justices who agree with the general decision, but for reasons other than or in addition to those stated in the majority opinion, may write **concurring opinions**, and those who disagree may write **dissenting opinions**. These other opinions often have lasting impact as well, especially if the Court changes its mind, as it often does over time and as its composition changes. When such a reversal occurs, the reasons for the about-face are sometimes to be found in the dissent or the concurrence for the original decision.

THE POLITICAL EFFECTS OF JUDICIAL DECISIONS

The last area in which we can see the Supreme Court as a political actor is in the effects of the decisions it makes. These decisions, despite the best intentions of those who adhere to the philosophy of judicial restraint, often amount to the creation of public policies as surely as do the acts of Congress. Chapters 4 and 5, on civil liberties and the struggle for equal rights, make clear that the Supreme Court, at certain points in its history, has taken an active lawmaking role. The history of the Supreme Court's policymaking role is the history of the United States, and we cannot possibly recount it here, but a few examples should show that rulings of the Court have had the effect of distributing scarce and valued resources among people, affecting decisively who gets what, when, and how.[51]

It was the Court, for instance, under the early leadership of John Marshall, that greatly enhanced the power of the federal government over the states by declaring that the Court itself has the power to invalidate state laws (and acts of Congress as well) if they conflict with the Constitution;[52] that state law is invalid if it conflicts with national law;[53] that Congress' powers go beyond those listed in Article I, Section 8, of the Constitution;[54] and that the federal government can regulate interstate commerce.[55] In the early years of the twentieth century, the Supreme Court was an ardent defender of the right of business not to be regulated by the federal government, striking down laws providing for maximum working hours,[56] regulation of child labor,[57] and minimum wages.[58] The role of the Court in making civil rights policy is well known. In 1857 it decided that slaves, even freed slaves, could never be citizens;[59] in 1896 it decided that separate accommodations for whites and blacks were constitutional;[60] and then it reversed itself, declaring separate but equal to be unconstitutional in 1954.[61] It is the Supreme Court that has been responsible for the expansion of due process protection for criminal defendants,[62] for instituting the principle of one person–one vote in drawing legislative districts,[63] and for creating the right of a woman to have an abortion in the first trimester of pregnancy.[64] And, of course, there was the case of *Bush v. Gore*, with which we began this chapter. Each of these actions has altered the distribution of power in American society in ways that some would argue should be done only by an elected body.

In many ways, the Roberts Court promises to be as political as those that have come before, although there have been some surprising twists that keep Court-watchers guessing. In 2010 the Court ruled five to four that campaign finance legislation could not limit the money spent by corporations on electioneering broadcasts because corporations have First Amendment protections.[65] Although we don't yet fully understand the impact of this case, as we will see in Chapter 11, the Super PACs it allows have changed the campaigning landscape. In 2012 the Court handed down rulings that, among other things, struck down most of Arizona's immigration law and upheld the constitutionality of President Obama's health care bill, albeit not on grounds that

concurring opinions documents written by justices expressing agreement with the majority ruling but describing different or additional reasons for the ruling

dissenting opinions documents written by justices expressing disagreement with the majority ruling

observers had anticipated. In 2013 the Court rolled back parts of the historic Voting Rights Act and then the next week struck down the Defense of Marriage Act that defined marriage as being between a man and a woman. And in 2014 the Court limited the president's ability to make appointments during congressional recesses, struck down overall limits on contributions individuals can make to campaigns, and ruled in a split decision that family-owned corporations do not have to provide health insurance that covers birth control to employees if it offends the owners' religious beliefs. In 2016 the Court, still down one member because of the Republicans' refusal to hold hearings on Obama's nominee, struck down a restrictive Texas abortion law, decided that a domestic violence conviction was grounds for denying an individual's right to own a gun, and reaffirmed that race can be used as a criterion in college admissions standards, giving new life to affirmative action. In none of those cases, except perhaps the affirmative action case, did the diminished numbers on the Court make a significant difference. Although this is by no means a comprehensive list of Supreme Court cases during Roberts's tenure, it shows that these decisions get right in the thick of determining who gets what, and how they get it.[66]

In Your Own Words Outline the institutional rules and political influences that shape the Supreme Court and the decisions it makes.

CITIZENSHIP AND THE COURTS

Equal treatment and equal access?

In this chapter we have been arguing that the legal system and the American courts are central to the maintenance of social order and conflict resolution, and are also a fundamental component of American politics—who gets what, and how they get it. This means that a crucial question for American democracy is, who takes advantage of this powerful system for allocating resources and values in society? An important component of American political culture is the principle of equality before the law. We commonly take that principle to mean that all citizens should be treated equally by the law, but it also implies that all citizens should have equal access to the law. In this concluding section we look at the questions of equal treatment and equal access.

EQUAL TREATMENT BY THE CRIMINAL JUSTICE SYSTEM

In Chapter 5, on civil rights, we examined in depth the issue of equality before the law in a constitutional sense. But what about the day-to-day treatment of citizens by the law enforcement and legal systems? Citizens are treated differently by these systems according to their race, their income level, and the kinds of crimes they commit. Experience has led African Americans and whites to develop very different narratives about the role the criminal justice system plays in their lives—narratives that are told and strengthened by the witness borne by social media. When law enforcement violations of civil rights are videotaped, posted in real time, and go viral before the official report has been made, the conventional, pro–law enforcement narratives are harder to maintain, although people's perceptions of the events are still often divided along racial lines.

The country was sadly reminded of that fact in the summer of 2014 through the very different reactions whites and blacks had to the shooting of Michael Brown, an unarmed teenager, by a police officer in Ferguson, Missouri. In the week following the killing, amid riots and demonstrations, curfews and the calling in of the National Guard by the governor,

80 percent of African Americans said they thought the incident raised important ideas about race. In contrast, 47 percent of whites said the issue of race was getting more attention than it deserved.[67] For African Americans, Brown was but the latest and not the last young man to be shot by police in suspect circumstances, highlighting the fear that many have that their sons are often targeted by the police out of fear or prejudice. Whites, by contrast, are accustomed to seeing the police as a source of safety rather than danger, and often fail to understand what such incidents look like from the other side of the racial divide. In fact, as Ferguson struggled for calm, sympathy for the police officer who shot Brown generated several online efforts to raise support and funds for him and his family. The Brown murder was not an exception but—as the social media–driven Black Lives Matter movement drove home—just one in a series of similar betrayals of the public trust by law enforcement officers who are predisposed to believe that black men are more dangerous than whites.

When San Francisco 49er Colin Kaepernick knelt during the national anthem in 2016 to protest police violence, he was ostracized within the NFL. Other players who followed his example were accused of protesting the flag or the anthem instead of the violence they were trying to highlight. President Trump weighed in targeting the players, and the NFL owners followed suit with a decision to fine players who took a knee during the anthem. Trump's congratulatory tweet suggested that perhaps protesting players did not belong in the country at all.[68]

All this makes it painfully clear that African Americans and white Americans do not experience our criminal justice system in the same ways, beginning with what is often the initial contact with the system, the police. Blacks are often harassed by police or treated with suspicion without any real cause—consider the practice of "stop-and-frisk" tactics in black neighborhoods in New York City, for example, technically random in nature but affecting mostly black men. As a result, blacks, and black men especially, tend to perceive the police as persecutors rather than protectors. In New York, specifically, reactions to stop-and-frisk tended to reflect race, with 48 percent of whites calling the practice "acceptable," compared to a mere 35 percent of blacks.[69] Federal courts weighed in on the practice in 2013, ruling that stop-and-frisk violated the constitutional rights of minorities in the city and amounted to "indirect racial profiling." Stopping short of ending the practice entirely, Justice Shira A. Sheindlin called for a range of reforms and a federal monitor to oversee them.[70]

Today the fact remains that blacks are more likely to be arrested than whites, and they are more likely to go to jail, where they serve harsher sentences. A study of marijuana use and arrests, for example, shows that while young whites use marijuana at higher rates than blacks, blacks are three times more likely to be arrested for marijuana possession.[71] Clearly, initial interactions with police play a role here—they are more likely to stop and frisk a black person. But race is not the only factor that divides American citizens in their experience of the criminal justice system.

Income also creates a barrier to equal treatment by the law. Over half of those convicted of felonies in the United States were defended by court-appointed lawyers.[72] These lawyers are likely to be less than enthusiastic about their assignments. For one thing, the pay is modest and sometimes irregular. Many lawyers do not like to provide free services *pro bono publico* ("for the public good") because they are afraid it will offend their regular corporate clients. Consequently the quality of the legal representation available to the poor is not of the same standard available to those who can afford to pay well. Yale law professor John H. Langbein is scathing on the role of money in determining the legal fate of Americans. He says, "Money is the defining element of our modern American criminal-justice system." The wealthy can afford crackerjack lawyers who can use the "defense lawyer's bag of tricks for sowing doubts, casting aspersions, and coaching witnesses," but "if you are not a person of means, if you cannot afford to engage the elite defense-lawyer industry—and that means most of us—you will be cast into a different system, in which the financial advantages of the state will overpower you and leave you effectively at the mercy of prosecutorial whim."[73]

EQUAL ACCESS TO THE CIVIL JUSTICE SYSTEM

Whereas the issue with respect to the criminal justice system is equal treatment, the issue for the civil justice system is equal access. Most of us in our lifetimes will have some legal problems. The Supreme Court has ruled that low-income defendants must be provided with legal assistance in state and federal criminal cases, but there is no such guarantee for civil cases. That doesn't mean, however, that less affluent citizens have no recourse for their legal problems. Both public and private legal aid programs exist. Among others, the Legal Services Corporation (LSC), created by Congress in 1974, is a nonprofit organization that provides resources to over 138 legal aid programs around the country with more than 900 local offices. The LSC helps citizens and some immigrants with legal problems such as those concerning housing, employment, family issues, finances, and immigration. This program has been controversial, as conservatives have feared that it has a left-wing agenda, and Republicans have tried to limit it when they have been in the congressional majority.

Scott Olson/Getty Images

Emotions, Boiling Over

After local police shot and killed an unarmed teenager named Michael Brown in August 2014, protestors, both peaceful and disruptive, took to the streets of Ferguson, Missouri, to express their anger over what they saw as a pattern of unfair—and too often fatal—treatment along racial lines. Public reactions, especially heightened attention to the Black Lives Matter movement, brought renewed focus to issues of race relations in the United States.

Does the fact that these services exist mean that more citizens get legal advice? Undoubtedly it does. Every year LSC programs handle nearly a million cases.[74] Still, there is no question that many of the legal needs of the less affluent are not being addressed through the legal system.[75]

Clearly a bias in the justice system favors those who can afford to take advantage of lawyers and other means of legal assistance. And since people of color and women are much more likely to be poor than are white males (although white men are certainly represented among the poor), the civil justice system ends up discriminating as well.

These arguments do not mean that the U.S. justice system has made no progress toward a more equal dispensation of justice. Without doubt, we have made enormous strides since the days of *Dred Scott*, when the Supreme Court ruled that blacks did not have the standing to bring cases to court, and since the days when lynch mobs dispensed their brand of vigilante justice in the South. But the lives of African Americans are still at risk at multiple points in our justice system. Since Michael Brown's murder, the Black Lives Matter movement that we discussed in Chapter 1 has created and spread a counternarrative about the justice system in the United States that has helped to bring the experience of African Americans home to whites in a new way.

In Your Own Words Describe the relationship between citizens and the courts in America.

Let's Revisit: What's at Stake . . . ?

In the years since the divisive outcome of *Bush v. Gore*, the nation has calmed down. The stunning national crisis that began with the terrorist attacks on September 11, 2001, put things into a broader perspective, and a Court-decided election no longer seemed as great a danger as the possibility of being caught without any elected leader at all at a critical time. Public opinion polls show that trust in all institutions of government, including the Supreme Court, ran high after September 11, and Bush's legitimacy no longer rested with the Court's narrow majority but rather with the approval ratings that hit unprecedented heights in the aftermath of the terrorist attacks and with his successful reelection in 2004. But changed national circumstances and subsequent elections do not mean that the Court's unusual and controversial move in resolving the 2000 election should go unanalyzed. What was at stake in this extraordinary case?

First, as Justice Stevens pointed out at the time, the long-term consequences of people's attitudes toward the Court were at risk. Indeed, polls have shown a somewhat steady decline in people's perceptions of the highest court in the land in the years since, but it remains unclear whether that is due to the Court's finding in *Bush v. Gore* or to later rulings—or to an overall decrease in faith in government institutions.[76] The Court, as we have seen, has often engaged in policymaking, and to believe that it is not a political institution would be a serious mistake. But part of its own legitimacy has come from the fact that most people do not perceive it as political, and it is far more difficult now to maintain that illusion. In the immediate aftermath of the decision, the justices, speaking around the country, tried to contain the damage and reassure Americans. Some of the dissenting justices even emphasized that the decision was not made on political or ideological grounds. But fifteen years later, retired Justice Sandra Day O'Connor expressed some regrets, not about the ruling itself or her vote in it, but about the Court's decision to get involved at all. Noting that the case had earned the court "a less-than-perfect reputation," O'Connor wondered if "maybe the court should have said, 'We're not going to take it, goodbye.'"[77]

Also at stake in such a deeply divided decision was the Court's own internal stability and ability to work together. While the confidentiality of the justices' discussions in arriving at the decision has been well guarded, the decision itself shows that they were acrimonious. Again, in the aftermath, the justices have tried to put a unified front on what was clearly a bitter split. Members of the majority have continued to socialize with dissenters, and as Justice Scalia himself told one audience, "If you can't disagree without hating each other, you better find another profession other than the law."[78] The stakes in this case may have been more directly political than in most other cases, but the members of the Supreme Court are used to disagreeing over important issues and probably handle the level of conflict more easily than do the Americans who look up to them as diviners of truth and right.

Another stake in the pivotal decision was the fundamental issue of federalism itself. The federal courts, as Justice Ruth Bader Ginsburg wrote in her dissent, have a long tradition of deferring to state courts on issues of state law. Indeed, many observers were astounded that the Court agreed to hear the case in the first place, assuming that the justices would have sent it back to be settled in Florida. Normally it would have been the ardent conservatives on the Court—Rehnquist, Scalia, and Thomas—whom one would have expected to leap to the defense of states' rights. Subsequent decisions have made clear, however, that the *Bush v. Gore* decision did not signal a reversal on their part.

Some observers argue that the majority of the Court saw something else at stake that led them to set aside their strong beliefs in states' rights and to run the risk that they might be seen as more Machiavelli than King Solomon, more interested in power than wisdom. The majority saw the very security and stability of the nation at stake. Anticipating a long recount of the votes that might even then be inconclusive, they thought it was better to act decisively at the start rather than to wait until a circus-like atmosphere had rendered impossible the most important decision a voting public can make. Whether they were right in doing so, and whether the stakes justified the risks they took, politicians, partisans, and historians will continue to debate for years to come.

for CQ Press

Want a better grade?

Get the tools you need to sharpen your study skills. **SAGE edge** offers practice quizzes, eFlashcards, video, and multimedia at **edge.sagepub.com/barbourbrief8e.**

Review

Law and the American Legal System

Laws serve five main functions in a democratic society. They offer security, supply predictability, provide for conflict resolution through the **courts** (294), reinforce society's values, and provide for the distribution of social costs and benefits. American law is based on legislation, but its practice has evolved from a **common law tradition** (295) and the use of **precedent** (295) by judges.

Laws serve many purposes and are classified in different ways. **Substantive law** (295) covers what we can or cannot do, while **procedural law** (295) establishes the procedures used to enforce law generally and guarantees us **procedural due process** (295). **Criminal law** (296) concerns specific behaviors considered undesirable by the government, while **civil law** (296) covers interactions between individuals. **Constitutional law** (296) refers to laws included in the Constitution as well as the precedents established over time by judicial decisions relating to these laws. **Statutory law** (296), **administrative law** (297), and **executive orders** (297) are established by Congress and state legislatures, the bureaucracy, and the president, respectively.

Constitutional Provisions and the Development of Judicial Review

The founders were deliberately vague in setting up a court system so as to avoid controversy during the ratification process. The Constitution never stated that courts could decide the constitutionality of legislation. The courts gained the extraconstitutional power of **judicial review** (298) when Chief Justice John Marshall created it in *Marbury v. Madison* (299).

Federalism and the American Courts

The United States has a dual court system, with state and federal courts each having different **jurisdictions** (300). Cases come directly to a court through its **original jurisdiction** (300) or on **appeal** (300) if it has **appellate jurisdiction** (300). Both court systems have three tiers; the federal courts range from district courts to the U.S. courts of appeals to the Supreme Court. Judges are appointed to the federal courts by a political process involving the president and the Senate and, often, the principle of **senatorial courtesy** (304).

The Supreme Court

The U.S. Supreme Court reigns at the top of the American court system. It is a powerful institution, revered by the American public, but it is as political an institution as the other two branches of government. Politics is involved in how the Court is chosen—a process that considers merit; ideology, especially focusing on whether the justices are believers in **strict constructionism** (307), **judicial interpretivism** (307), **judicial activism** (314), or **judicial restraint** (314); reward; and representation. The work of the Court is also political, as the justices decide whether to issue **writs of certiorari** (310) based on the application of the **Rule of Four** (311), and as they decide cases influenced by their own values, the **solicitor general** (311), and a variety of **amicus curiae briefs** (311). These influences show up in the writing of the **opinion** (315), and both **concurring opinions** (316) and **dissenting opinions** (316). These opinions are decisive in determining who gets what in American politics.

You and 1,000,000 people like this.

Image created by Patricia Mann; icon by Thomas Pajot/Shutterstock.com

10

Public Opinion

In Your Own Words

After you've read this chapter, you will be able to

10.1 Explain the role of public opinion in a democracy.

10.2 Evaluate how well American citizens measure up to notions of an ideal democratic citizen.

10.3 Identify key factors that influence our individual and collective political opinions.

10.4 Describe different techniques used to gauge public opinion.

10.5 Give examples of ways in which public opinion enhances or diminishes the relationship between citizens and government.

What's at Stake . . . When We Move to More Direct Democracy?

It was late May 2018, and #hometovote was trending. Irish expats from all over the world were coming home to cast a constitutional vote on whether or not to repeal Ireland's Eighth Amendment banning abortions. Ireland's abortion laws were so restrictive that in 2012 a young woman, Savita Halappanavar, died of complications from a miscarriage after a hospital refused her a medically necessary abortion. Polls showed that the vote would be close, and so people were coming home to register their views. Because Ireland's voting laws for the most part require you to vote in person, in person they were voting, alongside many of their fellow countrypeople. Turnout was the highest it had been for a social issue in Ireland—64.1 percent of Irish voters showed up. And in the end, the close vote wasn't close after all. With a 66.4 percent majority, the Eighth Amendment was overturned, allowing for the passage of less restrictive laws.

It wasn't the first time a popular referendum had upended the social order in Ireland. In 2015, 61 percent of the country's voters turned out to decide, by a 62 percent majority, to allow marriage equality. In a country whose Constitution reflected the conservative principles of the Catholic Church, public opinion has been shifting faster than the wheels of government could turn. Politicians needed the Constitution amended to allow them to pass laws reflecting the shifts, and the people came out in droves to make it happen.

Direct votes on policy, like these two Irish referenda, are not unusual, but the results can be unpredictable and often shocking. For instance, on the morning of June 24, 2016, British citizens woke up to the unexpected news that they were on their way out of the European Union (EU)—an economic and political union of twenty-eight European countries that dated in some form back to the days after World War II. A nonbinding but politically important popular vote on whether the United Kingdom should withdraw from the EU (popularly called "Brexit") found that 51.9 percent of the U.K. voters (the United Kingdom consists of England, Scotland, Northern Ireland, Wales, and its overseas territory, Gibraltar) wanted out. Although Scotland, Northern Ireland, and Gibraltar voted to remain, they were stuck with the result.[1] By the evening of the 24th, Britain's prime minister, David Cameron, who had opposed Brexit but called the vote to appease political opponents, had resigned, the British pound was in free fall, several politicians who had advocated leaving were admitting they had played a little fast and loose with the facts about the consequences of a Brexit, and a number of British voters were expressing misgivings about the way they had voted. Some were so sure the measure would fail they had voted for it as a "protest." Brexit remorse or "Bregret" was setting in quickly.[2]

Referenda can have unexpected consequences. Are they a good idea? "Letting the people decide" is an attractive idea in a country like the United States that prides itself on its democracy. But how much responsibility do you want to take for the way you are governed? Most of us are pretty comfortable with the idea that we should vote for those who make our rules (although we don't all jump at the chance to do it), but how about voting on the rules themselves? Citizens of some states—California, for instance—have become used to being asked for their votes on new state laws through referenda and voter initiatives. Other states, too, hold popular votes on issues it is hard to get politicians to take action on. In May 2018, for example, Ohio passed an initiative rejecting partisan gerrymandering in favor of a less partisan method of redistricting. But what about national politics—do you know enough or care enough to vote on laws for the country as a whole, just as if you were a member of Congress or a senator? Are you confident that your political strings aren't being pulled by the authors of the social media you tune in to? Should we be governed more by public opinion than by the opinions of our elected leaders? This is the question that drives the debate about whether U.S. citizens should be able to participate in such forms of direct democracy as the national referendum or initiative.

All American states employ some degree of direct democracy (although it is generally much weaker in the South), but as we saw with Ireland and the United Kingdom, many other countries do as well. In the past several years alone, voters in Slovenia were asked to decide about the establishment of a tribunal to resolve a border dispute with Croatia, in Bolivia about whether there should be limits to individual landholdings, in Azerbaijan about amending the constitution, in Sierra Leone about choosing a president (in the first democratic elections since 1967), and in Iceland about terms of payment on the national debt.

Back in 1995 former senator Mike Gravel, D-Alaska, proposed that the United States join many of the world's nations in adopting a national plebiscite, or popular vote on policy. He argued that Americans should support a national initiative he called "Philadelphia II" (to evoke "Philadelphia I," which was, of course, the Constitutional Convention), which would set up procedures for direct popular participation in national lawmaking.[3] Such participation could take place through the ballot box (the Swiss go to the polls four times a year to vote on national policy) or even electronically, as some have suggested, with people voting on issues by computer at home. Experts agree that the technology exists for at-home participation in government. And public opinion is overwhelmingly in favor of proposals to let Americans vote for or against major national issues before they become law.[4]

Do you agree with Gravel and the roughly three-quarters of Americans who support more direct democracy at the national level? Should we have rule by public opinion in the United States? How would the founders have responded to this proposal? And what would be the consequences for American government if a national plebiscite were passed? Just what is at stake in the issue of direct democracy at the national level?

IT is fashionable these days to denounce the public opinion polls that claim to tell us what the American public thinks about this or that political issue. The American people themselves are skeptical—65 percent of them think that the polls are "right only some of the time" or "hardly ever right."[5] (You might believe that finding, or you might not.) Politicians can be leery of polls, too—or even downright scornful of them. Disdainful of the Bill Clinton years, when the president's team of pollsters openly tested the public on various issues, including his approval ratings, the George W. Bush administration was cagey about the fact that they watched polls at all. Bush himself frequently said things like, "I really don't worry about polls or focus groups; I do what I think is right."[6] Matthew Dowd, the Bush administration's chief of polling at the Republican National Committee, echoed that stance with an emphatic "We don't poll policy positions. Ever."[7]

Of course, the Bush administration did look at polls, and conducted them, too, just like every other administration has since the advent of modern polling. When in 2002 a reporter visited Karl Rove, Bush's chief political adviser, and asked about the impact of the corporate scandals of the time on Bush's effectiveness as president, Rove pulled out a bundle of polls and started reading off data to support his claim that people continued to support Bush. Then he caught the reporter's quizzical look. "'Not that we spend a lot of time on these,' he said quickly. . . ."[8] These reactions to public opinion raise an interesting question: What is so bad about being ruled by the polls in a democracy, which, after all, is supposed to be ruled by the people? If politics is about who gets what, and how they get it, shouldn't we care about what the "who" thinks? **Public opinion** is just what the public thinks (although as we have argued throughout this book, it is subject to mediation from a variety of sources). It is the aggregation, or collection, of individual attitudes and beliefs on one or more issues at any given time. **Public opinion polls** are nothing more than scientific efforts to measure that opinion—to estimate what an entire group of people thinks about an issue by asking a smaller sample of the group for their opinions. If the sample is large enough and chosen properly, we have every reason to believe that it will provide a reliable estimate of the whole. Today's technology enables us to keep a constant finger on the pulse of America, and to know what its citizens are thinking at almost any given time. Yet at least some Americans seem torn about the role of public opinion in government today. On the one hand, we want to believe that what we think matters, but on the other hand, we'd like to think that our elected officials are guided by unwavering standards and principles. Reflected in this dilemma are not just different views of public opinion but also different narratives about what constitutes "good leadership."

In this chapter we argue that public opinion *is* important for the proper functioning of democracy, that the expression of what citizens think and what they want is a prerequisite for their ability to use the system and its rules to get what they want from it. But the quality of the public's opinion on politics—the degree to which it is influenced by our demographics, our circumstances, and the channels through which we get information—and the ways that it actually influences policy may surprise us greatly. Specifically, in this chapter you will learn about the role of public opinion in a democracy, where our opinions come from, what our opinions are, how public opinion can be measured, and whether we think like the ideal democratic citizen.

THE ROLE OF PUBLIC OPINION IN A DEMOCRACY

Keeping the government of the people informed by the people

Public opinion is important in a democracy for at least two reasons. The first reason is normative: we believe public opinion *should* influence what government does. The second is empirical: a lot of people actually behave as though public opinion does matter, and to the degree that they measure, record, and react to it, it does indeed become a factor in American politics.

WHY PUBLIC OPINION *SHOULD* MATTER

The story of the American founding is about the rejection of aristocracy and monarchy and the rise of popular sovereignty—the idea that the people matter above all. The presence of "the people" is pervasive in the documents and narratives that created and support the American government. In the Declaration of Independence, Thomas Jefferson wrote that a just government must get its powers from "the consent of the governed." Our Constitution begins, "We, the People. . . ." And Abraham Lincoln's Gettysburg Address hails our nation as "government of the people, by the people, and for the people." What all of this tells us is that the very legitimacy of the U.S. government, like that of all other democracies, rests on the idea that government exists to serve the interests of its citizens. As political scientist V. O. Key observed, "Unless mass views have some place in the shaping of policy, all talk about democracy is nonsense."[9]

But how to determine whose views should be heard? As we saw in Chapter 1, different theories of democracy prescribe different roles for "the people," in part because these theories disagree about how competent the citizens of a country are to govern themselves. Elitists suspect that citizens are too ignorant, ill-informed, or subject to manipulation to be trusted with major political decisions. Pluralists trust groups of citizens to be competent on those issues in which they have a stake, but they think that individuals may be too busy to gather all the information they need to make informed decisions. Finally, proponents of participatory democracy have faith that the people are both smart enough and able to gather enough information to be effective decision makers.

As Americans, we are also somewhat confused about what we think the role of the democratic citizen should be. We introduced these conflicting notions of citizenship in Chapter 1. One view, public-interested citizenship, which describes what we might call the *ideal democratic citizen*, is founded on the vision of a virtuous citizen activated by concern for the common good, who recognizes that democracy carries obligations as well as rights. In this familiar model, a citizen should be attentive to and informed about politics, exhibit political tolerance and a willingness to compromise, and practice high levels of participation in civic activities.

A competing view of self-interested American citizenship holds that Americans are apolitical, self-absorbed actors. According to this view, Americans are almost the opposite of the ideal citizen: inattentive and ill informed, politically intolerant and rigid, and unlikely to get involved in political life.

In the current age, all forms of citizenship are subject to the power inherent in the channels through which we acquire information. An inquisitive citizen who reads widely, explores the web, and debates people with whom he or she disagrees is more likely to escape the perils of living in an information bubble and to demonstrate the values of public-interested citizenship. A citizen who ignores the news altogether or gets it only from sources he or she agrees with is more likely to be focused on less universal, more personal issues.

> **What traits of the ideal democratic citizen described here are most important for the health of democracy?**

We argue in this chapter, as we have earlier, that the American public displays all of these visions of citizenship. But we also argue that mechanisms in American politics buffer the impact of apolitical, self-interested behavior, so that government by public opinion does not have disastrous effects on the American polity. Although it may seem like some kind of magician's act, we show that Americans as a *group* often behave as ideal citizens, even though as *individuals* they do not.

WHY PUBLIC OPINION *DOES* MATTER

Politicians and media leaders act as though they agree with Key's conclusion, which is the practical reason why, regardless of the founding narrative, public opinion matters in

Dennis Drenner/MCT/MCT via Getty Images

Tell Me What You Really Think

Our elected officials may seem disconnected from popular opinion, but they are in fact keenly sensitive to their constituents, knowing that their votes on major bills may come back to haunt them when it's time for reelection. Members of Congress pay attention to public opinion polls, and most try to provide some face time in their districts as well. Here, Democratic senator Amy Klobuchar chats with constituents over coffee at a weekly "Minnesota Mornings" meet-and-greet event.

American politics. Elected politicians have their own narrative, which is that the public is keeping tabs on them. When voting on major bills, members of Congress worry quite a lot about public opinion in their districts.[10] Presidents, too, pay close attention to public opinion. In fact, recent presidents have invested major resources in having an in-house public opinion expert whose regular polls are used as an important part of presidential political strategies. And, indeed, the belief that the public is paying attention is not totally unfounded. Although the public does not often act as if it pays attention or cares very much about politics, it can change its mind and act decisively if the provocation is sufficient.

For instance, in the 2006 midterm election, voters showed their frustration with Republicans' support for the war in Iraq (despite polls that said a majority of Americans had come to oppose the war) by handing the Democrats enough seats in the House and the Senate to give them control in both chambers.[11] And in 2008 and 2010, elections were primarily about voter angst over a depressed economy, a worry that first enhanced and then diminished the Democrats' control of Congress. Multiple protest marches in the year and a half after Trump's inauguration made it clear that women's issues, immigration issues, and gun control were very much on the minds of millions of Americans. In special elections held to fill seats that became unexpectedly vacant, Democrats far outperformed Hillary Clinton's share of the presidential vote and Democrats succeeded in taking control of the House of Representatives in the 2018 midterms, as well as flipping seven governorships and six state legislative chambers.

Politicians are not alone in their tendency to monitor public opinion as they do their jobs. Leaders of the media also focus on public opinion, making huge investments in polls and devoting considerable coverage to reporting what the public is thinking. Polls are used to measure public attitudes toward all sorts of things and then are interpreted by the media, who set the narrative about what they mean. Of course, we are familiar with "horse-race" polls that ask about people's voting intentions and lend drama to media coverage of electoral races. Sometimes these polls themselves become the story the media covers, with results tweeted and retweeted as soon as they are available, and competing narratives quickly generated online to explain what they might mean. With the availability of a twenty-four-hour news cycle and the need to find something to report on all the time, it is not surprising that the media have fastened on their own polling as a newsworthy subject. Public opinion, or talk about it, seems to pervade the modern political arena.

In Your Own Words Explain the role of public opinion in a democracy.

CITIZEN VALUES

American reality far from the ideal

In the preceding section, we reminded you of the two competing visions of citizenship in America: one, the ideal democratic citizen who is knowledgeable, tolerant, and engaged in politics; and two, the apolitical, self-interested actor who does not meet this ideal. Not surprisingly, our behavior frequently combines aspects of each. For instance, some citizens tune out political news but are tolerant of others and vote regularly. Many activist citizens are informed, opinionated, and participatory but are intolerant of others' views, which can make the give and take of democratic politics difficult. We are not ideal democratic citizens, but we know our founders did not expect us to be. As we will see by the end of this chapter, our democracy has so far survived fairly well despite our lapses.

The ideal democratic citizen understands how government works, who the main actors are, and what major principles underlie the operation of the political system. Public opinion pollsters periodically take readings on what the public actually knows about politics, and the conclusion is always the same: Americans are not very well informed about their political system.[12]

Knowledge of key figures in politics is important for knowing whom to thank—or blame—for government policy, key information if we are to hold our officials accountable. For instance, virtually everyone (99 percent of Americans) can name the president, but in 2017, fewer than half (45 percent) knew that Neil Gorsuch was a justice on the Supreme Court and only 62 percent knew that Paul Ryan was the Speaker of the House of Representatives, a position that is third in line for succession to the presidency, directly after the vice president.[13] Americans have a reasonable understanding of the most prominent aspects of the government system and the most visible leaders but are ignorant about other central actors and key principles of American political life.

Interest in politics is also highly variable in the United States; only about a quarter of Americans say they follow public affairs "most of the time."[14] Taken together, the moderate levels of political knowledge and interest indicate that the American public does not approach the high levels of civic engagement recommended by civics texts, but neither are they totally ignorant and unconcerned.

Another key value for our ideal citizen is tolerance. In a democracy, with many people jockeying for position and many competing visions of the common good, tolerance for ideas different from one's own and respect for the rights of others provide oil to keep the democratic machinery running smoothly. Tolerance is a prerequisite for compromise, which is an essential component of politics generally and of democratic politics particularly.

How do Americans measure up on the important democratic requirement of respect for others' rights? The record is mixed. As we saw in Chapter 5, America has a history of denying basic civil rights to some groups, but clearly tolerance in general has been on the rise since the civil rights movement of the 1960s. Small pockets of intolerance persist, primarily among extremist groups, although as we saw in the *What's at Stake . . . ?* in Chapter 5, more and more of it has bubbled to the surface since the 2016 election cycle. The anonymity of channels of communication on the Internet, from Twitter to Snapchat, allows people to express "socially inappropriate" and even downright racist views without fear of retribution. In fact, the idea that we should conform to respectful ways of referring to each other has been condemned as rampant political correctness, and its opposite blossoms on some social networks and even in one-to-one personal and social relationships.

FIGURE 10.1

Comparison of Voter Turnout Among Select Nations

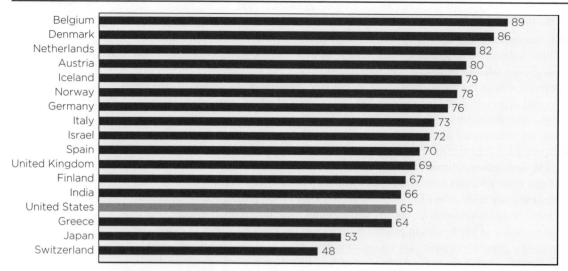

Source: Data calculated by authors with data from the Institute for Democracy and Electoral Assistance, www.idea.int/vt/.

In terms of general principles, most Americans support the values of freedom of speech, freedom of religion, and political equality. For instance, 90 percent of respondents told researchers that they believed in "free speech for all, no matter what their views might be." However, when citizens are asked to apply these principles to particular situations in which specific groups have to be tolerated (especially unpopular groups like the American Nazi Party preaching race hatred or atheists preaching against God and religion), the levels of political tolerance drop dramatically.[15]

In studies of political tolerance, the least politically tolerant are consistently the less educated and less politically sophisticated. For example, one study found that, on a civil liberties scale designed to measure overall support for First Amendment rights, only 24 percent of high school graduates earned high scores, compared with 52 percent of college graduates.[16] In practice, the mass public's record has not been bad, and some of the worst offenses of intolerance in our history, from slavery to the internment of Japanese Americans during World War II, were led by elites, not the mass public.

A final characteristic of ideal citizens is, not surprisingly, that they participate in the system. One of the most consistent criticisms of Americans by those concerned with the democratic health of the nation is that we do not participate enough. And indeed, as participation is usually measured, the critics are right. For instance, among industrialized nations, the United States ranks among the last in voter turnout (see Figure 10.1). Various explanations have been offered for the low U.S. turnout, including the failure of parties to work to mobilize turnout and obstacles to participation such as restrictive registration laws, limited voting hours, and the frequency of elections. We examine who votes and why in Chapter 12, but for now the fact remains that among industrialized nations, the United States has one of the lowest levels of voter turnout in national elections, although greater levels of participation are seen among those with more education and higher income.

WHAT INFLUENCES OUR OPINIONS ABOUT POLITICS?

Sources of differing opinions in the American public

Clearly many, but by no means all, Americans approximate the characteristics of our so-called ideal democratic citizen, and the traits of ideal democratic citizenship are not distributed equally across the population. But the fact that education and socioeconomic status have something to do with our political opinions and behaviors still does not tell us where our opinions come from. There are forces around us that bring most of us to consensus on the basics of the political culture we learned about in Chapter 1, and more complex forces that guide us into adopting the more divisive ideologies we studied in the same chapter.

MECHANISMS OF EARLY POLITICAL SOCIALIZATION: HOW WE LEARN SHARED NARRATIVES ABOUT THE RULES OF THE GAME

Democracies and, indeed, all other political systems depend for their survival on each new generation's picking up the values and allegiances of previous generations—beliefs in the legitimacy of the political system and its leaders, and a willingness to obey the laws and the commands of those leaders. Children in France or China support their leaders as surely as children of the United States support theirs. Sharing an essential narrative about the founding of a country and the values that support it and deserve loyalty is key here.

We learn our earliest opinions through a process called **political socialization**, whereby values, beliefs, and attachments to political ideals are transferred from generation to generation. Early on, those values are supportive of the political system as we learn patriotism and good citizenship skills. The key agents of socialization are family, school, and houses of worship—all of which have an interest in turning out well-behaved children with loyalty to country. Socialization is like mediation in the sense that the information we pick up comes through channels that may be controlled by people or organizations with interests in having us behave in particular ways. In the "olden days," of course, socialization was face to face, or maybe face to pastor or face to teacher, but now the possible agents of socialization have multiplied with the growth of the Internet and social media. Our fundamental values may be shaped in part by people we never see, never meet, and may not even be aware of.

The family is probably the biggest influence on our political development. Children typically develop an emotional response to some fundamental objects of government before they really understand much about those objects. They learn that the police are good (in most communities), the president is important, and the flag deserves respect. Thus one of the important orientations that develops in the preschool years is **patriotism**, a strong emotional attachment to the political community. Children saluting the flag or watching fireworks at Independence Day celebrations easily absorb the idea that being American is something special. Children also tend to choose the same political party as their parents.[17]

political socialization the process by which we learn our political orientations and allegiances

patriotism a strong emotional attachment to one's political community

Schools—where many children begin their day with the Pledge of Allegiance, and where schoolbooks explicitly emphasize stirring narratives about national origins, founding heroes, and patriotism—are also an important agent of political learning and the development of citizen orientations. Most school districts include as part of their explicit mission that the schools should foster good citizenship.[18] In many districts, U.S. history or civics is a required course, and some state legislatures require a course or two in U.S. and state politics for all college students in the state system.

The media we are exposed to can also help build common values. When there were fewer television stations, most children watched the same cartoons, many of which reinforced patriotic themes. Even today children watch videos and play video games that do the same things.

The groups we belong to also foster in us basic values. Peer groups have a lot of influence on individuals' social and political attitudes. People who attend the same church tend to have similar political attitudes, as do individuals who live in the same neighborhoods. These tendencies can be traced in part to the ways people select themselves into groups, but they are reinforced by social contacts and by the social media connections that allow us to expand the numbers of peers we can contact and to build on and participate in the stories about who we are. The processes of talking, working, and worshiping together lead people to see the world similarly.[19]

The appearance of consensus on rules of the game and basic values can be exaggerated by simple peer pressure. Researchers have documented a phenomenon they call the **spiral of silence**, a process by which minority voices silence themselves in the face of majority consensus.[20] This relative silence tends to embolden the advocates of the majority opinion to speak even more confidently. Thus, through this spiral of silence, what may begin as a bare majority for a group's position can become the overwhelming voice of the group.

DIFFERENCES IN PUBLIC OPINION

Political socialization produces a citizenry that largely agrees with the rules of the game and accepts the outcomes of the national political process as legitimate. That does not mean, however, that we are a nation in agreement on most or even very many things. As we get older and are exposed to more influences, our opinions become more complex. Our demographics (including race and ethnicity, gender, and age); partisanship and ideology; education; economic self-interest; and religion, as well as where we live, affect the way we come to see politics, what we believe we have at stake in the political process, and the kind of citizenship we practice. In the process we move from consensus on the basics of American political culture to more divisive beliefs.

Those divisive beliefs work against the positive feelings toward government we build in our early years. In fact, at any given time, large numbers of Americans express distrust in government to do the right thing, a reflection of the fact that the post–New Deal philosophy that there are public solutions to our problems means that when government acts there will be winners and losers. As conflict among different groups in society fluctuates, so do levels of trust that government will do the right thing. Occasionally we solidify behind our government and our leaders, especially when we perceive that we are under threat, as we did in the days after 9/11, but otherwise our trust in government reflects the divisions in our opinions and our loyalties to population subgroups.

spiral of silence the process by which a majority opinion becomes exaggerated because minorities do not feel comfortable speaking out in opposition

RACE AND ETHNICITY As we saw in Chapter 5, race has been a deep and consistent cleavage in American politics. Only in recent decades have blacks achieved the same political rights as the white majority, and disparity in income between whites and blacks continues. Even the early socialization experiences of whites and blacks are different, since for African American children it is not always clear that the police are their friends or that the system deserves their loyalty. Some of the most significant effects of the Obama presidency in this regard have been the opportunities for black kids to realize that the American dream of growing up to be president can actually belong to them, too.

The root of the differences between political attitudes of blacks and whites most certainly lies in the racial discrimination historically experienced by African Americans. Blacks tend to see much higher levels of discrimination and racial bias in the criminal justice system, in education, and in the job market. A large gulf exists between the races in their perceptions about the continuing frequency and severity of racial discrimination.[21]

Race also divides us on social policy. For instance, compared to whites, African Americans are more favorable to social spending that improves conditions for blacks and are more likely to oppose discrimination in housing. These differences are typical of a general pattern. On issues of economic policy and race, African Americans are substantially more liberal than whites. However, on social issues like abortion and prayer in schools, the racial differences are more muted.

Reflecting the very different stands on racial and economic issues the parties have taken, African Americans are the most solidly Democratic group in terms of both party identification and voting. Interestingly, as income and other status indicators rise for whites, they become more conservative and Republican. The same does not happen among African Americans. Better-educated and higher-income blacks actually have stronger racial identifications, which results in distinctly liberal positions on economic and racial issues and solid support for Democratic candidates.[22]

The increasing number of black conservatives indicates that the assumptions once made about African Americans and the Democratic Party are not universally true. Even so, the rise of Obama to become the first black president of the United States undoubtedly reinforced the bond between African Americans and the Democratic Party, and the racialization of politics in the Trump era has cemented it.

Americans differ by ethnicity as well as by race, and these factors interact in interesting ways to influence the opinions we hold on different policies. Although Asian Americans as a group have traditionally expressed little consensus across a wide range of issues, in the hyperpartisan times in which we now live they are becoming much more liberal.[23]

In general, whites, blacks, and Latinos are not consistent in terms of contemporary liberalism-conservatism. For example, whites are most conservative on the death penalty, with almost three-quarters favoring capital punishment, compared to about half of African Americans and Latinos. Blacks are most liberal in the belief that too little is spent on health care but most conservative in favoring prayer in the schools. Latinos stand out in their opposition to abortion and in not favoring a reduction in the numbers of immigrants allowed into the country. Although the pattern is not one of ideological consistency, these differences make sense in terms of the particular histories and contexts of America's racial and ethnic mix.

GENDER For many years, one's gender had almost no predictive power in explaining opinions and behavior—except that women were less active in politics and usually less warlike in their political attitudes. Since the 1960s, however, there has been a revolution in our expectations about the role of women in society and in politics. As women gained more education and entered the workforce, they also increased their levels of participation in politics. Whereas in the 1950s women trailed men in voter turnout by over 12 percent, since 2006 women have voted at a slightly higher rate than men.[24]

Interestingly, in the last quarter of the twentieth century, as men and women approached equality in their levels of electoral participation, their attitudes on issues diverged. This tendency for men and women to take different issue positions or to evaluate political figures differently is called the **gender gap**. In almost all cases, it means that women are more liberal than men. The ideological stances of women overall have not changed significantly since the 1970s, but those of men have shifted steadily, as more call themselves conservatives. On a number of specific policy issues, the gender gap is substantial: women are more liberal on social welfare policies, that is, programs of aid for children, the elderly, and the poor; and women are less favorable to the death penalty and less willing than men to go to war. On so-called women's issues, such as abortion or women having an equal role in business (where we might expect the greatest gender gap), the differences between the sexes are surprisingly small.[25] The gender gap has important electoral consequences. In fact, in every presidential election from 1980 to 2016, women were more supportive of the Democratic candidate than were men, and interestingly, in recent elections, this gap has been largest among young people (those aged eighteen to twenty-nine).[26] The Women's Marches following the election of Donald Trump and the rapid spread of the #MeToo movement across professions helped generate solidarity among women in favor of defending women's rights.

The differences between men and women might be explained by their different socialization experiences and by the different life situations they face. The impact of one's life situation has emerged recently in what observers are calling the **marriage gap**. This refers to the tendency for those who are married or widowed to express different opinions from those who have never been married. "Marrieds" tend toward more traditional and conservative values; "never marrieds" tend to have a more liberal perspective. The "never marrieds" are now sufficiently numerous that in many localities they constitute an important group that politicians must consider in deciding which issues to support.

STAGES OF LIFE We might expect that people change their opinions as they age, that our experiences over time affect how we see the political world, but there is precious little evidence for the common view that masses of people progress from youthful idealism to mature conservatism. Indeed, extensive research shows that, on most political issues, only small differences in policy preferences are related to age.[27]

One exception is the finding of consistent age differences in political engagement. Middle-age and older citizens are typically more attentive to and more active in politics: they report more frequent efforts to persuade others, they vote more often, and they are more likely to write letters to public officials and to contribute to political campaigns. It seems that acting out one's political role may be part and parcel of the array of activities that we associate with "settling down," such as marrying, having children, and establishing a career. This exception was mitigated somewhat in 2008 with the unusual response of young people to

gender gap the tendency of men and women to differ in their political views on some issues

marriage gap the tendency of married and unmarried people to differ in their political views on some issues

Barack Obama's candidacy for president. The Obama candidacy brought record numbers of young people to the polls, and at the same time created one of the sharpest age-vote relationships we have seen, with younger voters supporting Obama in overwhelming numbers.[28] Similarly, but not quite as dramatically, in 2016 young voters chose Hillary Clinton over Donald Trump 55 to 27 percent. However, millennials are far more likely to be Democrats than their parents, and in 2018, at least, both candidates and voters were looking younger than in previous elections.

Another area in which age plays a role in public opinion is in the creation of **political generations**, groups of citizens who have been shaped by particular events, usually in their youth, and whose shared experience continues to identify them throughout their lives. Having grown up in the years after 9/11, for instance, can give a generation a set of shared values as surely as did having grown up during the civil rights movement of the sixties, the Vietnam War, World War II, or the Great Depression.[29] One of the most distinctive of such groups was the New Deal generation—those who came of age during the 1930s. They were more Democratic in their party orientations than preceding generations, but they are also a generation that is almost gone.[30] They were followed by the Silent Generation and then the Baby Boomers—the huge eclectic group born in the postwar years between 1946 and 1964 who have entered late middle age and are beginning to collect Social Security and Medicare, expensive programs that end up being paid for in part by succeeding generations.

Larger even than the Baby Boomer generation are the millennials, born between about 1980 and 1997. Compared to their parents' generation, millennials are far more diverse, less religious, and more likely to be cynical about the media, possibly because they face a media landscape more complex, more multifaceted, and harder to master than any in history.[31] These young people do not fit the mold of their elders any more than previous generations did. Millennials, for example, favor legalization of marijuana, environmental protection, and LGBTQ rights, whereas their elders find those issues more controversial. They are also more likely to vote Democratic.[32] As we saw in Chapter 1, the post-millennial generation— iGen, Gen Z, or whatever name finally sticks—are politically similar to millennials, only more so. For many of them, the defining generational characteristics are a thoroughly mediated life and a fearful environment in school. iGen members are media savvy, opinionated, and ready to take on establishment powers (like the NRA) that they see as threatening their lives and safety.

As we can see in *Snapshot of America: What Do We Think, by Age?*, younger citizens are markedly more liberal on social issues than older Americans, for whom accepted attitudes on these issues were rather different when they came of age politically. Political events and age thus intersect, forming lasting imprints on each new, young group as it develops political views and enters the electorate. As older groups die, overall opinion among the citizenry changes. This is the process of generational replacement.

PARTISANSHIP AND IDEOLOGY Much of the division in contemporary American public opinion can be described in ideological (liberal or conservative) or partisan (Democrat or Republican) terms. How we adopt the labels of current political conflict has a good deal of influence on the policy positions we take, and even on how we perceive political personalities and events.

As we saw in Chapter 1, ideologies are sets of ideas about politics, the economy, and society that help us deal with the political world. For many Americans today, liberalism stands

political generations groups of citizens whose political views have been shaped by the common events of their youth

Snapshot of America: *What Do We Think, by Age?*

Policy Preference, by Age

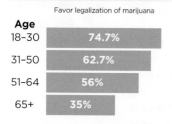

Favor legalization of marijuana

Age	
18–30	74.7%
31–50	62.7%
51–64	56%
65+	35%

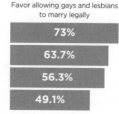

Favor allowing gays and lesbians to marry legally

73%
63.7%
56.3%
49.1%

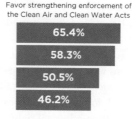

Favor strengthening enforcement of the Clean Air and Clean Water Acts

65.4%
58.3%
50.5%
46.2%

Favor deporting illegal immigrants

31.5%
43.5%
49.4%
50.6%

On Some Policies, Age Does Not Matter Much

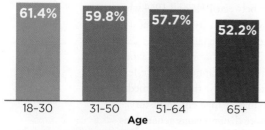

Agree that a woman should always be allowed to obtain an abortion as a matter of choice

18–30	31–50	51–64	65+
61.4%	59.8%	57.7%	52.2%

Age

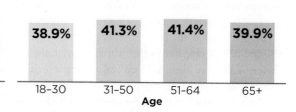

Agree that we should make it easier to obtain concealed gun carry permits

18–30	31–50	51–64	65+
38.9%	41.3%	41.4%	39.9%

Age

Behind the Numbers

As the graphs show, on a number of issues, younger people are more liberal than their elders. But on others, age groups split about the same. What is it about each of these issues, or different age groups' experiences, that might account for why age does or does not make a difference?

Source: Calculated by authors from the 2016 Cooperative Congressional Election Survey.

for faith in government action to bring about equitable outcomes and social tolerance, while conservatism represents a preference for limited government and traditional social values. A whole host of policy controversies in contemporary American politics are widely discussed in liberal-conservative terms, and those ideologies are pretty closely associated with one or the other political party.

Party identification, as we will see in Chapter 11, refers to our relatively enduring allegiances to one of the major political parties. For many of us it is part of what defines us and it comes from our very early years.[33] Party labels provide mental cues that we use in interpreting and responding to personalities and news.

Identification as a Democrat or a Republican strongly influences how we see the political world. Research shows that we resolve uncertainty about new policies or personalities or even objective events to be consistent with our partisanship. Toward the end of Republican president Ronald Reagan's second term in office, a poll asked Americans whether inflation and unemployment had gotten better or worse over the eight years of his administration. In fact, both had improved, but Democrats and Republicans were miles apart in their perceptions of the objective facts: a majority of the Democrats said inflation was worse and only 8 percent acknowledged it was better. By the end of Obama's second term, we saw the same phenomenon in reverse. Democrats recognized, accurately, that unemployment was way down; Republicans thought it had gone up.[34] Perceptions of whether the country was headed in the right direction immediately flipped after Trump was elected. Clearly we see the world through a partisan lens.

Because, as we have noted throughout this book, we are living in an age of hyperpartisanship, with party elites and candidates increasingly polarized, citizens have found it easier to sort themselves into one party or the other, especially as we are able to separate not just our residences and social lives but also our cultures, news, and entertainment.[35] This process of **partisan sorting** means that average Democrats and Republicans are much farther apart ideologically than was the case in previous decades. The impact on politics has been quite profound. For one thing, fewer people are likely to swing between candidates because fewer come to contemporary elections with a fully open mind.

We see this in the "red state versus blue state" phenomenon in presidential elections, in which the outcomes of all but a handful of states are perfectly predictable due to the states' being predominantly Republican and conservative, or Democratic and liberal.[36] Another consequence of the great partisan sort is that citizens (following the lead of politicians and commentators) find it much easier to demonize the opposition. Social scientists have coined the term **negative partisanship** to refer to the fact that for some people, hatred of the other party is the main cause of their allegiance to their own. This has contributed to the nastiness, anger, and general incivility of contemporary politics, which in turn has contributed to citizens' disgust with politics in general, and those rising levels of distrust in government we saw earlier.[37]

EDUCATION As we suggested earlier in our discussion of the ideal democratic citizen, a number of political orientations change as a person attains more education. One important study looked in depth at how education influences aspects of citizenship, separating citizen values into "democratic enlightenment" and "democratic engagement."[38] Democratic enlightenment refers to a citizen's ability to hold democratic beliefs, including the idea that politics is about compromise and that sometimes the needs of the whole community will conflict with and override one's individual preferences. Democratic engagement refers to a citizen's ability to understand his or her own interests and how to pursue those interests in politics. As you might expect, both democratic dimensions are boosted by education: better-educated citizens are more likely to be informed about politics, to be tolerant and committed to democratic principles, and to vote and to participate at all levels of the political system (see *Snapshot of America: What Do We Think, by Education and Income?*).[39] Those who graduate from college have many more of the attributes of the idealized active democratic citizen than do those who do not graduate from high school.

ECONOMIC SELF-INTEREST People's political preferences often come from an assessment of what is best for them economically, from asking, "What's in it for me?" They may be the victims of manipulation by groups who don't share their interests but who are trying to convince them they are on their side, but the essential individual calculation is that they will be better off, even if they are mistaken. So, for instance, those in the lowest income

partisan sorting the process through which citizens align themselves ideologically with one of the two parties, leaving fewer citizens remaining in the center and increasing party polarization

negative partisanship loyalty to a party driven by hatred of the other party

Snapshot of America: *What Do We Think, by Education and Income?*

Democratic Enlightenment

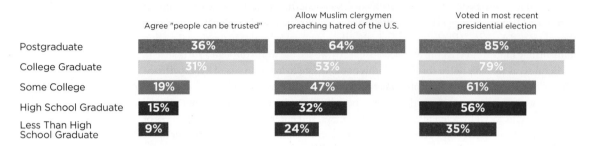

	Agree "people can be trusted"	Allow Muslim clergymen preaching hatred of the U.S.	Voted in most recent presidential election
Postgraduate	36%	64%	85%
College Graduate	31%	53%	79%
Some College	19%	47%	61%
High School Graduate	15%	32%	56%
Less Than High School Graduate	9%	24%	35%

Economic and Self-Interest

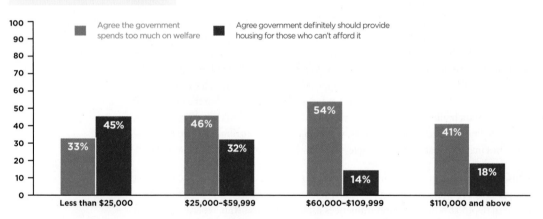

Agree the government spends too much on welfare

Agree government definitely should provide housing for those who can't afford it

	Less than $25,000	$25,000–$59,999	$60,000–$109,999	$110,000 and above
Welfare	33%	46%	54%	41%
Housing	45%	32%	14%	18%

*Some people think that the government in Washington should do everything possible to improve the standard of living of all poor Americans; other people think it is not the government's responsibility and that each person should take care of him- or herself.

Behind the Numbers

Americans' exercise of citizenship has long reflected a mix of concerns about community and self-interest. How do the democratic values of knowledge, participation, and enlightenment vary with levels of education? And can self-interest explain the differences in feelings about helping the poor and welfare among income groups?

Source: 2014 General Social Survey, calculated by authors.

brackets are the least likely to agree that too much is being spent on welfare or that they are paying too much in taxes; those with higher incomes are more likely to agree with these assessments. Similarly, those with lower incomes are generally more favorable than the wealthy to government attempts to narrow the income gap between rich and poor. These patterns are only tendencies, however. Some wealthy people favor the redistribution of wealth and more spending on welfare; some people living in poverty oppose these policies. Even on these straightforward economic questions, other factors are at work.

RELIGION Many political issues touch on matters of deep moral conviction or values. In these cases the motivation for action or opinion formation is not self-interest but one's view of what is morally right. The question of morals and government, however, is tricky. Many people argue that it is not the government's business to set moral standards, although it is increasingly becoming the position of social conservatives that government policy ought to reflect traditional moral values. In addition, government gets into the morals business by virtue of establishing policies on issues of moral controversy, like abortion, assisted suicide, and organ transplants. These questions are often referred to as social issues, as opposed to economic issues, which center more on how to divide the economic pie.

Our views of morality and social issues are often rooted in our differing religious convictions and the values with which we were raised. Following the New Deal realignment, there were major political differences in the preferences of the major American religious groups: Protestants, Catholics, and Jews. Non-southern Protestants were predominantly Republican, and Catholics and Jews were much more likely to be Democrats and to call themselves liberals. Over the years those differences have softened quite a bit, but today Catholics are less conservative than Protestants, and more Democratic, while Jews and those calling themselves "not religious" are clearly more liberal and Democratic than the other groups.

Specific religious affiliations may no longer be the most important religious cleavage for understanding citizen opinions on social issues. Since the 1970s a new distinction has emerged in U.S. politics, between those in whose lives traditional religion plays a central role and those for whom it is less important. In this alignment, those who adhere to traditional religious beliefs and practices (frequent churchgoers, regular Bible readers, "born-again Christians," and those who pray frequently) tend to take conservative positions on an array of social issues (such as homosexuality and abortion), compared with more liberal positions taken on those issues by what may be called "seculars," those who say they have no religious affiliation. Among those who say they are agnostic, Democrats far outnumber Republicans and liberals outnumber conservatives.

GEOGRAPHIC REGION Where we live matters in terms of our political beliefs. People in the Farm Belt talk about different things than do city dwellers in Manhattan. Politicians who come from these areas represent people with different preferences, and much of the politics in Congress is about being responsive to differing geography-based opinions.[40] For instance, scholars have long argued that "the South is different." The central role of race and its plantation past for a long time gave rise to different patterns of public opinion compared to the non-southern states. The South today is not the Old South, but the region does retain some distinctive values. Opinions in the South—by which we mean the eleven states of the Confederacy—remain more conservative on civil rights but also on other social issues, and more hierarchical—that is, they are more likely to see a substantive social order that government should maintain.

Whether we live in the city, the suburbs, or the country also has an effect on our opinions. City dwellers are more Democratic in their party affiliations and voting and are more liberal, both in their ideology and across most issues, from regulation of business to opposing capital punishment and favoring more environmental regulation. In fact, since the 1980s, the urban areas have become distinctly more Democratic while the Republican Party has gained strength in the suburbs and rural areas.[41] This is consistent with analyses finding that rural areas have become the anchor for the contemporary Republican Party, with its stress on limited government, individual responsibility, and traditional values.

In Your Own Words Identify key factors that influence our individual and collective political opinions.

MEASURING AND TRACKING PUBLIC OPINION

Using science to discover what people are thinking about political issues

Long before the beginning of modern scientific polling, politicians gauged what their constituents wanted through talking and listening to them. They still learn constituent opinion from the letters, phone calls, and email messages they receive. They visit constituents, make speeches, attend meetings, and talk with community leaders and interest group representatives. Direct contact with people puts politicians in touch with concerns that could be missed entirely by a scientifically designed public opinion poll. That poll might focus on issues of national news that are on the minds of national politicians or pollsters, but citizens may be far more concerned about the building of a dam upriver from their city or about teacher layoffs in their school district. (For a history of polling, see this chapter's *The Big Picture.*)

THE QUALITY OF OPINION POLLING TODAY

Politicians who don't like the results of public opinion polls may discount them, but the truth is that most social scientists and political pollsters conduct public opinion surveys according to the highest standards of scientific accuracy, and their results are for the most part reliable. Informal soundings of public opinion may be useful to a politician for some purposes, but they are not very reliable for gauging how everyone in a given population thinks because they are subject to sampling problems.

A sample is the portion of the population a politician or pollster surveys on an issue. Based on what that sample says, the surveyor then makes an estimation of what everyone else thinks. This may sound like hocus-pocus, but if the sample is scientifically chosen to be representative of the whole population, sampling actually works very well. No sample matches exactly the population from which it is drawn, but it should be close. Confronted with a critic who did not trust the notion of sampling, George Gallup is said to have responded, "Okay, if you do not like the idea of a sample, then the next time you go for a blood test, tell them to take it all!" It might seem counterintuitive, but statisticians have determined that a sample of only 1,000 to 2,000 people can be very representative of the more than 300 million residents of the United States, if it is randomly drawn from that population.

Pollsters are trained in how to select a truly **random sample**—that is, one that does not overrepresent any portion of the population and whose responses can therefore be safely generalized to the whole. When a sample is not chosen scientifically and has too many people in it from one portion of the population, we say it has a problem of **sample bias**. When trying to judge public opinion from what they hear among their supporters and friendly interest groups, politicians must allow for the bias of their own sampling. If they are not effective at knowing how those they meet differ from the full public, they will get a misleading idea of public opinion.

Because reputable survey firms use scientific sampling strategies, sampling bias is not generally a problem that plagues modern pollsters, but there is one way it can sneak in through the back door. The chief form of sample bias in current surveys is **nonresponse bias**, which occurs when the opinions of those who choose to participate in a survey differ from the opinions of those who do not. Response rates to telephone surveys have dropped considerably over the years; in current surveys sometimes as few as one-quarter of those intended to be included in surveys actually participate. The reasons for this drop include hostility to telemarketers; the increasing use of caller ID; the growing use of cell phones; and the simple fact that people are busier, are working more, and have less time and inclination to talk to strangers on the phone.[42] As a result, most telephone polls, unless corrected, will have too many elderly women and too few younger men because the former are typically at home to answer the phone when the interviewer calls, and the latter are more frequently out or have only a cell phone. One consequence of the nonresponse problem is that the most reluctant respondents—those likely to be missed in a typical survey—seem to be less racially tolerant than the average population, meaning that a standard survey might yield responses that are slightly more liberal on racial matters than might be the case for the population as a whole.[43]

Pollsters deal with the problem of differential response rates, which yield a sample that does not look demographically like the population being sampled—perhaps there are too many whites or old people, or not enough college graduates or young adults—by **weighting** the sample to match what the census says the population looks like. This is done during analysis of the results; under- or overrepresented groups are multiplied by values that bring them into line with their actual numbers in the population.

No matter how well drawn the sample or how fastidious the post-polling analysis, no poll is perfect. Pollsters cope with this lack of perfection by including a measure of **sampling error**, a number that indicates the poll's reliability. Based on the size of the sample, it tells within what range the actual opinion of the whole population would fall. Typically a report of a poll will say that its "margin of error" is plus or minus 3 percentage points. That means that, based on sampling theory, there is a 95 percent chance that the real figure for the whole population is within 3 percentage points of that reported. For instance, when a poll reports a presidential approval rating of 60 percent and a 3 percentage points margin of error, this means there is a 95 percent chance that between 57 and 63 percent of the population approve of the president's job performance. A poll that shows one candidate leading another by 2 percentage points of the projected vote is really too close to call since the 2 percentage points might be due to sampling error. The larger the sample, the smaller the sampling error, but samples larger than 2,000 add very little in the way of reliability.

Sampling is not the only challenge faced by modern pollsters; asking the right questions is also key. Getting the questions right in surveys is a surprisingly tricky business. Researchers

random sample a sample chosen in such a way that any member of the population being polled has an equal chance of being selected

sample bias the effect of having a sample that does not represent all segments of the population

nonresponse bias skewing of data that occurs when there is a difference in opinion between those who choose to participate and those who do not

weighting adjustments to surveys during analysis so that selected demographic groups reflect their values in the population, usually as measured by the census

sampling error a number that indicates within what range the results of a poll are accurate

THE BIG PICTURE:
How We Know What the Public Really Thinks

Public opinion polling is hard to get our minds around—how can we know what the public thinks without asking everyone? It seems beyond counterintuitive that we can estimate what an entire nation thinks by asking as few as 1,500 people, and yet, we can. While polling can feel mysterious, the truth is it is anything but—the science of polling allows us to make very educated estimates of what the public thinks.

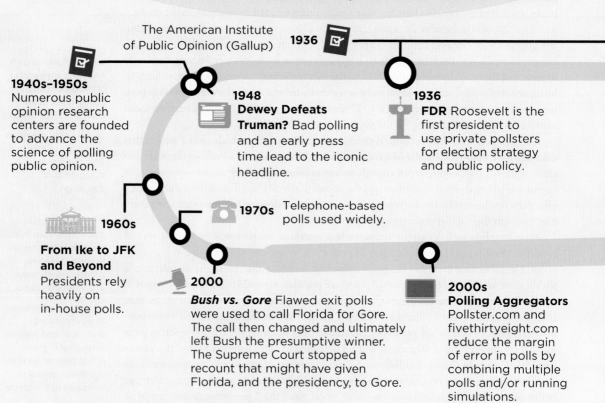

The History of Polling

JULY 4, 1776

"When in the course of human events, it becomes necessary for one people to dissolve the political bands that have connected them with another. . . a decent respect to the opinions of mankind requires that they should declare the causes that impel them to the separation."

The American Institute of Public Opinion (Gallup)

1936

1940s–1950s
Numerous public opinion research centers are founded to advance the science of polling public opinion.

1948
Dewey Defeats Truman? Bad polling and an early press time lead to the iconic headline.

1936
FDR Roosevelt is the first president to use private pollsters for election strategy and public policy.

1960s

From Ike to JFK and Beyond
Presidents rely heavily on in-house polls.

1970s Telephone-based polls used widely.

2000
Bush vs. Gore Flawed exit polls were used to call Florida for Gore. The call then changed and ultimately left Bush the presumptive winner. The Supreme Court stopped a recount that might have given Florida, and the presidency, to Gore.

2000s
Polling Aggregators
Pollster.com and fivethirtyeight.com reduce the margin of error in polls by combining multiple polls and/or running simulations.

"We all do no end of feeling and we mistake it for thinking. And out of it we get an aggregation which we consider a boon. Its name is public opinion. It is held in reverence. It settles everything. Some think it is the voice of God."
—Mark Twain, "Corn-pone Opinions," 1900

1824

First Straw Poll The poll showed a lead for Andrew Jackson over John Quincy Adams and two others. Jackson did win the popular vote but failed to get a majority in the Electoral College. The race was thrown to the House of Representatives, which picked Adams as the next president.

 1936 George Gallup calls the election correctly for FDR, using probability theory to generalize from a small sample.

 1920s–1930s
The Blossoming of Market Research Opinion researchers used sampling, survey techniques, and statistical methods to delve into consumers' minds.

 1916–1936
Literary Digest **Straw Poll** The bigger the sample size, the better? The poll was sent to 10 million people in 1936, and the 2 million who responded indicated that Republican Alf Landon was winning the presidency. But it was a bad sample, drawn from a list of people more likely to be Republican.

 2010s
Polling Techniques in Flux Cell phone-only households, call screening, low response rates, the rise of Internet polling, robo polling, and online panels are among the new considerations.

 2012
Unskewing the Polls Convinced that turnout would not match that of 2008, Romney's pollsters assumed that polls showing an Obama lead must be wrong and altered their polls turnout model. Romney was reportedly "shell shocked" when he lost.

 2016
The Polls Are Rigged Believing he would lose, Republican nominee Donald Trump tried to change the narrative by stressing to his base that the polls were "rigged," a claim that more than two-thirds of them believed.

Pollsters Get a Black Eye

Harry Truman laughed last and loudest after one of the biggest mistakes in American journalism. The Chicago Daily Tribune *relied on a two-week-old Gallup poll to predict the outcome of the 1948 presidential race, damaging the image of polling for decades. With polls today conducted all the way up to Election Day—and exit polls tracking how ballots are actually cast—similar goofs are much less likely.*

have emphasized several concerns with respect to constructing survey questions. For instance, respondents should be asked about things they know and have thought about. Otherwise, they will often try to be helpful but will give responses based on whatever cues they can pick up from the context of the interview or the particular question. Questions should not be ambiguous and should not lead respondents to a conclusion (for example, surveys should not use phrases like "wouldn't you agree . . . ?"). Questions should also avoid using words that evoke strong emotional responses, like *affirmative action* or *welfare*, that might prevent the respondent from giving an objective answer. In addition, studies have shown that the order in which questions are asked can change the results (respondents can be primed to remember that things are going well in the country or be reminded of a president they don't like by a prior question, which can change the answers they give later), as can a simple factor such as the number of choices offered for responses.

NEW TECHNOLOGIES AND CHALLENGES IN POLLING

Technology is a pollster's friend, but it can also create unexpected challenges. With the advent of computer technology has come the substitution of computers for humans to do the telephone interviewing. The computers dial the numbers (autodialing) and deliver recorded messages, even "interacting" by asking questions that are answered by pushing buttons on a touch-tone phone. This technology, called "robo calling," is much cheaper than using human interviewers, but it is also controversial. It is easily abused, especially when combined with push poll methods (described in the next section).[44] Legitimate polling firms also use robo calls and have collected more information on more political subjects than has been available in the past, such as the state-by-state results provided by SurveyUSA.[45]

Computers provide another challenge (and opportunity) for pollsters in the form of online surveys. Here we do not mean the polls that CNN or others put up asking for volunteers to click in their opinions on some issue. Pollsters create panels of Internet users who regularly log in to deliver their opinions on matters the pollsters select. Although some critics argue that the online polls have no scientific basis because they do not rely on strict probability samples, proponents argue that with appropriate adjustments, the Internet polls nicely match results from traditional telephone interviewing. They have the advantage of garnering fewer refusals, and for some kinds of questions, respondents to online surveys appear to be more candid in admitting to things that might be embarrassing to confess to a human interviewer.[46]

Pollsters also face a growing challenge as increasing numbers of citizens, especially younger people, rely on cell phones. The U.S. Telephone Consumer Protection Act limits the technologies that can be used to contact cell phone users—forbidding autodialing, for instance. Those contacted by cell phones are also more likely to refuse to answer polls. As pollsters adapt to these newer technologies, research and regulations are likely to lead to changes in how cell phone users are contacted.[47]

TYPES OF POLLS

Many people and organizations report the results of what they claim are measures of public opinion. To make sense of this welter of claims, it is useful to know some basic polling terminology and the characteristics of different types of polls.

NATIONAL POLLS National polls are efforts to measure public opinion within a limited period of time using a national representative sample. The time period of interviewing may be as short as a few hours, with the results reported the next day, or extended over a period of weeks, as in academic polls. The underlying goal, however, is the same: to achieve scientifically valid measures of the knowledge, beliefs, or attitudes of the adult population. Many national polls are conducted by the media in conjunction with a professional polling organization.

CAMPAIGN POLLS Polling is an important part of candidates' efforts to win election or reelection. Most well-funded campaigns begin with a **benchmark poll** to gather baseline information on how well the candidate is known, what issues people associate with the candidate, what issues people are concerned about, as well as assessments of the opposition, especially if the opponent is an incumbent. Benchmark polls are instrumental in designing campaign strategy.

Presidential contests and a few of the better-funded statewide races (for example, those for governor or U.S. senator) also conduct **tracking polls**. These follow changes in attitudes toward the candidates through ongoing sets of interviews. The daily samples are too small to allow for reliable generalization, but when they are averaged over time, with the oldest interviews dropped as newer ones are added, they provide a dynamic view of changes in voters' preferences and perceptions. A sudden change in a tracking poll might signal that the opponent's new ads are doing damage or that interest group endorsements are having an effect. Campaign strategies can be revised accordingly. More recently the news media have undertaken tracking polls as part of their election coverage. Their predictive performance is very good, especially when the results are aggregated. In 2016 the polling averages came close to predicting the popular vote, which went to Hillary Clinton slightly short of the three points the polls predicted. But the models failed to estimate turnout correctly when it came to the states, leading most analysts to think that Clinton would win the Electoral College as well. Only Nate Silver of fivethirtyeight.com felt there was uncertainty in the predictions, given the third-party vote and a relatively high number of undecided voters (see this chapter's *Profiles in Citizenship*). In the end, enough states that were predicted to go to Clinton slid over to Trump by just one point, and he won the Electoral College vote.[48]

On election night the media commentators often "call" a race, declaring one candidate a winner, sometimes as soon as the voting booths in a state are closed but well before the official vote count has been reported. These predictions are made, in part, on the basis of **exit polls**, which are short questionnaires administered, often by a consortium of news outlets, to samples of people who have just voted in selected precincts. Exit polls focus on

benchmark poll an initial poll on a candidate and issues on which campaign strategy is based and against which later polls are compared

tracking polls an ongoing series of surveys that follow changes in public opinion over time

exit polls election-related questions asked of voters right after they vote

Nate Silver

David E. Klutho/Sports Illustrated/
Getty Images

Nate Silver is a very smart guy. The young statistician wasn't long out of college before he had developed the PECOTA (Player Empirical Comparison and Optimization Test Algorithm) system—a model for predicting the performance of baseball players. Baseball is a long way from politics, however, and by 2008 Silver had given up sports and was concentrating his mathematical prowess on primaries and electoral votes, writing on the new blog that he called fivethirtyeight.com (after the total number of votes in the Electoral College).

What Silver added that other analysts didn't was a model that aggregated the existing polling and, based on those numbers as well as demographic and other data, ran computerized simulations of the various primary and general election races. His predictions were uncannily accurate, and soon Silver's readership soared and he was on cable TV, analyzing polls and races.

In 2010 Silver signed a three-year contract with the *New York Times*, and then left to start his own web empire at ESPN, where you can currently find fivethirtyeight.com. There, he blogs regularly on politics and elections—with occasional forays into sports, economics, and popular culture. He's also written a book, *The Signal and the Noise: Why So Many Predictions Fail—But Some Don't*.

What does he want people to get from his work? "I want to inform people, I want people to think more critically about things. Basically, I want people to not be intimidated by numbers and statistics, to not just assume that something that they hear, whether it's from a politician or from Fox News or from [another] writer in the *New York Times*, is necessarily true. I just want to encourage people to use their brains."

Here's some other advice from Nate Silver:

On patriotism

"You probably have some family members who have their flaws and idiosyncrasies and probably a few distant relatives who are even fairly screwed-up people, but you still love them, anyway. I think that's what patriotism is really, saying, 'Look, this is where I was born, or I migrated to the United States, this is where my loyalty is. . . .' You don't have a choice, it doesn't matter how unhappy you are, you know? It's your family, and you are stuck with it."

On keeping the republic

"People just have to be willing to put in the work. It's a big, complicated world now, and as many people that there are, there are more things to be done. Don't underestimate your ability to come up with an idea that nobody else has. It happens all the time. Quit being a consumer and be a producer. Start your own blog, start your own political organization. Have fun with it—there is nothing wrong with that at all."

Source: Nate Silver spoke with Christine Barbour in July 2010.

vote choice, a few demographic questions, some issue preferences, and evaluations of candidates. In addition to helping the networks predict the winners early, exit polls are used by network broadcasters and journalists to add explanatory and descriptive material to their election coverage.

Exit polls, however, have proved embarrassingly faulty in recent elections. In 2000, flawed data led the networks to mistakenly "call" Florida for Vice President Al Gore (which would have meant that he'd won the presidency), then to switch the call to George W. Bush, and finally, late in the evening, to conclude that the state was too close to call at all. Exit poll defenders argue that these polls are being misused by the public and the media; they are not intended to predict the elections in progress but to explain the vote after the election by providing information on what groups voted for which candidates. As a result of recent problems with these polls, networks are now relatively cautious in declaring winners without corroborating evidence from the actual vote returns. There were no mistakes in calling the states in the 2004 or 2008 presidential elections,[49] but in 2008 the pollsters took the precaution of embargoing their results until 5:00 p.m. on Election Day, in an effort to keep them out of the hands of people who didn't know how to interpret them.

PSEUDO-POLLS A number of opinion studies are wrongly presented as polls. More deceptive than helpful, these pseudo-polls range from potentially misleading entertainment to outright fraud. Examples of self-selection polls include viewer or listener call-in polls and Internet polls. These polls tell you only the opinions of that portion of the media outlet's audience (self-selected in the first place by their choice of a particular outlet) who care enough to call in or click a mouse (self-selected in the second place by their willingness to expend effort).

A second and increasingly common kind of pseudo-poll is the **push poll**, which poses as a legitimate information-seeking effort but is really a shady campaign trick to change people's attitudes. Push polls present false or highly negative information, often in a hypothetical form, and ask respondents to react to it. The information, presented as if true or at least possible, can raise doubts about a candidate and even change a voter's opinion about him or her. Such polls are often conducted without any acknowledgment of who is sponsoring them (usually the opponents of the person being asked about) and at the last minute so that the candidate cannot rebut the charges being circulated. Legislation against push polling has been introduced in several state legislatures, and the practice has been condemned by the American Association of Political Consultants.[50] There is a real question, however, about whether efforts to regulate push polls can survive a First Amendment test before the Supreme Court.

SURVEY EXPERIMENTS A final category of polls are those conducted by social scientists not so much to gauge and measure public opinion about elections or current events as to deepen our understanding of public attitudes, especially on controversial issues such as race, gender, and civil liberties, where respondents know what the socially acceptable answers to the survey questions are and so are less likely to disclose their true opinions. In survey experiments, the survey questions are manipulated in an effort to get respondents to disclose more information than they think they are disclosing. The number of survey experiments is increasing because the technology of the Internet allows the use of images, sounds, and other multimedia in addition to the words used in a typical survey.[51]

> *Do frequent opinion polls enhance or weaken democracy?*

push polls polls that ask for reactions to hypothetical, often false, information in order to manipulate public opinion

HOW ACCURATE ARE POLLS?

For many issues, such as attitudes toward the environment or presidential approval, we have no objective measure against which to judge the accuracy of public opinion polls.

With elections, however, polls do make predictions, and we can tell by the vote count whether the polls are correct.

The record of most polls, in general, is quite good. For example, almost all the major polls have predicted the winner of presidential elections correctly since 1980, except in the incredibly close 2000 election. They are not correct to the percentage point, nor would we expect them to be, given the known levels of sampling error, preelection momentum shifts, and the usual 15 percent of voters who claim to remain "undecided" up to the last minute. Polls taken closer to Election Day typically become more accurate as they catch more of the late deciders.[52] Even in 2016, they had Hillary Clinton's popular victory margin within one point, although the results for several of the states were slightly off.

In Your Own Words Describe different techniques used to gauge public opinion.

CITIZENSHIP AND PUBLIC OPINION

Informational shortcuts that save democracy from our lack of care and attention

Politicians may act as if citizens are informed and attentive, but we have seen ample evidence that only some Americans live up to our model of good citizenship, and those who do often belong disproportionately to the ranks of the well-educated, the well-off, and the older portions of the population. This disparity between our ideal citizen and reality raises some provocative questions about the relationship between citizens, public opinion, and democracy: Were the founders right to limit the influence of the masses on government? Do we want less informed and less coherent opinions represented in politics? Can democracy survive if it is run only by an educated elite? Can it work if many of us are subject to "fake news" or live in information bubbles, untouched by the issues and values that impact our fellow citizens?

Earlier in this chapter we suggested that all would not be lost for American democracy if only some of us turned out to be ideal citizens, and that although Americans as individuals might not fit the ideal, Americans as a group might behave as that ideal would predict. How is such a trick possible?

The argument goes like this: It may not be rational for all people to be deeply immersed in the minutiae of day-to-day politics. Our jobs, families, hobbies, and other interests leave us little time for in-depth study of political issues, and unless we get tremendous satisfaction from keeping up with politics (and some of us certainly do), it might be rational for us to leave the political information gathering to others. Social scientists call this idea **rational ignorance**.

This does not mean that we are condemned to make only ignorant or mistaken political decisions. Citizens are generally pretty smart. In fact, studies show that voters can behave much more intelligently than we could ever guess from their answers to surveys about politics. A great many of us, sometimes without thinking about it, use shortcuts called *heuristics* to get political information. Such heuristics often serve us quite well, in the sense that they help us make the same decisions we might have made had we invested considerable time and energy in collecting that political information ourselves.[53]

rational ignorance the state of being uninformed about politics because of the cost in time and energy

SHORTCUTS TO POLITICAL KNOWLEDGE

One such shortcut is the **on-line processing** of information.[54] (*On-line* here does not refer to time spent on the Internet, as you will see.) Many of the evaluations we make of people, places, and things in our lives (including political figures and ideas) are made on the fly. We assemble impressions and reactions while we are busy leading our lives. When queried, we might not be able to explain why we like or dislike a thing or a person, and we might sound quite ignorant in the sense of not seeming to have reasons for our beliefs. But we do have reasons, and they may make a good deal of sense, even if we can't identify what they are.

A second important mental shortcut that most of us use is the **two-step flow of information**. Politicians and the media send out massive amounts of information—multiple narrative streams that compete for our attention. We can absorb only a fraction of this information, and even then it is sometimes hard to know how to interpret it. In these circumstances, we tend to rely on **opinion leaders**, people who are more or less like us, who share our values, but who know more about the subject than we do, to mediate the information and make sense of it for us.[55] Opinion leaders and followers can be identified in all sorts of realms besides politics. When we make an important purchase, say, a computer or a car, most of us do not research all the scientific data and technical specifications. We ask people who are like us, who we think should know, and whom we can trust. We get others' opinions online, from those we follow on social media, from blogs, and from comments and reviews made by others; technology allows us to gather information from multiple "experts."[56] We compile their advice, consult our own intuition, and buy. The result is that we get pretty close to making an optimal purchase without having to become experts ourselves. The same thing happens politically. The two-step flow allows us to feel that we are very well informed without requiring us to expend all the resources that being informed entails.

Given the effectiveness of this process, something to consider is that, as part of the college-educated elite and a person who has taken an American politics class, you may be the opinion leader for your family or friends. Throughout the book we have emphasized the many ways that technology allows you to construct and disseminate narratives that compete with the powerful. Consider that with this status and opportunity comes responsibility as well, to be sure that the stories you create and pass on are factually correct and well (and critically) thought out.

A new wrinkle in the two-step flow is the practice of going online for others' opinions. Whether this is feedback ratings on eBay or the "likes" of Facebook, the process uses technology to gather information from "experts" (or at least those with a bit of experience and an opinion) about everything from airlines to zoos.[57] Interestingly, however, although many observers hoped that a computer-literate younger generation would become more

Frederick M. Brown/Getty Images

Ironically Informative

John Oliver takes the biting humor he honed at The Daily Show *to an entirely new level on HBO's* Last Week Tonight, *which provides thoroughly researched reports that are at once informative, creative, interactive, sarcastic, and of course, hilarious.*

on-line processing the ability to receive and evaluate information as events happen, allowing us to remember our evaluation even if we have forgotten the specific events that caused it

two-step flow of information the process by which citizens take their political cues from more well-informed opinion leaders

opinion leaders people who know more about certain topics than we do and whose advice we trust, seek out, and follow

politically engaged as a result of its heavy use of social media, it does not seem that users of Facebook or other new media are any more likely to participate or express opinions than those who do not engage in the digital social world.[58]

THE RATIONAL ELECTORATE

Politicians deal with citizens mostly in groups and only rarely as individuals. Elected officials think about constituents as whole electorates ("the people of the great state of Texas") or as members of groups (women, environmentalists, developers, workers, and so forth). Groups, it turns out, appear to be better behaved, more rational, and better informed than the individuals who make up the groups, precisely because of the sorts of shortcuts we discussed in the previous section. This doesn't seem to make sense, so perhaps a nonpolitical example will clarify what we mean.

Consider the behavior of fans at a football game. People seem to cheer at the appropriate times. They know pretty much when to boo the referees. They *oooh* and *aaah* more or less in unison. We would say that the crowd understands the game and participates effectively in it. However, what do the individual spectators know? If we were to do a football survey, we might ask about the players' names, the teams' win-loss records, the different offensive and defensive positions, the meaning of the referees' signals, and so forth. Some fans would do well, but many would probably get only a few questions right. From the survey, we might conclude that many people in this crowd do not know football at all. But because they take their cues from others, following the behavior of those who cheer for the same team, they can act as if they know what they are doing. Despite its share of football-ignorant individuals, in the aggregate—that is, as a group—the crowd acts remarkably football-intelligent.

Similarly, if we were to ask people when national elections are held, for instance, only a handful would be able to say it is the Tuesday after the first Monday in November of evenly numbered years. Some people would guess that they occur in November, others might say in the fall sometime, and others would admit they didn't know. Based on the level of individual ignorance in this matter, it would be surprising if many people ever voted at all, since you can't vote if you don't know when Election Day is. But somehow, as a group, the electorate sorts it out, and almost everyone who is registered and wants to vote finds his or her way to the polling place on the right day. By using shortcuts and taking cues from others, the electorate behaves just as if it knew all along when the election was. More substantively, even though many voters may be confused about which candidates stand where on specific issues, groups of voters do a great job of sorting out which party or candidate best represents their interests. Members of the religious right vote for Republicans, and members of labor unions vote for Democrats, for instance. Even though there are undoubtedly quite a few confused voters in the electorate in any particular election, they tend to cancel each other out in the larger scheme of things, although, understandably, some biases remain.[59] As a whole, from the politician's point of view, the electorate appears to be responsive to issues and quite rational in evaluating an incumbent's performance in office.[60]

So even though citizens do not spend a lot of time learning about politics, politicians are smart to assume that the electorate is attentive and informed. In fact, this is precisely what most of them do. For example, studies have shown that state legislators vote in accordance with the ideological preferences of their citizens, just as if the citizens were instructing them on their wishes.[61] The states with the most liberal citizens—for example, New York,

> *Is a democracy that depends on citizen "shortcuts" weaker than one that does not?*

Massachusetts, and California—have the most liberal policies. And the most conservative states—those in the South and the Rocky Mountains—have the most conservative policies. Other studies confirm a similar pattern in national elections.[62]

We began this chapter by asking why politicians routinely disparage polling. Why don't we have more confidence in being ruled by public opinion? After all, in a democracy, where the people's will is supposed to weigh heavily with our elected officials, we have uncovered some conflicting evidence. Many Americans do not model the characteristics of the ideal democratic citizen, but remember that the United States has two traditions of citizenship— one much more apolitical and self-interested than the public-spirited ideal. The reality in America is that the ideal citizen marches side by side with the more self-interested citizen, who, faced with many demands, does not put politics ahead of other daily responsibilities. But we have also argued that there are mechanisms and shortcuts that allow even some of the more apolitical and self-interested citizens to cast intelligent votes and to have their views represented in public policy. This tells us that at least one element of democracy— responsiveness of policies to public preferences—is in good working order, if the people the majority choose can make it through the institutional barriers to power (for example, gerrymandering, the Electoral College).

We should not forget that political influence goes hand in hand with opinion formation. Those who are opinion leaders have much more relative clout than do their more passive followers. And opinion leaders are not distributed equally throughout the population. They are drawn predominantly from the ranks of the well-educated and the well-off. Similarly, even though the shortcuts we have discussed allow many people to vote intelligently without taking the time to make a personally informed decision, many people never vote at all. Voters are also drawn from the more privileged ranks of American society. The poor, the young, and minorities—all the groups who are underrepresented at the voting booth—are also under-represented in policymaking. There cannot help but be biases in such a system.[63]

In Your Own Words Give examples of ways in which public opinion enhances or diminishes the relationship between citizens and government.

Let's Revisit: What's at Stake . . . ?

We have argued in this chapter that public opinion is important in policymaking and that politicians respond to it in a variety of ways. But what would happen if we more or less bypassed elected officials altogether and allowed people to participate directly in national lawmaking through the use of a national referendum or initiative? What is at stake in rule by public opinion?

On the one hand, voters would seem to have something real to gain in such lawmaking reform. It would give new meaning to government "by the people," and decisions would have more legitimacy with the public. Certainly it would be harder to point the finger at those in Washington as being responsible for bad laws. In addition, as has been the experience in states with initiatives, citizens might succeed in getting legislation passed that legislators themselves refuse to vote for. Prime examples are term limits and balanced budget amendments. Term limits would cut short many congressional careers, and balanced budget amendments would force politicians into hard choices about taxation and spending cuts that they prefer to avoid.

On the other side of the calculation, however, voters might be worse off. While policies like the two just mentioned clearly threaten the jobs of politicians, they also carry unintended consequences that might or might not be very good for the nation as a whole. The Irish referendum shows how voters can free politicians to pass laws in line with changing times and values; the experience of the Brexiteers in the United Kingdom provides an example of the kind of decision that citizens make when they want to send a message but do not, perhaps, want to live with all the consequences.[64] Not only policymaking but also the protection of individual freedoms might suffer under increased direct democracy; the majority is not always the best safeguard of civil liberties and civil rights.

Who should decide—politicians who make a career out of understanding government, or people who pay little attention to politics and current events and who vote from instinct and outrage? Politicians who have a vested interest in keeping their jobs, or the public who can provide a check on political greed and self-interest? The answer changes with the way you phrase the question, but the public might well suffer if left to its own mercy on questions of policy it does not thoroughly understand.

There is no doubt that the founders of the Constitution, with their limited faith in the people, would have rejected such a national referendum wholeheartedly. Not only does it bring government closer to the people, but it wreaks havoc with their system of separation of powers and checks and balances. Popular opinion was supposed to be checked by the House and the Senate, which were in turn to be checked by the other two branches of government. Bringing public opinion to the fore upsets this delicate balance.

In addition, many scholars warn that the hallmark of democracy is not just hearing what the people want, but allowing the people to discuss and deliberate over their political choices. Home computer voting or trips to the ballot box do not necessarily permit such key interaction.[65] Majority rule without the tempering influence of debate and discussion can deteriorate quickly into majority tyranny, with a sacrifice of minority rights.

The flip side may also be true, however. Since voters tend to be those who care more intensely about political issues, supporters of a national referendum also leave themselves open to the opposite consequence of majority tyranny: the tyranny of an intense minority who care enough to campaign and vote against an issue that a majority prefer, but only tepidly.

Finally, there are political stakes for politicians in such a reform. As we have already seen, the passage of laws they would not have themselves supported would make it harder for politicians to get things done. But on the positive side, a national referendum would allow politicians to avoid taking the heat for decisions that are bound to be intensely unpopular with some segment of the population. One of the reasons national referenda are often used in other countries is to diffuse the political consequences for leaders of unpopular or controversial decisions.

Direct democracy at the national level would certainly have a major impact on American politics, but it is not entirely clear who the winners and losers would be, or even if there would be any consistent winners. The new rules would benefit different groups at different times. The American people believe they would enjoy the power, and various groups are confident they would profit, but in the long run the public interest might be damaged in terms of the quality of American democracy and the protections available to minorities. Politicians have very little to gain. If such a reform ever does come about, it will be generated not by the elite but by public interest groups, special interest groups, and reformers from outside Washington.

for CQ Press

Want a better grade?

Get the tools you need to sharpen your study skills. **SAGE edge** offers practice quizzes, eFlashcards, video, and multimedia at **edge.sagepub.com/barbourbrief8e**.

Review

The Role of Public Opinion in a Democracy

The American public and politicians alike are divided about how much **public opinion** (326) should matter in democratic politics. Politicians and the media watch public opinion, as measured in **public opinion polls** (326), very closely. Elected officials look for job security by responding to immediate public desires or by skillfully predicting future requests. The media make large investments in polls, sometimes covering public attitudes on a candidate or an issue as a story in itself.

Citizen Values

There are two competing visions of citizenship in America. The ideal democratic citizen demonstrates political knowledge, tolerates different ideas, and votes consistently. At the other extreme lies the apolitical, self-interested citizen. Most Americans fall somewhere between these extremes.

What Influences Our Opinions About Politics?

Political socialization (331)—the transfer of fundamental democratic values from one generation to the next—is affected by demographic characteristics, including race, gender, age, and income—as evidenced, for example, by the **gender gap** (334) and the **marriage gap** (334)—and by other factors such as education, religion, and geographic region. But life experiences also play an important role: young children are typically taught to value **patriotism** (331) shaped by particular events, usually in their youth and whose shared experience continues to identify them throughout their lives, and watershed events experienced during people's youths can affect entire **political generations** (335). At the same time, the process of **partisan sorting** (337) has led to increased political polarization and **negative partisanship** (337) and has contributed to the phenomenon known as the **spiral of silence** (332).

Measuring and Tracking Public Opinion

Modern polling science surveys a **random sample** (341) of the population, controlling for **sample bias** (341), including **nonresponse bias** (341), with methods such as **weighting** (341) in order to minimize **sampling errors** (341). **Benchmark polls** (345), **tracking polls** (345), and **exit polls** (345) are used in running and covering campaigns to varying degrees. Pseudo-polls like call-in polls, most Internet polls, or **push polls** (347) are used to manipulate rather than measure public opinion.

11

Parties and Interest Groups

In Your Own Words

After you've read this chapter, you will be able to

11.1 Describe the role that parties play in making government policy.

11.2 Outline the evolution of the party system in the United States.

11.3 Identify four types of interest groups and the kinds of interests they represent.

11.4 Describe how interest groups use lobbying and campaign activities to get the public policy they want.

11.5 Identify specific resources that interest groups bring to bear when attempting to influence public policy.

11.6 Summarize the ways in which citizens interact with their government through membership in parties and interest groups.

What's at Stake . . . When "Outsiders" Challenge Establishment Party Candidates?

It happened to both parties in 2016, albeit in different ways and with different results.

In the Democratic Party it was at the primary stage—the early elections to determine who the party's presidential nominee would be. Hillary Clinton entered the race as the front-runner—the one everyone expected to win easily. When it came to party ideology, she was a moderate left Democrat, a liberal at heart who had been toughened to practicality by years of service to her party as first lady, senator from New York, and secretary of state under Barack Obama. In terms of her ties to her party, Clinton was as establishment as they come. Not only had she helped shape its modern identity, but she was well connected, well liked, and the clear party favorite.[1]

The challenge Clinton didn't predict came from her left. The independent senator from Vermont, Bernie Sanders, declared his intention to run in the Democratic primary on April 30, 2015. Running in a major party's primary instead of as an independent comes with huge advantages—media attention, a debate stage, ballot position. What it doesn't do is make you loyal to the party's goals or make the party establishment loyal to you.[2]

Although Clinton won the nomination eventually, Sanders's challenge was serious. He did particularly well with young voters, the white working class, and voters who themselves did not identify with a party. His best states were those where the candidate selection mechanism was the caucus—a discussion-based process that rewards intensity of support and willingness to spend time to choose the candidate—or the open primary—an election in which non–party members are allowed to participate. Sanders attacked Clinton's positions on trade and ended up pulling her to the left on a number of policy issues, such as college tuition, trade, and Wall Street reform, to name a few.

In the process, Sanders left Clinton battle scarred, with a reputation for being inauthentic and untrustworthy on important issues that some of his supporters never forgave. Despite his subsequent endorsement and his enthusiastic campaigning on Clinton's behalf, many of the young people who backed Sanders never enthusiastically transferred their support to her, and a number defected to third-party candidates. The white working-class support Sanders had drawn appealed to Democrats who felt the party had ignored them in favor of propping up the banks and corporations and supporting social programs to aid minorities. Many of them were angry and resentful, ripe for the picking by an anti-establishment candidate, and when Sanders left the stage, there was another in the wings.

The same outsider infiltration that happened to the Democrats was happening to the Republicans. A crowded field of primary hopefuls seeking the nomination was already deeply divided, like their party, between establishment economic conservatives (Jeb Bush and Chris Christie, Rand Paul, Carly Fiorina, Lindsey Graham, John Kasich, Scott Walker, and George Pataki) and social conservative, Tea Party/Freedom Caucus types (Marco Rubio, Ted Cruz, Ben Carson, Mike Huckabee, Bobby Jindal, Rick Perry, and Rick Santorum). As the establishment candidates took aim at each other, another outsider, a former Democrat turned original birther, a successful real estate developer and reality-show host, stepped in and stole the show.[3]

The field barely had a chance. Donald Trump's entertainment value was such that he garnered hours of free media time as the cable stations covered his rallies, hoping he would say something outrageous as he sought to persuade voters that he was running against the "political correctness" that kept them from expressing their true feelings. Aiming straight for the disaffected voters who felt abandoned by the party that had promised them much (control of immigration, the repeal of Obamacare, the end of abortion and gay marriage) but delivered little, Trump promised to "make America great again," and in the process decimated the field. With withering scorn, he called Jeb Bush, the establishment favorite, front-runner, and heir to the Bush family dynasty, "low energy," and Bush's quiet and restrained demeanor seemed to prove him right. "Little Marco" diminished Rubio, "Lyin' Ted Cruz" took care of the Texan, as one by one Trump mocked them and bullied them and knocked them out of the race.

There was a policy debate to be had in the Republican Party, an important one between the establishment and the Freedom Caucus that had been brewing for years and immobilizing Congress, but it never got a hearing. Instead, the primary was reduced to a clown show of name calling and one-upmanship as each candidate tried to outdo himself or herself on the issues Trump brought front and center—mainly immigration (he promised to build a huge wall between the United States and Mexico that Mexico would pay for) and the undoing of the Obama agenda. Trump's rallies drew large crowds, drawn to hear him talk about how he would deport undocumented workers, ban Muslims from entering the country, and bring back jobs he claimed were stolen by the Chinese, all while generally signaling disrespect for social norms of respectful language and politically correct behavior. Those signals, as we noted in *What's at Stake . . . ?* in Chapter 5, were interpreted as not-so-subtle dog whistles that freed up an underbelly of American culture to use crude sexist, racist, anti-Semitic, and xenophobic language at his rallies and in social media forums that Trump did not repudiate. Social media became an echo chamber that repeated the sentiments, or gave them attention by disparaging them. In either case, social media amplified them.

But like Sanders, Trump's outsider, anti-establishment stance appealed to those who felt that Washington had gotten too corrupt and full of itself, too dysfunctional and too removed from their concerns. He drew support not just from bigots but also from the same white working class to which Sanders appealed. By the end of the primary season, against everyone's best guesses and predictions, Trump was the Republican Party's nominee, and he went on to win the Electoral College in a squeaker of a surprise victory in November.

What just happened here? How did two outside candidates have such an impact on the nomination process to which they barely had any ties? What impact is that having on the parties' futures? Just what is at stake when party establishments are challenged from outside like this? We will return to that question after we look more closely at the role parties play in American politics and how they work.

THE old adage says there is safety in numbers, but more important in politics, there is also power in numbers. In *Federalist* No. 10, James Madison wasn't worried about the odd voter getting antsy and voting for a harebrained candidate or idea. He was concerned that large numbers of voters would come to define themselves as being opposed to what he thought was good for the public. He was worried about the political power of *groups* that would use the rules of politics to get what they wanted at the expense of everyone else.

And small wonder. Madison saw what happened under the Articles of Confederation, when individuals banded together to make claims on their government. Since then, we have seen innumerable examples of group power, everything from Republican attempts to restore the South after the Civil War, to the women's suffrage movement, to the National Rifle Association's (NRA's) efforts to limit gun control, to liberal and conservative groups' attempts to influence who sits on the Supreme Court. For many Americans, this group action is the meaning of modern democracy. In fact, we saw in earlier chapters that although some people argue that the individual voter in America cannot make a difference, many others believe in pluralist democracy, the idea that individuals can find their political strength only in numbers, by joining with other like-minded people to get the representation they want.

In this chapter we examine two central kinds of groups that Americans form: political parties and interest groups. Both types of groups form on the basis of common political ideas and goals, and use the system to realize those goals. The key difference is in what is at stake for the groups: political parties seek to elect their members to office in order to control government, and interest groups seek only to influence what government does. Specifically, you will learn about the role of political parties in a democracy, the American party system, the various roles interest groups play, the types of interest groups that exist in the U.S. political system, how interest groups attempt to exert their political influence, and the resources that different interest groups bring to bear in influencing government decisions.

WHAT ARE POLITICAL PARTIES?

Organizations seeking to influence policy by controlling the apparatus of government

Probably because Madison hoped that political parties would not thrive, parties—unlike Congress, the presidency, the Supreme Court, and even the free press—are not mentioned in the Constitution. As we will see, in fact, many of the rules that determine the establishment and role of parties have been created by party members themselves. Although the founding documents of American politics are silent on the place of political parties, keen political observers have long appreciated the fundamental role that parties play in our system of government.[4] According to one scholar, "Political parties created democracy, and . . . democracy is unthinkable save in terms of parties."[5]

THE ROLE OF POLITICAL PARTIES IN A DEMOCRACY

Remembering that politics is about who gets what, and how they get it, helps us understand what parties are about. **Political parties** are organizations that seek, under a common banner, to promote their ideas and policies by gaining control of government through the nomination and election of candidates for office. Each major party represents a different ideological perspective about the way that government should be used to solve problems. Ideologies, as we have said before, are broad sets of ideas about politics that help to organize our views of the political world, the information that regularly bombards us, and the positions we take on various issues. Parties are important mediators of those views—passing them on to us and letting

political party a group of citizens united by ideology and seeking control of government in order to promote their ideas and policies

us know which views are acceptable from the party's perspective and which are not. In addition, parties provide support for democratic government in three crucial ways:

- They *provide a linkage* between voters and elected officials, helping to tell voters what candidates stand for and providing a way for voters to hold their officials accountable for what they do in office, both individually and collectively.
- They *overcome some of the fragmentation in government* that comes from separation of powers and federalism by linking members in all branches and levels of government.
- They *provide an articulate opposition* to the ideas and policies of those elected to serve in government. Some citizens and critics may decry the **partisanship**, or taking of political sides, that sometimes seems to be motivated by the possibilities for party gain as much as by principle or public interest. Others, however, see partisanship as providing the necessary antagonistic relationship that keeps politicians honest and allows the best political ideas and policies to emerge.

COURTESY RONALD REAGAN LIBRARY

It's a Party for the Party
The national nominating conventions have evolved into full-blown spectacles, as carefully orchestrated as a Super Bowl halftime show or the Oscars. Here, Ronald Reagan and his vice president, George H. W. Bush, stand with their wives, watching balloons drop to celebrate the end of the 1984 Republican National Convention in Dallas.

To highlight the multiple tasks that parties perform to make democracy work and to make life easier for politicians, political scientists find it useful to divide political parties into three separate components: the party organization, the party-in-government, and the party-in-the-electorate.[6]

PARTY ORGANIZATION The **party organization** is what most people think of as a political party. It represents the system of central committees at the national, state, and local levels. At the top of the Democratic Party organization is the Democratic National Committee. Likewise, the Republican National Committee heads the Republican Party. Underneath these national committees are state-level party committees, and below them are county-level party committees, or county equivalents. The party organization performs the central party function of electioneering. **Electioneering** involves recruiting and nominating candidates, defining policy agendas, and getting candidates elected.

Each party's electioneering activities begin months before the general election. The first step is simply finding candidates to run. Fulfilling this responsibility is often difficult because, in many instances, the organizations must recruit candidates to run against a current officeholder—the incumbent—and incumbents are hard to beat.

The nomination phase is a formal process through which the party chooses a candidate for each elective office to be contested that year. Today, party primaries, or preliminary elections between members of the same party vying for the party's nomination, are the dominant means

partisanship loyalty to a party that helps shape how members see the world, define problems, and identify appropriate solutions

party organization the official structure that conducts the political business of parties

electioneering the process of getting a person elected to public office

of choosing candidates for congressional, statewide, state legislative, and local offices. Some candidates are nominated at a convention. A nominating convention is a formal party gathering that is bound by a number of strict rules relating to the selection of voting participants—called *delegates*—and the nomination of candidates. The most prominent conventions are the national presidential nominating conventions for the Democratic and Republican Parties,[7] which are held the summer before the election, after the state presidential primaries. Usually the presidential nominating convention merely rubber-stamps the primary victor.

After a political party nominates its candidates, one of the party's main roles is to develop a policy agenda, which represents policies that the party's candidates agree to promote when campaigning and to pursue when governing. The development of such an agenda involves much politicking and gamesmanship as each faction of the party tries to get its views written into the party platform. Whoever wins control of the party platform has decisive input into how the campaign will proceed.

In the election phase, the role of the party changes from choosing among competing candidates within the party and developing policy agendas to getting its nominated candidates elected. Traditionally the party's role here was to "organize and mobilize" voters, but increasingly parties also provide extensive services to candidates, including fundraising, training in campaign tactics, instruction in compliance with election laws, public opinion polling, and professional campaign assistance.[8]

PARTY-IN-GOVERNMENT The party-in-government includes all the candidates for national, state, and local office who are elected. A key function of political parties is governing, or controlling government by organizing and providing leadership for the legislative and executive branches, enacting policy agendas, mobilizing support for party policy, and building coalitions.

When a party "controls" government at the national level and in the states, it means that the party determines who occupies the leadership positions in the branch of government in which it has a majority. Thus when Barack Obama won the presidency in 2008, Obama, and by extension the Democrats, controlled the top leadership positions in the executive branch of government (cabinet secretaries and undersecretaries and the White House staff). Because the Democrats enhanced the majority of the U.S. House and Senate contests they had won in 2006, their continued majority status won them the right to organize their respective houses of Congress by occupying the major leadership roles. In the Senate and the House, this meant selecting the majority leader in the Senate and the Speaker of the House, controlling committee assignments, selecting chairs of legislative committees, and having a majority of seats on each committee. When the Republicans won back control of the House in 2010, they in turn selected the leaders—the Speaker, the House majority leader, and the majority whip—and took over the committee chairmanships. Since they didn't quite achieve a majority in the Senate, those leadership positions remained in Democratic hands until 2015.

Of course, the ultimate goal of a political party is not only to fill the leadership positions in government but also to execute its policy agenda—the party's solutions to the nation's problems. Whether the problems concern affordable health care, welfare abuse, taxes, distressed communities, low-skill jobs moving to developing countries, undocumented immigrants, or the economy, each party represents an alternative vision for how to approach and solve these problems. About two-thirds of the promises of the party that controls the presidency are implemented, compared to about half of the promises of the party that does not control the presidency.[9]

nominating convention the formal party gathering to choose candidates

party-in-government party members who have been elected to serve in government

governing activities directed toward controlling the distribution of political resources by providing executive and legislative leadership, enacting agendas, mobilizing support, and building coalitions

FIGURE 11.1
Party Identification, 1952–2018

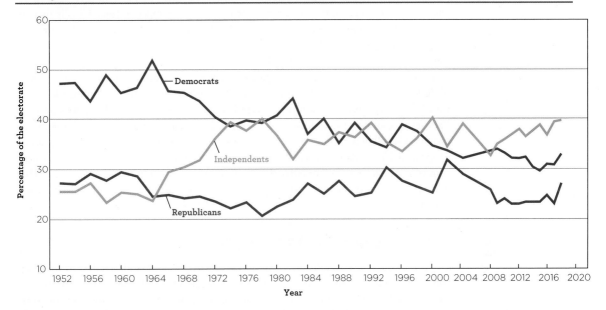

Source: American National Election Studies, University of Michigan; data made available by the Inter-University Consortium for Political and Social Research; for 2009–2013, data from Pew Research Center, "Party Identification," www.pewresearch.org/data-trend/political-attitudes/party-identification/. Extended with authors' calculations using Pew Research Center national adult surveys, 2014 and 2016. Data accessed through the Roper Center for Public Opinion Research.

PARTY-IN-THE-ELECTORATE The **party-in-the-electorate** represents ordinary citizens who identify with or have some feeling of attachment to one of the political parties. Public opinion surveys determine **party identification**, or party ID, by asking respondents whether they think of themselves as Democrats, Republicans, or independents. Over time, voter attachment to the two parties has declined; the percentages identifying as independents increased in the 1960s and 1970s so that today more people consider themselves independents than identify with either major party (see Figure 11.1). The Democratic Party, which had a large numerical advantage among identifiers in the 1950s, lost ground after peaking in the 1960s. The parties were about even by 2002, but the Democrats have recovered and held a modest lead in party affiliation that has grown slightly since 2016. Most voters who identify with one of the political parties "inherit" their party IDs from their parents, as we suggested in our discussion of political socialization in Chapter 10.[10] Party identifiers generally support the party's basic ideology and policy principles. These principles usually relate to the party's stance on the use of government to solve various economic and social problems.

Although voters do not have a strong formal role to play in the party organization, parties use identifiers as a necessary base of support during elections. In virtually every presidential election, both of the major-party candidates win the votes of an overwhelming percentage

party-in-the-electorate ordinary citizens who identify with the party

party identification voter affiliation with a political party

of those who identify with their respective parties. But just capturing one's **party base** is not sufficient to win a national election since neither party has a majority of the national voters. As we will see later in this chapter, candidates are often pulled between the ideological preferences of their base and the more moderate preferences of independents. Usually they try to capture those moderates during the general election campaign, but in 2004 George W. Bush took the opposite tack, focusing on appeals to his conservative activist base. Although John Kerry won more of the independent vote, the much higher turnout rate and very small number of defections among Republicans were enough to return Bush to the White House. In 2008 Republican John McCain, worried that his own independent "maverick" status would not stir enthusiasm among his base, picked social conservative Alaskan governor Sarah Palin as his running mate. Although she did get the base more excited, overall Republican turnout was still down from 2004, and Barack Obama, with outsized turnout among young people and African Americans and an energized Democratic base, easily won the independent vote and the election. In 2016 Hillary Clinton kept much of the Obama coalition but didn't get as much of the white, working-class vote as Donald Trump, who doubled down on attracting his base.

THE RESPONSIBLE PARTY MODEL

Earlier we said that one of the democratic roles of parties is to provide a link between voters and elected officials—or, to use the terms we just introduced, between the party-in-the-electorate and the party-in-government. There are many ways in which parties can link voters and officials, but for the link to truly enhance democracy—that is, the control of leaders by citizens—certain conditions have to be met. Political scientists call the fulfillment of these conditions the **responsible party model**.[11] These conditions are as follows:

- Each party should present a coherent set of programs to the voters, consistent with the party's ideology and clearly different from the other party's programs.
- The candidates for each party pledge to support and implement the programs if elected.
- Voters should make their choices based on which party's programs most closely reflect their own ideas and hold the parties responsible for unkept promises by voting their members out of office.
- Each party, then, should exercise control over its elected officials to ensure that party officials are promoting and voting for its programs, thereby providing accountability to voters.

The responsible party model proposes that democracy is strengthened when voters are given clear alternatives and hold the parties responsible for keeping their promises. Voters can, of course, hold officials accountable without the assistance of parties, but it takes a good deal more of their time and attention. Furthermore, several political scientists have noted that although individuals can be held accountable for their own actions, many, if not most, government actions are the products of many officials. Political parties give us a way of holding officials accountable for what they do collectively as well as individually.[12]

The responsible party model fits some systems, especially parliamentary systems such as in Great Britain, quite well. Strong, disciplined, and determined parties are appropriate for a parliamentary system where the majority party controls, by definition, both the legislative and

party base members of a political party who consistently vote for that party's candidates

responsible party model party government when four conditions are met: clear choice of ideologies, candidates pledged to implement ideas, party held accountable by voters, and party control over members

executive branches, and can control the government without minority obstruction like our Senate filibuster. The model is more problematic when used, as political scientists in the past have done, to critique the American parties, which during the middle decades of the twentieth century were seen as too unfocused and undisciplined to fit the model.[13] Changes in our system over the past twenty years or so have brought the American parties closer to a responsible party system—especially in the distinctive policy programs the parties have come to represent. But even as our parties have become more highly polarized, there is a growing disconnect between their behavior and the demands of our constitutional system. This means that the parties often share power and cooperate to get things done, yet such polarized parties in our systems of shared powers are a recipe for gridlock and frustration.[14] In practice the American system also falls short of the idealized responsible party model because American voters don't fit the model's conditions; they do not vote solely on party or issues, relying on other considerations like candidate experience and personality. Still, even though it doesn't fit the American case perfectly, the responsible party model is valuable because it underscores the importance of voters holding the parties accountable for governing, and it provides a useful yardstick for understanding fundamental changes in the U.S. two-party system.

In Your Own Words Describe the role that parties play in making government policy.

THE AMERICAN PARTY SYSTEM

From party machines to effective political organizations

For James Madison, parties were just an organized version of that potentially dangerous political association, the faction. He had hopes that their influence on American politics would be minimal, but scarcely was the ink dry on the Constitution before the founders were organizing themselves into groups to promote their political views.

THE HISTORY OF PARTIES IN AMERICA

In the 1790s a host of disagreements among politicians led Alexander Hamilton and John Adams to organize the Federalists, a group of legislators who supported their views. Later, Thomas Jefferson and James Madison would do the same with the Democratic-Republicans. Over the course of the next decade, these organizations expanded beyond their legislative purposes to include recruiting candidates to run under their party label for both Congress and the presidency. The primary focus, however, was on the party-in-government and not on the voters.[15]

In 1828 Martin Van Buren and Andrew Jackson turned the Democratic Party away from a focus on the party-in-government, creating the country's first mass-based party and setting the stage for the development of the voter-oriented party machine. **Party machines** were tightly organized party systems at the state, county, and city levels that kept control of voters by getting them jobs, helping them out financially when necessary, and in fact becoming part of their lives and their communities. This mass organization was built around one principal goal: taking advantage of the expansion of voting rights to all white men (even those without property) to elect more Democratic candidates.[16]

party machines mass-based party systems in which parties provided services and resources to voters in exchange for votes

The Jacksonian Democrats enacted a number of party and government reforms designed to enhance the control of party leaders, known as **party bosses**, over candidates, officeholders, and campaigns. During the nomination process, the party bosses would choose the party's candidates for the general election. Winning candidates were expected to hire only other party supporters for government positions and reward only party supporters with government contracts, expanding the range of people with a stake in the party's electoral success. This system of **patronage**, which we discussed in Chapter 8, rewarded faithful party supporters with public offices, jobs, and government contracts and ensured that the party's candidates were loyal to the party or at least to the party bosses.

Because the Democratic Party machine was so effective at getting votes and controlling government, the Whig Party (1830s through 1850s), and later the Republican Party (starting in the mid-1850s), used these same techniques to organize. Party bosses and their party machines were exceptionally strong in urban areas in the East and Midwest. These urban machines, designed to further the interests of the parties themselves, had the important democratic consequence of integrating into the political process the masses of new immigrants coming into the urban centers at the turn of the twentieth century. Because parties were so effective at mobilizing voters, the average voter participation rate exceeded 80 percent in most U.S. elections prior to the 1900s.

The strength of these party machines was also their weakness. In many cases, parties would do almost anything to win, including buying votes, mobilizing new immigrants who could not speak English and were not U.S. citizens, and resurrecting dead people to vote. In addition, the whole system of patronage, based on doling out government jobs, contracts, and favors, came under attack by reformers in the early 1900s as representing favoritism and corruption. Political reforms such as **party primaries**, in which the party-in-the-electorate rather than the party bosses chose between competing party candidates for a party's nomination, and civil service reform, under which government jobs were filled on the basis of merit instead of party loyalty, did much to ensure that party machines went the way of the dinosaur.

REALIGNMENT

A striking feature of American history is that although we have not had a revolution since the 1700s, we have changed our political course several times and in rather dramatic ways. One of the many advantages of a democratic form of government is that dramatic changes in policy direction can be effected through the ballot box rather than through bloody revolution. Over the course of two centuries, the two-party system in the United States has been marked by periods of relative stability lasting twenty-five to forty years, with one party tending to maintain a majority of congressional seats and controlling the presidency. These periods of stability are called **party eras**. Short periods of large-scale change—peaceful revolutions, as it were, signaled by one major critical election in which the majority of people shift their political allegiance from one party to another—mark the end of one party era and the beginning of another. Scholars call such a shift in party dominance a **realignment**. In a realignment, the coalitions of groups supporting the parties change. Although it is not always the case, realignments generally result in parallel changes in government policies, reflecting the policy agenda of each party's new coalition. Realignments have been precipitated by critical events like the Civil War and the Great Depression. The United States has gone through five

party bosses party leaders, usually in an urban district, who exercised tight control over electioneering and patronage

patronage the system in which successful party candidates reward supporters with jobs or favors

party primary an election in which party candidates are nominated by registered party members rather than party bosses

party eras extended periods of relative political stability in which one party tends to control both the presidency and Congress

realignment a substantial and long-term shift in party allegiance by individuals and groups, usually resulting in a change in policy direction

party eras in its history and perhaps is in a sixth now (see this chapter's *The Big Picture*).

For much of the twentieth century, the United States was in the midst of the fifth party era, ushered in by Franklin Roosevelt's New Deal and marked by the congressional domination of the Democratic Party. Most analysts agree that the New Deal coalition supporting the fifth party era has changed, but there is much controversy over the timing and character of that change and, in fact, about whether we have entered a new party era at all.[17] Although there have been many incremental changes, there has been no defining critical election. The dramatic but slow nature of this change can be seen in how the geographic centers of the two parties have moved since the New Deal. We used to be able to talk about the "solid Democratic South," because the southern states, though conservative on many issues, voted Democratic so as not to support the "party of Lincoln." But today the southern states are reliably Republican in presidential elections, and the Democrats' geographic strength lies in the industrial Northeast and Midwest and on the Pacific Coast.

"THAT'S WHAT'S THE MATTER."

BOSS TWEED. "As long as I count the Votes, what are you going to do about it? say?"

Set to Win
Party bosses like New York City's Boss Tweed controlled the political process and ruled the ballot box.

Although these realigning changes have undoubtedly taken place, because no solid new majority has emerged, some analysts believe that we are really in a period of **dealignment**, a dissolving of the old era of party dominance, in which voters are more likely to call themselves independents and no party is clearly dominant.[18] What no one knows is whether this period of highly competitive parties is one of transition to a new party era or whether we are already in the sixth party era.

THE PARTIES TODAY

As *The Big Picture* in this chapter indicates, the New Deal coalition supporting the fifth party era has changed, but no single critical election has marked a clear realignment. Rather, we have had an incremental realignment across a relatively long series of elections that has included the massive migration of white southerners to the Republican Party and the less massive but still notable trend for Catholics to be less solidly Democratic than they were at the formation of the New Deal. Similarly, African Americans have shifted from somewhat favoring the Democratic Party to overwhelming Democratic identification, a trend solidified with Barack Obama's nomination as the Democratic candidate for the presidency in 2008. The geographic bases of the parties have also changed: the South used to be solidly Democratic; it is now the most dependable region for the Republican Party in presidential elections. In recent elections, Democrats have been more likely to win in New England and the mid-Atlantic states—areas where the Republicans were stronger in the 1940s.

Since the 1980s, party identification has strengthened, but more along ideological lines and less along regional lines.[19] In recent years these changes have been labeled as differences

dealignment a trend among voters to identify themselves as independents rather than as members of a major party

THE BIG PICTURE:
How the American Political Parties Have Evolved

James Madison may have been suspicious of political parties, lumping them in with the dreaded "factions" that he thought were so destructive to liberty, but the fact is that they have always been with us, even in Madison's time. What has varied over time is not the tendency of Americans to form umbrella groups with their ideological fellows to try to effect political change from inside the system, but the particular configurations of those parties. This Big Picture shows how American parties have evolved over time and, since 1879, when data on the current parties begin, just how polarized those parties have been at various times in our history.

First Party Era

In the U.S. party system's elite-driven formative stage, the issue of federal versus states' rights provided the central political cleavage. The Federalists, supporters of a stronger national government, were led by John Adams and Alexander Hamilton, while the Democratic-Republicans (also called Jeffersonian Republicans) supported states' rights and were led by Thomas Jefferson and James Madison.

Second Party Era

Buoyed by an explosion in the number of voters—which swelled from 350,000 in 1824 to well over a million in 1828—Andrew Jackson prevailed in the bitter election of 1828, solidifying the coalition of states' rights supporters (lower classes and southern states) over those advocating more power for the national government (business interests and northern states). From the ashes of Adams's failed candidacy came a new party—the Whigs, led by Henry Clay and Daniel Webster, who competed with the Democrats until the mid-1850s.

Third Party Era

Republicans took control of the House of Representatives in 1858, and by 1860 the party's presidential candidate, Abraham Lincoln, had won the presidency as well. After the Civil War, an era of regionalism pitted Republicans (northern and western states) against Democrats (southern and pro-slavery states). Presidential elections were closely contested, but the Republicans tended to hold the edge.

Political Parties in Power

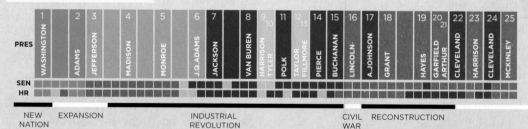

Ideological Difference Between Parties in Congress

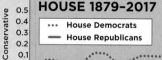

Fourth Party Era

Although William Jennings Bryan, a Nebraska Democrat, attempted to merge the Democratic Party with the People's Party in the presidential election of 1896, he failed to amass enough farmers and industrial labor voters to win. The splitting of votes between the People's Party and the Democrats strengthened the Republican Party. As economic issues subsided in the late 1890s, the regional bases of Republicans and Democrats intensified.

Fifth Party Era

The coalition of voters supporting the New Deal included southern Democrats, Catholic immigrants, blue-collar workers, and farmers. Republicans maintained support among business owners and industrialists, and strengthened their regional support in the Northeast and Plains states.

Sixth Party Era

While there is much controversy about whether we have entered a new partisan era at all, and no single critical election has marked the realignment, incremental changes have occurred that are large and so far long-lasting. A realigning process has mobilized African Americans and other minorities into the Democratic Party and southern whites into the Republican Party, creating a greater consistency between partisanship and ideological and issue preferences. The current era is characterized by a narrowly divided nation, intense party competition, and increased gridlock in government.

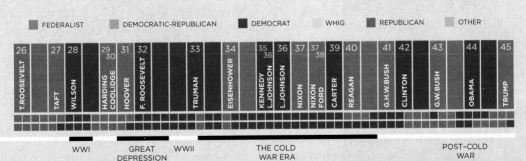

FEDERALIST   DEMOCRATIC-REPUBLICAN   DEMOCRAT   WHIG   REPUBLICAN   OTHER

26 T. ROOSEVELT | 27 TAFT | 28 WILSON | 29 30 HARDING COOLIDGE | 31 HOOVER | 32 F. ROOSEVELT | 33 TRUMAN | 34 EISENHOWER | 35 36 KENNEDY L. JOHNSON | 36 L. JOHNSON | 37 NIXON | 37 38 NIXON FORD | 39 CARTER | 40 REAGAN | 41 G.H.W.BUSH | 42 CLINTON | 43 G.W.BUSH | 44 OBAMA | 45 TRUMP

WWI   GREAT DEPRESSION   WWII   THE COLD WAR ERA   POST–COLD WAR

2018

between "Red" and "Blue" America, which refers to the southern, midwestern, and mountain states' (red states') support for the Republican Party set against a pattern of coastal and industrial Northeast (blue states) support for Democrats (see *Snapshot of America: How Did We Vote in the 2016 Presidential Election?* in Chapter 12).

The current party era is thus characterized by major changes that have mobilized African Americans, Latinos, Asian Americans, and other minorities into the Democratic Party and southern whites into the Republican Party, and a system in which neither party has a clear, enduring majority. These phenomena have led to a much higher incidence of divided government at the national and state levels, with the executive and legislative branches in the hands of different parties. One consequence of divided government is that it makes it difficult for voters to know which party to hold accountable.

WHAT DO THE AMERICAN PARTIES STAND FOR?

A key feature of the responsible party model is that the parties should offer voters a choice between different visions of how government should operate. Barry Goldwater, the 1964 Republican presidential nominee, stated this more bluntly: political parties, he said, should offer "a choice, not an echo." Offering voters a choice is the primary means through which parties make representative democracy work. In many countries, particularly those with more than two parties, the choices offered by parties can range from radical communist to ultraconservative. In America, however, the ideological range of the two major parties, the Democrats and the Republicans (often also called the GOP, for "Grand Old Party"), is much narrower. In fact, among many American voters, there is a perception that the two parties do not offer real choices.

Although it may seem to voters that members of the two parties are not very different, they are really quite distinct in their ideologies, their memberships, and the policies for which they stand. At least since the New Deal of the 1930s, the Democratic Party, especially outside the South, has been aligned with a liberal ideology. As we saw in Chapter 1, liberals encourage government action to solve economic and social problems but want government to stay out of their personal, religious, and moral lives, except as a protector of their basic rights. The Republican Party, by contrast, has been associated with a conservative perspective, looking to government to provide social and moral order but demanding that the economy remain as unfettered as possible in the distribution of material resources. This is not to say that all Democrats are equally liberal or that all Republicans are equally conservative. Each party has its more extreme members and its more moderate members. Democrats and Republicans who hold their ideologies only moderately might be quite similar in terms of what they believe and stand for. As we saw in Chapter 6, however, in today's era of **hyperpartisanship** and polarization, all Republicans are more conservative than the most conservative Democrat, yielding two completely distinct ideological encampments with little basis for compromise. The differences among the public are not as great, but they are still quite notable.

Since the 1960s the parties have become more consistent internally with respect to their ideologies. The most conservative region in the country is the South, but because of lingering resentment of the Republican Party for its role in the Civil War, the South was for decades tightly tied to the Democratic Party. In the 1960s, however, conservative southern Democratic voters began to vote for the Republican Party, and formerly Democratic politicians were switching their allegiances as well. By the 1990s the South had become predominantly Republican. This swing made the Democratic Party more consistently liberal and the Republicans more consistently conservative, and gave the

hyperpartisanship a commitment to party so strong that it can transcend other commitments

party activist bases more power within each party, because they did not have to do battle with people of different ideological persuasions.

Party ideologies attract and are reinforced by different coalitions of voters. This means that the Democrats' post–New Deal liberal ideology reflects the preferences of its coalition of working- and lower-class voters, including union members, minorities, women, the elderly, and more educated urban dwellers. The Republicans' conservative ideology reflects the preferences of upper- and middle-class whites, those who belong to evangelical and Protestant religions, and rural and suburban voters. There is nothing inevitable about these coalitions, and they are subject to change as the parties' stances on issues change and as the opposing party offers new alternatives. Working-class whites (non-Hispanic whites without a college education) were once the bedrock constituency of the Democratic Party. However, the Republicans' more conservative appeals on racial and social issues have won over enough of this group that they are likely to support Republicans in a given election, although as we saw in the 2016 primaries by their choice of Donald Trump as their candidate, they do not feel that the establishment party has been responsive to their concerns.[20] Partisan differences between men and women used to be insignificant, but the gender gap we discussed in Chapter 10 has grown in recent years.

> *Are the American people well represented by a two-party system?*

When the parties run slates of candidates for office, those candidates run on a **party platform**—a list of policy positions the party endorses and pledges its elected officials to enact. A platform is the national party's campaign promises, usually made only in a presidential election year. If the parties are to make a difference politically, their platforms have to reflect substantial differences that are consistent with their ideologies. The responsible party model requires that the parties offer distinct platforms, that voters know about them and vote on the basis of them, and that the parties ensure that their elected officials follow through in implementing them. A guide for interpreting and understanding party platforms is provided in *Don't Be Fooled by . . . Political Party Platforms.*

FORCES DRAWING THE PARTIES APART AND PUSHING THEM TOGETHER

Political parties in our system have a dilemma—how to keep the core ideological base satisfied while appealing to enough more moderate voters that they can win elections in diverse constituencies. This is not likely to be a problem in a small, homogeneous district. Conservative Republicans and liberal Democrats can be nominated and elected and party members are happy. As constituencies get larger and more diverse, parties have a choice. They can be moderate and win elections, or stay ideologically pure and lose. In other words, there are internal forces that draw the parties away from each other, to the opposite ends of the ideological spectrum, but external, electoral forces can push them together. These forces are central to understanding electoral politics in America today.

On any policy or set of policies, voters' opinions range from very liberal to very conservative. In the American two-party system, however, most voters tend to be in the middle, holding a moderate position between the two ideological extremes (see Figure 11.2). The party that appeals best to the moderate voters usually wins most of the votes. Thus even though the ideologies of the parties are distinct, the pressures related to winning a majority of votes can lead both parties to campaign on the same issue positions, making them appear more alike to voters.[21] For instance, Republicans have moved from their initial opposition to join the majority of voters in supporting Social Security, Medicare, and Medicaid. Similarly, Democrats

party platform a list of policy positions a party endorses and pledges its elected officials to enact

Political Party Platforms

Are you a member of a political party, or thinking about becoming one? If so, you've got some homework to do. Each major party (and most minor ones, too) has put together a party platform—a document that outlines the party's political positions and agenda for the coming years. You can think of the party platform as a political dating profile, filled with information that can help you make sound decisions about whether you want to pursue a relationship with one party or another.

You can find the full text of the 2016 platforms on the web sites of each of the two major parties' national committees:

- The Democratic Party: www.democrats.org/party-platform
- The Republican Party: www.gop.com/the-2016-republican-party-platform/

Before you become "involved" with a party, we encourage you to read the platforms of your preferred party—and perhaps consider alternatives as well.

WHAT TO WATCH OUT FOR

When you read a party's platform, keep these questions in mind:

- **Whose platform is it?** Established parties like the Democratic and Republican Parties want to excite their bases, while upstarts like the Greens and the Libertarians might be more concerned with attracting new members. Consider how these goals might influence how each party presents itself in its party platform.

- **Who is this platform directed to?** Is it catering to the mainstream party members or to the party's more extreme factions? Where do you fit in?

- **How did the political climate affect this platform?** Platforms are created as part of the national conventions—which come at the tail end of the presidential primary season. Do you think the events (and players) of this party's primary influenced the platform? If so, how does that influence relate to you and your political priorities?

- **What does this party—and the other parties!—have to say about issues you care about?** The beauty of digital information is that you can quickly and easily search for key words that matter most to you. Do a quick search for terms that are high on your political priority list—for example, *health care, abortion, firearms, terrorism, taxes, the Supreme Court*—to find out where each party stands on the issue.

- **Do you think the party can deliver on its policy proposals?** What resources (money, power, and so on) would it need? Can it get them? Would enacting the promised policies achieve what the party claims it would? Who would win, and who would lose?

- **Does this platform deserve your support?** Membership in a political party is a form of political power: by voting in party primaries, you can help to shape the party of the future, along with its agenda. Think carefully about how you can best wield that power. Supporting a party need not mean that you endorse the party line on every single issue—but it is a useful way of identifying a clear set of priorities for political action.

- **What are your alternatives?** In the end, you may determine that membership in a party is not important to you at all, and that you wish to remain an independent voter. But remember that, come November, you will be choosing among candidates who *are* affiliated with parties. Knowing what each party stands for can help you to make better decisions in the voting booth—especially in state and local elections, where you may not have access to the kind of information made available about national candidates.

have dropped their resistance to a balanced federal budget and have become advocates of fiscal responsibility.

Although the need to appeal to the many moderate voters in the middle of the American political spectrum has brought the two major parties together, powerful forces within the parties still keep them apart. These are the need to placate party activists and the need to raise money. The main players in a political party are often called the "party faithful," or **party activists**—people who are especially committed to the values and policies of the party and who devote more of their resources, both time and money, to the party's cause. Although these activists are not an official organ of the party, they represent its lifeblood. Compared to the average voter, party activists tend to be more ideologically extreme (more conservative or more liberal than the average party identifier) and to care more intensely about the party's issues. They can have a significant influence on the ideological character of the party.[22]

Party activists play a key role in keeping the parties ideologically distinct, because one of their primary purposes in being active in the party is to ensure that the party advocates their issue positions (see Figure 11.2). Because they tend to be concerned with keeping the party pure, they are reluctant to compromise on these issues, even if it means losing an election.[23] Liberal activists kept the Democratic Party to the left of most Americans during the 1970s and 1980s. The only Democratic candidate who won a presidential election during that time was Jimmy Carter, in the immediate aftermath of the Watergate scandal that drove Republican Richard Nixon from office. The Democratic Party dealt with this problem by restructuring its internal politics and giving more weight to moderates like Bill Clinton and Al Gore. They also responded by relabeling themselves as "progressives," with fewer and fewer candidates and on-air leftists embracing the "liberal" label.[24] In 2008 Barack Obama appealed to moderates with his insistence that politics need not be ideological and divisive, but in 2012, after four years of partisan gridlock in Washington, he ran instead on helping the middle class, and his campaign focused on turning out the Democratic base. Even under President Obama the party stayed relatively moderate. It was not until 2016 that the liberal wing of the party reappeared, fully energized in support of Bernie Sanders. The Democratic Party was ultimately forced to include much of Sanders's policy preferences in the party's platform.

The Republicans got caught in the same trap of appearing to be as conservative as their most activist members in the religious right and, later, in the Tea Party. The Democrats were consequently able to capture the presidency by appealing to the moderate middle—focusing on the economic problems of Americans in 1992 and appropriating and giving less extreme meaning to the label "family values" in 1996. The Republicans responded by moving to the middle in 2000, choosing in George W. Bush a candidate who could appeal to moderate voters. As we saw in *What's at Stake . . . ?*, the Republicans have been struggling with an establishment at odds with its most conservative members, first, in the religious right and, later, in the Tea Party. The 2016 primaries revealed internal schisms among party activists divided between those holding economic conservative views, those holding social conservative views, and a new populism that found its voice in supporting the candidacy of Donald Trump. Since the election, the party as a whole has lost some identifiers who felt strongly about their ideological principles, and the ones who remain have moved closer to Trump's positions.[25]

The need to please party activists gives candidates a powerful incentive to remain true to the party's causes. Candidates who are moderate too much or too often risk alienating the activists who are a key component of their success. Thus, even though many nominees temper their stances to win a majority of the votes, winning candidates, mindful of their bases, tend to return to their roots once in office.[26] This means that few politicians are

party activists the "party faithful"; the rank-and-file members who actually carry out the party's electioneering efforts

FIGURE 11.2
External and Internal Forces on the Parties

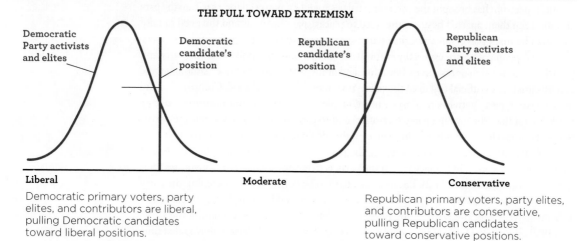

THE PULL TOWARD EXTREMISM

Democratic Party activists and elites

Democratic candidate's position

Republican candidate's position

Republican Party activists and elites

Liberal   Moderate   Conservative

Democratic primary voters, party elites, and contributors are liberal, pulling Democratic candidates toward liberal positions.

Republican primary voters, party elites, and contributors are conservative, pulling Republican candidates toward conservative positions.

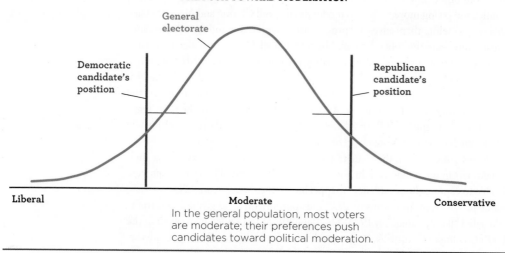

THE PUSH TOWARD MODERATION

General electorate

Democratic candidate's position

Republican candidate's position

Liberal   Moderate   Conservative

In the general population, most voters are moderate; their preferences push candidates toward political moderation.

willing to be truly moderate and work with the other side. Since the 1980s we have seen increased partisanship in politics, which often leads to gridlock and inaction. As mentioned in Chapter 10, the pull toward polarization has been increased further by a recent trend toward what political scientists call **negative partisanship**, the tendency to hate the other party even more than one likes one's own.[27] In an environment of negative partisanship, it is hard to find a unifying policy position because the parties are like two rival sports teams whose rabid fans can't stand each other and they don't *want* to find common ground. This is different from both polarization and hyperpartisanship because it goes beyond commitment to the party's ideological or policy positions; partisanship actually becomes part of one's personal identity.

negative partisanship loyalty to a party driven by hatred of the other party

Under normal circumstances, the parties can deal with the tension between activists and the larger body of moderates in ways other than by changing the party positions. One strategy is simply to emphasize partisan issues that are popular with moderates or to reframe the issues in ways that are palatable to more voters. In the 2004 election, George W. Bush focused on the dangers inherent in the war on terror, on which moderates favored him strongly over John Kerry; however, in 2008 and 2012 the need to appease the party base kept John McCain and Mitt Romney to the right of center for most of their campaigns. By 2016 we were well outside the bounds of party politics as usual. Hillary Clinton tried to find a unifying theme with her "Stronger Together" message but had to spend much of her time reacting to the things said and done by Donald Trump. Trump made little effort to run to the middle or to dissociate himself from the base that had given him his primary victory. Negative partisanship, for the most part, kept both parties in their lanes, but so many other variables were at work in that election that it is hard to fit it into the usual party narratives.

CHARACTERISTICS OF THE AMERICAN PARTY SYSTEM

Party systems vary tremendously around the world. The American party system is distinctive: it is predominantly a two-party system, it tends toward ideological moderation, it has decentralized party organizations, and its parties-in-government are undisciplined.

TWO PARTIES The United States has a two-party system. Throughout most of our history, in fact, the Democrats and the Republicans have been the only parties with a viable chance of winning the vast majority of elective offices. The most important reason the United States maintains a two-party system is that the rules of the system—in most cases designed by members of the two parties themselves—make it very difficult for third parties to do well on a permanent basis.[28] The U.S. Constitution prescribes a single-member-district electoral system for choosing members of Congress. This means that the candidate who receives the most votes in a defined district wins that seat and the loser gets nothing, except perhaps some campaign debt. This type of winner-take-all system creates strong incentives for voters to cast their ballots for one of the two established parties, because many voters believe that they are effectively throwing away their votes when they vote for a third-party candidate.

Does partisanship have to lead to divisiveness?

The United States has other legal barriers that reinforce the two-party system. In most states, legislators from both parties have created election laws that regulate each major party's activities, but these laws also protect the parties from competition. For example, state election laws ensure the place of both major parties on the ballot and make it difficult for third parties to gain ballot access. Many states require that potential independent or third-party candidates gather a large number of signatures before their names can be placed on the ballot. Another common state law requires a third party to have earned some minimum percentage of the votes in the previous election in order to conduct a primary to select its candidates.

As campaigns have become more dependent on money and television, both major parties have sought to limit third-party candidates' access to these vital resources, although social media has helped to erase some of the practical limitations. Thanks to 1974 campaign reforms, federal election laws now dictate the amount of campaign contributions that presidential candidates can receive from individuals and political action committees. These laws also provide dollar-for-dollar federal matching money for both major parties' nominees, if they agree to limit their spending to a predetermined amount. Third-party candidates cannot claim federal campaign funds until after the election is over, however, and even then their funds are limited by the percentage of past and current votes they received. In practice, they need to have gained about 5 percent or more of the national vote to be eligible for federal funds.[29] In 1992 billionaire Ross Perot funded his presidential campaign out of his own fortune, refusing the limits set by federal law and making himself ineligible to receive matching funds. This gesture, which few third-party candidates can afford to make, enabled him to receive a large enough percentage of the votes that he qualified for federal campaign funds in the 1996 election, when he did limit his spending. In addition, his party, the Reform Party, was eligible to receive such funds in 2000.

Just because the Democrats and the Republicans have dominated our party system does not mean that they have gone unchallenged. Over the years, numerous third parties have tried to alter the partisan makeup of American politics. These parties have usually arisen either to address specific issues that the major parties failed to address, like Prohibition in 1869 or the environment in 1972, or to promote ideas that were not part of the ideological spectrum covered by the existing parties, like socialist parties or the Libertarian Party. In general, third parties have sprung up from the grassroots or have broken off from an existing party (the latter are referred to as splinter parties). In the case of the current Tea Party movement, the new party is not actually distinct from the Republican Party (most Tea Party members identify as conservative Republicans), and as long as the Republican Party adopts most of the issues the Tea Partiers care about, they are not likely to separate and form an organized party of their own. In many cases third parties have been headed by a strong leader who carried much of the burden of the party's success on his or her shoulders. Teddy Roosevelt's Bull Moose Party (1912) and Ross Perot's Reform Party (1992) are prime examples.

Although no third-party candidate has ever won the presidency, by no means is the impact of third parties on presidential elections negligible. For example, if Ralph Nader had not run as a third-party candidate in 2000, Al Gore probably would have won the Electoral College vote as well as the popular vote. The 2016 election was so close it is entirely likely that third-party candidacies by Gary Johnson and Jill Stein had an impact at the margin, contributing to Hillary Clinton's Electoral College loss. When a third-party candidate changes the results of an election in such a way, he or she is said to have played the role of a spoiler.

INCREASING IDEOLOGICAL POLARIZATION Compared to many other party systems—for instance, India, the global leader in political parties, which in 2015 had at least 1,866 registered partisan groups—the United States has traditionally had a rather limited menu of viable parties: the moderately liberal Democratic Party versus a moderately conservative Republican Party. Both parties continue to agree on the fundamental features of American politics—including the Bill of Rights, the Constitution, and a capitalist free-enterprise system—but the policy differences between the parties have grown. Rather than the 1950s characterization of the parties as "Tweedledum and Tweedledee," today there stands, as we saw in Chapter 2, an ideological gulf between the parties on a host of central issues of the economy, the distribution of the nation's resources, and the role of government in our private lives. As much as ever in our history, the Democratic Party holds that government policy should actively promote the welfare of the middle class and the poor, largely by extending the enlarged role of the state that defined the New Deal. Today's Republicans, in contrast, want to greatly reduce the role of government in the market and let individual initiative and the workings of unfettered capitalism settle questions of resource allocation while giving the states a stronger role in legislating conformance to "traditional family values." The result is a country that has consensus on the fundamentals of government structure but with parties that are divided sharply over the role of government in the economy and our lives.

DECENTRALIZED PARTY ORGANIZATIONS   In American political parties, local and state party organizations make their own decisions. They have affiliations to the national party organization but no obligation to obey its dictates other than selecting delegates to the national convention. Decision making is dispersed across the organization rather than centralized at the national level; power tends to move from the bottom up instead of from the top down. This means that local concerns and politics dominate the lower levels of the party, molding its structure, politics, and policy agendas.

Several major divisions characterize the organization of American parties. Each party has a national committee, the Republican National Committee (RNC) and the Democratic National Committee (DNC), whose members come from every state. These committees run the party business between conventions and expend enormous sums of money to get their candidates elected to office at every level. The congressional campaign committees are formed by both parties for the sole purpose of raising and distributing campaign funds for party candidates in the House and the Senate. At the more localized level, state party committees generally focus their efforts on statewide races and, to a lesser extent, state legislative contests, whereas local party organizations come together when an election approaches but are not permanently organized.

There are several reasons for the decentralized structure of American parties. One reason is that the federal electoral system makes it difficult for any national coordinating body to exercise control. Federalism also leads to decentralized parties because state laws have historically dictated the organizational structures and procedures of the state and local parties. In addition, U.S. parties lack strong organizational tools to exercise centralized control of candidates for office. In most cases, each party's candidates are chosen in direct primaries. Direct primaries, in which local party voters rather than party leaders control the nomination process, make strong centralized control an almost impossible task. When former Ku Klux Klan member David Duke ran as a Republican for governor of Louisiana in 1991 and for the state's senator in 2016, Republican leaders were outraged but powerless to stop him (he lost both elections).

CHANGES IN PARTY DISCIPLINE OVER TIME   Not only are American party organizations notable for their lack of a hierarchical (top-down) power structure, but the officials who have been elected to government from the two parties do not necessarily take their orders from the top. Party leaders have often had trouble getting their members to follow the party line, a necessary component of the responsible party model. Beginning in the 1980s, however, and perhaps best illustrated by Newt Gingrich's House Speakership (1994–1998), party discipline began to play a much stronger role in legislative politics. Gingrich made party loyalty a condition for leadership positions in committees and for his support, a pattern that continued under Speaker Dennis Hastert, R-Ill. Democrats have had more trouble holding their members to a party line, but as their frustration with President George W. Bush grew, they were more likely to vote as a block to try to stop his policies. From 2006 to 2010, Democrat Nancy Pelosi, the first woman Speaker of the House, led the Democrats with a firm and expert hand, gaining the reputation among some as "one of the most powerful Speakers in modern history."[30] Pelosi's ability to lead the House Democrats and to pass President Obama's program was made possible by the increased ideological homogeneity within the Democratic Party, which is an important aspect of the polarized political parties of the contemporary era.[31] The Republican victories in 2010 made John Boehner, R-Ohio, the new Speaker of the House. His freshman class was largely supported by the Tea Party movement (now known as the Freedom Caucus), and their energy and unbending commitment to conservative principles repeatedly made it difficult for Boehner to reach compromises with his Democratic colleagues or the Obama administration, frequently causing him to back off of positions he had taken to keep his party base happy.[32] He finally quit in frustration in 2015 and was replaced by Paul Ryan, R-Wisc., who was more trusted by the party base, but who quit amid his own frustrations in 2018.

In Your Own Words   Outline the evolution of the party system in the United States.

THE ROLES, FORMATION, AND TYPES OF INTEREST GROUPS

Organizing around common political goals to influence policy from outside the apparatus of government

Americans have long been addicted not only to political parties but also to membership in other groups. As the French observer Alexis de Tocqueville noted when he traveled in America in the early 1830s, "Americans of all ages, all conditions, and all dispositions, constantly form associations. They have not only commercial and manufacturing companies, in which all take part, but associations of a thousand other kinds—religious, moral, serious, futile, general or restricted, enormous or diminutive."[33]

This tendency of Americans to form groups disturbed James Madison, who worried about the power of factions, or citizens united by some interest or passion that might be opposed to the common good. Most political scientists, however, have a different take on factions, which they call by the more neutral term *interest groups*. An **interest group** is an organization of individuals who share a common political goal and unite for the purpose of influencing public policy decisions.[34] We saw in Chapter 1 that interest groups play a central role in the pluralist theory of democracy, which argues that democracy is enhanced when citizens' interests are represented through group membership. Group interaction becomes a central mechanism in who gets what in American politics. It ensures that members' interests are represented, but also that no group can become too powerful.

ROLES OF INTEREST GROUPS

Negative images of interest groups abound in American politics and the media. Republicans speak of the Democrats as "pandering" to special interest groups like labor unions and trial lawyers, hoping to give the impression that the Democrats give special treatment to some groups at the expense of the public good. In turn, Democrats claim that the Republican Party has been captured by big business or the religious right, again suggesting that they do not have the national interest at heart but rather the specialized interests of small segments of society. In truth, interest groups have become an integral part of American politics, and neither party

interest group an organization of individuals who share a common political goal and unite for the purpose of influencing government decisions can afford to ignore them. They play six important roles in American politics, enhancing citizens' ability to use the system to achieve the stakes they value:[35]

- *Representation.* Interest groups help represent their members' views to Congress, the executive branch, and administrative agencies. Representation in this case is not geographic, as it is in Congress, but rather is based on common interests. Whether an interest group represents teachers, manufacturers of baby food, people concerned with the environment, or the elderly, it ensures that its members' concerns are adequately heard in the policymaking process. The activity of persuading policymakers to support an interest group's positions is called lobbying.
- *Participation.* Interest groups provide an avenue for citizen participation in politics that goes beyond voting in periodic elections. They are a mechanism for people sharing the same interests or pursuing the same policy goals to pool their resources and channel their efforts for collective action. Whereas individual political action might seem futile, participation in a group can be much more effective.
- *Education.* One of the more important functions of interest groups is to educate policymakers regarding issues that are important to the groups.
- *Agenda building.* Interest groups alert the proper government authorities about their issues, get the issues on the political agenda, and make those issues a high priority for action.
- *Provision of program alternatives.* Interest groups can be effective in supplying alternative suggestions for how issues should be dealt with once they have been put on the agenda. From this mix of proposals, political actors choose a solution.[36]
- *Program monitoring.* Once laws are enacted, interest groups keep tabs on their consequences, informing Congress and the regulatory agencies about the effects, both expected and unexpected, of federal policy.

WHY DO INTEREST GROUPS FORM?

Many of us can imagine public problems that we think need to be addressed. But despite our reputation as a nation of joiners, most of us never act, never organize a group, and never even join one. What makes the potential members of an interest group come together in the first place? Several conditions make organization easier. It helps if the potential members share a perception of a problem that needs to be solved or a threat to their interests that needs to be addressed. It also helps if the members have the resources—time, money, and leadership—to organize.

Even though external threats, financial resources, and effective leadership can all spur interest group formation, these factors are usually not enough to overcome what political scientists call the *problem of collective action.* Another name for this is the free rider problem: Why should people join a group to solve a problem when they can free ride—that is, reap the benefits of the group's actions—whether they join or not?[37] The free rider problem affects interest groups because most of the policies that these groups advocate involve the distribution of a collective good. A collective good is a good or benefit that, once provided, cannot be denied to others. Public safety, clean air, peace, and lower consumer prices are all examples of collective goods that can be enjoyed by anyone. When collective goods are involved, it is difficult to persuade people to join groups, because they are going to reap the benefits anyway. The larger the number of potential members involved, the more this holds true, because each member will have trouble seeing that his or her efforts will make a difference.

lobbying interest group activities aimed at persuading policymakers to support the group's positions

free rider problem the difficulty groups face in recruiting when potential members can gain the benefits of the group's actions whether they join or not

collective good a good or service that, by its very nature, cannot be denied to anyone who wants to consume it

Many groups overcome the free rider problem by supplying **selective incentives**—benefits available to their members that are not available to the general population. They might include **material benefits**, tangible rewards that members can use. One of the most common material benefits is information. For example, many groups publish a magazine or newsletter packed with information about issues important to the group and pending legislation relevant to the group's activities. **Solidary benefits**, which come from interaction and bonding among group members, are another type of selective incentive. For many individuals, politics is an enjoyable activity, and the social interactions occurring through group activities provide high levels of satisfaction and are a strong motivating force. Finally, **expressive benefits** are those rewards that come from doing something that you believe in strongly—essentially from the expression of your values and interests.

Group leaders often use a mixture of incentives to recruit and sustain members. Thus the National Rifle Association (NRA) recruits many of its members because they are committed to protecting an individual's right to bear arms. The NRA reinforces this expressive incentive with material incentives, such as its magazine, and solidary incentives resulting from group fellowship. The combination of all these incentives helps make the NRA one of the strongest interest groups in Washington.

TYPES OF INTEREST GROUPS

There are potentially as many interest groups in the United States as there are interests, which is to say the possibilities are endless. Therefore, it is helpful to divide these groups into different types, based on the kind of benefit they seek for their members. Here we distinguish among economic, equal opportunity, public, and government (both foreign and domestic) interest groups. Depending on the definitions they use, scholars have come up with different schemes for classifying interest groups, so don't be surprised if you come across these groups under other labels.

Economic interest groups seek to influence government for the economic benefit of their members. Generally these groups are players in the productive and professional activities of the nation. The economic benefits they seek may be higher wages, lower tax rates, bigger government subsidies, or more favorable regulations, for example. What all economic interest groups have in common is that they focus primarily on pocketbook issues. Such groups include corporations and business associations, unions and professional associations, and agricultural interest groups. Increasingly in the post–*Citizens United* world, rich individuals are also spending politically—either on behalf of the industries that made them rich or for pet causes they have come to support.

Equal opportunity interest groups organize to promote the civil rights of people who believe that their interests are not being adequately represented and protected in national politics through traditional means. These groups also advocate for their members because, in many cases, they are economically disadvantaged or are at risk of becoming so. Equal opportunity groups believe that they are underrepresented not because of *what they do* but because of *who they are*. They may be the victims of discrimination or see themselves as threatened. These groups organize on the basis of age, race, ethnic group, gender, and sexual orientation. Membership is not limited to people who are part of the demographic group, because many people believe that promoting the interests and rights of various groups in society is in the broader interest of all. For this reason, some scholars classify these groups as public interest groups. Because these are often groups who feel that they

selective incentives benefits that are available only to group members as an inducement to get them to join

material benefits selective incentives in the form of tangible rewards

solidary benefits selective incentives related to the interaction and bonding among group members

expressive benefits selective incentives that derive from the opportunity to express values and beliefs and to be committed to a greater cause

economic interest groups groups that organize to influence government policy for the economic benefit of their members

equal opportunity interest groups groups that organize to promote the civil and economic rights of underrepresented or disadvantaged groups have been marginalized by and excluded from the system, they may seek to influence policy by going around traditional channels and using less conventional means like protests, sit-ins, and demonstrations. Black Lives Matter marches, demonstrations in support of young undocumented immigrants who were brought to the country as children, the Women's Marches and the #MeToo social media protest, as well as the marches organized by young people who do not feel safe at school because of gun violence have become powerful social movements that policymakers pay close attention to because they energize so many voters.

A **public interest group** tries to influence government to produce noneconomic benefits that cannot be restricted to the interest group's members or denied to any member of the general public. The benefits of clean air, for instance, are available to all, not just the members of the environmental group that fights for them. In a way, all interest group benefits are collective goods that all members of the group can enjoy, but public interest groups seek collective goods that are open to all members of society or, in some cases, everyone in the world.

Activism for Animals
People for the Ethical Treatment of Animals (PETA) promotes animal welfare and a vegan lifestyle, often with attention-grabbing stunts, including locking activists in cages outside a fur coat store in Philadelphia.

Public interest group members are usually motivated by a view of the world that they think everyone would be better off to adopt. They believe that the benefit they seek is good for everyone, even if individuals outside their groups disagree or even reject the benefit. Although few people would dispute the value of clean air, peace, and the protection of human rights internationally, there is no such consensus about protecting the right to an abortion, the right to carry a concealed weapon, or the right to smoke marijuana. Yet public interest groups are involved in procuring and enforcing these rights for all Americans.

Because public interest groups are involved in the production of collective goods for very large populations and the incentive to contribute on an individual basis may be particularly difficult to perceive, these groups are especially vulnerable to the free rider problem. That has not stopped them from organizing, however. There are more than twenty-five hundred public interest groups in the United States today.[38] People are drawn to a particular group because they support its values and goals; that is, expressive benefits are the primary membership draw. Although many members are attracted initially by expressive benefits, public interest groups seek to keep them active by offering material benefits and services, ranging from a free subscription to the group's magazine to discount insurance packages. Public interest groups include environmental groups, consumer groups, religious groups, Second Amendment groups, reproductive rights groups, and human rights groups.

Government interest groups—representing both foreign and domestic governments—also lobby Congress and the president. Typically some lobbyists' most lucrative contracts come from foreign governments seeking to influence foreign trade policies. In recent years, ethics rules have been initiated to prevent former government officials from working as foreign government lobbyists as soon as they leave office, but lobbying firms continue to hire them when they can because of their contacts and expertise.[39]

public interest groups groups that organize to influence government to produce collective goods or services that benefit the general public

government interest groups groups that organize to represent foreign or domestic governments, and to lobby Congress and the president on their behalf

Domestic governments have become increasingly involved in the business of influencing federal policy. With the growing complexities of American federalism, state and local governments have an enormous stake in what the federal government does and often try to gain resources, limit the impact of policy, and otherwise alter the effects of federal law. All fifty states have government relations offices in Washington to attempt to influence federal policy directly.[40]

Donald Trump's presidency has presented new challenges to government lobbying laws since he continues to be interested in advancing his wide business interests, many of which require the cooperation of foreign governments. As the many scandals haunting members of his family business and his administration make clear, foreign governments found the Trumps to be attractive and potentially lucrative lobbying targets.[41]

In Your Own Words Identify four types of interest groups and the kinds of interests they represent.

INTEREST GROUP POLITICS

Different strategies for influencing different branches of government

The term *lobbying* comes from seventeenth-century England, where representatives of special interests would meet members of the English House of Commons in the large anteroom, or lobby, outside the House floor to plead their cases.[42] Contemporary lobbying reaches far beyond the lobby of the House or the Senate, however. Interest groups contact lawmakers directly, but they no longer confine their efforts to chance meetings in the legislative lobby—or to members of the legislature. Today they target all branches of government, and the American people as well. The ranks of those who work with lobbyists also have swelled. Beginning in the 1980s, interest groups, especially those representing corporate interests, have been turning to a diverse group of political consultants, including professional Washington lobbyists, campaign specialists, advertising and media experts, pollsters, and academics. Lobbying today is a big business in its own right, creating narratives to persuade the public, weaponizing social media, and backing candidates whose narratives fit with their own.

There are two main types of lobbying strategy: **direct lobbying** (sometimes called "inside lobbying"), or interaction with actual decision makers within government institutions, and **indirect lobbying** (also called "outside lobbying"), or attempts to influence public opinion and mobilize interest group members or the general public to contact their elected representatives on an issue. Some groups have resorted to more confrontational indirect methods, using political protests (often developing into full-blown social movements) to make their demands heard by policymakers. Recently, corporations and other more traditional interest groups have been combining tactics—joining conventional lobbying methods with the use of email, computerized databases, talk radio, and twenty-four-hour cable TV—to bring unprecedented pressure to bear on the voting public to influence members of government.

direct lobbying direct interaction with public officials for the purpose of influencing policy decisions

indirect lobbying attempts to influence government policymakers by encouraging the general public to put pressure on them

DIRECT LOBBYING

Direct lobbying involves face-to-face interaction between lobbyists and members of government. We tend to think of Congress as the typical recipient of lobbying efforts, but the president, the bureaucracy, and even the courts are also the focus of efforts to influence policy.

LOBBYING CONGRESS When interest groups lobby Congress, they rarely concentrate on all 435 members of the House or all 100 members of the Senate. Rather, lobbyists focus their efforts on congressional committees, because that is where most bills are written and revised. Because the committee leadership is relatively stable from one Congress to the next (unless a different party wins a majority), lobbyists can develop long-term relationships with committee members and their staffs. These personal contacts, which might take place at meetings, banquets, parties, or lunches, or simply in casual meetings in the hallways of Congress, are important because they represent a major means through which interest groups provide information to members of Congress. This is the most common and most effective form of lobbying strategy.

Much of modern-day lobbying also involves the use of "hired guns," or professional lobbyists, many of them former government officials, put on retainer by a client to lobby for that client's interests. Rotating into lobbying jobs from elected or other government positions is known as passing through the revolving door, a concept we encounter again in Chapter 13. It refers to public officials who leave their posts to become interest group representatives (or media figures), parlaying the special knowledge and contacts they gathered in government into lucrative salaries in the private sector. Revolving-door activity is subject to occasional attempts at regulation and frequent ethical debate, because it raises questions about whether people should be able to convert public service into private profit, and whether such an incentive draws people into public office for motives other than serving the public interest.

President Obama felt so strongly that the revolving door was a breach of the public trust that early in his administration he signed an executive order prohibiting presidential appointees from working as lobbyists for two years after leaving their posts and from returning to lobby the executive branch during his time in office.[43] In support of his oft-repeated intention to "drain the swamp," Donald Trump signed an executive order requiring administration appointees to pledge not to lobby the agencies for which they worked for five years. Nonetheless, one investigation found that of the nearly two hundred people who left his administration in his first year and a half in office, several had gone on to lobbying jobs by obtaining waivers allowing them to do so, by working part time so that they didn't have to register as lobbyists, or, in one case, by refusing to sign the pledge at all.[44] On the flip side of the revolving door, ProPublica, a nonprofit public watchdog, found that 187 members of the Trump administration had previously tried to influence the agencies they were now hired to lead.[45]

Interest groups also lobby congressional decision makers by providing testimony and expertise, and sometimes they even draft legislation on the many issues on which policymakers cannot take the time to become expert.[46] Information is one of the most important resources lobbyists can bring to their effort to influence Congress.

Giving money to candidates is another lobbying technique that helps interest groups gain access and a friendly ear (see Figure 11.3). The 1974 Federal Election Campaign Act, passed in an effort to curb campaign spending abuses, sought to regulate the amount of money an interest group can give to candidates for federal office by providing for political action committees (PACs), which serve as fundraisers for interest groups. There are strict limitations on how much money PACs can donate to a candidate, but a number of loopholes allow them to get around some of the restrictions. These loopholes have been enhanced since 2010, when the Supreme Court's ruling in *Citizens United v. Federal Election Commission* essentially removed any limits on political expenditures by corporations and unions.

revolving door the tendency of public officials, journalists, and lobbyists to move between public- and private-sector (media, lobbying) jobs

political action committee (PAC) the fundraising arm of an interest group

FIGURE 11.3
Contributions to Political Parties, by Economic Sector, 2013–2016

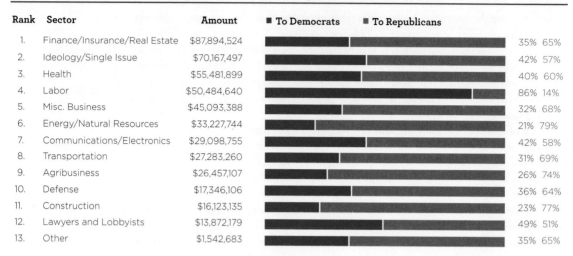

Rank	Sector	Amount	To Democrats	To Republicans
1.	Finance/Insurance/Real Estate	$87,894,524	35%	65%
2.	Ideology/Single Issue	$70,167,497	42%	57%
3.	Health	$55,481,899	40%	60%
4.	Labor	$50,484,640	86%	14%
5.	Misc. Business	$45,093,388	32%	68%
6.	Energy/Natural Resources	$33,227,744	21%	79%
7.	Communications/Electronics	$29,098,755	42%	58%
8.	Transportation	$27,283,260	31%	69%
9.	Agribusiness	$26,457,107	26%	74%
10.	Defense	$17,346,106	36%	64%
11.	Construction	$16,123,135	23%	77%
12.	Lawyers and Lobbyists	$13,872,179	49%	51%
13.	Other	$1,542,683	35%	65%

Which economic sectors are financing our elected officials? This figure shows how much different sectors of the economy are contributing to which political parties. Although contributions do not necessarily guarantee politicians' votes or support, they certainly let politicians know what issues their political friends are concerned about. Notice that the finance/insurance/real estate sector outspends any other group by a wide margin. What is this likely to mean when issues of financial reform or consumer protection legislation are considered?

Source: Center for Responsive Politics, "PACs by Industry," www.opensecrets.org/pacs/list.php.

Interest groups also attempt to bolster their lobbying efforts by forming coalitions with other interest groups. These coalitions tend to be based on single issues, and building such coalitions has become an important strategy in lobbying Congress.

Many attempts have been made to regulate the tight relationships between lobbyists and lawmakers. The difficulty, of course, is that lawmakers benefit from their relationships with lobbyists in many ways and are not enthusiastic about curtailing their opportunities to get money and support. In 1995 Congress completed its first attempt in half a century to regulate lobbying when it passed the Lobbying Disclosure Act. The act requires lobbyists to report how much they are paid, by whom, and what issues they are promoting.[47] Also in 1995, both the Senate and the House passed separate resolutions addressing gifts and travel opportunities given by interest groups to senators and representatives.[48]

These reforms have not closed the door on lavish spending by lobbyists, although initially the rule changes cast a definite chill on lobbyists' activities.[49] As lobbyists and members of Congress have learned where they can bend the rules, however, relations between them have returned to a more familiar footing. The 2005 scandals involving lobbyist Jack Abramoff touched a number of Congress members, including the powerful Republican Tom DeLay, showing that the potential for corrupt relationships between lawmakers and lobbyists is as great as ever. Partly in reaction, in September 2007, after the Democrats took back the majority in the House and the Senate in 2006, Congress passed and President Bush signed the Honest Leadership and Open Government Act, which tightened travel and gift restrictions.[50] The combination of the 2007 reform and President Obama's limitations on lobbyists' access to the White House led to a significant drop in lobbying. The number of registered lobbyists dropped from 14,840 to 12,340 between 2007 and 2013.[51] Nevertheless, lobbying groups scrambled to find new ways to provide travel for lawmakers they wanted to influence, and ways to make free meals acceptable.[52]

LOBBYING THE PRESIDENT, THE BUREAUCRACY, AND THE COURTS

Lobbyists also target the president and the White House staff to try to influence policy. As with Congress, personal contacts within the White House are extremely important, and the higher up, the better. The official contact point between the White

House and interest groups is the Office of Public Engagement. The basic purpose of this office is to foster good relations between the White House and interest groups in order to mobilize these groups to support the administration's policies.

In the case of the Trump White House, lobbying is slightly different because the president has retained his private business interests. It is relatively easy for groups seeking to gain access to the president to do so by staying at one of his many properties, especially Mar-a-Lago, where he himself spends so much of his time. Public Citizen, a public watchdog group, found that in the president's first year in office, sixty-four industry groups, corporations, foreign governments, and political groups and candidates spent money at Trump properties.[53] It is probably impossible to trace any explicit quid pro quo arrangements without seeing more financial records, but one of the reasons presidents have historically divested themselves of their financial interests or put them into blind trusts is to avoid any appearance of conflict of interest.

Whereas opportunities for lobbying the president are normally somewhat limited, opportunities for lobbying the rest of the executive branch abound. Interest groups know that winning the legislative battle is only the first step. The second, and sometimes more important, battle takes place in the bureaucracy, where Congress has delegated rule-making authority to federal agencies that implement the law.[54]

Interest groups often try to gain an advantage by developing strong relations with regulating agencies. Because many of the experts on a topic are employed by the interests being regulated, it is not unusual to find lobbyists being hired by government agencies, or vice versa, in an extension of the revolving-door situation we discussed earlier. The close relationships that exist between the regulated and the regulators, along with the close relationships between lobbyists and congressional staffs, lead to the creation of iron triangles (see Chapter 8).

Interest groups try to influence government policy by challenging the legality of laws or administrative regulations in the courts. These legal tactics have been used by groups like the National Association for the Advancement of Colored People (antidiscrimination cases); the American Civil Liberties Union (freedom of speech, freedom of religion, and civil liberties cases); the Sierra Club (environmental enforcement); and Common Cause (ethics in government). Sometimes groups bring cases directly, and sometimes they file amicus curiae ("friend of the court") briefs asking the courts to rule in ways favoring their positions.

INDIRECT LOBBYING

One of the most powerful and fastest-growing kinds of lobbying is indirect lobbying, in which lobbyists use public opinion to put pressure on politicians to do what the lobbyists want.[55] Interest groups use the public to lobby and influence government decision makers in a variety of ways. In a mediated world, the possibilities for informing and activating citizens have exploded.

Many interest group leaders are sure that people will rally to their side once they know the "truth" about their causes, and so they set out to educate the public. They conduct extensive research to make their cases and court the media and hire public relations firms to get their ideas across.[56] An increasingly popular way for interest groups to promote their message has been by using **issue advocacy ads**, which encourage constituents to support or oppose a certain policy or candidate without directly telling them how to vote. Such ads skirted campaign finance law that limited the money groups could spend to advocate for candidates directly, but since the 2010 Supreme Court case *Citizens United*, groups can raise funds and spend freely to support their favored candidates.

Groups can also get information to the public through the skillful use of the Internet, whether through carefully designed advocacy web sites and blogs, through social networks, or through web-based videos, creating messages that go "viral," spreading quickly by email and hitting targeted audiences. Internet-savvy interest groups are increasingly turning to YouTube for a cheap and efficient way to get their message out. Lobbyists have used YouTube on behalf of such diverse interests as The Science Coalition, a group of research universities; Concerned Families for ATV Safety; and the Competitive Enterprise Institute, which lobbies against U.S. government energy standards.[57]

The point of disseminating information, hiring public relations firms, and running issue advocacy ads is to motivate the public to lobby politicians themselves. As you might expect, groups like AARP, the Christian Coalition, and the NRA, which are blessed with large memberships, have an advantage because they can mobilize a large contingent of citizens from all over the country to lobby representatives, senators, and the president. Generally this mobilization involves encouraging members to write letters, send email messages or faxes, or make phone calls to legislators about a pending issue.

A discussion of interest group politics would not be complete without mention of the unconventional technique of social protest. Throughout our history, groups have turned to **social protest**—activities ranging from planned, orderly demonstrations to strikes and boycotts, to acts of civil disobedience—when other techniques have failed to bring attention to their causes. Like other grassroots lobbying techniques, the techniques of social protest provide a way for people, often those closed out from more traditional avenues of political action, to publicly disseminate a narrative expressing their disagreement with a government policy or action. Thus demonstrations and protests have frequently served an important function for those who have been excluded from the political process because of their minority, social, or economic status. While social protest may have the same objective as other types of indirect lobbying—that is, spreading the narrative, educating the public, and mobilizing the group's members—demonstrations and spontaneous protests also aim to draw in citizens who have not yet formed an opinion or to change the minds of those who have. Such actions may turn a political action into a mass movement, attracting formerly passive or uninterested observers to the cause. The media explosion of the modern age,

issue advocacy ads advertisements that support issues or candidates without telling constituents how to vote

social protest public activities designed to bring attention to political causes, usually generated by those without access to conventional means of expressing their views

especially the advent of the Internet, has given social protesters many more ways to find each other and organize. Social analysts also have observed that the Internet has facilitated the growth of groups like militias and white supremacist organizations that previously dwelled on the fringes of society.[58]

More recently, women engaged in social demonstrations against the Trump administration's policies toward women by marching the day after his inauguration and again one year later. The #MeToo movement, focused on holding men (or, more rarely, women) accountable for sexual harassment and sexual assault, spread through social media and resulted in the indictments or firings of such powerful men as Hollywood producer Harvey Weinstein, NBC anchor Matt Lauer, and PBS and CBS host Charlie Rose. These movements have energized women to become politically involved, running for office in numbers the United States has never seen. In 2018, following the shootings at Marjory Stoneman Douglas High School, students organized walkouts from schools and a day of national protest against the ease with which military-style assault weapons could be obtained. As we saw in Chapter 1, organized under the hashtag #NeverAgain, thousands of people marched to bring awareness to the problem of the easy accessibility of assault-style weapons. The March for Our Lives students spent the summer crossing the country, registering young people to vote and creating a social movement that is becoming part of the American political environment. Although it isn't possible to gauge the impact they had on the 2018 election turnout, young voters turned out at a rate that was usually high for a midterm election, which many often skip.

"ASTROTURF" POLITICAL CAMPAIGNS: DEMOCRATIC OR ELITE DRIVEN?

The indirect lobbying we just discussed is often called **grassroots lobbying**, meaning that it addresses people in their roles as ordinary citizens. It is the wielding of power from the bottom (roots) up, rather than from the top down. Most of what we refer to as grassroots lobbying, however, does not spring spontaneously from the people but is orchestrated by elites, leading some people to call it **astroturf lobbying**—indicating that it is not genuine.

Often the line between real grassroots and astroturf lobbying is blurred, however. A movement may be partly spontaneous but partly orchestrated. MoveOn is an example of a group that started out as a spontaneous expression of the popular will to lobby Congress against the impeachment of President Bill Clinton but that spread by "word of mouse" over the Internet. Similarly, the current Tea Party movement has been, in part, the project of Dick Armey, a former Republican House majority leader whose organization, FreedomWorks, promotes low taxes and small government. FreedomWorks and several other conservative groups, as well as prominent individuals including some commentators at Fox News, have lent their organizational expertise to the Tea Partiers but deny that they are orchestrating an astroturf movement.[59] Regardless of how it started out, the Tea Party movement has certainly acquired a life and mind, perhaps several minds, of its own.

At the astroturf extreme, there was nothing spontaneous at all about the pharmaceutical industry's 2003 efforts to oppose the importation of cheaper drugs from Canada. The Pharmaceutical Research and Manufacturers Association (PhRMA), the industry's lobbying group, spent over $4 million on tactics such as persuading seniors that their access to medicine would be limited if reimportation of these American-made drugs were allowed and convincing members of a Christian advocacy group that prescription drug importation

grassroots lobbying indirect lobbying efforts that spring from widespread public concern

astroturf lobbying indirect lobbying efforts that manipulate or create public sentiment, "astroturf" being artificial grassroots

Are there any lobbying techniques that should be off limits in a democracy?

might lead to easier access to the controversial morning-after pill.[60] Such a strategy is obviously an attempt to create an opinion that might not otherwise even exist, playing on popular fears about drug availability and sentiments about abortion in order to achieve corporate ends.

Corporate interests seeking to take advantage of astroturf techniques employ expensive armies of lobbyists, media experts, and political strategists to conduct polls; craft multimedia advertising campaigns; and get the message out to "the people" through cable and radio talk shows, the Internet, outbound call centers, or fax machines. One media consultant has predicted that direct lobbying will become less important as indirect lobbying increases in effectiveness and popularity.[61] Although indirect lobbying seems on its face to be more democratic, to the extent that it manipulates public opinion, it may in fact be less so. At the same time, to the extent that Americans can become more sophisticated mediated citizens, there are ever more tools for them to create their own narratives and to take on powerful interests, as the students from Parkland did with the NRA.

In Your Own Words   Describe how interest groups use lobbying and campaign activities to get the public policy they want.

INTEREST GROUP RESOURCES

Using money, leadership, membership, and information to make their voices heard

Interest group success depends in large part on the resources a group can bring to the project of influencing government. The pluralist defense of interest groups is that all citizens have the opportunity to organize, and thus all can exercise equal power. But all interest groups are not created equal. Some have more money, more effective leadership, more members, or better information than others, and these resources can translate into real power differences in the high-stakes world of American politics, and consequently into real winners and losers. In this section we examine the resources that interest groups can draw on—money, leadership, membership, and information—to get what they want from government.

MONEY

Interest groups need money to conduct the business of trying to influence government policymakers. Money can buy an interest group the ability to put together a well-trained staff, to hire outside professional assistance, and to make campaign contributions in the hopes of gaining access to government officials. Having money does not guarantee favorable policies, but not having money just about guarantees failure.

One of the reasons money is important is that it enables an interest group to hire a professional staff, usually an executive director, assistants, and other office support personnel. The main job of this professional staff is to take care of the group's day-to-day operations, including pursuing policy initiatives; recruiting and maintaining membership; providing membership services; and, of course, getting more money through direct mailings, telemarketing, and organizational functions. Money is important for creating an organizational infrastructure that can in turn be used to raise additional support and resources.

FIGURE 11.4

PAC Contributions to All Congressional Candidates, by Type of PAC and Candidate Party, 2015–2016

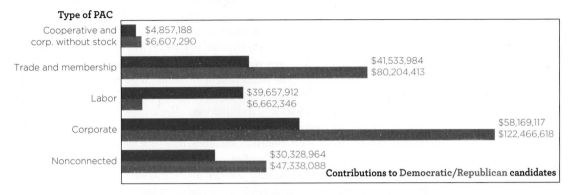

Type of PAC

Cooperative and corp. without stock: $4,857,188 / $6,607,290

Trade and membership: $41,533,984 / $80,204,413

Labor: $39,657,912 / $6,662,346

Corporate: $58,169,117 / $122,466,618

Nonconnected: $30,328,964 / $47,338,088

Contributions to Democratic/Republican **candidates**

Source: Federal Election Commission, "PAC Table 2: PAC Contributions to Candidates: January 1, 2015 through December 31, 2016," https://transition.fec.gov/press/summaries/2016/tables/pac/PAC2_2016_24m.pdf.

Money also enables the interest group to hire the services of professionals, such as a high-powered lobbying firm. Such firms have invested heavily to ensure that they have connections to members of Congress.[62] A well-endowed group also can hire a public relations firm to help shape public opinion on a particular policy.

Interest groups live by the axiom that to receive, one must give—and give a lot to important people. The maximum that any PAC can give to a congressional campaign is $5,000 for each separate election. While some PACs give millions to campaigns, most PACs give less than $50,000 to candidates for each election cycle, focusing their contributions on members of the committees responsible for drafting legislation important to their groups.[63] In the wake of the *Citizens United* decision, however, considerable money can be spent by groups on a candidate's behalf, and the groups don't have to disclose the donors' identities. It has become apparent that although the *Citizens United* decision made only small changes to campaign finance law, it had the psychological effect of giving a "green light" to those who wanted to spend lavishly on an election.[64] In 2016 the so-called Super PACs unleashed by *Citizens United* spent more than $1 billion, though it wasn't clear that all that money had a real impact on the outcome of the election, at least in the presidential and senate races.[65]

PAC spending is usually directed toward incumbents of both parties, with incumbents in the majority party, especially committee chairs, getting the greatest share. About 80 percent of PAC contributions go to incumbent members of Congress.[66] Although most PACs want to curry favor with incumbents of either party, some tend to channel their money to one party. For instance, business interests, the American Medical Association, pro-life groups, Christian groups, and the NRA tend to support Republican candidates; and labor groups, the Association of Trial Lawyers of America, the National Education Association, and environmental and pro-choice groups give primarily to Democrats.

The ability to make sizable and strategically placed campaign contributions buys an interest group access to government officials.[67] Access gives the interest group the ability to talk to a representative and members of his or her staff and to present information relevant to the policies they seek to initiate, change, or protect. Access is important because representatives have any number of competing interests vying for their time. Money is meant to oil the door hinge of a representative's office so that it swings open for the interest group. For instance, a $175,000 donation to the Republican National Committee over four years yielded a three-day private event between the donors and the Republican leadership of Congress.[68] The Clinton administration was known in its early years for allowing major donors to stay in the Lincoln bedroom of the White House. The access bought by campaign contributions is usually less blatant, but officials know who has supported their campaigns, and they are unlikely to forget it when interest groups come knocking at their doors.

The relationship between money and political influence is extremely controversial. Many critics argue that this money buys more than just access; they say it buys votes. The circumstantial evidence for this contention is strong. For instance, in the Senate deliberations on a public option in health care, which would have provided individuals with an alternative to private health care insurance, the thirty senators who supported the public option had received an average of $15,937 in contributions from the health care industry in the previous six years, compared to the $37,322 that was received, on average, by the seventy senators who opposed it.[69]

However, in the matter of vote buying, systematic studies of congressional voting patterns are mixed. These studies show that the influence of campaign contributions is strongest in committees, where most bills are drafted. Once a bill reaches the floor of the House or the Senate, though, there is no consistent link between campaign contributions and roll-call voting.[70] This

> **Does it distort democracy for interest groups to bring different resources to the political process?**

suggests that campaign contributions influence the process of creating and shaping legislation, and thus defining the policy alternatives. Nonetheless, the final outcome of a bill is determined by political circumstances that go beyond the campaign contributions of interest groups.

LEADERSHIP

Leadership is an intangible element in the success or failure of an interest group. The strong, effective leadership of what one scholar has called *interest group entrepreneurs* can help a group organize even if it lacks other resources.[71] Such a leader can keep a group going when it seems to lack support from other sources. Cesar Chavez's leadership of the United Farm Workers in the mid-1950s through the early 1990s is an excellent case in point.

MEMBERSHIP: SIZE AND INTENSITY

The size of any interest group is an important resource. For instance, with nearly 38 million members, AARP can mobilize thousands of people in an attempt to influence elected officials' decisions regarding issues like mandatory retirement, Social Security, and Medicare. In addition, if an interest group's members are spread throughout the country, as are AARP's, that group can exert its influence on almost every member of Congress.

The level of intensity that members exhibit in support of a group's causes also is critical. If a group's members are intensely dedicated to its causes, the group may be far stronger than its numbers would indicate. Members represent the lifeblood of an interest group because they generally fund its activities and they can be mobilized to write letters, send email messages, and engage in other forms of personal contact with legislators or administrative officials. For instance, even though a majority of Americans favor some form of gun control, they are outweighed in the political process by the intense feeling of the just over four million members who the NRA claims strongly oppose gun control.

INFORMATION AND COMMUNICATION

Information is one of the most powerful resources in an interest group's arsenal. Often the members of a group are the only sources of information on the potential or actual impact of a law or regulation. The long struggle to regulate tobacco is a case in point. While individuals witnessed their loved ones and friends suffering from lung disease, cancer, and heart problems, it took public health interest groups like the American Cancer Society, the Public Health Cancer Association, and the American Heart Association to conduct the studies, collect the data, and show the connection between these life-threatening illnesses and smoking. Of course, the tobacco industry and its interest group, the American Tobacco Institute, presented their own research to counter these claims. Not surprisingly, the tobacco industry's investigations showed "no causal relationship" between tobacco use and these illnesses.[72] Eventually the volume of information showing a strong relationship overwhelmed industry research suggesting otherwise. In 1998 the tobacco industry reached a settlement with states to pay millions of dollars for the treatment of tobacco-related illnesses.

But information that isn't circulated cannot be a powerful tool. In a mediated era like ours—when most of us experience politics, if not life itself, through channels we do not control—it is imperative for those wanting to lobby government effectively to master the use of those channels. For a group to build and disseminate a moving narrative, it has to know who its audience is and how that audience accesses and shares information. There are increasing generational effects at work—while older people remain glued to the local news or maybe a cable outlet like Fox News, younger people curate the information they get. Cracking the code and using all available media will increasingly be crucial to an interest group's success at getting what it wants.

In Your Own Words   Identify specific resources that interest groups bring to bear when attempting to influence public policy.

CITIZENSHIP AND POLITICAL GROUPS

Power in numbers

Defenders of pluralism believe that group formation helps give more power to more citizens, and we have seen that it certainly can enhance democratic life. Parties and interest groups offer channels for representation and participation, and they help to keep politicians accountable. Pluralists also believe that the system as a whole benefits from group politics. They argue that groups will compete with one another and ultimately must form coalitions to create a majority. In the process of forming coalitions, groups compromise on policy issues, leading to final policy outcomes that reflect the general will of the people, as opposed to the narrow interests of specific groups or individuals.[73] In this final section we examine the claims of critics who argue that the politics of groups

Paul Markow Photography

Wayne Pacelle was the CEO of the Humane Society of the United States, the nation's largest animal rights organization, and worked to expand the group's membership and influence Washington in behalf of creatures great and small. Each law enacted by Congress to protect animals, each state bill passed, each statewide ballot measure approved—he tallies them all.

Pacelle has felt that kind of enormous, compassionate connection to animals ever since he was two or three years old. He carried that empathy and awareness with him as he got older and he began to fit it into a broader context of what it meant to him to be a responsible citizen. "I'm broadly interested in making the world a better place," he says. "That's the bottom line. Public policy is just the means to achieve the end of a more fair, a more just society."

He may be an optimist, but he's a realist, too. "You'd be naive to think money doesn't have an impact," he says. "It does. It gains access, and it builds loyalty. But, ultimately, money is a means to an end."

On the positive side of lobbying

"There's a reason in Washington, D.C., that there are thousands of lobbyists and thousands of interest groups. They're not here for fun; it's not just a big party. They're here because it does make a difference, and participation can have a measurable impact on public policy... I mean when we're not on defense, we're on the offense. It's almost a very crusading sort of attitude. I don't like to infuse it with religious sorts of notions, but it's a powerful, ethical construct. And having enough imagination to see that things can be different. That we're not just locked into our present set of social relationships and circumstances, that we can aspire to do things better."

On keeping the republic

"No one's going to hand you a key to change everything, but if you're smart and if you're determined you can make a real difference in the world. I've seen it happen thousands and thousands of times. And anybody who tells me differently just isn't paying attention to what's going on. And don't count on somebody else to do it, you know, don't count on a group like the Humane Society of the United States to do it. When I go around and I talk to people I say, 'Listen, we can help.' And our staff of four hundred, we've got great experts and we do a lot of amazing stuff, but you make the difference. It's the collective action of people of conscience that really can have a meaningful impact on society. And again, the history is of people stepping up and calling themselves to action. And leadership and citizenship are such important values in this culture. And if not them, who?"

Source: Wayne Pacelle talked with Christine Barbour on March 10, 2005.

skews democracy—gives more power to some people than to others—and particularly discriminates against segments of society that tend to be underrepresented in the first place (the poor and the young, for instance).

We have seen in this chapter that a variety of factors—money, leadership, membership, and information—can make a group successful. But this raises a red flag for American democracy. In American political culture, we value political equality, which is to say the principle of one person, one vote. And as far as voting goes, this is how we practice democracy. Anyone who attempts to visit the polls twice on Election Day is turned away, no matter how rich that person is, how intensely she feels about the election, or how eloquently he begs for another vote. But policy is not made only at the ballot box. It is also made in the halls and hearing rooms of Congress, the conference rooms of the bureaucracy, corporate boardrooms, private offices, restaurants, and bars. In these places, parties and interest groups speak loudly, and since some groups are vastly more successful than others, they have the equivalent of extra votes in the policymaking process.

We are not terribly uncomfortable with the idea that interest groups with large memberships should have more power. After all, democracy is usually about counting numbers. But when it comes to the idea that the wealthy, those who feel intensely, or those who have more information have an advantage, we balk. What about the rest of us? Should we have relatively less power over who gets what because we lack these resources?

It is true that the major parties and interest groups with money have the distinct advantages of organization and access. Many critics suggest that business interests represent a small, wealthy, and united set of elites who dominate the political process,[74] and there is much evidence to support the view that business interests maintain a special relationship with government and tend to unite behind basic conservative issues (less government spending and lower taxes). Other evidence, however, suggests that business interests are often divided regarding government policies and that other factors, such as membership, can counterbalance their superior monetary resources. Corporate money may buy access, but politicians ultimately depend on votes. Groups with large memberships have more voters. When a group's membership is highly motivated and numerous, it can win despite the opposition's lavish resources.[75] Thus what helps to equalize the position of powerful groups in American politics is the willingness on the part of citizens to fight fire with fire, politics with politics, and organization with organization, an effort made more accessible with the widespread use of the Internet. It is, finally, the power of participation and democracy that can make pluralism fit the pluralists' hopes. For some groups, such as the poor, such advice may be nearly impossible to follow. Other groups left out of the system, such as the merely indifferent or young people who regard current issues as irrelevant, will pay the price of inattention and disorganization when the scorecards of interest group politics are finally tallied.

In Your Own Words Summarize the ways in which citizens interact with their government through membership in parties and interest groups.

Let's Revisit: What's at Stake . . . ?

We began this chapter by looking at the way two outside candidates had an outsized impact on the 2016 election results. Bernie Sanders helped weaken Hillary Clinton in ways she was unable to recover from, and Donald Trump decimated his primary field and ended up winning the presidency. That's a lot of power for people outside a party establishment to leverage—clearly both candidates spoke to something in the electorate that the establishment candidates missed. We asked what was at stake when outside candidates take on the establishment.

For the parties, the answer is clearly, a lot. That's why party machines thrived—they could keep an iron check on insurrection, and the establishment *was* the party. Democratic reforms of the party system helped rid the parties of corruption, made them more transparent and democratic, but also rendered them more fragile, more open to the influence of outside challengers. That's why, despite the fact that open primaries can help recruit new members, parties are cautious about them.

For the Democratic Party, the Sanders campaign opened up a schism that had long simmered beneath the surface but had been relatively quiet since the Bill Clinton years—a division between those who sought more radical economic transformation to overturn the existing power structure and those who were focused on more incremental change to expand rights and economic security. Those who take the former view argue that Democrats have forgotten their roots as supporters of the working class and have instead become a detached party of intellectual and entertainment elites. More moderate Democrats argue that the way to get things done is by working closer to the middle and trying to find compromise solutions that bring Americans together. Hidden in this split is a disagreement about whether economic transformation would bring with it racial and gender equality or whether those problems are systemic and must be addressed as such. On this point, too, Bernie Sanders and Hillary Clinton disagreed, with Clinton focusing much more on race and diversity, and perhaps further alienating the white working class who felt ignored by the party.

Those divisions in the Democratic Party, which have been quiet for several decades, are likely to be more explosive now that Sanders supporters are blaming Hillary Clinton for the loss of an election they think their candidate would have won. (Since no one seriously ran against Sanders, we can't know how that hypothetical match would have turned out.) But it is difficult to respond simultaneously to white working-class constituencies who feel some degree of racial grievance, and communities of color who have been one of the stalwart supporters of the party.

For the Republican Party, the stakes of the Trump election are mixed. On the one hand, they won! Republicans of all stripes are thrilled to be in charge of two branches of government, with the prospect of cementing their control over the third. On the other hand, few Republicans wanted Trump to be their nominee. They don't want the racial and gender baggage he brings with him. And they know that a long-term breach with Hispanics is bad for the party, given the changing national demographics. Their agenda is not Trump's agenda, and they can only hope that he doesn't care enough to challenge them on the policies they want to pass. However, Trump doesn't think he owes the party anything (and in most respects, he's right), so he probably feels little obligation to play nice if his will conflicts with theirs. Trump's electoral behavior would not indicate that playing nice is one of his strengths, and the party is likely to be the loser if conflict ensues.

At the same time, the Trump election is a distraction from the party's internal divisions that it's been struggling to resolve. The Republican Party houses both procedural economic conservatives and more substantive social conservatives, and their preferred policies are not the same. Some of the social conservatives are the white working class that chose Trump as the nominee and voted for his election— possibly some of the same people who supported Bernie Sanders, since we know that Hillary Clinton lost some white working-class support to Trump. Clearly those internal divisions are not harming the party's existence now, and if they hang on to state legislatures in 2020 and continue to gerrymander their way to a congressional majority, they may not in the future.

But the Republican Party is a party that has lost the popular vote in six of the last seven presidential elections. Only the vagaries of the Electoral College have given them the presidencies in two of those elections. If their goal is to build an enduring majority, they need to follow the advice of their 2012 "autopsy" report to be more inclusive, something a Trump presidency so far does not seem to have in the cards.

The stakes in outside infiltration of parties clearly vary by party. For voters, it can open up more choices. But for a system that depends on two strong parties to work, it carries risks of weakening the parties internally, or undermining their agendas altogether. Our history shows that the parties have survived worse threats, but we are certainly in challenging times today.

for CQ Press

Want a better grade?

Get the tools you need to sharpen your study skills. **SAGE edge** offers practice quizzes, eFlashcards, video, and multimedia at **edge.sagepub.com/barbourbrief8e.**

Review

Theories of pluralist democracy emphasize the importance of political groups, what Madison referred to as factions, in enhancing representation and helping people get what they want from the political system. Two key kinds of groups in American politics are political parties, which organize in order to seek control of government, and interest groups, whose goal is to influence government decisions.

What Are Political Parties?

Political parties (358) link voters and elected officials; overcome government fragmentation; and help provide, through the promotion of **partisanship** (359), a coherent ideological opposition to the party in power. Parties have three components. The official party structure, or **party organization** (359), gets people elected to office through the process of **electioneering** (359), which includes, among other steps, the formal **nominating conventions** (360). The officials, once elected, form the **party-in-government** (360), whose job includes **governing** (360). The **party-in-the-electorate** (361) encompasses all the people whose **party identification** (361) ties them to the party, including the most active and loyal members, who form the **party base** (362). These three components come together in the **responsible party model** (362)—an ideal model of how parties can provide an essential linkage in democratic politics.

The American Party System

The history of parties in the United States has evolved from an age of **party machines** (363), where **party bosses** (364) controlled candidates and officeholders, partly through the practice of **patronage** (364). Reforms, including the introduction of the **party**

primary (364), made the old machines obsolete by making the parties more democratic. Periods when one party has majority control of most elements of government are called **party eras** (364), signaled by a critical election and in existence until citizens switch their allegiance to another party through a political **realignment** (364). **Dealignment** (365) takes place if voters change their party ID to identify as independents instead. The parties stand for different ideologies and policies, as can be seen in their **party platforms** (369). The preferences of their bases, or **party activists** (371), and the influence of **hyperpartisanship** (368) and **negative partisanship** (372) make them more different, while the need to win moderate voters in national campaigns pushes them back to the middle.

The Roles, Formation, and Types of Interest Groups

Interest groups (376) can enhance democracy by increasing citizens' opportunities for representation and participation; by **lobbying** (377) and educating policymakers; and by assisting in building agendas, providing program alternatives, and monitoring programs. But many groups, especially when their goals involve the provision of **collective goods** (377) accessible to all, have difficulty getting members to join and contribute to their efforts because of the **free rider problem** (377). They try to combat this problem by offering **selective incentives** (378): **material** (378), **solidary** (378), or **expressive benefits** (378). Interest groups take several forms. Depending on the type of representation they are seeking to enhance and the kind of goals they pursue, they can be **economic interest groups** (378), **equal opportunity interest groups** (378), **public interest groups** (379), or **government interest groups** (379).

Interest Group Politics

Interest groups seek to influence policymakers through an activity called lobbying. Lobbyists, many of whom worked for the government at one time in a practice called the **revolving door** (381), may engage in **direct lobbying** (380), targeting Congress—through a variety of strategies including contributions to **political action committees** (381)—the president, the bureaucracy, and the Courts. **Indirect lobbying** (380) involves influencing the public to pressure lawmakers to do what the groups want. Techniques include the use of **issue advocacy ads** (384) and **social protest** (384). When such lobbying by the public is spontaneous, we call it **grassroots lobbying** (385). When it is manipulated by corporate or organized interests, it is called **astroturf lobbying** (385).

Interest Group Resources

Interest groups' success at getting what they want can depend on their access to resources—primarily money, leadership, members, and information.

12

Voting, Campaigns, and Elections

In Your Own Words

After you've read this chapter, you will be able to

12.1 Summarize the influences on who votes and who doesn't.

12.2 Describe factors that affect citizens' decisions on whether and how to vote.

12.3 Identify the organizational and strategic tactics employed in presidential campaigns.

12.4 Recognize the importance of elections for citizens.

What's at Stake . . . in the Electoral College?

Oh, the irony! The candidate who throughout the election accused the process of being rigged won in the end, not because he got more votes but because of an ancient and vestigial appendage of election law that distorted the popular vote results so that his losing margin was enough to deliver to him the presidency.

For Republicans who watched election results late into the night on November 8, 2016, it was a lightning bolt of good luck that managed to strike twice in twenty years, though it had happened only four times in our history. For Democrats it felt like the crazy, upending election of 2000 all over again, minus the Supreme Court and the recount. A candidate who had trailed in the national poll averages for the entire election cycle and who continued to trail in the popular vote was about to win the presidency of the United States. When all the votes were counted, Donald Trump was nearly three million popular votes behind Hillary Clinton. Yet he—not she—became president of the United States.

How does that happen? Stunned and tearful Democrats were in shock, feeling their votes hadn't counted, feeling disenfranchised. Crowds took to the streets in cities across the nation to protest the election results. Petitions circulated demanding that the people's vote be honored.

Jubilant Republicans thanked their lucky stars for an institution they often felt was rigged against them but that had managed to give them the presidency in three of the last seven elections, even though they had won the popular vote in only one of them.

The Democrats' demon and the Republicans' savior? The Electoral College.

The Electoral College is like the appendix of American politics. It's an organ you don't really need any more and that is generally so quiet and unobtrusive you don't even realize it's there. But when it gets inflamed, it's painful, and if it bursts, it threatens a systemwide failure.

The emergency caused by the Electoral College has so far not threatened the life of the republic, but it can pose a crisis of legitimacy. Twice in this very young century, Democratic winners of the popular vote had to give gracious concession speeches, respecting the procedures of American politics and the results they produced, even while they and their supporters felt robbed of a victory that seemed by every other rule of democracy to be theirs.

What is this evolutionary appendage that intervenes periodically to save the bacon of the party that lost the popular vote and throw the winning party into mourning? Where did it come from, and why doesn't some political surgeon just remove it before it causes more chaos?

The U.S. founders faced a dilemma about how the executive of the new republic should be chosen. Remember, in the days after Shays's Rebellion, they were filled with doubt about the wisdom that the people could be counted on to exercise. Direct popular election of the president felt too risky—they might pick a rabble-rousing demagogue like Daniel Shays, who wouldn't demonstrate the wisdom and stability that the founders valued. Besides, the South would object; since slaves were not citizens and couldn't vote, the North would always have a population advantage. But the alternative, giving Congress the ability to choose the executive like in a parliamentary system, meant doing away with their cherished principle of separation of powers. The Electoral College seemed to be one of those compromises that had worked so well for them throughout the constitution-writing process.

Electors would be chosen at the state level, originally by state legislators (who had been elected by the people) and eventually by the people themselves. The number of electors awarded to each state would be based on the total number of representatives that that state had in Congress (House plus Senate). This removed any objections the South would have since it had already been decided that slaves would count as three-fifths of a person for purposes of determining how many representatives a state received. Electors would cast votes for the presidency based on their independent judgment about who would be the better presidential candidate. In the 68th *Federalist Paper*, Alexander Hamilton wrote, "A small number of persons, selected by their fellow-citizens from the general mass, will be most likely to possess the information and discernment requisite to such complicated [tasks]."

And that is the ancient history of today's Electoral College. Since then our ideas about democracy have changed. We no longer see the people as the threat to stability that the founders worried about, and we have introduced more popular control into our political process. We amended the Constitution to directly elect senators, when once they too were chosen by state legislators, so that the entire Congress is directly elected by the people.

Even the Electoral College has evolved a bit. In the early 1800s, states figured they would have more leverage if, rather than voting independently, their electors all voted the same way. When they began to cast their votes for the popular vote winner in their state, the founders who felt this violated the check provided by independent electors were dismayed. Some very unorthodox election results ensued when states were using different methods of elector selection, including Andrew Jackson winning both the popular vote for president and the Electoral College in 1824 and *still* losing the presidency in the House of Representatives. By the late 1800s, all states were choosing their electors by popular vote.

Still, even with electors popularly chosen, the matter of how to distribute them remains, and that too is up to the states. Today all states but two give all their votes to the popular vote winner in their state. The other two, Maine and Nebraska, use a system based on congressional districts. In this chapter's *The Big Picture,* we show you how different state rules for distributing the votes could have resulted in different winners in the 2012 presidential election.

Ironically, the winner-take-all distribution of electoral votes generally exaggerates the advantage of the winner, turning even a slight popular vote lead into a landslide in the Electoral College. In the few cases like 2000 and 2016, however, it has a different, antidemocratic consequence. Since Hillary Clinton lost some crucial states, such as Wisconsin, Florida, and Pennsylvania, by a point or less, and won other, big states like California and New York by millions of votes, her popular vote number was enough to win easily, but she lost the Electoral College vote by a narrow margin in enough places to lose out on the presidency.

Coincidentally, back when Al Gore lost the Electoral College vote while winning the popular majority in 2000, the newly elected junior senator from New York, Hillary Clinton, said, "I believe strongly that in a democracy, we should respect the will of the people and to me that means it's time to do away with the Electoral College and move to the popular election of our president."[1] In fact, in 2012, Trump himself called the Electoral College "a disaster for a democracy."[2] There have been schemes for change that avoid the complicated and unlikely process of constitutional amendment, such as the National Popular Vote Interstate Compact that aims to create a contract among states controlling at least 270 electoral votes. Under the compact they would cast their votes for the popular vote winner. It has been enacted in twelve states controlling 172 electoral votes and is pending in several others (see www.nationalpopularvote.com). Yet, until enough states sign on, the Electoral College is still with us and still thwarting the popular will at awkward intervals.

So in this "enlightened democratic" day and age, the question is why? Why do we still have this archaic institution whose original purpose, like that of the human appendix, has long since been lost to history, but, like the appendix, still flares up occasionally in unexpected ways? For a voter who cast a ballot for a person who won more votes but lost the election, it can feel a bit like a democratic backfire. What is at stake in keeping the Electoral College after all this time? We will return to this question after we look more closely at how voting and elections work in American politics.

ALTHOUGH we pride ourselves on our democratic government, Americans seem to have a love-hate relationship with the idea of campaigns and voting. As a result, we engage in competing narratives about the worth of elections. On the one hand, many citizens believe that elections do not accomplish anything, that elected officials ignore the wishes of the people, and that government is rigged to benefit the elite at the expense of the many. There are exceptions, of course, but typically only about half of the eligible electorate votes.

On the other hand, however, when it is necessary to choose a leader or make a decision, whether picking the captain of a football team or deciding where to have dinner with a group of friends, the first instinct of many Americans is to look for a show of hands. Even though there are other ways to choose leaders—picking the oldest, the wisest, or the strongest; holding a lottery; or asking for volunteers—Americans almost always prefer an election. We elect over half a million public officials in America.[3] This means we have a lot of elections—more elections more often for more officials than in any other democracy.

In this chapter we examine the complicated place of elections in American politics and American culture. You will learn about Americans' ambivalence about the vote and the reasons why only about half of the citizenry even bother to exercise what is supposed to be a precious right; how voters go about making decisions and how this in turn influences the character of presidential elections; and the organizational and strategic aspects of running for the presidency.

EXERCISING THE RIGHT TO VOTE IN AMERICA

Easy for some; difficult or impossible for others

We argued in Chapter 10 that even without being well informed and following campaigns closely, Americans can still cast intelligent votes reflecting their best interests. But in a typical presidential election, barely half of the adult population votes and in off-year congressional elections, primaries, and many state and local elections, the rates of participation drop even lower. Some observers argue that that is just fine—ill-informed voters *should* stay home. The question of how easy we should make voting is one with important philosophical and partisan implications.

REGULATING THE ELECTORATE

One factor with a significant impact on whether people exercise their right to vote is the legal obstacle course they face. Voter turnout provides a dramatic illustration of our theme that rules make a difference in who wins and who loses in politics. Election rules define who can vote and how easy it will be for those legally eligible to vote to actually do so. In many countries the government takes responsibility for registering citizens to vote, and in some—Australia, Belgium, and Italy, for example—voting is required by law. As a result, turnout rates in these countries are high.[4] Traditionally the United States has had a set of rules that puts a brake on voting participation by making registration a burdensome activity and by making voting more difficult than it is in other places. Election rules act as a set of valves that make it easier or harder for people to vote, a process we call **regulating the electorate**.

HOW EASY SHOULD VOTING BE? A PARTISAN DIVIDE Even people who are deeply committed to democratic norms debate whether voting ought to be made so easy that uninformed voters go to the polls. For those who think voters should pass some minimum threshold of involvement in the system, the existence of some hurdles, in the form of registration laws and limited voting opportunities, helps to weed out those who really do not know much about the issues or the candidates they are voting for. Those who reject this idea say that everyone who is obligated under the law ought to have easy access to making that law, and that individuals might not know the nuances of public policy but they do know their own interests best. This is a philosophical debate that is unlikely to be solved any time soon.

Alongside this philosophical debate is an ongoing and recently intensified partisan battle about who should be encouraged to vote. At the heart of this debate (if not in its rhetoric) is not so much what is good for the democracy as a whole, as much as what is most beneficial to each political party. Substantial demographic differences are found in the primary supporters of the parties. In general, Republicans have been wealthier, whiter, and better educated; Democrats less wealthy, less educated, and much more diverse. In recent years, those with more education have swung to the Democratic Party, especially those with advanced degrees. Republicans are still more likely to vote, and restrictions on voting like voter ID laws, fewer voting hours, or longer registration periods are widely believed to have a greater impact on Democratic supporters. Thus, at least since the battle over the Voting Rights Act of 1965, there has been a consistent split between Democrats,

regulating the electorate the process of setting rules that define who can vote and how difficult or easy it will be to cast a ballot in an election

who tend to favor laws that make voting easier, since their voters are those most likely to be dissuaded by cumbersome regulations, and Republicans, who favor tighter rules, knowing that most of their voters will turn out anyway. This battle has intensified in recent years as the parties have become more polarized.

And so, the debate over how easy it should be to exercise one's right to vote, instead of being fought over philosophical grounds about the nature of democracy, has become a partisan power struggle. When Democrats were in charge of Congress in the 1990s, they attempted to address the problem at the federal level. In 1993, for instance, Congress passed the so-called **Motor Voter Act**, which requires the states to take a more active role in registering people to vote, including providing registration opportunities when people are applying for driver's licenses or at the welfare office. A number of states followed up with laws that allowed extended periods of early voting; same-day registration; and, in the case of Oregon, voting by mail. Each reform has marginally increased the numbers of people voting, but on the whole the results have been a disappointment to Democratic reformers. An exhaustive review of the research concluded that, even with obstacles to voting removed, "for many people, voting remains an activity from which there is virtually no gratification—instrumental, expressive, or otherwise."[5] Even though regulating the electorate makes little apparent difference to electoral outcomes, it has not gone away as a partisan issue.

STATE CONTROL OF ELECTIONS AND THE ROLE OF THE SUPREME COURT

Although constitutional amendments set fundamental voting protections based on race, gender, and age, and federal legislation like the 1993 Motor Voter Act is the law of the land, the Constitution gives to the states the primary responsibility for determining how elections are held. Most of the rules that regulate the electorate—how early and where voters need to register, whether early voting or voting by mail is permitted, how long polls are open, and the like—are made at the state level, and over time we have seen substantial fluctuations in how easy various states make it for citizens to exercise their constitutional right to vote.

Since 2008, and especially following the 2010 Republican successes in state elections, state laws have been passed that require various forms of identification to vote and that cut back on the existing trend of permitting early voting. The Supreme Court cleared the way for the election rule battles in its 2008 decision that Indiana's voter ID law—at the time the strictest in the nation—does not violate the Constitution. Encouraged by that decision, almost half of the states, mostly those under Republican control, have instituted voting restrictions. These include various voter ID requirements, restrictions of voter registration drives, elimination of election-day registration, and a cutting back on opportunities for early voting.[6] (See *Snapshot of America: How Did We Vote in the 2016 Presidential Election?*)

The Voting Rights Act of 1965 put some southern states under scrutiny to be sure they were not continuing to discriminate against African Americans. But in 2013 the drive to tighten the voting rules was made much easier by the Supreme Court's decision in *Shelby County v. Holder*, which blunted the Voting Rights Act's requirement for states with histories of racial discrimination to have changes in their election laws cleared by the federal courts or the Department of Justice. Following that decision, a number of states in the deep South implemented restrictive provisions that would be or had been denied under the preclearance requirement. Recent changes in Virginia provide an illustration of the measures

Motor Voter Act legislation allowing citizens to register to vote at the same time they apply for a driver's license or other state benefit

the Republican-controlled state governments have adopted: the state eliminated same-day registration, reduced the early voting period, ended preregistration for sixteen- and seventeen-year-olds, and instituted a photo ID requirement. Republicans insist that these measures are intended to reduce voter fraud, but there is little or no evidence that such fraud exists and the real agenda is clearly to restrict the voting of constituents (minorities, the poor, and the young) who are seen as sympathetic to Democrats.

But the electoral rules are not settled. Citizen and partisan groups are contesting efforts to restrict voting in the legislatures and in the courts. Although the justification for greater restrictions is generally stated in terms of ensuring the integrity of the electoral process—a goal few would disagree with, whether Democrats or Republicans—the sharp partisan divide on electoral restrictions supports the idea that this is really a battle to regulate the electorate for partisan advantage. Before the 2016 election the courts struck down restrictive state election laws in Texas, North Carolina, Wisconsin, Kansas, and North Dakota. Although the Supreme Court struck down a North Carolina voter ID law as too restrictive, it has also signaled its intent to leave all but the most egregious cases to the states. With the new firm conservative majority on the Court, that is unlikely to change.[7]

WHO VOTES AND WHO DOESN'T?

Many political observers, activists, politicians, and political scientists worry about the extent of nonvoting in the United States.[8] When people do not vote, they have no voice in choosing their leaders, their policy preferences are not registered, and they do not develop as active citizens. Some observers fear that their abstention signals an alienation from the political process.

From survey data, we know quite a lot about who votes and who doesn't in America in terms of their age, gender, income, education, and racial and ethnic make-up.

For instance, older citizens consistently vote at higher rates than younger ones do.[9] Gender also makes a difference. Since 1984, women have been voting at a higher rate than men, although the differences are typically only three or four percentage points. The likelihood of voting goes up steadily with income and education.

Finally, race and ethnicity matter. Turnout among members of racial and ethnic minority groups has traditionally been lower than that of whites. But that changed in 2008 (and 2012), with an African American as the Democratic nominee.

When we add these characteristics together, the differences are substantial. For example, the turnout among eighteen- to twenty-four-year-old males with less than a high school education is about a third of the turnout rate for females aged sixty-five to seventy-four years with advanced degrees.[10] By virtue of their different turnout rates, some groups in American society are receiving much better representation than others. The upshot is that our elected officials are indebted to and hear much more from the higher socioeconomic ranks in society. They do not hear from and are not elected by the low-participation "have nots."[11]

WHAT IF WE DON'T VOTE?

Despite all the good reasons for doing so, many people do not vote. Does it matter? There are two ways to tackle this question. One approach is to ask whether election outcomes would be different if nonvoters were to participate. The other approach is to ask whether higher levels

Snapshot of America: *How Did We Vote in the 2016 Presidential Election?*

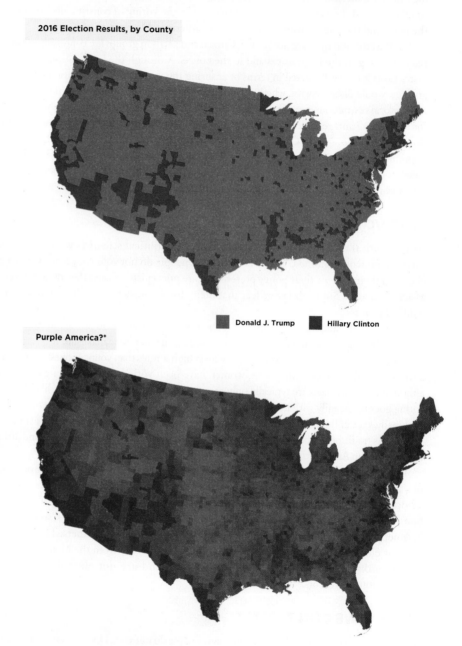

2016 Election Results, by County

■ Donald J. Trump ■ Hillary Clinton

Purple America?*

*Counties in purple reflect a mix of Democratic and Republican votes.
Source: Map by M. E. J. Newman, http://www-personal.umich.edu/~mejn/election/2016/. Licensed under Creative Commons CC-BY-2.0: https://creativecommons.org/licenses/by/2.0/.

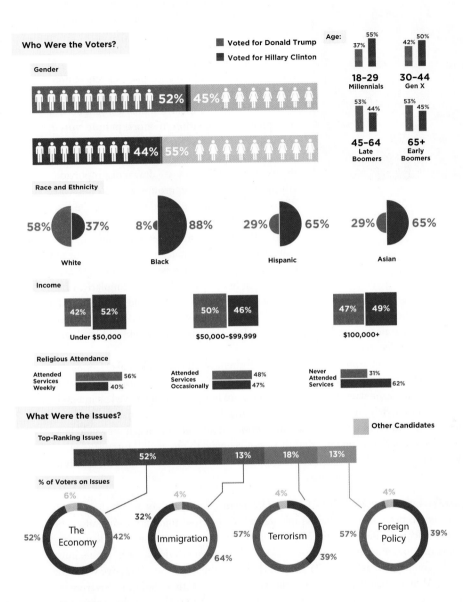

Who Were the Voters?

Legend: Voted for Donald Trump / Voted for Hillary Clinton

Age:
- 18–29 Millennials: 37% / 55%
- 30–44 Gen X: 42% / 50%
- 45–64 Late Boomers: 53% / 44%
- 65+ Early Boomers: 53% / 45%

Gender
- Male: 52% / 45%
- Female: 44% / 55%

Race and Ethnicity
- White: 58% / 37%
- Black: 8% / 88%
- Hispanic: 29% / 65%
- Asian: 29% / 65%

Income
- Under $50,000: 42% / 52%
- $50,000–$99,999: 50% / 46%
- $100,000+: 47% / 49%

Religious Attendance
- Attended Services Weekly: 56% / 40%
- Attended Services Occasionally: 48% / 47%
- Never Attended Services: 31% / 62%

What Were the Issues?

Other Candidates

Top-Ranking Issues
52% | 13% | 18% | 13%

% of Voters on Issues
- The Economy: 52% / 42% / 6%, 32%
- Immigration: 57% / 64% / 4%, 32%
- Terrorism: 57% / 39% / 4%
- Foreign Policy: 57% / 39% / 4%

Behind the Numbers

We hear a lot about Red and Blue America, but it is more complicated. On the maps, notice most states are a mix of Democratic and Republican counties. Within this, which groups tend to be Democratic or Republican? Can you think of any issues that could be the basis for the partisan tendencies between different groups of voters?

Source: CNN Exit Polls, November 9, 2016, http://www.cnn.com/election/results/exit-polls

Exercising the Right to Vote

Students wait in line to vote on the campus of the University of Central Arkansas in 2016. Young people tend to vote at lower rates than older citizens, while women vote at higher rates than men. Many people, however, don't vote, and convenience, such as having a polling station nearby, may be a contributing factor.

of nonvoting indicate that democracy is not healthy. Both questions, of course, concern important potential consequences of low participation in our elections.

CONSEQUENCES FOR ELECTION OUTCOMES Studies of the likely effects of nonvoting come up with contradictory answers, but the upshot is that it is unclear whether it would benefit one party or the other if more people voted. Republicans tend to fear that encouraging more people to vote would result in more Democrats in the electorate since they are drawn disproportionally from demographic groups who do not vote. There is some evidence that this might be the case. One political scholar found some evidence of this for the 1980 presidential election and concluded that a much higher turnout among nonvoters would have made the election closer and that Jimmy Carter might even have won reelection.[12] Similarly, when political scientists have run simulations to test whether full turnout would alter the results in elections for the U.S. Senate, the share of the vote for Democratic candidates is increased, but given that these elections are not particularly close, the extra votes would seldom change the winner of the elections.[13]

Undermining this interpretation are findings from most other presidential elections that nonvoters' preferences are quite responsive to short-term factors, so they disproportionately prefer the winning candidate. Because these voters are less partisan and have less intensely held issue positions, they are moved more easily by the short-term campaign factors favoring one party or the other. In most presidential elections, nonvoters' participation would have increased the winner's margin only slightly or not changed things at all.[14] Interviews taken shortly after recent presidential elections suggest that those who did not vote would have broken for the winner, regardless of party.[15]

CONSEQUENCES FOR DEMOCRACY Low turnout might not affect who wins an election, but elections do more than simply select leaders. How might nonvoting affect the quality of democratic life in America? Nonvoting can influence the stability and legitimacy of democratic government. The victor in close presidential elections, for example, must govern the country, but as little as 25 percent of the eligible electorate may have voted for the winner. When a majority of the electorate sits out of an election, the entire governmental process may begin to lose legitimacy in society at large. Nonvoting can also have consequences for the nonvoter. To the extent that nonvoters have different policy goals, they are underrepresented by not voting. Politicians are more attentive to the voice of voters (and contributors). And then psychologically, as we noted, failure to participate politically can aggravate already low feelings of efficacy and produce higher levels of political estrangement. To the extent that being a citizen is an active pursuit, unhappy, unfulfilled, and unconnected citizens seriously damage the quality of democratic life for themselves and for the country as a whole.

In Your Own Words Summarize the influences on who votes and who doesn't.

HOW AMERICA DECIDES

Making the choice about whether and how to vote

Obviously, voting varies dramatically in its importance to different citizens. For some, it is a significant aspect of their identities as citizens: 87 percent of American adults believe that voting in elections is a "very important obligation" for Americans, although about half that many actually vote.[16] Citizens decide about whether and how to vote based on a variety of factors.

If we do choose to go to the polls, a number of considerations go into our decision about how to vote, including our partisan identification and social group membership; our gender, race, and ethnicity; our stance on the issues and our evaluation of the job government has been doing generally; and our opinions of the candidates. In this section we examine how these factors play out in the simple act of voting.

DECIDING WHETHER TO VOTE

Deciding whether and how to vote is enormously complex. We may not consciously consider each of these factors, but most play a role in our final decision. One choice is whether to vote at all. As we noted elsewhere, compared with citizens of other democratic nations, Americans have markedly lower voter turnout levels. Despite overall increases in education, age, and income, which generally increase the number of voters, presidential election turnout rates have barely gotten over the 60-percent mark for more than thirty years (and midterm congressional turnout rates have been much lower).[17] (See Figure 12.1.)

ATTITUDE CHANGES Political scientists have found that some of the low voter turnout we can see in Figure 12.1 is accounted for by changes over time in psychological orientations or attitudes toward politics.[18] For one thing, if people feel that government is corrupt, or the system is rigged, or they cannot make a difference, they often don't bother to vote. Lower feelings of political efficacy lead to less participation.

Attitudes, of course, do not change without some cause; they reflect citizens' reactions to what they see in the political world. It is easy to understand why attitudes have changed since the relatively tranquil 1950s. Amid repeated scandal and increasing partisanship, our public airwaves have been dominated by negative information about and images of the leadership in Washington, D.C. Turnout was down, for instance, in the generation that came of age during the Nixon Watergate scandal. President Obama ran successfully by raising expectations for a more inclusive, cleaner, and less partisan politics, and the United States saw the highest turnout levels in decades. However, the hyperpartisanship that followed lowered people's estimation of the president, Congress, and politics in general. Democratic voter turnout was down in 2010, especially among young voters, as discussed earlier, in part because midterm election turnout always drops but also possibly reflecting frustration with Obama's inability to change the tone as he had promised

> *Should there be penalties for those who don't vote?*

FIGURE 12.1

Voter Turnout in Presidential and Midterm House Elections, 1932–2018

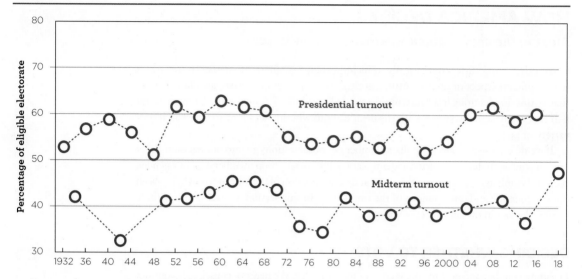

Source: Presidential data from 2000 through 2005, *The New York Times* Almanac, 114; midterm data through 1998 from U.S. Census Bureau, *2000 Statistical Abstract,* 291; 2004 data and beyond from United States Election Project, www.electproject.org/home/voter-turnout/voter-turnout-data.

and with the continued partisanship in politics. In 2016, both Vermont senator Bernie Sanders and billionaire Donald Trump appealed to feelings of frustration, cynicism, and rancor and drew some of these voters to the polls.

VOTER MOBILIZATION Another factor that political scientists argue has led to lower turnout from the 1960s into the 2000s is a change in the efforts of politicians, interest groups, and especially political parties to make direct contact with people during election campaigns.[19] **Voter mobilization** includes contacting people—especially supporters—to inform them about the election and to persuade them to vote. It can take the form of making phone calls, knocking on doors, or even supplying rides to the polls. As the technology of campaigns, especially the use of television, developed and expanded in the 1980s and 1990s, fewer resources were used for the traditional shoe-leather efforts of direct contact with voters, but solid evidence now indicates that personal contacts do a better job of getting out the vote than do mass mailings and telephone calls.[20] Both Democrats and Republicans have invested heavily in high-tech, sophisticated get-out-the-vote (GOTV) efforts that have led to increases in participation, at least in presidential elections (see Figure 12.1).[21] High-tech voter mobilization efforts were instrumental in both of President Obama's victories, but Hillary Clinton was not able to build on his efforts in 2016.

voter mobilization a party's efforts to inform potential voters about issues and candidates and to persuade them to vote

DECREASE IN SOCIAL CONNECTEDNESS

Some of the overall decline in voter turnout toward the end of the last century is due to larger societal changes rather than to citizen reactions to parties and political leaders. Social connectedness refers to the number of organizations people participate in and how tightly knit their communities and families are—that is, how well integrated they are into the society in which they live. As people increasingly leave the communities in which they grew up, live alone, and join fewer groups like religious and social organizations, they lose their ties to the larger community and have less of a stake in participating in communal decisions. Lower levels of social connectedness have been an important factor in accounting for the low turnout in national elections.[22]

COSTS AND BENEFITS OF VOTING

A final element in the decision of whether or not to vote is whether an individual gets enough in turn from voting to make it worth the costs he or she has to pay to do so. Voting demands our resources, time, and effort. Given those costs, if someone views voting primarily as a way to influence government and doesn't believe his or her vote counts, it becomes a largely irrational act.[23] Indeed, no one individual's vote is likely to change the course of an election unless the election would otherwise be a tie, and the probability of that happening in a presidential election is small (though, as the 2000 election showed, it is not impossible).

For many people, however, the benefits of voting go beyond the likelihood that they will affect the outcome of the election. In fact, studies have demonstrated that turnout decisions are not really based on our thinking that our votes will determine the outcome. Rather, we achieve other kinds of less tangible benefits from voting. Just like the expressive benefits that many people get from joining an interest group, there are expressive benefits from voting as well. It feels good to do what we think we are supposed to do or to help, however little, the side or the causes we believe in.[24] Plus, we get social rewards from our politically involved friends for voting (and avoid sarcastic remarks for not voting). These benefits accrue no matter which side wins.

It is useful to remember, however, that even these psychological benefits are not distributed equally in the electorate. For example, the social pressures to be engaged and the rewards from voting are substantially higher for those in the middle class than for the working class and the unemployed. That is, the socially (and economically) connected receive greater expressive as well as "instrumental" or policy benefits from voting.

Souls to the Polls
Congregants from Day Springs Missionary Baptist Church in Gainesville, Florida, head to polling sites to cast their ballots in October 2012, one of many "souls to the polls" events organized by black churches. Voters are more likely to cast ballots when barriers to voting—including transportation to polling sites—are low. Strong social connections such as those provided by membership in a church or civic group also increase voter participation.

> **Is our democracy stronger if more Americans vote?**

social connectedness citizens' involvement in groups and their relationships to their communities and families

DECIDING WHOM TO VOTE FOR

The decision to vote is only part of the voter's calculus. There is also the question of whom to vote for, a decision that is shaped by party loyalty and group identity as much as by the candidates and the issue positions they take.

PARTISANSHIP AND SOCIAL GROUP MEMBERSHIP The single biggest factor accounting for how people decide to vote is party identification, a concept we discussed in Chapter 11. For most citizens, party ID is relatively stable, carrying over from one election to the next in what one scholar has called "a standing decision."[25] In 2016, 89 percent of those identifying with the Democratic Party voted for Hillary Clinton, and 90 percent of those identifying with the Republican Party voted for Donald Trump.[26]

Scholars have demonstrated that party ID also has an important indirect influence on voting decisions, because voters' party ID also colors their views on policy issues and their evaluation of candidates, leading them to judge their party's candidate and issue positions as superior.[27] Under unusual circumstances, social group characteristics can exaggerate or override traditional partisan loyalties. The 1960 election, for instance, was cast in terms of whether the nation would elect its first Catholic president. In that context, religion was especially salient, and fully 82 percent of Roman Catholics supported John F. Kennedy, compared to just 37 percent of Protestants—a difference of 45 percentage points. Compare that to 1976, when the Democrats ran a devout Baptist, Jimmy Carter, for president. The percentage of Catholics voting Democratic dropped to 58 percent, while Protestants voting Democratic increased to 46 percent. The difference shrank to just 12 percentage points.

GENDER, RACE, AND ETHNICITY The impact of gender on voting decisions is not clear. In Chapter 10 we discussed the gender gap in the positions men and women take on the issues, which has generally led women to be more likely to support the Democratic candidate. Since 1964, women have been more supportive of the Democratic candidate in every presidential election but one (they were not more likely to support Carter in 1976), and the Democrats clearly wanted to put women's issues at the forefront during the 2016 campaign.[28] But women do not vote monolithically; for instance, married women are more conservative than single women.

It's an open question whether the gender of a candidate affects the women's vote. Despite the speculation that the nomination of Sarah Palin as the Republican vice presidential candidate might have swayed some women to support the McCain-Palin ticket, there was little evidence in the 2008 exit polls to support that idea. According to exit polls, Hillary Clinton benefited from a gender gap, but no larger than Barack Obama's. College-educated women voted for her in much greater numbers than those without a degree.[29]

African Americans have tended to vote Democratic since the civil rights movement of the 1960s. In fact, just under 90 percent of African American voters cast votes for the Democratic candidate in recent presidential elections (1988 to 2004).[30] The nomination of Barack Obama, the first African American to receive a major party's presidential nomination, increased the solidarity of the African American vote even further. African American support for the Democratic ticket reached a record 95 percent in 2008 and 93 percent in 2012.[31]

Ethnicity is less predictive of the vote than race, partly because ethnic groups in the United States become politically diverse as they are assimilated into the system. Although immigrant groups have traditionally found a home in the Democratic Party, dating back to the days when the party machine would provide a one-stop shop for new immigrants seeking jobs, homes, and social connections, recent immigrant groups today include Asians and Hispanics, both of which comprise diverse ethnic communities with distinct identities and varying partisan tendencies.[32] These diverse groups tend to support the Democratic Party, but each has subgroups that are distinctly more Republican: Vietnamese, in the case of Asians, and Cubans, among Latino groups.[33] That said, in 2016, Clinton received the overwhelming majority of Hispanic votes. Nationally 65 percent of Latino voters supported Clinton (down from 71 percent for Obama in 2012), as did 65 percent of Asian Americans, and 56 percent of all other racial and ethnic minorities. One observer calls these groups the "coalition of the ascendant," meaning that these are growing portions of the population whose support for the Democratic Party spells trouble for the Republicans if they cannot broaden their appeal.[34] Even so, Trump was able to make up the difference with white support in 2016.

ISSUES AND POLICY An idealized view of elections would have highly attentive citizens paying careful attention to the different policy positions offered by the candidates and then, perhaps aided by informed policy analyses from the media, casting their ballots for the candidates who best represent their preferred policy solutions. In truth, as we know by now, American citizens are not "ideal," and the role played by issues is less obvious and more complicated than the ideal model would predict. The apparent role of issues in electoral decision making is limited by the following factors:

- People are busy and, in many cases, rely on party labels to tell them what they need to know about the candidates.[35]
- People know where they stand on "easy" issues like capital punishment or gay marriage, but some issues, like economic and tax policy, health care, Social Security reform, or foreign policy in the Middle East, are complicated. Many citizens tend to tune out these more complicated issues or, confused, fail to vote in their own interests.[36]
- The media do not generally cover issues in depth. Instead, they much prefer to focus on the horse-race aspect of elections, looking at who is ahead in the polls rather than what substantive policy issues mean for the nation.[37]
- As we discussed in Chapter 10, people process a lot of policy-relevant information in terms of their impressions of candidates (on-line processing) rather than as policy information. They are certainly influenced by policy information, but they cannot necessarily articulate their opinions and preferences on policy.

Although calculated policy decisions by voters are rare, policy considerations do have a real impact on voters' decisions. To see that, it is useful to distinguish between prospective and retrospective voting. The idealized model of policy voting with which we opened this section is prospective voting, in which voters base their decisions on what will happen in the future if they vote for a candidate—what policies will be enacted, what values will be emphasized in policy. Prospective voting requires a good deal of information that average voters, as we have seen, do not always have or even want. While all voters do some prospective voting and, by election time, are usually aware of the candidates' major issue positions, it is primarily party activists and political elites who engage in the full-scale policy analysis that prospective voting entails.

Instead, most voters supplement their spotty policy information and interest with their evaluation of how they think the country is doing, how the economy has performed, and how well the incumbents have carried out their jobs. They engage in retrospective voting, casting their votes as signs of approval based on past performance to signal their desire for more of the same or for change.[38]

In presidential elections, this means that voters look back at the state of the economy; at perceived successes or failures in foreign policy; and at domestic issues like education, gun control, or welfare reform. In 1980 Ronald Reagan skillfully focused on voter frustration in

prospective voting basing voting decisions on well-informed opinions and consideration of the future consequences of a given vote

retrospective voting basing voting decisions on reactions to past performance; approving the status quo or a desire for change

the presidential debate by asking voters this question: "[A]re you better off than you were four years ago?"[39] Politicians have been reprising that question ever since.

In 2012 the central strategic campaign objective of the Republican challenger, Mitt Romney, was to cast the election as a referendum on Obama's culpability for a slow economic recovery, hoping that this strategy would push voters to cast a ballot for change. The Obama campaign had the challenge of changing the subject and making the election a choice between the president's and Romney's visions for the country. The Obama campaign began a concerted effort to shape public views of Romney in the summer of 2012, running commercials that painted the Republican as a rich venture capitalist who was out of touch with middle-class America. By the time Romney began to answer those ads in the fall campaign, many people had made up their minds. Similarly, Hillary Clinton ran in 2016 on the strength of the Obama record and sought to make Trump's temperament and inexperience a focal point of her campaign. In the end, it turned out that a sufficient number of voters recognized his flaws but voted for him anyway because they either didn't like Clinton or believed that Trump would shake up Washington.

Retrospective voting is considered to be "easy" decision making, as opposed to the more complex decision making involved in prospective voting because one only has to ask, "How have things been going?" as a guide to whether to support the current party in power. Retrospective voting is also seen as a useful way of holding politicians accountable, not for what they said or are saying in a campaign, but for what they or members of their party in power did. Some scholars believe that this type of voting is all that is needed for democracy to function well.[40] In practice, voters combine elements of both voting strategies.

THE CANDIDATES In addition to considerations of party, personal demographics, and issues, voters also base their decisions on judgments about candidates as individuals. What influences voters' images of candidates? Some observers have claimed that voters view candidate characteristics much as they would a beauty or personality contest. There is little support, however, for the notion that voters are won over merely by good looks or movie-star qualities. Consider, for example, that Richard Nixon almost won against John F. Kennedy, who had good looks, youth, and a quick wit in his favor. Then, in 1964, the awkward, gangly Lyndon Johnson defeated the more handsome and articulate Barry Goldwater in a landslide. In fact, ample evidence indicates that voters form clear opinions about candidate qualities that are relevant to governing, such as trustworthiness, competence, experience, and sincerity. Citizens also make judgments about the ability of the candidates to lead the nation and withstand the pressures of the presidency. Ronald Reagan, for example, was admired widely for his ability to stay above the fray of Washington politics and to see the humor in many situations. By contrast, his predecessor, Jimmy Carter, seemed overwhelmed by the job.

The 2012 campaign allowed voters to develop distinct images of Barack Obama and Mitt Romney. First, voters had four years of almost daily experience with Obama as president, and one thing that the polls showed was that voters generally liked him, even in an economy that virtually everyone agreed had not recovered fast enough. In January 2012 one poll found that fully 71 percent agreed that the president was "warm and friendly" rather than "cold and aloof."[41] Similarly, Obama stacked up well as a "good communicator" and one who "cares about people like me." Among voters who valued this attribute most in their voting decisions, 81 percent cast their ballots for Obama.[42] Obama's challenger, Mitt Romney, decided early on to stress his success in business as qualification for dealing with the economy. He did manage to hold an edge on who could manage the economy better (just 49 percent to Obama's

48 percent in the exit polls), but, with the help of a lot of Democratic and Obama ads, he came to be seen as a rich plutocrat who was unconcerned about the average person. In 2016 the Clinton campaign started early to define Donald Trump as a man temperamentally unsuited to the presidency—xenophobic, racist, and sexist. Trump used the methods that had served him well during the primary—seizing on a perceived weakness in his opponent and reinforcing it with name-calling—and started calling her "Crooked Hillary Clinton." Although polls showed voters mistrusted Clinton, they also thought she was more qualified to hold the office. A majority agreed, but enough voters in a handful of states ultimately decided differently and elected Trump to the presidency.

In Your Own Words Describe factors that affect citizens' decisions on whether and how to vote.

PRESIDENTIAL CAMPAIGNS
The long, expensive road to the White House

Being president of the United States is undoubtedly a difficult challenge, but so is getting the job in the first place. It is a long, expensive, and grueling "road to the White House," as the media like to call it.

GETTING NOMINATED

Each of the major parties (and the minor parties, too) needs to come up with a single viable candidate from the long list of party members with ambitions to serve in the White House. How the candidate is chosen will determine the sort of candidate chosen. Remember, in politics the rules are always central to shaping the outcome. Prior to 1972, primary election results were mostly considered "beauty contests" because their results were not binding. But since 1972, party nominees for the presidency have been chosen in primaries, taking the power away from the party elite and giving it to the activist members of the party who care enough to turn out and vote in the party primaries.

THE PRE-PRIMARY SEASON It is hard to say when a candidate's presidential campaign actually begins. Potential candidates may begin planning and thinking about running for the presidency in childhood. Bill Clinton is said to have wanted to be president since high school, when he shook President Kennedy's hand. At one time or another, many people in politics consider going for the big prize, but there are several crucial steps between wishful thinking and actually running for the nomination. Candidates vary somewhat in their approach to the process, but most of those considering a run for the White House follow similar steps.

Potential candidates usually test the waters unofficially. They talk to friends and fellow politicians to see just how much support they can count on, and they often leak news of their possible candidacy to the press to see how it is received in the media. This period of jockeying for money, lining up top campaign consultants, generating media buzz, and getting commitments of potential support from party and interest group notables—even before candidates announce they are running—is called the **invisible primary**. If these efforts have positive results, candidates file with the Federal Election Commission (FEC) to set up a committee to

invisible primary early attempts to raise money, line up campaign consultants, generate media attention, and get commitments for support even before candidates announce they are running

receive funds so that they can officially explore their prospects. The candidate can exploit the formation of an *exploratory committee* as a media event, using the occasion to get free publicity for the launching of the still-unannounced campaign. Candidates then need to acquire a substantial war chest to pay for the enormous expenses of running for the nomination. With the money in the bank, the potential candidate must use the pre-primary season to position himself or herself as a credible prospect with the media. It is no coincidence that in most election years (2016 was a notable exception), the parties' nominees have all held prominent government offices and have entered the field with some media credibility. Incumbents especially have a huge advantage here. The final step of the pre-primary season is the official announcement of candidacy. Like the formation of the exploratory committee, this statement is part of the campaign itself. Promises are made to supporters, agendas are set, media attention is captured, and the process is under way.

PRIMARIES AND CAUCUSES The actual fight for the nomination takes place in the state party caucuses and primaries in which delegates to the parties' national conventions are chosen. In a **party caucus**, grassroots members of the party in each community gather in selected locations to discuss the current candidates. They then vote for delegates from that locality who will be sent to the national convention, or who will go on to larger caucuses at the state level to choose the national delegates. Attending a caucus is time consuming, and other than in the 2004 Iowa caucus, where the turnout doubled from its 2000 level, participation rates are frequently in the single digits.[43] However, 2008 marked a big change, with most states setting records for primary and caucus turnout, especially on the Democratic side, where the heated nomination battle between Barack Obama and Hillary Clinton sparked unusual levels of interest. Most states still hold primary elections, but in recent years there has been a trend toward caucuses, the method used in thirteen states.[44]

The most common device for choosing delegates to the national conventions is the **presidential primary**. Primary voters cast ballots that send to the conventions those delegates who are committed to voting for a particular candidate. Presidential primaries can be either open or closed, depending on the rules the state party organizations adopt, and these can change from year to year. Any registered voter may vote in an **open primary**, regardless of party affiliation. At the polling place, the voter chooses the ballot of the party whose primary he or she wants to vote in. Only registered party members may vote in a **closed primary**. A subset of this type of primary is the semi-open primary, open only to registered party members and those not registered as members of another party.

The Democrats also send elected state officials, including Democratic members of Congress and governors, to their national conventions. Some of these officials are "superdelegates," able to vote as free agents, but the rest must reflect the state's primary vote.[45]

The parties' primary rules differ not only in terms of whom they allow to vote but also in how they distribute delegates among the candidates. The Democrats generally use a method of proportional representation, in which the candidates get the percentage of delegates equal to the percentage of the primary vote they win (provided they get at least 15 percent). Republican rules run from proportional representation, to winner take all (the candidate with the most votes gets all the delegates, even if he or she does not win an absolute majority), to direct voting for delegates (the delegates are not bound to vote for a particular candidate at the convention), to the absence of a formal system (caucus participants may decide how to distribute the delegates).

party caucus a local gathering of party members to choose convention delegates

presidential primary an election by which voters choose convention delegates committed to voting for a certain candidate

open primary a primary election in which eligible voters do not need to be registered party members

closed primary a primary election in which only registered party members may vote

State primaries also vary in the times at which they are held, with various states engaged in **front-loading**, vying to hold their primaries first in order to gain maximum exposure in the media and power over the nomination. By tradition and state law, the Iowa caucuses and the New Hampshire primary are the first contests for delegates. As a result, they get tremendous attention, from both candidates and the media—much more than their contribution to the delegate count would justify. This is why in 1998 other states began moving their primaries earlier in the season.[46] The process of moving primary dates up continued in 2012, with the Iowa caucuses held on January 3 and twenty-three states holding primaries or caucuses by Super Tuesday, which was on March 6, 2012.

The consequence of such front-loading is that candidates must have a full war chest and be prepared to campaign nationally from the beginning. Traditionally, winners of early primaries could use that success to raise more campaign funds to continue the battle. With the primaries stacked at the beginning, however, this becomes much harder. When the winner can be determined within weeks of the first primary, it is less likely that a dark horse, or unknown candidate, can emerge. The process favors well-known, well-connected, and especially well-funded candidates. Again, incumbents have an enormous advantage here. The heavily front-loaded primary has almost no defenders, but it presents a classic example of the problems of collective action that politics cannot always solve.[47] No single state has an incentive to hold back and reduce its power for the good of the whole; each state is driven to maximize its influence by strategically placing its primary early in the pack.

In most of the crowded primaries in recent years there has been a clear **front-runner**, a person who many assume will win the nomination before the primaries even begin. Early front-runner status is positive because it means the candidate has raised significant money, has a solid organization, and receives more media coverage than his or her opponents. But success in primaries comes not just from getting a majority of the votes but also from being perceived as a winner, and front-runners are punished if they fail to live up to lofty expectations—the fate shared by Republican Rudy Giuliani and Democrat Hillary Clinton in 2008. The goal for all the other candidates is to attack the front-runner so as to drive down his or her support, while maneuvering into position as the chief alternative. Then, if the front-runner stumbles, as often happens, each of the attacking candidates hopes to emerge from the pack.

Generally a candidate's campaign strategy becomes focused on developing **momentum**, the perception by the press, the public, and the other candidates in the field that one is on a roll, and that polls, primary victories, endorsements, and funding are all coming one's way. Considerations of electability—which candidate has the best chance to triumph in November—are important as voters decide whom to support, and here candidates who seem to have momentum can have an advantage.

It Always Starts in Iowa

Candidates eyeing the presidential nominations of their parties tend to spend a lot of time in Iowa, where crucial first votes take place. In 2018, Congressman John Delaney, D-Md., became the first candidate to visit the state ahead of the 2020 election. Unlike many of his peers in years past, who came up with unrelated excuses for their visits, Delaney was clear about his reason for the trip, which earned him some respect among election-weary Iowans.

front-loading the process of scheduling presidential primaries early in the primary season

front-runner the leading candidate and expected winner of a nomination or an election

momentum the widely held public perception that a candidate is gaining electoral strength

Increasingly important in the primary season are debates among the contenders for a party's nomination. These are televised nationally, giving the whole country exposure to each party's candidates. It is arguable that in 2008, the many debates among candidates for the Democratic nomination gave Barack Obama national media exposure, and the united effort of the candidates to weaken Hillary Clinton in those debates was costly to her as well. In 2016, the crowded debate stage enabled Donald Trump to lay low while the other candidates battled each other. Meanwhile, Hillary Clinton found a surprisingly adept debate opponent in Sen. Bernie Sanders that helped boost his candidacy to prominence.

THE CONVENTION Since 1972, delegates attending the national conventions have not had to decide who the parties' nominees would be. However, two official actions continue to take place at the conventions. First, as we discussed in Chapter 11, the parties hammer out and approve their platforms, the documents in which parties set out their distinct issue positions. Second, the vice presidential candidate is named officially. The choice of the vice president is up to the presidential nominee. There is no clear evidence that the vice presidential choice has significant electoral consequences, but the presidential nominees weigh it carefully nonetheless.

Traditionally, the choice was made to balance the ticket (ideologically, regionally, or even, when Democrat Walter Mondale chose Geraldine Ferraro in 1984, by gender). Bill Clinton's choice of Al Gore was a departure from this practice, as he tapped a candidate much like himself—a Democratic moderate from a southern state. In 2000 George W. Bush picked Dick Cheney, a man whose considerable experience in the federal government was expected to offset Bush's relative lack of it.

In 2008 Barack Obama chose Delaware senator Joe Biden as his running mate, going for an experienced hand with foreign policy background to shore up his own record. Democrats applauded his pick of Biden as one who would balance the ticket and showcased Obama's own judgment and decision-making skills. They had barely finished cheering their new nominee, however, when John McCain upstaged Obama with his own pick, Alaska governor Sarah Palin, who he felt would bolster his maverick credentials, help him energize his base, and bolster his standing with women. The choice was immediately controversial; wildly popular with religious conservatives, it was viewed with surprise and skepticism by Democrats and media commentators. In 2016 Donald Trump picked Indiana governor Mike Pence as a nod to the party establishment he had just beaten, then reportedly wondered if he could change his mind.[48] Hillary Clinton irritated many more progressive voters by going with what many considered the "safe," moderate pick of Virginia senator Tim Kaine, but she maintained that her key criteria were having a running mate she was comfortable with and who had the governing experience to step in and take over the job. If nothing else, the caliber of the nominee's choice for vice president is held to be an indication of the kind of appointments the nominee would make if elected.

Although their actual party business is limited, the conventions still usually provide the nominee with a "convention bump" in the polls. The harmonious coverage, the enthusiasm of party supporters, and even the staged theatrics seem to have a positive impact on viewers. The result is that candidates have usually, though not always, experienced a noticeable rise in the polls immediately following the conventions.

THE GENERAL ELECTION CAMPAIGN

After the candidates are nominated in late summer, there is a short break, at least for the public, before the traditional fall campaign. When the campaign begins, the goal of each side is to convince supporters to turn out and to get undecided voters to choose its candidate. Most voters, the party identifiers, will usually support their party's candidate, although they need to be motivated by the campaign to turn out and cast their ballots. Most of the battle in a presidential campaign is for the swing voters, the one-third or so of the electorate who have not made up their minds at the start of the campaign and who are open to persuasion by either side. As one would expect, given the forces described in Chapter 11, this means that for both parties the general election strategy differs considerably from the strategy used to win a primary election. Traditionally the logic has been that to win the general election, the campaigns move away from the sharp ideological tone used to motivate the party faithful in the primaries and "run to the middle" by making less ideological appeals. However, in this era of hyperpartisanship, especially since the second George W. Bush campaign, the tendency has been for a campaign to stay with the party's ideological message, putting at least as much emphasis on mobilizing its base as on appealing to independents and uncommitted voters.

In the general campaign, each side seeks to get its message across, to define the choice in terms that give its candidate the advantage. This massive effort to influence the information to which citizens are exposed requires a clear strategy, which begins with a plan for winning the states where the candidate will be competitive.

THE ELECTORAL COLLEGE Because our founders feared giving too much power to the volatile electorate, we do not actually vote for the president and vice president in presidential elections. Rather, we cast our votes in November for electors (members of the Electoral College), who in turn vote for the president in December. The Constitution provides for each state to have as many electoral votes as it does senators and representatives in Congress. Thus Alaska has three electoral votes (one for each of the state's U.S. senators and one for its sole member of the House of Representatives). By contrast, California has fifty-five electoral votes (two senators and fifty-three representatives). In addition, the Twenty-third Amendment gave the District of Columbia three electoral votes. There are 538 electoral votes in all; 270 are needed to win the presidency.

Electors are generally activist members of the party whose presidential candidate carried the state (see *The Big Picture* for an overview of how the Electoral College works). In December, following the election, the electors meet and vote in their state capitals. In the vast majority of cases, they vote as expected, but there are occasional "faithless electors" who vote for their own preferences. The results of the electors' choices in the states are then sent to the Senate, where the ballots are counted when the new session opens. If no candidate achieves a majority in the Electoral College, the Constitution calls for the House of Representatives to choose from the top three electoral vote winners. In this process, each state has one vote. If the vote goes to the House, then the Senate decides on the vice president, with each senator having a vote. This has happened only twice (the last time was in 1824), although some observers of the 2000 election speculated that that election, too, could have been decided in the House of Representatives if Florida's election had not been decided in the courts.

The importance of the Electoral College is that all the states but Maine and Nebraska operate on a winner-take-all basis. Thus the winner in California, even if he or she has less than half of the popular vote, wins all of the state's fifty-five electoral votes. Similarly, the loser in California may have won 49 percent of the popular vote but gets nothing in the Electoral College. It is possible, then, for the popular vote winner to lose in the Electoral College. This has happened only four times in our history. Usually, however, the opposite happens: the Electoral College exaggerates the candidate's apparent majority. The 2012 election is typical

swing voters the approximately one-third of the electorate who are undecided at the start of a campaign

Electoral College an intermediary body that elects the president

THE BIG PICTURE:
How the Electoral College Works, and How It Might Work

The founding fathers intended the Electoral College to be a compromise between direct election of the president (they weren't sure they trusted us?) and selection of the president by Congress (they didn't want him to be indebted). Consequently, the Electoral College is selected once every four years, those members meet in November to choose the president, and then they disband, never to meet again. Good idea, or bad? Look at how it works and decide for yourself.

How It Works   Each state is allotted a set number of electors but can decide how to allocate them among the presidential candidates.

 + **=** **#**

# of Representatives	2 Senators	Total Allotted Votes Per State	538 Votes in total

What Your Vote Means   When you cast your vote you are really voting for an elector chosen by the state party who will cast a vote for president on your behalf.

 ▶ ▶

Electors pledged to a candidate are chosen by state parties

Citizens vote for electors pledged to their preferred candidate

States allocate their electoral votes to the candidate(s) according to that state's formula

How the States Allocate Their Votes

48 states have a winner-take-all system where the candidate who wins the popular vote in the state gets ALL the state's electoral votes. But Maine and Nebraska award their votes proportionally.

In 2016, the Electoral Vote Looked Like This...

On election night, news networks use returns and exit poll interviews to estimate who won each state and its electoral votes. A simple majority, or 270, is sufficient to win.

270*

Trump 304 ☑	Clinton 227

Source: "Presidential Election Results," *New York Times*, www.nytimes.com/elections/results/president.

Two "faithless electors" declined to cast their electoral votes for Trump and five refused to vote for Clinton, despite their states' results.

But It Could Be Different

The winner-take-all system seems unfair to some people, and it concentrates presidential contests in just a few "battleground states." But states could allocate their votes differently. Here are a few of the options, with a look at how they would have affected the results of the 2016 election.

In 2016, the Electoral Vote Looked Like This...

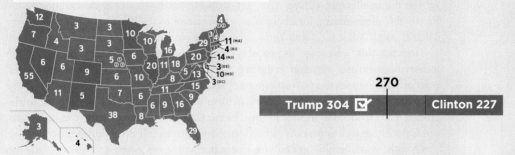

270

| Trump 304 ☑ | Clinton 227 |

If States Could Allocate Their Votes Differently...

Congressional District — Popular

270

| Trump 290 ☑ | Clinton 248 |

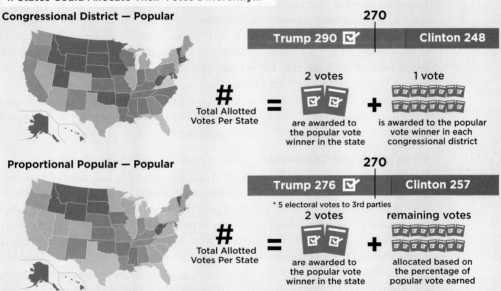

#
Total Allotted Votes Per State

=

2 votes
are awarded to the popular vote winner in the state

+

1 vote
is awarded to the popular vote winner in each congressional district

Proportional Popular — Popular

270

| Trump 276 ☑ | Clinton 257 |

* 5 electoral votes to 3rd parties

#
Total Allotted Votes Per State

=

2 votes
are awarded to the popular vote winner in the state

+

remaining votes
allocated based on the percentage of popular vote earned

Popular Vote — Eliminate the Electoral College (because the popular vote winner has lost 5 times!)

| Trump 62,979,636 (48.88%) | Clinton 65,844,610 (51.11%) ☑ |

National Popular Vote Interstate Compact A budding agreement among the states would commit each state to cast all of its electoral votes for the national popular vote winner, ensuring that the popular vote winner becomes president, but without amending the Constitution. It will take effect if states with 270 combined electoral votes commit to be bound by it. As of 2018, twelve states plus the District of Columbia, accounting for more than half of the required 270 votes, had passed legislation to join the compact.

Source: 270toWin, www.270towin.com/alternative-electoral-college-allocation-methods/

of this exaggeration of the victory margin in the Electoral College. Obama got more than 51 percent of the two-party popular vote, but his majority in the Electoral College was 61.7 percent. This exaggeration of the winning margin has the effect of legitimizing winners' victories and allowing them to claim that they have a mandate—a broad popular endorsement—even if they won by a smaller margin of the popular vote.

The rules of the Electoral College give greater power to some states over others. The provision that all states get at least three electoral votes in the Electoral College means that citizens in the smaller-population states get proportionately greater representation in the Electoral College. Alaska, for example, sent one elector to the Electoral College for every 240,000 people, while California had one elector for every 679,000 residents.

However, this "advantage" is probably offset by the practice of winner take all, which focuses the candidates' attention on the largest states with the biggest payoff in electoral votes, especially the competitive or "battleground" states. Small states with few electoral votes or those that are safely in the corner of one party or the other are ignored. In 2016 the battleground map expanded to include Florida, North Carolina, Virginia, Pennsylvania, Nevada, and Colorado, as well as typically red and blue states that usually don't find themselves close.

Over the years, hundreds of bills have been introduced in Congress to reform or abolish the Electoral College.[49] Major criticisms of the current system include the claims that the Electoral College is undemocratic because it is possible for the popular winner not to get a majority of the electoral votes, that in a very close contest the popular outcome could be dictated by a few "faithless electors" who vote their conscience rather than the will of the people of their states, and that the Electoral College distorts candidates' campaign strategies. The winner-take-all provision in all but two states puts a premium on a few large, competitive states, which get a disproportionate share of the candidates' attention.

Few people deny the truth of these charges, and hardly anyone believes that if we were to start all over, the current Electoral College would be chosen as the best way to elect a president. Nevertheless, it's not clear it will ever be changed.

WHO RUNS THE CAMPAIGN? Running a modern presidential campaign has become a highly specialized profession. Most presidential campaigns are led by an "amateur," a nationally prestigious chairperson who may serve as an adviser and assist in fundraising. However, the real work of the campaign is done by the professional staff the candidate hires. These may be people the candidate knows well and trusts, or they may be professionals who sign on for the duration of the campaign and then move on to another. Campaign work in the twenty-first century is big business. Donald Trump's campaign was not an orthodox one and broke many of the rules of modern campaigning. He relied heavily on his children, especially his son-in-law; on his campaign CEO (which is not a traditional position), Steven Bannon from Breitbart News; on his campaign manager, Kellyanne Conway; and on Republican National Committee chair Reince Priebus.

Some of the jobs include not only the well-known ones of campaign manager and strategist but also more specialized components tailored to the modern campaign's emphasis on information and money. For instance, candidates need to hire research teams to prepare position papers on issues so that the candidate can answer any questions posed by potential supporters and the media. But researchers also engage in the controversial but necessary task of oppo research—delving into the background and vulnerabilities of the opposing candidate with an eye to exploiting his or her weaknesses. Central to the modern campaign's efforts to get and control the flow of information are pollsters and focus group administrators, who are critical for testing the public's reactions to issues and strategies. Media consultants try to get

oppo research
investigation of an opponent's background for the purpose of exploiting weaknesses or undermining credibility

free coverage of the campaign whenever possible and to make the best use of the campaign's advertising dollars by designing commercials and print advertisements.

Candidates also need advance teams to plan and prepare their travel agendas, to arrange for crowds (and the signs they wave) to greet the candidates at airports, and even to reserve accommodations for the press. Especially in the primaries, staff devoted to fundraising are essential to ensure the constant flow of money necessary to grease the wheels of any presidential campaign. They work with big donors and engage in direct-mail campaigns to solicit money from targeted groups. Finally, of course, candidates need to hire a legal team to keep their campaigns in compliance with FEC regulations and to file the required reports. In general, campaign consultants are able to provide specialized technical services that the parties' political committees cannot.[50]

PRESENTING THE CANDIDATE An effective campaign begins with a clear understanding of how the candidate's strengths fit with the context of the times and the mood of the voters. To sell a candidate effectively, the claims to special knowledge, competence, or commitment must be credible.[51] As the campaigns struggle to control the flow of information about their candidates and influence how voters see their opponents, oppo research comes into play, sometimes complete with focus groups and poll testing. In fact, oppo research has become a central component in all elections, leading to the negative campaigning so prevalent in recent years.[52] Research on one's opponent, however, cannot compensate for the failure to define oneself in clear and attractive terms. Again, in 2016, the Trump campaign broke with all the conventional wisdom. The candidate did not release his tax returns; produced a superficial medical report; spoke offensively about women, Latinos, and Muslims; and refused to acknowledge that Barack Obama was a citizen. Shortly after he kicked off his campaign, Trump was recorded mocking a disabled reporter. And tapes surfaced in which he had earlier bragged in a radio interview about walking in on beauty pageant contestants while they were undressed and in which he boasted that his fame allowed him to assault women without any consequences. Trump's supporters mostly acknowledged that those things happened but either admired them or just didn't care.[53]

THE ISSUES Earlier we indicated that issues matter to voters as they decide how to vote. This means that issues must be central to the candidate's strategy for getting elected. From the candidate's point of view, there are two kinds of issues to consider when planning a strategy: valence issues and position issues.

Valence issues are policy matters on which the voters and the candidates share the same preference. These are what we might call "motherhood and apple pie" issues, because no one opposes them. Everyone is for a strong, prosperous economy; for America having a respected leadership role in the world; for fighting terrorism; for thrift in government; and for a clean environment. Similarly, everyone opposes crime and drug abuse, government waste, political corruption, and immorality.

Position issues have two sides. On abortion, there are those who are pro-life and those who are pro-choice. On military engagements such as Vietnam or Iraq, there are those who favor pursuing a military victory and those who favor just getting out. Many of the hardest decisions for candidates are on position issues: although a clear stand means that they will gain some friends, it also guarantees that they will make some enemies. Realistic candidates, who want to win as many votes as possible, try to avoid being clearly identified with the losing side of important position issues. One example is abortion. Activists in the Republican Party fought to keep their strong pro-life plank in the party platform in 2000. However, because a majority of the electorate is opposed to the strong pro-life position, George W. Bush seldom

valence issues issues on which most voters and candidates share the same position

position issues issues on which the parties differ in their perspectives and proposed solutions

mentioned the issue during the campaign, even though one of his first acts as president was to cut federal funding to overseas groups that provide abortions or abortion counseling. John McCain, needing to solidify his Republican base in 2008, was more explicit about his party's pro-life stance, and it appeared to cost him with independent voters, as it did with Mitt Romney in 2012. When two Republican senate candidates made news by arguing that abortion should not be legal even in the case of rape, President Obama was able to paint Romney as extreme on the issue by association.

When candidates or parties do take a stand on a difficult position issue, the other side often uses it against them as a wedge issue. A **wedge issue** is a position issue on which the

wedge issue a controversial issue that one party uses to split the voters in the other party

parties differ and that proves controversial within the ranks of a particular party. For a Republican, an anti–affirmative action position is not dangerous, since few Republicans actively support affirmative action. For a Democrat, though, it is a dicey issue, because liberal party members endorse it but more moderate members do not. An astute strategy for a Republican candidate, then, is to raise the issue, hoping to drive a wedge between the Democrats and to recruit to his or her side the Democratic opponents of affirmative action.

The idea of **issue ownership** helps to clarify the role of policy issues in presidential campaigns. Because of their past stands and performance, each of the parties is widely perceived as better able to handle certain kinds of problems. For instance, the Democrats are seen as better able to deal with the economy while the Republicans are held to be more effective at foreign policy. The voter's decision, then,

A Strong Position

The race for governor of Virginia in 2017 turned ugly when Republican candidate Ed Gillespie ran campaign ads equating support for sanctuary cities by his Democratic opponent, Ralph Northam, with support for undocumented immigrant members of the violent Salvadoran gang MS-13. Northam supporters and others accused Gillespie of drawing on the tradition of the famous Willie Horton ad and playing on some white voters' fears of Latinos and immigrants.

involves not so much evaluating positions on those issues, as deciding which problem is more important. In 2008, when the economy foundered as a result of the subprime mortgage crisis, it benefited Barack Obama since voters believed his party was better able to cope.[54] From the candidate's point of view, the trick is to convince voters that the election is about the issues that his or her party "owns." Sometimes a party will try to take an issue that is "owned" by the other party and redefine it in order to claim ownership of it. Bush did this successfully in 2000 with the education issue, just as Clinton reversed the advantage Republicans usually held on crime.[55]

Because valence issues are relatively safe, candidates stress them at every opportunity. They also focus on the position issues that their parties "own" or on which they have majority support. This suggests that the real campaign is not about debating positions on issues—how to reduce the deficit or whether to restrict abortion—but about which issues should be considered. Issue campaigning is to a large extent about setting the agenda.

THE MEDIA It is impossible to understand the modern political campaign without appreciating the pervasive role of the media. Even though many voters tend to ignore campaign ads—or at least they tell survey interviewers that they do—we know that campaign advertising matters. It has increased dramatically with the rise of television as people's information source of choice. Studies show that advertising provides usable information for voters. Political ads can heighten the loyalty of existing supporters, and they can educate the public about what candidates stand for and what issues candidates believe are most important. Ads also can be effective in establishing the criteria on which voters choose between candidates. Although **negative advertising** may turn off some voters and give the perception that politics is an unpleasant business, the public accepts accurate attacks on the issues. As long as it does not go too far, an attack ad that highlights negative aspects of an opponent's record actually registers more quickly and is remembered more frequently and longer by voters than are positive ads.[56] Experts suggested that requiring candidates to appear in their own ads would discourage negativity, but that doesn't seem to be the case. For instance, by early October 2008, nearly all the

issue ownership the tendency of one party to be seen as more competent in a specific policy area

negative advertising campaign advertising and other forms of communication that emphasize negative characteristics of opponents rather than one's own strengths

Viral Media

Verbal accusations, negative attacks, and rumor mongering have characterized American election campaigns since the days of George Washington. *George Washington?* His opponents called him a "dictator" who would "debauch the nation."[1] Thomas Jefferson was accused of having an affair with a slave, a controversy that has outlived any of the people involved and Abraham Lincoln was claimed to have had an illegitimate child.

Like it or not (and most Americans say they do not), in the Internet age such negative and deeply personal attacks are more prevalent than ever. Once, negative attacks were limited to soap box speeches and debates, and quotes that accusers hoped would get picked up by the news media. The age of television made attack advertisements—sometimes paid for by candidates but more often by third parties—a choice weapon in the battle for the hearts and minds of the electorate. Today such groups don't need to pay for airtime or space in newspapers—they can create videos, memes, or even just pithy but potent tweets, and release them into the wild. The more outrageous the claims made in them, the more likely they are to go viral. And they're effective: people remember negative messages far more than they do positive ones. Tracking polls show that after a voter has seen a negative ad eight times, he or she begins to move away from the attacked candidate.[3]

Candidates, operatives, and interest groups usually claim that their messages are not really negative, but rather that they are "comparative," and indeed a candidate often needs to compare his or her record with another's in order to make the case that he or she is the superior choice. But negative ads and media attacks are nonetheless unpopular with voters, who often see them as nasty, unfair, and false. In fact, claims that are proven untrue can frequently backfire on the person making them.

WHAT TO WATCH OUT FOR

How is a savvy media consumer to know what to believe? Be careful, be critical, and be fair in your assessment of the messages that pop up on your screens. Ask yourself these questions:

- **How did this message find you?** Did it come up in your social media feeds? Was it a paid advertisement? Was it forwarded, posted, or tweeted by a friend? As we've discussed elsewhere, social media are designed to connect you with content that will appeal to you and your deeply held beliefs. If a claim seems to be tailor made to make you feel outraged, consider whether you are being manipulated by an algorithm.

- **Who created the message?** If it's a glossy video, chances are it was professionally produced—and someone had to pay for it. Was it paid for by a candidate's campaign? What do they have at stake, and how might that affect their charges? If it's a rougher or more rudimentary meme (the kind that your nephew could create on his phone in about thirty seconds), think hard before you lend it any credence at all. If you can't tell who created it, you should probably dismiss it.

- **Are the accusations relevant to the campaign or the office in question?** If character is a legitimate issue, questions of adultery or drug use might have bearing on the election. If not, they might just be personal details used to smear this candidate's reputation. Ask yourself, What kind of person should hold the job? What kinds of qualities are important?

- **Is the accusation or attack timely?** If a person is accused of youthful experimentation or indiscreet behavior in his or her twenties but has been an upstanding lawyer and public servant for twenty-five years, do the accusations have bearing on how the candidate will do the job?

- **Does the message convey a fair charge that can be answered, or does it evoke unarticulated fears and emotions?** A 1964 ad for Lyndon Johnson's presidential campaign showed a little girl counting as she plucked petals from a daisy. An adult male voice gradually replaced hers, counting down to an explosion resulting in a mushroom cloud that obliterated the picture. The "Daisy" commercial never even mentioned Johnson's opponent, Barry Goldwater, though the clear implication was that the conservative, pro-military Goldwater was likely to lead the nation to a nuclear war. The ad was aired only once, but it became a classic example of the sort of ad that seeks to play on the fears of its viewers.

- **Is there any truth to the message?** Before you click "share" on that scathing accusation against a candidate you don't like, study the message and evaluate its truthfulness. Valuable resources for fact-checking messages in the media—including ads, reporting, claims made by candidates and their surrogates, and viral messages—include FactCheck .org, Snopes.com, and Politifact.com.

---

1. Alexandra Marks, "Backlash Grows Against Negative Political Ads," *Christian Science Monitor*, September 28, 1995, 1.
2. Ibid.

ads run by Republican John McCain were negative. Although only 35 percent of Barack Obama's advertising was negative, the fact that he was outspending McCain by running more ads meant that the gap wasn't as large as those numbers would indicate.[57]

Because paid media coverage is so expensive, a campaign's goal is to maximize opportunities for free coverage while controlling, as much as possible, the kind of coverage they get. The major parties' presidential candidates are accompanied by a substantial entourage of reporters who need to file stories on a regular basis, not only for the nation's major newspapers and television networks but also to keep busy the reporters and commentators on the cable news stations like CNN, MSNBC, and Fox. These media have substantial influence in setting the agenda—determining which issues are important and, hence, which candidates' appeals will resonate with voters.[58] As a result, daily campaign events are planned more for the press and the demands of the evening news than for the in-person audiences, who often seem to function primarily as a backdrop for the candidates' efforts to get favorable airtime each day. The campaigns also field daily conference calls with reporters to attack their opponents and defend their candidates and to try to control, or "spin," the way they are covered. In recent election cycles, a strategy for getting on the news without spending a lot of money has been to produce negative "web ads" designed for Internet circulation, which, if catchy enough, could get endless coverage by the networks, the cable stations, and the blogs (see *Don't Be Fooled by . . . Viral Media*).

Although the candidates want the regular exposure, they do not like the norms of broadcast news, which they see as perpetuating horse-race journalism, focusing on who is ahead rather than on substantive issues.[59] In addition, the exhausting nature of campaigns, and the mistakes and gaffes that follow, are a source of constant concern because of the media's tendency to zero in on them and replay them endlessly. The relationship between the campaigns and the media is testy. Each side needs the other, but the candidates want to control the message, and the media want stories that are "news"—controversies, changes in the candidates' standings, or stories of goofs and scandals. We discuss the complex relationship between the media and the candidates at greater length in Chapter 13.

Candidates in recent elections have turned increasingly to "soft news" and entertainment programming to get their messages across. Candidates have been especially effective at appealing across party lines to reach the less engaged voters in the soft news formats. Since Bill Clinton appeared on *The Arsenio Hall Show* to play his saxophone in 1992, candidates have made late night television one of their go-to places to show their human side and demonstrate their senses of humor. NBC's *Saturday Night Live*, Comedy Central's *The Daily Show* (previously with Jon Stewart and now with Trevor Noah), and *The Late Show with Stephen Colbert* have been favored destinations for candidates (even Michelle Obama stopped in to visit *The Daily Show with Jon Stewart* and *The Colbert Report*). In 2016 both Hillary Clinton and Donald Trump made appearances on *SNL* and various talk shows, and Clinton even appeared on *Between Two Ferns* with Zach Galifianakis.

In 2008 the Internet really came into its own as a source of news. Mainstream media outlets like the *New York Times*, the *Washington Post, Time* magazine, and the major networks maintained blogs that joined independent bloggers like Josh Marshall of talkingpointsmemo .com and *National Review Online* in updating campaign news and poll results throughout the day. And now that there's a cell phone in every pocket, YouTube has helped to transform the electoral landscape as well. A recorded gaffe or misstatement by a candidate or a campaign surrogate could go viral—reaching millions of viewers with the quick swipes of many fingers. Politicians accustomed to a more conventional way of campaigning were often caught in the YouTube trap. Bill Clinton, for instance, campaigning for his wife in the Democratic primary in 2008, was several times recorded saying something ill-advised that spread quickly before he could attempt damage control. Even the more media-savvy Obama found a recording of his words about frustrated voters becoming bitter, spoken at what he thought was a closed fundraiser, making the Internet and then the mainstream media rounds at lightning speed. And Mitt Romney was recorded in 2012 at a private fundraiser speaking about how 47 percent of Americans, who pay no taxes, would never vote for him or be persuaded to take responsibility for their lives. His poll numbers dipped after this, and although they improved after the first debate, he was haunted by the image of being unsympathetic to the plight of almost half of Americans. In 2016 there seemed to be nothing Donald Trump could say that would offend his supporters enough to change their votes, and many admired his brash authenticity.

PRESIDENTIAL DEBATES Since 1976 the presidential debates have become one of the major focal points of the campaign. The first televised debate was held in 1960 between John F. Kennedy and Richard Nixon. The younger and more photogenic Kennedy came out on top in those televised debates, but interestingly, those who heard the debates on the radio thought that Nixon did a better job.[60] In general, leading candidates find it less in their interest to participate in debates because they have more to lose and less to win, and so for years debates took place on a sporadic basis.

In the past twenty-five years, however, media and public pressure have all but guaranteed that at least the major-party candidates will participate in debates, although the number, timing, and format of the debates are renegotiated for each presidential election season. Recent elections have generated two or three debates, with a debate among the vice presidential contenders worked in as well. Third-party candidates, who have the most to gain from the free media exposure and the legitimacy that debate participation confers on a campaign, lobby to

Presidential Debates, Then and Now

The 1960 presidential debate between Vice President Richard Nixon and Sen. John F. Kennedy was the first to be televised, benefitting the young, charismatic Kennedy, who appeared poised and relaxed in comparison to a brooding Nixon. A half-century later, many analysts argue that debates have little influence on election outcome, but the 2016 election may have proved to be the exception. For instance, while many felt that Hillary Clinton won the 2016 presidential debates, she lost the election to opponent Donald Trump.

be included but rarely are. Ross Perot was invited in 1992 because both George H. W. Bush and Bill Clinton hoped to woo his supporters, but neither Gary Johnson nor Jill Stein made the 15 percent polling threshold to participate in 2016.

Do the debates matter? Detailed statistical studies show, not surprisingly, that many of the debates have been standoffs. However, some of the debates, especially those identified with significant candidate errors or positive performances, have moved vote intentions 2 to 4 percent, which in a close race could be significant.[61] In addition, there is a good deal of evidence, including from 2004, that citizens learn about the candidates and their issue positions from the debates.[62] In 2008, with Barack Obama an unknown quantity to many voters, the debates helped to introduce him to the general electorate in a way that voters found reassuring, and media "insta-polls" unanimously proclaimed him the winner over John McCain in all three. Interest in the debates varies with how much suspense surrounds the outcome of the election. When the seat is open or the candidates are less well known, more people are likely to watch the debates.[63] In 2012 President Obama was familiar to voters, but his challenger, Mitt Romney, was known mostly as the plutocratic caricature that had been painted of him in Obama advertisements. During their first debate, Romney looked relaxed, confident, and presidential, while the president looked grumpy and passive. Polls showed a huge win for Romney, and many of the Republican-leaning voters who had been turned off by Romney's 47 percent gaffe returned to his camp. Obama's poll numbers dipped, and Romney even took the lead in the polls for a short while. Mad at himself for his sleepy performance in the first debate, Obama snapped back in the second and third debates, and polls showed that voters considered him the winner. By Election Day he had returned to his pre-debate standing in the polls.

Hillary Clinton and Donald Trump faced off in three debates in 2016, with Clinton a strong winner in all scientific post-debate polls. Her extensive debate prep paid off and she was able to needle the less prepared Trump into making responses that made him seem short-tempered and irritable. Since Clinton was trying to make the election about temperament, this played well into her narrative. Unfortunately, the debates were generally thin on substance.

MONEY Winning—or even losing—a presidential campaign involves serious money. The two major-party presidential candidates in 2016 spent over $1 billion each, money that was supplemented by PAC spending. Figure 12.2 shows this striking upward trend, which came about despite significant fundraising limits put into place by the Bipartisan Campaign Reform Act (BCRA).

This torrent of cash is used to cover the costs of all of the activities just discussed: campaign professionals, polling, travel for the candidates and often their spouses (along with the accompanying staff and media), and the production and purchase of media advertising. Where does all this money come from?

Government matching funds are given, in the primary and general election campaigns, to qualified presidential candidates who choose to accept it and to spend only that money. The funds come from citizens who have checked the box on their tax returns that sends $3 ($6 on joint returns) to fund presidential election campaigns. The idea behind the law is to more easily regulate big money influence on campaign finances, ensure a fair contest, and free up candidates to communicate with the public. For primary elections, if a candidate raises at least $5,000 in each of twenty states and agrees to abide by overall spending limits (about $55 million in 2012), as well as state-by-state limits, the federal government matches every contribution up to $250.

This same fund fully finances both major-party candidates' general election campaigns and subsidizes the two national party nominating conventions. John McCain opted to participate in the 2008 federal campaign financing and faced a spending limit of $84.1 million. Barack Obama was the first presidential nominee not to participate in the general election federal financing, arguing that by relying on small donors, his campaign was essentially publicly funded anyway. This meant that his campaign had to raise all the funds it would spend rather than receive the federal subsidy, but it also meant that the Obama campaign was not limited in the amount it could spend. If presidential candidates accept this public funding, they may not raise any other funds or use any leftover funds raised during the primary campaign. In 2012 both parties' candidates anticipated raising and spending at least $1 billion each, so both campaigns passed up the option of receiving government matching funds (about $94 million available in 2012) and the limitations that accepting those funds would impose.[64] Third parties that received at least 5 percent of the vote in the previous presidential campaign may also collect public financing. Unlike the two major parties, however, the money a third party receives depends on the number of votes the party received in the previous election. Obama's decision to self-fund pretty much spelled the death of public funding of presidential general election campaigns, as neither candidate in 2012 or 2016 accepted it, and few taxpayers were donating funds to keep it going in any case.[65]

Hard money refers to the funds given *directly* to candidates by individuals, political action committees (PACs), the political parties, and the government. The spending of hard money is under candidates' control, but its collection is governed by the rules of the Federal Election Campaign Act of 1972, 1974, and its various amendments. This act established the FEC and was intended to stop the flow of money from, and the influence of, large contributors by outlawing contributions by corporations and unions, and by restricting contributions from individuals. The campaign finance reform bill passed in 2002 actually raised the hard money limits. Under that law, individuals can give a federal candidate up to $2,300 per election and

government matching funds money given by the federal government to qualified presidential candidates in the primary and general election campaigns

hard money campaign funds donated directly to candidates; amounts are limited by federal election laws

FIGURE 12.2

Increase in Total Spending in Presidential Campaigns, 1976–2016

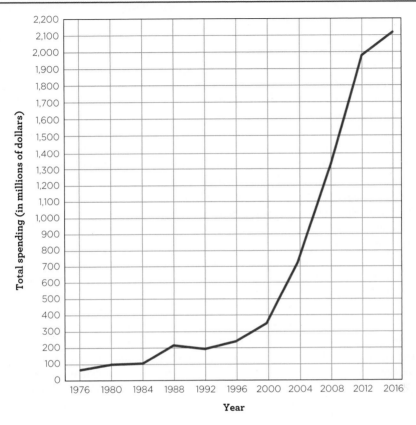

Source: Center for Responsive Politics, "Presidential Fund-raising and Spending, 1976–2008," www.opensecrets.org/pres08/totals.php?cycle=2008; "Banking on Becoming President," www.opensecrets.org/pres08/index.php; "2012 Presidential Race," www.opensecrets.org/pres12/index.php?ql3; "2016 Presidential Race," www.opensecrets.org/pres16/.

can give a total of $108,200 to all federal candidates and parties in a two-year election cycle.[66] The limit on the parties' hard money contributions to candidates was held to be unconstitutional in a 1999 Colorado district federal court decision but was later upheld in a five-to-four Supreme Court decision.[67]

However, in the 2010 decision in *Citizens United v. Federal Election Commission*,[68] the Supreme Court struck down a provision of BCRA (also known as the McCain-Feingold Act) that prohibited corporations (and, by implication, unions and interest groups) from sponsoring broadcast ads for or against specific candidates. Corporations and unions are thus free to engage in broadcast campaigns, although provisions requiring disclosure and limitations on direct contributions to candidates were retained. Experts disagreed about the likely consequences of the far-reaching decision, but mirroring the Court's five-to-four breakdown on the ruling, it was generally decried by liberals and supported by conservatives.[69]

Soft money is unregulated money collected by parties and interest groups in unlimited amounts to spend on party-building activities, GOTV drives, voter education, or issue position advocacy. Prior to the passage of campaign reform in 2002, as long as the money was not spent to tell people how to vote or coordinated with a specific candidate's campaign, the FEC could not regulate soft money. This allowed corporate groups, unions, and political parties to raise unlimited funds often used for television and radio advertising, especially in the form of **issue advocacy ads**. As we discussed in Chapter 11, issue advocacy ads are television or radio commercials during an election campaign that promote a particular issue, usually by attacking the character, views, or position of the candidate the group running the ad wishes to defeat. The courts have considered these ads protected free speech and have held that individuals and organizations could not be stopped from spending money to express their opinions about issues, or even candidates, so long as they did not explicitly tell viewers how to vote.

Most observers thought that BCRA would remove unregulated money from campaigns and curb negative advertising. It limited the spending of PACs and parties, but new groups, called 527 groups after the loophole (section 527) in the Internal Revenue Code that allows them to avoid the regulations imposed by the law, sprang up in their stead (see Chapter 11). Like groups that raised and spent soft money prior to BCRA, 527s can raise unlimited funds for issue advocacy or voter mobilization so long as they do not openly promote or try to defeat any particular candidate. BCRA forbade all groups, even 527s, from running such ads funded by soft money within sixty days of a general election or thirty days of a primary election. The 2010 *Citizens United* case loosened the regulations further, lifting the sixty-day limit.

Interest groups, corporations, and unions have greater leeway in how and when they campaign for candidates. They are still limited in making direct (hard money) contributions but most of their efforts will be as independent expenditures (efforts that cannot be coordinated with the candidates' campaigns). Given that such contributors do not share a single common ideology or set of issue preferences, some observers argue that any effects will largely cancel each other out but there is no doubt that we have seen a huge influx of private money into elections.[70]

GETTING OUT THE VOTE As we mentioned earlier, voter mobilization efforts are an increasingly important part of any presidential campaign. In the 1980s and 1990s, such efforts concentrated mostly on television advertising. Parties have not decreased their television advertising, but they have found that increasing their volunteer corps on the ground, in conjunction with the efforts of sympathetic interest groups (unions and liberal groups for Democrats, Christian conservative groups for Republicans), is a successful strategy for mobilizing voters. In an analysis of the 2002 midterm elections, Republicans found that they could turn out 2 to 3 percent more of their voters by having precinct chairs knock on doors than by using advertising and phone calling alone.[71] Today mobilization efforts combine old-school door-to-door campaigning with modern technology,[72] including the use of vast computer databases to tell volunteers whose doors to knock on.[73] The Clinton team followed the model established by Obama. It had hundreds of offices and deployed thousands of volunteers across the battleground states. They ran a high-tech, professional campaign. Donald Trump did not have a ground game, relying on his rallies to build enthusiasm and the Republican National Committee, which had made a major effort to up its game after 2012.

soft money
unregulated campaign contributions by individuals, groups, or parties that promote general election activities but do not directly support individual candidates

issue advocacy ads advertisements that support issues or candidates without telling constituents how to vote

INTERPRETING ELECTIONS

After the election is over, when the votes are counted, and we know who won, it would seem that the whole election season is finally finished. In reality, the outcomes of our collective decisions cry for interpretation. Probably the most important interpretation is the one articulated by the victor. The winning candidate in presidential elections inevitably claims an **electoral mandate**, maintaining that the people want the president to do the things he campaigned on and that the election is all about the voters' preference for the president's leadership and policy programs. Presidents who can sell the interpretation that their election to office is a ringing endorsement of their policies can work with Congress from a favored position.[74] To the extent that presidents are able to sell their interpretation, they will be more successful in governing. In contrast, the losing party will try to argue that its loss was due to the characteristics of its candidate or specific campaign mistakes. Party members will, predictably, resist the interpretation that the voters rejected their message and their vision for the nation.

The media also offer their interpretations. In fact, research shows that of the many possible explanations that are available, the mainstream media quickly—in just a matter of weeks—home in on an agreed-upon standard explanation of the election.[75] In 2016 it was that both candidates were unlikable and that the campaign was negative, exhausting, and issue free. The media's difficulty in calling Trump out on his many fabrications and their attempts to create a false equivalence in their treatment of the two candidates were in part due to Clinton's long, difficult relationship with the media and what they perceive as her secretiveness, as well as the fact that, believing Clinton would win, few in the media took Trump seriously until the very end. When investigative reports finally began to dig into Trump's background, it was late in the game. Then, ten days before Election Day, FBI director James Comey said he was looking into Clinton's emails again, and that became the focus of the media coverage. By the time Comey cleared Clinton a week later, many people had already voted.

In Your Own Words Identify the organizational and strategic tactics employed in presidential campaigns.

CITIZENSHIP AND ELECTIONS

Do too many informed voters lead to too much conflict?

At the beginning of this chapter, we acknowledged that the American citizen does not bear a strong resemblance to the ideal citizen of classic democratic theory. Nothing we have learned here leads us to think otherwise, but that does not mean that Americans are doomed to an undemocratic future. Scholars who conducted the earliest studies of voting based on survey research were surprised at the low levels of interest most citizens showed in presidential election campaigns. These studies of the 1944 and 1948 presidential elections found that most citizens had their minds made up before the campaigns began and that opinions changed only slightly in response to the efforts of the parties and candidates. Instead of people relying on new information coming from the campaigns, they voted according to the groups to which they belonged. Income, occupation, religion, and similar factors structured whom people talked to, what they learned, and how they voted. The authors of these studies concluded that democracy is probably safer without a single type of citizen who matches the civic ideal of high levels of participation, knowledge, and commitment.[76]

electoral mandate the perception that an election victory signals broad support for the winner's proposed policies

In this view, such high levels of involvement would indicate a citizenry fraught with conflict. Intense participation comes with intense commitment and strongly held positions, which make for an unwillingness to compromise. This revision of the call for classic "good citizens" holds that our democratic polity is actually better off when it has lots of different types of citizens: some who care deeply, are highly informed, and participate intensely; many more who care moderately, are a bit informed, and participate as much out of duty to the process as out of commitment to one party or candidate; and some who are less aware of politics until some great issue or controversy awakens them from their political slumber.

The virtue of modern democracy in this *political specialization view* is that citizens play different roles and that together these combine to form an electoral system that has the attributes we prefer: it is reasonably stable; it responds to changes of issues and candidates, but not too much; and the electorate as a whole cares, but not so intensely that any significant portion of the citizenry will challenge the results of an election. Its most obvious flaw is that it is biased against the interests of those who are least likely to be activist or pluralist citizens—the young, the poor, the uneducated, and minorities.[77]

In Your Own Words Recognize the importance of elections for citizens.

Let's Revisit: What's at Stake . . . ?

We began this chapter asking how, in a modern democracy, an archaic constitutional institution, long altered from its original purpose, managed to throw an election from a popular vote winner to her opponent. What is at stake in keeping the Electoral College in an age when its use seems to have outlived the intentions and concerns of the founders and when, in fact, it might have preserved the fate of exactly the unexperienced, populist kind of candidate they were seeking to avoid?

As we have seen in this chapter, and all through this book, politics is about rules, and jockeying to get the rules that give you an advantage. To understand the stakes in keeping the Electoral College, we need to be clear on the fact that its major job is to produce winners and losers.

There is the most agitation to change a rule when it is perceived to produce a result that makes you a loser. Then you have a stake in changing it. In the case of the Electoral College, when it produces a president other than the popular vote winner, there is one side losing and feeling aggrieved, ready to change the rules, but there is also a side that won, and, what's more, a side that won *only* because of the Electoral College. That side has a stake in keeping the institution. Finding consensus for change at that point is impossible.

There is far less agitation to change the rules when, like a quiet appendix, it's not causing any trouble. At that time we hardly notice it. And when change probably means a constitutional amendment, which is hard work even during times of passionate desire for transformation, it's even less likely.

Uncontested states—the non-swing states that generally go consistently for one party or the other—would normally have a stake in changing the Electoral College because most of them receive hardly any attention by campaigners for the White House. The National Public Vote project claims that 94 percent of the 2016 presidential campaign was fought in just twelve states.[78]

But that means that the twelve states that received all the attention have a large stake in keeping things just as they are. Candidate visits, promises, ad spending, rallies, news coverage—all those are plusses to the states that are used to figuring as the important swing states.

What was curious about the 2016 election is that the electoral map began to shift in subtle ways. With demographic changes it's possible that today's solid red or blue states will be tomorrow's swing states, and that gives all states a stake in waiting to see how things turn out.

One clear possessor of stakes in this process is the American people who, as we have seen, are by and large proceduralists, accepting the outcome of the rules whether they like them or not, because they recognize that a rule-based procedural system is preferable to the alternative. At the same time, we *are* a democracy. And we have a stake in having rules that are seen as fair and representative of the people's will—which may be why the National Popular Vote Interstate Compact continues to gather support, and why the 2016 election resulted in renewed calls for reform.

for CQ Press

Want a better grade?

Get the tools you need to sharpen your study skills. **SAGE edge** offers practice quizzes, eFlashcards, video, and multimedia at **edge.sagepub.com/barbourbrief8e.**

Review

Exercising the Right to Vote in America

Voting enhances the quality of democratic life by legitimizing the outcomes of elections, but election rules can make it more or less difficult to vote, in a process known as **regulating the electorate** (399). However, American voter turnout levels are typically among the lowest in the world and may endanger American democracy. Factors such as age, income, education, and race affect whether a person is likely to vote, as do legal obstacles (though measures like the **Motor Voter Act** [400] try to overcome these).

How America Decides

Varying levels of **social connectedness** (407) and **voter mobilization** (406) play a role in whether or not Americans choose to vote. Those who do participate cannot realistically investigate every policy proposal on their own. Therefore, voters make their decisions by considering party identification and peer viewpoints; prominent issues, employing elements of both **prospective voting** (409) and **retrospective voting** (409); as well as candidate image.

Presidential Campaigns

The "road to the White House" is long, expensive, and grueling. It begins with planning and early fundraising, a sort of **invisible primary** (411) stage, and develops into more active campaigning during the **presidential primary** (412)—where primaries may be **open** (412) or **closed** (412)—and the **party caucus** (412) phase, a period considerably shortened these days due to the practice of **front-loading** (413). Candidates want to be perceived to have **momentum** (413) in the race, but being considered the **front-runner** (413) has both advantages and disadvantages. Each party's choice of a candidate is announced officially at the party conventions, and the general election campaign is launched after Labor Day.

The general election campaign is shaped by the battle for large states with significant votes in the **Electoral College** (415) and the quest to find and convert **swing voters** (415). Professional staff run the campaign—coordinating activities, engaging in **oppo research** (418), managing the media and running ads, including **negative advertising** (421). An essential part of campaign strategy is the consideration of issues—**valence issues** (419) on which most candidates agree; **position issues** (419) on which they differ; **wedge issues** (420), which can be used against the other side; and **issue ownership** (421), which can give one party or the other an edge.

Raising and spending money is also a key part of campaigns. Campaign money can be in the form of **government matching funds** (426) given to candidates of the major parties and to candidates of the minor parties who performed well in the previous election, **hard money** (426) donations collected by the candidates, or **soft money** (428) collected by parties and interest groups. Soft money, used for get-out-the-vote efforts and the funding of **issue advocacy ads** (428), was supposed to be regulated by campaign finance legislation in 2002, but loopholes have allowed it to flourish in a different form. All this campaign activity is geared toward winning the election, so that the victorious candidate can claim an **electoral mandate** (429).

Bill Hinton/Contributor

13

Media, Power, and Political Communication

In Your Own Words

After you've read this chapter, you will be able to

13.1 Discuss changes over the past several decades in the ways in which Americans get their news and information.

13.2 Describe the ways in which media ownership and government regulation influence the news we get.

13.3 Explain the roles and responsibilities of journalists and the tools they use to shape and perpetuate political narratives.

13.4 Identify the strategies politicians use to counter the influence of the media and shape and perpetuate their own political narratives.

13.5 Summarize the relationship between citizens and the media.

What's at Stake . . . in Living in an Information Bubble?

From the moment Americans woke up on June 12, 2016, to the horrific news that forty-nine people had been shot at the Pulse nightclub in Orlando, Florida, two competing stories about the tragedy took root in the American psyche. Spawned by the ideological assumptions we began with, fed by the media sources we turned to for information, and nurtured by the social media connections through which we shared what we learned, the stories grew. They were symbolized by two very different speeches by the 2016 presidential candidates and perfectly illustrated by the ongoing chatter on two competing morning talk shows throughout the week: *Morning Joe* on MSNBC and *Fox & Friends* on Fox.

One story said that the shooter was a mentally disturbed American of Afghan heritage, born in New York, conflicted about his own sexuality, violent at home, and unpopular at work for his homophobic and racist language. The big question for the people for whom this narrative made sense was how this unbalanced man, three times interviewed by the FBI for possible terrorist sympathies and on the terror watch list for a period of time, was able to be licensed as a security guard and managed to buy the AR-15 assault weapon that allowed him to mow down partiers at Pulse.

In her speech, presumptive Democratic nominee Hillary Clinton embraced the LGBTQ community, emphasized the importance of reaching out to the American Muslim population to enlist their cooperation in detecting radicalized "lone-wolf" terrorists, and talked about the importance of putting an assault weapon ban in place so that the same weapon that had been used in multiple mass shootings could not be easily purchased by people with suspicious backgrounds or histories of mental illness.

The themes Clinton set out were talked about, repeated, and woven into a common story about the Orlando shooting that was discussed endlessly on MSNBC's *Morning Joe*, as well as on innumerable other shows and through newspaper stories and social media communications that were shared like wildfire, for days after the massacre.

But that was not the only narrative. A competing story said that the shooting was conducted by a member of ISIS, committed to exterminating gays and other Americans in an act of radical Islamic terrorism. In this view the president of the United States was complicit in the attack by not using the phrase "radical Islamic terrorism" and perhaps for suspected Muslim sympathies. The big question for people persuaded by this narrative was how the shooter had gotten into the country in the first place and how he and people like him could be kept out. In his speech, given shortly after Clinton's, presumptive Republican nominee Donald Trump also expressed sympathy for the LGBTQ community, but he reiterated his call for a ban on immigration from countries where there was a perceived threat to Americans. He referred to the shooter as an Afghan born to immigrant parents, not as an American, and said the major problem we faced was that Hillary Clinton wanted to let huge numbers of Muslim immigrants into the country without proper vetting. He deplored a lack of leadership that he said was destroying the country.

Trump was not lauded by his party leadership for his accusations about President Obama or his call for a ban on Muslim immigration, but his views clearly resonated with his base. The morning show *Fox & Friends* reinforced the narrative, as did other Fox shows and talk radio, and it too took off on wings of social media.

A Gallup poll captured the difference: 60 percent of Democrats saw the issue as gun violence; 70 percent of Republicans said it was terrorism.[1]

Two narratives, focused on one objective event, explaining the world in diametrically opposed ways (and neither one true, apparently, as more evidence emerged in later years).[2] If you lived in one world, you would not even recognize the other. Your media-viewing habits, your connections with family and friends, and the news you would forward to each other would create the impression that all right-thinking people saw the world the way you did. You would be in an information bubble, the kind we discussed back in Chapter 1, a closed loop of self-reinforcing evidence supporting a particular interpretation of events.

Does it make a difference to your life or to the republic we all try to keep if citizens are living in virtually separate worlds of so-called facts and information? Do democracies require that we share some fundamental understanding of the world? Are information bubbles merely a version of the ideologies we have discussed throughout this book, or do they threaten the integrity of the common political culture itself? Can we communicate without the common foundation provided by referencing the same understanding of facts? Just what is at stake in a world of citizens locked in information bubbles?

IN this book we have seen that a major component of power is control of information, or the way information is assembled into narratives, and we have come to recognize the truth right under all of our noses—information is no longer a scarce resource. It is an abundant resource and the clamour of the information marketplace is the sound of many people seeking to tell and sell their narratives at increasing volume. The phenomenal increase of channels through which information can flow—that is, the explosion of the media in the past century but especially in the digital age—has made understanding the relationships among power, narratives, and political communication all the more central. Indeed, as citizens and scholars, we ignore it at our peril.

In every chapter in this book we have tried to be clear that power is not just something that is leveraged at us, but something that we, as citizens, can lay claim to. It may not be easy, the decks may be stacked against us, but it is possible. In the mediated age in which we now live, that is truer than ever, which is why we began our discussion of the media in Chapter 1—so that you would be able to think about how the channels through which information is delivered affect all of our lives and how we, in turn, can affect the information. This chapter, more so than most in this book, is almost as much about us as it is about institutions and process.

Today we are bombarded by a constant competition of narratives, spewing from every television and radio show, web site, blog, Twitter feed, Facebook page, or Instagram story. In this chapter we look at the modern media world, the impact it has on shaping our political beliefs, and the ways in which we can take hold of the narrative ourselves to be more critical consumers of the information we receive.

WHERE DO WE GET OUR INFORMATION?

A hybrid of traditional and interactive sources

Narratives are built from information, and increasingly we get that information from a wide array of media sources. *Media* is the plural of *medium*, meaning in this case an agency through which communication between two different entities can take place. Just as a medium can be a person who claims to transmit messages from the spiritual world to earthbound souls, today's **mass media**, whether through printed word or electronic signal, convey information cheaply and efficiently from the upper reaches of the political world to everyday citizens. Today we do far more than just watch and listen to the media, which are increasingly multimedia, digital, available on demand, and often interactive in nature. Communication scholars refer to this merging of traditional and digital media as **media convergence**, and it has implications for our political as well as social lives.[3] Politicians scramble to stay on top of electronic innovations that continually shape and alter the political world. And what is just as important in a democratic society, the media help carry information back from citizens to the politicians who lead, or seek to lead, them.

The news media in the twenty-first century increasingly rely on new technology. The printing press may have been invented in China over a thousand years ago, but almost all of the truly amazing innovations in information technology—telegraphs, telephones, photography, radio, television, computers, faxes, cell phones, and the Internet—have been developed in the past two hundred years, and just over half of them have come into common use only in the past fifty. What that means is that our technological capabilities sometimes outrun our sophistication about how that technology ought to be used or how it may affect the news it transfers.

Understanding who gets information, where it comes from, and how that information is affected by the technology that brings it to us is crucial to being a knowledgeable student of politics, not to mention an effective democratic citizen. In this section we examine the sources that we in America turn to for the news and the consequences that follow from our choices.

THE MASS MEDIA TODAY

Once upon a time, news entered the average American's life at only a couple of neatly defined and very predictable points during the day. The local morning paper arrived before dawn, there to be read over coffee and breakfast. The afternoon paper (yes, most cities had two papers back then) was waiting for you when you came home from work. Big-city papers like the *New York Times* and the *Washington Post* were available only to those who lived in New York or Washington, D.C., unless you ordered a copy of the paper to be mailed to you, at great expense, arriving several days late (no FedEx, no overnight delivery). In 1960 the evening news came on at 7:30 p.m., and TV-owning America (87 percent of households in 1960) got their last news of the day from one of only three channels. That was pretty much it for news in 1960s America, unless a special event (a space shot, for instance) or a tragedy (like John F. Kennedy's assassination) occurred that required a special bulletin.

Today media convergence defines how we get our news—we get at least a little news from a lot of sources. Only 18 percent of Americans report often getting news from print newspapers, 25 percent from radio, 33 percent from news web sites and apps, 26 percent from network news, 28 percent from cable TV, and 37 percent from local TV.[4] But overall, 67 percent of adults get some news on social media, 50 percent sometimes or often. They are likeliest to

mass media the means of conveying information to large public audiences cheaply and efficiently

media convergence the merging of traditional media with digital communication technologies such as telecommunications and the Internet

Bettmann/Getty Images

Charles Ommanney/Getty Images

One Hour of Nightly News to 24/7

In 1968, television news was limited to evening broadcasts on the three networks—only a few relatively powerful people, like President Lyndon Johnson, had the luxury of tuning in to all three of them simultaneously. Today it's easy to create your own custom media diet from a variety of sources—and carry them all around in your pocket—but ironically, President Obama was one of the later adopters of this new technology, due to security concerns.

get news from, in descending order, Twitter, Reddit, Facebook, Tumblr, YouTube, Snapchat, Instagram, LinkedIn, and WhatsApp, although Facebook is by far the most popular social media site in general, followed by YouTube, Instagram, LinkedIn, and Snapchat.[5]

There are sharp generational divides in these habits. Millennials (those born between about 1980 and 1997) are far more likely to rely on Facebook for news than are their elders (although they are less likely to be interested in political news); Baby Boomers (born between 1946 and 1964) rely more on local television; and Gen Xers (born in between) split the difference.[6]

Consider what this means. Younger generations are more likely to get their news from sources they curate themselves—that is, they choose the source of the news directly, or they choose the people with whom they associate, who in turn share the news with them. By contrast, older Americans watch whatever is served up to them by the media elite. That means that younger people are participating in the choice of narratives they wish to engage in, but they also have the option of eliminating all the ones they don't like. *Snapshot of America: Where Do We Get Our News?* shows the demographics behind this changing media landscape.

Although most of the American public is exposed to some news, and some people are exposed to quite a lot of it, levels of political information in this country are not high. In one study, only about half of the public could correctly answer basic questions about domestic politics and public figures.[7] These politically informed people are not evenly distributed throughout the population, either. Older Americans, those with more education, and men were more likely to answer the questions correctly.[8]

THE DEMISE OF THE PRINT MEDIA

No less a grand thinker than Thomas Jefferson said, "The basis of our governments being the opinion of the people, the very first object should be to keep that right; and were it left to me to decide whether we should have a government without newspapers or newspapers without a government, I should not hesitate a moment to prefer the latter."[9] A look at some survey results, however, shows that print media are in deep trouble, and 2015 was the worst year for newspapers since the Great Recession.[10] Many venerable newspapers have ceased publication

Snapshot of America: *Where Do We Get Our News?*

News Consumers

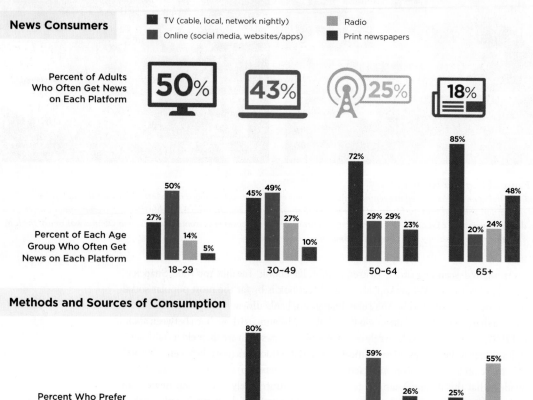

■ TV (cable, local, network nightly)
■ Online (social media, websites/apps)
■ Radio
■ Print newspapers

Percent of Adults Who Often Get News on Each Platform

50% 43% 25% 18%

Percent of Each Age Group Who Often Get News on Each Platform

18–29
- 27%
- 50%
- 14%
- 5%

30–49
- 45%
- 49%
- 27%
- 10%

50–64
- 72%
- 29%
- 29%
- 23%

65+
- 85%
- 20%
- 24%
- 48%

Methods and Sources of Consumption

Percent Who Prefer Getting Their News on Each Platform

Those who prefer...

Watching the news
- 80%
- 12%
- 3%
- 4%

Reading the news
- 10%
- 59%
- 4%
- 26%

Listening to news
- 25%
- 14%
- 55%
- 3%

Online News Sources

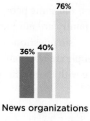

Percent of Online News Consumers Who "Often" or "Sometimes" Get News Online From...

■ Often
■ Sometimes
■ Often + Sometimes

News organizations
- 36%
- 40%
- 76%

People they are close with
- 15%
- 54%
- 69%

People they are not particularly close with
- 6%
- 28%
- 34%

Source: Pew Research Center, "The Modern News Consumer," July 7, 2016, www.journalism.org/2016/07/07/the-modern-news-consumer/; Jeffrey Gottfried and Elisa Shearer, "Americans' Online News Use Is Closing in on TV News Use," Pew Research Center, September 7, 2017, www.pewresearch.org/fact-tank/2017/09/07/americans-online-news-use-vs-tv-news-use/.

Behind the Numbers

The Pew Research Center derived these categories of news consumers from their surveys. Given the descriptions of each, where do you fit? In what ways does where one gets one's news affect one's knowledge of political leaders?

or moved to a print-online hybrid or simply an online existence, most notably the *Christian Science Monitor*.[11] Today most towns have only one paper, if they have any at all.

What aspects of journalism are fundamental to keeping the republic?

Near the end of the second decade of the century, it is not unusual to hear people say that the day of the print media is over.[12] If you are feeling inclined to irony, you can Google "newspapers are dead" and you will get over 60,000,000 hits, all with people insisting (1) that it is true, (2) that it isn't, (3) that it matters, and (4) that it doesn't. In further irony, many of the most thriving news web sites—from "viral news sites" like *BuzzFeed* to online journals like the *Drudge Report* and the *Huffington Post* that traffic in "breaking news"—are often merely linking to reporting done by those same dinosaur newspapers whose deaths they are quick to proclaim.

The demise of those newspapers carries a cost that has little to do with whether their reporting is accessed at a newsstand or on a phone. As Internet expert and writer Clay Shirky says, "Society doesn't need newspapers. What we need is journalism."[13] By this he means information, well researched and objective, about the world we live in, about the things our elected officials are doing in our name, and about the consequences of the public choices we make.

That kind of journalism has traditionally been paid for by newspapers that have either had their own news bureaus around the world or subscribed to and supported a news service like the Associated Press (AP). The money they paid for news-gathering came from advertisers who today have multiple, cheap, or even free outlets through which to reach customers. The loss of those crucial revenue streams hit newspapers—and thus journalism—hard (see *Don't Be Fooled by . . . Clickbait* later in this chapter). Shirky argues that we are in the midst of a revolution, "where the old stuff gets broken faster than the new stuff is put in its place,"[14] so we don't know what journalism will look like in a new, post-newspaper age, but he thinks it's quite likely that that is where we are headed.

RADIO AND TELEVISION

Radios, once state-of-the-art communication, have become commonplace. Ninety-one percent of Americans say they listen weekly[15] to one or more of the 15,000-plus radio stations broadcast over the airwaves in the United States.[16] Since the 1980s, "talk radio" has provided an interactive political platform, allowing the radio hosts and their guests, as well as the audience, to air their opinions on politics and creating a sense of political community among their primarily conservative listeners. There are also two noncommercial networks, National Public Radio and Public Radio International, funded in small part by the U.S. government but primarily by private donations from corporations and individuals.[17]

But the impact of radio on the American public, initially dramatic, cannot compare with the effects of television. American ownership of television sets skyrocketed from 9 percent of households in 1950 to 97 percent in 1975, a statistic that continues to hold firm. In fact, 58 percent of American homes have one or two television sets and 39 percent own three or more; about 84 percent of U.S. adults subscribe to cable or satellite services, although that percentage is falling as streaming services become more popular.[18] Live television viewership has declined over the past decade, but Americans remain voracious viewers of videos, whether live on television, delayed on a digital recording device, or streamed from the Internet. Nielsen, a marketing firm that tracks audience share, reports that the average American watches five hours of live television each day, and another half hour of "time shifted" television.[19] That doesn't count the hours they spend watching videos, many of which originated for television, that they stream on another device. Considering that Americans spend six to eight hours a day at school or at work, this is an astounding figure, accounting for much of America's leisure time.

Television is primarily an entertainment medium; news has always been a secondary function. Once given a choice of only three networks, the typical American home today receives nearly 189 television channels, although they each might watch only about 17 of them.[20] Rather than pursuing broad markets, stations are now often focusing on specific audiences such as people interested in health and fitness, sports, or travel. This practice of targeting a small, specialized broadcast market is called **narrowcasting**.[21] The competition for viewers is fierce, and as we will see, the quality of the news available can suffer as a consequence.

Politicians were quick to realize that, even more than radio, television allowed them to reach a broad audience without having to deal with print reporters and their adversarial questions. The Kennedy administration was the first to make real use of television, a medium that might have been made for the young, telegenic president. And it was television that brought the nation together in a community of grief when Kennedy was assassinated. Television carried the Vietnam War (along with its protesters) and the civil rights movement into Americans' homes, and the images that it created helped build popular support to end the war abroad and segregation at home. Television can create global as well as national communities, an increasingly familiar experience to many Americans as they watch their TVs in the wake of jubilant international celebrations, natural disasters, or human-made mayhem.

A number of television shows today focus on politics. Many cable stations and C-SPAN, sometimes called "America's Town Hall," offer news around the clock, although not all the news concerns politics. Weekend shows like *Meet the Press* highlight the week's coverage of politics, and the cable news stations frequently showcase debates between liberals and conservatives on current issues. Political shows target particular age groups or ideologies. And politics is often the subject of the jokes on such shows as *Full Frontal*, *Saturday Night Live*, *The Daily Show*, *The Late Show*, and *Last Week Tonight*.

Since at least 2000, the major presidential candidates and their wives have appeared on these comedy/entertainment shows to try to demonstrate that they are regular, likable people and to reach audiences that might not otherwise tune in to politics. President Obama was particularly adept at using unorthodox outlets, for instance, appearing on the online show *Between Two Ferns* in 2014 to encourage young people to sign up for health insurance. Hillary Clinton appeared on the show in 2016 while suffering from pneumonia.

In 2016, Donald Trump let Jimmy Fallon tousle his hair, revealing an extensive comb-over. These appearances have the effect of humanizing the candidates and making them seem approachable, often by getting them to laugh at themselves.

THE INTERNET

The reach of print media, radio, and television is dwarfed by the scope and possibilities of the Internet, which connects home or business computers to a global network of digital sites and an ever-expanding array of media content. In 2018 some 89 percent of American adults used the Internet (up from 46 percent in 2000).[22] A full 65 percent of households have a broadband connection at home, down from a high of 70 percent in 2016, and more than 80 percent of Americans are able to access the Internet from smartphones and other devices.[23] We have already seen the numbers of Americans who get news online and

narrowcasting the targeting of specialized audiences by the media

particularly from social media. Thirty-seven percent of Internet users have socially interacted with others concerning the news—creating it, commenting on it, or disseminating it through social networking sites like Facebook or Twitter.[24] The Internet has revolutionized the way we get information.

The digital age in which we live today has made politics immediate and personal. For much of our history, we haven't known our fellow citizens outside of our own communities, we have been unable to directly investigate the issues ourselves, and we've had no idea what actions our government has taken to deal with issues unless the media told us. We are still dependent on the mass media to connect us to our government, and to create the only real space we have for public deliberation of issues. But technological developments make possible ever-newer forms of political community and more immediate access to information. Government officials can communicate with us directly, bypassing the traditional press. Networking sites like Facebook, LinkedIn, and Twitter allow people to reach out and interact socially, and politicians have not been shy about using such strategies to create networks of supporters. Chat rooms and blogs allow people with common interests to find each other from the far reaches of the world, allowing debate and discussion on a scale never before imagined.

Some visionaries talk of the day when we will all vote electronically on individual issues from our home computers (or maybe even our phones). If we have not yet arrived at that day of direct democratic decision making, changes in the media are nonetheless revolutionizing the possibilities of democracy, much as the printing press and television did earlier, bringing us closer to the Athenian ideal of political community in cyberspace, if not in real space.

Today, most major **news organizations**—including all the major newspapers and broadcast news organizations—are multimedia ventures. All the major newspapers, magazines, and news networks (both TV and radio), along with news services like the AP, have web sites where all or most of the news in their print versions can be found, often with additional content, including blogs and podcasts. Access to these sites is sometimes available for free, although that clearly provides a disincentive for people to subscribe, thus damaging these news organizations' bottom line and hindering their ability to report the news. Increasingly, they are putting most of their content behind a pay wall, like the *New York Times* and *Wall Street Journal* have done, as they search for a viable business model that will keep them solvent.

By searching for the topics we want and connecting to links with related sites, we can customize our web news. Politics buffs can bypass nonpolitical news, and vice versa. True politics junkies can go straight to the source: the federal government makes enormous amounts of information available at its www.whitehouse.gov, www.house.gov, and www.senate.gov sites.

The web has also provided fertile ground for myriad other sources of news to take root. While print and broadcast media were faced with a scarcity of space and airtime, the wide open web has space for seemingly endless content and a low barrier to entry for new voices seeking a platform. For example, online news sites like *Slate*, *Vox*, *Salon*, the *Huffington Post*, and the *Drudge Report* exist solely on the Internet and may or may not adopt the conventions, practices, and standards of the more traditional media. Also in the mix are **news aggregators**—sites and software that cull content from other web sites to produce "newsfeeds." Editors on some news aggregators, like Google News, the *Huffington Post*, *BuzzFeed*, and *theSkimm*, choose articles from other sites to share with their readers, sometimes in combination with original content. Other news aggregators allow readers to customize their own news feeds through web-based applications. Anyone

news organizations businesses (and occasionally nonprofits) devoted to reporting and disseminating news via print, broadcast, or digital media—or a multimedia combination

news aggregators web sites, applications, and software that cull content from other digital sources

with a smartphone can set up a blog, podcast, or video channel via simple and inexpensive (or even free) applications such as WordPress, Stitcher, and YouTube. This new technology provides open platforms for individuals to create content that is personal, political, cultural, or anything in between—running the gamut from individual diaries to investigative journalism.

The proliferation of web sites professing to provide news can make processing the information on the web challenging. As we discussed in Chapter 1, these overlapping sources give us access to more information than ever before, but the task of sorting and evaluating that information is solely our own responsibility.

Not only does the web provide information, but it is also interactive to a degree that far surpasses talk radio or television. Most social media, web sites, and blogs offer discussion opportunities through which all sorts of information can be shared, topics debated, and people met. Although this can allow the formation of communities based on specialized interests or similar views, it can also make it very easy for people with fringe or extreme views to find each other and organize.[25] Political campaigns began to take advantage of this in 2008, using online technology and social networking principles to organize, raise funds, and get out the vote. Barack Obama's campaign proved to be skilled at using the new technology, setting the gold standard for future candidates to beat.[26] The Internet has the potential to increase the direct participation of citizens in political communities and political decisions, though the fact that not all Americans have equal access to the web means that multiple classes of citizenship could form.

Some observers believe that the new media landscape is fertile ground for positive changes. Media critic Dan Gillmor argues that a powerful, citizen-driven journalism is taking the place of a complacent, ratings-driven corporate journalism, that information is gathered and disseminated in real time with multiple researchers on the job to correct and assist each other, a sort of Wikipedia journalism, perhaps.[27] This is the model, for instance, of Andrew Sullivan, who "live blogged" the Iranian uprising in 2009, passing on to his readers information tweeted to him from the front lines, information that could not have been easily gathered even with a news bureau in Tehran. Sullivan would agree with Gillmor, arguing that blogging is "the first journalistic model that actually harnesses rather than exploits the true democratic nature of the web."[28] (See *Profiles in Citizenship* for more from Andrew Sullivan.)

For Sullivan, the demise of the old media and the rise of the new was a positive development, making him more hopeful for democracy, not less. He said,

But what distinguishes the best of the new media is what could still be recaptured by the old: the mischievous spirit of journalism and free, unfettered inquiry. Journalism has gotten too pompous, too affluent, too self-loving, and too entwined with the establishment of both wings of American politics to be what we need it to be.

We need it to be fearless and obnoxious, out of a conviction that more speech, however much vulgarity and nonsense it creates, is always better than less speech. In America, this is a liberal spirit in the grandest sense of that word—but also a conservative one, since retaining that rebelliousness is tending to an ancient American tradition, from the Founders onward.[29]

Andrew Sullivan

Andrew H. Walker/Getty Images

Andrew Sullivan was a blogging pioneer, a man who described his job as "having a conversation with 1.2 million people a month." By the time her retired his blog in 2015, he had transformed the way a writer could crowd-source information and interact with an audience. In the beginning, it seemed to be a perfect medium for Sullivan. It allowed him combine advocacy and fact-sifting in a form that broke with the old models of news-gathering. He wrote "what bloggers do is completely new—and cannot be replicated on any other medium . . . And it harnesses the web's real genius—its ability to empower anyone to do what only a few in the past could genuinely pull off . . . It's a new medium finally finding a unique voice."[1]

Here are some other thoughts from Andrew Sullivan:

On patriotism

"It's not the same thing as nationalism. It is not that your country is always right. . . . I think at some level it is simply loving—and I mean that in a deep sense—the culture, tradition, constitution, and people of the place you call home. In a way I must say I have two patriotisms—of the country I came from and the country I'm still trying to become a citizen of. And patriotism, yes, does mean sometimes dissenting from one's country's leadership, but I think it's too facile to say it's the highest form. I think another equally valid form is supporting your country when the chips are down, even when it isn't perfect, even when it does make mistakes, because it's yours."

On keeping the republic

"America is actually in I think a quite extraordinary crisis right now—spiritually, politically, and economically. I don't think it's been this acute since maybe the late 70s or 60s. . . . I do think people have to understand if they are not there the discourse will be captured by someone else. And you have a responsibility—I've lived long enough to understand that. And it's easy to insulate oneself and delude oneself into thinking it doesn't really matter or I don't have to do something—but in fact you do.

One of the ways this really struck home for me was, personally, in the late 80s, early 90s, the AIDS crisis. I realized if I didn't help these people who were dying no one would. . . . And then when I contracted it, and thought I was given a few years, I sat down and wrote [his book] *Virtually Normal*, because I wanted to leave behind a contribution to an argument [about gay rights]. . . . I had nothing to lose because I thought I was going to die. But why should I have had to get to that point? So imagine that you have a couple of years left on this Earth, what are you waiting for?"

Source: Andrew Sullivan talked with Christine Barbour in August 2010.

1. Andrew Sullivan, "A Blogger's Manifesto," *Sunday Times of London*, February 24, 2002.

Shirky is optimistic as well:

For the next few decades, journalism will be made up of overlapping special cases. Many of these models will rely on amateurs as researchers and writers. Many of these models will rely on sponsorship or grants or endowments instead of revenues. Many of these models will rely on excitable 14 year olds distributing the results. Many of these models will fail. No one experiment is going to replace what we are now losing with the demise of news on paper, but over time, the collection of new experiments that do might give us the journalism we need.[30]

And then again, they may not—Shirky's optimism does not seem misplaced in light of the work of writers such as Gillmor and Sullivan, but it's undeniable that the changing ways in which information is shared will have some effects on our democracy. The jury is out on this one, but the open, innovative nature of the medium allows each of us to engage in the experimentation and work that might bring the answers. The late media critic Marshall McLuhan wrote in the 1960s that "the medium is the message." In the Internet age, that has the potential to be true as never before.

In Your Own Words Discuss changes over the past several decades in the ways in which Americans get their news and information.

HOW DOES MEDIA OWNERSHIP AFFECT CONTROL OF THE NARRATIVE?

A complex system of corporate and independent gatekeepers

As we saw in Chapter 1, the people who control the news we get are gatekeepers—they are in charge of what information gets to us. We have also seen that the gatekeeping structure of the American media has changed radically since the days of the nation's founding. Back then, newspapers were partisan instruments dependent on government for their very existence. But today, most news comes from—or at least through—massive, corporate-owned sources—whether conventional news sources like the *New York Times* and CBS or through Facebook and Google. In this section we look at ownership of the modern media complex, the ways in which government regulates (or does not regulate) the media, and how it all affects the media's gatekeeping function.

WHO OWNS THE MEDIA?

Today the media are big business, but on a scale undreamed of by such early journalism entrepreneurs as Joseph Pulitzer and William Hearst, whose fiercely competitive tabloid wars in 1890s New York gave birth to what is known as *yellow journalism*, as each rushed to attract readers with sensational headlines and stories.

The traditional mainstream media still exist but all the major circulation newspapers in this country, as well as commercial radio and television networks, are owned by major conglomerates and have huge digital presences. Overall this has meant that there are fewer and fewer media outlets owned by fewer and fewer corporations, with content more and more the same.[31] In fact, just six corporations—Time-Warner (currently in the process of merging with AT&T), Disney, Viacom, CBS Corporation, News Corp, and Comcast—own most of the major national newspapers, the leading news magazines, the national television networks including CNN and other cable stations, as well as publishing houses, movie studios, telephone companies, entertainment firms, and other multimedia operations. Most of these corporations are also involved in other businesses, as their familiar names attest.

Often editorial decisions are matters of corporate policy, not individual judgment. And if profit was an overriding concern for the editor-entrepreneurs a century ago, it is gospel for

gatekeepers journalists and the media elite who determine which news stories are covered and which are not

the conglomerates today. *The Big Picture* in this chapter gives you an idea of what this corporate ownership of the media looks like, but keep in mind that it is a constantly changing picture. What troubles critics is that many Americans don't know that most of their news and entertainment comes from just a few corporate sources and are unaware of the consequences that this corporate ownership structure has for all of us.[32]

But the modern conventional media have a lot of competition in the area of creating narratives. Startups like *VICE, Vox, FiveThirtyEight, BuzzFeed*, and the *Huffington Post* on the center-left—all of which have developed fresh, diverse, often edgy brands—have become media empires themselves or been gobbled up by other outlets. Sites like *Breitbart* have done the same on the far right. Many journalists who began as bloggers have found their way into the bigger media picture as well. And corporate forces like Google, Facebook, and Apple, while not journalistic producers in their own right, aggregate and distribute news via algorithms that decide who gets what information. As we suggested earlier, social media are rapidly becoming favored news sources, even though they are not news producers. Though sites like Facebook, Twitter, and YouTube are big business and may use their own formulas to decide what news to expose us to, they, as well as blogs and crowd-sourced sites, like Medium, allow citizen participation to an unprecedented degree.

Importantly, even though social media outlets post articles and news on our pages that their formulas think we will be interested in, they are based on our own profiles—we decide who our friends are on Facebook or whose tweets fill our feed or who we follow on Instagram—and the algorithms are based on what the social media outlets judge to be our taste. We end up creating, with a little artificial intelligence assistance, a curated base of knowledge that essentially tells us what we have decided we want to hear. We are not helpless, but in order not to be caught in a bubble, we cannot be passive, either.

According to the Pew Center's Project for Excellence in Journalism, which has studied YouTube in particular,

> the data reveal that a complex, symbiotic relationship has developed between citizens and news organizations on YouTube, a relationship that comes close to the continuous journalistic "dialogue" many observers predicted would become the new journalism online. Citizens are creating their own videos about news and posting them. They are also actively sharing news videos produced by journalism professionals. And news organizations are taking advantage of citizen content and incorporating it into their journalism. Consumers, in turn, seem to be embracing the interplay in what they watch and share, creating a new kind of television news.[33]

In addition, the growing number of cell phone users offers another way for people to access their customized news streams (a whopping 92 percent of millennials own smartphones), with owners of smartphones notable for their heavy news consumption and people who access their news on mobile devices spending longer with the news and getting it from more sources.[34] The fact that these tech-savvy news readers are disproportionately well educated and young suggests that America's news-reading habits may be changing dramatically, and that the web may come closer to realizing its potential for offering a truly democratic, practical, and "free" alternative to the corporate-produced news we now receive.

THE BIG PICTURE:
Who Owns (and Controls) Today's Information Networks?

Today most of our news comes from a handful of powerful sources. While some, like the *New York Times*, are still independent, others are part of massive media conglomerates, or like the *Washington Post*, owned by Amazon's Jeff Bezos, tied in other ways to the information world. What implication does this ownership structure have for the news we get?

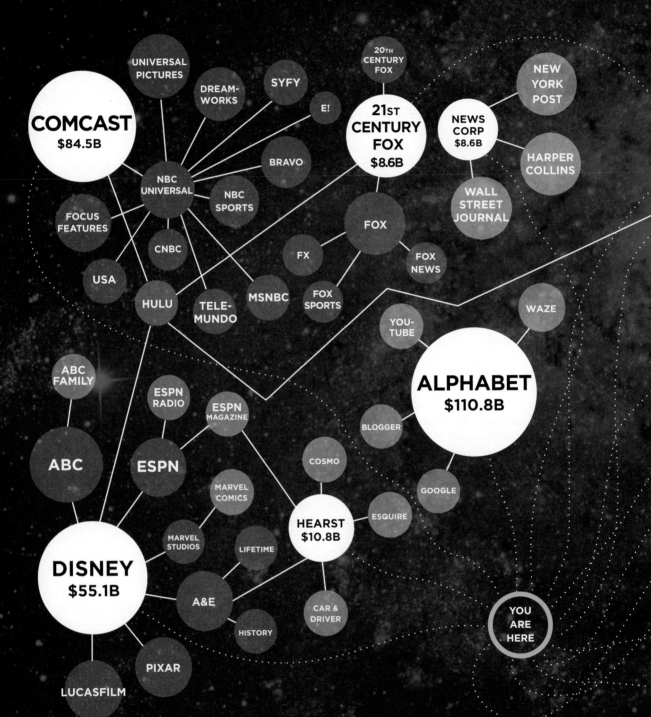

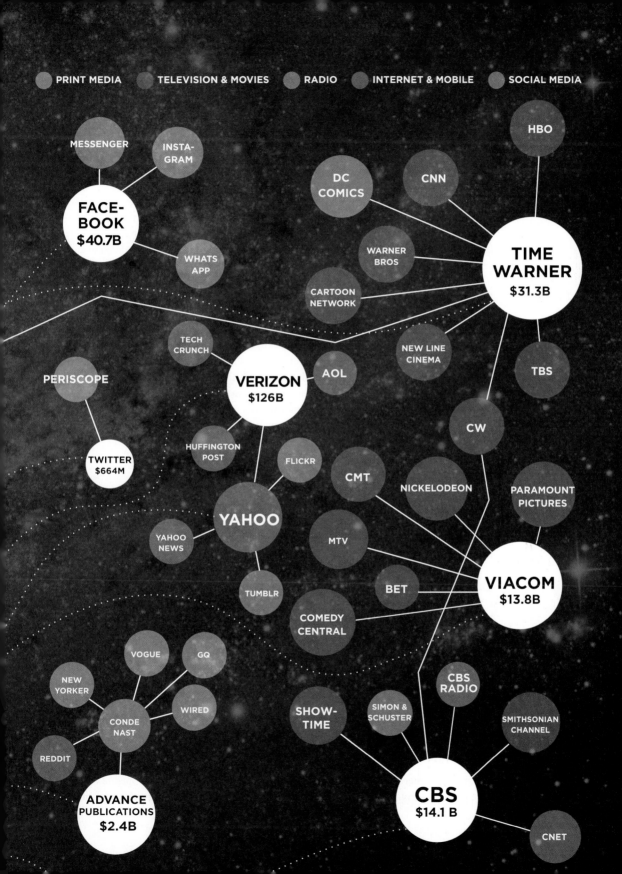

HOW DOES MEDIA OWNERSHIP
IMPACT THE NEWS WE GET?

What does the concentrated corporate ownership of the traditional mass media mean to us as consumers of the news? We should be aware of at least five major consequences:

- There is a **commercial bias** in the media today toward what will increase advertiser revenue and audience share. Journalistic judgment and ethics are often at odds with the imperative to turn a profit.
- The effort to get and keep large audiences, and to make way for increased advertising, means a reduced emphasis on political news. This is especially true at the local television level, where older Americans, in particular, tend to get their information.[35]
- The content of the news we get is lightened up, dramatized, and streamlined to keep audiences tuned in.[36] Some web sites like *BuzzFeed* specialize in **clickbait** pieces—sensational headlines that tease you into clicking a link to find some intriguing-sounding information. Other news web sites tell you in advance how many minutes it will take to read an article so that you know what you are committing to before you start.
- The corporate ownership of today's media means that the media outlets frequently face conflicts of interest in deciding what news to cover or how to cover it.
- Breaking a news story has always been a point of pride for editors and journalists. (It is the *Washington Post* that gets kudos for breaking the Watergate scandal—nobody remembers the second newspaper to chime in.) In the rush to avoid getting "scooped" by another station or newspaper, reporters and editors alike have sometimes jumped the gun, disseminating incorrect information or flat-out lies without taking the time to fact check or analyze them.

ALTERNATIVES TO THE CORPORATE MEDIA

Today the giant corporate media conglomerations do not define all of our alternatives for getting news, and they cannot control all the narratives as effectively as they once did. Still, the explosion of online publishing gives more people more alternatives for getting (and sharing) information that is not subject to a corporate agenda.

Because the drive for profit affects the news we get in serious ways, it's important to note that some forms of media have chosen a different route to financial survival. Government-owned radio and television, of course, can provide an alternative to the for-profit media world. A small independent press does continue to thrive outside the for-profit world. A few investigative magazines, like *Mother Jones* (published by the Foundation for National Progress) and *Consumer Reports* (published by Consumers Union), and web sites like factcheck.org (University of Pennsylvania) and ProPublica rely on funding from subscribers and members of their nonprofit parent organizations.[37] However, unless they are completely free of advertising (as is *Consumer Reports*), even these independent publications are not entirely free from corporate influence.

REGULATION OF THE MEDIA

The media in America are almost entirely privately owned, but they do not operate without some public control. Although the principle of freedom of the press keeps the print media

commercial bias the tendency of the media to make coverage and programming decisions based on what will attract a large audience and maximize profits

clickbait sensational headlines designed to tempt Internet users to click through to a specific web site

Clickbait

You're trolling through your newsfeeds and see a link that is just irresistible: a revolutionary diet secret, a terrifying news headline, or a top ten list just begging you to select the "five greatest" songs/athletes/movies of all time. Do you click? Do you read? Do you share?

Web sites depend on web traffic to generate revenue, and web traffic is measured in clicks. Much of the content on the Internet today is designed specifically to go viral—to be circulated widely and quickly. And it's not just cat videos that go viral—sometimes, it's news. Donald Trump's use of Twitter is a case in point: the reality star propelled himself to the front of the Republican presidential field on the back of tweets that provoked either outrage or praise, and which were quickly reposted, parsed, and commented on by a news media hungry for clicks.[1] By the end of the election, Trump's campaign had gotten nearly $6 billion in free media coverage, much of it in viral coverage.[2]

WHAT TO WATCH OUT FOR

Here are a few tips for savvy web surfing:

- **Is this headline manipulating you?** Savvy headline writers know that writers can drum up what researchers call "manufactured emotions" over what is often pretty benign content. The most effective headlines will provoke anxiety, outrage, fear, or curiosity.[3] That doesn't mean that there's no real news hidden behind clickbait headlines—but it doesn't mean that there *is* real news there, either.

- **Is this news, or is it fluff?** Some important news stories can rise to the top on the back of clicks, making their way from independent publications or citizen journalists into the mainstream media. Videos capturing police shootings are just one example of real news stories that spread via viral sharing. But sometimes important news stories can fall through the cracks while the Internet explodes over viral stories, such as the "what color is this dress?" meme that seemed to take over the web in 2015[4]. There's nothing wrong with entertainment on the web—just make sure you're not missing out on real news.

- **Is this "sponsored content"?** Seeking to shore up diminishing revenue streams, many news outlets (not to mention your social media feeds) include advertising, often presented in the same style and format as the site's original content. Many articles with buzzy headlines, sitting alongside regular reporting on respected news sites, are actually long-form advertisements, written specifically to change perceptions about a product or company, and are designed to be shared via social media.[5] Look out for tags like "sponsored content," "recommended post," or "advertisement."

- **Is this troll fodder?** Internet trolls—individuals who intentionally disrupt online discourse with arguments and commentary that is inflammatory, abusive, or off-topic—don't generate much sympathy. But they do generate clicks, and publishers know it. Even sites that malign or claim to ban such activity simultaneously try to attract trolls, knowing that an online controversy will push even more browsers toward their site.[6] Trolling can be a political tool, as well—late in the election season of 2016, the news broke that Russia had hired Internet trolls to try to sway American public opinion.[7] Avoid getting sucked into online sparring matches with Internet trolls.

- **Is this an article, or a listicle?** There's something about a top five list that's just hard to resist. Psychologists theorize that we like lists because they pique our curiosity (we want to see if we can guess what's on it) and because of the ease with which we can scan and digest information when it's presented in this easy and predictable format.[8]

(Continued)

(Continued)

If you look for listicles that offer links to deeper sources of information, you'll find they can be a useful jumping-off point.[9] More often than not, however, they are just another route to lure you to advertising and multiple clicks.

- Are people reading this, or just sharing it? A 2016 study showed that more than half of the links shared on social media were not actually clicked on—that is, people shared the story without having read it. The study also found that this kind of sharing plays an outsize role in shaping political narratives and agendas.[10] Don't engage in blind sharing: before you recommend (or comment on) a story, read it!

1. Michael Barbaro, "Pithy, Mean and Powerful: How Donald Trump Mastered Twitter for 2016," *New York Times*, October 5, 2015, www.nytimes.com/2015/10/06/us/politics/donald-trump-twitter-use-campaign-2016.html.

2. Nicholas Confessore and Karen Yourish, "$2 Billion Worth of Free Media for Donald Trump," *New York Times*, March 15, 2016, www.nytimes.com/2016/03/16/upshot/measuring-donald-trumps-mammoth-advantage-in-free-media.html.

3. Bryan Gardiner, "You'll Be Outraged at How Easy It Was to Get You to Click on This Headline," *Wired*, December 18, 2015, www.wired.com/2015/12/psychology-of-clickbait/.

4. Johnathan Mahler, "The White and Gold (No, Blue and Black) Dress That Melted the Internet," *New York Times*, February 27, 2015, www.nytimes.com/2015/02/28/business/a-simple-question-about-a-dress-and-the-world-weighs-in.html.

5. Jeff Sonderman and Millie Tran, "The Definition of 'Sponsored Content,'" American Press Institute, November 13, 2013, www.americanpressinstitute.org/publications/reports/white-papers/the-definition-of-sponsored-content/.

6. Lene Bech Sillesen, "Trolls Make Good Clickbait," *Columbia Journalism Review*, August 21, 2014, www.cjr.org/behind_the_news/trolls_make_good_clickbait_-_t.php.

7. Natasha Bertrand, "It Looks Like Russia Hired Internet Trolls to Pose as Pro-Trump Americans," *Business Insider*, July 27, 2016, www.businessinsider.com/russia-internet-trolls-and-donald-trump-2016-7.

8. Claudia Hammond, "Nine Psychological Reasons Why We Love Lists," BBC, April 13, 2015, www.bbc.com/future/story/20150410-9-reasons-we-love-lists.

9. Rachel Edidin, "5 Reasons Listicles Are Here to Stay, and Why That's OK," *Wired*, January 8, 2014, www.wired.com/2014/01/defense-listicle-list-article/.

10. Caitlin Dewey, "6 in 10 of You Will Share This Link Without Reading It, a New, Depressing Study Says," *Washington Post*, June 16, 2016, www.washingtonpost.com/news/the-intersect/wp/2016/06/16/six-in-10-of-you-will-share-this-link-without-reading-it-according-to-a-new-and-depressing-study/.

nearly free of restriction (see Chapter 4), the broadcast media have been treated differently and control of the Internet has become controversial and complex.

In the early days of radio, great public enthusiasm for the new medium resulted in so many radio stations that signal interference threatened to damage the whole industry. Broadcasters asked the government to impose some order, which it did with the passage of the Federal Communications Act, creating the Federal Communications Commission (FCC), an independent regulatory agency, in 1934. Because access to the airwaves was considered a scarce public resource, the government acted to ensure that radio and television serve the public interest by representing a variety of viewpoints. Accordingly, the 1934 bill contained three provisions designed to ensure fairness in broadcasting—the equal time rule (if one candidate speaks, all must have the opportunity); the fairness doctrine (requiring stations to give free airtime to issues of public concern); and the right of rebuttal (allowing people whose reputations were damaged on air to respond)—all of which have been limited or eliminated since.

Can a corporately owned press be a free press?

These rules remain somewhat controversial. Politicians would like to have the rules enforced because they help them to air their views publicly. Media owners see these rules as forcing them to air unpopular speakers who damage their ratings and as limiting their abilities to decide station policy. They argue that access to broadcast time is no longer such a scarce resource, given all the cable and satellite outlets, and that the broadcast media should be subject to the same legal protections as the print media.

Many of the limitations on station ownership that the original act established were abolished with the 1996 Telecommunications Act in order to open up competition and promote diversity in media markets. The act failed to rein in the media giants, however, and ended up facilitating mergers that concentrated media ownership even more. The law permits ownership of multiple stations as long as they do not reach more than 35 percent of a market, and nothing prevents the networks themselves from reaching a far larger market through their collective affiliates. The 1996 legislation also opened up the way for ownership of cable stations by network owners, and it allows cable companies to offer many services previously supplied only by telephone companies. The overall effect of this deregulation has been to increase dramatically the possibilities for media monopoly.

As we saw in *What's at Stake . . . ?* in Chapter 4, some Internet users favor a policy of net neutrality that would prevent telecommunication companies from using their control over Internet access to restrict or limit content with price discrimination and would keep the Internet unfettered and open to innovation. Opponents argue that such a policy would reduce incentives for companies to innovate. In 2015, at President Obama's urging, the FCC ruled in favor of net neutrality, ensuring that all Internet traffic must be treated equally (see Chapter 8). Although the ruling had no chance of becoming law, the Republican House immediately voted to oppose it and the ruling was challenged in court as well. The Trump administration overturned it in 2018.

In Your Own Words Describe the ways in which media ownership and government regulation influence the news we get.

SPINNING POLITICAL NARRATIVES
The stories we tell that legitimize or delegitimize power

Think about the narrative that northerners tell about the Civil War or the one told by native southerners: was it a war to end slavery and restore national unity, or a war of secession because states' rights were violated? Same war, different narrative, in a battle of competing meanings that has not yet been settled today.

When CBS News anchor Walter Cronkite went to Vietnam in 1968 and said we were losing the war there, that report clashed with the narrative the government was telling. President Lyndon Johnson knew he'd lost the support of the country because Cronkite was seen as a trustworthy gatherer and reporter of the facts. Today there is no consensus on who is the trusted reporter of facts. The saying that "you are entitled to your own opinion but not your own facts," once the gold standard of debate, is laughable in the face of some of today's realities. Some candidates and officials, and indeed, the president of the United States, lie so fast that the fact checkers can't keep up with them; cable stations, web sites, and commentators on Twitter herald facts based on very different assumptions of reality; and many journalists follow an ethic that "fairness" requires finding "equivalence" between two sides, which are often not equivalent at all.

We like to think that journalism is all about facts and in its purest sense, it is. A fact is simply a verifiable piece of information that can be shown to be empirically true. If it isn't true, it isn't a fact. Control of the facts itself can confer power. Discovering and reporting facts in a timely way is power. What we think of as the job of the news media is a powerful part of a democratic society. Without the facts, we cannot make the good, informed decisions about our governance that we need to make.

But control of the facts can be directed toward goals other than the health of a democracy. Withholding factual information that someone needs to make a decision, or releasing that information at a strategic time, or refusing to invest resources in uncovering the facts—all of those are powerful actions that do not lead to good, informed decision making. The thing about facts is that by themselves they don't always tell us what we need to know. They often need to be put into context and interpreted so that we know what to make of them, and at that point, they begin to be part of a narrative, a story that imparts meaning and value. In this section we look at the major weavers of political narratives and the ways in which political narratives are shaped.

THE FACT GATHERERS

The basic fabric of our national narratives is woven by journalists—professional reporters or fact gatherers whose job it is to tell us *what happened*. They may interpret facts, but they don't speculate, or insert their own judgment for that of their audience, or traffic in known untruths. If they make a mistake, which happens, they correct it. Journalists aren't perfect—their demographic profile alone suggests they may be predisposed to see the world in one way or another (see *Snapshot of America: Who Are the Journalists?*), but their job is to try to discover and disseminate the facts.

THE ANALYSTS

Some journalists take great pride in sticking to reporting. But the greater the access to and contact with those in power, the harder it is to maintain a distance and to refrain from putting one's analysis in with the facts. Providing analysis doesn't mean a journalist is not reporting facts, it just means that the journalist's own expertise, values, ideas, beliefs, understandings, and even political agenda might get included in the narrative. It can be very difficult for experts not to want to share their expertise—great humility does not generally spring from contact with great power.

What is fascinating about living in an age of widespread social networks, however, is that although the media elite have an easier time of controlling the narrative than the rest of us, the Internet gives everyone with a computer or a smartphone a bit part in spreading a compelling story, or even attempting to challenge it. The extensive sharing, tweeting, clicking, and even trolling that we have noted throughout this chapter means that the mainstream corporate media do not maintain the monopoly of control they once had. Such criticism of the narrative in real time at least opens the possibility that the story will be influenced from multiple sources. And we have seen already that the democratizing effects of the Internet have weakened the mainstream corporate chokehold on determining what the news is.

THE REVOLVING DOOR As former *Washington Post* journalist David Broder pointed out, the concentration of politics, politicians, and reporters in Washington leads to "a complex but cozy relationship between journalists and public officials," a trend that Broder calls

Snapshot of America: *Who Are the Journalists?*

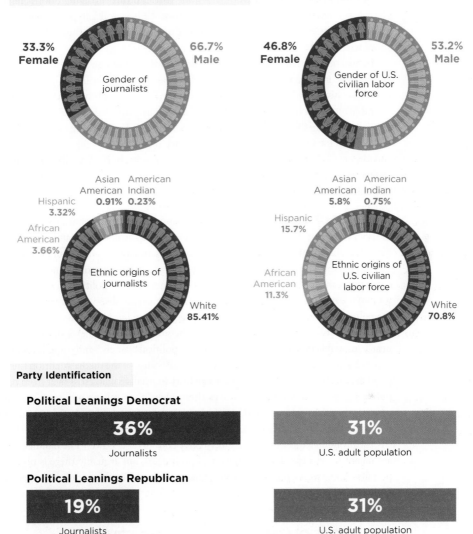

How Journalists Compare to the Rest of Us

33.3% Female — Gender of journalists — **66.7% Male**

46.8% Female — Gender of U.S. civilian labor force — **53.2% Male**

Ethnic origins of journalists:
Hispanic 3.32%
Asian American 0.91%
American Indian 0.23%
African American 3.66%
White 85.41%

Ethnic origins of U.S. civilian labor force:
Hispanic 15.7%
Asian American 5.8%
American Indian 0.75%
African American 11.3%
White 70.8%

Party Identification

Political Leanings Democrat

36%	**31%**
Journalists	U.S. adult population

Political Leanings Republican

19%	**31%**
Journalists	U.S. adult population

Behind the Numbers

Compare the backgrounds and political leanings of journalists with the larger U.S population. Who is underrepresented? Is this a problem for the kind of news that Americans hear and read? Would greater diversity among journalists affect how events are reported and interpreted in the news?

Source: Lars Willnat and David H. Weaver. *The American Journalist in the Digital Age: Key Findings.* Bloomington: School of Journalism, Indiana University. 2014.

the "revolving door."[38] The **revolving door**, like the similar interest group phenomenon we discussed in Chapter 11, refers to the practice of journalists taking positions in government and then returning to journalism again, or vice versa, perhaps several times over. The number of prominent journalists who have gone through this revolving door is legion, as any glimpse of a cable news panel will make obvious.[39] These folks, in permanent or temporary exile from politics themselves, are only sometimes agenda-free as they help weave narratives about what current political events mean.

To take one particularly glaring example, Karl Rove, George W. Bush's policy adviser and currently a commentator on Fox, even while he heads a Republican PAC, was heavily invested in the narrative that Mitt Romney would win the 2012 election, an outcome he had put considerable money behind. His adherence to his own narrative led him to support the story that the polls showing Obama ahead were wrong and, when Fox called the state of Ohio and thus the election for Obama on election night, Rove blew an on-air fuse, calling for a retraction and forcing anchor Megyn Kelly to reconfirm the results. In 2016, CNN hired former Trump campaign manager Corey Lewandowski as a commentator, even as he was still under contractual ties to Trump.

THE ROLE OF THE PUNDIT Many of those analysts who return to the media through the revolving door find themselves joining the ranks of the journalists and academics who have earned the unofficial and slightly tongue-in-cheek title of **pundit**. A pundit is traditionally a learned person, someone professing great wisdom. In contemporary media parlance, it has come to mean a professional observer and commentator on politics—a person skilled in the ways of the media and of politics who can make trenchant observations and predictions about the political world and help us untangle the complicated implications of political events.

The twenty-four-hour news cycle and the growth in cable news shows mean there is a nearly insatiable demand for bodies to fill the political "panels," and sometimes the ones who appear have pretty tenuous claims to expertise. Because of the media attention they get, many pundits join the unofficial ranks of the celebrity journalists who cross over from reporting on public figures to being public figures themselves, thus raising a host of questions about whether they themselves should be subject to the same standards of criticism and scrutiny that they apply to politicians. Because they receive wide media coverage from their fellow journalists, the pronouncements of the punditry carry considerable power. The pundits, as journalists, are meant to be a check on the power of politicians, but arguably there is no check on the pundits as they weave their stories about the meaning of American politics, except an increasingly cynical public.

THE CREATION OF POLITICAL NARRATIVES

The media are among the main agents of what we called *political socialization* in Chapter 10: they help to transfer political values from one generation to the next and to shape political views in general by the narratives they create about the meaning of politics. We have already looked at the question of bias in the media and noted not only that there is a corporate or commercial bias but also that Americans are increasingly convinced that the news media are ideologically biased. Political scientists acknowledge that ideological bias may exist, but they conclude that it isn't so much that the media tell us what to think as that they tell us what to think *about* and how to think about it. Scholars have documented several kinds of related

revolving door the tendency of public officials, journalists, and lobbyists to move between public- and private-sector (media, lobbying) jobs

pundit a professional observer and commentator on politics

media effects on our thinking: agenda setting, framing, persuasion by professional communicators, and a tendency to reduce politics to issues of conflicts and superficial image rather than substantive policy disputes.[40]

AGENDA SETTING Even the Internet is limited in the number of the many daily political events it can cover, which means that reporters, especially television reporters, perform the function of agenda setting—defining for the public the relative importance of an issue through the amount and prominence of coverage it receives.[41] When television reporters choose to cover an event, they are telling us that out of all the events happening, this one is important and we should pay attention. They are priming us to focus on it and to evaluate politicians in light of it. It gives our national storytellers immense power to decide what is important enough for us to pay attention to, although the Internet dilutes that effect somewhat.

FRAMING Just as a painting's appearance can be altered by changing its frame, a political event can look different to us depending on the media's framing of the event—that is, what they choose to emphasize in their coverage. For example, people view a war differently depending on whether the coverage highlights American casualties or military victories. To return to the issue we opened this chapter with, the media can portray a massacre in a nightclub as the action of a disturbed young man with a gun he should not have been able to buy, or as the action of an international terrorist who had no business being in this country. The important point about framing is that how the media present a political issue or event may affect how the public perceives that issue, whether they see it as a problem, and who they view as responsible for solving it.

PERSUASION BY PROFESSIONAL COMMUNICATORS Some political scientists argue that the media affect public opinion because viewers, who often don't have the time or background to research issues themselves, rely on *opinion leaders* (see Chapter 10).[42] Often, however, especially in the age of Internet news, social media, twenty-four-hour cable, and multiple broadcast choices, the communicators on whom the media rely are people who regularly pass through the revolving door and whose objectivity cannot be taken for granted.

REDUCTION OF POLITICS TO SOUND AND FURY Reporting on the details of policy wonkery is hard work, and delving into the nitty gritty of a story requires diligence and toughness. Some journalists have these qualities and demonstrate them daily, whether they are *Vox*'s Ezra Klein giving full rein to his inner policy wonk in an evaluation of economic policy, or NPR's Sarah Koenig doing long-form investigations on the hit podcast *Serial*. But such hard work is just that, and in a nonstop, twenty-four-hour news cycle, journalists don't always have the ability or the luxury to do the long-form piece or the deep dive into a story. Being under constant pressure to produce something that people will tune in to or click on means that a lot of what is reported is shallow and meaningless, unless reporters can peg it to a quick and dirty narrative. Who is ahead? How does it look? Is she corrupt? Did he cheat? These are default narratives that consume much of American political coverage and cause a weary public to view it with a cynical eye.

Horse-race journalism refers to the media's tendency to see politics as a competition between individuals. Rather than reporting on the policy differences between politicians or

agenda setting the media's role in defining the relative importance of an issue or event via the amount and prominence of coverage they devote to it

framing the process through which the media emphasize particular aspects of a news story, thereby influencing the public's perception of the story

horse-race journalism the media's focus on the competitive aspects of politics rather than on actual policy proposals and political decisions

the effects their proposals will have on ordinary Americans, today's media tend to create narratives based on who is ahead, what they need to do to catch up, and what various events will do to the poll numbers, the visible (though not always reliable) indicator of who is ahead. When you report on politics as if it were a battle between individual gladiators or a game of strategy and wit but not substance, it tends to increase citizen cynicism, as if politicians cared only to score victories off one another in a never-ending fight to promote their own self-interests, and it also ignores the concerns that citizens have about politics. The obsession with who is winning may keep bored reporters engaged, but it's a narrative that trivializes what is at stake in campaigns, or partisan battles in Congress, or disputes between the president and Congress, and it doesn't help educate the American public.

Television is primarily an entertainment medium and, by its nature, is focused on image: what people look like, what they sound like, and how an event is staged and presented. Television, and to some extent its competition in the print and digital media, concentrates on doing what it does well: giving us pictures of politics instead of delving beneath the surface. Political players respond by focusing on optics—the way a situation, person, or event is presented by the media and perceived by the public—rather than on substantive issues. This, along with the horse-race metaphor we just mentioned, has the effect of leading us to value the more superficial aspects of politics, even if only subconsciously.

In a similar way, the necessities of the media turn the words of politicians into the audio equivalent of a snapshot, the sound bite. A sound bite is a short block of speech by a politician that makes it on the news. The amount of time that the electronic media devote to the actual words a politician utters is shrinking. In 2000 the average length for a sound bite from a presidential candidate on the nightly network news was 7.3 seconds, down from 10 seconds in 1992 and 42 seconds in 1968.[43] Journalists use the extra time to interpret what we have heard and often to put it into the horse-race metaphor we just discussed.[44]

In an implicit acknowledgment that the public's attention span has been trained to require instant and speedy gratification, social media cater to this penchant for bite-sized ideas. Instagram and Snapchat encourage people to communicate through single (and, in the case of Snapchat, transient) images, and Twitter has managed to turn a bug into a feature, forcing politicians and journalists alike to condense their thoughts to a mere 280 characters.

The emphasis on image and simplified narratives also means that reporters tend to concentrate on developing scandals to the exclusion of other, possibly more relevant, news events. Political scientist Larry Sabato refers to this behavior as a feeding frenzy: "the press coverage attending any political event or circumstance where a critical mass of journalists leap to cover the same embarrassing or scandalous subject and pursue it intensely, often excessively, and sometimes uncontrollably."[45] Many such feeding frenzies have been over scandals that have proved not to be true or seemed insignificant with the passing of time, and yet the media have treated them with the seriousness of a world crisis. After such attacks, the media frequently indulge in introspection and remorse, until the next scandal starts to brew.

Political scientist Thomas Patterson argues that the zest for catching politicians in a lie or a "gaffe" means that the press treat most presidents and presidential candidates as fundamentally untrustworthy, when in fact most do precisely what they say they are going to do. Because it takes time and energy to investigate all the claims that a president or a candidate makes, the media evaluate political claims not with their own careful scrutiny but with statements from political opponents. This makes politics appear endlessly adversarial and, as Patterson says, replaces investigative journalism with attack journalism.[46]

optics the way a situation, person, or event is presented by the media and perceived by the public

sound bite a brief, snappy excerpt from a public figure's speech that is easy to repeat on the news

feeding frenzy excessive press coverage of an embarrassing or scandalous subject

THE POWER OF THE MAINSTREAM MEDIA'S NARRATIVE

The effects of agenda setting; framing; expert persuasion; and shallow, overly dramatized reporting should not be taken to mean that we are all unwitting dupes of the media. In the first place, these are not iron-clad rules; they are tendencies that scholars have discovered and confirmed with experimentation and public opinion surveys. That means that they hold true for many but not all people. Members of the two major political parties, for instance, are less affected by agenda setting than are independents, perhaps because the latter do not have a party to rely on to tell them what is important,[47] although as the media become more partisan, the partisan narratives can themselves be reinforced by media effects.

Second, we bring our own armor to the barrage of media effects we face regularly. We all filter our news watching through our own narratives constructed on the ideas, values, and distinct perspectives we bring to politics. That is, we exercise **selective perception**.[48] If people do not seem to be well informed on the issues emphasized by the media, it may be that they do not see them as playing a role in a narrative they value or as having an effect on their lives. The point is that, as consumers, we do more than passively absorb the messages and values provided by the media.

A serious consequence of the superficial and negative content of political coverage is that voters' opinions of candidates have sunk, and citizen dissatisfaction with the electoral process has risen.[49] Not only is the public becoming more cynical about the political world, but it is also becoming more cynical about the media. A recent public opinion poll shows that half or more of the American public now thinks that the news is too biased, sensationalized, and manipulated by special interests, and that reporters offer too many of their own opinions, quote unnamed sources, and are negative.[50] If people cease to trust the media, the media become less effective in playing their legitimate roles as well as their more controversial ones, and democracy becomes more difficult to sustain.

It would be good for democracy if the growing dominance of online media sources could counteract some of the media's negativity by allowing interactivity, but all it takes is a look at the comments on an online article or blog post to realize that much of the media's negative view of politics either reflects or has animated a similar public perspective. The difference, of course, is that the mainstream media tend to be negative about the process in general and the animus of members of the public tends to be more tribal—elevating the party or side they agree with and being vitriolic about the one they don't.

In fact, although researchers have tried to look at whether the ideological slant of a news source makes a difference to one's perception of the news, it is a difficult question to answer since people seem to gravitate to the sources with which they agree. Are their views shaped by bias in the news, or do they choose the bias they prefer to be exposed to? A 2003 study looking at misperceptions about the Iraq war (specifically, beliefs that there was evidence of links between al Qaeda and Saddam Hussein, that weapons of

selective perception
the phenomenon of filtering incoming information through personal values and interests

THE CHRISTIAN SCIENCE MONITOR BENNETT

'...Political campaigns have become so simplistic and superficial...
In the 20 seconds we have left, could you explain why?..

mass destruction had been found in Iraq, and that world opinion favored U.S. action in Iraq) concluded that the frequency with which those beliefs were held varied dramatically with the primary source of a person's news. Watchers of Fox News (which tended to be more supportive of the Bush administration) held those misperceptions much more frequently than did those who got their news from other sources.[51]

In Your Own Words Explain the roles and responsibilities of journalists and the tools they use to shape and perpetuate political narratives.

POLITICS AS PUBLIC RELATIONS
Waging the permanent campaign

There is no doubt that the media portray politics in a negative light and that news reporting emphasizes personality, superficial image, and conflict over substantive policy issues. Some media figures argue, however, that this is not the media's fault, but rather the responsibility of politicians and their press officers who are so obsessed with their own images on television that they limit access to the media, speak only in prearranged sound bites, and present themselves to the public in carefully orchestrated "media events."[52] That is, in their own effort to control the political narrative, politicians are limiting the ability of journalists to do their jobs properly.

Media events are designed to limit the ability of reporters to put their own interpretation on the occasion. The rules of American politics, which require a politician to have high public approval to maximize his or her clout, mean that politicians have to try to get maximum exposure for their ideas and accomplishments while limiting the damage the media can do with their intense scrutiny, investigations, and critical perspectives. This effort to control the media can lead to an emphasis on short-term gain over long-term priorities and the making of policy decisions with an eye to their political impact—a tendency that has come to be known as the **permanent campaign**.[53]

NEWS MANAGEMENT

News management describes the chief mechanism of the permanent campaign, the efforts of a politician's staff—media consultants, press secretaries, pollsters, campaign strategists, and general advisers—to control the news about the politician. The staff want to put their own issues on the agenda, determine for themselves the standards by which the politician will be evaluated, frame the issues, and supply the sources for reporters, so that they will put their client, the politician, in the best possible light. In contemporary political jargon, they want to put a **spin**, or an interpretation, on the news that will be most flattering to the politician whose image is in their care, to build the narrative that the media representatives will repeat as fact. To some extent, modern American politics has become a battle between the press and the politicians and among the politicians themselves to control the agenda and the narratives that reach the public. It has become a battle of the "spin doctors."

The classic example of news management is the rehabilitation of the image of Richard Nixon after he lost the 1960 election to the more media-savvy Kennedy campaign. Inspired

permanent campaign the idea that governing requires a continual effort to convince the public to sign on to the program, requiring a reliance on consultants and an emphasis on politics over policy

news management the efforts of a politician's staff to control news about the politician

spin an interpretation of a politician's words or actions, designed to present a favorable image

by the way the Kennedy administration had managed the image of Kennedy as war hero, patriot, devoted father, and faithful husband, when at least one of those characterizations wasn't true, Nixon speechwriter Ray Price saw his mission clearly. Noting that Nixon was personally unpopular with the public, he wrote in a 1967 memo, "We have to be very clear on this point: that the response is to the image, not to the man, since 99 percent of the voters have no contact with the man. It's not what's there that counts, it's what's projected—and it's not what he projects but rather what the voter receives. It's not the man we have to change, but rather the received impression."[54] With the help of an advertising executive and a television producer, among others, Nixon was repackaged and sold to voters as the "New Nixon." He won election as president in 1968 and 1972, and that he had to resign in 1974 is perhaps less a failure of his image makers than the inevitable revelation of the "real" Nixon underneath.

NEWS MANAGEMENT TECHNIQUES

The techniques of political communication that Nixon's handlers developed for managing his image have become part of the basic repertoire of political staffs, particularly in the White House but even to some extent for holders of lesser offices. They can include any or all of the following:[55]

- *Tight control of information.* Staffers pick a "line of the day"—for instance, a focus on education or child care—and orchestrate all messages from the administration around that theme. This strategy frustrates journalists who are trying to follow independent stories. But it recognizes that the staff must "feed the beast" by giving the press something to cover, or they may find the press rebelling and covering stories they don't want covered at all.[56]
- *Tight control of access to the politician.* If the politician is available to the press for only a short period of time and makes only a brief statement, the press corps is forced to report the appearance as the only available news.
- *Elaborate communications bureaucracy.* The Nixon White House had four offices handling communications. In addition to the White House press secretary, who was frequently kept uninformed so that he could more credibly deny that he knew the answers to reporters' questions, there was an Office of Communications, an Office of Public Liaison, and a speechwriting office.
- *A concerted effort to bypass the White House press corps.* During Nixon's years this meant going to regional papers that were more easily manipulated. Today it can also include television talk shows and late-night television, and other forums that go directly to the public, such as town hall meetings and digital opportunities to reach the public through outlets like Facebook, Reddit, and YouTube. Part and parcel of this approach is the strategy of rewarding media outlets that provide friendly coverage and punishing those that do not.
- *Prepackaging the news in sound bites.* If the media are going to allow the public only a brief snippet of political language, the reasoning goes, let the politician's staff decide what it will be. In line with this, the press office will repeat a message often, to be sure the press and the public pick up on it, and it will work on phrasing that is catchy and

> ### Should journalists always protect their sources?

memorable. Not incidentally, almost every serious politician now has a Twitter account that he, she, or the staff uses regularly.

- *Leaks.* A final and effective way that politicians attempt to control the news is with the use of **leaks**, secretly revealing confidential information to the press. Leaks can serve a variety of purposes. For instance, a leak can be a **trial balloon**, in which an official leaks a policy or plan in order to gauge public reaction to it. If the reaction is negative, the official denies he or she ever mentioned it, and if it is positive, the policy can go ahead without risk.

NEWS MANAGEMENT SINCE NIXON

Not all presidential administrations are equally accomplished at using these techniques of news management, of course. Nixon's was successful, at least in his first administration, and Ronald Reagan's has been referred to as a model of public relations.[57] President Bill Clinton did not manage the media effectively in the early years of his first administration; consequently, he was at the mercy of a frustrated and annoyed press corps. Within a couple of years, however, the Clinton staff had become much more skilled, and by his second administration they were adeptly handling scandals that would have daunted more seasoned public relations experts.

The George W. Bush administration did a superb job of news management, especially in Bush's first term. For instance, most of Bush's public events were open only to Bush supporters; where there was audience interaction, he received questions only from those who endorsed his programs and goals, and reporters who could be trusted to ask supportive questions were favored in White House news briefings and press conferences.[58] Supporters defended the Bush White House's news management strategy as efficient and praiseworthy. Critics, by contrast, claimed that the White House had become a "propaganda machine" to serve the president's political goals.[59]

Barack Obama's White House was as disciplined as Bush's, although his public events were not vetted for supporters and the president faced more negative questions because of it. During the presidential campaign, the Obama camp was famous for avoiding leaks and controlling its message, and although that perfect discipline was not maintained in the White House, it was still remarkably free of public infighting and leaks. Obama's first press secretary, Robert Gibbs, was a senior adviser to the president and had uncommon access and a dedication to protecting Obama's interests, though his second, Jay Carney, and his third, Josh Earnest, were more traditional spokespeople.[60] One difference between the Obama administration and its predecessors was the elaborate electronic communication network it had set up, which allowed administration officials to talk directly to supporters and to bypass the traditional media if they wanted to, texting and tweeting as well as sending emails and posting information, videos, and pictures to the White House web site.

Donald Trump did not begin his presidency on a good footing with the press.[61] During his campaign he had made them a target, limiting the access of outlets whose coverage he didn't like, telling them he would sue them, and calling them out at his rallies, saying they were dishonest. Trump has always preferred to provide his own coverage of events via Twitter, a habit that did not change with his ascension to the presidency. More than any other president, he has felt free to create his own narratives, even when they bear no relationship to widely validated facts; to chart his own course; and to suggest that media coverage of him that is unflattering is false and that journalists should be punished for publishing what he calls fake news.

leaks confidential information secretly revealed to the press

trial balloon an official leak of a proposal to determine public reaction to it without risk

Trump's supporters delight in his brash disregard for the norms of truth telling and free speech and sometimes there is entertainment value in his politics as performance art—but even more than the Nixon administration's news management, it also poses a real threat to the fundamental principles of democratic governance.

REDUCTION IN POLITICAL ACCOUNTABILITY

There is a real cost to the transformation of politics into public relations, no matter whose administration is engaging in the practice (and with varying degrees of expertise, they all do). Not only does it mean that politicians must spend time and energy on image considerations that do not really help them serve the public, but the skills required by an actor and a statesperson are not the same. The current system may encourage us to choose the wrong leaders for the wrong reasons and discourage the right people from running at all.

The transformation of politics into professional storytelling also means that we suffer from a loss of **political accountability**. Such accountability is the very hallmark of democracy: political leaders must answer to the public for their actions. If our leaders do something we do not like, we can make them bear the consequences of their actions by voting them out of office. The threat of being voted out of office is supposed to encourage them to do what we want in the first place. If politics is reduced to image, if we don't know what our leaders are doing, and if it becomes a game of cat and mouse with the media over what story should be told to the public, then accountability is weakened and so is democracy.[62]

In Your Own Words Identify the strategies politicians use to counter the influence of the media and shape and perpetuate their own political narratives.

CITIZENSHIP AND THE MEDIA

Growing citizen access increases engagement but blurs lines of journalism

In this chapter we have been unable to talk about the media without talking about citizenship. Citizens have been a constant "who" in our analysis because the media exist largely to give information to citizens and to mediate their relationship to government. But if we evaluate the traditional role of the media with respect to the public, the relationship that emerges is not a particularly responsive one. Almost from the beginning, control of the American media has been in the hands of an elite group, whether party leaders, politicians, wealthy entrepreneurs, or corporate owners. Financial concerns have meant that the media in the United States have been driven more by profit motive than by public interest. Not only are ownership and control of the media far removed from the hands of everyday Americans, but the reporting of national news is done mostly by reporters who do not fit the profile of those "average" citizens and whose concerns often do not reflect the concerns of their audience.

Citizens' access to the media has been correspondingly remote. The primary role available to them has been passive: that of reader, listener, or watcher. The power they wield is the power of switching newspapers or changing channels, essentially choosing among competing elites; but this is not an active, participatory role. While freedom of the press is a right technically held by all citizens, there is no right of access to the press. Citizens have difficulty

political accountability the democratic principle that political leaders must answer to the public for their actions

Capturing History With a Cell Phone

The arrest of two black men in a Philadelphia Starbucks—they were waiting for a friend before ordering—was captured in this blurry photo, taken on a bystander's phone. Widespread use of smartphones and access to mass audiences through social networking platforms has enabled citizen journalists to shed light on events and experiences that the traditional news media either ignored or had difficulty reporting.

citizen journalism
reporting and commentary by everyday citizens unaffiliated with traditional media outlets, and distributed via the web in the form of blogs, podcasts, or video uploads

making their voices heard, and, of course, most do not even try. Members of the media holler long and loud about their right to publish what they want, but only sporadically and briefly do they consider their obligations to the public to provide the sort of information that can sustain a democracy. If active democracy requires a political community in which the public can deliberate about important issues, it would seem that the American media are failing miserably at creating that community.

The rapid changes in information technology that we have discussed throughout this chapter offer some hope that the media can be made to serve the public interest more effectively. The media are in flux and, although the future of the print media is in question, some of the new media that are replacing it are remarkably more open and responsive. Along with social networks, some of these new media—such as cable news, specialized television programs, and Internet news—allow citizens to get fast-breaking reports of events as they occur and even to customize the news that they get. Talk radio and call-in television shows—new uses of the "old" media—allow citizen interaction, as do Internet chat rooms and other online forums. Many web sites allow users to give their opinions of issues in unscientific straw polls (see Chapter 10). Some analysts speculate that it is only a matter of time until we can all vote on issues from our home computers. The one thing that the new media have in common is that they bypass the old, making the corporate journalistic establishment less powerful than it was but perhaps giving rise to new elites and raising new questions about participation and how much access we really want citizens to have.

One of the most significant developments in the new media is the proliferation of **citizen journalism**, reporting and commentary by everyday citizens unaffiliated with traditional media outlets, and distributed via the web in the form of blogs, podcasts, and video sharing. These new platforms are, essentially, the modern equivalent of giving citizens their own printing presses and the means to publish their views. Although these resources can be devoted to any subject, the ones that interest us here are the ones that focus on politics and media criticism. As is true of any unregulated media source, a good deal of inaccurate and unsubstantiated information is posted on the web. There is no credentialing process for citizen reporters or bloggers, they are not usually admitted to the White House or other official news conferences unless they also report for a more traditional media outlet, and they generally lack the resources required to do a great deal of investigative reporting.

But citizen journalists can also do many things that their more mainstream colleagues cannot, and there is some truly first-rate journalism to be found on the web. Since these writers and reporters are not (usually) indebted to deep corporate pockets, they can hold the mainstream media accountable. For example, the prevalence of smartphones (77 percent of Americans own them today, as opposed to only 35 percent in 2011)[63] has resulted in firsthand evidence of police brutality toward African Americans being captured on video and used to counter police narratives. For instance, the shooting death of Philando Castile was recorded by his girlfriend, Diamond Reynolds, on her smartphone and streamed via Facebook Live. Because of the live stream, nearly 2.5 million viewers witnessed an event that they would normally hear about only through victim and eyewitness testimony. As the digital divide closes and even more Americans are able to document the events of their lives and their interactions with public officials, such transparency will only increase.[64]

Should the media be driven by what consumers want to know or what they need to know?

It is the job of consumers to scrutinize the reporting of citizens as scrupulously as they do the rest of the media, especially as it becomes easier and easier for anyone to post anything to the Internet. There is no substitute for critical evaluation of the news, but citizen journalism provides a new kind of content that is truly independent, open, and democratic in a way that traditional media sources never could be.

In Your Own Words Summarize the relationship between citizens and the media.

Let's Revisit: What's at Stake . . . ?

We began this chapter by asking what's at stake in the job of keeping the republic if we're locked in separate media bubbles, curating our own news, and creating or believing narratives that fit our preconceived ideas rather than challenging us to think critically. Is it just that we are divided ideologically, or is the integrity of the political culture we share at stake?

The results of the contentious 2016 election were so close that, even though Hillary Clinton won by the metric of the popular vote, the official rules of the Electoral College gave the presidency to Donald Trump. Having survived that election, barely, it is tempting to answer the question of what's at stake by saying that living in our closed information bubbles brings us very close to losing the common understanding and shared beliefs about the political world that make a peaceful resolution of our differences possible.

Perhaps the best example is a fundamental one. Donald Trump's campaign slogan was "Make America Great Again," or #MAGA as he frequently tweeted out to his many supporters. He elaborated on the narrative of what that slogan stood for at rallies of people who fully shared his views: immigration was destroying the country, trade had stolen our jobs, Muslims threatened our security, the military was terrible, inner cities were war zones, and we were a loser of a country. Only Trump could fix this mess of a nation and restore us to greatness.

Supporting Trump's narrative were Trump himself, in rallies, on Twitter, and on Fox News's *The Sean Hannity Show*; other commentators on Fox; the rightwing Breitbart News, whose publisher left to become CEO of Trump's campaign; and innumerable social media sites. It was a gloomy, downright scary apocalyptic vision. To half the population, that vision was as alien as Mars. But it resonated with Trump's supporters, figuratively if not literally. Their America wasn't great any more. There were too many people who looked different, too many people not speaking English, too many people telling them that the language they used to describe their life experiences was off-limits and crude, too many people upending gender roles and the very idea of gender itself, too many people getting fat off of government without doing any work. Too many people looking down on them for being who they were, when who they were—upstanding white, working-class citizens—used to mean something. Making America great again meant restoring their dignity, making them whole, and soothing the sense of grievance that convinced them the rules of life were rigged against them.

Clinton's supporters, by contrast, were in an entirely different bubble. Also supported through social media as well as in most outlets of popular culture, their idea was that, sure, America had a ways to go, but it was so much *greater* than it had been. The picture was rosy. A popular African American president was leaving office after two full terms, breaking a barrier many thought they would never see. People of color were optimistic about their futures. Cops were still killing black men, but Black Lives Matter had organized and there was power in that organization. A woman was running for president, and many people thought she might win. Diversity meant interesting people, widened horizons, great restaurants, a vivid and colorful world. Gays were free to marry, transgender people were free to be themselves, people could even smoke pot legally in a handful of states. With a Democrat in the White House for four more years (they hoped), many of the changes that Obama had enacted to protect the environment, provide security to immigrants, and provide health care to all would be locked in, and liberals on the Supreme Court would secure reproductive rights for women and rights for gays. America was a wonderful country; it seemed it could only get better.

How on earth to reconcile these two narratives? Ironically, the great equalizer was the election. Both sides could feel that their narrative won, but only one side could claim the presidency, and with Trump on his way to the White House, the optimistic, rose-colored-glasses people began to feel that maybe they did, in fact, live in an apocalyptic world. And things for the Trump supporters began to look brighter. Whether the two narratives would meet somewhere in the middle or pass each other on forever-separate paths is an open question with open consequences. The stakes of living in separate narrative bubbles are critical to us all.

for CQ Press

Want a better grade?

Get the tools you need to sharpen your study skills. **SAGE edge** offers practice quizzes, eFlashcards, video, and multimedia at **edge.sagepub.com/barbourbrief8e.**

Review

Where Do We Get Our Information?

An increasing number of Americans have access to the **mass media** (436) via any number of devices, and in the age of **media convergence** (436), much of our news comes to us via **news aggregators** (441) that connect us with information from traditional **news organizations** (441) along with other sources. Media outlets try to distinguish themselves through **narrowcasting** (440) in the face of a vastly increased number of news sources and consumers' ability to cultivate their own news feeds.

How Does Media Ownership Affect Control of the Narrative?

Today's media are largely profit driven, and although small and independent news sources are gaining traction through digital media, the biggest news organizations are still owned by a few large corporate interests that function as **gatekeepers** (444). This profit motive can lead to a **commercial bias** (448) in reporting and has contributed to the rise of **clickbait** (448) journalism. Although the modern new media landscape allows for more content and more diverse voices, those voices are still largely intertwined with big media on many levels. The government also plays a role, with regulations on broadcast media, including the 1934 Federal Communications Act.

Spinning Political Narratives

Public skepticism of the media has increased in recent decades. Some critics claim that the **revolving door** (454) damages news objectivity, with government insiders and lobbyists taking jobs as political **pundits** (454) and vice versa. In any case, the media influence politics by shaping public opinion through **agenda setting** (455), **framing** (455), and persuasion, although citizens have their own armor against this influence, called **selective perception** (457). Journalists also tend to reduce politics to conflict and image, especially through the widespread practice of **horse-race journalism** (455), an overemphasis on **optics** (456) and **sound bites** (456), and engagement in a **feeding frenzy** (456) at the whiff of scandal.

Politics as Public Relations

Politicians respond to the media by turning politics into public relations, running what amounts to a **permanent campaign** (458), and by mastering the techniques of **news management** (458), attempting to control the narrative with **trial balloons** (460), **leaks** (460), and **spin** (458). The result of this complex relationship between the media and politicians is a reduction in **political accountability** (461).

14

Domestic and Foreign Policy

In Your Own Words

After you've read this chapter, you will be able to

14.1 Explain what policy is, who makes it, and how it is made.

14.2 Identify four government policy programs that attempt to improve citizens' lives.

14.3 Explain the difference between fiscal and monetary policy.

14.4 Identify the basic goals and types of foreign policy.

14.5 Describe ways in which policymaking reflects public opinion.

What's at Stake . . . in a Shrinking Middle Class?

In 2010 Bernie Sanders took the floor of the U.S. Senate to address what he saw as patent unfairness in the United States' economic system. The Vermont senator ended up talking for eight and a half hours—one of the longest nonstop speeches in the chamber's recent history. Seven years later, Sanders was still talking, and his devotion to the matter of income inequality struck a chord with struggling Americans as the long-time independent mounted a formidable (but ultimately unsuccessful) bid for the Democratic Party's presidential nomination in 2016. Just over a year after that election put Donald Trump in office, Sanders took aim at the Republicans' $1.5 trillion plan for tax cuts that they said would spur economic growth for all Americans, but that he considered a giveaway to the rich. "We have a nation today that has a grotesque level of income and wealth inequality—worse than at any time since the late 1920s," Sanders said before the Senate passed the tax-cut bill. "The top one-tenth of 1 percent now owns almost as much wealth as the bottom 90 percent, and 62 percent of all new income is going to the top 1 percent. The Republicans' solution is to make this grotesque inequality even worse by giving 62 percent of the tax benefits to the top 1 percent."[1]

Decades ago, there was a common belief in American society that hard work could enable anyone to reach the middle class, or move from the middle class into the higher economic reaches of society. In addition, there was a strong sense that those in the middle of the income distribution table shared a middle-class identity. That group included blue-collar workers, who owned homes, held steady jobs, and could reasonably expect that their children would someday find better-paying work. But rapid changes over the past several decades have challenged that middle-class ideal. A May 2018 poll asked people if the middle class had gotten a boost from President Trump's policies. Just 14 percent said middle-class families had been helped a lot, 45 percent said they had been helped a little, and 36 percent said those families hadn't benefited at all.[2]

Although narratives about income inequality are often spun as divisions between rich and poor, the shift in the distribution has had perhaps its most profound effects on the middle class. A growing number of academic studies, analyses of data, and scholarly commentaries have warned that the wealth of the American middle class is being outpaced by the holdings of the rich. The Pew Research Center, a nonpartisan organization in Washington, D.C., found that the share of adults in middle-income households fell from 61 percent of the population in 1971 to 50 percent in 2015. Meanwhile, wealthy households earned almost half of the nation's household income, even though they represented only about one-fifth of the actual U.S. population. That was more than the 29 percent of income earnings they held in 1970.[3] The three richest Americans—Microsoft founder Bill Gates, Amazon founder Jeff Bezos, and investor Warren Buffett—owned more wealth in 2017 than the entire bottom half of the U.S. population combined, roughly 160 million people.[4] The income divide is especially pronounced between those who have college degrees and those who do not. Although the slow recovery after the recession of 2008 is partially to blame for the stagnation of wages for middle-class workers, analysts also point to rapid shifts in technology, which increases demand for high-skilled workers and decreases the number of low-skill jobs available.[5] "The sharpest class division is between people with four-year college degrees and everybody else," said Andrew J. Cherlin, a sociologist at Johns Hopkins University in Baltimore, Maryland.[6]

Clearly, this issue has gained traction since 2011, when the Occupy Wall Street movement vividly protested the vast gap between America's wealthiest people and the rest of society. Adding fuel to the Occupy fire was the popularity of French economist Thomas Piketty's 2014 book *Capital in the Twenty-first Century*, in which he argued that capitalism inevitably will lead to a growing concentration of economic power into the hands of those fortunate enough to inherit large sums of money from their parents, a state Piketty calls "patrimonial capitalism."[7] By 2016, alarms were going off across the American political spectrum. Sean McElwee, a policy analyst at the liberal think tank Demos, predicted that "rising inequality of income and wealth will be the most important political battleground over the next few decades."[8] Eric Schnurer, the president of a public policy consulting firm, agreed that the world would see a "tidal wave . . . welling up from widespread disaffection with the grossly uneven—and, more important, unfair—distribution of pain and gain."[9] On the political right, commentator Ramesh Ponnuru said that although conservatives do not share that view, they should pay substantially more attention to the fate of middle-class Americans. "Republicans have grown increasingly aware, since their defeat in the 2012 election, that their party has a damaging reputation for caring only about the economic interests of the rich," he wrote.[10]

The issue came up often during the 2016 presidential race. Voters such as Sediena Barry, 34, of Reynoldsburg, Ohio, said their frustration about having to pay more in taxes than some wealthy people inspired them to vote for Sanders. "Young people were told, 'Get an education and work hard and you'll get ahead,' and none of us are," she said.[11] Some Republicans sought to reframe the discussion. Edward Conard, a former partner at Bain Capital—the investment firm where 2012 Republican presidential candidate Mitt Romney once worked—argued in a best-selling book that it was wrong to adopt Sanders's approach of faulting the wealthiest Americans. Those individuals' risk-taking, Conard argued, had accelerated economic growth. "Blaming the success of America's 1 percent for the slow growth of middle- and working-class incomes leads to policies that slow an already slow-growing economy," Conard said.[12]

Republicans promoted their 2017 tax-cut overhaul as something that would help spur middle-class growth. But they saw little immediate public enthusiasm for the law. An NBC News/*Wall Street Journal* poll in April 2018 said just 27 percent of Americans thought the law was a good idea, down 3 percentage points since January.[13] The situation led some Republicans to question if they needed to do more than just cut taxes to help average Americans. One of them was Marco Rubio, the Florida senator who unsuccessfully challenged Trump for the Republican nomination in 2016. "There is still a lot of thinking on the right that if big corporations are happy, they're going to take the money they're saving [from tax cuts] and reinvest it in American workers," Rubio said in April 2018. "In fact . . . there's no evidence whatsoever that the money's been massively poured back into the American worker." Rubio called for the government, not companies, to take the lead in expanding the middle class. "If we basically say everyone is on their own and the market's going to take care of it, we will rip the country apart, because millions of good, hard-working people lack the means to adapt," he said.[14]

But hearing similar observations from both ends of the political spectrum doesn't mean that there's a whole lot of agreement on what to do to grow and lift the middle class. If everyone agrees that the increased income inequality in general, and a shrinking middle class in particular, are problems, why is it so hard to implement policy solutions? Is inequality caused by economic policy—and can it be fixed by such policy? Just what is at stake when the middle class is shrinking? We'll revisit these questions after we take a closer look at how policy—in this case, economic policy—works.

THE quality of this air is horrible," we say as we gasp for breath while jogging in a local park. "Someone ought to *do* something about this."

"It's intolerable that homeless people have to sleep in the public library. Why doesn't somebody *do* something?"

"How tragic that so many young children don't have health care. Can't anyone *do* anything about it?"

When we utter such cries of disgust, frustration, or compassion, we are not calling on the heavens to visit us with divine intervention. Usually the general somebody/anybody we call on for action is our government, and what government does or doesn't do, at the end of the day, is called public policy. In fact, public policy has been a focus of discussion throughout this book. When we ask what's at stake, as we do throughout this book, the *what* is almost always a government action or policy. When we talk about political narratives, as we have frequently done, they almost always involve a justification or a challenge to government action, or to policy. The study of public policy is inseparable from the study of American politics.

In this chapter we focus specifically on what public policy is and how the parts of government we have studied come together to create it. But government is not something "out there," something external to us. We have seen in this book that we are increasingly drawn into the political decisions of our government through the media by which we get our information and that in many ways American government is very responsive to us as citizens, either individually as voters or collectively as interest groups. In some policy areas, such as social welfare reform and crime policy, politicians have responded to public opinion by limiting welfare and getting tougher on criminals. In other areas, notably Social Security and health care, politicians have responded to the powerful demands of organized interest groups. In still other policy areas, primarily economic policy, some of the political decisions have been taken out of the hands of elected officials precisely because these individuals tend to respond to what voters and interest groups want, or what they imagine they want.

In this chapter we look at what policy is, who makes it, who benefits (the winners), who pays (the losers), and how it is made. You will learn about specific domestic policy areas—social policy such as Social Security, welfare, and health care policy; economic policy such as fiscal, monetary, and tax policy—as well as the less familiar world of foreign policy.

MAKING PUBLIC POLICY

How government attempts to solve collective problems

Our lives are regulated by policies that influence nearly everything we do. For example, many stores have a no-return *policy* on discounted merchandise. Restaurant owners alert customers to their *policy* toward underdressed diners with the sign "No shirt, no shoes, no service." Your college or university may have a policy requiring a minimum grade point average for continued enrollment.

These are private, nongovernmental policies, adopted by individuals, businesses, or organizations to solve problems and to advance individual or group interests. Stores want to sell their new merchandise, not last season's leftovers; restaurant owners want a certain clientele to dine in their establishments; and institutions of higher education want to maintain standards and give students an incentive to excel. The problems of the clothing store, the restaurant, and the university are straightforward. Addressing these problems with a policy is pretty easy. Creating public policies, however, is more difficult than creating policies on merchandise returns, dining attire, and acceptable grades.

Public policy is a government plan of action to solve a problem that people share collectively or that they cannot solve on their own. That is not to say that the intended problem is always solved, or that the plan might not create more and even worse problems. Sometimes government's plan of action is to do nothing; that is, it may be a plan of *in*action, with the expectation (or hope) that the problem will go away on its own, or in the belief that it is not or should not be government's business to solve it. Some issues may be so controversial that policymakers would rather leave them alone, confining the scope of a policy debate to relatively "safe" issues.[15] But, by and large, we can understand public policy as a purposeful course of action intended by public officials to solve a public problem.[16] When that problem occurs here in the United States, we say that the government response is domestic policy; when it concerns our relations with other nations, we call it foreign policy.

SOLVING PUBLIC PROBLEMS

Public policies differ from the restaurant's "No shirt, no shoes, no service" policy because they are designed to solve common problems, not to address the concerns of a single business or institution. We think of problems as public when they cannot be handled by individuals, groups, businesses, or other actors privately, or when they directly or indirectly affect many citizens. Public problems might include the need for collective goods that individuals alone cannot or will not produce, such as highways, schools, and welfare. Public problems can include harm caused to citizens by the environment, foreign countries, dangerous products, or each other. When people suggest that government ought to do something about violent crime, or about drug use, or about poor school quality, they are suggesting that government should create a policy to address a public problem. Generally speaking, the suggestion takes hold when it fits with a preexisting narrative (for example, "international trade takes away Americans' jobs") or helps create a compelling new one (for example, "America's crumbling infrastructure poses public safety problems").

Sometimes the very question of whether or not a problem is public becomes the subject of political debate, or of conflicting narratives. If the prevailing narrative is that a large gap between rich and poor is just a normal result of the market, then it won't be perceived as a problem in need of a solution. If a group like Occupy Wall Street or an individual like Bernie Sanders can change the narrative, as we saw in *What's at Stake . . . ?*, politicians may react in different ways: by offering counternarratives that claim there really isn't a problem or that the problem is something other than what is claimed, or if they buy the narrative, they may compete to offer solutions to the problem.

Government can address public problems directly, by building schools, prisons, or highways, for example, but a great deal of public problem solving entails offering incentives to individuals or groups to get them to behave the way government wants them to behave. In other words, public policy can encourage or discourage behaviors in order to solve a problem that already exists or to avoid creating a future problem. For instance, government has an interest in having well-educated, property-owning citizens, since the conventional wisdom is that such people are more stable and more likely to obey the laws—in short, to be good citizens. Consequently, government policy encourages students to go to college by offering low-interest college loans and generous tax credits. It encourages homeownership in the same way. These various forms of federal assistance provide incentives for us to behave in a certain way to avoid creating the problem of an uneducated, rootless society.

public policy a government plan of action to solve a problem

DIFFICULTIES IN SOLVING PUBLIC PROBLEMS

Despite the good intentions of policymakers, however, public problems can be difficult to solve. First, as we have already suggested, people have different narratives about what constitutes a problem in the first place. The definition of a public problem is not something that can be looked up in a book. It is the product of the values and beliefs of political actors and, consequently, is frequently the subject of passionate debate. Even something that seems to be as obviously problematic as poverty can be controversial. To people who believe that poverty is an inevitable though unfortunate part of life, or to those who feel that poor people should take responsibility for themselves, poverty may not be a problem requiring a public solution.

A second reason that solving public problems can be hard is that solutions cost money—often a lot of money. Finding the money to address a new problem usually requires shifting it out of existing programs or raising taxes. With an eye toward the next election, politicians are reluctant to spend tax dollars to support new initiatives. This is especially true when these new initiatives are not widely supported by citizens, which is often the case with policies that take money from some citizens in order to benefit others, such as welfare policy.

Public problems can also be difficult to solve because their solutions often generate new problems. Policies tough on crime can jam up the courts and slow the criminal justice system. Policies to help the poor can create dependence on government among the disadvantaged. And environmental policies can impair a business's ability to compete. Often the problems caused by policy require new policies to solve them in turn.

> *What problems require public solutions, and what problems should be left to individuals to solve?*

A final reason that problems can be hard to solve has to do with their complexity. Seldom are there easy answers to any public dilemma. Even when policymakers can agree on a goal, they often lack sufficient knowledge about how to get there. Competing solutions may be proposed, with no one knowing definitively which will best solve the problem. And some public problems may in reality be multiple problems with multiple causes—further muddying the effort to find adequate solutions. Policymaking in the American context is made even more complex by the federal system. Whose responsibility is it to solve a given problem—the federal, state, or local government's?

TYPES OF PUBLIC POLICY

In an effort to make sense of all the policies in contemporary politics, some political scientists divide them into types—redistributive, distributive, or regulatory—depending on who benefits and who pays, what the policy tries to accomplish, and how it is made.[17] Although this classification, summarized in Table 14.1, is not perfect (for instance, sometimes a policy can fit into more than one category), it does help us to think about policy in a coherent way.

Redistributive policies attempt to shift wealth, income, and other resources from the "haves" to the "have-nots." Like Robin Hood, government acting through redistributive policies seeks to help its poorer citizens. The U.S. government's income tax policy is redistributive because it is based on a progressive tax rate. People who earn more pay a higher percentage of their incomes to the federal government in taxes. (The progressivity of the income tax, however, is tempered by other elements of the U.S. tax code.) Programs such as housing or food assistance are redistributive policies because they shift dollars away from people with relatively larger incomes to people with smaller or no incomes. As we see later in this chapter,

redistributive policies policies that shift resources from the "haves" to the "have-nots"

TABLE 14.1

Types of Policy

TYPE OF POLICY	POLICY GOAL	WHO PROMOTES THIS POLICY?	WHO BENEFITS? (WINS)	WHO PAYS? (LOSES)	EXAMPLES
Redistributive	To help the have-nots in society	Public interest groups; officials motivated by values	Disadvantaged citizens	Middle- and upper-class taxpayers	Medicaid; food assistance
Distributive	To meet the needs of various groups	Legislators and interest groups	Members of interest groups and the legislators they support	All taxpayers	Homeowners' tax deductions; veterans' benefits; anticrime policies; education reform
Regulatory	To limit or control actions of individuals or groups	Public interest groups	Public	Targeted groups	Environmental policy

U.S. social welfare policy is largely redistributive. Health care policy in the United States is also redistributive, since the government, through taxation, provides for the cost of health care for some of those who cannot afford it.

Redistributive policies are generally politically difficult to put in place because they take resources away from the affluent segments of society who are most likely to be politically active, to vote regularly, and to contribute to political campaigns or interest groups. These attentive constituents individually or collectively contact their congressional representatives to express their views. In contrast, the recipients of redistributive policies, far lower on the socioeconomic scale, tend to vote less often and lack the resources to donate to political campaigns or form interest groups. Their causes may be taken up by public interest groups, professional organizations representing social workers, or legislators who believe that it is government's job to help the needy. In the battle of who gets what in politics, policies that redistribute wealth are relatively rare because the people who must pay for the policy are better equipped than the poor to fight political battles.

distributive policies policies funded by the whole taxpayer base that address the needs of particular groups

Distributive policies, by contrast, are much easier to make, because the costs are not perceived to be borne by any particular segment of the population. Tax deductions for interest on home mortgage payments, agriculture price supports, interstate highway policies, federal grants for higher education, even programs that provide for parks and recreation, are examples of distributive policies. The common feature of distributive policies is that although they provide benefits to a recognizable group (such as homeowners or the families of college students), the costs are widely distributed. In other words, all taxpayers foot the bill.

regulatory policies policies designed to restrict or change the behavior of certain groups or individuals

Regulatory policies differ from redistributive and distributive policies in that they are designed to restrict or change the behavior of certain groups or individuals. Whereas redistributive and distributive policies work to increase assistance to particular groups, regulatory policies tend to do just the opposite. They limit the actions of the regulatory target group—the group whose behavior government seeks to control. Most environmental policies, for example, are regulatory in nature. Business owners face myriad air emissions limitations and permit requirements that must be met in order to avoid government sanctions, including the possibility of civil fines or a criminal trial. Since the groups being regulated frequently have greater resources at their disposal than the groups seeking the regulation (often public interest groups), the battle to regulate business can be lopsided.

The politics surrounding the creation of regulatory policies is highly confrontational. The "losers" in regulatory policy are often the target groups. Business doesn't want to pay for environmental controls; nor do manufacturers want to be monitored for compliance by government. By contrast, interest groups representing the beneficiaries of the policy argue just as strongly for the need for regulatory control. To continue our environmental policy example, the Environmental Defense Fund and the American Lung Association are repeat players in policy developments under the Clean Air Act. These groups have frequently sued the U.S. Environmental Protection Agency to compel it to lower the acceptable levels of airborne pollutants.[18]

WHO MAKES POLICY?

All the political actors we have studied in this book have a hand in the policymaking process. Government actors inside the system—members of Congress, the president, the courts, and bureaucrats—are involved, as are actors outside the system—interest groups, the media, and members of the public themselves.

Policies are usually created by members of Congress in the form of one or more new laws. Sometimes what we think of as a single policy is really a bundle of several laws or amendments to laws. Environmental policy and social welfare policy are prime examples of bundles of programs and laws. National environmental policy is included in more than a dozen laws, among them the Clean Air Act, the Clean Water Act, and the Safe Drinking Water Act. Social welfare policy consists of more than direct financial assistance to poor families. Also included are programs that subsidize food purchases, provide day care for children, and offer job training and education for the parents.

The role of Congress in creating and legitimating policy through its laws is critically important to understanding national public policy. As we discussed in Chapter 6, members of Congress are often most attentive to what their constituencies and the interest groups that support their campaigns want. Nonetheless, many members of Congress also follow their own values and consciences when making difficult political decisions.

The president may also create policy, perhaps by putting an issue on the public agenda, by including it (or not) in his budget proposal, by vetoing a law made by Congress, or by issuing an executive order that establishes a new policy or augments an existing one. Executive orders sometimes make profound changes in policy. One such executive order created affirmative action. When Congress passed the Civil Rights Act in 1964 banning employment discrimination against women and minorities, the law did not require that employers actively seek to employ persons within these protected classes. Arguing that America must seek "equality as a fact and equality as a result," President Lyndon Johnson issued executive orders requiring federal contractors to develop affirmative action programs to promote the hiring and advancement of minorities and women. Donald Trump has made frequent use of executive orders in a wide range of areas in his first two years. By March 2018, he had issued 54 executive orders—the highest of any president since Democrat Jimmy Carter.[19]

Government bureaucracies at the federal, state, or local level may also create or enhance policy through their power to regulate. Administrative agencies are crucial to the policymaking process, helping to propose laws, lobbying for their passage, making laws of their own under authority delegated from Congress, and implementing laws. Moreover, agencies have enormous control over policy simply by how they enforce it.

Finally, the courts are policymakers as well. We saw in Chapter 9 that the Supreme Court has been responsible for some of the major changes in policy direction in this country with respect to business regulation, civil rights, and civil liberties, to name just a few. When the courts rule on what the government can or should do (or not do), they are clearly taking an active policymaking role. In addition, they are often asked to rule on the implementation of policy decisions made elsewhere in the government—on affirmative action, for example, or welfare policy, or education.

National policies are best thought of as packages made by several actors. Congress passes a law that establishes a policy. In turn, federal or state agencies respond by writing regulations and working with individuals and groups who are affected by the policy. Presidents may want to emphasize (or deemphasize) a policy in several ways. They may publicize the new policy through public statements—most notably the State of the Union address. They may issue formal (executive orders) or informal instructions to agencies that highlight policy goals. So, although a law may initially establish a plan of action for a public problem, policies tend to evolve over time and contain many elements from all branches of government. Taken as a whole, these various components (laws, regulations, executive orders, agency actions, and so on) form the government's policy.

STEPS IN THE POLICYMAKING PROCESS

Political scientists have isolated five steps that most policymakers follow in the process of trying to solve a public problem. Figure 14.1 illustrates the policymaking process.

The first step in creating policy is *agenda setting*. Agenda setting occurs when problems come to the attention of people who can address them (usually members of Congress). These problems can be brought to Congress' attention by individual members, the president, interest groups, the media, or public opinion polls.

The second step in the policymaking process is called *policy formulation*. At this step, several competing solutions to the policy problem or objective are developed and debated in Congress. These alternative strategies often take the form of bills—perhaps proposed by the president or an administrative agency—introduced into Congress and sent to committees for deliberation.

If a preferred policy alternative emerges from the policy formulation stage, it must be legitimized through formal government action, referred to as the *policy adoption* stage. Policies—some trivial, some enormously important—are continually being adopted by all three branches of government through congressional legislation, executive orders, agency regulation, or court ruling.

Once policies are adopted they must be put into practice. During the *policy implementation* stage, federal or state agencies interpret the policy by writing regulations, creating guidance documents, or drafting memorandums of agreement with other agencies. Agency staff meet with the beneficiaries of the policy, staff in other departments, citizens, and interest groups in an attempt to devise a workable plan for putting the policy into action. Implementation of public policy is neither easy nor guaranteed; those charged with implementing it can often derail the policy by not enforcing it.

FIGURE 14.1

The Policymaking Process

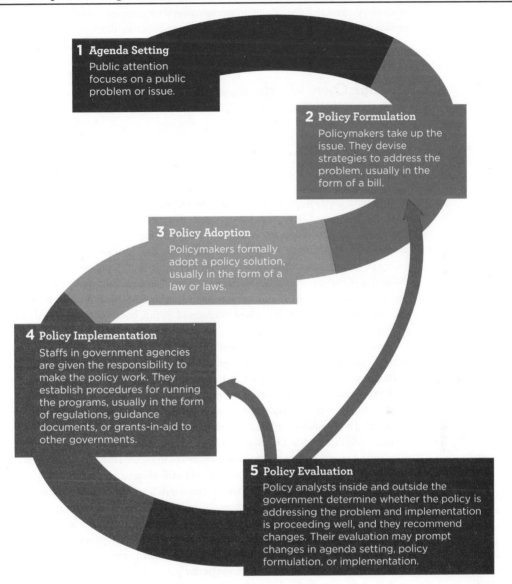

1 Agenda Setting
Public attention focuses on a public problem or issue.

2 Policy Formulation
Policymakers take up the issue. They devise strategies to address the problem, usually in the form of a bill.

3 Policy Adoption
Policymakers formally adopt a policy solution, usually in the form of a law or laws.

4 Policy Implementation
Staffs in government agencies are given the responsibility to make the policy work. They establish procedures for running the programs, usually in the form of regulations, guidance documents, or grants-in-aid to other governments.

5 Policy Evaluation
Policy analysts inside and outside the government determine whether the policy is addressing the problem and implementation is proceeding well, and they recommend changes. Their evaluation may prompt changes in agenda setting, policy formulation, or implementation.

Policymaking begins with agenda setting and ends with policy evaluation, which often cycles back to the creation of new policy initiatives.

The last step in the policymaking process is to evaluate the policy. *Policy evaluation* requires the policy analyst to ask several fundamental questions: Does the policy, as currently constructed, address the initial public problem? Does it represent a reasonable use of public resources? Would other strategies be more effective? Has it produced any undesirable effects?

Policy evaluation is conducted inside government by agencies such as the U.S. Government Accountability Office, the Congressional Budget Office, the Office of Management and Budget, and the Congressional Research Service. Congress also conducts oversight hearings in which agencies that implement programs report their progress toward policy goals. Groups outside government also evaluate policy to determine whether the desired outcomes are being achieved. Some of these groups are nonpartisan and are funded by philanthropic organizations.

In Your Own Words Explain what policy is, who makes it, and how it is made.

SOCIAL POLICY

Government efforts to improve citizens' lives

In the United States we have public policies to address every imaginable public problem, from transportation, to crime, to education. We can't discuss every public policy in this short chapter, but we can zero in on a few in order to give you a clearer idea of how the policy process works—who the actors are, what they want, and how they go about getting it.

Social policies are primarily distributive and redistributive policies that seek to improve the quality of citizens' lives. They focus on a variety of quality-of-life problems—most of them centered on the problem of improving people's standards of living. As we will see, social policies can benefit people at all levels of income and wealth, but most frequently they deal with the issue of poverty.

Poverty is a particularly difficult issue for societies to deal with because there is no universally accepted understanding of who is poor. In fact, defining poverty is itself a policy decision made by a government agency, the U.S. Census Bureau, which determines the poverty threshold, or the poverty line for American families.

Whether they address poverty by ignoring it and leaving the issue to private charities or by building an extensive welfare state, all societies have a policy on how to take care of the economically vulnerable. One way to address the problem is with social welfare policies, government programs that provide for the needs of those who cannot, or sometimes will not, provide for themselves—needs for shelter, food and clothing, jobs, education, old age care, and medical assistance. Most social welfare policies are redistributive; they transfer resources, in the form of financial assistance or essential services, from those with resources to those without. Policies such as these are usually means-tested programs; that is, beneficiaries must prove that they lack the necessary means to provide for themselves, according to the government's definitions of eligibility. As we said earlier, redistributive programs can be politically divisive and can open the way to partisan battle.

A second way societies deal with the problem of caring for the economically vulnerable is through social insurance programs that offer benefits in exchange for contributions made by citizens to offset future economic need. Social Security is an example of a social insurance program. Whereas welfare policies are usually designed to be temporary solutions for helping the poor, social insurance programs cover longer-range needs. Social insurance programs are distributive because everyone pays, but only a certain segment of the population—in the case of Social Security, the elderly—receives benefits.

social policies distributive and redistributive policies that seek to improve the quality of citizens' lives

social welfare policies public policies that seek to meet the basic needs of people who are unable to provide for themselves

means-tested programs social programs whose beneficiaries qualify by demonstrating need

social insurance programs programs that offer benefits in exchange for contributions

Social Security a social insurance program under which individuals make contributions during working years and collect benefits in retirement

Although both welfare and Social Security were designed to aid the needy—poor children in the first case and the elderly poor in the second—they have evolved in different directions because of who is involved and how they go about trying to get what they want from the system. Today the differences are substantial.

Social Security is a hugely popular program whose benefit levels are guarded jealously, whereas welfare has been reformed to end its long-term guarantee that no American child would go hungry. Social Security promises a lifetime of benefits to recipients, even though most draw far more money out of the system than they ever put in. Welfare laws now limit recipients to two years at a time in the program, with a lifetime total of five years. Why the differences? The answer lies in the identity of the beneficiaries of the two programs and those who pay for them (the *who*), what the two programs try to accomplish (the *what*), and the politics under which each policy is produced (the *how*). In this section we look at each of these elements more closely.

SOCIAL SECURITY

Social Security was born in the midst of the Great Depression, when so many older Americans found themselves facing an impoverished retirement that Franklin Roosevelt's New Deal administration passed the Social Security Act of 1935. Social Security provides what is essentially a guaranteed pension for workers. Lyndon Johnson's amendment to the act added health care benefits for the elderly in the form of Medicare. These programs have brought financial security to many retired people, but they are costly programs, especially with the Baby Boomer generation reaching retirement age.

It Pays to Stay Alive

Social Security has been an immensely popular program in the United States, guaranteeing benefits to Americans once they hit age sixty-five. But when the program launched in 1935, the life expectancy of the average American male was just fifty-nine years. An aging population has put a strain on the system, but its immense popularity makes reform difficult.

Social Security is a social insurance program: people contribute to Social Security during their working lives in order to receive benefits when they retire. Consequently, most people see Social Security in a positive light—as if they are receiving something they have earned and to which they are entitled, not a government handout. As we will see, that is only part of the story.

On its face, Social Security looks very different from the social welfare programs in which income or resources are transferred from one group to another. Recipients contribute a portion of their income, matched by their employers, directly into a fund for Social Security. Their Social Security contribution appears on their paycheck as a withholding called FICA

Social Security Act the New Deal Act that created AFDC, Social Security, and unemployment insurance

(Federal Insurance Contributions Act). Current workers pay the Social Security of current retirees, with any leftover money going into the Social Security Trust Fund. When workers retire they receive monthly checks from the Social Security Administration, based on how much money they have paid into the system.

Social Security looks like an insurance program, and as we noted earlier that's what we call it. But Social Security differs from real insurance in critical ways. Insurance allows us to pool our resources with others to cover the uncertainties of life—illness, accidents, and the like. Those of us who are lucky end up subsidizing those of us who aren't. But we will all get old (at least we hope we will), and we will all receive Social Security benefits, so there will be no lucky retirees subsidizing the lives of unlucky retirees. Social Security has to pay for all of us, so it is really more like a forced savings plan than an insurance plan. The government requires that we save our money each month so that we can draw on it in our retirement.

But if Social Security is a forced savings account, it is a magical one indeed because it never runs out as long as we or our spouses are alive. We continue to receive payments long after we've gotten back the money we put in, even including the interest we might have earned had our money been in a real savings account. And since there is no means test for Social Security, not only poor recipients but also billionaires can continue to collect this direct subsidy from taxpayers.

So far this system has worked because the number of people in the workforce has been able to cover the retirement expenses of those leaving it. The Social Security Trust Fund has gotten fat because the pool of workers has grown faster than the pool of retirees. The Social Security Trust Fund now receives more in FICA taxes than is paid out in benefits, but by 2020 that will change as the number of retirees grows and the fund is tapped to pay their benefits.[20] If nothing is done to change the way Social Security works (for example, by cutting benefits, increasing Social Security taxes, or raising the retirement age), the Social Security Board of Trustees estimates that the trust fund will run out of money by the year 2034. Money coming in each year from FICA taxes is expected to cover only about three-quarters of what Social Security will be obligated to pay out, according to the current promise of the program.[21]

Unless Congress acts, the remaining quarter will be paid from the government's general coffers. This is because Social Security is an **entitlement program**, which means that benefits must be paid to people who are entitled to receive them. Funding entitlement programs is nondiscretionary for government: once the entitlement is created, recipients who qualify must receive their benefits. Entitlements comprise an increasing share of the federal budget. By 2018, entitlement spending was more than 60 percent of the budget, and it continues to grow. Social Security itself is the government's largest program, paying approximately $916 billion in benefits, or about 24 percent of the federal budget, in 2016.[22]

Many older Americans continue to need the economic protection that Social Security provides, but the system is not sustainable into the indefinite future in its present form. It could be made sustainable, but the remedies we just discussed—cutting benefit levels, increasing taxes, or raising the retirement age—are politically unpalatable. If they were enacted, people would have to pay more or get less or both, and no one wants to do those things.

Social Security has been shielded from hard decisions by AARP, a powerful organization of older Americans that protects the interests of retirees. While Republicans have favored programs converting Social Security, in whole or in part, to private savings accounts, the 2008 stock market crash took away much of the enthusiasm for that. In 2016 the Democrats argued that not only should Social Security *not* be privatized but that the program should be expanded. When he campaigned for president, Trump repeatedly promised not to cut Social Security. Even

entitlement program
a federal program that guarantees benefits to qualified recipients

as budget deficits rose in 2017, he told his budget director he would not do so.[23] An April 2018 *Economist*/YouGov poll found that Social Security came in third behind the economy and health care as the issue Americans most cared about, well ahead of immigration, the environment, terrorism, and education.[24] Although the issue of Social Security is likely to stay on the public agenda until its financial problems are addressed, the question of how to finance the program remains a controversial area of debate.[25]

WELFARE POLICY IN THE UNITED STATES

Social Security is a program designed to protect people's long-term financial futures; it is not designed to alleviate poverty in the short term. In fact, through the greater part of our history, poverty was not considered a public problem requiring government action. It was not until the Great Depression of the 1930s forced large numbers of previously successful working- and middle-class people into poverty that the public view shifted and citizens demanded that government step in. Today the American government tries to improve the quality of life for its poorest citizens through social welfare policies, focusing particularly on economic security for children.

The same New Deal Social Security Act that guaranteed pensions for older Americans included a program called Aid to Families With Dependent Children (AFDC), based on the commitment that no child would ever go hungry in America. AFDC was a means-tested program that provided benefits for families with children who could demonstrate need, to keep the children fed and to tide over the adults until they could find work and provide for their children themselves. The federal government contributed more than half the AFDC payments, and the states supplied the balance, managed the program, and determined who was eligible and how much they received. Even though states retained a role, with AFDC, for the first time, the federal government assumed responsibility for the economic well-being of its citizens.

It is important to note, however, what AFDC did not promise. Assistance here was primarily to dependent children—their parents were aided only secondarily, and the intention was to get them back to work. We had not become a society that easily accepted the notion that the haves are responsible for the have-nots. Redistributive policies that transfer money from the working person to children might seem acceptable; policies that subsidize able-bodied adults, much less so. The United States has never kept pace with the western European welfare states that have promised their citizens security from cradle to grave (or from womb to tomb, as some observers have put it more graphically). American welfare policy has had far more limited aspirations, and even those have been controversial. By the 1990s even liberals were clamoring for reform of a welfare system that seemed to have lost sight of its ideals and that, rather than propping up people until they could return to work, produced a culture of dependency that became increasingly difficult for recipients to escape.

At the center of the controversy was AFDC. By 1996 over four million families were receiving aid, and the majority of AFDC recipients in the 1990s were young, unmarried mothers (aged nineteen to thirty), unemployed, residing in central cities.[26] AFDC had been designed to raise above the poverty line those families hurt by economic downturns. President Roosevelt and the New Deal architects believed that the government should provide some temporary support when the economy slumped. Opponents of AFDC posed the question: how long is "temporary"?

AFDC was criticized because it contained no work requirements and set no time limits for remaining on welfare. As a redistributive program, it was viewed as a transfer of money from a hard-working segment of the population to one that did nothing to earn it. Public opinion polls showed that many Americans believed that welfare recipients were unwilling to work, living off the generosity of hard-working taxpayers. Since lower-income people are less likely to organize for political purposes, welfare recipients put up no coordinated defense of their benefits. Republicans had traditionally been more critical of welfare policy, but even some Democrats began to heed the calls of their constituents for welfare reform, arguing that the welfare system created disincentives for recipients to become productive members of society. On August 22, 1996, President Bill Clinton signed the Personal Responsibility and Work Opportunity Reconciliation Act, fulfilling his promise to "end welfare as we know it."

With Clinton's signature, AFDC was replaced by the **Temporary Assistance to Needy Families (TANF)** block grant to state governments. This reform gives states greater control over how they spend their money but caps the amount that the federal government will pay for welfare. The law requires work in exchange for time-limited benefits. Most recipients must find a job within two years of going on welfare and cannot stay on the welfare rolls for more than a total of five years altogether or less, depending on the state. Moreover, many states cap family benefits when an additional child is born to a family on welfare. The 1996 legislation expired in October 2002 and had to be renewed by Congress. After a lengthy and contentious reauthorization process, Congress finally enacted changes to TANF three years later in the Deficit Reduction Act of 2005. The reforms enacted in the Deficit Reduction Act increased further the work focus of the TANF program, by increasing the proportion of recipients who must be working and by defining more narrowly what counts as "work."[27] More than a decade after the heated debates surrounding its adoption, the controversy over welfare reform has resurfaced. Many conservatives, who favor sharply cutting spending on social programs, have argued that in a time of tight budgets, government can no longer play such a dominant role in providing assistance. Several Republicans have urged new approaches to the issue, such as phasing out government's involvement and replacing it with greater involvement from community organizations and private businesses.[28]

Few observers dispute that the reforms have successfully reduced the welfare rolls—the Department of Health and Human Services reports that, from August 1996 to December 2017, the number of welfare recipients fell from 12.2 million to 3.2 million (see Figure 14.2). Although studies of families who have left welfare have found that nearly two-thirds are employed in any given month and that more than three-fourths have worked since leaving welfare,[29] some critics argue that even when jobs are found, wages are so low that many people are unable to lift their families out of poverty.[30] The inadequacy of work as a means of raising low-wage workers out of poverty is even more pronounced in the current economic climate characterized by stagnant wages, which has led to a reevaluation of the 1996 welfare reform by some Democrats, who now argue that more should be done to help needy Americans.[31] These challenges were the focus of a recent national poverty conference in which one expert reported, "We have a work-based safety net without work. We're really in a pickle."[32]

TANF is not the only policy designed to solve the problem of poverty in the United States. The largest food assistance program is the **Supplemental Nutrition Assistance Program (SNAP)**, previously called the Food Stamp program. In 2017, more than 42 million Americans participated in SNAP each month.[33] SNAP provides low-income families with vouchers to purchase food (typically dispersed via an electronic system using a plastic card similar to a bank card). For most poor families, SNAP benefits are only part of the food budget. Families also spend some of their own cash to buy enough food for the month. The amount of SNAP benefits that households receive is indexed to family income. In 2015 these benefits averaged nearly $127 per person.

Temporary Assistance to Needy Families (TANF) a welfare program of block grants to states that encourages recipients to work in exchange for time-limited benefits

Supplemental Nutrition Assistance Program (SNAP) a federal program that provides vouchers to the poor to help them buy food

FIGURE 14.2

Population Receiving Welfare (AFDC and TANF), 1960–2017

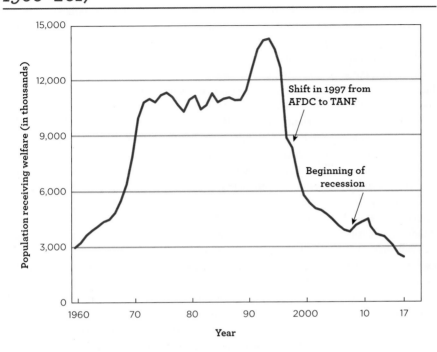

Source: Data obtained from the U.S. Department of Health and Human Services, Administration for Children and Families, Office of Family Assistance, www.acf.hhs.gov/programs/ofa/programs/tanf/data-reports.

Another approach to poverty policy in the United States is Head Start, a major component of Lyndon Johnson's War on Poverty. The program provides preschool education for low-income children and assistance and education to pregnant women. Head Start is a different approach to helping the poor; it aims at making welfare unnecessary by giving low-income children many of the advantages that their more affluent peers take for granted, and that can be significant in determining one's chances in life. Head Start prepares children for elementary school by putting them in environments that encourage learning and help them develop social skills. Most people agree with the goal of Head Start, but much controversy exists over how successful the program has been. Because of the increasing costs[34] and perceived limited return on the investment, conservatives often recommend scaling back Head Start.

HEALTH CARE

Although in 2010 Congress passed and President Obama signed the Patient Protection and Affordable Care Act, which made access to health insurance more available and affordable for most Americans by 2014, the United States stands out among industrialized nations as the only one that doesn't have a universal health care system guaranteeing minimum basic care to all. Ironically, of those nations, it also spends the most on health care: 17.2 percent of the U.S. gross domestic product (GDP) went to health care in 2016, far ahead of second place, Switzerland (12.4 percent), and third place, Germany (11.3 percent). And this spending is expected to increase to 19.7 percent of the GDP by 2026.[35]

Before health care reform was passed in 2010, the federal government's only role in health care was confined to the provision of Medicare and Medicaid. Like Social Security, Medicare is a social insurance program designed to help the elderly pay their medical costs. Like TANF, Medicaid is a means-tested welfare program to assist the poor—especially children—with their medical costs. Between these two programs, many Americans were left uninsured. Indeed, an estimated 49.9 million Americans, or 16.3 percent of the population, were without coverage in 2010.[36]

Signed into law by President Johnson in 1965 as an amendment to the Social Security Act, Medicare extended health care coverage to virtually all Americans who are over sixty-five, disabled, or suffering from permanent kidney failure. The idea was that workers would pay a small Medicare tax (collected as a payroll tax like FICA) while they were healthy in order to receive medical health insurance when they retired.

As the population ages and lives longer, and as medical costs skyrocket, Medicare has become an extraordinarily expensive program. Medicare is the nation's fourth largest expenditure, and the trustees for the Medicare Trust Fund estimate that full benefit payments can be made only until 2027, seven years before the Social Security Trust Fund is expected to experience a shortfall.[37] Because of this, many people argue that policymakers need to deal urgently with Medicare as well as Social Security.[38]

In 2003 Congress passed and President Bush signed the Medicare Modernization Act, which provided the elderly with prescription drug coverage under Medicare for the first time and gave private insurance companies a much greater role in the program. Democrats criticized the cost of the program (estimated to be $724 billion over the next ten years), argued that the plan gave too much power to health maintenance organizations (HMOs), and attacked Bush for not allowing the importation of less expensive drugs from Canada, claiming that the plan is a windfall for the pharmaceutical industry. In the 2012 presidential campaign, Medicare became a focal point because of vice presidential candidate Paul Ryan's plan for converting Medicare to a voucher program and removing the guarantee of coverage, a plan the Democrats rejected.

Medicaid was also enacted as an amendment to the Social Security Act in 1965, as part of President Johnson's Great Society program. A federally sponsored program that provides free medical care to the poor, Medicaid is funded jointly by the national and state governments and covers hospitalization, prescription drugs, doctors' visits, and long-term nursing care.

The problems with Medicare and Medicaid give some clues about why U.S. policymakers have consistently hesitated to create a national health care system to serve all Americans. Fears of excessive government control, large costs, and inefficient services have doomed reform efforts. Proponents of universal health care find it difficult to eliminate the perception that government control will harm the quality and raise the cost of health care services. The rise of HMOs in the 1990s raised hopes that the phenomenal costs could be controlled and health care standards maintained. However, in response to HMOs, doctors frequently lament the loss of autonomy and patients complain of diminishing quality of care and ever-rising costs.[39]

Rising health care costs for everyone and concern over the high number of Americans who had no health care insurance at all made federal health care reform a key issue in the 2008 election, both in the Democratic primary campaign and later in the general election. Although

Medicare the federal government's health insurance program for the elderly and disabled

Medicaid a federally sponsored program that provides medical care to the poor

Obama, an advocate of making health insurance available to all, won the presidency, there was no guarantee that health care reform would proceed as he had hoped. The economic crash of 2008 and the expensive financial bailout and stimulus plans that followed made spending money on social programs much less attractive to politicians. Even so, the Obama administration continued to push health care reform as its primary domestic policy priority. Adopting lessons from failed efforts to reform our nation's complex health care insurance and delivery system, Obama did not propose the creation of a single-payer or unified national health care plan like those in Europe. Instead, he endorsed a range of separate policy changes that he argued would combine together to expand access to health insurance, slow the growth of health care costs, and provide more patient protections—particularly for the hard-to-insure such as those with preexisting conditions.[40]

After a contentious yearlong debate, a massive reform bill—the Patient Protection and Affordable Care Act (ACA, now widely known as Obamacare)—was signed into law in March 2010. It did not include a public option, a proposed government-sponsored health insurance plan that would compete with the plans offered by private health insurance companies, because the Speaker of the House and the Senate majority leader were unable to put together a winning coalition to vote for its inclusion. However, the law included many provisions aimed at expanding insurance coverage: it required that employers with fifty or more employees provide health insurance and that most Americans outside that system purchase health insurance for themselves or pay a penalty, and it prohibited insurers from denying coverage to those with preexisting conditions. To make these mandates affordable, the bill expanded Medicaid to more low-income individuals and provided subsidies and tax credits to individuals and small businesses to reduce the burden of insurance premiums.

Based on ideas generated by a conservative think tank, the reform bill also created state-based American Health Benefit Exchanges and Small Business Health Options Exchanges to serve as vehicles for individuals and small businesses to purchase qualified health insurance in a competitive market. These exchanges are administered by a government agency or nonprofit organization—under governance of the states. Additionally, Consumer Operated and Oriented Plan (CO-OP) programs allow for the creation of nonprofit, member-run health insurance companies in all fifty states.[41]

The hard-won victory for the Democrats was made more difficult by the refusal of any Republican to support the bill and by the death of longtime health care reform advocate Sen. Ted Kennedy of Massachusetts. After a grueling battle in the House and the subsequent legislative maneuvers required to align the House bill with the Senate version, the public was

SAUL LOEB/AFP/Getty Images

Stamp of Approval

President Obama signs the Patient Protection and Affordable Care Act into law on March 23, 2010. The legislation provided national health care reform, one of the Obama administration's main domestic policy priorities and one subject to great controversy. Although the Supreme Court upheld the law in 2012, Republicans continued to call for its repeal.

frustrated with the partisan debate. Although Republicans decried the law and insisted they would work to repeal it, Democrats scrambled to get some key provisions into effect before the 2010 midterm elections so that voters could see what the reforms might mean in their lives. Though experts said the law would mean long-term savings for the health care system, a recession-weary nation, tired of government spending and leery of giving too much power to federal officials, voted heavily against the Democrats in the 2010 midterm elections, in many places costing them control at the state level that would have eased implementation of the health care plan.[42]

The issue eventually went to the U.S. Supreme Court, which held several days of hearings in March 2012 on whether the law was constitutional. The ruling, handed down at the end of that June, was a surprise, with the conservative chief justice, John Roberts, joining the more center-left justices in upholding the law in a five-to-four vote. The majority did not say that Congress could require people to buy insurance through its commerce clause powers, but rather that the individual mandate constituted a tax on those who chose not to buy insurance and as such was a constitutional exercise of congressional power. The Court did, however, weaken the law's requirement that states participate in the Medicaid expansion. By July 2018, thirty-three states and the District of Columbia agreed to participate and expand Medicaid coverage. Another fourteen states had decided against expansion and three were still considering expansion.[43]

The Supreme Court issued another ruling in June 2015 that helped keep the Affordable Care Act intact. The court ruled in *King v. Burwell* that the law allowed the government to provide nationwide tax subsidies to help the poor and middle class buy health insurance. The ruling in this case was a more decisive six to three, prompting President Obama to predict it would permanently survive. "After multiple challenges to this law before the Supreme Court, the Affordable Care Act is here to stay," Obama said, adding: "What we're not going to do is unravel what has now been woven into the fabric of America."[44]

With Donald Trump's assumption of office in 2017, Republicans believed their opportunity to overturn the law had arrived. A repeal bill was introduced that put in place various provisions attractive to Republicans, such as giving states more flexibility in establishing essential health benefits and ending various ACA taxes and fees. Various House committees approved it on party-line votes. But when Republican leaders tried to bring the bill to the House floor, they faced vocal objections from a faction of ardent conservatives known as the Freedom Caucus, who were holding out for a full repeal of the ACA. Several Republican governors also came out against the bill, arguing that they wanted more of a say in how it was crafted. The House finally passed the bill in May on a 217-to-213 vote, with twenty Republicans—most of them moderates from districts that voted for Hillary Clinton in 2016—joining all of the House's Democrats in opposition.[45]

The focus shifted to the Senate, where Republican leaders drafted their own version of the repeal bill behind closed doors. That approach angered some of the Senate's Republicans, who said the regular process of developing legislation in committee should have been followed. Senate leaders decided in July to bring a repeal-only bill without any replacement language, but that vote failed. The leadership next said it would bring up a scaled-down version of the repeal. Three Republican senators—Maine's Susan Collins, Lisa Murkowski of Alaska, and John McCain of Arizona—voted against it, causing it to fail 49 to 51.[46] In a statement, McCain decried the unwillingness of Republicans to collaborate with Democrats on a compromise:

I've stated time and time again that one of the major failures of Obamacare was that it was rammed through Congress by Democrats on a strict-party line basis without a single Republican vote. We should not make the mistakes of the past that has led to Obamacare's collapse. . . . We must now return to the correct way of legislating and send the bill back to committee, hold hearings, receive input from both sides of the aisle, heed the recommendations of nation's governors, and produce a bill that finally delivers affordable health care for the American people.[47]

Despite their failure to overturn the Affordable Care Act, Republicans did succeed in 2017 in passing, as part of their tax overhaul bill, a repeal of the "individual mandate," the requirement that most Americans have insurance or pay a fine. Most people who do not have health coverage that complies with the act's minimum standards faced a tax penalty of $695 per adult or 2.5 percent of their household income, whichever is higher. The mandate's repeal is scheduled to take effect in 2019.[48] The nonpartisan Congressional Budget Office estimated that, in 2019, the move would raise insurance premiums in the individual market by 10 percent.[49] Then, in February 2018, the Trump administration called for expanding short-term health insurance plans. Those plans are intended as temporary insurance coverage, generally to help people manage transitions between different sources of coverage. The administration's rule called for expanding the plans' duration, making them a long-term source of coverage.[50] The Affordable Care Act's supporters criticized the move as another way to drive up premiums in the individual insurance market and thus weaken the law.[51]

At the end of the Obama administration, the ACA had lived up to its supporters' expectations: the percentage of adults who were uninsured for at least part of the previous year plummeted from 51 million in 2010 to 33.2 million in the first nine months of 2017.[52] How it will fare under the Trump administration remains to be seen.

MIDDLE-CLASS AND CORPORATE WELFARE

Social policies include not only what we typically think of as welfare—programs to assist the poor—but also programs that increase the quality of life for the middle class. Clearly this is true of the social insurance programs of Social Security and Medicare, which go to all contributors, rich and poor, in amounts that generally exceed their contributions. But a number of other distributive policies benefit workers, middle-class homeowners, students, and members of the military. These policies help a particular group in society at the expense of all taxpayers by giving that group a subsidy. Subsidies are financial incentives such as cash grants, tax deductions, or price supports given by the government to corporations, individuals, or other governments usually to encourage certain activities or behaviors (such as homeownership or college attendance). Even though these subsidies are designed to achieve government's ends, they have long since fallen into the category of benefits to which groups feel entitled.

Among the subsidies that benefit groups we wouldn't typically associate with social welfare policies are those that support education. A well-educated citizenry is a valuable asset for a nation, and government uses subsidies in a number of ways to try to achieve one. For instance, the federal government provides funds to local school systems for certain types of educational programs, provides direct student loans and guarantees loans made to students by private lenders such as banks and credit unions, and provides some relief to families with dependents in college by allowing tax credits as long as the taxpayer's adjusted gross income is below a certain amount.

subsidy a financial incentive given by the government to corporations, individuals, or other governments

Another kind of subsidy that benefits the middle class encourages homeownership through the mortgage interest tax deduction, which allows homeowners to deduct the cost of their mortgage interest payments from their taxable income. Because homeowners must meet a certain income level to receive this tax break, the policy in effect helps only taxpayers in the middle- and upper-class income brackets. A similar government program provides student and home mortgage loans to veterans and those currently serving in the military.

Finally, U.S. corporations are also beneficiaries of social subsidies. According to some analysts, an estimated $170 billion is funneled to American corporations through direct federal subsidies and tax breaks each year.[53] Many subsidies are linked to efforts to create jobs. However, there is little oversight for many of these programs, and there are many instances of subsidies going to companies that are downsizing or—in the case of many high-tech companies—moving jobs overseas. Business leaders also claim that subsidies for research and development are needed to keep American companies afloat in the global marketplace. The biggest winners are agribusiness, the oil industry, and energy plants.

In Your Own Words Identify four government policy programs that attempt to improve citizens' lives.

ECONOMIC POLICY

Promoting the nation's financial stability

Another kind of public policy is **economic policy**, which addresses the problem of economic security, not for a particular group or segment of society, but for society itself. In Chapter 1 we said that the United States has an economic system of regulated capitalism. That is, the U.S. economy is a market system in which the government intervenes to protect rights and make procedural guarantees. All the different strategies that government officials, both elected and appointed, employ today to solve economic problems, to protect economic rights, and to provide procedural guarantees to help the market run smoothly are called economic policy.

For much of our history, policymakers have felt that government should pursue a hands-off economic policy, in effect letting the market take care of itself, guided only by the laws of supply and demand. This attitude was in keeping with a basic tenet of capitalism, which holds that the economy is already regulated by millions of individual decisions made each day by consumers and producers in the market. The Great Depression of the 1930s, however, changed the way government policymakers viewed the economy. Since that economic disaster, the goal of economic policymakers has been to even out the dramatic cycles of inflation and recession without undermining the vitality and productivity of a market-driven economy.

FISCAL POLICY AND MONETARY POLICY

economic policy the strategies that government officials employ to solve economic problems

Even before the stock market crash of 1929 that precipitated the Great Depression, economic reformers had begun to question the ability of the unregulated market to guard the public interest. They argued that some government intervention in the economy might be necessary—not only to improve the public welfare and protect people from the worst effects of the business cycle but also to increase the efficiency of the market itself. Such intervention could take one of two forms: fiscal policy, which enables government to regulate the economy through its powers to tax and spend, or monetary policy, which allows government to manage the economy by controlling the money supply through the regulation of interest rates (the cost of borrowing money). Both strategies, as we will see, have political advantages and costs, and both play an important role in contemporary economic policy. (See *The Big Picture: Rising Economic Inequality in America—The New Gilded Age*.)

One of the strongest advocates of government action in the 1930s was British economist John Maynard Keynes (pronounced "canes"), who argued that government can and should step in to regulate the economy by using **fiscal policy**—the government's power to tax and spend. According to Keynes, government could stimulate a lagging economy by putting more money into it (increasing government spending and cutting taxes) or cool off an inflationary economy by taking money out (cutting spending and raising taxes).

Keynes argued, contrary to most other economists at the time, that achieving a **balanced budget** in the national economy—in which government spends no more money than it brings in through taxes and revenues—is not essential. Rather, for Keynes, **deficits** (shortfalls due to the government spending more in a year than it takes in) and **surpluses** (extra funds because government revenues are greater than its expenditures) were tools to be utilized freely to fine-tune the economy.

The Keynesian strategy of increasing government spending during recessionary periods and cutting back during expansionary periods gradually became the primary tool of economic policy in the period between 1930 and the 1970s. Franklin Roosevelt used it to lead the country out of the Depression in the 1930s, and subsequent presidents made fiscal policy the foundation of their economic programs until the late 1970s, when the economy took a turn that fiscal policy seemed unable to manage. During this period the U.S. economy was characterized by inflation and, *at the same time*, unemployment. Keynesian theory was unable to explain this odd combination of economic events, and economists and policymakers searched for new theories to help guide them through this difficult economic period.

In recent years, some conservative Republican members of Congress have rejected Keynesianism in favor of what is known as the "Austrian school" of economic theory. Austrian economist Friedrich Hayek argued the economy is too complicated for politicians to avert recessions and unemployment without unintended consequences that could be worse. The Republicans have used this argument as a basis for contending the government shouldn't try to regulate the economy.[54]

Many people looking at the high inflation and growing unemployment of the 1970s began to turn to monetary policy as a way to manage the economy. **Monetary policy** regulates the economy by controlling the money supply (the sum of all currency on hand in the country plus the amount held in bank accounts) by manipulating **interest rates**. The monetarists believed that the high inflation of the 1970s was caused by too much money in the economy, and they advocated cutting back on the supply by raising interest rates to take some money out of circulation. When money is scarce (and interest rates are high), people borrow less because it costs more; thus they spend less and drive down aggregate demand. When there is a lot of money, people can borrow it cheaply—that is, at low interest rates—and they are more likely to spend it, raising aggregate demand. By raising and lowering interest rates, government can regulate the cycles of the market economy just as it does by taxing and spending. As a tool of economic policy, however, monetary policy can be somewhat hard to control. Small changes can have big effects. Reducing the money supply might lower inflation, but too great a reduction can also cause a recession, which is what happened in the early 1980s. Changes need to be made in narrow increments rather than in broad sweeps.

fiscal policy economic policy in which government regulates the economy through its powers to tax and spend

balanced budget a budget in which expenditures equal revenues

deficits shortfalls in the budget due to the government's spending more in a year than it takes in

surplus the extra funds available because government revenues are greater than its expenditures

monetary policy economic policy in which government regulates the economy by manipulating interest rates to control the money supply

interest rates the cost of borrowing money calculated as a percentage of the money borrowed

There was a time when the American dream of working hard and achieving a better life was a realistic aspiration. That dream becomes an illusion for many as more and more of the national income becomes concentrated at the top 1% and higher. Globalization, the transition from a manufacturing to a service economy, and government policies all contribute to this growing economic inequality.

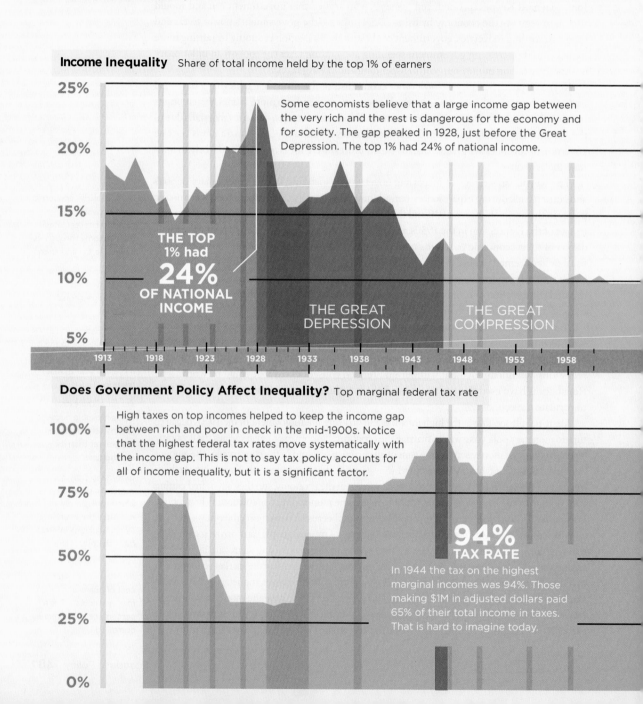

Income Inequality Share of total income held by the top 1% of earners

Some economists believe that a large income gap between the very rich and the rest is dangerous for the economy and for society. The gap peaked in 1928, just before the Great Depression. The top 1% had 24% of national income.

THE TOP 1% had **24%** OF NATIONAL INCOME

THE GREAT DEPRESSION

THE GREAT COMPRESSION

Does Government Policy Affect Inequality? Top marginal federal tax rate

High taxes on top incomes helped to keep the income gap between rich and poor in check in the mid-1900s. Notice that the highest federal tax rates move systematically with the income gap. This is not to say tax policy accounts for all of income inequality, but it is a significant factor.

94% TAX RATE

In 1944 the tax on the highest marginal incomes was 94%. Those making $1M in adjusted dollars paid 65% of their total income in taxes. That is hard to imagine today.

■ The Great Depression era	■ Recession/depression
■ Peak income inequality eras	■ Top marginal tax rates
■ The Great Compression era	■ Highest/lowest tax rates

Source: Thomas Piketty and Emmanuel Saez, "Income Inequality in the United States, 1913-1998," Quarterly Journal of Economics, 118 (1), 2003: 1-39, updated to 2012 by Saez, http://eml.berkeley.edu/~saez/lecture_saez_arrow.pdf. Series based on pre-tax cash market income, including realized capital gains and excluding government transfers. 2012 data based on preliminary statistics; The Nation, June 30, 2008, "Plutocracy Reborn," www.thenation.com/article/plutocracy-reborn.

The period from the end of WWII into the 1970s is known as the "Great Compression," with relative equality in income and in income growth. We still had rich, middle class, and poor, but they were not that far apart. The top 1% share was just 9% in 1978.

THE TOP 1% had
22%
OF NATIONAL INCOME

The period since the early 1980s has seen the rich getting richer. The top 1% had 22% of income in 2015. From 1978 to 2012 the top 20% saw income increase by 75% while the bottom 20% saw a 12% decrease (in constant $).

THE TOP 1% had
9% **OF NATIONAL INCOME**

1963   1968   1973   1978   1983   1988   1993   1998   2003   2008   2013

In 2018 the tax on the highest marginal incomes will drop to 37% from 39.6%. In addition, many of the richest get a significant portion of their income from capital gains, which are taxed at 15%.

Top rates for the estate tax (on inheritances) follow the pattern set by income tax rates. The top rate for estate taxes peaked at 77% from 1941 to 1978. The current rate is 45%.

28%
TAX RATE
Top marginal tax rates lowest since the Great Depression.

Today policymakers use a combination of fiscal and monetary policy to achieve economic goals, and the highs and lows of boom and bust have been tempered greatly. Fluctuations in inflation, unemployment, and GDP continue to occur, but they lack the punishing ferocity of the earlier unregulated period (see *Don't Be Fooled by . . . Economic Indicators*). The two kinds of policy are not equally easy for government to employ, however. Most significantly, unlike the heavily political tools of fiscal policy, the instruments of monetary policy are removed from the political arena and are wielded by actors who are not subject to electoral pressures.

We can thank the politicians of the early twentieth century for divorcing monetary policy from politics. Controlling interest rates is a regulatory policy that would generate heavy lobbying from businesses and corporations, which have a huge stake in the cost of money. After a series of financial panics, Congress established the **Federal Reserve System** in 1913, as an independent commission, to control the money supply. The Fed, as it is known, is a system of twelve federal banks run by a Board of Governors. The Fed chair is appointed by the president and serves a four-year term that overlaps but does not necessarily coincide with the president's term of office. The Fed controls the supply of money by controlling the interest rates at which banks borrow money, by limiting the amount of money the banks have to hold in reserve, and by buying government securities.

Monetary policy, while subject to its own challenges, can at least avoid the political pitfalls that those making fiscal policy must regularly watch out for. This is primarily because fiscal policymakers, as elected officials, try to respond to their constituents' demands or what they anticipate their constituents' demands will be. For instance, most of us do not want our taxes increased, even if it means that the national economy will be better off, and we may threaten to punish politicians who try to raise them.

Fiscal policy is made by Congress and the president through the budget process. Government budgets are where we find, in black and white, the clearest indications of politics—who gets what, and who pays for it. The government budget process also exemplifies the conflict we discussed in Chapter 6 between the needs for lawmaking and the electoral imperatives of representation. Members of Congress and the president, as lawmakers, have an interest in maintaining a healthy economy and should be able to agree on appropriate levels of taxes and spending to see that the economy stays in good shape. But as elected leaders they are also accountable to constituencies and committed to ideological or partisan goals. From a politician's perspective the budget is a pie to be divided and fought over.

The preparation of the president's budget begins over a year before it is submitted to Congress by the Office of Management and Budget (OMB). OMB acts as the president's representative and negotiates for months with the agencies and departments in fashioning a budget that reflects the president's priorities but does not inflame entrenched constituencies at the same time. (See the *Profiles in Citizenship* feature on former OMB director Peter Orszag.)

Congress' job is to approve the budget, but it does not accept everything that the president requests. Members' ability to use fiscal policy in a responsible way is hampered by the desire to increase spending for the folks back home at the same time that they are disinclined to raise their taxes. Caught as they are between the demands of lawmaking and representation, and their own divergent ideological goals, they are unable to use the budget as a very effective tool of fiscal policy.

Increased spending without corresponding tax increases, of course, raises the federal deficit; and interest payments on the money we borrow to pay the deficit constrain our future choices. In the 1990s the deficit problem disappeared briefly when, due in large part to general national economic prosperity and cooperation between President Bill Clinton and the

Federal Reserve System the independent commission that controls the money supply through a system of twelve federal banks

FIGURE 14.3

U.S. Federal Budget Deficit/Surplus and Debt

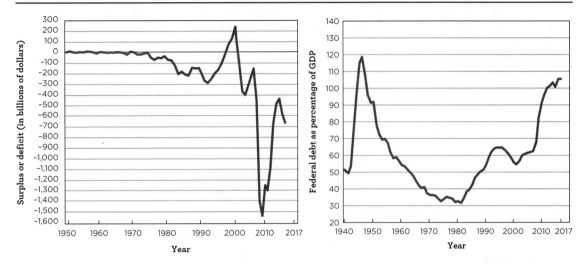

The annual budget deficit (left) is the amount by which government spending exceeds tax revenues. If tax revenue is greater than the government spending, a budget surplus results. In the 1970s and 1980s the United States ran larger budget deficits (in the billions), but the trend was reversed briefly in the 1990s. What stands out, however, is the result of the government's efforts to stimulate the economy to fight the 2008 Great Recession with recent very large deficits. The federal debt (right) represents the total amount of outstanding loans owed by the U.S. government, here presented as a percentage of our GDP. The current debt is above 100 percent of the GDP, which has not occurred since the massive national spending that financed our participation in World War II.

Source: Office of Management and Budget, Historical Tables, "Table 1.1: Summary of Receipts, Outlays, and Surpluses or Deficits: 1789-2023" and "Table 7.1: Federal Debt at the End of Year: 1940–2023," www.whitehouse.gov/omb/historical-tables/.

Fed, the federal government balanced its budget and began to run a surplus in 1998.[55] (See Figure 14.3.) Politically this changed the process dramatically. National politicians now began to debate which priorities should be the target of government spending.

The problem of how to spend the surplus, however, was short lived. The 2001 tax cut, promised by George W. Bush in his campaign and passed by a Republican-led House and Senate soon after he became president, sharply reduced the surplus. As economic growth slowed and the prosperity of the 1990s began to wind down, government revenues dropped from earlier estimates, shrinking the anticipated surplus further. By mid-2002 the deficit had returned. To help stimulate the economy, the president endorsed additional tax cuts in 2003, which contributed further to the rising deficit. Finally, the wars in Afghanistan and Iraq cost the government over $500 billion during the Bush administration (headed toward $1 trillion by 2010).[56]

The deficit was destined to grow quickly. With economic disaster on the immediate horizon, the Bush administration oversaw the passage of the Troubled Assets Relief Program (TARP) in October 2008 to bail out financial institutions deemed "too big to fail." Much of the funds had been repaid by 2010, but the program still cost about $30 billion; nevertheless, it might ultimately end up making a profit for the government.[57] The American Recovery and

Economic Indicators

Keeping up with the economy, in good times or bad, can be a challenge, especially when politicians are trying to persuade you to see things their way. As one guide to understanding the economy put it, "Economic figures can be manipulated to demonstrate almost anything."[1] Politicians are wont to spin those figures to support their arguments and to attract voters to their side. An understanding of the economic indicators used to assess the economy can help you figure out how the economy is really doing and can arm you against the persuasive words of politicians.

Here we examine just a few of literally dozens of these variables. You can find the most recent data from these leading economic indicators and others at www.esa.doc.gov. For a more complete guide to understanding a wide range of economic indicators, you might want to consult a reference book, such as *The Economist's Guide to Economic Indicators*.[2]

- **Real GDP.** The real gross domestic product (GDP) is the total economic activity in constant prices. Because of inflation, it is important to put all prices on the same scale. In other words, to see how much the economy has grown from 2000 to 2018, you would want to convert 2018 dollars into 2000 dollars. Because real GDP uses constant prices, it is a useful measure to track economic growth over time. A real GDP growth of around 3 percent per year is a good sign for the U.S. economy.[3] A rise in real GDP shows that production and consumption are increasing.
- **Unemployment rate.** The unemployment rate is the percentage of the labor force that is not currently employed but is actively seeking work. An unemployment rate of 5 percent or less is generally considered to be a sign of a strong economy and a growing GDP. However, the unemployment rate can be misleading because it

includes only people who are available for and actively seeking work—so the real percentage of those unemployed is usually higher than the unemployment rate because some people are not actively seeking jobs.

- **Job growth.** Narratives that focus entirely on the number of people looking for work don't provide a clear picture of the job market. Job growth is the gross number of jobs added to the economy, and it is tracked each month by the Bureau of Labor Statistics. But more jobs doesn't always mean less unemployment. Robust job growth will often prompt people who had given up on job searches (and thus were not included in the unemployment rate) to start looking again. This can increase the unemployment rate even though the total number of people working has increased.
- **Personal income and personal disposable income.** Personal income is an individual's income received from many sources but primarily from wages and salaries. It also includes interest, dividends, and Social Security. Personal disposable income is a person's income after taxes and fees are deducted. A growth rate of 3 percent per year is considered to be a healthy increase in personal income, although growth should be steady. Too rapid an increase in personal income can lead to inflation.[4] These two measures predict the ability of citizens to consume and save.
- **Consumer spending.** The amount of goods that people are buying is another way to measure the health of the economy because it is the key factor in the increase or decrease of the GDP. One way to measure consumer spending is by the Department of Labor's Consumer Expenditure Survey, which asks American consumers questions about their buying habits on items such as food, apparel, housing, and entertainment. Consumer spending accounts for approximately 70 percent of the GDP and has a big impact on job growth.[5]
- **Stock market price indexes.** A stock market price index measures the overall change in stock prices

of corporations traded on U.S. stock markets. There are many different stock market price indexes, including the New York Stock Exchange (NYSE) Composite Index, the NASDAQ Composite Index, and the Dow Jones Industrial Average Index. The Dow Jones Industrial Average Index, for instance, provides the average price per share of thirty large companies' stocks on the NYSE. The NYSE Composite Index covers the prices of about 1,900 companies listed on the NYSE. A strongly performing stock market affects consumer and investment spending. If the stock market is performing well, people are more optimistic about the economy and are more likely to buy or invest.

- **Home and motor vehicle sales.** The purchases of these major items are good indicators of consumer demand, as well as of construction and manufacturing activity. The number of homes and motor vehicles sold can change depending on the time of year (for example, car sales are likely to increase when companies decrease prices to sell older models to make way for the new models), which makes it a smart idea to take two or three months together and compare that with similar periods of previous years.

WHAT TO WATCH OUT FOR

To avoid being duped, ask yourself the following questions when you hear these indicators bandied about by a politician with an agenda:

- **Whose numbers are they?** Always consider the source of economic indicators. Government sources like the Office of Management and Budget (OMB), the Bureau of Labor Statistics (BLS), and the Federal Reserve (whose economic data site, FRED, is beloved by economists) are generally considered reliable sources of objective economic information. Numbers that come from private institutions and think tanks may also be useful, but take the time to investigate sources that may have an ideological or political agenda.

- **Who is interpreting the data?** Numbers may be neutral, but those who report them invariably have ideas, opinions, or agendas that will lead them to look at data in different ways. When you read economic news, take care to differentiate between the objective numbers and the subjective analysis that almost always accompanies them.

- **What were the expectations?** Whether the numbers met the expectations of economic forecasters is as important as the numbers themselves. An increase of 50,000 new jobs might seem like positive growth, but not if forecasters projected an increase of 250,000. Again, it's important to remain a vigilant critical thinker. Ask yourself who the forecasters are, and what agenda they might have.

- **Are the numbers affected by seasonality?** Consumer spending and sales rise and fall at certain times of the year. For example, few people are building houses in the winter, which means that a decline in the number of home sales from August to December does not necessarily mean a drop-off in the economy. Be wary of financial news that makes such comparisons. For seasonal variables, it is best to compare numbers to previous years.

1. *The Economist's Guide to Economic Indicators: Making Sense of Economics*, 5th ed. (Princeton, N.J.: Bloomberg Press, 2003), 1.
2. Ibid.
3. Ibid., 47.
4. Ibid., 85.
5. Norman Frumkin, *Guide to Economic Indicators*, 3rd ed. (Armonk, N.Y.: M. E. Sharpe, 2000).

Reinvestment Act of 2009 (commonly known as the stimulus bill) added nearly $900 billion in spending on tax relief for individuals and businesses, extensions of unemployment insurance, infrastructure development, and various other projects designed in the Keynesian economic tradition to kick the economy into gear. Supporters of these efforts to soften the blow of economic recession and jump-start the economy claimed that TARP and the stimulus package headed off a much worse decline in the economy. Detractors from the right argued that they simply bailed out big corporations while leaving the taxpayers to pay a mounting load of debt, whereas critics on the left asserted that the stimulus needed to be even bigger than it was.[58] The nonpartisan Congressional Budget Office estimated that the program had added as many as 3.3 million jobs by the summer of 2011.[59]

With the 2010 deficit projected to be $1.3 trillion (just below the record $1.42 trillion of 2009), the issues of spending and taxing were back at the heart of partisan battles as the 2010 midterm elections approached.[60] Republicans declared the stimulus bill a failure because it hadn't created enough jobs to pump up the economy, saying further that a recession was no time for government to spend money. They deplored the recklessness of running up the deficit by spending, while insisting that the Bush tax cuts, scheduled to lapse in 2010, be made permanent.[61] The Democrats, by contrast, argued that a recession was the very time that government should spend money and demanded an end to the Bush tax cuts for the top 2 percent of the population.[62]

The elections were a disaster for Democrats. Republicans, many of them allied with the low-tax, limited-government Tea Party movement, regained control of the House of Representatives while picking up seats in the Senate. They vowed to balance the budget by reining in spending without raising taxes. House Budget Committee chair Paul Ryan, R-Wis., proposed a controversial long-term budget that called for overhauling Medicare for all those Americans currently under age fifty-five, turning Medicaid into a series of block grants to states, and switching the Social Security system to guaranteed private accounts. Even though the bill had no chance of passing in the Democratic-led Senate, the House adopted the Ryan plan in 2011 with only four Republican "no" votes and over unanimous Democratic opposition.[63]

That action set the stage for one of the most politically volatile debates of recent years. During the summer of 2011, President Obama and congressional Democrats engaged in a fierce battle with Republicans over raising the federal debt limit, a measure necessary to allow the government to pay off debts it had already incurred. Between 1960 and August 2011, Congress had voted to raise the debt ceiling seventy-eight times as a way to make government borrowing easier. But Republicans in the House openly called for the government to default on its debts as a way of forcing lawmakers to become serious about addressing longer-term budget problems. They thwarted an attempt by President Obama to forge a "grand bargain" with House Speaker John Boehner, R-Ohio, when it became clear that such a deal might include tax increases, something most House Republicans opposed unconditionally. Eventually an agreement was struck to raise the debt limit, but the chaotic process took a heavy toll on the federal government's credibility. The bond rating house Standard & Poor's downgraded the U.S. credit rating for the first time in history, and a *New York Times* poll showed the highest disapproval ratings for Congress since the newspaper began recording them. Veteran political scientists Norman Ornstein and Thomas Mann said the incident exemplified Congress' deep dysfunction and led them to call their 2012 book about Capitol Hill *It's Even Worse Than It Looks*.[64]

With the unemployment rate stuck at around 8 percent in 2012, Republicans were eager to make Obama's handling of the economy the central issue in his reelection bid. Obama's Republican opponent, former Massachusetts governor Mitt Romney, continually attacked the president for not doing more to help Americans find jobs and keep more of their incomes. To underscore the issue's importance, he picked Ryan as his vice presidential running mate. But Obama portrayed the wealthy Romney as someone with an inability to understand average Americans. He cast the race as an opportunity to expand on the achievements of his first term—which included reinvigorating the domestic automobile industry—while giving people of all incomes as much chance as the wealthy to succeed. Obama won reelection with ease, getting 51 percent of the vote to Romney's 47 percent.[65]

In his second term, Obama tried to make good on his promise to help lower-income Americans by proposing an increase in the federal minimum wage to $10.10 an hour. He then issued an executive order raising the wage for federal workers on new contracts to $10.10 beginning in 2015. "It's time to give America a raise," Obama said at a rally the following month. "It's not bad business to do right by your workers; it's good business."[66]

The move had strong public approval, with various polls showing the idea had backing from more than two-thirds of those surveyed. But the idea met with skepticism from some economists who believed that setting a higher minimum wage reduces employment and from conservatives who remained resolutely against it. The Senate's Democrats sought to increase the wage in April 2014, but only one Republican joined them and they fell six votes shy of the sixty votes required to overcome GOP objections.[67] Democrats called for a $15 an hour minimum wage at their 2016 national convention.

Meanwhile, partisan battling over the budget during Obama's final months in office only grew more intense. The president submitted a budget proposal in February 2016 calling for a $10 a barrel tax on oil, which could fund new roads, bridges, and other transportation projects. He also called for significant spending increases for cancer research and to fight prescription-drug abuse. But Republicans, breaking with a forty-one-year tradition, announced that they not only wouldn't consider the budget proposal; they would not hold any hearings on it. Ryan, who had become Speaker of the House, said that the House and Senate Budget Committees' chairs made that decision, but that he supported them.[68]

The American public has grown less concerned about the budget deficit in recent years. A poll in January 2016 found that 56 percent said reducing the deficit should be a top priority for the president and Congress, down from 64 percent in 2015 and 72 percent in 2013, when it was named one of the country's biggest priorities, along with jobs and the economy. In 2016 the deficit ranked ninth out of eighteen policy areas.[69] Without popular pressure to curtail spending and balance the budget, politicians are unlikely to make the hard choices such action would entail.

TAX POLICY

Technically, taxation is part of the federal budgetary process. The U.S. government takes in a lot of money in taxes every year, estimated to be more than $3.4 trillion in 2018.[70] The largest single source of revenue for the federal government is individual federal income taxes. The next largest is contributions to social insurance, of which Social Security is the largest component by far, with funds coming equally from our paychecks and employers.

Personal income taxes in the United States are **progressive taxes**, which means that people with higher incomes not only pay more taxes but they also pay at a higher rate. Taxes are paid on all the income an individual or household receives, including wage and salary income, interest and dividends, rents on property owned, royalties, even game show winnings. Everyone is subject to the same rate of taxation for some base amount, and incomes over that amount are subject to progressively higher percentages of tax. The range of taxable income at each tax bracket determines your marginal tax rate. For example, if you are in a 35 percent tax bracket, it does not mean that you pay 35 percent of all your income in taxes, but that you pay 35 percent on everything you make above a certain threshold—and a lower percentage on the income made under that base amount.

Other taxes are called **regressive taxes**, even if they are fixed percentages, because they take a higher proportion of income from a poor person's income than from those who are well-off. Sales taxes are often argued to be regressive, particularly when they are levied on necessities like food and electricity. Furthermore, poor people spend a higher portion of their incomes on

progressive taxes
taxes whose rates increase with income

regressive taxes taxes that require poor people to pay a higher proportion of their income than do the well-off

consumables that are subject to the sales tax; the wealthy, in contrast, spend a significant portion of their income on investments, stocks, or elite education for their children, which are not subject to sales taxes. Other regressive taxes include excise taxes and Social Security taxes.

The two parties have very different ideas about what kinds of tax should be levied on whom. In general, Democrats focus on easing the tax burden on lower-income groups in the name of fairness and equity. As a matter of fiscal policy, they tend to want to put money into the hands of workers and the working poor on the assumption that this will translate quickly into consumer spending, which increases demand and stimulates the whole economy. This is the "trickle-up" strategy. Give benefits to those with less, and let the effects percolate upward throughout the economic system.

In contrast, Republicans focus more on lowering the high rates of taxation on those with larger incomes. Their sentiments are motivated by a different view of fairness, that those who make more money should have the freedom to keep it. Republicans argue that the wealthy are more likely to save or invest their extra income (from a tax break), thus providing businesses with the capital they need to expand—an argument that some observers call supply-side economics. Not only do they believe that the rate of taxation on the top tax brackets should be reduced, but they also argue for a reduction in the **capital gains tax**, the tax levied on the returns that people earn from capital investments, like the profits from the sale of stocks or a home. The notion here is that if wealthy people are taxed at lower rates, they will invest and spend more, the economy will prosper, and the benefits will "trickle down" to the rest of the members of society. The debate between trickle-up and trickle-down theories of taxation represents one of the major partisan battles in Congress, and not only reveals deep ideological divisions between the parties but also demonstrates the very real differences in the constituencies to which they respond.

As all tax-paying Americans know, the system of tax regulations—known as the tax code—is extremely complex. The complexity stems in part from the fact that you don't pay tax on your entire salary. Many expenses are deductible—that is, you can subtract them from your salary before you calculate the tax you owe. To pay no more taxes than you should, you need to be aware of all the deductions you can take—for instance, for mortgage interest, interest on college loans, business expenses, and charitable contributions. Furthermore, the government often gives tax benefits to promote certain behaviors. Businesses might receive tax credits if they buy environmentally friendly equipment, or farmers might be able to write off the expenses of a new tractor. Knowing which deductions you are entitled to can save you hundreds or thousands of dollars at tax time.

What would a just tax code look like?

capital gains tax a tax levied on the returns that people earn from capital investments, like the profits from the sale of stocks or a home

flat tax a tax system in which all people pay the same percentage of their income

The tax code is so frustrating to so many taxpayers that politicians periodically propose reforms to make filing taxes easier and, they argue, fairer. After his reelection in 2004, for instance, President George W. Bush made reforming the tax code a central piece of his second term. Perhaps the most common change proposed by tax reform groups is the institution of a flat tax. Under a **flat tax**, all people would pay the same percentage of their incomes in taxes, regardless of how much money they made or what their expenses were. According to advocates, the plan would vastly simplify the tax code and almost everyone would be able to file their taxes on their own.

However, much more is at stake here than just making it easier to file taxes; there are ideological reasons for a flat tax as well. Recall that we said earlier that progressive taxes are redistributive policies. As a result, wealthier people pay a greater percentage of their salary in taxes. Not only do conservatives argue against this redistribution on grounds of fairness, but advocates of lower, flatter taxes usually align with the conservative notion of limited government.

Karen Bleier/AFP/Getty Images

PROFILES IN CITIZENSHIP:
Peter Orszag

Economist Peter Orszag knows that getting the right *policy* answer while balancing the pressure from politicians to get the right *political* answer was a challenge. The former director of the Congressional Budget Office (CBO) and the Office of Management and Budget (OMB). On the difference between the two, he says, "CBO is correctly seen by the press as being a pretty impartial neutral arbiter and playing it straight, so that was not hard. The OMB job is a more challenging combination because it's got part where you are supposed to be analytical and rigorous and bringing evidence to bear, but you are also part of the president's economics team, and you're a West Wing staffer."

At OMB, Orszag was instrumental in shaping the health care reform bill that Obama signed in 2010. Since his stint in Washington, he's back in the private sector. He told us: "...I have always found that people who have a breadth of experience are the most interesting and can bring a lot to whatever task that they are currently doing."

On public versus private service

"The thing I would say about government versus business and applying what you have learned...the breadth and depth is unmatched compared to most other settings. In terms of getting exposure to lots of different areas, it's difficult to beat. On top of that is, of course,

whatever benefit one derives psychologically from a sense of public service. What I say is as long as you feel like you are contributing to forward progress, the return in terms of your sense of self is extraordinarily high."

On keeping the republic

"I think the single most important thing at this point is to resist the strong trend towards polarization that is hollowing out the middle of the political spectrum and making evidence-based debate difficult. So that means toning down the volume on either left or right medium streams on cable news and on the blogosphere.

And there is a broader point to that, too, which is that most of us have grown up, and I think it's still the case for college freshmen ... We've been trained that if we read something in the newspaper or see it on the Internet it must be true. The probability that it is correct is not anywhere as near as high as it was at some point. We need to move to an attitude where when we see something or hear something or read something we don't automatically assume and give it the benefit of the doubt, unless it's coming from a certain trusted source.... [T]his is a huge problem, I think, because it is difficult to have the kind of democracy that we want and need when the debate often occurs at this level, where it's just kind of bombs being thrown back and forth."

Source: Peter Orszag spoke with Christine Barbour and Gerald C. Wright on December 3, 2010.

In their eyes, government is providing too many unnecessary services—cutting taxes would force the government to shrink for lack of resources.

Another option proposed occasionally is a national sales tax—otherwise known as a **consumption tax**. Currently all but five states have their own sales tax, but a national tax would apply in addition to these sales taxes. Under such a plan, the national income tax would be abolished and people would be taxed not on what they earn but on what they spend. Again, proponents argue that a consumption tax would simplify the tax code. European countries have a version of a consumption tax called a **value-added tax (VAT)**. Unlike the consumption

consumption tax a tax on what people spend rather than on what they earn

value-added tax (VAT) a consumption tax levied at each stage of production, based on the value added to the product at that stage

tax proposed in the United States, where the tax is implemented at the point of sale, the VAT is levied at each stage of production based on the value added to the product at that stage.

The adoption of either a flat income tax or a consumption tax would dramatically simplify tax-paying for Americans, but there is significant resistance to implementing these reforms. Some opponents argue that the taxes are unfair to the less well-off because they are regressive. Other opponents of reforming the current tax code fear that such reforms will seriously reduce donations to charitable organizations. Although many Americans would like to see the tax code made less complex, few can agree on how to make this happen because, for all their complaints, no one really wants to give up the advantages they have under the current system.

When the Republicans won the White House, the Senate, and the House in 2016, they thought their moment for tax reform had come, but as is usually the case, they were able to make only minor changes around the system's edges. After failing to overturn Obama's Affordable Care Act, they adopted tax reform as their top priority. Large-scale reform proved too much for even Republicans to agree on. Although they billed their tax-reform legislation as a strategy to help the middle class, the chief beneficiaries turned out to be corporations. Republicans claimed that corporations would turn their excess revenue back to workers in the form of raises. This proved not to be the case, as predicted by Democrats, who argued that the bill was skewed too far toward corporations and wealthy Americans.[71]

ECONOMIC REGULATORY POLICY

Whereas fiscal policies tend to be redistributive in nature, most economic policy, including monetary policy, is regulatory. A regulatory policy is designed to restrict or change the behavior of certain groups or individuals. Government can regulate business in the interests of consumer safety, for instance, or impose environmental standards and limit the impact industry might have on the environment. When it comes to the American system of regulated capitalism, economic regulatory policy aims to protect economic rights and make procedural guarantees. So far we have been discussing government's role in regulating the markets to even out the highs and lows and encourage the growth of prosperity. Government can also intervene for other purposes as well.

Economic regulation can be an extremely controversial issue in a capitalist economy. Those who favor it argue that the market, left to its own devices, can be unfair and unpredictable, wreaking havoc in individual lives and having the potential for systemwide disaster. They point to problems such as the subprime mortgage crisis in 2008, in which thousands of loans were made to high-risk homebuyers without adequate background checks. When the economy soured, foreclosures soared as buyers could not make their home payments. The crisis extended to legions of other homeowners facing declining property values and to failing mortgage companies and the collapse of some of the largest financial corporations on Wall Street.[72] (This situation was dramatized in journalist Michael Lewis's book *The Big Short*, which was made into a movie in 2015 with an all-star cast that included Steve Carell, Brad Pitt, Ryan Gosling, and Christian Bale.) Opponents of regulation argue that when industries face more regulation, it increases their costs of production, which in turn makes prices rise and limits consumer choice.

Both sides often cite the classic example of the airline industry to make their point. In 1938 the government began to make laws determining how the airline industry would run, on the grounds that it was a new industry in need of regulation and a public utility. The Civil

Aeronautics Board was established to set prices, determine routes, and set up schedules while ensuring the airlines earned a fair rate of return. By the 1970s the system was bogged down in bureaucratic rules. Flying was not easily accessible to many Americans. Airfares were expensive because competition was limited, parts of the country had no easy access to air service, and consumers were unhappy. Under President Jimmy Carter, the process of **deregulation**—the removal of excessive regulations in order to improve economic efficiency—was begun, to be completed by Congress in 1978. Under deregulation, airfares dropped, new routes opened, low-cost airlines started up, and scheduling became more flexible.

Proponents of deregulation insist that the increased efficiency is reason enough to reduce regulation. At the same time, opponents point to the costs of deregulation—bankruptcies that left many airline workers unemployed and without pensions, and continuing labor problems as the remaining airlines struggled to stay in business.[73] In general, because it helps some groups and hurts others, the issue of regulation remains controversial in American politics. Both political parties tend to support making business more efficient by removing excessive regulations, but Republicans, with their closer ties to business, tend to push for more deregulation, whereas Democrats, with a traditional alliance with labor, push for less.

Following the collapse of the subprime mortgage market in 2008, however—a crisis brought on in part by a lack of regulation in the first place—Congress passed, and President Obama signed, a financial reform bill in 2010. Called the Dodd-Frank Wall Street Reform and Consumer Protection Act, it established a consumer protection agency, set in place some banking reform, and increased federal oversight and control over derivatives trading, the financial instrument that allowed mortgage speculation and that brought down financial giants such as AIG.[74] That it was passed at all under the partisan conditions of 2010 politics in America is notable itself, but Dodd-Frank is not a dramatic change in the way banks do business. As the *Wall Street Journal* wrote after the bill passed, "From the beginning, lawmakers opted against a dramatic reshaping of the country's financial architecture. Instead, they moved to create new layers of regulation to prevent companies from taking on too much risk."[75]

In any case, Dodd Frank did not survive long—with Trump's election in 2016, a deregulatory process began that seemed aimed at undoing everything the Obama administration had accomplished, from financial, to environmental, to labor regulation.

In Your Own Words Explain the difference between fiscal and monetary policy.

FOREIGN POLICY

Dealing with issues that cross national borders

Foreign policy is official U.S. policy designed to solve problems that take place between us and actors outside our borders. It is crucial to our domestic tranquility; without a strong and effective foreign policy, our security as a rich and peaceful country could be blown away in a heartbeat. Our foreign policy is almost always carried out for the good of American citizens or in the interest of national security. Even foreign aid, which to some critics seems like giving away American taxpayers' hard-earned money to people who have done nothing to deserve it, is part of a foreign policy to stabilize the world, to help strengthen international partnerships and alliances, and to keep Americans safe. Similarly, humanitarian intervention, like the NATO (North Atlantic

deregulation the elimination of regulations in order to improve economic efficiency

foreign policy a country's official positions, practices, and procedures for dealing with actors outside its borders

Treaty Organization) military action in Kosovo in 1999, is ultimately conducted to support our values and the quality of life we think other nations ought to provide for their citizens.

Many politicians have tried to encourage Americans to turn their backs on the rest of the world, promoting a foreign policy called isolationism, which holds that Americans should put themselves and their problems first and not interfere in global concerns. The United States has tried to pursue an isolationist policy before, perhaps most notably after World War I, but this experiment was seen largely as a failure. Most recently, the events of September 11, 2001, have put to rest the fiction that what happens "over there" is unrelated to what is happening "over here." In opposition to isolationism, interventionism holds that to keep the republic safe, we must be actively engaged in shaping the global environment and be willing to intervene in order to shape events. The United States has had a long history of interventionism—in the Americas and Asia in the 1800s; in World Wars I and II; and, since September 11, in the Middle East.

Foreign policy exists to support American interests, but determining what American interests are can be very difficult. In crisis situations, as we will see, foreign policy decisions are often made in secret. When situations are not critical, however, foreign policy decisions are made in the usual hubbub of American politics. Here, as we know, many actors with competing interests struggle to make their voices heard and to get policy to benefit themselves. Foreign policy, just like domestic policy, is about who gets what, and how they get it. The difference is that in foreign policy the stakes can be a matter of life and death, and we have far less control over the other actors involved.

UNDERSTANDING FOREIGN POLICY

The outward focus of foreign policy separates it from domestic policy, although sometimes the distinction between "foreign" and "domestic" is not so clear. Consider, for example, how environmental policy in the United States can have foreign repercussions. American industries located on the border with Canada have been the source of some tensions between the two countries because pollution from U.S. factories is carried into Canada by prevailing winds. This pollution can damage forests and increase the acidity of lakes, killing fish and harming other wildlife. Environmental regulations are largely a domestic matter, but because pollution is not confined to the geography of the United States, the issue takes on unintended international importance. Still, foreign policy is generally understood to be intentionally directed at external actors and the forces that shape these actions.

External actors can include many different entities. They could be other countries—sovereign bodies with governments and territories, like Mexico or the Republic of Ireland. Intergovernmental organizations—bodies that have countries as members, such as the United Nations, which has 193 member countries; NATO, which has 29 members from North America and Europe; the Organization of Petroleum Exporting Countries (OPEC), which has 15 member countries from Africa, Asia, the Middle East, and Latin America; and the European Union (EU), which has 28 members from across Europe and more waiting to join—are also the focus of foreign policy interactions, as are nongovernmental organizations, or NGOs. NGOs are organizations that focus on specific issues and whose members are private individuals or groups from around the world. Greenpeace (environmental), Amnesty International (human rights), International Committee of the Red Cross (humanitarian relief), and Doctors Without Borders (medical care) are all NGOs.

U.S. foreign policy also can be directed toward other nongovernmental groups, such as multinational corporations—large companies that do business in multiple countries and that

isolationism a foreign policy view that nations should stay out of international political alliances and activities, and focus on domestic matters

interventionism a foreign policy view that the United States should actively engage in the affairs of other nations in order to try to shape events in accordance with U.S. interests

intergovernmental organizations bodies, such as the United Nations, whose members are countries

nongovernmental organizations organizations comprising individuals or interest groups from around the world focused on a special issue

multinational corporations large companies that do business in multiple countries

often wield tremendous economic power, like Nike or General Motors. Miscellaneous other actors—groups that do not fit the other categories, including those that have a "government" but no territory, like the Middle East's Palestinians or Ireland's Irish Republican Army, and groups that have no national ties, such as terrorist groups like al Qaeda and ISIS (although ISIS tries to claim territory like a state)—often have much at stake in U.S. foreign policy, too.

American foreign policy toward these actors falls into three broad categories.[76] **Crisis policy** deals with emergency threats to our national interests or values. Such situations often come as a surprise, and the use of force is one way to respond.[77] **Strategic policy** lays out the basic U.S. stance toward another country or a particular problem. **Structural defense policy** focuses largely on the policies and programs that deal with defense spending and military bases. These policies usually focus on, for example, buying new aircraft for the air force and navy or deciding which military bases to consolidate or close down.

THE POST–COLD WAR SETTING OF AMERICAN FOREIGN POLICY

To get to the present, let us think about the past. At the end of World War II, when the common purpose of fighting Adolf Hitler and ending German fascism no longer held the United States and the Soviet Union in an awkward alliance, fissures developed between the two largest and strongest superpowers in global politics. Nearly all of Europe was divided between allies of the Soviets and allies of the United States, a division seen most graphically in the splitting of postwar Germany into a communist East and a capitalist West.

For nearly fifty years following World War II, tensions between the two superpowers shaped U.S. foreign policy and gave it a predictable order. The **Cold War**, waged between the United States and the Soviet Union from 1945 to 1989, was a bitter global competition between democracy and authoritarianism, capitalism and communism. It never erupted into a "hot" war of military action, due in large part to the deterrent effect provided by a policy of "mutual assured destruction." Each side spent tremendous sums of money on nuclear weapons to make sure it had the ability to wipe out the other side. During this era, American foreign policy makers pursued a policy of **containment**, in which the United States tried to prevent the Soviet Union from expanding its influence, especially in Europe.

But as dangerous as the world was during the Cold War, it seemed easy to understand, casting complicated issues into simple choices of black and white. Countries were either with us or against us: they were free societies or closed ones, had capitalist or communist economies, were good or bad. Although the world was hardly that simple, it seemed that way to many people, and much of the complexity of world politics was glossed over—or perhaps bottled up—only to explode after the end of the Cold War in 1989.[78]

In 1991 the Soviet Union finally fell apart, to be replaced by more than a dozen independent states. Although most Westerners hailed the fall of the Soviet Union as an end to the tension that kept the Cold War alive, Russia inherited the Soviet nuclear arsenal, and a majority of its citizens hold a negative view of the leaders of the United States. Russians' views of American citizens have also become more critical recently.[79] (Americans' views of Russia have also been declining, to points as low as ever since the end of the Cold War.[80])

Russia's attitude toward the United States is not irrational. When the Cold War ended, many of the countries that had been under Soviet control and part of the Soviet defense alliance called the Warsaw Pact started looking to the United States and NATO for security. Over the years that followed, many of these countries joined NATO and the European Union.

crisis policy foreign policy, usually made quickly and secretly, that responds to an emergency threat

strategic policy foreign policy that lays out a country's basic stance toward international actors or problems

structural defense policy foreign policy dealing with defense spending, military bases, and weapons procurement

Cold War the half-century of competition and conflict after World War II between the United States and the Soviet Union (and their allies)

containment the U.S. Cold War policy of preventing the spread of communism

Official White House Photo by Pete Souza

Killing bin Laden

President Obama and his national security team, including Secretary of State Clinton, watch the Navy Seal raid on Osama bin Laden's compound from the White House Situation Room on May 1, 2011.

When the United States sought to put part of a new ballistic missile defense system in the Czech Republic, Russian leaders became particularly irritated. The prospect of Ukraine moving closer to NATO upset Russian president Vladimir Putin greatly. With conflict breaking out in Ukraine, followed by U.S. sanctions on Russia, talk of a renewed Cold War between the old superpowers has increased. The Russian assault on the U.S. electoral system in 2016, their effort to boost the chances of Donald Trump's victory, as well as to destabilize faith in western democracy generally, have underscored this point for many in both parties—although President Trump has, inexplicably, tried to remain close to President Putin.

This post–Cold War era has eluded easy description in terms of global organization and threats to the United States, especially in the days since September 11.[81] Who is likely to be our most dangerous adversary? What threats must we prepare for? How much should we spend on military preparedness? Are we the world's police officer, a global banker, or a humanitarian protector? We have experimented with all of these roles in the past several years.[82] In September 2002 President George W. Bush asserted that the United States' role is to maintain its military supremacy and take preemptive action against hostile and threatening states. The president also said that the United States would make no distinction between terrorist groups that threaten or attack the United States and countries that harbor those groups. In identifying an "axis of evil" of Iran, Iraq, and North Korea, President Bush set out a vision of American foreign policy that was rooted in taking active steps to promote democracy and to use force, alone if necessary, to eliminate perceived threats before they could more fully develop. This **Bush Doctrine** joined a long list of presidential foreign policy doctrines that have tried to define and protect U.S. interests in the world.

President Obama's approach was markedly different from his predecessor's. Obama emphasized diplomatic over military solutions, keeping communications channels with our

Bush Doctrine the policy that supported preemptive attacks as a legitimate tactic in the U.S. war on state-sponsored terrorism

enemies open and trying to find common interests on which to build. Although Obama pulled troops out of Iraq, a war he opposed from the start, he ramped up the war effort in Afghanistan in the hopes of creating a stable system there that wouldn't provide cover to those who wish our country harm, and he stepped up the use of drone strikes and Special Forces to try to target ISIS when it was clear that the terrorist group meant harm to the United States.

What shape a Trump Doctrine might take is as yet unknown: Donald Trump's campaign positions had elements of several different kinds of foreign policy, some very aggressive (toward ISIS and even China), others more conciliatory (such as toward Russia).

WHO MAKES FOREIGN POLICY?

Consider the following headlines: "U.S. Opens Relations With China" and "U.S. Attacks al Qaeda Base in Afghanistan." They make it sound as if a single actor—the United States—makes foreign policy. Even as a figure of speech, this is misleading in two important ways. First, the image of the United States as a single actor suggests that the country acts with a single, united mind, diverting our attention from the political reality of conflict, bargaining, and cooperation that takes place *within* the government over foreign policy.[83] Second, it implies that all foreign policies are essentially the same—having the same goals and made by the same actors and processes. Our earlier description of the three different policy types indicates that this is not so; and in fact, as we will see, each type of policy is made by different actors in different political contexts.

The political dynamics behind crisis policy, for instance, are dominated by the president and the small group of advisers around the Oval Office. Congress tends not to be much engaged in crisis policy but often watches with the rest of the public (and the world) as presidents and their advisers decide how to respond to international crises. The choice of going to war in Iraq in 2003, for example, was made by President Bush and a number of key government policymakers around him.

Strategic policy tends to be formulated in the executive branch, but usually deep in the bureaucracy rather than at the top levels. This gives interest groups and concerned members of Congress opportunities to lobby for certain policies. The public usually learns about these policies (and responds to and evaluates them) once the president announces them. The U.S. policy of containment of communism in the 1940s, for example, was developed mostly in the State Department and was then approved by President Harry Truman.[84]

Finally, structural defense policy, which often starts in the executive branch, is crafted largely in Congress, whose members tend to have their fingers on the pulses of their constituents, with much input from the bureaucracy and interest groups. When a plan to build and deploy a new fighter jet is developed, for example, it is made with coordination between Congress and the Defense Department—usually with members of Congress keeping a close eye on how their states and districts will fare from the projects.

Clearly a variety of actors are involved in making different types of foreign policy. What they all have in common is that they are officially acting on behalf of the federal government. It is not official foreign policy when New York City and San Francisco impose economic sanctions on Burma, or when private citizens like former president Jimmy Carter or the Reverend Jesse Jackson attempt to help resolve conflicts in Africa or Serbia.[85]

THE PRESIDENT AND THE EXECUTIVE BRANCH As we saw in Chapter 7, the president is the chief foreign policy maker. The president is more likely to set the foreign policy agenda than other actors in American politics because of his or her constitutional powers,

FIGURE 14.4
Key Foreign Policy Agencies

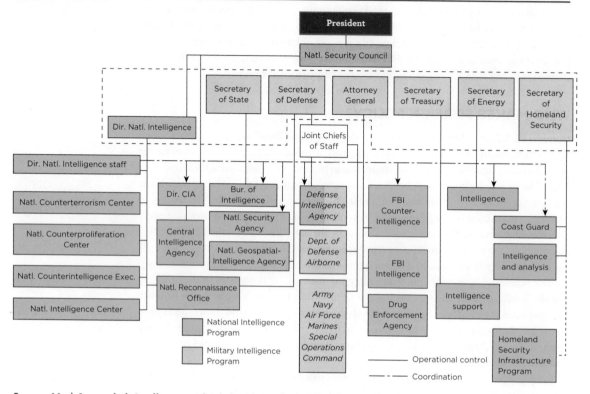

Source: Mark Lowenthal, *Intelligence*, 6th ed. (Washington, D.C.: CQ Press, 2015).

the informal powers that come with this high-profile job, and the chief executive's opportunities to communicate directly with the public.

The president sits at the top of a large pyramid of executive agencies and departments that assist in making foreign policy (see Figure 14.4). If the president does not take time to manage the agencies, other individuals may seize the opportunity to interpret foreign policy in terms of their own interests and goals. In a sense, the president provides a check on the power of the executive agencies, and without the president's leadership, foreign policy can drift. President Ronald Reagan didn't pay a lot of attention to foreign affairs, and so staff members in the National Security Council began to make foreign policy themselves. The result was the Iran-contra affair in the mid-1980s.

The **National Security Council (NSC)** is part of the president's inner circle, the Executive Office of the President. It was created in 1947 by the National Security Act to advise the president on matters of foreign policy and is coordinated by the national security adviser. By law the NSC includes the president, vice president, secretary of state, and secretary of defense. Additionally, the director of national intelligence (who is also the head of the Central Intelligence Agency) and the chair of the Joint Chiefs of Staff (the head of the

National Security Council (NSC) the organization within the Executive Office of the President that provides foreign policy advice to the president

commanders of the military services) sit as advisers to the NSC. Beyond this, the president has wide discretion to decide what the NSC will look like and how he will use it by appointing other members and deciding how the council will function.

In addition to the NSC, several executive departments and agencies play a critical role in foreign policy making. The Department of State is charged with managing foreign affairs. It is often considered to be "first among equals" in its position relative to the other departments because it was the first department established by the Constitution in 1789. The State Department is headed by the secretary of state, who is part of the president's cabinet and fulfills a variety of foreign policy roles, including maintaining diplomatic and consular posts around the world, sending delegates and missions (groups of government officials) to a variety of international organization meetings, and negotiating treaties and executive agreements with other countries. Among the employees of the State Department are the foreign service officers, the most senior of which are the U.S. ambassadors.

The second major department involved in foreign policy is the Department of Defense, headquartered in the Pentagon. The main job of this department is to manage American soldiers and their equipment in order to protect the United States. The Defense Department is headed by the secretary of defense, whose job in part is to advise the president on defense matters and who, it is important to note, is a civilian.

The Joint Chiefs of Staff is part of the Defense Department. This group consists of the senior military officers of the armed forces: the army and navy chiefs of staff, the chief of naval operations, the commandant of the Marine Corps, and the chief of the National Guard Bureau. The chair is selected by the president. The Joint Chiefs of Staff advises the secretary of defense, although the chair also may offer advice directly to the president and is responsible for managing the armed forces of the United States.

Another executive actor in foreign policy making is the intelligence community, which comprises several government agencies and bureaus. This community's job is to collect, organize, and analyze information. Information can be gathered in a number of ways, from the mundane (such as reading foreign newspapers) to the more clandestine (for instance, spying both by human beings and through surveillance satellites). Until 2004 the community was coordinated by the director of central intelligence, who was also the head of the Central Intelligence Agency (CIA). In the wake of many studies and hearings about the events leading up to September 11, as well as current security concerns, President George W. Bush signed legislation that altered how the intelligence community is managed. The job of the director of central intelligence was limited to directing the CIA. The job of coordinating the entire network of agencies now falls to the director of national intelligence.

In addition to the State Department, the Defense Department, and the intelligence community, other departments have roles to play in foreign policy. For instance, the Treasury Department and the Commerce Department are concerned with America's foreign economic policy, and the Department of Agriculture is interested in promoting American agricultural products abroad.

CONGRESS As we saw in Chapter 6, Congress has a variety of constitutional roles in making foreign policy, including the powers to make treaties, to declare war, and to appropriate money. But Congress faces obstacles in its efforts to play an active role in foreign policy. It must deal with the considerable powers of the president, for instance, and it is more oriented toward domestic than foreign affairs, given the ever-present imperative of reelection. Congressional organization also can hamper Congress' role in foreign policy.

Department of State the executive department charged with managing foreign affairs

Department of Defense the executive department charged with managing the country's military personnel, equipment, and operations

Joint Chiefs of Staff the senior military officers from four branches of the U.S. armed forces

intelligence community the agencies and bureaus responsible for obtaining and interpreting information for the government

Central Intelligence Agency (CIA) the government organization that oversees foreign intelligence gathering and related classified activities

director of national intelligence the overseer and coordinator of the activities of the many agencies involved in the production and dissemination of intelligence information in the U.S. government, as well as the president's main intelligence adviser

FIGURE 14.5

The Executive-Legislative "Struggle" Over Foreign Policy

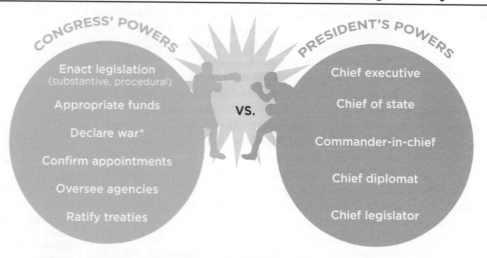

CONGRESS' POWERS

Enact legislation
(substantive, procedural)

Appropriate funds

Declare war*

Confirm appointments

Oversee agencies

Ratify treaties

VS.

PRESIDENT'S POWERS

Chief executive

Chief of state

Commander-in-chief

Chief diplomat

Chief legislator

* War has not been declared since World War II, but American forces have been involved in multiple military actions, including these:

Korea

When President Truman ordered U.S. troops into Korea in June 1950, he did so without a declaration of war—or any other form of congressional approval. Instead, Truman relied on his power as president and on our role as part of the United Nations, which authorized military action to repel the invasion of South Korea by the North. More than 30,000 U.S. troops were killed in this "forgotten war."

Vietnam

Lyndon Johnson relied on the 1964 Tonkin Gulf Resolution as a congressional "functional equivalent" of a declaration of war—a blank check, really, that led to about half a million U.S. forces in the region at the height of the war and about 50,000 U.S. deaths.

Iraq

By the time the United States invaded Iraq in 2003, the pattern of presidents going to Congress for an "Authorization for the Use of Military Force" had become the new pattern. Over fifteen years, more than 4,000 U.S. deaths, and trillions of dollars later, Iraq remains a troublesome situation.

The fragmentation of Congress, the slow speed of deliberation, and the complex nature of many foreign issues can make it difficult for Congress to play a big role, particularly in fast-moving foreign events.

The foreign policy tension between the president and Congress is illustrated by the complex issues surrounding the use of military force (see Figure 14.5). The president is in charge of the armed forces, but only Congress can declare war. Presidents try to get around the power of Congress by committing troops to military actions that do not have the official status of a war, but this can infuriate legislators. Presidents have sent troops abroad without a formal declaration of war on a number of occasions—for example, to Korea (1950), the Dominican Republic (1965), Vietnam (1965), Lebanon (1982), Grenada (1983), Panama (1989), the Persian Gulf (1990), Afghanistan (2001), and Iraq (2003). As the United States became more involved in the Vietnam War, however, Congress became increasingly unhappy with the president's role. When, in the early 1970s, public opinion against the war became increasingly vocal, Congress turned on the commander-in-chief, passing the War Powers Act (WPA) of 1973 over President Richard Nixon's veto. The act includes the following provisions:

1. The president must inform Congress of the introduction of forces into hostilities or situations where imminent involvement in hostilities is clearly indicated by the circumstances.
2. Troop commitments by the president cannot extend past sixty days without specific congressional authorization.
3. Any time American forces become engaged in hostilities without a declaration of war or specific congressional authorization, Congress can direct the president to disengage such troops by a concurrent resolution of the two houses of Congress.

The WPA has not stopped presidents from using force abroad, however. Chief executives have largely sidestepped the act through a simple loophole: they don't make their reports to Congress exactly as the act requires, and therefore they never trigger the sixty-day clock. They generally report "consistent with but not pursuant to" the act, a technicality that allows them to satisfy Congress' interest in being informed without tying their hands by starting the clock.

Despite its difficulties in enforcing the WPA, Congress has tried to play a fairly active role in foreign policy making, sometimes working with presidents and sometimes at odds with them. The calculation for Congress is fairly straightforward: let presidents pursue risky military strategies. If they succeed, take credit for staying out of their way. If they fail, blame them for not consulting and for being "imperial." Either way, Congress wins.

HOW DO WE DEFINE A FOREIGN POLICY PROBLEM?

The actors we have just discussed work in a very distinctive political environment that helps them decide when a foreign situation constitutes a problem and when it should be acted on. Most foreign policy is either action to correct something we don't like in the world or reaction to world events. The United States could try to meddle in almost any country's affairs and could react to almost anything that happens in the world. How do policymakers in Washington, members of the media, and average Americans decide what is sufficiently important to Americans and American interests to require a foreign policy? What makes the United States act or react?

The answer is complex. First, a distinctive American approach to foreign policy has developed over the years that reflects the United States' view of its global role, its values, and its political goals. For instance, American foreign policy makers are divided about the United States' role in the world: should it be an interventionist actor, or should it focus on problems closer to home and leave the global community to solve its own problems? A second tension comes from the question of whether U.S. foreign policy should be driven by moral concerns (doing what is right—for instance, with respect to human rights) or by practical concerns (ignoring what is right in favor of what is expedient—for instance, ensuring U.S. access to foreign oil or other natural resources). A final tension arises from the conflict between the desire of the United States to

> *How much should foreign policy reflect the will of the people?*

promote its own national security and economic growth and its desire to promote the spread of democracy in the world. Because of inherent tensions among these roles, values, and goals, our country's approach to defining foreign policy problems is not always consistent.

Foreign policy also is shaped by politics. The political context in which American foreign policy is forged involves the actors we have just met, in combination with pressures both global and domestic. Global pressures involve the actions of other nations, over which we have no control other than brute force, and international organizations, like the United Nations and NATO. Other global pressures concern economic issues. In an increasingly interdependent global economy, ups and downs in one country tend to reverberate throughout the world. Foreign policy makers are influenced by these international forces, but also by domestic pressures. Just as in domestic policy, the media, public opinion, and interest groups weigh in and try to influence what policymakers do. To the extent that the policymakers are elected officials, these domestic actors can carry considerable weight.

In Your Own Words   Identify the basic goals and types of foreign policy.

CITIZENSHIP AND POLICY

The influence of the public's opinions on policymaking

In this book we have discussed elite, pluralist, and participatory theories of democracy. This chapter has shown that each theory explains some aspect of policymaking in the United States. Clearly some foreign and domestic policies are the products of a closely guarded elite policymaking process that could not be less democratic at its core. Foreign policy, especially when dealing with crisis situations, takes place in secrecy, with the details kept even from other policymakers at the elite level. Monetary policy is designed specifically to protect the economy from the forces of democracy—from the short-term preferences of citizens and the eagerness of elected officials to give citizens what they want. Other policy areas, like Social Security policy, are very pluralistic. Even though society as a whole might be better off with more stringent rules concerning who gets what from Social Security, older Americans, in the guise of AARP, have lobbied successfully to maintain the generous and universal benefits that make Social Security so expensive. But the power of political groups does not negate the power of citizens. Individual Americans, in their roles as voters and participants in public opinion polls, have a decisive influence on policymaking, both domestic and foreign. Although they may not participate in the sense of getting deeply involved in the process themselves, there is no doubt that politicians respond to the public's preferences in creating public policy.

As we saw in Chapter 10, public opinion matters in politics. State legislators, for instance, vote in accordance with the ideological preferences of their constituents.[86] States with more liberal citizens, such as New York, Massachusetts, and California, have more liberal policies, and more conservative states, like those in the South and the Rocky Mountains, have more conservative state policies. Other studies have found a similar pattern in national elections.[87] What these findings tell us is that for all the cynicism in politics today, when it comes to who gets what, when, and how, American federalism works to a remarkable degree.

In Your Own Words   Describe ways in which policymaking reflects public opinion.

Let's Revisit: What's at Stake . . . ?

At the beginning of this chapter, we heard voices from opposite ends of the political spectrum sounding the alarm about income inequality—and in particular, about the challenges posed to what has become a rapidly shrinking middle class—and asked what is at stake in creating policy to address the issue. In the pages since, we've taken a look at the basic mechanisms of the American economy, and the different types of policy tools that lawmakers can use to manage it.

Some observers on the left claim that the solution is for the government to raise taxes on the wealthy to redistribute income in a fairer manner; those on the right generally say that the answer is to cut taxes, which would encourage spending and investment by well-off people, creating jobs and opportunity for all Americans in the process. In between are countless policy proposals—from increasing tax credits and raising the minimum wage for the working poor, to increasing access to higher education, to changing the tax code, to placing tariffs on imported goods in order to encourage manufacturing jobs here at home.

After Donald Trump's election, Democrats were split over how to proceed. Some politicians representing parts of the country that went heavily for Trump, such as Ohio congressman Tim Ryan, warned against tilting too far in favor of government action that could stifle the private sector. "We can be hostile to monopolies, oligarchies and concentrations of wealth," he said. "But we can't be hostile to capitalism." But some of the Democrats seen as potential challengers to Trump in 2020, including Senators Cory Booker of New Jersey, Kirsten Gillibrand of New York, Kamala Harris of California, and Jeff Merkley of Oregon, remained in favor of an activist approach. They signed on to a bill that would create a pilot program offering guaranteed jobs paying at least $15 an hour in fifteen high-unemployment communities.[88] Sanders, meanwhile, called for an even more sweeping way to create jobs by establishing 2,500 job centers nationwide.[89] He also unveiled a bill in May 2018 that would make it easier for workers to join unions and bolster unions' negotiating power by, among other things, allowing unions to boycott suppliers and companies associated with a business in a labor dispute. "Declining unionization has fueled rising inequality," Sanders said. "Today, corporate profits are at an all-time high, while wages as a percentage of the economy are near an all-time low. The middle class is disappearing, and the gap between the very rich and everyone else is growing wider and wider."[90] Former vice president Joe Biden framed the debate differently. "I don't think 500 billionaires are the reason we're in trouble," Biden said in May 2018. "The folks at the top aren't bad guys." Even so, Biden added, more attention should be paid to the middle class: "But this gap is yawning, and it's having the effect of pulling us apart."[91]

SAGE edge™
for CQ Press

Want a better grade?

Get the tools you need to sharpen your study skills. **SAGE edge** offers practice quizzes, eFlashcards, video, and multimedia at **edge.sagepub.com/barbourbrief8e.**

Review

Making Public Policy

Public policy (470) is a government plan of action to solve problems that people share collectively or that they cannot solve by themselves. Policies that address these problems can be **redistributive policies** (471), which shift resources from those who have them to those who do not; **distributive policies** (472), which use the resources of all to benefit a segment of society; or **regulatory policies** (472), which seek to modify the behavior of groups or individuals.

Public policy is made by actors in all branches and levels of government. The policymaking process involves agenda setting, policy formulation, policy adoption, policy implementation, and policy evaluation.

Social Policy

Social policies (476) are mostly redistributive and distributive policies that work to improve individuals' quality of life. They include **social welfare policies** (476), usually **means-tested programs** (476) directed toward those who cannot care for themselves, and **social insurance programs** (476), like **Social Security** (477), that offer benefits in exchange for contributions. Social Security is currently in financial straits because it is an **entitlement program** (478) whose benefits must be paid whether or not the money is there. The older Americans who receive those benefits are well organized politically. Social welfare programs are easier to reform because poor people do not organize effectively to defend their interests, and in 1996 the guarantees of the **Social Security Act** (477) were eliminated with the advent of **Temporary Assistance to Needy Families (TANF)** (480). Other social welfare policies include the **Supplemental Nutrition Assistance Program (SNAP)** (480) and Head Start. Social policy also covers health care policy, including **Medicare** (482) and **Medicaid** (482), and various programs that supply **subsidies** (485) to citizens and corporations to encourage behaviors that the government values, like buying a home, going to college, and providing jobs.

Economic Policy

Economic policy (486) refers to government strategies to provide for the health of the economy as a whole and to solve economic problems. One of its main tools is **fiscal policy** (487), which involves regulating the ups and downs of the economy through government's power to tax and spend. Practitioners of fiscal policy believe that it is not necessary for government to pursue a **balanced budget** (487) but that **deficits** (487) and **surpluses** (487) are tools to be used strategically to help regulate the economy. A second tool of economic policy is **monetary policy** (487), which tries to regulate the economy by controlling the money supply through manipulation of **interest rates** (487). Congress is the main agent of fiscal policy, which means that it is often subject to political pressure. Monetary policy, made by the **Federal Reserve System** (490), is much more insulated from politics.

Part of the nation's tax policy, federal income taxes are **progressive taxes** (495), meaning that people with more income are taxed at a higher rate; other taxes are **regressive taxes** (495), meaning that they impose a greater burden on the less well-off. Conservatives in the United States would rather have fewer progressive taxes and seek to eliminate the **capital gains tax** (496) on investments altogether. Liberals prefer the wealthy to bear a larger share to lighten the load on the poor. Current proposals for reforming the tax code include a **flat tax** (496) and a **consumption tax** (497) such as a **value-added tax (VAT)** (497). Although Democrats and Republicans disagree on what exactly its role should be, government also seeks to keep the economy healthy through regulatory policy, including **deregulation** (499).

Foreign Policy

Foreign policy (499) is designed to solve problems between us and foreign actors. Sometimes the United States has tried to ignore the rest of the world, a policy known as **isolationism** (500), but more often it has tried to reach its goals by engaging other nations with a more active policy of **interventionism** (500). The actors the United States engages with are many other countries, **intergovernmental organizations** (500), **nongovernmental organizations** (500), and **multinational corporations** (500), among others. Foreign policies can be **crisis policy** (501), dealing with emergency threats; **strategic policy** (501), dealing with our basic stance toward a foreign actor or problem; or **structural defense policy** (501), dealing with defense and military issues. Throughout the latter half of the twentieth century, our foreign policy was defined by the **Cold War** (501) with the Soviet Union, in which we pursued a policy of **containment** (501) to limit the USSR's influence. Our policy in a post–Cold War era is more difficult to define, as the threats to us are not necessarily from other nations but from groups like al Qaeda and ISIS.

American foreign policy is made by a variety of actors—executive, legislative, and judicial—acting on behalf of the federal government. The president is the chief foreign policy maker, with the assistance of a huge network of federal agencies, among them the **National Security Council (NSC)** (504), the **Department of State** (505), the **Department of Defense** (505), the **Joint Chiefs of Staff** (505), and the **intelligence community** (505), including the **Central Intelligence Agency (CIA)** (505) and the **director of national intelligence** (505). With different constitutional responsibilities, the president and Congress often wrangle for control over foreign policy. The **Bush Doctrine** (502) is the latest in a long line of presidential foreign policy doctrines.

APPENDIX MATERIAL

1
ARTICLES OF CONFEDERATION

Articles of Confederation and perpetual Union between the states of New Hampshire, Massachusetts-bay, Rhode Island and Providence Plantations, Connecticut, New York, New Jersey, Pennsylvania, Delaware, Maryland, Virginia, North Carolina, South Carolina and Georgia.

ARTICLE I

The Stile of this Confederacy shall be "The United States of America."

ARTICLE II

Each state retains its sovereignty, freedom, and independence, and every power, jurisdiction, and right, which is not by this Confederation expressly delegated to the United States, in Congress assembled.

ARTICLE III

The said States hereby severally enter into a firm league of friendship with each other, for their common defense, the security of their liberties, and their mutual and general welfare, binding themselves to assist each other, against all force offered to, or attacks made upon them, or any of them, on account of religion, sovereignty, trade, or any other pretense whatever.

ARTICLE IV

The better to secure and perpetuate mutual friendship and intercourse among the people of the different States in this Union, the free inhabitants of each of these States, paupers, vagabonds, and fugitives from justice excepted, shall be entitled to all privileges and immunities of free citizens in the several States; and the people of each State shall free ingress and regress to and from any other State, and shall enjoy therein all the privileges of trade and commerce, subject to the same duties, impositions, and restrictions as the inhabitants thereof respectively, provided that such restrictions shall not extend so far as to prevent the removal of property imported into any State, to any other State, of which the owner is an inhabitant; provided also that no imposition, duties or restriction shall be laid by any State, on the property of the United States, or either of them.

If any person guilty of, or charged with, treason, felony, or other high misdemeanor in any State, shall flee from justice, and be found in any of the United States, he shall, upon demand of the Governor or executive power of the State from which he fled, be delivered up and removed to the State having jurisdiction of his offense.

Full faith and credit shall be given in each of these States to the records, acts, and judicial proceedings of the courts and magistrates of every other State.

ARTICLE V

For the most convenient management of the general interests of the United States, delegates shall be annually appointed in such manner as the legislatures of each State shall direct, to meet in Congress on the first Monday in November, in every year, with a power reserved to each State to recall its delegates, or any of them, at any time within the year, and to send others in their stead for the remainder of the year.

No State shall be represented in Congress by less than two, nor more than seven members; and no person shall be capable of being a delegate for more than three years in any term of six years; nor shall any person, being a delegate, be capable of holding any office under the United States, for which he, or another for his benefit, receives any salary, fees or emolument of any kind.

Each State shall maintain its own delegates in a meeting of the States, and while they act as members of the committee of the States.

In determining questions in the United States in Congress assembled, each State shall have one vote.

Freedom of speech and debate in Congress shall not be impeached or questioned in any court or place out of Congress, and the members of Congress shall be protected in their persons from arrests or imprisonments, during the time of their going to and from, and attendence on Congress, except for treason, felony, or breach of the peace.

ARTICLE VI

No State, without the consent of the United States in Congress assembled, shall send any embassy to, or receive any embassy from, or enter into any conference, agreement, alliance or treaty with any King, Prince or State; nor shall any person holding any office of profit or trust under the United States, or any of them, accept any present, emolument, office or title of any kind whatever from any King, Prince or foreign State; nor shall the United States in Congress assembled, or any of them, grant any title of nobility.

No two or more States shall enter into any treaty, confederation or alliance whatever between them, without the consent of the United States in Congress assembled, specifying accurately the purposes for which the same is to be entered into, and how long it shall continue.

No State shall lay any imposts or duties, which may interfere with any stipulations in treaties, entered into by the United States in Congress assembled, with any King, Prince or State, in pursuance of any treaties already proposed by Congress, to the courts of France and Spain.

No vessel of war shall be kept up in time of peace by any State, except such number only, as shall be deemed necessary by the United States in Congress assembled, for the defense of such State, or its trade; nor shall any body of forces be kept up by any State in time of peace, except such number only, as in the judgement of the United States in Congress assembled, shall be deemed requisite to garrison the forts necessary for the defense of such State; but every State shall always keep up a well-regulated and disciplined militia, sufficiently armed and accoutered, and shall provide and constantly have ready for use, in public stores, a due number of field pieces and tents, and a proper quantity of arms, ammunition and camp equipage.

No State shall engage in any war without the consent of the United States in Congress assembled, unless such State be actually invaded by enemies, or shall have received certain advice of a resolution being formed by some nation of Indians to invade such State, and the danger is so imminent as not to admit of a delay till the United States in Congress assembled can be consulted; nor shall any State grant commissions to any ships or vessels of war, nor letters of marque or reprisal, except it be after a declaration of war by the United States in Congress assembled, and then only against the Kingdom or State and the subjects thereof, against which war has been so declared, and under such regulations as shall be established by the United States in Congress assembled, unless such State be infested by pirates, in which case vessels of war may be fitted out for that occasion, and kept so long as the danger shall continue, or until the United States in Congress assembled shall determine otherwise.

ARTICLE VII

When land forces are raised by any State for the common defense, all officers of or under the rank of colonel, shall be appointed by the legislature of each State respectively, by whom such forces shall be raised, or in such manner as such State shall direct, and all vacancies shall be filled up by the State which first made the appointment.

ARTICLE VIII

All charges of war, and all other expenses that shall be incurred for the common defense or general welfare, and allowed by the United States in Congress assembled, shall be defrayed out of a common treasury, which shall be supplied by the several States in proportion to the value of all land within each State, granted or surveyed for any person, as such land and the buildings and improvements thereon shall be estimated according to such mode as the United States in Congress assembled, shall from time to time direct and appoint.

The taxes for paying that proportion shall be laid and levied by the authority and direction of the legislatures of the several States within the time agreed upon by the United States in Congress assembled.

ARTICLE IX

The United States in Congress assembled, shall have the sole and exclusive right and power of determining on peace and war, except in the cases mentioned in the sixth article—of sending and receiving ambassadors—entering into treaties and alliances, provided that no treaty of commerce shall be made whereby the legislative power of the respective States shall be restrained from imposing such imposts and duties on foreigners, as their own people are subjected to, or from prohibiting the exportation or importation of any species of goods or commodities whatsoever—of establishing rules for deciding in all cases, what captures on land or water shall be legal, and in what manner prizes taken by land or naval forces in the service of the United States shall be divided or appropriated—of granting letters of marque and reprisal in times of peace—appointing courts for the trial of piracies and felonies committed on the high seas and establishing courts for receiving and determining finally appeals in all cases of captures, provided that no member of Congress shall be appointed a judge of any of the said courts.

The United States in Congress assembled shall also be the last resort on appeal in all disputes and differences now subsisting or that hereafter may arise between two or more States concerning boundary, jurisdiction or any other causes whatever; which authority shall always be exercised in the manner following. Whenever the legislative or executive authority or lawful agent of any State in controversy with another shall present a petition to Congress stating the matter in question and praying for a hearing, notice thereof shall be given by order of Congress to the legislative or executive authority of the other State in controversy, and a day assigned for the appearance of the parties by their lawful agents, who shall then be directed to appoint by joint consent, commissioners or judges to constitute a court for hearing and determining the matter in question: but if they cannot agree, Congress shall name three persons out of each of the United States, and from the list of such persons each party shall alternately strike out one, the petitioners beginning, until the number shall be reduced to thirteen; and from that number not less than seven, nor more than nine names as Congress shall direct, shall in the presence of Congress be drawn out by lot, and the persons whose names shall be so drawn or any five of them, shall be commissioners or judges, to hear and finally determine the controversy, so always as a major part of the judges who shall hear the cause shall agree in the determination: and if either party shall neglect to attend at the day appointed, without showing reasons, which Congress shall judge sufficient, or being present shall refuse to strike, the Congress shall proceed to nominate three persons out of each State, and the secretary of Congress shall strike in behalf of such party absent or refusing; and the judgement and sentence of the court to be appointed, in the manner before prescribed, shall be final and conclusive; and if any of the parties shall refuse to submit to the authority of such court, or to appear or defend their claim or cause, the court shall nevertheless proceed to pronounce sentence, or judgement, which shall in like manner be final and decisive, the judgement or sentence and other proceedings being in either case transmitted to Congress, and lodged among the acts of Congress for the security of the parties concerned: provided that every commissioner, before he sits in judgement, shall take an oath to be administered by one of the judges of the supreme or superior court of the State, where the cause shall be tried, 'well and truly to hear and determine the matter in question, according to the best of his judgement, without favor, affection or hope of reward': provided also, that no State shall be deprived of territory for the benefit of the United States.

All controversies concerning the private right of soil claimed under different grants of two or more States, whose jurisdictions as they may respect such lands, and the States which passed such grants are adjusted, the said grants or either of them being at the same time claimed to have originated antecedent to such settlement of jurisdiction, shall on the petition of either party to the Congress of the United States, be finally determined as near as may be in the same manner as is before prescribed for deciding disputes respecting territorial jurisdiction between different States.

The United States in Congress assembled shall also have the sole and exclusive right and power of regulating the alloy and value of coin struck by their own authority, or by that of the respective States—fixing the standards of weights and measures throughout the United States—regulating the trade and managing all affairs with the Indians, not members of any of the States, provided that the legislative right of any State within its own limits be not infringed or violated—establishing or regulating post offices from one State to another, throughout all the United States, and exacting such postage on the papers passing through the same as may be requisite to defray the expenses of the said office—appointing all officers of the land forces, in the service of the United States, excepting regimental officers—appointing all the officers of the naval forces, and commissioning all officers whatever in the service of the United States—making rules for the government and regulation of the said land and naval forces, and directing their operations.

The United States in Congress assembled shall have authority to appoint a committee, to sit in the recess of Congress, to be denominated 'A Committee of the States,' and to consist of one delegate from each State; and to appoint such other committees and civil officers as may be necessary for managing the general affairs of the United States under their direction—to appoint one of their members to preside, provided that no person be allowed to serve in the office of president more than one year in any term of three years; to ascertain the necessary sums of money to be raised for the service of the United States, and to appropriate and apply the same for defraying the public expenses—to borrow money, or emit bills on the credit of the United States, transmitting every half-year to the respective States an account of the sums of money so borrowed or emitted—to build and equip a navy—to agree upon the number of land forces, and to make requisitions from each State for its quota, in proportion to the number of white inhabitants in such State; which requisition shall be binding, and thereupon the legislature of each State shall appoint the regimental officers, raise the men and cloath, arm and equip them in a solid-like manner, at the expense of the United States; and the officers and men so cloathed, armed and equipped shall march to the place appointed, and within the time agreed on by the United States in Congress assembled. But if the United States in Congress assembled shall, on consideration of circumstances judge proper that any State should not raise men, or should raise a smaller number of men than the quota thereof, such extra number shall be raised, officered, cloathed, armed and equipped in

the same manner as the quota of each State, unless the legislature of such State shall judge that such extra number cannot be safely spread out in the same, in which case they shall raise, officer, cloath, arm and equip as many of such extra number as they judge can be safely spared. And the officers and men so cloathed, armed, and equipped, shall march to the place appointed, and within the time agreed on by the United States in Congress assembled.

The United States in Congress assembled shall never engage in a war, nor grant letters of marque or reprisal in time of peace, nor enter into any treaties or alliances, nor coin money, nor regulate the value thereof, nor ascertain the sums and expenses necessary for the defense and welfare of the United States, or any of them, nor emit bills, nor borrow money on the credit of the United States, nor appropriate money, nor agree upon the number of vessels of war, to be built or purchased, or the number of land or sea forces to be raised, nor appoint a commander in chief of the army or navy, unless nine States assent to the same: nor shall a question on any other point, except for adjourning from day to day be determined, unless by the votes of the majority of the United States in Congress assembled.

The Congress of the United States shall have power to adjourn to any time within the year, and to any place within the United States, so that no period of adjournment be for a longer duration than the space of six months, and shall publish the journal of their proceedings monthly, except such parts thereof relating to treaties, alliances or military operations, as in their judgement require secrecy; and the yeas and nays of the delegates of each State on any question shall be entered on the journal, when it is desired by any delegates of a State, or any of them, at his or their request shall be furnished with a transcript of the said journal, except such parts as are above excepted, to lay before the legislatures of the several States.

ARTICLE X

The Committee of the States, or any nine of them, shall be authorized to execute, in the recess of Congress, such of the powers of Congress as the United States in Congress assembled, by the consent of the nine States, shall from time to time think expedient to vest them with; provided that no power be delegated to the said Committee, for the exercise of which, by the Articles of Confederation, the voice of nine States in the Congress of the United States assembled be requisite.

ARTICLE XI

Canada acceding to this confederation, and adjoining in the measures of the United States, shall be admitted into, and entitled to all the advantages of this Union; but no other colony shall be admitted into the same, unless such admission be agreed to by nine States.

ARTICLE XII

All bills of credit emitted, monies borrowed, and debts contracted by, or under the authority of Congress, before the assembling of the United States, in pursuance of the present confederation, shall be deemed and considered as a charge against the United States, for payment and satisfaction whereof the said United States, and the public faith are hereby solemnly pledged.

ARTICLE XIII

Every State shall abide by the determination of the United States in Congress assembled, on all questions which by this confederation are submitted to them. And the Articles of this Confederation shall be inviolably observed by every State, and the Union shall be perpetual; nor shall any alteration at any time hereafter be made in any of them; unless such alteration be agreed to in a Congress of the United States, and be afterwards confirmed by the legislatures of every State.

And Whereas it hath pleased the Great Governor of the World to incline the hearts of the legislatures we respectively represent in Congress, to approve of, and to authorize us to ratify the said Articles of Confederation and perpetual Union. Know Ye that we the undersigned delegates, by virtue of the power and authority to us given for that purpose, do by these presents, in the name and in behalf of our respective constituents, fully and entirely ratify and confirm each and every of the said Articles of Confederation and perpetual Union, and all and singular the matters and things therein contained: And we do further solemnly plight and engage the faith of our respective constituents, that they shall abide by the determinations of the United States in Congress assembled, on all questions, which by the said Confederation are submitted to them. And that the Articles thereof shall be inviolably observed by the States we respectively represent, and that the Union shall be perpetual.

In Witness whereof we have hereunto set our hands in Congress. Done at Philadelphia in the State of Pennsylvania the ninth day of July in the Year of our Lord One Thousand Seven Hundred and Seventy-Eight, and in the Third Year of the independence of America.

Agreed to by Congress 15 November 1777
In force after ratification by Maryland,
1 March 1781

2

DECLARATION OF INDEPENDENCE

On June 11, 1776, the responsibility to "prepare a declaration" of independence was assigned by the Continental Congress, meeting in Philadelphia, to five members: John Adams, Benjamin Franklin, Thomas Jefferson, Robert Livingston, and Roger Sherman. Impressed by his talents as a writer, the committee asked Jefferson to compose a draft. After modifying Jefferson's draft the committee turned it over to Congress on June 28. On July 2 Congress voted to declare independence; on the evening of July 4, it approved the Declaration of Independence.

In Congress, July 4, 1776.

The unanimous Declaration of the thirteen United States of America,

When in the Course of human events, it becomes necessary for one people to dissolve the political bands which have connected them with another, and to assume among the Powers of the earth, the separate and equal station to which the Laws of Nature and of Nature's God entitle them, a decent respect to the opinions of mankind requires that they should declare the causes which impel them to the separation.

We hold these truths to be self-evident, that all men are created equal, that they are endowed by their Creator with certain unalienable Rights, that among these are Life, Liberty and the pursuit of Happiness. That to secure these rights, Governments are instituted among Men, deriving their just powers from the consent of the governed. That whenever any form of Government becomes destructive of these ends, it is the Right of the People to alter or to abolish it, and to institute new Government, laying its foundation on such principles and organizing its powers in such form, as to them shall seem most likely to effect their Safety and Happiness. Prudence, indeed, will dictate that

Government long established should not be changed for light and transient causes; and accordingly all experience hath shown, that mankind are more disposed to suffer, while evils are sufferable, than to right themselves by abolishing the forms to which they are accustomed. But when a long train of abuses and usurpations, pursuing invariably the same Object evinces a design to reduce them under absolute Despotism, it is their right, it is their duty, to throw off such Government, and to provide new Guards for their future security. Such has been the patient sufferance of these Colonies; and such is now the necessity which constrains them to alter their former Systems of Government. The history of the present King of Great Britain is a history of repeated injuries and usurpations, all having in direct object the establishment of an absolute Tyranny over these States. To prove this, let Facts be submitted to a candid world.

He has refused his Assent to Laws, the most wholesome and necessary for the public good.

He has forbidden his Governors to pass Laws of immediate and pressing importance, unless suspended in their operation till his Assent should be obtained; and when so suspended, he has utterly neglected to attend to them.

He has refused to pass other Laws for the accommodation of large districts of people, unless those people would relinquish the right of Representation in the Legislature, a right inestimable to them and formidable to tyrants only.

He has called together legislative bodies at places unusual, uncomfortable, and distant from the depository of their Public Records, for the sole purpose of fatiguing them into compliance with his measures.

He has dissolved Representative Houses repeatedly, for opposing with manly firmness his invasions on the rights of the people.

He has refused for a long time, after such dissolutions, to cause others to be elected; whereby the Legislative Powers, incapable of Annihilation, have returned to the People at large for their exercise; the State remaining in the mean time exposed to all the dangers of invasion from without, and convulsions within.

He has endeavored to prevent the population of these States; for that purpose obstructing the Laws of Naturalization of Foreigners; refusing to pass others to encourage their migration hither, and raising the conditions of new Appropriations of Lands.

He has obstructed the Administration of Justice, by refusing his Assent to Laws for establishing Judiciary Powers.

He has made Judges dependent on his Will alone, for the tenure of their offices, and the amount and payment of their salaries.

He has erected a multitude of New Offices, and sent hither swarms of Officers to harass our People, and eat out their substance.

He has kept among us, in times of peace, Standing Armies without the Consent of our legislature.

He has affected to render the Military independent of and superior to the Civil Power.

He has combined with others to subject us to a jurisdiction foreign to our constitution, and unacknowledged by our laws; giving his Assent to their acts of pretended legislation:

For quartering large bodies of armed troops among us:

For protecting them, by a mock Trial, from Punishment for any Murders which they should commit on the Inhabitants of these States:

For cutting off our Trade with all parts of the world:

For imposing taxes on us without our Consent:

For depriving us in many cases, of the benefits of Trial by Jury:

For transporting us beyond Seas to be tried for pretended offences:

For abolishing the free System of English Laws in a neighbouring Province, establishing therein an Arbitrary government, and enlarging its Boundaries so as to render it at once an example and fit instrument for introducing the same absolute rule into these Colonies:

For taking away our Charters, abolishing our most valuable Laws, and altering fundamentally the Forms of our Governments:

For suspending our own Legislature, and declaring themselves invested with Power to legislate for us in all cases whatsoever.

He has abdicated Government here, by declaring us out of his Protection and waging War against us.

He has plundered our seas, ravaged our Coasts, burnt our towns, and destroyed the lives of our people.

He is at this time transporting large armies of foreign mercenaries to compleat the works of death, desolation and tyranny, already begun with circumstances of Cruelty & perfidy scarcely parallel in the most barbarous ages, and totally unworthy the Head of a civilized nation.

He has constrained our fellow Citizens taken Captive on the high Seas to bear Arms against their Country, to become the executioners of their friends and Brethren, or to fall themselves by their Hands.

He has excited domestic insurrections amongst us, and has endeavoured to bring on the inhabitants of our frontiers, the merciless Indian Savages, whose known rule of warfare, is an undistinguished destruction of all ages, sexes and conditions.

In every stage of these Oppressions We have Petitioned for Redress in the most humble terms: Our repeated Petitions have been answered only by repeated injury. A Prince, whose character is thus marked by every act which may define a Tyrant, is unfit to be the ruler of a free People.

Nor have We been wanting in attention to our British brethren. We have warned them from time to time of attempts by their legislature to extend an unwarrantable jurisdiction over us. We have reminded them of the circumstances of our emigration and settlement here. We have appealed to their native justice and magnanimity, and we have conjured them by the ties of our common kindred to disavow these usurpations, which would inevitably interrupt our connections and correspondence. They too have been deaf to the voice of justice and of consanguinity. We must, therefore, acquiesce in the necessity, which denounces our Separation, and hold them, as we hold the rest of mankind, Enemies in War, in Peace Friends.

We, therefore, the Representatives of the United States of America, in General Congress, Assembled, appealing to the Supreme Judge of the world for the rectitude of our intentions, do, in the Name, and by Authority of the good People of these Colonies, solemnly publish and declare, That these United Colonies are, and of Right ought to be Free and Independent States; that they are Absolved from all Allegiance to the British Crown, and that all political connection between them and the State of Great Britain, is and ought to be totally dissolved; and that as Free and Independent States, they have full Power to levy War, conclude Peace, contract Alliances, establish Commerce, and to do all other Acts and Things which Independent States may of right do. And for the support of this Declaration, with a firm reliance on the Protection of Divine Providence, we mutually pledge to each other our Lives, our Fortunes and our sacred Honor.

3

CONSTITUTION OF THE UNITED STATES

The United States Constitution was written at a convention that Congress called on February 21, 1787, for the purpose of recommending amendments to the Articles of Confederation. Every state but Rhode Island sent delegates to Philadelphia, where the convention met that summer. The delegates decided to write an entirely new constitution, completing their labors on September 17. Nine states (the number the Constitution itself stipulated as sufficient) ratified by June 21, 1788.

The framers of the Constitution included only six paragraphs on the Supreme Court. Article III, Section 1, created the Supreme Court and the federal system of courts. It provided that "[t]he judicial power of the United States, shall be vested in one supreme Court," and whatever inferior courts Congress "from time to time" saw fit to establish. Article III, Section 2, delineated the types of cases and controversies that should be considered by a federal—rather than a state—court. But beyond this, the Constitution left many of the particulars of the Supreme Court and the federal court system for Congress to decide in later years in judiciary acts.

We the People of the United States, in Order to form a more perfect Union, establish Justice, insure domestic Tranquility, provide for the common defence, promote the general Welfare, and secure the Blessings of Liberty to ourselves and our Posterity, do ordain and establish this Constitution for the United States of America.

ARTICLE I

Section 1. All legislative Powers herein granted shall be vested in a Congress of the United States, which shall consist of a Senate and House of Representatives.

Section 2. The House of Representatives shall be composed of Members chosen every second Year by the People of the several States, and the Electors in each State shall have the Qualifications requisite for Electors of the most numerous Branch of the State Legislature.

No Person shall be a Representative who shall not have attained to the age of twenty five Years, and been seven Years a Citizen of the United States, and who shall not, when elected, be an Inhabitant of that State in which he shall be chosen.

[Representatives and direct Taxes shall be apportioned among the several States which may be included within this Union, according to their respective Numbers, which shall be determined by adding to the whole Number of free Persons, including those bound to Service for a Term of Years, and excluding Indians not taxed, three fifths of all other Persons.][1] The actual Enumeration shall be made within three Years after the first Meeting of the Congress of the United States, and within every subsequent Term of ten Years, in such Manner as they shall by Law direct. The Number of Representatives shall not exceed one for every thirty Thousand, but each State shall have at Least one Representative; and until such enumeration shall be made, the State of New Hampshire shall be entitled to chuse three, Massachusetts eight, Rhode-Island and Providence Plantations one, Connecticut five, New-York six, New Jersey four, Pennsylvania eight, Delaware one, Maryland six, Virginia ten, North Carolina five, South Carolina five, and Georgia three.

When vacancies happen in the Representation from any State, the Executive Authority thereof shall issue Writs of Election to fill such Vacancies.

The House of Representatives shall chuse their Speaker and other Officers; and shall have the sole Power of Impeachment.

Section 3. The Senate of the United States shall be composed of two Senators from each State, [chosen by the Legislature thereof,][2] for six Years; and each Senator shall have one Vote.

Immediately after they shall be assembled in Consequence of the first Election, they shall be divided as equally as may be into three Classes. The Seats of the Senators of the first Class shall be vacated at the Expiration of the second Year, of the second Class at the Expiration of the fourth Year, and of the third Class at the Expiration of the sixth Year, so that one third may be chosen every second Year; [and if Vacancies happen by Resignation, or otherwise, during the Recess of the Legislature of any State, the Executive thereof may make temporary Appointments until the next Meeting of the Legislature, which shall then fill such Vacancies.][3]

No Person shall be a Senator who shall not have attained to the Age of thirty Years, and been nine Years a Citizen of the United States, and who shall not, when elected, be an Inhabitant of that State for which he shall be chosen.

The Vice President of the United States shall be President of the Senate, but shall have no Vote, unless they be equally divided.

The Senate shall chuse their other Officers, and also a President pro tempore, in the Absence of the Vice President, or when he shall exercise the Office of President of the United States.

The Senate shall have the sole Power to try all Impeachments. When sitting for that Purpose, they shall be on Oath or Affirmation. When the President of the United States is tried, the Chief Justice shall preside: And no Person shall be convicted without the Concurrence of two thirds of the Members present.

Judgment in Cases of Impeachment shall not extend further than to removal from Office, and disqualification to hold and enjoy any Office of honor, Trust or Profit under the United States: but the Party convicted shall nevertheless be liable and subject to Indictment, Trial, Judgment and Punishment, according to Law.

Section 4. The Times, Places and Manner of holding Elections for Senators and Representatives, shall be prescribed in each State by the Legislature thereof; but the Congress may at any time by Law make or alter such Regulations, except as to the Places of chusing Senators.

The Congress shall assemble at least once in every Year, and such Meeting shall [be on the first Monday in December],[4] unless they shall by Law appoint a different Day.

Section 5. Each House shall be the Judge of the Elections, Returns and Qualifications of its own Members, and a Majority of each shall constitute a Quorum to do Business; but a smaller Number may adjourn from day to day, and may be authorized to compel the Attendance of absent Members, in such Manner, and under such Penalties as each House may provide.

Each House may determine the Rules of its Proceedings, punish its Members for disorderly Behaviour, and, with the Concurrence of two thirds, expel a Member.

Each House shall keep a Journal of its Proceedings, and from time to time publish the same, excepting such Parts as may in their Judgment require Secrecy; and the Yeas and Nays of the Members of either House on any question shall, at the Desire of one fifth of those Present, be entered on the Journal.

Neither House, during the Session of Congress, shall, without the Consent of the other, adjourn for more than three days, nor to any other Place than that in which the two Houses shall be sitting.

Section 6. The Senators and Representatives shall receive a Compensation for their Services, to be ascertained by Law, and paid out of the Treasury of the United States. They shall in all Cases, except Treason, Felony and Breach of the Peace, be privileged from Arrest during their Attendance at the Session of their respective Houses, and in going to and returning from the same; and for any Speech or Debate in either House, they shall not be questioned in any other Place.

No Senator or Representative shall, during the Time for which he was elected, be appointed to any civil Office under the Authority of the United States, which shall have been created, or the Emoluments whereof shall have been encreased during such time; and no Person holding any Office under the

United States, shall be a Member of either House during his Continuance in Office.

Section 7. All Bills for raising Revenue shall originate in the House of Representatives; but the Senate may propose or concur with Amendments as on other Bills.

Every Bill which shall have passed the House of Representatives and the Senate, shall, before it become a Law, be presented to the President of the United States; If he approve he shall sign it, but if not he shall return it, with his Objections to that House in which it shall have originated, who shall enter the Objections at large on their Journal, and proceed to reconsider it. If after such Reconsideration two thirds of that House shall agree to pass the Bill, it shall be sent, together with the Objections, to the other House, by which it shall likewise be reconsidered, and if approved by two thirds of that House, it shall become a Law. But in all such Cases the Votes of both Houses shall be determined by yeas and Nays, and the Names of the Persons voting for and against the Bill shall be entered on the Journal of each House respectively. If any Bill shall not be returned by the President within ten Days (Sundays excepted) after it shall have been presented to him, the Same shall be a Law, in like Manner as if he had signed it, unless the Congress by their Adjournment prevent its Return, in which Case it shall not be a Law.

Every Order, Resolution, or Vote to which the Concurrence of the Senate and House of Representatives may be necessary (except on a question of Adjournment) shall be presented to the President of the United States; and before the Same shall take Effect, shall be approved by him, or being disapproved by him, shall be repassed by two thirds of the Senate and House of Representatives, according to the Rules and Limitations prescribed in the Case of a Bill.

Section 8. The Congress shall have Power To lay and collect Taxes, Duties, Imposts and Excises, to pay the Debts and provide for the common Defence and general Welfare of the United States; but all Duties, Imposts and Excises shall be uniform throughout the United States;

To borrow Money on the credit of the United States;

To regulate Commerce with foreign Nations, and among the several States, and with the Indian Tribes;

To establish an uniform Rule of Naturalization, and uniform Laws on the subject of Bankruptcies throughout the United States;

To coin Money, regulate the Value thereof, and of foreign Coin, and fix the Standard of Weights and Measures;

To provide for the Punishment of counterfeiting the Securities and current Coin of the United States;

To establish Post Offices and post Roads;

To promote the Progress of Science and useful Arts, by securing for limited Times to Authors and Inventors the exclusive Right to their respective Writings and Discoveries;

To constitute Tribunals inferior to the supreme Court;

To define and punish Piracies and Felonies committed on the high Seas, and Offences against the Law of Nations;

To declare War, grant Letters of Marque and Reprisal, and make Rules concerning Captures on Land and Water;

To raise and support Armies, but no Appropriation of Money to that Use shall be for a longer Term than two Years;

To provide and maintain a Navy;

To make Rules for the Government and Regulation of the land and naval Forces;

To provide for calling forth the Militia to execute the Laws of the Union, suppress Insurrections and repel Invasions;

To provide for organizing, arming, and disciplining, the Militia, and for governing such Part of them as may be employed in the Service of the United States, reserving to the States respectively, the Appointment of the Officers, and the Authority of training the Militia according to the discipline prescribed by Congress;

To exercise exclusive Legislation in all Cases whatsoever, over such District (not exceeding ten Miles square) as may, by Cession of particular States, and the Acceptance of Congress, become the Seat of the Government of the United States, and to exercise like Authority over all Places purchased by the Consent of the Legislature of the State in which the Same shall be, for the Erection of Forts, Magazines, Arsenals, dock-Yards, and other needful Buildings;—And

To make all Laws which shall be necessary and proper for carrying into Execution the foregoing Powers, and all other Powers vested by this Constitution in the Government of the United States, or in any Department or Officer thereof.

Section 9. The Migration or Importation of such Persons as any of the States now existing shall think proper to admit, shall not be prohibited by the Congress prior to the Year one thousand eight hundred and eight, but a Tax or duty may be imposed on such Importation, not exceeding ten dollars for each Person.

The Privilege of the Writ of Habeas Corpus shall not be suspended, unless when in Cases of Rebellion or Invasion the public Safety may require it.

No Bill of Attainder or ex post facto Law shall be passed.

No Capitation, or other direct, Tax shall be laid, unless in Proportion to the Census or Enumeration herein before directed to be taken.[5]

No Tax or Duty shall be laid on Articles exported from any State.

No Preference shall be given by any Regulation of Commerce or Revenue to the Ports of one State over those of another; nor shall Vessels bound to, or from, one State, be obliged to enter, clear, or pay Duties in another.

No Money shall be drawn from the Treasury, but in Consequence of Appropriations made by Law; and a regular Statement and Account of the Receipts and Expenditures of all public Money shall be published from time to time.

No Title of Nobility shall be granted by the United States: And no Person holding any Office of Profit or Trust under them, shall, without the Consent of the Congress, accept of any present, Emolument, Office, or Title, of any kind whatever, from any King, Prince, or foreign State.

Section 10. No State shall enter into any Treaty, Alliance, or Confederation; grant Letters of Marque and Reprisal; coin Money; emit Bills of Credit; make any Thing but gold and silver Coin a Tender in Payment of Debts; pass any Bill of Attainder, ex post facto Law, or Law impairing the Obligation of Contracts, or grant any Title of Nobility.

No State shall, without the Consent of the Congress, lay any Imposts or Duties on Imports or Exports, except what may be absolutely necessary for executing its inspection Laws: and the net Produce of all Duties and Imposts, laid by any State on Imports or Exports, shall be for the Use of the Treasury of the United States; and all such Laws shall be subject to the Revision and Controul of the Congress.

No State shall, without the Consent of Congress, lay any Duty of Tonnage, keep Troops, or Ships of War in time of Peace, enter into any Agreement or Compact with another State, or with a foreign Power, or engage in War, unless actually invaded, or in such imminent Danger as will not admit of delay.

ARTICLE II

Section 1. The executive Power shall be vested in a President of the United States of America. He shall hold his Office during the Term of four Years, and, together with the Vice President, chosen for the same Term, be elected, as follows:

Each State shall appoint, in such Manner as the Legislature thereof may direct, a Number of Electors, equal to the whole Number of Senators and Representatives to which the State may be entitled in the Congress: but no Senator or Representative, or Person holding an Office of Trust or Profit under the United States, shall be appointed an Elector.

[The Electors shall meet in their respective States, and vote by Ballot for two Persons, of whom one at least shall not be an Inhabitant of the same State with themselves. And they shall make a List of all the Persons voted for, and of the Number of Votes for each; which List they shall sign and certify, and transmit sealed to the Seat of the Government of the United States, directed to the President of the Senate. The President of the Senate shall, in the Presence of the Senate and House of Representatives, open all the Certificates, and the Votes shall then be counted. The Person having the greatest Number of Votes shall be the President, if such Number be a Majority of the whole Number of Electors appointed; and if there be more than one who have such Majority, and have an equal Number of Votes, then the House of Representatives shall immediately chuse by Ballot one of them for President; and if no Person have a Majority, then from the five highest on the list the said House shall in like Manner chuse the President. But in chusing the President, the Votes shall be taken by States, the Representation from each State having one Vote; A quorum for this Purpose shall consist of a Member or Members from two thirds of the States, and a Majority of all the States shall be necessary to a Choice. In every Case, after the Choice of the President, the Person having the greatest Number of

Votes of the Electors shall be the Vice President. But if there should remain two or more who have equal Votes, the Senate shall chuse from them by Ballot the Vice President.][6]

The Congress may determine the Time of chusing the Electors, and the Day on which they shall give their Votes; which Day shall be the same throughout the United States.

No Person except a natural born Citizen, or a Citizen of the United States, at the time of the Adoption of this Constitution, shall be eligible to the Office of President; neither shall any Person be eligible to that Office who shall not have attained to the Age of thirty five Years, and been fourteen Years a Resident within the United States.

In Case of the Removal of the President from Office, or of his Death, Resignation, or Inability to discharge the Powers and Duties of the said Office,[7] the Same shall devolve on the Vice President, and the Congress may by Law provide for the Case of Removal, Death, Resignation or Inability, both of the President and Vice President, declaring what Officer shall then act as President, and such Officer shall act accordingly, until the Disability be removed, or a President shall be elected.

The President shall, at stated Times, receive for his Services, a Compensation, which shall neither be encreased nor diminished during the Period for which he shall have been elected, and he shall not receive within that Period any other Emolument from the United States, or any of them.

Before he enter on the Execution of his Office, he shall take the following Oath or Affirmation:—"I do solemnly swear (or affirm) that I will faithfully execute the Office of President of the United States, and will to the best of my Ability, preserve, protect and defend the Constitution of the United States."

Section 2. The President shall be Commander in Chief of the Army and Navy of the United States, and of the Militia of the several States, when called into the actual Service of the United States; he may require the Opinion, in writing, of the principal Officer in each of the executive Departments, upon any Subject relating to the Duties of their respective Offices, and he shall have Power to grant Reprieves and Pardons for Offences against the United States, except in Cases of Impeachment.

He shall have Power, by and with the Advice and Consent of the Senate, to make Treaties, provided two thirds of the Senators present concur; and he shall nominate, and by and with the Advice and Consent of the Senate, shall appoint Ambassadors, other public Ministers and Consuls, Judges of the supreme Court, and all other Officers of the United States, whose Appointments are not herein otherwise provided for, and which shall be established by Law: but the Congress may by Law vest the Appointment of such inferior Officers, as they think proper, in the President alone, in the Courts of Law, or in the Heads of Departments.

The President shall have Power to fill up all Vacancies that may happen during the Recess of the Senate, by granting Commissions which shall expire at the End of their next Session.

Section 3. He shall from time to time give to the Congress Information of the State of the Union, and recommend to their Consideration such Measures as he shall judge necessary and expedient; he may, on extraordinary Occasions, convene both Houses, or either of them, and in Case of Disagreement between them, with Respect to the Time of Adjournment, he may adjourn them to such Time as he shall think proper; he shall receive Ambassadors and other public Ministers; he shall take Care that the Laws be faithfully executed, and shall Commission all the Officers of the United States.

Section 4. The President, Vice President and all civil Officers of the United States, shall be removed from Office on Impeachment for, and Conviction of, Treason, Bribery, or other high Crimes and Misdemeanors.

ARTICLE III

Section 1. The judicial Power of the United States, shall be vested in one supreme Court, and in such inferior Courts as the Congress may from time to time ordain and establish. The Judges, both of the supreme and inferior Courts, shall hold their Offices during good Behaviour, and shall, at stated Times, receive for their Services, a Compensation, which shall not be diminished during their Continuance in Office.

Section 2. The judicial Power shall extend to all Cases, in Law and Equity, arising under this Constitution, the Laws of the United States, and Treaties made, or which shall be made, under their Authority; —to all Cases affecting Ambassadors, other public Ministers and Consuls; —to all Cases of admiralty and maritime Jurisdiction; —to Controversies to which the United States shall be a Party; —to Controversies between two or more States; —between a State and Citizens of another State; —between Citizens of different States; —between Citizens of the same State claiming Lands under Grants of different States, and between a State, or the Citizens thereof, and foreign States, Citizens or Subjects.[8]

In all Cases affecting Ambassadors, other public Ministers and Consuls, and those in which a State shall be Party, the supreme Court shall have original Jurisdiction. In all the other Cases before mentioned, the supreme Court shall have appellate Jurisdiction, both as to Law and Fact, with such Exceptions, and under such Regulations as the Congress shall make.

The Trial of all Crimes, except in Cases of Impeachment, shall be by Jury; and such Trial shall be held in the State where the said Crimes shall have been committed; but when not committed within any State, the Trial shall be at such Place or Places as the Congress may by Law have directed.

Section 3. Treason against the United States, shall consist only in levying War against them, or in adhering to their Enemies, giving them Aid and Comfort. No Person shall be convicted of Treason unless on the Testimony of two Witnesses to the same overt Act, or on Confession in open Court.

The Congress shall have Power to declare the Punishment of Treason, but no Attainder of Treason shall work Corruption of Blood, or Forfeiture except during the Life of the Person attainted.

ARTICLE IV

Section 1. Full Faith and Credit shall be given in each State to the public Acts, Records, and judicial Proceedings of every other State. And the Congress may by general Laws prescribe the Manner in which such Acts, Records and Proceedings shall be proved, and the Effect thereof.

Section 2. The Citizens of each State shall be entitled to all Privileges and Immunities of Citizens in the several States.

A Person charged in any State with Treason, Felony, or other Crime, who shall flee from Justice, and be found in another State, shall on Demand of the executive Authority of the State from which he fled, be delivered up, to be removed to the State having Jurisdiction of the Crime.

[No Person held to Service or Labour in one State, under the Laws thereof, escaping into another, shall, in Consequence of any Law or Regulation therein, be discharged from such Service or Labour, but shall be delivered up on Claim of the Party to whom such Service or Labour may be due.][9]

Section 3. New States may be admitted by the Congress into this Union; but no new State shall be formed or erected within the Jurisdiction of any other State; nor any State be formed by the Junction of two or more States, or Parts of States, without the Consent of the Legislatures of the States concerned as well as of the Congress.

The Congress shall have Power to dispose of and make all needful Rules and Regulations respecting the Territory or other Property belonging to the United States; and nothing in this Constitution shall be so construed as to Prejudice any Claims of the United States, or of any particular State.

Section 4. The United States shall guarantee to every State in this Union a Republican Form of Government, and shall protect each of them against Invasion; and on Application of the Legislature, or of the Executive (when the Legislature cannot be convened) against domestic Violence.

ARTICLE V

The Congress, whenever two thirds of both Houses shall deem it necessary, shall propose Amendments to this Constitution, or, on the Application of the Legislatures of two thirds of the several States, shall call a Convention for proposing Amendments, which, in either Case, shall be valid to all Intents and Purposes, as Part of this Constitution, when ratified by the Legislatures of three fourths of the several States, or by Conventions in three fourths thereof, as the one or the other Mode of Ratification may be proposed by the Congress; Provided [that no Amendment which may be made prior to the Year One thousand eight hundred and eight shall in any Manner affect the first and fourth Clauses in the Ninth Section of the first Article; and][10] that no State, without its Consent, shall be deprived of its equal Suffrage in the Senate.

ARTICLE VI

All Debts contracted and Engagements entered into, before the Adoption of this Constitution, shall be as valid against the United States under this Constitution, as under the Confederation.

This Constitution, and the Laws of the United States which shall be made in Pursuance thereof; and all Treaties made, or which shall be made, under the Authority of the United States, shall be the supreme Law of the Land; and the Judges in every State shall be bound thereby, any Thing in the Constitution or Laws of any State to the Contrary notwithstanding.

The Senators and Representatives before mentioned, and the Members of the several State Legislatures, and all executive and judicial Officers, both of the United States and of the several States, shall be bound by Oath or Affirmation, to support this Constitution; but no religious Test shall ever be required as a Qualification to any Office or public Trust under the United States.

ARTICLE VII

The Ratification of the Conventions of nine States, shall be sufficient for the Establishment of this Constitution between the States so ratifying the Same.

Done in Convention by the Unanimous Consent of the States present the Seventeenth Day of September in the Year of our Lord one thousand seven hundred and Eighty seven and of the Independence of the United States of America the Twelfth. IN WITNESS whereof We have hereunto subscribed our Names,

George Washington, President and deputy from Virginia, and thirty-eight other delegates.

[The language of the original Constitution, not including the Amendments, was adopted by a convention of the states on September 17, 1787, and was subsequently ratified by the states on the following dates: Delaware, December 7, 1787; Pennsylvania, December 12, 1787; New Jersey, December 18, 1787; Georgia, January 2, 1788; Connecticut, January 9, 1788; Massachusetts, February 6, 1788; Maryland, April 28, 1788; South Carolina, May 23, 1788; New Hampshire, June 21, 1788.

Ratification was completed on June 21, 1788.

The Constitution subsequently was ratified by Virginia, June 25, 1788; New York, July 26, 1788; North Carolina, November 21, 1789; Rhode Island, May 29, 1790; and Vermont, January 10, 1791.]

AMENDMENTS
AMENDMENT I

(First ten amendments ratified December 15, 1791.)

Congress shall make no law respecting an establishment of religion, or prohibiting the free exercise thereof; or abridging the freedom of speech, or of the press; or the right of the people peaceably to assemble, and to petition the Government for a redress of grievances.

AMENDMENT II

A well regulated Militia, being necessary to the security of a free State, the right of the people to keep and bear Arms, shall not be infringed.

AMENDMENT III

No Soldier shall, in time of peace be quartered in any house, without the consent of the Owner, nor in time of war, but in a manner to be prescribed by law.

AMENDMENT IV

The right of the people to be secure in their persons, houses, papers, and effects, against unreasonable searches and seizures, shall not be violated, and no Warrants shall issue, but upon probable cause, supported by Oath or affirmation, and particularly describing the place to be searched, and the persons or things to be seized.

AMENDMENT V

No person shall be held to answer for a capital, or otherwise infamous crime, unless on a presentment or indictment of a Grand Jury, except in cases arising in the land or naval forces, or in the Militia, when in actual service in time of War or public danger; nor shall any person be subject for the same offence to be twice put in jeopardy of life or limb; nor shall be compelled in any criminal case to be a witness against himself, nor be deprived of life, liberty, or property, without due process of law; nor shall private property be taken for public use, without just compensation.

AMENDMENT VI

In all criminal prosecutions, the accused shall enjoy the right to a speedy and public trial, by an impartial jury of the State and district wherein the crime shall have been committed, which district shall have been previously ascertained by law, and to be informed of the nature and cause of the accusation; to be confronted with the witnesses against him; to have compulsory process for obtaining witnesses in his favor, and to have the Assistance of Counsel for his defence.

AMENDMENT VII

In Suits at common law, where the value in controversy shall exceed twenty dollars, the right of trial by jury shall be preserved, and no fact tried by a jury, shall be otherwise re-examined in any Court of the United States, than according to the rules of the common law.

AMENDMENT VIII

Excessive bail shall not be required, nor excessive fines imposed, nor cruel and unusual punishments inflicted.

AMENDMENT IX

The enumeration in the Constitution, of certain rights, shall not be construed to deny or disparage others retained by the people.

AMENDMENT X

The powers not delegated to the United States by the Constitution, nor prohibited by it to the States, are reserved to the States respectively, or to the people.

AMENDMENT XI (RATIFIED FEBRUARY 7, 1795)

The Judicial power of the United States shall not be construed to extend to any suit in law or equity, commenced or prosecuted against one of the United States by Citizens of another State, or by Citizens or Subjects of any Foreign State.

AMENDMENT XII (RATIFIED JUNE 15, 1804)

The Electors shall meet in their respective states and vote by ballot for President and Vice-President, one of whom, at least, shall not be an inhabitant of the same state with themselves; they shall name in their ballots the person voted for as President, and in distinct ballots the person voted for as Vice-President, and they shall make distinct lists of all persons voted for as President, and of all persons voted for as Vice-President, and of the number of votes for each, which lists they shall sign and certify, and transmit sealed to the seat of the government of the United States, directed to the President of the Senate; — The President of the Senate shall, in the presence of the Senate and House of Representatives, open all the certificates and the votes shall then be counted; — The person having the greatest number of votes for President, shall be the President, if such number be a majority of the whole number of Electors appointed; and if no person have such majority, then from the persons having the highest numbers not exceeding three on the list of those voted for as President, the House of Representatives shall choose immediately, by ballot, the President. But in choosing the President, the votes shall be taken by states, the representation from each state having one vote; a quorum for this purpose shall consist of a member or members from two-thirds of the states, and a majority of all the states shall be necessary to a choice. [And if the House of

Representatives shall not choose a President whenever the right of choice shall devolve upon them, before the fourth day of March next following, then the Vice-President shall act as President, as in the case of the death or other constitutional disability of the President. —][11] The person having the greatest number of votes as Vice-President, shall be the Vice-President, if such number be a majority of the whole number of Electors appointed, and if no person have a majority, then from the two highest numbers on the list, the Senate shall choose the Vice-President; a quorum for the purpose shall consist of two-thirds of the whole number of Senators, and a majority of the whole number shall be necessary to a choice. But no person constitutionally ineligible to the office of President shall be eligible to that of Vice-President of the United States.

AMENDMENT XIII
(RATIFIED DECEMBER 6, 1865)

Section 1. Neither slavery nor involuntary servitude, except as a punishment for crime whereof the party shall have been duly convicted, shall exist within the United States, or any place subject to their jurisdiction.

Section 2. Congress shall have power to enforce this article by appropriate legislation.

AMENDMENT XIV
(RATIFIED JULY 9, 1868)

Section 1. All persons born or naturalized in the United States, and subject to the jurisdiction thereof, are citizens of the United States and of the State wherein they reside. No State shall make or enforce any law which shall abridge the privileges or immunities of citizens of the United States; nor shall any State deprive any person of life, liberty, or property, without due process of law; nor deny to any person within its jurisdiction the equal protection of the laws.

Section 2. Representatives shall be apportioned among the several States according to their respective numbers, counting the whole number of persons in each State, excluding Indians not taxed. But when the right to vote at any election for the choice of electors for President and Vice President of the United States, Representatives in Congress, the Executive and Judicial officers of a State, or the members of the Legislature thereof, is denied to any of the male inhabitants of such State, being twenty-one years of age,[12] and citizens of the United States, or in any way abridged, except for participation in rebellion, or other crime, the basis of representation therein shall be reduced in the proportion which the number of such male citizens shall bear to the whole number of male citizens twenty-one years of age in such State.

Section 3. No person shall be a Senator or Representative in Congress, or elector of President and Vice President, or hold any Office, civil or military, under the United States, or under any State, who, having previously taken an oath, as a member of Congress, or as an officer of the United States, or as a member of any State legislature, or as an executive or judicial officer of any State, to support the Constitution of the United States, shall have engaged in insurrection or rebellion against the same, or given aid or comfort to the enemies thereof. But Congress may by a vote of two-thirds of each House, remove such disability.

Section 4. The validity of the public debt of the United States, authorized by law, including debts incurred for payment of pensions and bounties for services in suppressing insurrection or rebellion, shall not be questioned. But neither the United States nor any State shall assume or pay any debt or obligation incurred in aid of insurrection or rebellion against the United States, or any claim for the loss or emancipation of any slave; but all such debts, obligations and claims shall be held illegal and void.

Section 5. The Congress shall have power to enforce, by appropriate legislation, the provisions of this article.

AMENDMENT XV
(RATIFIED FEBRUARY 3, 1870)

Section 1. The right of citizens of the United States to vote shall not be denied or abridged by the United States or by any State on account of race, color, or previous condition of servitude.

Section 2. The Congress shall have power to enforce this article by appropriate legislation.

AMENDMENT XVI
(RATIFIED FEBRUARY 3, 1913)

The Congress shall have power to lay and collect taxes on incomes, from whatever source derived, without apportionment among the several States, and without regard to any census or enumeration.

AMENDMENT XVII
(RATIFIED APRIL 8, 1913)

The Senate of the United States shall be composed of two Senators from each State, elected by the people thereof, for six years; and each Senator shall have one vote. The electors in each State shall have the qualifications requisite for electors of the most numerous branch of the State legislatures.

When vacancies happen in the representation of any State in the Senate, the executive authority of such State shall issue writs of election to fill such vacancies: Provided, That the legislature of any State may empower the executive thereof to make temporary appointments until the people fill the vacancies by election as the legislature may direct.

This amendment shall not be so construed as to affect the election or term of any Senator chosen before it becomes valid as part of the Constitution.

AMENDMENT XVIII
(RATIFIED JANUARY 16, 1919)

Section 1. After one year from the ratification of this article the manufacture, sale, or transportation of intoxicating liquors within, the importation thereof into, or the exportation thereof from the United States and all territory subject to the jurisdiction thereof for beverage purposes is hereby prohibited.

Section 2. The Congress and the several States shall have concurrent power to enforce this article by appropriate legislation.

Section 3. This article shall be inoperative unless it shall have been ratified as an amendment to the Constitution by the legislatures of the several States, as provided in the Constitution, within seven years from the date of the submission hereof to the States by the Congress.[13]

AMENDMENT XIX
(RATIFIED AUGUST 18, 1920)

The right of citizens of the United States to vote shall not be denied or abridged by the United States or by any State on account of sex.

Congress shall have power to enforce this article by appropriate legislation.

AMENDMENT XX
(RATIFIED JANUARY 23, 1933)

Section 1. The terms of the President and Vice President shall end at noon on the 20th day of January, and the terms of Senators and Representatives at noon on the 3d day of January, of the years in which such terms would have ended if this article had not been ratified; and the terms of their successors shall then begin.

Section 2. The Congress shall assemble at least once in every year, and such meeting shall begin at noon on the 3d day of January, unless they shall by law appoint a different day.

Section 3.[14] If, at the time fixed for the beginning of the term of the President, the President elect shall have died, the Vice President elect shall become President. If a President shall not have been chosen before the time fixed for the beginning of his term, or if the President elect shall have failed to qualify, then the Vice President elect shall act as President until a President shall have qualified; and the Congress may by law provide for the case wherein neither a President elect nor a Vice President elect shall have qualified, declaring who shall then act as President, or the manner in which one who is to act shall be selected, and such person shall act accordingly until a President or Vice President shall have qualified.

Section 4. The Congress may by law provide for the case of the death of any of the persons from whom the House of Representatives may choose a President whenever the right of choice shall have devolved upon them, and for the case of the death of any of the persons from whom the Senate may choose a Vice President whenever the right of choice shall have devolved upon them.

Section 5. Sections 1 and 2 shall take effect on the 15th day of October following the ratification of this article.

Section 6. This article shall be inoperative unless it shall have been ratified as an amendment to the Constitution by the legislatures of three-fourths of the several States within seven years from the date of its submission.

AMENDMENT XXI (RATIFIED DECEMBER 5, 1933)

Section 1. The eighteenth article of amendment to the Constitution of the United States is hereby repealed.

Section 2. The transportation or importation into any State, Territory, or possession of the United States for delivery or use therein of intoxicating liquors, in violation of the laws thereof, is hereby prohibited.

Section 3. This article shall be inoperative unless it shall have been ratified as an amendment to the Constitution by conventions in the several States, as provided in the Constitution, within seven years from the date of the submission hereof to the States by the Congress.

AMENDMENT XXII (RATIFIED FEBRUARY 27, 1951)

Section 1. No person shall be elected to the office of the President more than twice, and no person who has held the office of President, or acted as President, for more than two years of a term to which some other person was elected President shall be elected to the office of the President more than once. But this Article shall not apply to any person holding the office of President when this Article was proposed by the Congress, and shall not prevent any person who may be holding the office of President, or acting as President, during the term within which this Article becomes operative from holding the office of President or acting as President during the remainder of such term.

Section 2. This article shall be inoperative unless it shall have been ratified as an amendment to the Constitution by the legislatures of three-fourths of the several States within seven years from the date of its submission to the States by the Congress.

AMENDMENT XXIII (RATIFIED MARCH 29, 1961)

Section 1. The District constituting the seat of Government of the United States shall appoint in such manner as the Congress may direct:

A number of electors of President and Vice President equal to the whole number of Senators and Representatives in Congress to which the District would be entitled if it were a State, but in no event more than the least populous State; they shall be in addition to those appointed by the States, but they shall be considered, for the purposes of the election of President and Vice President, to be electors appointed by a State; and they shall meet in the District and perform such duties as provided by the twelfth article of amendment.

Section 2. The Congress shall have power to enforce this article by appropriate legislation.

AMENDMENT XXIV (RATIFIED JANUARY 23, 1964)

Section 1. The right of citizens of the United States to vote in any primary or other election for President or Vice President, for electors for President or Vice President, or for Senator or Representative in Congress, shall not be denied or abridged by the United States or any State by reason of failure to pay any poll tax or other tax.

Section 2. The Congress shall have power to enforce this article by appropriate legislation.

AMENDMENT XXV
(RATIFIED FEBRUARY 10, 1967)

Section 1. In case of the removal of the President from office or of his death or resignation, the Vice President shall become President.

Section 2. Whenever there is a vacancy in the office of the Vice President, the President shall nominate a Vice President who shall take office upon confirmation by a majority vote of both Houses of Congress.

Section 3. Whenever the President transmits to the President pro tempore of the Senate and the Speaker of the House of Representatives his written declaration that he is unable to discharge the powers and duties of his office, and until he transmits to them a written declaration to the contrary, such powers and duties shall be discharged by the Vice President as Acting President.

Section 4. Whenever the Vice President and a majority of either the principal officers of the executive departments or of such other body as Congress may by law provide, transmit to the President pro tempore of the Senate and the Speaker of the House of Representatives their written declaration that the President is unable to discharge the powers and duties of his office, the Vice President shall immediately assume the powers and duties of the office as Acting President.

Thereafter, when the President transmits to the President pro tempore of the Senate and the Speaker of the House of Representatives his written declaration that no inability exists, he shall resume the powers and duties of his office unless the Vice President and a majority of either the principal officers of the executive departments or of such other body as Congress may by law provide, transmit within four days to the President pro tempore of the Senate and the Speaker of the House of Representatives their written declaration that the President is unable to discharge the powers and duties of his office. Thereupon Congress shall decide the issue, assembling within forty-eight hours for that purpose if not in session. If the Congress, within twenty-one days after receipt of the latter written declaration, or, if Congress is not in session, within twenty-one days after Congress is required to assemble, determines by two-thirds vote of both Houses that the President is unable to discharge the powers and duties of his office, the Vice President shall continue to discharge the same as Acting President; otherwise, the President shall resume the powers and duties of his office.

AMENDMENT XXVI
(RATIFIED JULY 1, 1971)

Section 1. The right of citizens of the United States, who are eighteen years of age or older, to vote shall not be denied or abridged by the United States or by any State on account of age.

Section 2. The Congress shall have power to enforce this article by appropriate legislation.

AMENDMENT XXVII
(RATIFIED MAY 7, 1992)

No law varying the compensation for the services of the Senators and Representatives shall take effect, until an election of Representatives shall have intervened.

Source: U.S. Congress, House, Committee on the Judiciary, The Constitution of the United States of America, as Amended, 100th Cong., 1st sess., 1987, H Doc 100-94.

NOTES

1. The part in brackets was changed by section 2 of the Fourteenth Amendment.
2. The part in brackets was changed by the first paragraph of the Seventeenth Amendment.
3. The part in brackets was changed by the second paragraph of the Seventeenth Amendment.
4. The part in brackets was changed by section 2 of the Twentieth Amendment.
5. The Sixteenth Amendment gave Congress the power to tax incomes.
6. The material in brackets was superseded by the Twelfth Amendment.

7. This provision was affected by the Twenty-fifth Amendment.
8. These clauses were affected by the Eleventh Amendment.
9. This paragraph was superseded by the Thirteenth Amendment.
10. Obsolete.
11. The part in brackets was superseded by Section 3 of the Twentieth Amendment.
12. See the Nineteenth and Twenty-sixth Amendments.
13. This amendment was repealed by Section 1 of the Twenty-first Amendment.
14. See the Twenty-fifth Amendment.

NOTES

CHAPTER 1

1. Emily Witt, "How the Survivors of Parkland Began the Never Again Movement," *The New Yorker*, February 19, 2018, www.newyorker.com/news/news-desk/how-the-survivors-of-parkland-began-the-never-again-movement.
2. Dahlia Lithwick, "They Were Trained for This Moment," *Slate*, February 28, 2018, slate.com/news-and-politics/2018/02/the-student-activists-of-marjory-stoneman-douglas-high-demonstrate-the-power-of-a-full-education.html.
3. Asma Khalid, "A New Generation's Political Awakening," NPR, April 21, 2018, www.npr.org/2018/04/21/604293152/a-new-generations-political-awakening.
4. Jonathan Bernstein, "Let Teenagers Vote," Bloomberg, February 21, 2018, www.bloomberg.com/view/articles/2018-02-21/expand-u-s-voting-rights-to-teenagers; Jonathan Bernstein, "Democracy Demands We Let Teenagers Vote," Bloomberg, March 13, 2018, www.bloomberg.com/view/articles/2018-03-13/democracy-demands-we-let-teenagers-get-the-vote.
5. E. J. Dionne, *Why Americans Hate Politics* (New York: Simon & Schuster, 1991), 354, 355.
6. Harold D. Lasswell, *Politics: Who Gets What, When, How* (New York: McGraw-Hill, 1938).
7. Joseph A. Schumpeter, *Capitalism, Socialism, and Democracy*, 3rd ed. (New York: Harper Colophon Books, 1950), 269–296.
8. Robert A. Dahl, *Pluralist Democracy in the United States* (Chicago, Ill.: Rand McNally, 1967).
9. Carole Pateman, *Participation and Democratic Theory* (New York: Cambridge University Press, 1970).
10. Bruce E. Johansen, *Forgotten Founders: Benjamin Franklin, the Iroquois and the Rationale for the American Revolution* (Ipswich, Mass.: Gambit, Inc., 1982).
11. Eli Pariser, "Beware Online 'Filter Bubbles,'" March 2011, www.ted.com/talks/eli_pariser_beware_online_filter_bubbles?language=en; Mandy Zibart, "How to Escape Your News Bubble," January 21, 2016, medium.com/extra-extra/how-to-escape-your-news-bubble-3187c83fa481#.5wbplmiye.
12. "The Danger of the Social Media Information Bubble," *Science Daily*, democracychronicles.com/social-media-information/.
13. Pariser, "Beware Online 'Filter Bubbles.'"
14. Philip Bump, "Why the Trump Administration Bears the Blame for Separating Children From Their Families at the Border," *Washington Post*, June 15, 2018, www.washingtonpost.com/news/politics/wp/2018/06/15/why-the-trump-administration-bears-the-blame-for-separating-children-from-their-families-at-the-border/.
15. *Graham v. Richardson*, 403 U.S. 532 (1971).
16. See, for instance, Nicole Cusano, "Amherst Mulls Giving Non-Citizens Right to Vote," *Boston Globe*, October 26, 1998, B1; "Casual Citizenship?" editorial, *Boston Globe*, October 31, 1998, A18.
17. Kate Zernike and Megan Thee-Brenan, "Poll Finds Tea Party Backers Wealthier and More Educated," *New York Times*, April 14, 2010.
18. Amanda Taub, "The Rise of American Authoritarianism," *Vox*, March 1, 2016, www.vox.com/2016/3/1/11127424/trump-authoritarianism.
19. NYU professor Jonathan Haidt, quoted in Taub, "The Rise of American Authoritarianism."
20. Matt Grossmann, "Racial Attitudes and Political Correctness in the 2016 Presidential Election," Niskanen Center, May 10, 2018, niskanencenter.org/blog/racial-attitudes-and-political-correctness-in-the-2016-presidential-election/.
21. Benjamin R. Barber, "Foreword," in Grant Reeher and Joseph Cammarano, eds., *Education for Citizenship: Ideas and Innovations in Political Learning* (New York: Rowman & Littlefield, 1997), ix.

CHAPTER 2

1. Kirk Johnson, Richard Pérez-Peña, and Erik Eckholm, "Cautious Response to Armed Oregon Protest," *New York Times*, January 4, 2016, www.nytimes.com/2016/01/05/us/in-oregon-law-enforcement-faces-dilemma-in-confronting-armed-group.html; Julie Turkewitz and Kirk Johnson, "Ammon Bundy and 7 Oregon Protesters Held; La Voy Finicum Is Reported Dead," *New York Times*, January 27, 2016, www.nytimes.com/2016/01/27/us/oregon-armed-group-arrest-bundy.html; Associated Press, "In Total Surrender, Ammon Bundy Urges Followers to Stand Down," *New York Post*, January 28, 2016, nypost.com/2016/01/28/in-total-surrender-ammon-bundy-urges-followers-to-stand-down/.
2. David Barstow, "Tea Party Lights Fuse for Rebellion on Right," *New York Times*, February 15, 2010, www.nytimes.com/2010/02/16/us/politics/16teaparty.html.
3. Tea Party, "About Us," www.teaparty.org/about-us/.
4. "Lubbock Co. Judge Warns of Potential Danger If Obama Is Re-elected," Fox 34 News, August 23, 2012, www.myfoxlubbock.com/news/local/story/Lubbock-tom-head-tax-rates-president-obama/PeO4Q8GeGEiy_FpxheUnmA.cspx.
5. Toni Lucy, "Anti-Government Forces Still Struggle to Recover From Oklahoma City Fallout," *USA Today*, May 9, 2000, 9A; Evan Thomas and Eve Conant, "Hate: Antigovernment Extremists Are on the Rise—and On the March," *Newsweek*, April 19, 2010.
6. See, for example, Jamelle Bouie, "How Trump Happened," March 13, 2016, www.slate.com/articles/news_and_politics/cover_story/2016/03/how_donald_trump_happened_racism_against_barack_obama.single.html.
7. There are many good illustrations of this point of view. See, for example, Gordon Wood, *The Creation of the American Republic, 1776–1787* (New York: Norton, 1969); Lawrence Henry Gipson, *The Coming of the Revolution, 1763–1775* (New York: Harper Torchbooks, 1962); Bernard Bailyn, *The Ideological Origins of the American Revolution* (Cambridge, Mass.: Belknap, 1967); and Jack P. Greene, ed., *The Reinterpretation of the American Revolution, 1763–1789* (New York: Harper and Row, 1968).
8. Cited in John L. Moore, *Speaking of Washington* (Washington, D.C.: Congressional Quarterly Press, 1993), 102–103.
9. John Locke, *A Second Treatise of Government*, C. B. Macpherson, ed. (Indianapolis, Ind.: Hackett, 1980), 31.
10. Donald R. Wright, *African Americans in the Colonial Era* (Arlington Heights, Ill.: Harlan Davidson, 1990), 122.
11. Ibid., 152.
12. Mary Beth Norton et al., *A People and a Nation* (Boston: Houghton Mifflin, 1994), 159.

13. Robert Darcy, Susan Welch, and Janet Clark, *Women, Elections, and Representation* (Lincoln: University of Nebraska Press, 1994), 8.

14. See, for example, Sally Smith Booth, *The Women of '76* (New York: Hastings House, 1973); and Charles E. Claghorn, *Women Patriots of the American Revolution: A Biographical Dictionary* (Metuchen, N.J.: Scarecrow Press, 1991).

15. Carl Holliday, *Woman's Life in Colonial Days* (Boston: Cornhill, 1922), 143.

16. Wood, *Creation of the American Republic*, 398–399.

17. Ibid.

18. Ibid., 404.

19. Alexander Hamilton, James Madison, and John Jay, *The Federalist Papers*, Clinton Rossiter, ed. (New York: New American Library, 1961), 84.

20. James Madison, *Notes of Debates in the Federal Convention of 1787* (New York: Norton, 1969), 86.

21. Baron de Montesquieu, *The Spirit of the Laws*, Thomas Nugent, trans. (New York: Hafner Press, 1949), 152.

22. *The Economist*, "America Might See a New Constitutional Convention in a Few Years," September 30, 2017, www.economist.com/news/briefing/21729735-if-it-did-would-be-dangerous-thing-america-might-see-new-constitutional-convention; Dennis Welch, "Lawmakers Converge on State Capitol to Talk Constitutional Convention," *AZ Family*, September 12, 2017, www.azfamily.com/story/36351851/lawmakers-converge-on-state-capitol-to-talk-constitutional-convention.

23. There are many collections of Anti-Federalist writings. See, for example, W. B. Allen and Gordon Lloyd, eds., *The Essential Antifederalist* (Lanham, Md.: University Press of America, 1985); Cecilia Kenyon, ed., *The Antifederalists* (Indianapolis, Ind.: Bobbs-Merrill, 1966); and Ralph Ketcham, *The Anti-Federalist Papers and the Constitutional Convention Debates* (New York: New American Library, 1986).

24. Clinton Rossiter, "Introduction," in Hamilton, Madison, and Jay, *Federalist Papers*, vii.

25. Hamilton, Madison, and Jay, *Federalist Papers*, 322.

26. Ketcham, *Anti-Federalist Papers*, 14.

27. Carl Hulse, "Recalling 1995 Bombing, Clinton Sees Parallels," *New York Times*, April 16, 2010.

CHAPTER 3

1. Andrew Harris, "Marijuana Mayhem Splits U.S. in Two as States Like Idaho Bust Travelers," *Idaho Statesman*, August 22, 2014, www.idahostatesman.com/2014/08/22/3336621/marijuana-mayhem-splits-us-in.html.

2. Dave Phillips, "Bid to Expand Medical Marijuana Business Faces Federal Hurdles," *New York Times*, August 23, 2014, www.nytimes.com/2014/08/24/us/bid-to-expand-medical-marijuana-business-faces-federal-hurdles.html; Joel Warner, "Charlotte's Web: Untangling One of Colorado's Biggest Cannabis Success Stories," *Westword*, December 3, 2014, www.westword.com/news/charlottes-web-untangling-one-of-colorados-biggest-cannabis-success-stories-6050830; Saundra Young, "Marijuana Stops Child's Severe Seizures," CNN, August 7, 2013, www.cnn.com/2013/08/07/health/charlotte-child-medical-marijuana/index.html.

3. James Higdon, "How a Pair of Kentucky Pols Are About to Legalize Hemp," *Politico*, August 4, 2018, https://www.politico.com/magazine/story/2018/08/04/mcconnell-comer-legalize-hemp-marijuana-kentucky-219156.

4. Carrie Johnson, "U.S. Eases Stance on Medical Marijuana," *Washington Post*, October 20, 2009.

5. Matt Laslo, "Why Is the White House Contradicting Trump's Pot Policy?," *Rolling Stone*, August 30, 2018, https://www.rollingstone.com/politics/politics-news/why-is-the-white-house-contradicting-trumps-pot-policy-717524/.

6. Lindsey Seavert, "Mom Charged After Giving Son Medical Marijuana," KARE (NBC affiliate), Minneapolis, MN, August 20, 2014, www.kare11.com/story/news/local/2014/08/20/mn-mom-charged-after-giving-son-medical-marijuana/14372025/.

7. Juliet Lapidos, "The Public Lightens Up About Weed," *New York Times*, July 26, 2014, www.nytimes.com/2014/07/27/opinion/sunday/high-time-the-public-lightens-up-about-weed.html.

8. For a full explanation of the bakery metaphors, see Morton Grodzins, *The American System* (Chicago, Ill.: Rand-McNally, 1966). A more updated discussion of federalism can be found in Joseph Zimmerman, *Contemporary American Federalism: The Growth of National Power* (New York: Praeger, 1992).

9. Justice Louis Brandeis, *New State Ice Co. v. Liebmann*, 285 U.S. 262 (1932).

10. Eliza Griswold, "The Fracturing of Pennsylvania," *New York Times*, November 11, 2011; Wenonah Hauter, "For Democrats Nationwide, Pennsylvania Offers a Lens on the Widening Rift Over Fracking," The Bog, Huff Post Politics, September 25, 2013, www.huffingtonpost.com/weno-nah-hauter/for-democrats-nationwide-_b_3981518.html.

11. James Dao, "Red, Blue and Angry All Over," *New York Times*, January 16, 2005.

12. *McCulloch v. Maryland*, 4 Wheat. 316 (1819).

13. *Gibbons v. Ogden*, 9 Wheat. 1 (1824).

14. *Cooley v. Board of Wardens of Port of Philadelphia*, 53 U.S. (12 How.) 299 (1851).

15. *Dred Scott v. Sanford*, 60 U.S. 393 (1857).

16. *Pollock v. Farmer's Loan and Trust Co.*, 1157 U.S. 429 (1895).

17. *Lochner v. New York*, 198 U.S. 45 (1905).

18. *Hammer v. Dagenhart*, 247 U.S. 251 (1918).

19. John Kincaid, "State-Federal Relations: Dueling Policies," in *The Book of the States 2008* (Lexington, Ky.: The Council of State Governments, 2008), 19.

20. Ibid.

21. Morris Fiorina, *Congress: Keystone of the Washington Establishment*, 2nd ed. (New Haven, Conn.: Yale University Press, 1989); John E. Chubb, "Federalism and the Bias for Centralization," in John E. Chubb and Paul E. Peterson, eds., *The New Directions in American Politics* (Washington, D.C.: Brookings Institution, 1985), 273–306.

22. U.S. Census Bureau, *Statistical Abstract of the United States, 2010* (Washington, D.C.: U.S. Census Bureau), Table 419.

23. Quote from Rochelle L. Stanfield, "Holding the Bag," *National Journal*, September 9, 1995, 2206.

24. David Walker, *The Rebirth of Federalism* (Chatham, N.J.: Chatham House, 1995), 232–234; Kincaid, "State-Federal Relations."

25. Martha Derthick, "Madison's Middle Ground in the 1980s," *Public Administration Review* (January–February 1987): 66–74.

26. Donald F. Kettl, "Mandates Forever," *Governing* (August 2003): 12; Tom Diemer, "Unfunded Mandate Bill Working Well," *Cleveland Plain Dealer*, February 8, 1998, 20A; Jonathan Walters, "The Accidental Tyranny of Congress," *Governing* (April 1997): 14.

27. "Keeping America Healthy," www.medicaid.gov/Medicaid-CHIP-Program-Information/By-Topics/Financing-and-Reimbursement/Financing-and-Reimbursement.html.

28. Alison Vekshin, "Tea Party Opposition to Stimulus Will Harm States, Kramer Says," *Business Week*, September 15, 2010, www.businessweek.com/news/2010-09-15/tea-party-opposition-to-stimulus-will-harm-states-kramer-says.html; Jeff Brady, "Stimulus Money Meets Mixed Reactions From States," Weekend Edition, National Public Radio, February 19, 2009, www.npr.org/templates/story/story.php?storyId=100731571; National Conference of State Legislatures, "State Budget Update, March 2011," www.ncsl.org/issues-research/budget/state-budget-update-march-2011.aspx.

29. Stephen C. Fehr, "Recession Could Reshape State Governments in Lasting Ways," Pew Center for the States, February 11, 2010, www.stateline.org/live/details/story?contentId=454018.

30. Ibid.

31. Pickerill J. Mitchell and Cynthia J. Bowling, "Polarized Parties, Politics, and Policies: Fragmented Federalism in 2013–2014," *Publius: The Journal of Federalism* 44 (2014): 369–398; Shanna Rose and Cynthia J. Bowling, "The State of American Federalism 2014–15: Pathways to Policy in an Era of Party Polarization," *Publius: The Journal of Federalism* 45 (2015): 351–379.

32. John Maggs, "Hizzoner, the Pizza Man," *National Journal*, November 21, 1998, 2796–2798.

33. *Gonzales v. Raich*, 545 U.S. 1 (2005).

34. Carrie Johnson, "U.S. Eases Stance on Medical Marijuana," *Washington Post*, October 20, 2009.

35. Jacob Sullum, "The Power to Regulate Anything," *Los Angeles Times*, April 22, 2008.

36. Warren Richey, "Showdown Over Medical Marijuana," *Christian Science Monitor*, November 29, 2004.

CHAPTER 4

1. The White House, "Net Neutrality, President Obama's Plan for a Free and Open Internet," obamawhitehouse.archives.gov/node/323681.

2. "FCC Approves Sweeping Internet Regulation Plan, Obama Accused of Meddling," Foxnews.com, February 26, 2015, www.foxnews.com/politics/2015/02/26/fcc-approves-sweeping-internet-regulation-plan-obama-accused-meddling.html.

3. The White House, "Net Neutrality."

4. Mario Trujillo, "House Passes Bill Barring FCC From Regulating Internet Rates," April 15, 2016, thehill.com/policy/technology/276454-house-passes-bill-barring-fcc-from-regulating-internet-rates.

5. "FCC Approves Sweeping Internet Regulation Plan."

6. Trujillo, "House Passes Bill Barring FCC From Regulating Internet Rates."

7. Jim Puzzanghera, "Senate Takes First Step to Save Net Neutrality Rules, Voting to Overturn FCC Action," *Los Angeles Times*, May 16, 2018, www.latimes.com/business/la-fi-net-neutrality-senate-20180516-story.html.

8. Harper Neidig, "Dems Push to Restore Net Neutrality Rules," *The Hill*, May 6, 2016, thehill.com/policy/technology/386313-dems-push-to-restore-net-neutrality-rules.

9. Ann Bowman and Richard Kearney, *State and Local Government*, 3rd ed. (Boston, Mass.: Houghton Mifflin, 1996), 39.

10. David M. O'Brien, *Constitutional Law and Politics*, vol. 2 (New York: Norton, 1995), 300.

11. *Barron v. The Mayor and City Council of Baltimore*, 7 Peters 243 (1833).

12. *Chicago, Burlington & Quincy Railroad Co. v. Chicago*, 166 U.S. 226 (1897).

13. *Gitlow v. New York*, 268 U.S. 652 (1920), cited in O'Brien, 304.

14. Peter Irons, *Brennan vs. Rehnquist: The Battle for the Constitution* (New York: Knopf, 1994), 116.

15. O'Brien, *Constitutional Law and Politics*, 646.

16. Irons, *Brennan vs. Rehnquist*, 137.

17. *Epperson v. Arkansas*, 393 U.S. 97 (1968); *Abington School District v. Schempp*, 374 U.S. 203, 83 S. Ct. 1560 (1963); *Murray v. Curlett*, 374 U.S. 203 (1963); *Engel v. Vitale*, 370 U.S. 421, 82 S. Ct. 1261 (1962).

18. *Lemon v. Kurtzman*, 403 U.S. 602, 91 S. Ct. 2105 (1971).

19. O'Brien, *Constitutional Law and Politics*, 661.

20. Charles C. Hayes, "State Lawmakers Reignite School Wars Over Religion," The First Amendment Center, at Vanderbilt University and the Newseum, Friday, April 6, 2012, www.firstamendmentcenter.org/state-lawmakers-reignite-school-wars-over-religion.

21. *Cantwell v. Connecticut*, 310 U.S. 296 (1940).

22. *Minersville School District v. Gobitis*, 310 U.S. 586 (1940); *West Virginia State Board of Education v. Barnette*, 319 U.S. 624 (1943).

23. *Sherbert v. Verner*, 374 U.S. 398 (1963).

24. *Employment Division, Department of Human Resources v. Smith*, 494 U.S. 872 (1990).

25. *City of Boerne v. Flores*, 521 U.S. 507 (1997).

26. *Gonzales v. O Centro Espirata Beneficente Uniao do Vegetal*, 546 U.S. 418 (2006).

27. Adam Liptak, "Religious Groups Given 'Exception' to Work Bias Law," *New York Times*, January 11, 2012, www.nytimes.com/2012/01/12/us/supreme-court-recognizes-religious-exception-to-job-discrimination-laws.html.

28. Rodney K. Smith, "Does Obama Really Care About Religious Freedom in America?" *Christian Science Monitor*, February 17, 2012, www.csmonitor.com/Commentary/Opinion/2012/0217/Does-Obama-really-care-about-religious-freedom-in-America.

29. John L. Sullivan, James Piereson, and George Marcus, *Political Tolerance and American Democracy* (Chicago, Ill.: University of Chicago Press, 1982), 203.

30. John Cassidy, "Demonizing Edward Snowden: Which Side Are You On?" *New Yorker* blog, June 24, 2013, www.newyorker.com/online/blogs/johncassidy/2013/06/demonizing-edward-snowden-which-side-are-you-on.html.

31. O'Brien, *Constitutional Law and Politics*, 373; Samuel Walker, *In Defense of American Liberties: A History of the ACLU* (New York: Oxford University Press, 1990), 14.

32. *Schenck v. United States*, 249 U.S. 47 (1919); *Debs v. United States*, 249 U.S. 211 (1919); *Frowerk v. United States*, 249 U.S. 204 (1919); *Abrams v. United States*, 250 U.S. 616 (1919).

33. *Brandenburg v. Ohio*, 395 U.S. 444 (1969).

34. *Street v. New York*, 394 U.S. 576 (1969).

35. *Texas v. Johnson*, 491 U.S. 397 (1989).

36. *United States v. Eichman*, 110 S.Ct. 2404 (1990).

37. *Virginia v. Black*, 538 U.S. 343 (2003).

38. *National Association for the Advancement of Colored People v. Alabama*, 357 U.S. 449 (1958).

39. *Sheldon v. Tucker*, 364 U.S. 516 (1960).

40. *Heart of Atlanta Motel v. United States*, 379 U.S. 241 (1964).

41. *Roberts v. United States Jaycees*, 468 U.S. 609 (1984).

42. *Jacobellis v. Ohio*, 378 U.S. 476 (1964).

43. *Miller v. California*, 413 U.S. 15 (1973).

44. *Cohen v. California*, 403 U.S. 15 (1971).

45. *Brown vs Entertainment Merchants Association* 564 U.S. (2011).

46. *Chaplinsky v. New Hampshire*, 315 U.S. 568 (1942).

47. *Terminello v. Chicago*, 337 U.S. 1 (1949).

48. *Cohen v. California*, 403 U.S. 15 (1971).

49. *Doe v. University of Michigan*, 721 F.Supp. 852 (E.D. Mich. 1989); *UMW Post v. Board of Regents of the University of Wisconsin*, 774 F.Supp. 1163, 1167, 1179 (E.D. Wis. 1991).

50. *R.A.V. v. City of St. Paul*, 60 LW 4667 (1992).

51. *Near v. Minnesota*, 283 U.S. 697 (1930).

52. *New York Times Company v. United States*, 403 U.S. 670 (1971).

53. *New York Times v. Sullivan*, 376 U.S. 254 (1964).

54. *Nebraska Press Association v. Stuart*, 427 U.S. 539 (1976).

55. *Reno v. ACLU*, 521 U.S. 1113 (1997).

56. *Ashcroft v. ACLU*, 124 S. Ct. 2783 (2004).

57. *United States v. American Library Association, Inc.*, 539 U.S. 194 (2003).

58. Pamela LiCalzi O'Connell, "Compressed Data: Law Newsletter Has to Sneak Past Filters," *New York Times*, April 2, 2001, C4.

59. Jeffery Seligno, "Student Writers Try to Duck the Censors by Going On-line," *New York Times*, June 7, 2001, G6.

60. Chloe Albanesius, "After Blackout, Congress Postpones Action on SOPA, PIPA," *PC Magazine*, January 20, 2012, www.pcmag.com/article2/0,2817,2399132,00.asp.

61. Robert J. Spitzer, *The Politics of Gun Control* (Chatham, N.J.: Chatham House, 1995), 47, 49.

62. *United States v. Lopez*, 514 U.S. 549 (1995); *Printz v. United States*, 521 U.S. 898 (1997).

63. Walter Hickey, "How the NRA Became the Most Powerful Special Interest in Washington," *Business Insider*, December 18, 2012, www.businessinsider.com/nra-lobbying-money-national-rifle-association-washington-2012–12.

64. Jugal K. Patel, "After Sandy Hook, More Than 400 People Have Been Shot in Over 200 School Shootings," *New York Times*, February 15, 2018, www.nytimes.com/interactive/2018/02/15/us/school-shootings-sandy-hook-parkland.html.

65. *United States v. Cruikshank*, 92 U.S. 542 (1876); *Presser v. Illinois*, 116 U.S. 252 (1886); *Miller v. Texas*, 153 U.S. 535 (1894); *United States v. Miller*, 307 U.S. 174 (1939).

66. Warren Richey, "Supreme Court Asserts Broad Gun Rights," *Christian Science Monitor*, June 27, 2008.

67. Adam Liptak, "Justices Extend Firearm Rights in 5-to-4 Ruling," *New York Times*, June 28, 2010, www.nytimes.com/2010/06/29/us/29scotus.html.

68. Robert Barnes and Dan Eggen, "Supreme Court Affirms Fundamental Right to Bear Arms," *Washington Post*, June 29, 2010.

69. Fredrick Kunkle, "Virginia Gun-rights Enthusiasts Celebrate Virginia Law on Firearms in Bars," *Washington Post*, July 3, 2010.
70. *Katz v. United States*, 389 U.S. 347 (1967).
71. *Jones v. NY*, 565 U.S. __ (2012).
72. Adam Liptak, "Major Ruling Shields Privacy of Cellphones, *New York Times*, June 25, 2014, www.nytimes.com/2014/06/26/us/supreme-court-cellphones-search-privacy.html.
73. *Skinner v. Railway Labor Executive Association*, 489 U.S. 602 (1989).
74. *Veronia School District v. Acton*, 515 U.S. 646 (1995).
75. Associated Press, "Supreme Court Upholds Invasive Strip Searches," National Public Radio, April 2, 2012, www.npr.org/2012/04/02/149849568/supreme-court-upholds-invasive-strip-searches.
76. *Weeks v. United States*, 232 U.S. 383 (1914).
77. *Wolf v. Colorado*, 338 U.S. 25 (1949).
78. *Mapp v. Ohio*, 367 U.S. 643 (1961).
79. *United States v. Calandra*, 414 U.S. 338 (1974).
80. *United States v. Janis*, 428 U.S. 433 (1976).
81. *Massachusetts v. Sheppard*, 468 U.S. 981 (1984); *United States v. Leon*, 468 U.S. 897 (1984); *Illinois v. Krull*, 480 U.S. 340 (1987).
82. *Herring v. United States*, No. 07–513. Argued October 7, 2008—Decided January 14, 2009.
83. *Miranda v. Arizona*, 382 U.S. 925 (1965); *Dickerson v. United States*, 530 U.S. 428, 120 S. Ct. 2326; 2000 U.S. LEXIS 4305.
84. *Johnson v. Zerbst*, 304 U.S. 458 (1938).
85. *Gideon v. Wainwright*, 372 U.S. 335 (1963).
86. *Ross v. Moffitt*, 417 U.S. 600 (1974); *Murray v. Giarratano*, 492 U.S. 1 (1989).
87. *Atkins v. Georgia*, 536 U.S. 304 (2002); *Roper v. Simmons*, 543 U.S. 551 (2005); *Kennedy v. Louisiana*, No. 07–343. Argued April 16, 2008—Decided June 25, 2008, modified October 1, 2008.
88. *Furman v. Georgia*, 409 U.S. 902 (1972); *Jackson v. Georgia*, 409 U.S. 1122 (1973); *Branch v. Texas*, 408 U.S. 238 (1972).
89. *Gregg v. Georgia*, 428 U.S. 153 (1976); *Woodson v. North Carolina*, 428 U.S. 280 (1976); *Roberts v. Louisiana*, 428 U.S. 325 (1976).
90. *McClesky v. Zant*, 111 S. Ct. 1454 (1991).
91. *Baze v. Rees*, 553 U.S. ___ (2008).
92. Jack Hitt, "The Moratorium Gambit," *New York Times Magazine*, December 9, 2001, 82.
93. Keith Richburg, "New Jersey Approves Abolition of Death Penalty," *Washington Post*, December 14, 2007, A3.
94. Baxter Oliphant, "Support for Death Penalty Lowest in More Than Four Decades," Pew Research Center, September 29, 2016, www.pewresearch.org/fact-tank/2016/09/29/support-for-death-penalty-lowest-in-more-than-four-decades/; Frank Newport, "In U.S., Two-Thirds Continue to Support Death Penalty," October 13, 2009, www.gallup.com/poll/123638/In-U.S.-Two-Thirds-Continue-Support-Death-Penalty.aspx.
95. *Griswold v. Connecticut*, 391 U.S. 145 (1965).
96. *Roe v. Wade*, 410 U.S. 113 (1973).
97. *Harris v. McRae*, 448 U.S. 297 (1980).
98. See, for example, *Webster v. Reproductive Health Services*, 492 U.S. 4090 (1989); *Rust v. Sullivan*, 111 S. Ct. 1759 (1991); and *Gonzales v. Carhart*, 550 U.S. 124 (2007).
99. Jeanne A. Conroy and Nancy L. Stanwood, "In 2014, Why Are We Still Arguing About Birth Control?" CNN, March 25, 2014, www.cnn.com/2014/03/25/opinion/conry-stanwood-contraception-hobby-lobby/.
100. Erik Eckholm, "Push for 'Personhood' Amendment Represents New Tack in Abortion Fight," *New York Times*, October 25, 2011, www.nytimes.com/2011/10/26/us/politics/personhood-amendments-would-ban-nearly-all-abortions.html.
101. Andrew Sullivan, "An Anti-Abortion Frenzy in the States," *The Daily Dish*, April 25, 2012, andrewsullivan.thedailybeast.com/2012/04/an-anti-abortion-frenzy-in-the-states.html; Erik Eckholm and Kim Severson, "Virginia Senate Passes Ultrasound Bill as Other States Take Notice," *New York Times*, February 28, 2012, www.nytimes.com/2012/02/29/us/virginia-senate-passes-revised-ultrasound-bill.html.
102. *Whole Woman's Health et al. v. Hellerstedt, Commissioner, Texas Department of State Health Services, et al.*, www.supremecourt.gov/opinions/15pdf/15-274_p8k0.pdf.
103. *Bowers v. Hardwick*, 478 U.S. 186 (1986).
104. *Lawrence v. Texas*, 539 U.S. 558 (2003).
105. *Romer v. Evans*, 517 U.S. 620 (1996).
106. *Cruzan by Cruzan v. Director, Missouri Department of Health*, 497 U.S. 261 (1990).
107. Soumya Karlamangla, "California's Physician-Assisted Suicide Law Is Overturned—At Least for Now," *Los Angeles Times*, May 25, 2018, www.latimes.com/health/la-me-ln-end-of-life-option-act-20180525-htmlstory.html.

CHAPTER 5

1. Rosie Gray, "Inside a White Nationalist Conference Energized by Trump's Rise," *Buzzfeed*, May 26, 2016, www.buzzfeed.com/rosiegray/inside-a-white-nationalist-conference-energized-by-trumps-ri.
2. Rosie Gray, "How 2015 Fueled the Rise of the Freewheeling, White Nationalist Alt Right Movement," *Buzzfeed*, December 27, 2015, www.buzzfeed.com/rosiegray/how-2015-fueled-the-rise-of-the-freewheeling-white-nationali.
3. Carly Mallenbaum, "Former KKK Grand Wizard David Duke Keeps Tweeting Support for Trump," USA Today, November 9, 2016, www.usatoday.com/story/news/politics/onpolitics/2016/11/09/david-duke-donald-trump-tweet/93526394/.
4. Conor Friedersdorf, "How to Take 'Political Correctness' Away From Donald Trump," *The Atlantic*, February 23, 2016, www.theatlantic.com/politics/archive/2016/02/how-to-take-political-correctness-away-from-donald-trump/470271/.
5. Carly Wayne, Nicholas Valentino, and Marzia Oceno, "How Sexism Drives Support for Donald Trump," *Washington Post*, October 23, 2016, www.washingtonpost.com/news/monkey-cage/wp/2016/10/23/how-sexism-drives-support-for-donald-trump/.
6. Sarah Posner and David Neiwert, "How Trump Took Hate Groups Mainstream," *Mother Jones*, October 14, 2016, www.motherjones.com/politics/2016/10/donald-trump-hate-groups-neo-nazi-white-supremacist-racism/.
7. Ben Jacobs and Oliver Laughland, "Charlottesville: Trump Reverts to Blaming Both Sides Including 'Violent Alt-Left,'" *The Guardian*, August 16, 2017, www.theguardian.com/us-news/2017/aug/15/donald-trump-press-conference-far-right-defends-charlottesville.
8. Cited in Ronald Brownstein, "Trump's Rhetoric of White Nostalgia," *The Atlantic*, June 2, 2016, www.theatlantic.com/politics/archive/2016/06/trumps-rhetoric-of-white-nostalgia/485192/.
9. Carol Graham, "Unhappiness in America," Brookings, May 27, 2016, www.brookings.edu/research/opinions/2016/05/27-unhappiness-in-america-graham.
10. Olga Khazan, "Middle-Aged White Americans Are Dying of Despair," *The Atlantic*, November 4, 2015, www.theatlantic.com/health/archive/2015/11/boomers-deaths-pnas/413971/.
11. Matthew Macwilliams, "The One Weird Trait That Predicts Whether You're a Trump Supporter," *Politico*, January 17, 2016, www.politico.com/magazine/story/2016/01/donald-trump-2016-authoritarian-213533.
12. Wendy Rahn and Eric Oliver, "Trump's Voters Aren't Authoritarians, New Research Says. So What Are They?" *Washington Post*, March 9, 2016, www.washingtonpost.com/news/monkey-cage/wp/2016/03/09/trumps-voters-arent-authoritarians-new-research-says-so-what-are-they/.
13. Michael Tesler, "In a Trump-Clinton Match-up, Racial Prejudice Makes a Striking Difference," *Washington Post*, May 25, 2016, www.washingtonpost.com/news/monkey-cage/wp/2016/05/25/in-a-trump-clinton-match-up-theres-a-striking-effect-of-racial-prejudice/; Michael Tesler, "Trump Is the First Modern Republican to Win the Nomination Based on Racial Prejudice," *Washington Post*, August 1, 2016, www.washingtonpost.com/news/monkey-cage/wp/2016/08/01/trump-is-the-first-republican-in-modern-times-to-win-the-partys-nomination-on-anti-minority-sentiments/.
14. Kathy Kiely, "These Are America's Governors. No Blacks. No Hispanics," *USA Today*, January 21, 2002, 1A.

15. Carol Graham, "Unhappiness in America," Brookings, May 27, 2016, www.brookings.edu/research/opinions/2016/05/27-unhappiness-in-america-graham.

16. David M. O'Brien, *Constitutional Law and Politics*, vol. 2 (New York: Norton, 1991), 1265.

17. American Civil Liberties Union, "Felon Enfranchisement and the Right to Vote," www.aclu.org/votingrights/exoffenders/index.html.

18. Scholars are divided about Lincoln's motives in issuing the Emancipation Proclamation; whether he genuinely desired to end slavery or merely used political means to shorten the war is hard to tell at this distance. Donald G. Nieman, *Promises to Keep: African-Americans and the Constitutional Order, 1776 to the Present* (New York: Oxford University Press, 1991), 55.

19. Bernard A. Weisberger, *Many Papers, One Nation* (Boston, Mass.: Houghton Mifflin Company, 1987), 200.

20. Nieman, *Promises to Keep*, 107.

21. *The Civil Rights Cases*, 109 U.S. 3 (1883).

22. *Plessy v. Ferguson*, 163 U.S. 537 (1896).

23. *Brown v. Board of Education of Topeka (I)*, 347 U.S. 483 (1954).

24. *Brown v. Board of Education of Topeka (II)*, 349 U.S. 294 (1955).

25. *Gayle v. Browder*, 352 U.S. 903 (1956).

26. *Heart of Atlanta Motel, Inc. v. United States*, 379 U.S. 241 (1964); *Katzenbach v. McClung*, 379 U.S. 294 (1964); *Harper v. Virginia Board of Elections*, 383 U.S. 663 (1966).

27. Nieman, *Promises to Keep*, 179.

28. Ibid., 180.

29. *Swann v. Charlotte-Mecklenberg Board of Education*, 402 U.S. 1 (1971).

30. *Milliken v. Bradley*, 418 U.S. 717 (1974).

31. "*Brown v. Board*'s Goals Unrealized," *Atlanta Journal-Constitution*, May 16, 2004, 6C; Gary Orfield and Chungmei Lee, "*Brown* at 50: King's Dream or *Plessy*'s Nightmare?" report conducted by the Harvard Civil Rights Project, 2004, www.civilrightsproject.harvard.edu/research/reseg04/brown50.pdf.

32. *Regents of the University of California v. Bakke*, 438 U.S. 265 (1978).

33. *Patterson v. McLean Credit Union*, 491 U.S. 164 (1989).

34. *Wards Cove Packing, Inc., v. Atonio*, 490 U.S. 642 (1989).

35. *City of Richmond v. J. A. Croson*, 488 U.S. 469 (1989).

36. Pew Research Center for People and the Press, "Public Backs Affirmative Action but Not Minority Preferences," June 2, 2009, www.pewresearch.org/pubs/1240/sotomayor-supreme-court-affirmative-action-minority-preferences.

37. *Gratz v. Bollinger*, 539 U.S. 244 (2003).

38. *Grutter v. Bollinger*, 539 U.S. 306 (2003).

39. Nick Anderson, "How Supreme Court's Michigan Affirmative Action Ruling Affects Colleges," *Washington Post*, April 23, 2014, www.washingtonpost.com/local/education/how-supreme-courts-michigan-affirmative-action-ruling-affects-colleges/2014/04/23/7b0c79ae-cad7-11e3-93eb-6c0037dde2ad_story.html.

40. Robert Barnes, "Supreme Court Upholds University of Texas Affirmative-Action Admissions," *Washington Post*, June 23, 2016, www.washingtonpost.com/politics/courts_law/supreme-court-upholds-university-of-texas-affirmative-action-admissions/2016/06/23/513bcc10-394d-11e6-8f7c-d4c723a2becb_story.html

41. Carmen DeNavas-Walt and Bernadette D. Proctor, "Income and Poverty in the United States: 2014," www.census.gov/content/dam/Census/library/publications/2015/demo/p60-252.pdf; Ruth Simon and Tom McGinty, "Loan Rebound Misses Black Businesses," *Wall Street Journal*, March 14, 2014, http://www.wsj.com/articles/SB10001424052702304585004579417021571596610.

42. Adam Liptak, "Supreme Court Invalidates Key Part of Voting Rights Act," *New York Times*, June 25, 2013, www.nytimes.com/2013/06/26/us/supreme-court-ruling.html.

43. Adam Liptak and Michael Wines, "Strict North Carolina Voter ID Law Thwarted After Supreme Court Rejects Case," May 15, 2017, www.nytimes.com/2017/05/15/us/politics/voter-id-laws-supreme-court-north-carolina.html.

44. National Conference of Black Mayors, "Leadership Development Program," www.aphia06dbl.org/files/NCBM.pdf.

45. Pew Research Center for the People and the Press, "Blacks Upbeat About Black Progress, Prospects," January 12, 2010, www.people-press.org/reports/576; Gallup, "One Third in US See Improved Race Relations Under Obama," August 24, 2011, www.gallup.com/poll/149141/one-third-improved-race-relations-obama.aspx; Pew Research Center, "Race in America: Key Data Points," August 27, 2013, www.pewresearch.org/key-data-points/race-in-america-key-data-points/.

46. Josiah Ryan, "'This Was a Whitelash,' Van Jones' Take on the Election Results," CNN, November 9, 2016, www.cnn.com/2016/11/09/politics/van-jones-results-disappointment-cnntv/.

47. J. Bretting and B. Morris, "Fry-Bread Federalism Revisited: A Model of American Indian Intergovernmental Relations," paper presented at the 2005 annual meeting of the Western Political Science Association, Oakland, CA.

48. U.S. Census Bureau, "American Indian and Alaskan Native Heritage Month," November 2017, www.census.gov/newsroom/facts-for-features/2017/aian-month.html.

49. Ibid.

50. Nicholas Kristof, "Poverty's Poster Child," *New York Times*, May 10, 2012, www.nytimes.com/2012/05/10/opinion/kristof-poverty sposter-child.html.

51. National Indian Gaming Commission web site, "2016 Indian Gaming Revenues Increased 4.4%," July 17, 2017, www.nigc.gov/news/detail/2016-indian-gaming-revenues-increased-4.4.

52. Americana Gaming Association, *State of the States: The AGA Survey of the Casino Industry*, 2017, www.americangaming.org/sites/default/files/research_files/2017%20State%20of%20the%20States.pdf.

53. National Caucus of Native American State Legislators web site, www.nativeamericanlegislators.org/Public%20Documents/Caucus%20 Membership.aspx.

54. U.S. Census Bureau, "Hispanic Heritage Month 2017," October 17, 2017, www.census.gov/content/dam/Census/newsroom/facts-for-features/2017/cb17-ff17.pdf.

55. U.S. Census Bureau, "2010 Census Shows Nation's Hispanic Population Grew Four Times Faster Than US Population," May 26, 2011, www.census.gov/newsroom/releases/archives/2010_census/cb11-cn146.html.

56. Pew Hispanic Center, "Country of Origin Profiles," May 26, 2011, www.pewhispanic.org/2011/05/26/country-of-origin-profiles/.

57. Pew Research Center, "5 Facts About Latinos and Education," July 28, 2016, www.pewresearch.org/fact-tank/2016/07/28/5-facts-about-latinos-and-education/.

58. Mark Falcoff, "Our Language Needs No Law," *New York Times*, August 5, 1996.

59. Douglas R. Hess and Jody Herman, "Representational Bias in the 2008 Electorate," November 2009, www.projectvote.org.

60. U.S. Census Bureau, "Press Kit: Voting and Registration in the Election of November 2016," Figure 3, May 10, 2017, www.census.gov/content/dam/Census/newsroom/press-kits/2017/voting-and-registration/figure03.png.

61. Ibid.

62. *Hirabayashi v. United States*, 320 U.S. 81 (1943); *Korematsu v. United States*, 323 U.S. 214 (1944).

63. Data from harvard.edu, stanford.edu, mit.edu, and berkeley.edu, compiled by the authors June 19, 2018.

64. U.S. Census Bureau, "Income, Poverty and Health Insurance Coverage: 2010," www.census.gov/newsroom/releases/archives/income_wealth/cb11-157.html.

65. Lena H. Sun, "Getting Out the Ethnic Vote," *Washington Post*, October 7, 1996, B5; K. Connie Kang, "Asian Americans Slow to Flex Their Political Muscle," *Los Angeles Times*, October 31, 1996, A18.

66. Ibid.

67. Ibid.

68. Chris Fuchs, "Nearly 40 Percent of Asian-American Voters Don't Favor a Party. Can the DNC Change That?" NBC News, May 15, 2018, www.nbcnews.com/news/asian-america/nearly-40-percent-asian-americans-voters-don-t-favor-party-n862806.

69. Eleanor Flexner, *Century of Struggle: The Woman's Rights Movement in the United States* (New York: Atheneum, 1973), 148–149.

70. Nancy E. McGlen and Karen O'Connor, *Women's Rights: The Struggle for Equality in the 19th and 20th Centuries* (New York: Praeger, 1983), 272–273.

71. Flexner, *Century of Struggle*, 296.

72. Jane Mansbridge, *Why We Lost the ERA* (Chicago, Ill.: University of Chicago Press, 1986), 13.

73. *Reed v. Reed*, 404 U.S. 71 (1971); *Craig v. Boren*, 429 U.S. 190 (1976).

74. *Weinberger v. Wiesenfeld*, 420 U.S. 636 (1975); *Califano v. Goldfarb*, 430 U.S. 199 (1977); *Califano v. Westcott*, 443 U.S. 76 (1979); *Orr v. Orr*, 440 U.S. 268 (1979).

75. Shelley Donald Coolidge, "Flat Tire on the Road to Pay Equity," *Christian Science Monitor*, April 11, 1997, 9; National Committee on Pay Equity, "The Wage Gap Over Time: In Real Dollars, Women See a Continuing Gap," www.pay-equity.org/info-time.html.

76. *Ledbetter v. Goodyear Tire & Rubber Co.*, 550 U.S. 618 (2007).

77. Clare O'Connor, "Trump Halting Equal Pay Measure 'A Blatant Attack on Women,' Activists Say," *Forbes*, August 30, 2017, www .forbes.com/sites/clareoconnor/2017/08/30/trump-halting-equal-pay-measure-a-blatant-attack-on-women-activists-say/#3a197352395b.

78. Joseph E. Abboud, "Salary History Not a Defense to Equal Pay Act Claims, 9th Circuit Says," May 16, 2018, www.lexology.com/library/ detail.aspx?g=7e17b8c1-680c-452c-b81f-b1339680c8fd.

79. Barbara Noble, "At Work: And Now the Sticky Floor," *New York Times*, November 22, 1992, 23.

80. Kenneth Gray, "The Gender Gap in Yearly Earnings: Can Vocational Education Help?" Office of Special Populations' Brief, University of California, Berkeley, vol. 5, no. 2.

81. Rasmussen Reports, "77% Think Woman President Likely in Next 10 Years," January 15, 2014, www.rasmussenreports.com/public_ content/politics general_politics/january_2014/77_think_woman_ president_likely_in_next_10_years.

82. *CQ Weekly*, "Guide to the New Congress," November 6, 2014, www .cq.com/graphics/weekly/2014/11/06/wr 20141106_CQWeekly.pdf; Center for American Women and Politics, fact sheets, www.cawp .rutgers.edu/fast_facts/.

83. Center for American Women and Politics, "Women in Elective Office 2015," www.cawp.rutgers.edu/women-elective-office-2015.

84. Center for American Women and Politics, "Women Mayors in U.S. Cities 2014," www.cawp.rutgers.edu/fast_facts/levels_of_office/Local-WomenMayors.php.

85. Amy Caiazza, "Does Women's Representation in Elected Office Lead to Women-Friendly Policy?" Research in Brief, Institute for Women's Policy Research, May 2002, www.thecocklebur.com/wp-content/ uploads/2010/12/One-2002-report.pdf; Kimberly Cowell-Meyers and Laura Langbein, "Linking Women's Descriptive and Substantive Representation in the United States," *Politics and Gender* 5 (2009): 491–518.

86. Kristin Eliasberg, "Making a Case for the Right to Be Different," *New York Times*, June 16, 2001, B11.

87. *Bowers v. Hardwick*, 478 U.S. 186 (1986).

88. *Romer v. Evans*, 115 S. Ct. 1092 (1996).

89. *Lawrence v. Texas*, 539 U.S. 558 (2003).

90. *Goodridge v. Dept. of Pub. Health*, 440 Mass. 309 (2003).

91. Ariane de Vogue, "Supreme Court Rules for Colorado Baker in Same-Sex Wedding Cake Case," CNN, June 4, 2018, www.cnn .com/2018/06/04/politics/masterpiece-colorado-gay-marriage-cake-supreme-court/index.html.

92. David W. Dunlap, "Gay Survey Raises a New Question," *New York Times*, October 18, 1994, B8.

93. National Gay and Lesbian Task Force, "The Gay, Lesbian, and Bisexual Vote: As Much as 5% of Presidential and Congressional Voters," 2004, www.thetaskforce.org/theissues/issue.cfm?issueID=32.

94. Nathaniel Frank, "What the Changes to DADT Mean: The Good, the Bad and the Politically Dangerous," *Huffington Post*, March 25, 2010, www.huffingtonpost.com/nathaniel-frank/what-the-changes-to-dadt_b_513665.html.

95. Pew Research Center, "Changing Attitudes on Gay Marriage," May 12, 2016, www.pewforum.org/2016/05/12/changing-attitudes-on-gay-marriage/.

96. *Massachusetts Board of Retirement v. Murgia*, 427 U.S. 307 (1976).

97. *Massachusetts Board of Retirement v. Murgia*; *Vance v. Bradley*, 440 U.S. 93 (1979); *Gregory v. Ashcroft*, 501 U.S. 452 (1991).

98. *Alabama v. Garrett*, 531 U.S. 356 (2001).

CHAPTER 6

1. Burgess Everett and Glenn Thrush, "McConnell Throws Down the Gauntlet: No Scalia Replacement Under Obama," *Politico*, February 13, 2016, www.politico.com/story/2016/02/mitch-mcconnell-antonin-scalia-supreme-court-nomination-219248#ixzz48Bb3zrNc.

2. Burgess Everett, "Flake Says It Might Be Garland Time," *Politico*, October 20, 2016, www.politico.com/story/2016/10/jeff-flake-merrick-garland-vote-supreme-court-230109.

3. John R. Hibbing and Elizabeth Theiss-Morse, *Congress as Public Enemy* (New York: Cambridge University Press, 1995), chs. 2, 3.

4. Glenn R. Parker and Roger H. Davidson, "Why Do Americans Love Their Congressmen So Much More Than Their Congress?" *Legislative Studies Quarterly* (February 1979): 52–61.

5. Heinz Eulau and Paul D. Karps, "The Puzzle of Representation: Specifying Components of Responsiveness," *Legislative Studies Quarterly* 2 (1977): 233–254.

6. Gary Jacobson, *The Politics of Congressional Elections*, 4th ed. (New York: Longman, 1997), ch. 8.

7. Pew Research Center poll, cited in John Avalon, "Hyper-partisanship Dragging Down Nation," CNN, June 7, 2012, www.cnn .com/2012/06/07/opinion/avlon-partisan-pew/index.html.

8. Keith Poole and Howard Rosenthal, "The Polarization of the Political Parties," May 10, 2012, voteview.com/political_polarization.asp.

9. David W. Brady, Hahrie Han, and Jeremy C. Pope, "Primary Elections and Candidate Ideology: Out of Step With the Primary Electorate?" *Legislative Studies Quarterly* 32 (2007): 79–105.

10. Thomas E. Mann and Norman J. Ornstein, *It's Even Worse Than It Looks: How the American Constitutional System Collided With the New Politics of Extremism* (New York: Basic Books, 2012); Thomas E. Mann and Norman J. Ornstein, "Let's Just Say It: The Republicans Are the Problem," *Washington Post*, April 27, 2012, https:// .washingtonpost.com/opinions/lets-just-say-it-the-republicans-are-the-problem/2012/04/27/gIQAxCVUIT_story.html.

11. Mann and Ornstein, "Let's Just Say It."

12. Ibid.

13. Charles Mahtesian and Jim VandeHei, "Congress: It's Going to Get Worse," *Politico*, May 1, 2012, www.politico.com/news/ stories/0412/75771.html; Steve LaTourette, "The Senate's 'Manchurian Candidates,'" *Politico*, November 11, 2012, www.politico .com/news/stories/1112/83703.html.

14. Megan Slack, "Here's How a Government Shutdown Hurts the American People," *The White House Blog*, September 30, 2013, www.whitehouse.gov/blog/2013/09/30/heres-how-government-shutdown-hurts-american-people; Jonathan Weisman and Ashley Parker, "Republicans Back Down, Ending Crisis Over Shutdown and Debt Limit," *New York Times*, October 16, 2013, www.nytimes .com/2013/10/17/us/congress-budget-debate.html.

15. Jonathan Miller, "Mourdock: Compromise Is Democrats Agreeing With Republicans," *National Journal*, May 9, 2012, www .nationaljournal.com/congress/mourdock-compromise-is-democrats-agreeing-with-republicans-20120509.

16. "Moderate GOP Rep. LaTourette Announces Retirement," MSNBC, July 31, 2012, www.msnbc.com/the-daily-rundown/moderate-gop-rep-latourette-announces.

17. Ella Nilsen, "'None of This Is Normal': Read the Full Transcript of Sen. Jeff Flake's Blistering Retirement Speech," *Vox*, October 24, 2017, www.vox.com/2017/10/24/16537284/full-transcript-flake-retirement-speech.

18. Ross K. Baker, *House and Senate* (New York: Norton, 1989).

19. D. C. W. Parker and M. Dull, "Divided We Quarrel: The Politics of Congressional Investigations, 1947–2004," *Legislative Studies Quarterly* 34 (2009): 319–345.

20. Jonathan Alter, "Obama Miracle Is White House Free of Scandal," Bloomberg News, October 27, 2011, www.bloomberg.com/ news/2011-10-27/obama-miracle-is-white-house-free-of-scandal-commentary-by-jonathan-alter.html.

21. Tim Fernholz, "Democrats, Meet Darrell Issa, Likely the Man With the Subpoena," *Newsweek*, September 7, 2010, www.thedailybeast .com/newsweek/2010/09/07/darrell-issa-could-investigate-

president-obama.html; Paul Waldman, "What Benghazi Is About: Scandal Envy," *The American Prospect*, November 15, 2012, prospect.org/article/what-benghazi-about-scandal-envy.

22. Tim Fernholz, "Democrats, Meet Darrell Issa, Likely the Man With the Subpoena," *Newsweek*, September 7, 2010, www.thedailybeast.com/newsweek/2010/09/07/darrell-issa-could-investigate-president-obama.html; Paul Waldman, "What Benghazi Is About: Scandal Envy," *The American Prospect*, November 15, 2012, prospect.org/article/what-benghazi-about-scandal-envy.

23. Neil A. Lewis, "Justice Dept. Nominee Avoids Confrontation at Hearing," *New York Times*, February 26, 2009, 23; Charlie Savage, "Long After Nomination, An Obama Choice Withdraws," *New York Times*, April 10, 2010, 16.

24. Adam Liptak, "Supreme Court Rebukes Obama on Right of Appointment," *New York Times*, June 24, 2014, www.nytimes.com/2014/06/27/us/supreme-court-president-recess-appointments.html.

25. Charles Cameron, Albert Cover, and Jeffrey Segal, "Senate Voting on Supreme Court Nominations," *American Political Science Review* 84 (1990): 525–534.

26. David Mayhew, *Congress: The Electoral Connection* (New Haven, Conn.: Yale University Press, 1974).

27. *Baker v. Carr*, 396 U.S. 186 (1962); *Westberry v. Sanders*, 376 U.S. 1 (1964).

28. Sandhya Somashekhar and Aaron Blake, "Census Data Realigns Congressional Districts in Key Political States," *Washington Post*, December 21, 2010, www.washingtonpost.com/wp-dyn/content/article/2010/12/21/AR2010122103084.html.

29. Roger H. Davidson and Walter J. Oleszek, *Congress and Its Members*, 9th ed. (Washington, D.C.: CQ Press, 2004), 48.

30. Sam Wang, "The Great Gerrymander of 2012," *New York Times*, February 2, 2013, www.nytimes.com/2013/02/03/opinion/sunday/the-great-gerrymander-of-2012.html.

31. Katie Sanders, "Steny Hoyer: House Democrats Won Majority of 2012 Popular Vote," Politifact, February 19, 2013, www.politifact.com/truth-o-meter/statements/2013/feb/19/steny-hoyer/steny-hoyer-house-democrats-won-majority-2012-popu/.

32. Lydia Wheeler, "Supreme Court Punts Partisan Gerrymandering Case," *The Hill*, June 25, 2018, thehill.com/regulation/court-battles/393926-supreme-court-punts-issue-of-partisan-gerrymandering; M. L. Schultze, "ACLU Revises Ohio Gerrymandering Lawsuit After Supreme Court Ruling," WOSU Public Media, June 27, 2018, radio.wosu.org/post/aclu-revises-ohio-gerrymandering-lawsuit-after-supreme-court-ruling#stream/0.

33. Charles Cameron, David Epstein, and Sharyn O'Halloran, "Do Majority–Minority Districts Maximize Substantive Black Representation in Congress?" *American Political Science Review* 90 (December 1996): 794–812; Kevin Hill, "Does the Creation of Majority Black Districts Aid Republicans? An Analysis of the 1992 Congressional Election in Eight Southern States," *Journal of Politics* 57 (May 1995): 384–401; D. Lublin, "Racial Redistricting and African-American Representation: A Critique of 'Do Majority-Minority Districts Maximize Substantive Black Representation in Congress?'" *American Political Science Review* 93 (1999): 183–186.

34. "How to Rig an Election," *The Economist*, April 25, 2002; Aaron Blake, "Name That District! (Gerrymandering Edition)," *Washington Post*, July 27, 2011, www.washingtonpost.com/blogs/the-fix/post/name-that-district-gerrymandering-edition/2011/07/25/gIQA17HucI_blog.html.

35. Richard L. Hasen, "Suppression of Minority Voting Rights Is About to Get Way Worse," *Slate*, June 25, 2018, slate.com/news-and-politics/2018/06/the-abbott-v-perez-case-echoes-shelby-county-v-holder-as-a-further-death-blow-for-the-voting-rights-act.html; Nina Totenberg, "Supreme Court Upholds Texas' Congressional, State Legislative Maps," NPR, June 25, 2018, www.npr.org/2018/06/25/623318888/supreme-court-upholds-texas-congressional-state-legislative-maps.

36. *Shaw v. Reno*, 509 U.S. 630 (1993); *Miller v. Johnson*, 115 S. Ct. 2475 (1995).

37. Peter Urban, "Congress Gets Lavish Benefits," *Connecticut Post*, January 16, 2005; Debra J. Saunders, "Perks of Office" [editorial], *San Francisco Chronicle*, November 19, 2000, 9.

38. Gary Jacobson, *The Politics of Congressional Elections*, 3rd ed. (New York: HarperCollins, 1992); Peverill Squire, "Challengers in Senate Elections," *Legislative Studies Quarterly* 14 (1989): 531–547; David Cannon, *Actors, Athletes and Astronauts: Political Amateurs in the United States Congress* (Chicago: University of Chicago Press, 1990).

39. Calculated by the authors from the Campaign Finance Institute data table, "Expenditures of House Incumbents and Challengers, by Election Outcome, 1974–2008," www.cfinst.org/pdf/vital/VitalStats_t3.pdf.

40. Michal McDonald, "Suspect When More Data Analyzed We'll See Not So Much a Republican Wave, but More a Democratic Trough," Twitter @ElectProject, November 5, 2014.

41. Glenn Parker, *Characteristics of Congress: Patterns in Congressional Behavior* (Englewood Cliffs, N.J.: Prentice Hall, 1989), 17–18, ch. 9.

42. Davidson and Oleszek, *Congress and Its Members*, 9th ed., 155–156.

43. Leroy Rieselbach, *Congressional Reform in the Seventies* (Morristown, N.J.: General Learning Press, 1977); Leroy Rieselbach, *Congressional Reform* (Washington, D.C.: Congressional Quarterly Press, 1986).

44. Ibid.

45. Ed Gillespie and Bob Schellhas, eds., *Contract With America: The Bold Plan by Rep. Newt Gingrich, Rep. Dick Armey and the House Republicans to Change the Nation* (New York: Random House, 1994); James G. Gimpel, *Legislating the Revolution* (Boston: Allyn & Bacon, 1996).

46. Perry Bacon Jr., "Don't Mess With Nancy Pelosi," *Time*, August 27, 2006.

47. Ronald Peters, coauthor of *Speaker Nancy Pelosi and the New American Politics*, quoted in Edward Epstein, "Pelosi Gets Good Marks in Two New Books," *CQ Weekly*, May 10, 2010, 1128.

48. Bill Weiss, "Call for Resignation of Speaker John Boehner," MoveOn.org, petitions.moveon.org/sign/call-for-resignation; Sean Davis, "Is It Time for John Boehner to Resign as Speaker?" *The Federalist*, October 16, 2013, thefederalist.com/2013/10/16/time-john-boehner-resign-speaker/.

49. Davidson and Oleszek, *Congress and Its Members*, 9th ed., 193.

50. Mathew McCubbins and Thomas Schwartz, "Congressional Oversight Overlooked: Police Patrols Versus Fire Alarms," *American Journal of Political Science* (February 1984): 165–179.

51. Barbara Sinclair, "Party Leaders and the New Legislative Process," in Dodd and Oppenheimer, eds., *Congress Reconsidered*, 6th ed., 229–245.

52. Davidson and Oleszek, *Congress and Its Members*, 9th ed., 204.

53. Steven Smith and Eric Lawrence, "Party Control of Committees in the Republican Congress," in Dodd and Oppenheimer, eds., *Congress Reconsidered*, 6th ed., 163–192.

54. Davidson and Oleszek, *Congress and Its Members*, 9th ed., 219–220.

55. Ramsey Cox, "Senate Rejects Amendment to End Tobacco Farm Subsidies," *The Hill*, May 23, 2013, thehill.com/blogs/floor-action/senate/301645-senate-rejects-amendment-to-end-tobacco-farm-subsidies.

56. Roger H. Davidson, Walter J. Oleszek, and Frances E. Lee, eds. *Congress and Its Members*, 11th ed. (Washington, D.C.: CQ Press, 2008), 276.

57. John Stewart, "A Chronology of the Civil Rights Act of 1964," in Robert Loevy, ed., *The Civil Rights Act of 1964: The Passage of the Law That Ended Racial Segregation* (Albany: SUNY Press, 1997), 358.

58. Stewart, "A Chronology of the Civil Rights Act of 1964," 358–360.

59. Barbara Sinclair, "The New World of U.S. Senators," in Dodd and Oppenheimer, eds., *Congress Reconsidered*, 8th ed., 11; Richard Beth and Stanley Bach, "Filibusters and Cloture in the Senate," *Congressional Research Service*, March 28, 2003, www.senate.gov/reference/resources/pdf/RL30360.pdf.

60. Burgess Everett and Seung Min Kim, "Senate Goes for 'Nuclear Option,'" *Politico*, November 21, 2013, www.politico.com/story/2013/11/harry-reid-nuclear-option-100199.html.

61. Sahil Kapur, "Nuclear Option Triggered: Dems Make Historic Change to Filibuster Rules," *Talking Points Memo*, November 21, 2013, talkingpointsmemo.com/dc/harry-reid-nuclear-option-senate.

62. Barbara Sinclair, "The New World of U.S. Senators," in Lawrence C. Dodd and Bruce I. Oppenheimer, eds., *Congress Reconsidered*, 8th ed. (Washington, D.C.: CQ Press, 2005), 11; Richard Beth and Stanley Bach, "Filibusters and Cloture in the Senate," Congressional Research Service, March 28, 2003, www.senate.gov/reference/resources/pdf/RL30360.pdf.

63. Barbara Sinclair, *Unorthodox Lawmaking: New Legislative Processes in the U.S. Congress*, 4th ed. (Washington, D.C.: CQ Press, 2011).

64. Donald R. Matthews and James A. Stimson, *Yeas and Nays* (New York: Wiley, 1975).

65. Richard Smith, "Interest Group Influence in the U.S. Congress," *Legislative Studies Quarterly* 20 (February 1995): 89–140.

66. Stephen C. Craig, *The Malevolent Leaders: Popular Discontent in America* (Boulder, Colo.: Westview Press, 1993); David Easton, "A Reassessment of the Concept of Political Support," *British Journal of Political Science* 5 (1975): 435–457; Glenn Parker, "Some Themes in Congressional Unpopularity," *American Journal of Political Science* 21 (1977): 93–110; E. J. Dionne Jr., *Why Americans Hate Politics* (New York: Simon & Schuster, 1991).

67. Parker and Davidson, "Why Do Americans Love Their Congressmen So Much More Than Their Congress?"; Richard F. Fenno Jr., "If, as Ralph Nader Says, Congress Is 'the Broken Branch,' How Come We Love Our Congressmen So Much?" in Norman J. Ornstein, ed., *Congress in Change* (New York: Praeger, 1975), 277–287.

68. Hibbing and Theiss-Morse, *Congress as Public Enemy.*

69. John R. Hibbing and Elizabeth Theiss-Morse, "Civics Is Not Enough: Teaching Barbarics in K–12," *Political Science & Politics* 29 (1996): 157.

70. Nina Totenberg, "Sen. McCain Says Republicans Will Block All Court Nominations If Clinton Wins," NPR, October 17, 2016, www.npr.org/2016/10/17/498328520/sen-mccain-says-republicans-will-block-all-court-nominations-if-clinton-wins.

71. Burgess Everett, "Flake Says It Might Be Garland Time," *Politico*, October 20, 2016, www.politico.com/story/2016/10/jeff-flake-merrick-garland-vote-supreme-court-230109.

72. Ed Pilkington, "Feel the love, feel the hate – my week in the cauldron of Trump's wild rallies," *The Guardian*, November 1, 2018, https://www.theguardian.com/us-news/2018/nov/01/trump-rallies-america-midterms-white-house.

73. Laila Lalalmi, "Does American 'Tribalism' End in a Compromise, or a Fight?," *New York Times*, June 26, 2018, https://www.nytimes.com/2018/06/26/magazine/does-american-tribalismend-in-a-compromise-or-a-fight.html.

CHAPTER 7

1. Jonathan Bernstein, "Trump Has Already Abdicated His Role as Head of State," Bloomberg, August 21, 2017, www.bloomberg.com/view/articles/2017-08-21/trump-has-already-abdicated-his-role-as-head-of-state-j6m413br; "Normalizing Trump: An Incredibly Brief Explainer," PressThink, September 17, 2017, pressthink.org/2017/09/normalizing-trump-incredibly-brief-explainer/.

2. Bruce Miroff, "Monopolizing the Public Space: The President as a Problem for Democratic Politics," in Bruce Miroff, Raymond Seidelman, and Todd Swanstrom, eds., *Debating Democracy* (Boston, Mass.: Houghton Mifflin, 1997), 294–303.

3. Max Farrand, *The Framing of the Constitution of the United States* (New Haven, Conn.: Yale University Press, 1913), 163.

4. David Montgomery, "S.D. Republican Party Calls for Obama Impeachment," *Sioux Falls Argus Leader*, June 23, 2014; Impeach Obama Petition, www.teaparty.org/impeach-obama-petition/; Reid J. Epstein, "Impeach Obama, Says Michael Burgess," *Politico*, August 9, 2011; Igor Volsky, "Top Republican Senator Suggests Impeaching Obama Over Immigration Policies," ThinkProgress, June 26, 2012, thinkprogress.org/politics/2012/06/26/506195/top-republican-senator-suggests-impeaching-obama-over-immigration-policies/; Jennifer Steinhauer, "Ignoring Qualms, Some Republicans Nurture Dreams of Impeaching Obama," *New York Times*, August 24, 2013; Tal Kopan, "Kerry Bentivolio: Impeachment 'a Dream,'" *Politico*, August 21, 2013.

5. Robert DiClerico, *The American President*, 4th ed. (Englewood Cliffs, N.J.: Prentice Hall, 1995), 374; Susan Milligan, "Democrats Scuttle Proposal to Impeach Bush: Move Avoids House Debate," *Boston Globe*, June 12, 2008, A5.

6. Joseph A. Pika and John Anthony Maltese, *The Politics of the Modern Presidency*, 6th ed. (Washington, D.C.: CQ Press, 2004), 3; Jeffrey K. Tulis, "The Two Constitutional Presidencies," in Michael Nelson, ed., *The Presidency and the Political System* (Washington, D.C.: Congressional Quarterly Press, 1995), 91–123.

7. Loch Johnson and James M. McCormick, "The Making of International Agreements: A Reappraisal of Congressional Involvement," *Journal of Politics* 40 (1978): 468–478.

8. Joseph J. Schatz, "With a Deft and Light Touch, Bush Finds Ways to Win," *CQ Weekly*, December 11, 2004, 2900–2904; and calculated by authors from Thomas, thomas.loc.gov/home/treaties/treaties.html.

9. D. Roderick Kiewiet and Mathew D. McCubbins, "Presidential Influence on Congressional Appropriations Decisions," *American Political Science Review* 32 (1988): 713–736.

10. Schatz, "With a Deft and Light Touch, Bush Finds Ways to Win."

11. Charlie Savage, "Shift on Executive Power Lets Obama Bypass Rivals," *New York Times*, April 22, 2012.

12. Jack L. Goldsmith, Office of Legal Counsel Under George W. Bush, quoted in Savage, "Shift on Executive Power Lets Obama Bypass Rivals"; see also Peter Baker, "Obama Making Plans to Use Executive Power," *The New York Times*, February 12, 2010, www.nytimes.com/2010/02/13/us/politics/13obama.html

13. Kenneth R. Mayer, *With the Stroke of a Pen: Executive Orders and Presidential Power* (Princeton, N.J.: Princeton University Press, 2002), 88–89.

14. Adam L. Warber, *Executive Orders and the Modern Presidency: Legislating From the Oval Office* (Boulder, Colo.: Lynne Rienner Publishers, 2006); William G. Howell, *Power Without Persuasion: The Politics of Direct Presidential Action* (Princeton, N.J.: Princeton University Press, 2003).

15. Robert A. Carp, Ronald Stidham, and Kenneth L. Manning, *Judicial Process in America*, 6th ed. (Washington, D.C.: CQ Press, 2004), 168.

16. Amy Goldstein, "Civil Rights Organizations Question Nominee Elena Kagan's Record on Race," *Washington Post*, June 27, 2010.

17. Charlie Savage, "Obama Backers Fear Opportunities to Reshape Judiciary Are Slipping Away," *New York Times*, November 14, 2009, www.nytimes.com/2009/11/15/us/politics/15judicial.html?scp=3&sq=Obama%20judicial%20appointments&st=cse.

18. Jennifer Bendery, "Obama Leaving His Mark on Judiciary as Senate Confirms Gay, Black Judges," *Huffington Post*, June 24, 2014, www.huffingtonpost.com/2014/06/17/obama-judges_n_5503075.html.

19. Jennifer Bendery, "Trump Is Remaking the Courts in His Image: White, Male and Straight," *Huffington Post*, March 11, 2018, www.huffingtonpost.com/entry/trump-judicial-nominees-white-male-straight_us_5aa2b9bee4b07047bec6107c.

20. Gerald Boyd, "White House Hunts for a Justice, Hoping to Tip Ideological Scales," *New York Times*, June 30, 1987; Alan I. Abramowitz and Jeffrey A. Segal, *Senate Elections* (Ann Arbor: University of Michigan Press, 1992), 1–6.

21. Russell Wheeler, "Prevent Federal Court Nomination Battles: De-Escalating the Conflict Over the Judiciary," Brookings Institution Working Paper, 2008, www.brookings.edu/~/media/Files/Projects/Opportunity08/PB_JudicialPolicy_Wheeler.ashx.

22. Jennifer Bendery, "As Senate Runs Out of Judges to Confirm, Dozens of Courts Still Sit Empty With No Nominees," *Huffington Post*, June 4, 2014, www.huffingtonpost.com/2014/06/04/obama-judicial-nominees_n_5439100.html.

23. Rebecca Mae Salokar, *The Solicitor General: The Politics of Law* (Philadelphia, Penn.: Temple University Press, 1992), 29.

24. Bob Woodward, *Shadow: Five Presidents and the Legacy of Watergate* (New York: Simon & Schuster, 1999), 212–217.

25. *In re Neagle*, 135 U.S. 546 (1890); *In re Debs*, 158 U.S. 564 (1895); *United States v. Curtiss-Wright Export Corp.*, 299 U.S. 304, 57 S. Ct. 216 (1936); *Youngstown Sheet & Tube v. Sawyer*, 343 U.S. 579 (1952).

26. Lyn Ragsdale, *Presidential Politics* (Boston, Mass.: Houghton Mifflin, 1993), 55.

27. *Historical Statistics of the United States: Colonial Times to 1970* (Washington, D.C.: U.S. Government Printing Office, 1975).

28. *Inaugural Addresses of the United States* (Washington, D.C.: U.S. Government Printing Office, 1982), quoted in Ragsdale, *Presidential Politics*, 71.

29. Suzanne Bilyeu, "FDR: How He Changed America—and Still Affects Your Life Today," *New York Times Upfront*, January 14, 2008.

30. Arthur M. Schlesinger Jr., *The Imperial Presidency* (Boston, Mass.: Mariner Books, 2004).

31. Richard Nixon interview with David Frost, May 20, 1977, cited in Charles Savage, *Takeover: The Return of the Imperial Presidency and the Subversion of American Democracy* (New York: Little, Brown, 2007), 21.

32. Dana Milbank, "Cheney Refuses Records' Release; Energy Showdown With GAO Looms," *Washington Post*, January 28, 2002, A1.

33. Charlie Savage, "Bush Challenges Hundreds of Laws," *Boston Globe*, April 30, 2006, www.bostonglobe.com.

34. Philip Cooper, cited in Savage, "Bush Challenges Hundreds of Laws."

35. Carrie Budoff Brown and Jennifer Epstein, "President Obama's 'Year of Action' Falls Short," *Politico*, October 8, 2014, www.politico.com/story/2014/10/president-obama-executive-action-111687.html.

36. Alexander Burns, Jonathan Martin, and Maggie Haberman, "Pence Is Trying to Control Republican Politics. Trump Aides Aren't Happy," *New York Times*, May 14, 2018, www.nytimes.com/2018/05/14/us/politics/pence-trump-midterms.html.

37. Richard E. Neustadt, *Presidential Power and the Modern Presidents* (New York: Free Press, 1990), 10.

38. George Edwards III, *The Strategic President: Persuasion and Opportunity in Presidential Leadership* (Princeton, N.J.: Princeton University Press, 2009).

39. Ibid.

40. Samuel Kernell, *Going Public: New Strategies of Presidential Leadership*, 2nd ed. (Washington, D.C.: Congressional Quarterly Press, 1996).

41. Barbara Hinckley, *The Symbolic Presidency* (London: Routledge, 1990), ch. 2.

42. See Hedrick Smith, *The Power Game: How Washington Works* (New York: Random House, 1988), 405–406, for similar reports on the Nixon and Reagan administrations.

43. Lee Sigelman, "Gauging the Public Response to Presidential Leadership," *Presidential Studies Quarterly* 10 (Summer 1980): 427–433; James A. Stimson, "Public Support for American Presidents: A Cyclical Model," *Public Opinion Quarterly* 40 (Spring 1976): 1–21; Michael MacKuen, "Political Drama, Economic Conditions, and the Dynamics of Presidential Popularity," *American Journal of Political Science* 27 (February 1983): 165–192.

44. John Sides, "Is Obama More Popular Than He Should Be?" *New York Times*, May 2, 2012, fivethirtyeight.blogs.nytimes.com/2012/05/02/is-obama-more-popular-than-he-should-be/.

45. John R. Hibbing and Elizabeth Theiss-Morse, *Stealth Democracy: Americans' Beliefs About How Government Should Work* (New York: Cambridge University Press, 2002).

46. Paul Brace and Barbara Hinckley, *Follow the Leader: Opinion Polls and the Modern Presidents* (New York: Basic Books, 1992), ch. 5.

47. Ibid., ch. 6.

48. Richard E. Neustadt, *Presidential Power and the Modern Presidents* (New York: Free Press, 1990), 50–72.

49. James L. Sundquist, "Needed: A Political Theory for a New Era of Coalition Government in the United States," *Political Science Quarterly* 103 (Winter 1988–1989): 613–635.

50. *Congressional Quarterly Weekly Report*, December 21, 1996, 3455.

51. Shawn Zeller, "Historic Success, at No Small Cost," *CQ Weekly*, January 11, 2010, 112.

52. David Mayhew, *Divided We Govern: Party Control, Lawmaking, and Investigations, 1946–1990* (New Haven, Conn.: Yale University Press, 1991).

53. Terry Moe, "Presidents, Institutions, and Theory," in George C. Edwards III, John H. Kessel, and Bert A. Rockman, eds., *Researching the Presidency: Vital Questions, New Approaches* (Pittsburgh, Penn.: University of Pittsburgh Press, 1993), 370.

54. Ibid.

55. The President's Committee on Administrative Management, *Report of the Committee* (Washington, D.C.: U.S. Government Printing Office, 1937).

56. Jane Meyer and Doyle MacManus, *Landslide: The Unmaking of the President, 1984–1988* (Boston, Mass.: Houghton Mifflin, 1988).

57. Tom Hamburger and Christi Parsons, "President Obama's Czar System Concerns Some," *Los Angeles Times*, March 5, 2009; Zachary Coile, "Obama's Big Task: Managing the Best, Brightest," *San Francisco Chronicle*, January 11, 2009; James Risen, "Obama Takes on Congress Over Policy Czar Positions," *New York Times*, April 16, 2011.

58. White House, "2013 Annual Report to Congress on White House Staff," www.whitehouse.gov/briefing-room/disclosures/annual-records/2013.

59. Harold Relyea, "Growth and Development of the President's Office," in David Kozak and Kenneth Ciboski, eds., *The American Presidency* (Chicago, Ill.: Nelson Hall, 1985), 135; James P. Pfiffner, *The Modern Presidency*, 2nd ed. (New York: St. Martin's, 1998), 122.

60. Sid Frank and Arden Davis Melick, *The Presidents: Tidbits and Trivia* (Maplewood, N.J.: Hammond, 1986), 103.

61. Timothy Walch, ed., *At the President's Side: The Vice-Presidency in the Twentieth Century* (Columbia: University of Missouri Press, 1997), 45.

62. Ann Devroy and Stephen Barr, "Reinventing the Vice Presidency: Defying History, Al Gore Has Emerged as Bill Clinton's Closest Political Advisor," *Washington Post National Weekly Edition*, February 27–March 5, 1995, 6–7.

63. Michelle Obama, "As Barack's First Lady, I Would Work to Help Working Families and Military Families," *U.S. News & World Report*, October 1, 2008.

64. Jeffrey M. Jones, "Michelle Obama Remains Popular in U.S.," www.gallup.com/poll/154952/michelle-obama-remains-popular.aspx.

65. Robert K. Murray and Tim H. Blessing, "The Presidential Performance Study: A Progress Report," *Journal of American History* 70 (December 1983): 535–555.

66. Jon R. Bond and Richard Fleisher, *The President in the Legislative Arena* (Chicago: University of Chicago Press, 1990); George C. Edwards III, *Presidential Influence in Congress* (San Francisco: Freeman, 1980).

67. James David Barber, *The Presidential Character*, 4th ed. (Englewood Cliffs, N.J.: Prentice Hall, 1992).

68. See Michael Nelson, "James David Barber and the Psychological Presidency," in David Pederson, ed., *The "Barberian" Presidency: Theoretical and Empirical Readings* (New York: Peter Lang, 1989), 93–110; Alexander George, "Assessing Presidential Character," *World Politics* (January 1974): 234–283; Jeffrey Tulis, "On Presidential Character," in Jeffrey Tulis and Joseph Bessette, eds., *The Presidency and the Constitutional Order* (Baton Rouge: Louisiana State University Press, 1981).

69. Joseph Califano, *A Presidential Nation* (New York: Norton, 1975), 184–188.

70. Joel Achenbach, "In a Heated Race, Obama's Cool Won the Day," *Washington Post*, November 6, 2008, A47.

71. Justin Frank, "Has Obama Had a Psychological Breakthrough?" *Time*, December 14, 2011, ideas.time.com/2011/12/14/has-obama-had-a-psychological-breakthrough/.

72. Joel Achenbach, "In a Heated Race, Obama's Cool Won the Day," *Washington Post*, November 6, 2008, A47.

CHAPTER 8

1. John Whitesides, "Beyond the Daily Drama and Twitter Battles, Trump Begins to Alter American Life," Reuters, September 28, 2017, www.reuters.com/article/us-trump-effect-rules/beyond-the-daily-drama-and-twitter-battles-trump-begins-to-alter-american-life-idUSKCN1C3261; Chase Gunter, "How Big Is the Federal Workforce, Really?" FCW, October 5, 2017, fcw.com/articles/2017/10/05/federal-workforce-volker-size.aspx; Clyde Wayne Crews, Jr., "Trump's 2018 Regulatory Reform Agenda by the Numbers," *Forbes*, May 10, 2018, www.forbes.com/sites/waynecrews/2018/05/10/trumps-2018-regulatory-reform-agenda-by-the-numbers/#36f294187cd2; Danny Vinik, "The Radical Idea Buried in Trump's State of the Union," *Politico*, February 1, 2018, www.politico.com/agenda/story/2018/02/01/trump-civil-service-reform-state-of-the-union-000635.

2. John Whitesides, "Beyond the daily drama and Twitter battles, Trump begins to alter American life," Reuters, September 28, 2017, https://

www.reuters.com/article/us-trump-effect-rules/beyond-the-daily-drama-and-twitter-battles-trump-begins-to-alter-american-life-idUSKCN1C3261.

3. Clyde Wayne Crews, "Trump's 2018 Regulatory Reform Agenda By the Numbers," Forbes, May 10, 2018, https://www.forbes.com/sites/waynecrews/2018/05/10/trumps-2018-regulatory-reform-agenda-by-the-numbers/#5d7366d97cd2; Noam Scheiber, "Trump Moves to Ease the Firing of Federal Workers," New York Times, May 25, 2018.

4. H. H. Gerth and C. Wright Mills, eds., From Max Weber (New York: Oxford University Press, 1946), 196–199.

5. Herbert Kaufman, "Emerging Conflicts in the Doctrines of Public Administration," American Political Science Review 50 (December 1956): 1057–1073.

6. Morris P. Fiorina, Congress: Keystone of the Washington Establishment (New Haven, Conn.: Yale University Press, 1977).

7. Louis Jacobson, "Taking the Measure of the Federal Workforce Under Donald Trump," PolitiFact, January 22, 2018, www.politifact.com/truth-o-meter/article/2018/jan/22/taking-measure-federal-workforce/.

8. Kenneth J. Meier, Politics and the Bureaucracy: Policymaking in the Fourth Branch of Government (Pacific Grove, Calif.: Brooks/Cole, 1993), 18.

9. Meier, Politics and the Bureaucracy, 18–24.

10. Best Places to Work in the Federal Government, "FEC," bestplacestowork.org/BPTW/rankings/detail/LF00; "Social Security Administration," bestplacestowork.org/BPTW/rankings/detail/SZ00.

11. William G. Howell and David E. Lewis, "Agencies by Presidential Design," Journal of Politics 64 (2002): 1095–1114.

12. Dennis D. Riley, Controlling the Federal Bureaucracy (Philadelphia, Penn.: Temple University Press, 1987), 139–142.

13. Office of Management and Budget, "2017 Draft Report to Congress on the Benefits and Costs of Federal Regulations and Agency Compliance With the Unfunded Mandates Reform Act," www.whitehouse.gov/wp-content/uploads/2017/12/draft_2017_cost_benefit_report.pdf; Clyde Wayne Crews, Jr., "How Many Federal Agencies Exist? We Can't Drain the Swamp Until We Know," Forbes, July 5, 2017, www.forbes.com/sites/waynecrews/2017/07/05/how-many-federal-agencies-exist-we-cant-drain-the-swamp-until-we-know/#70fbbe331aa2.

14. U.S. News & World Report, February 11, 1980, 64.

15. David E. Lewis, "The Adverse Consequences of the Politics of Agency Design for Presidential Management in the United States: The Relative Durability of Insulated Agencies," British Journal of Political Science 34 (2004): 377–404.

16. Noam Scheiber, "Trump Moves to Ease the Firing of Federal Workers," New York Times, May 25, 2018, www.nytimes.com/2018/05/25/business/economy/trump-federal-workers.html.

17. John B. Judis, "The Quiet Revolution: Obama Has Reinvented the State in More Ways Than You Can Imagine," New Republic, February 1, 2010, www.tnr.com/article/politics/the-quiet-revolution.

18. Ibid.

19. Emily Stephenson, "Postal Service Downsizing Plan Cuts 35,000 Jobs," February 23, 2012, www.msnbc.msn.com/id/46501840/ns/business-us_business/t/postal-service-downsizing-plan-cuts-jobs/#.T80IVr9Xsb1; Emily Stewart, "Trump's Trying to Fight Amazon and Jeff Bezos From the White House," Vox, May 21, 2018, www.vox.com/policy-and-politics/2018/5/19/17371780/donald-trump-amazon-jeff-bezos-postal-service.

20. Bureau of Labor Statistics, "Employment Projections: Civilian Labor Force by Age, Sex, Race and Ethnicity," www.bls.gov/emp/ep_table_304.htm; FedSmith, Inc., "Federal Work Force 2014: Key Figures," www.scribd.com/doc/220100041/Federal-Workforce-2014-Key-Figures.

21. Meier, Politics and the Bureaucracy, 177–181.

22. Donald F. Kettl, System Under Stress: Homeland Security and American Politics (Washington, D.C.: CQ Press, 2004), 48.

23. "The 9/11 Commission Report: Final Report of the National Commission on Terrorist Attacks Upon the United States, Executive Summary," www.c-span.org/pdf/911final reportexecsum.pdf.

24. Quoted in Kettl, System Under Stress, 53.

25. Catherine Rampell, "Whistle-blowers Tell of Cost of Conscience," USA Today, November 24, 2006, 13A; Peter Eisler, "Whistle-blowers' Rights Get Second Look; Bills to Strengthen Protections Now Have Better Chance to Pass, Backers Say," USA Today, March 15, 2010, 6A.

26. Terry Moe, "The President's Cabinet," in James Pfiffner and Roger J. Davidson, eds., Understanding the Presidency, 3rd ed. (New York: Longman, 2003), 208.

27. Office of Personnel Management, Federal Workforce Statistics: The Fact Book, 2003 Edition (Washington, D.C.: Office of Personnel Management, 2003), 10, www.opm.gov/feddata/03factbk.pdf.

28. Francis E. Rourke, Bureaucracy, Politics and Public Policy, 3rd ed. (Boston, Mass.: Little, Brown, 1984), 106.

29. Albert B. Crenshaw, "Cash Flow," Washington Post, June 28, 1998, H1.

30. Anthony E. Brown, The Politics of Airline Regulation (Knoxville: University of Tennessee Press, 1987).

31. David E. Lewis, "Staffing Alone: Unilateral Action and the Politicization of the Executive Office of the President, 1988–2004," Presidential Studies Quarterly 35 (2005): 496–514.

32. Charlie Savage, "Bush Aide Admits Hiring Boasts; Says He Broke No Rules Giving Jobs to Conservatives," Boston Globe, June 6, 2007, A9; Charlie Savage, "Scandal Puts Spotlight on Christian Law School; Grads Influential in Justice Dept.," Boston Globe, April 8, 2007, A1; Eric Lipton, "Colleagues Cite Partisan Focus by Justice Officials," New York Times, May 12, 2007, A1.

33. Robert Barnes, "Supreme Court Rebukes Obama on Recess Appointments," Washington Post, June 26, 2014.

34. Sonam Sheth and Skye Gould, "Who's Running the Government?" Business Insider, April 22, 2017, www.businessinsider.com/whos-running-the-government-trump-unfilled-executive-branch-positions-2017-4.

35. Riley, Controlling the Federal Bureaucracy, ch. 2.

36. Harold Seidman and Robert Gilmour, Politics, Position, and Power: From the Positive to the Regulatory State, 4th ed. (New York: Oxford University Press, 1986), 3; Mark Landler and Annie Lowrey, "Obama Bid to Cut Government Tests Congress," New York Times, January 13, 2012, www.nytimes.com/2012/01/14/us/politics/obama-to-ask-congress-for-power-to-merge-agencies.html.

37. Lorraine Woellert and John Bresnahan, "Sweeping Trump proposal seeks to shrink government, merge agencies," Politico, June 21, 2018, https://www.politico.com/story/2018/06/21/trump-shrink-federal-agencie-661976.

38. Quoted in Riley, Controlling the Federal Bureaucracy, 43.

39. Edmund L. Andrews, "Blowing the Whistle on Big Oil," New York Times, December 3, 2006.

40. Quoted in Jason DeParle, "Minerals Service Had a Mandate to Produce Results," New York Times, August 7, 2010.

41. Center for Responsive Politics, "Oil and Gas," www.opensecrets.org/industries/indus.php?ind=e01.

42. Hugh Heclo, "Issue Networks and the Executive Establishment," in Anthony King, ed., The New American Political System (Washington, D.C.: American Enterprise Institute, 1978), 87–124.

43. Deborah Zabarenko, "Environmental Group to Sue U.S. Over Oil Permits," Reuters, May 14, 2010, www.reuters.com/article/idUSTRE64D64320100515.

44. Thomas E. Mann, Molly Reynolds, and Peter Hoey, "Is Congress on the Mend?" New York Times, April 28, 2007.

45. Felicity Barringer, "Limits on Logging Are Reinstated," New York Times, July 16, 2009, www.nytimes.com/2009/07/17/science/earth/17forest.html.

46. Emily Shugerman, "Donald Trump Signs Executive Order That Could Allow Companies to Mine and Drill for Oil at National Monuments," The Independent, April 26, 2017, www.independent.co.uk/news/world/americas/donald-trump-order-national-monuments-oil-mining-logging-federal-land-protections-latest-a7703866.html.

47. Matthew Crenson and Francis E. Rourke, "By Way of Conclusion: American Bureaucracy Since World War II," in Louis Galambois, ed., The New American State: Bureaucracies and Policies Since World War II (Baltimore, Md.: Johns Hopkins University Press, 1987), 137–177.

48. Charles Lane, "High Court Rejects Detainee Tribunals: 5 to 3 Ruling Curbs President's Claim of Wartime Power," Washington Post, June 30, 2006, A1; Robert Barnes, "Justices Say Detainees Can Seek Release," Washington Post, June 13, 2008, A1.

49. UN Environment, "Rapid and unprecedented action required to stay within 1.5°C says UN's Intergovernmental Panel on Climate Change," October 8, 2018, https://www.unenvironment.org/news-and-stories/press-release/rapid-and-unprecedented-action-required-stay-within-15oc-says-uns.

CHAPTER 9

1. This list is based loosely on the discussion of the functions of law in James V. Calvi and Susan Coleman, *American Law and Legal Systems* (Upper Saddle River, N.J.: Prentice Hall, 1997), 2–4; Steven Vago, *Law and Society* (Upper Saddle River, N.J.: Prentice Hall, 1997), 16–20; and Lawrence Baum, *American Courts: Process and Policy*, 2nd ed. (Boston, Mass.: Houghton Mifflin, 1998), 4–5.

2. Alexander Hamilton, James Madison, and John Jay, *The Federalist Papers*, ed. Clinton Rossiter (New York: New American Library, 1961).

3. Robert A. Carp and Ronald Stidham, *The Federal Courts* (Washington, D.C.: CQ Press, 1991), 4.

4. Lawrence Baum, *The Supreme Court*, 5th ed. (Washington, D.C.: CQ Press, 1995), 13.

5. *Marbury v. Madison*, 5 U.S. (1 Cranch) 137 (1803).

6. *Dred Scott v. Sanford*, 19 How. 393 (1857).

7. Lawrence Baum, *The Supreme Court*, 12th ed. (Washington, D.C.: CQ Press, 2016), 159, 162.

8. Lawrence Baum, *The Supreme Court*, 5th ed. (Washington, D.C.: CQ Press, 1995), 22–24.

9. Joan Biskupic, "Making a Mark on the Bench," *Washington Post National Weekly Edition*, December 2–8, 1996, 31.

10. Sheldon Goldman, Sara Schiavoni, and Elliot Slotnick, "George W. Bush's Judicial Philosophy: Mission Accomplished," *Judicature* 92 (May/June 2009): 276.

11. John Schwartz, "For Obama, a Record on Diversity but Delays on Judicial Confirmations," *New York Times*, August 6, 2011, www.nytimes.com/2011/08/07/us/politics/07courts.html?_r=2.

12. Jennifer Bendery, "Obama Leaving His Mark on Judiciary as Senate Confirms Gay, Black Judges," *Huffington Post*, June 24, 2014, www.huffingtonpost.com/2014/06/17/obama-judges_n_5503075.html; Kevin Liptak, "Obama Nominates First Muslim Federal Judge," *Huffington Post*, June 17, 2016, www.cnn.com/2016/09/07/politics/obama-nominates-first-muslim-judge/.

13. Charlie Savage, "Ratings Shrink President's List for Judgeships," *New York Times*, November 22, 2011, www.nytimes.com/2011/11/23/us/politics/screening-panel-rejects-many-obama-picks-for-federal-judgeships.html.

14. Rorie Spill Solberg and Eric N. Waltenburg, "Trump's Judicial Nominations Would Put a Lot of White Men on Federal Courts," *Washington Post*, November 28, 2017, www.washingtonpost.com/news/monkey-cage/wp/2017/11/28/this-is-how-trump-is-changing-the-federal-courts/; John Gramlich, "Trump's Appointed Judges are a Less Diverse Group Than Obama's," Pew Research Center, March 20, 2018, www.pewresearch.org/fact-tank/2018/03/20/trumps-appointed-judges-are-a-less-diverse-group-than-obamas/.

15. Biskupic, "Making a Mark on the Bench."

16. Jeffrey Toobin, "Obama's Unfinished Judicial Legacy," *New Yorker*, July 31, 2012, www.newyorker.com/online/blogs/comment/2012/07/why-judges-matter.html; Charlie Savage, "Ratings Shrink President's List for Judgeships," *New York Times*, November 22, 2011, www.nytimes.com/2011/11/23/us/politics/screening-panel-rejects-many-obama-picks-for-federal-judgeships.html; Max Ehrenfreund, "The Number of White Dudes Becoming Federal Judges Has Plummeted Under Obama," *Washington Post*, February 18, 2016, www.washingtonpost.com/news/wonk/wp/2016/02/18/the-number-of-white-dudes-becoming-federal-judges-has-plummeted-under-obama/.

17. Doug Kendall, "The Bench in Purgatory: The New Republican Obstructionism on Obama's Judicial Nominees," *Slate*, October 26, 2009, www.slate.com/id/2233109/.

18. Susan Davis and Kelsey Snell, "Mitch McConnell on Filling the Federal Bench: 'This Is My Top Priority,'" NPR, May 24, 2018, www.npr.org/2018/05/24/614228261/mitch-mcconnell-on-filling-the-federal-bench-this-is-my-top-priority.

19. David G. Savage, "Conservative Courts Likely Bush Legacy," *Los Angeles Times*, January 2, 2008, A11.

20. David M. O'Brien, "Ironies and Disappointments: Bush and Federal Judgeships," in Colin Campbell and Bert Rockman, eds., *The George W. Bush Presidency* (Washington, D.C.: CQ Press, 2004), 139–143.

21. Manu Raju, "Republicans Warn Obama on Judges," *Politico*, March 2, 2009, www.politico.com/news/stories/0309/19526.html.

22. Al Weaver, "Schumer Blasts 'Appalling' Senate GOP Flip-Flop on Judicial Nominees," *Washington Examiner*, May 7, 2018, www.washingtonexaminer.com/news/congress/schumer-blasts-appalling-senate-gop-flip-flop-on-judicial-nominees.

23. Greg Gordon, "Federal Courts, Winner Will Make a Mark on the Bench," *Minneapolis Star Tribune*, September 27, 2004, 1A.

24. Savage, "Ratings Shrink President's List for Judgeships."

25. Allan Smith, "Trump Is Bypassing Judicial Ratings Agencies Before Making His Nominations—and It Has Led to a Substantial Increase in 'Not Qualified' Nominees," *Business Insider*, November 15, 2017, www.businessinsider.com/trump-judicial-nominees-increase-in-aba-not-qualified-ratings-2017-11.

26. Gallup Organization, *Polls, Topics & Trends: Trust in Government*, various dates through 2004, www.gallup.com/poll/content/?ci=5392&pg=1; Linda Greenhouse, "The Nation: Vote Count Omits a Verdict on the Court," *New York Times*, November 18, 2001, sec. 4, 4.

27. Davis and Snell, "Mitch McConnell on Filling the Federal Bench."

28. Although the president has no official "list" of criteria, scholars are mostly agreed on these factors. See, for instance, Henry J. Abraham, *The Judiciary* (New York: New York University Press, 1996), 65–69; Lawrence Baum, *American Courts* (Boston, Mass.: Houghton Mifflin, 1998), 105–106; Philip Cooper and Howard Ball, *The United States Supreme Court: From the Inside Out* (Upper Saddle River, N.J.: Prentice Hall, 1996), 49–60; and Thomas G. Walker and Lee Epstein, *The Supreme Court of the United States* (New York: St. Martin's Press, 1993), 34–40.

29. Baum, *American Courts*, 4th ed., 105.

30. From the filmstrip *This Honorable Court* (Washington, D.C.: Greater Washington Educational Telecommunications Association, 1988), program 1.

31. Ibid.

32. Peter Baker, "Kagan Nomination Leaves Longing on the Left," *New York Times*, May 10, 2010, www.nytimes.com/2010/05/11/us/politics/11nominees.html.

33. Oyez, "Neil Gorsuch," https://www.oyez.org/justices/neil_gorsuch.

34. CBS News, September 29, 2018, "Brett Kavanaugh's attack on Democrats could pose risk to Supreme Court," https://www.cbsnews.com/news/brett-kavanaugh-attack-on-democrats-poses-risk-to-supreme-court/.>

35. Baum, *American Courts*, 4th ed., 105.

36. Walker and Epstein, *The Supreme Court of the United States*, 40.

37. Sonia Sotomayor, "A Latina Judge's Voice," address at U.C. Berkeley, October 26, 2001, www.berkeley.edu/news/media/releases/2009/05/26_sotomayor.shtml.

38. Baum, *The Supreme Court*, 8th ed., 103.

39. U.S. Supreme Court, "2013 Year-End Report on the Federal Judiciary," www.supremecourt.gov/publicinfo/year-end/2013year-endreport.pdf.

40. Federal Judicial Center, "Supreme Court Caseloads, 1880–2015," www.fjc.gov/history/exhibits/graphs-and-maps/supreme-court-caseloads-1880-2015.

41. Cooper and Ball, *The United States Supreme Court*, 104.

42. Ibid., 134.

43. Walker and Epstein, *The Supreme Court of the United States*, 90.

44. Ibid., 91–92.

45. Walker and Epstein, *The Supreme Court of the United States*, 129–130.

46. Adam Cohen, "Psst . . . Justice Scalia . . . You Know, You're an Activist Too," *New York Times*, April 19, 2005, www.nytimes.com/2005/04/19/opinion/psst-justice-scalia-you-know-youre-an-activist-judge-too.html.

47. What follows is drawn from the excellent discussion in Cohen, "Psst . . . Justice Scalia," 131–139.

48. Baum, *The Supreme Court*, 8th ed., 82; Greg Stohr, "Record Number of Amicus Briefs Filed in Health Care Cases," Bloomberg News, March 15, 2012, go.bloomberg.com/health-care-supreme-court/2012-03-15/record-number-of-amicus-briefs-filed-in-health-care-cases/.

49. Max Lerner, *Nine Scorpions in a Bottle: Great Judges and Cases of the Supreme Court* (New York: Arcade Publishing, 1994).

50. Philip J. Cooper, *Battles on the Bench: Conflict Inside the Supreme Court* (Lawrence: University Press of Kansas, 1995), 42–46.

51. For a provocative argument that the Court does not, in fact, successfully produce significant social reform and actually damaged the civil rights struggles in this country, see Gerald N. Rosenberg,

The Hollow Hope: Can Courts Bring About Social Change? (Chicago, Ill.: University of Chicago Press, 1991).

52. *Marbury v. Madison* (1803).

53. *Martin v. Hunter's Lessee*, 14 U.S. 304 (1816).

54. *McCulloch v. Maryland*, 4 Wheat. 316 (1819).

55. *Gibbons v. Ogden*, 9 Wheat. 1 (1824).

56. *Lochner v. New York*, 198 U.S. 45 (1905).

57. *Hammer v. Dagenhart*, 247 U.S. 251 (1918).

58. *Adkins v. Children's Hospital*, 261 U.S. 525 (1923).

59. *Dred Scott v. Sanford*, 19 How. 393 (1857).

60. *Plessy v. Ferguson*, 163 U.S. 537 (1896).

61. *Brown v. Board of Education*, 347 U.S. 483 (1954).

62. For example, *Mapp v. Ohio*, 367 U.S. 643 (1961); *Gideon v. Wainwright*, 372 U.S. 335 (1963); and *Miranda v. Arizona*, 382 U.S. 925 (1965).

63. *Baker v. Carr*, 396 U.S. 186 (1962).

64. *Roe v. Wade*, 410 U.S. 113 (1973).

65. *Citizens United v. Federal Election Commission*, 558 U.S. ____ (2010).

66. Tom McCarthy, "The Supreme Court Has Already Reshaped America—Here's How," *Guardian*, July 2, 2018, www.theguardian.com/law/2018/jul/02/supreme-court-donald-trump-anthony-kennedy-conservative-nominee-republicans.

67. Pew Research Center for the People and the Press, "Stark Racial Divisions in Reactions to Ferguson Police Shooting," August 18, 2014, www.people-press.org/2014/08/18/stark-racial-divisions-in-reactions-to-ferguson-police-shooting/.

68. Jeremy Stahl, "The NFL Just Gave Donald Trump Everything He Wanted," *Slate*, May 23, 2018, slate.com/culture/2018/05/the-nfls-new-anthem-policy-is-a-political-gift-from-roger-goodell-to-donald-trump.html; Tom Schad, "'#Winning': Mike Pence Hails NFL's New Anthem Policy as a Victory for Donald Trump," *USA Today*, May 23, 2018, www.usatoday.com/story/sports/nfl/2018/05/23/mike-pence-nfl-new-national-anthem-policy-win-donald-trump/637826002/.

69. "New Yorkers' Views of the Mayor and the Police," *New York Times*, August 20, 2012, www.nytimes.com/interactive/2012/08/20/nyregion/new-yorkers-views-of-the-mayor-and-the-police.html.

70. Joseph Goldstein, "Judge Rejects New York's Stop and Frisk Policy," *New York Times*, August 12, 2013, www.nytimes.com/2013/08/13/nyregion/stop-and-frisk-practice-violated-rights-judge-rules.html.

71. Dylan Matthews, "The Black/White Marijuana Arrest Gap, in Nine Charts," *Washington Post Wonkblog*, June 4, 2013, www.washingtonpost.com/blogs/wonkblog/wp/2013/06/04/the-blackwhite-marijuana-arrest-gap-in-nine-charts/.

72. Bureau of Justice Statistics, "Indigent Defense Systems," www.bjs.gov/index.cfm?ty=tp&tid=28#top.

73. John H. Langbein, "Money Talks, Clients Walk," *Newsweek*, April 17, 1995, 32.

74. Legal Services Corporation, "Fact Sheet: What Is LSC?", www.lsc.gov/about/factsheet_whatislsc.php.

75. Consortium on Legal Services and the Public, *Agenda for Success: The American People and Civil Justice* (Chicago, Ill.: American Bar Association, 1996); see also Legal Services Corporation, "Serving the Civil Legal Needs of Low-Income Americans," April 30, 2000, www.lsc.gov/pressr/exsum.pdf.

76. Justin McCarthy, "Americans Losing Confidence in All Branches of U.S. Government," Gallup Politics, June 30, 2014, www.gallup.com/poll/171992/americans-losing-confidence-branches-gov.aspx.

77. Dahleen Glanton, "O'Connor Questions Court's Decision to Take Bush v. Gore," *Chicago Tribune*, April 27, 2013, articles.chicagotribune.com/2013-04-27/news/ct-met-sandra-day-oconnor-edit-board-20130427_1_o-connor-bush-v-high-court.

78. Linda Greenhouse, "*Bush v. Gore*: A Special Report," *New York Times*, February 20, 2001.

CHAPTER 10

1. Brian Wheeler and Alex Hunt, "Brexit: All You Need to Know About the UK Leaving the EU," BBC, August 10, 2016, www.bbc.com/news/uk-politics-32810887.

2. Lizzie Dearden, "Brexit Research Suggests 1.2 Million Leave Voters Regret Their Choice in Reversal That Could Change Result," *Independent*, July 1, 2016, www.independent.co.uk/news/uk/politics/brexit-news-second-eu-referendum-leave-voters-regret-bregret-choice-in-millions-a7113336.html.

3. Mike Gravel, "Philadelphia II: National Initiatives," *Campaigns and Elections* (December 1995/January 1996): 2.

4. According to a September 1994 Roper poll, 76 percent favor a national referendum.

5. Survey by Fox News and Opinion Dynamics, May 24–May 25, 2000. Retrieved from the iPOLL database, The Roper Center for Public Opinion Research, University of Connecticut, www.ropercenter.uconn.edu/ipoll.html.

6. "Exchange With Reporters in Waco, Texas, August 7, 2001," in *Public Papers of the Presidents: George W. Bush—2001*, vol. 2, p. 945. U.S. Government Printing Office via GPO Access.

7. Joshua Green, "The Other War Room," *Washington Monthly*, April 2002, 16.

8. Matt Bai, "Rove's Way," *New York Times Magazine*, October 20, 2002, 56.

9. V. O. Key Jr., *Public Opinion and American Democracy* (New York: Knopf, 1961), 7.

10. John Kingdon, *Congressmen's Voting Decisions*, 2nd ed. (New York: Harper & Row, 1981), ch. 2.

11. Gary C. Jacobson, "The War, the President, and the 2006 Midterm Congressional Elections," paper presented at the annual meeting of the Midwest Political Science Association, Chicago, April 12–15, 2007.

12. Many works repeat this theme of the uninformed and ignorant citizen. See, for example, Bernard Berelson, Paul F. Lazarsfeld, and William N. McPhee, *Voting: A Study of Opinion Formation in a Presidential Campaign* (Chicago, Ill.: University of Chicago Press, 1954); Angus Campbell, Philip E. Converse, Warren E. Miller, and Donald E. Stokes, *The American Voter* (New York: Wiley, 1960); W. Russell Neuman, *The Paradox of Mass Politics* (Cambridge, Mass.: Harvard University Press, 1986); and Michael X. Delli Carpini and Scott Keeter, *What Americans Know About Politics and Why It Matters* (New Haven, Conn.: Yale University Press, 1996).

13. Pew Research Center, "From Brexit to Zika: What Do Americans Know?", July 25, 2017, www.people-press.org/2017/07/25/from-brexit-to-zika-what-do-americans-know/.

14. Pew Research Center for the People and the Press, October 2011 Knowledge Survey.

15. Herbert McClosky and Alida Brill, *Dimensions of Tolerance* (New York: Russell Sage Foundation, 1983), 50.

16. Ibid.

17. M. Kent Jennings and Richard G. Niemi, *The Political Character of Adolescence* (Princeton, N.J.: Princeton University Press, 1974); Robert C. Luskin, John P. McIver, and Edward Carmines, "Issues and the Transmission of Partisanship," *American Journal of Political Science* 33 (May 1989): 440–458; Christopher H. Achen, "Parental Socialization and Rational Party Identification," *Political Behavior* 24 (June 2002): 151–170.

18. Shirley Engle and Anna Ochoa, *Education for Democratic Citizenship: Decision Making in the Social Studies* (New York: Teachers College of Columbia University, 1988).

19. Kenneth D. Wald, Dennis E. Owen, and Samuel S. Jill Jr., "Political Cohesion in Churches," *Journal of Politics* 52 (1990): 197–215; Robert Huckfeldt, Paul Allen Beck, Russell J. Dalton, and Jeffrey Levine, "Political Environments, Cohesive Social Groups, and the Communication of Public Opinion," *American Journal of Political Science* 39 (1995): 1025–1054; David C. Leege, Kenneth D. Wald, Brian S. Krueger, and Paul D. Mueller, *The Politics of Cultural Differences: Social Change and Voter Mobilization in the Post–New Deal Period* (Princeton, N.J.: Princeton University Press, 2002).

20. Elisabeth Noelle-Neumann, *The Spiral of Silence: Public Opinion, Our Social Skin* (Chicago, Ill.: University of Chicago Press, 1984).

21. Lee Sigelman and Susan Welch, *Black Americans' Views of Racial Equality—The Dream Deferred* (Cambridge, U.K.: Cambridge University Press, 1991).

22. Katherine Tate, "Black Political Participation in the 1984 and 1988 Presidential Elections," *American Political Science Review* 85 (December 1991): 1159–1176.

23. Thomas B. Edsall, "Why Are Asian-Americans Such Loyal Democrats?", *New York Times*, November 4, 2015, www.nytimes.com/2015/11/04/opinion/why-are-asian-americans-such-loyal-democrats.html.

24. Figure calculated by the authors from National Election Studies data.

25. Rosalee A. Clawson and Zoe M. Oxley, *Public Opinion: Democratic Ideal and Democratic Practice*, 2nd ed. (Washington, D.C.: CQ Press, 2013).

26. "Trends in Voter Turnout," Social Science Data Analysis Network analysis of Current Population Survey data, www.ssdan.net/sites/default/files/briefs/vtbrief.pdf; Center for Information and Research on Civic Learning and Engagement, "Voter Turnout Among Young Women and Men in the 2012 Presidential Election," www.civicyouth.org/wp-content/uploads/2013/05/fs_gender_13_final.pdf.

27. Christine L. Day, *What Older Americans Think: Interest Groups and Aging Policy* (Princeton, N.J.: Princeton University Press, 1990).

28. Scott Helman, "Obama Strikes Chord With Generation Next: Campaign Targets Youth Vote in Ind," *Boston Globe*, May 3, 2008; Cynthia Burton and Joseph A. Gambardello, "Turnout for N.J. Primary Highest in Half a Century," *Philadelphia Inquirer*, February 7, 2008.

29. Paul R. Abramson and Ada W. Finifter, "On the Meaning of Political Trust: New Evidence From Items Introduced in 1978," *American Journal of Political Science* 25 (May 1981): 295–306; Arthur H. Miller, "Is Confidence Rebounding?" *Public Opinion* (June/July 1983); Robert S. Erikson and Kent L. Tedin, *American Public Opinion*, 7th ed. (New York: Pearson-Longman, 2005), 162–166.

30. Warren E. Miller and J. Merrill Shanks, *The New American Voter* (Cambridge, Mass.: Harvard University Press, 1996), ch. 7.

31. Hannah Fingerhut, "Millennials' Views of News Media, Religious Organizations Grow More Negative," Pew Research Center, January 4, 2016, www.pewresearch.org/fact-tank/2016/01/04/millennials-views-of-news-media-religious-organizations-grow-more-negative/; David Masci, "Q&A: Why Millennials Are Less Religious Than Older Americans," Pew Research Center, January 8, 2016, www.pewresearch.org/fact-tank/2016/01/08/qa-why-millennials-are-less-religious-than-older-americans/; Eileen Patten, "The Nation's Latino Population Is Defined by Its Youth," Pew Research Center, April 20, 2016, www.pewhispanic.org/2016/04/20/the-nations-latino-population-is-defined-by-its-youth/.

32. "A Deep Dive Into Party Affiliation, Pew Research Center, April 7, 2015, www.people-press.org/2015/04/07/a-deep-dive-into-party-affiliation/.

33. Campbell et al., *The American Voter*; Donald P. Green, Bradley Palmquist, and Eric Schickler, *Partisan Hearts and Minds: Political Parties and the Social Identities of Voters* (New Haven, Conn.: Yale University Press, 2002).

34. CBS News poll, February 2–4, 2009; telephone survey of 864 respondents, calculated by the authors from data obtained from the Roper Center; Janell Ross, "How Come 53% of Republicans Think the Unemployment Rate Has Risen Under Obama?", *Washington Post*, November 20, 2015, www.washingtonpost.com/news/the-fix/wp/2015/11/20/the-amount-of-misinformation-about-our-economy-is-amazing/.

35. M. J. Hetherington, "Resurgent Mass Partisanship: The Role of Elite Polarization," *American Political Science Review* 95 (2001): 619–631; Alan Abramowitz, *The Disappearing Center: Engaged Citizens, Polarization and American Democracy* (New Haven, Conn.: Yale University Press, 2010); Matthew S. Levendusky, *The Partisan Sort: How Liberals Became Democrats and Conservatives Became Republicans* (Chicago, Ill.: University of Chicago Press, 2010).

36. Gerald C. Wright and Nathan Birkhead, "The Macro Sort of State Partisanship," *Political Research Quarterly* 67 (2014): 426–439.

37. Lilliana Mason, "The Rise of Uncivil Agreement: Issue Versus Behavioral Polarization in the American Electorate," *American Behavioral Scientist* 57 (2013): 140–159; Daniel M. Shea and Morris P. Fiorina, *Can We Talk? The Rise of Rude, Nasty, Stubborn Politics* (New York: Pearson, 2013).

38. Norman H. Nie, Jane Junn, and Kenneth Stehlik-Barry, *Education and Democratic Citizenship in America* (Chicago, Ill.: University of Chicago Press, 1996).

39. For more on the effects of education, see Delli Carpini and Keeter, 188–189; Erikson and Tedin, 7th ed., 152–159; and Herbert H. Hyman, Charles R. Wright, and John Shelton Reed, *The Enduring Effects of Education* (Chicago, Ill.: University of Chicago Press, 1975). For a dissenting view that formal education is just a mask for intelligence and native cognitive ability, see Robert Luskin, "Explaining Political Sophistication," *Political Behavior* 12 (1990): 3298–3409.

40. Robert S. Erikson, Gerald C. Wright, and John P. McIver, *Statehouse Democracy* (New York: Cambridge University Press, 1993), 18.

41. Philip Bump, "There Really Are Two Americas, An Urban One and a Rural One," *Washington Post*, October 21, 2014, www.washingtonpost.com/news/the-fix/wp/2014/10/21/there-really-are-two-americas-a-urban-one-and-a-rural-one/.

42. Richard Morin, "Don't Ask Me: As Fewer Cooperate on Polls, Criticism and Questions Mount," *Washington Post*, October 28, 2004, C1.

43. Pew Research Center for the People and the Press, "Opinion Poll Experiment Reveals Conservative Opinions Not Underestimated, But Racial Hostility Missed," March 27, 1998, www.people-press.org/content.htm; Andrew Rosenthal, "The 1989 Elections: Predicting the Outcome; Broad Disparities in Votes and Polls Raising Questions," *New York Times*, November 9, 1989, A1; Adam Clymer, "Election Day Shows What the Opinion Polls Can't Do," *New York Times*, November 12, 1989, sec. 4, 4; George Flemming and Kimberly Parker, "Race and Reluctant Respondents: Possible Consequences of Non-Response for Pre-Election Survey," May 16, 1998, www.people-press.org/content.htm.

44. William Saletan, "Phoning It In," *Slate*, December 7, 2007, www.slate.com/iod/2179395/.

45. SurveyUSA home page, www.surveyusa.com.

46. David Sanders, Harold D. Clarke, Marianne C. Stewart, and Paul Whiteley, "Does Mode Matter for Modeling Political Choice? Evidence From the 2005 British Election Study," *Political Analysis* 15 (2007): 257–285; Robert P. Berrens, Alok K. Bohara, Hank Jenkins-Smith, Carol Silva, and David L. Weimer, "The Advent of Internet Surveys for Political Research: A Comparison of Telephone and Internet Samples," *Political Analysis* 11 (2003): 1–22; Taylor Humphrey, "The Case for Publishing (Some) Online Polls," *Polling Report*, January 15, 2007; Linchiat Chang and Jon A. Krosnick, "National Surveys via RDD Telephone Interviewing Versus the Internet," *Public Opinion Quarterly* 2009 (73): 641–678.

47. J. Michael Brick, Pat D. Brick, Sarah Dipko, Stanley Presser, Clyde Tucker, and Yangyang Yuan, "Cell Phone Survey Feasibility in the U.S.: Sampling and Calling Cell Numbers Versus Landline Numbers," *Public Opinion Quarterly* 71 (Spring 2007): 23–39. See the special issue of *Public Opinion Quarterly* (Winter 2007) for perspectives on the challenges that cell phones pose for surveys.

48. Nate Silver, "Which Polls Fared Best, and Worst, in the 2012 Presidential Race," FiveThirtyEight, November 10, 2012, fivethirtyeight.blogs.nytimes.com/2012/11/10/which-polls-fared-best-and-worst-in-the-2012-presidential-race/.

49. Adam Lisberg, "Exit Polls Out of Whack: Early Numbers Told Wrong Story," *New York Daily News*, November 4, 2002, 11; "Evaluation of Edison/Mitofsky Election System 2004," prepared by Edison Media Research and Mitofsky International for the National Election Pool (NEP), January 19, 2005.

50. "Pollsters Seek AAPC Action," *Campaigns and Elections* (July 1996): 55.

51. TESS Time-Sharing Experiments for the Social Sciences, tess.experimentcentral.org.

52. Robert S. Erikson and Kent Tedin, *American Public Opinion*, 5th ed. (Boston, Mass.: Allyn & Bacon, 1995), 42–47.

53. Research suggests that use of information shortcuts does allow the electorate to make decisions that are more in line with their values than if they did not have such shortcuts; see Samuel Popkin, *The Reasoning Voter* (Chicago, Ill.: University of Chicago Press, 1991); and Paul Sniderman, Richard Brody, and Philip Tetlock, *Reasoning and Choice: Exploration in Political Psychology* (New York: Cambridge

University Press, 1991). However, this is not the same as saying that, if fully informed, everyone would make the same decision as they do without information. Indeed, information really does count; see Larry Bartels, "Uninformed Votes: Information Effects in Presidential Elections," *American Journal of Political Science* 40 (February 1996): 194–230; and Scott Althaus, "Information Effects in Collective Preferences," *American Political Science Review* 92 (September 1998): 545–558.

54. Milton Lodge, Kathleen McGraw, and Patrick Stroh, "An Impression-Driven Model of Candidate Evaluation," *American Political Science Review* 82 (June 1989): 399–419.

55. Berelson, Lazarsfeld, and McPhee, *Voting*, 109–115.

56. Philip Meyer, "The Elite Newspaper of the Future," *American Journalism Review* (October/November 2008), www.ajr.org/article.asp?id=4605.

57. Ibid.

58. J. C. Baumgartner and J. S. Morris, "MyFaceTube Politics: Social Networking Web Sites and Political Engagement of Young Adults," *Social Science Computer Review* 28 (2009): 24–44.

59. Larry M. Bartels, "Uninformed Votes: Information Effects in Presidential Elections," *American Journal of Political Science* 40 (1996): 194–230.

60. Gerald C. Wright, "Level of Analysis Effects on Explanations of Voting," *British Journal of Political Science* 18 (July 1989): 381–398; Popkin, *The Reasoning Voter*; Benjamin Page and Robert Shapiro, *The Rational Public* (Chicago, Ill.: University of Chicago Press, 1993).

61. Erikson, Wright, and McIver, *Statehouse Democracy*, 18.

62. Michael B. MacKuen, Robert S. Erikson, and James A. Stimson, "Macropartisanship," *American Political Science Review* 89 (December 1989): 1125–1142.

63. Larry M. Bartels, *Unequal Democracy: The Political Economy of the New Gilded Age* (Princeton, N.J.: Princeton University Press, 2008), ch. 9; Martin Gilens, "Inequality and Democratic Responsiveness," *Public Opinion Quarterly* 69 (2005): 778–796.

64. Dearden, "Brexit Research Suggests 1.2 Million Leave Voters Regret Their Choice."

65. Jean Bethke Elshtain, "A Parody of True Democracy," *Christian Science Monitor*, August 13, 1992, 18.

CHAPTER 11

1. Brian Stelter, "Reid and Angle Campaigns Fight Over Web Site," The Caucus, July 6, 2010, thecaucus.blogs.nytimes.com/2010/07/06/reid-and-angle-campaigns-fight-over-web-site/?ref=politics; Adam Weinstein, "Nevada Tea Partiers' Memory Hole," *Mother Jones*, June 9, 2010, motherjones.com/mojo/2010/06/nevada-tea-partier-memoryhole-website-sharron-angle-harry-reidsenate.

2. Stelter, "Reid and Angle Campaigns Fight Over Web Site."

3. Jessica Taylor, "Mason-Dixon Poll: Reid Rises Again," *Politico*, July 16, 2010, www.politico.com/news/stories/0710/39842.html.

4. See, for example, James Bryce, *The American Commonwealth*, vol. 2 (Chicago, Ill.: Sergel, 1891), pt. 3.

5. E. E. Schattschneider, *Party Government* (New York: Holt, Rinehart & Winston, 1942), 1.

6. This definition and the following discussion are based on Frank Sorauf, *Party Politics in America* (Boston, Mass.: Little, Brown, 1964), ch. 1; and V. O. Key, *Politics, Parties, and Pressure Groups*, 5th ed. (New York: Corwell, 1964).

7. The discussion of national conventions is based on David Price, *Bring Back the Parties* (Washington, D.C.: Congressional Quarterly Press, 1984), chs. 6 and 7; and Leon D. Epstein, *Political Parties in the American Mold* (Madison: University of Wisconsin Press, 1986), ch. 4.

8. C. P. Cotter, J. L. Gibson, J. F. Bibby, and R. J. Huckshorn, *Party Organizations in American Politics* (New York: Praeger, 1984); John J. Coleman, "Resurgent or Just Busy? Party Organizations in

9. Gerald Pomper with Susan Lederman, *Elections in America*, 2nd ed. (New York: Longman, 1980), 145–150, 167–173.

10. Richard G. Niemi and M. Kent Jennings, "Issues of Inheritance in the Formation of Party Identification," *American Journal of Political Science* 35 (1991): 970–988.

11. The discussion of the responsible party model is based on Austin Ranney, *The Doctrine of the Responsible Party Government* (Urbana: University of Illinois Press, 1962), chs. 1 and 2; and Frank J. Sorauf and Paul Allen Beck, *Party Politics in America*, 6th ed. (Glenview, Ill.: Scott, Foresman, 1988), ch. 16.

12. Morris P. Fiorina, "The Decline of Collective Responsibility in American Politics," *Daedalus* 109 (Summer 1980): 24–45; John H. Aldrich, *Why Parties: The Origin and Transformation of Party Politics in America* (Chicago, Ill.: University of Chicago Press, 1995), 3.

13. American Political Science Association, "Toward a More Responsible Two-Party System: A Report of the Committee on Political Parties of the American Political Science Association," *American Political Science Review* 44 (1950; 3, pt. 2): 1–99.

14. Thomas E. Mann and Norman J. Ornstein, *It's Even Worse Than It Looks* (New York: Basic Books, 2012).

15. Aldrich, *Why Parties*, 69.

16. This discussion of the Jacksonian Democrats and machine politics and patronage is based on Aldrich, *Why Parties*, ch. 4; Epstein, *Political Parties in the American Mold*, 134–143; and Sorauf and Beck, *Party Politics in America*, 6th ed., 83–91.

17. Marjorie Randon Hershey, *Party Politics in America*, 11th ed. (New York: Longman, 2004), 130–135.

18. William H. Flanigan and Nancy H. Zingale, *Political Behavior of the American Electorate*, 9th ed. (Washington, D.C.: Congressional Quarterly Press, 1998), 59–66.

19. Gerald C. Wright, John P. McIver, Robert S. Erikson, and David B. Holian, "Stability and Change in State Electorates, Carter Through Clinton," paper presented at the Midwest Political Science Association meetings, Chicago, 2000; Larry Bartels, "Partisanship and Voting Behavior, 1952–1996," *American Journal of Political Science* 44 (2000): 35–50.

20. Ruy A. Teixeira and Joel Rogers, *America's Forgotten Majority: Why the White Working Class Still Matters* (New York: Basic Books, 2000); Thomas Frank, *What's the Matter With Kansas? How Conservatives Won the Heart of America* (New York: Metropolitan Books, 2004).

21. Anthony Downs, *An Economic Theory of Democracy* (New York: Harper & Row, 1957).

22. James L. Gibson and Susan E. Scarrow, "State Organizations in American Politics," in Eric M. Uslaner, ed., *American Political Parties: A Reader* (Itasca, Ill.: Peacock, 1993), 234.

23. James Q. Wilson, *The Amateur Democrat: Club Politics in Three Cities* (Chicago: University of Chicago Press, 1965).

24. Godfrey Hodgson, *The Myth of American Exceptionalism* (New Haven: Yale University Press, 2009).

25. Thomas Carsey, Geoffrey Layman and Mark Brockway, "Donald Trump and Conflict Extension in American Public Opinion" Paper presented at the annual meeting of the Southern Political Science Association, New Orleans, January 4–6, 2017.

26. Gerald C. Wright and Michael B. Berkman, "Candidates and Policy in U.S. Senatorial Elections," *American Political Science Review* 80 (1986): 576–590.

27. Alan Abramowitz and Steven Webster, "'Negative Partisanship' Explains Everything," *Politico*, September/October 2017, www.politico.com/magazine/story/2017/09/05/negative-partisanship-explains-everything-215534.

28. This section is based on Alan Ware, *Political Parties and Party Systems* (Oxford, U.K.: Oxford University Press, 1996).

29. L. Sandy Maisel, *Parties and Elections in America*, 2nd ed. (New York: McGraw-Hill, 1993), ch. 10; Price, *Bring Back the Parties*, 284.

30. Michelle Cottle, "House Broker," *New Republic*, June 11, 2008, www.tnr.com.

31. John Aldrich and David Rohde, "The Logic of Conditional Party Government: Revisiting the Electoral Connection," in L. Dodd and B. I. Oppenheimer, eds., *Congress Reconsidered*, 7th ed. (Washington, D.C.: CQ Press, 2001).

32. Ed Hornick, "The 'Big Headache': Boehner Backed Into Corner by Tea Party, Obama," CNN News, July 26, 2011, articles.cnn .com/2011-07-26/politics/tea.party.boehner_1_tea-party-debt-ceiling-debt-limit-vote?_s=PM:POLITICS.

33. Alexis de Tocqueville, *Democracy in America*, Richard D. Heffner, ed. (New York: New American Library, 1956), 198.

34. This definition is based on Jeffrey M. Berry, *The Interest Group Society*, 3rd ed. (New York: Longman, 1997); and David Truman, *The Governmental Process*, 2nd ed. (New York: Knopf, 1971).

35. Berry, *The Interest Group Society*, 6–8; John W. Kingdon, *Agendas, Alternatives, and Public Policy* (Boston, Mass.: Little, Brown, 1984).

36. Kingdon, *Agendas, Alternatives, and Public Policy*.

37. Mancur Olson Jr., *The Logic of Collective Action* (New York: Schocken, 1971).

38. Allan J. Cigler and Anthony J. Nowns, "Public Interest Entrepreneurs and Group Patrons," in Allan J. Cigler and Burdett A. Loomis, eds., *Interest Group Politics*, 4th ed. (Washington, D.C.: Congressional Quarterly Press, 1995), 77–78.

39. Pamela Fessler, "Ethics Standards Announced," *Congressional Quarterly Weekly Report*, December 12, 1992, 3792; Allison Mitchell, "A New Form of Lobbying Puts Public Face on Private Interests," *New York Times on the Web*, September 30, 1998.

40. Beverly A. Cigler, "Not Just Another Special Interest: Intergovernmental Representation," in Cigler and Loomis, eds., *Interest Group Politics*, 4th ed., 134–135.

41. Nyshka Chandran, "Foreign Officials From Four Countries Tried to Figure Out Ways to Manipulate Jared Kushner, Report Says," CNBC, February 28, 2018, www.cnbc.com/2018/02/28/foreign-officials-want-to-influence-jared-kushner-report.html; Chris Riotta, "Jared Kushner Hid One of His Companies on a Disclosure Form—Then Profited," *Newsweek*, October 12, 2017, www.newsweek.com/jared-kushner-ivanka-trump-white-house-forms-omissions-cadre-millions-679231; Jeremy Venook, "Is Kushner Companies Taking Advantage of Its Connection to the President?," *The Atlantic*, May 9, 2017, www.theatlantic.com/business/archive/2017/05/jared-kushner-conflict-of-interest/525897/.

42. William Safire, *Safire's New Political Dictionary* (New York: Random House, 1993), 417–418.

43. Dan Eggen and R. Jeffrey Smith, "Lobbying Rules Surpass Those of Previous Administrations, Experts Say," *Washington Post*, January 22, 2009, www.washingtonpost.com/wp-dyn/content/article/2009/01/21/AR2009012103472.html.

44. Derek Kravitz and Alex Mierjeski, "Trump Promised His Appointees Wouldn't Become Lobbyists. Guess How That Turned Out," *Mother Jones*, May 6, 2018, www.motherjones.com/politics/2018/05/trump-promised-his-appointees-wouldnt-become-lobbyists-guess-how-that-turned-out/.

45. Ben Mathis-Lilley, "Swamp-Draining Trump Administration Has Hired 187 Lobbyists, New Report Finds," *Slate*, March 7, 2018, slate .com/news-and-politics/2018/03/trump-administration-has-hired-187-lobbyists-propublic-finds-swamp-much.html.

46. See Diana M. Evans, "Lobbying the Committee: Interest Groups and the House Public Works and Transportation Committee," in Allan J. Cigler and Burdett A. Loomis, eds., *Interest Group Politics*, 3rd ed. (Washington, D.C.: Congressional Quarterly Press, 1991), 264–265. For a graphic example of this practice, see Michael Weisskopf and David Maraniss, "Forging an Alliance for Deregulation; Rep. DeLay Makes Companies Full Partners in the Movement," *Washington Post*, March 12, 1995, A1.

47. Adam Clymer, "Congress Passes Bill to Disclose Lobbyists' Roles," *New York Times*, November 30, 1995, 1.

48. Adam Clymer, "Senate, 98–0, Sets Tough Restriction on Lobbyist Gifts," *New York Times*, July 29, 1995, 1; "House Approves Rule to Prohibit Lobbyists' Gifts," *New York Times*, November 17, 1995, 1.

49. David S. Cloud, "Three-Month-Old Gift Ban Having Ripple Effect," *Congressional Quarterly Weekly Report*, March 23, 1996, 777–778.

50. Jeff Zeleny and David D. Kirkpatrick, "House, 411–8, Passes a Vast Ethics Overhaul," *New York Times*, August 1, 2007.

51. Megan R. Wilson, "Bombshell: Ethics Office Alleges Illegal Lobbying," *The Hill*, July 25, 2014, thehill.com/business-a-lobbying/business-a-lobbying/213394-bombshell-ethics-office-alleges-illegal-lobbying.

52. Zeleny and Kirkpatrick, "House, 411–8, Passes a Vast Ethics Overhaul."

53. Alan Zibel, "Presidency for Sale: 64 Trade Groups, Companies, Candidates, Foreign Governments and Political Groups Spending Money at Trump's Properties," Public Citizen, January 16, 2018, https://corporatepresidency.org/presidencyforsale/.

54. See Douglas Yates, *Bureaucratic Democracy* (Cambridge, Mass.: Harvard University Press, 1982), ch. 4.

55. Samuel Kernell, *Going Public: New Strategies of Presidential Leadership* (Washington, D.C.: Congressional Quarterly Press, 1986), 34.

56. Berry, *The Interest Group Society*, 121–122.

57. Cindy Skrzycki, "The Newest Lobbying Tool: Underwear," *Washington Post*, May 29, 2007, D1.

58. Susan Dodge and Becky Beaupre, "Internet Blamed in Spread of Hate," *Chicago Sun-Times*, July 6, 1999, 3; Jennifer Oldham, "Wiesenthal Center Compiles List of Hate-Based Web Sites," *Los Angeles Times*, December 18, 1999, A1; Victor Volland, "Group Warns of Hate on Internet," *St. Louis Post-Dispatch*, October 22, 1997, 8A; Becky Beaupre, "Internet Pumps Up the Volume of Hatred," *USA Today*, February 18, 1997, 6A.

59. Chris Good, "The Tea Party Movement: Who's in Charge?" *The Atlantic*, April 13, 2009, www.theatlantic.com/politics/archive/2009/04/the-tea-party-movement-whos-in-charge/13041/.

60. Mark Brunswick, "Prescription Politics; Drug Lobby Intensifies Fight on Price Controls and Imports," *Minneapolis Star Tribune*, November 16, 2003, 1A; Jim VandeHei and Juliet Eilperin, "Drug Firms Gain Church Group's Aid; Claim About Import Measure Stirs Anger," *Washington Post*, July 23, 2003, A01.

61. Mike Murphy, quoted in Alison Mitchell, "A New Form of Lobbying Puts Public Face on Private Interest," *New York Times*, September 30, 1998, A1.

62. Bill McAllister, "Rainmakers Making a Splash," *Washington Post*, December 4, 1997, A21.

63. Federal Election Commission, "PAC's Grouped by Total Spent," April 13, 2005, www.fec.gov/press/press2005/20050412pac/groupbyspending2004.pdf; Richard L. Hall and Frank W. Wayman, "Buying Time: Money Interests and the Mobilization of Bias in Congressional Committees," *American Political Science Review* 84 (1990): 797–820.

64. Michael Luo, "Money Talks Louder Than Ever in Midterms," *New York Times*, October 7, 2010, www.nytimes.com/2010/10/08/us/politics/08donate.html; *Citizens United v. Federal Election Commission*, 558 U.S. 50 (2010).

65. Dan Eggen and T. W. Farnam, "Spending by Independent Groups Had Little Election Impact, Analysis Finds," *Washington Post*, November 7, 2012, www.washington post.com/politics/decision 2012/spending-by-independent-groups-had-little-election-impact-analysis-finds/2012/11/07/15fd30ea-276c-11e2-b2a0-ae18d6159439_story.html.

66. Jeffrey H. Birnbaum, "To Predict Losers in a Power Shift, Follow the Money," *Washington Post*, October 16, 2006, D1.

67. Andrew Bard Schmookler, "When Money Talks, Is It Free Speech?" *Christian Science Monitor*, November 11, 1997, 15; Nelson W. Polsby, "Money Gains Access. So What?" *New York Times*, August 13, 1997, A19.

68. Sara Fritz, "Citizen Lobby's Call to Arms," *International Herald-Tribune*, January 4–5, 1997; Katharine Q. Seelye, "G.O.P.'s Reward for Top Donors: 3 Days With Party Leaders," *New York Times*, February 20, 1997, A6.

69. "Senators Supporting Public Option Received Half as Much Money From Health Insurers," October 9, 2009, maplight.org/senators-supporting-public-option-got-half-as-much-money-from-health-insurers.

70. See John R. Wright, *Interest Groups and Congress* (Boston, Mass.: Allyn & Bacon, 1996), 136–145; "Contributions, Lobbying, and Committee

Voting in the U.S. House of Representatives," *American Political Science Review* 84 (1990): 417–438; Richard L. Hall and Frank W. Wayman, "Buying Time: Money Interests and the Mobilization of Bias in Congressional Committees," *American Political Science Review* 84 (1990): 797–820.

71. Robert Salisbury, "An Exchange Theory of Interest Groups," *Midwest Journal of Political Science* 13 (1969): 1–32.

72. Lee Fritscheler and James M. Hoefler, *Smoking and Politics*, 5th ed. (Upper Saddle River, N.J.: Prentice Hall, 1996), 20–35.

73. Truman, *The Governmental Process*, 2nd ed., 519.

74. See C. Wright Mills, *The Power Elite* (New York: Oxford University Press, 1956); G. William Domhoff, *The Powers That Be* (New York: Vintage, 1979).

75. The problem is that a relatively small number of groups have large memberships. Labor unions, some environmental groups like the Sierra Club, some social movements revolving around abortion and women's rights, and the NRA currently have large memberships spread across a number of congressional districts.

CHAPTER 12

1. Jonathan Mahler and Steven Edder, "The Electoral College Is Hated by Many. So Why Does It Endure?" *New York Times*, November 201, 2016, www.nytimes.com/2016/11/11/us/politics/the-electoral-college-is-hated-by-many-so-why-does-it-endure.html.

2. Ibid.

3. Gerald Pomper, *Elections in America* (New York: Dodd, Mead, 1970), 1.

4. International Institute for Democracy and Electoral Assistance, "Turnout in the World, Country by Country Performance," 2005, www.idea.int/vt/survey/voter_turnout_pop2.cfm.

5. Benjamin Highton, "Voter Registration and Turnout in the United States," *Perspectives on Politics* 2 (2004): 507–515.

6. Brennan Center for Justice, "States With New Voting Restrictions Since 2010 Election," www.brennancenter.org/new-voting-restrictions-2010-election.

7. Camila Domonoske, "As November Approaches, Courts Deal Series of Blows to Voter ID Laws," NPR, August 2, 2016, www.npr.org/sections/thetwo-way/2016/08/02/488392765/as-november-approaches-courts-deal-series-of-blows-to-voter-id-laws; Ariane de Vogue, "Voting Challenges Head Toward the Supreme Court: 4 Cases to Watch," CNN, July 19, 2016, www.cnn.com/2016/07/19/politics/voting-rights-supreme-court/; Adam Liptak and Michael Wines, "Strict North Carolina Voter ID Law Thwarted After Supreme Court Rejects Case," *New York Times*, May 15, 2017, www.nytimes.com/2017/05/15/us/politics/voter-id-laws-supreme-court-north-carolina.html; Joan Biskupic, "How the Supreme Court Is Changing the Rules on Voting," CNN, June 25, 2018, www.cnn.com/2018/06/25/politics/supreme-court-voting-rights-gerrymandering/index.html.

8. Steven J. Rosenstone and John Mark Hansen, *Mobilization, Participation, and Democracy in America* (New York: Macmillan, 1993); Ruy A. Teixeira, *The Disappearing American Voter* (Washington, D.C.: Brookings Institution, 1992); Raymond E. Wolfinger and Steven J. Rosenstone, *Who Votes?* (New Haven, Conn.: Yale University Press, 1980); Richard J. Timpone, "Structure, Behavior, and Voter Turnout in the United States," *American Political Science Review* 92 (March 1998): 145–158.

9. All of the figures in this section are taken from, or calculated by, the authors from the tables in U.S. Bureau of the Census, "Voting and Registration," thedataweb.rm.census.gov/TheDataWeb_HotReport2/voting/voting.html.

10. Ibid.

11. Kay Lehman Schlozman, Sidney Verba, and Henry E. Brady, "Civic Participation and the Inequality Problem," in *Civic Engagement in American Democracy*, Theda Skocpol and Morris P. Fiorina, eds. (New York: Russell Sage, 1999); Henry E. Brady, Kay Lehman Schlozman, and Sidney Verba, "Prospecting for Participants: Rational Expectations and the Recruitment of Political Activists," *American Political Science Review* 93 (1999): 153–168.

12. John Petrocik, "Voter Turnout and Electoral Preference: The Anomalous Reagan Elections," in Kay Lehman Schlozman, ed., *Elections in America* (Boston, Mass.: Allen & Unwin, 1987), 239–260.

13. Jack Citrin, Eric Schickler, and John Sides, "What If Everyone Voted? Simulating the Impact of Increased Turnout in Senate Elections," *American Journal of Political Science* 47 (January 2003): 75–90.

14. Petrocik, "Voter Turnout and Electoral Preference," 243–251; Stephen Earl Bennett and David Resnick, "The Implications of Nonvoting for Democracy in the United States," *American Journal of Political Science* 34 (August 1990): 795.

15. Calculated by the authors from the 2004 and 2008 Pre- and Post-American National Election Studies.

16. Roper Center for Public Opinion Research, Community Consensus Survey, February 12–14, 1999.

17. Richard Brody, "The Puzzle of Political Participation in America," in Anthony King, ed., *The New American Political System* (Washington, D.C.: American Enterprise Institute, 1978), 287–324.

18. Teixeira, *The Disappearing American Voter*, ch. 2; Paul R. Abramson, John H. Aldrich, and David W. Rohde, *Change and Continuity in the 1996 and 1998 Elections* (Washington, D.C.: CQ Press, 1999).

19. Rosenstone and Hansen, *Mobilization, Participation, and Democracy in America*.

20. Alan S. Gerber and Donald P. Green, "The Effects of Canvassing, Direct Mail, and Telephone Contact on Voter Turnout: A Field Experiment," *American Political Science Review* 94 (2000): 653–663.

21. Gerald Pomper, "The Presidential Election: The Ills of American Politics After 9/11," in Michael Nelson, ed., *The Elections of 2004* (Washington, D.C.: CQ Press, 2005), 46.

22. Teixeira, *The Disappearing American Voter*, 36–50; Robert Putnam, *Bowling Alone: The Collapse and Revival of American Community* (New York: Simon & Schuster, 2000), 31–47.

23. Anthony Downs, *An Economic Theory of Democracy* (New York: Harper & Row, 1957), 260–276.

24. Morris P. Fiorina, "The Voting Decision: Instrumental and Expressive Aspects," *Journal of Politics* 38 (1976): 390–415.

25. V. O. Key Jr., *The Responsible Electorate: Rationality in Presidential Voting, 1936–1960* (Cambridge, Mass.: Harvard University Press, 1966); Warren E. Miller and J. Merrill Shanks, *The New American Voter* (Cambridge, Mass.: Harvard University Press, 1996), ch. 7.

26. CNN, "Election 2016: Exit Polls," http://edition.cnn.com/election/results/exit-polls/national/president.

27. Angus Campbell, Phillip Converse, Warren Miller, and Donald Stokes, *The American Voter* (New York: Wiley, 1960); Donald Green, Bradley Palmquist, and Eric Schickler, *Partisan Hearts and Minds* (New Haven, Conn.: Yale University Press, 2002); Larry M. Bartels, "Beyond the Running Tally: Partisan Bias in Political Perceptions," *Political Behavior* 24 (2002): 117–150.

28. M. Margaret Conway, Gertrude A. Steuernagel, and David W. Ahern, *Women and Political Participation: Cultural Change in the Political Arena*, 2nd ed. (Washington, D.C.: CQ Press, 2005).

29. Calculated from Harold W. Stanley and Richard G. Niemi, *Vital Statistics on American Politics, 2007–2008* (Washington, D.C.: CQ Press, 2008), 127.

30. These figures are taken from media exit polls for the 2004 and 2008 presidential elections; Ron Brownstein, "The American Electorate Has Changed, and There's No Turning Back," *National Journal*, November 8, 2012, www.nationaljournal.com/magazine/the-american-electorate-has-changed-and-there-s-no-turning-back-20121108.

31. Wendy K. Tam, "Asians—A Monolithic Voting Bloc?" *Political Behavior* 17 (1995): 223–249; Pie-Te Lein, M. Margaret Conway, and Janelle Wong, *The Politics of Asian-Americans: Diversity and Community* (New York: Routledge, 2004); Atiya Kai Stokes, "Latino Group Consciousness and Political Participation," *American Politics Research* 41 (2003): 361–378; Benjamin Highton and Arthur L. Burris, "New Perspectives on Latino Voter Turnout in the United States," *American Politics Research* 30 (2002): 285–306.

32. Pei-Te Lien, Christian Collet, Janelle Wong, and S. Karthick Ramakrishnan, "Asian Pacific American Public Opinion and

Participation," *PS: Political Science and Politics* 34 (2001): 628; David L. Leal, Matt A. Barreto, Jongho Lee, and Rodolfo O. de la Garza, "The Latino Vote in the 2004 Election," *PS: Political Science and Politics* 38 (2005): 41–49.

33. CNN, "Election 2016: Exit Polls," edition.cnn.com/election/results/exit-polls/national/president.

34. Downs, *An Economic Theory of Democracy.*

35. Edward Carmines and James Stimson, "Two Faces of Issue Voting," *American Political Science Review* 74 (March 1980): 78–91; Larry Bartels, *Unequal Democracy* (Princeton, N.J.: Princeton University Press, 2008).

36. James Fallows, "Why Americans Hate the Media," *Atlantic Monthly*, February 1996, 45–64.

37. Morris P. Fiorina, *Retrospective Voting in American National Elections* (New Haven, Conn.: Yale University Press, 1981).

38. "The Candidates' Confrontation: Excerpts From the Debate," *Washington Post*, October 30, 1980, A14.

39. Fiorina, "The Voting Decision"; Benjamin I. Page, *Choice and Echoes in Presidential Elections* (Chicago, Ill.: University of Chicago Press, 1978).

40. Pew Poll cited in John Sides and Lynn Vavreck, *The Gamble: Choice and Chance in the 2012 Presidential Election* (Princeton, N.J.: Princeton University Press, 2012), 28.

41. Fox News, "2012 Exit Polls."

42. Thomas R. Marshall, "Turnout and Representation: Caucuses Versus Primaries," *American Journal of Political Science* 22 (1978): 169–182; Gerald C. Wright, "Rules and the Ideological Character of Primary Electorates," in Steven S. Smith and Melanie J. Springer, eds., *Reforming the Presidential Nomination Process* (Washington, D.C.: Brookings Institution Press, 2009).

43. Barry Burden, "The Nominations: Technology, Money, and Transferable Momentum," in Michael Nelson, ed., *The Elections of 2004* (Washington, D.C.: CQ Press), 21–22.

44. Rhodes Cook, "Steps to the Nomination: Earlier Voting in 1996 Forecasts Fast and Furious Campaigns," *Congressional Quarterly Weekly*, August 19, 1995, 24487; Andi O'Rourke, "How Many States Have Caucuses Instead of Primaries? Here's Exactly What to Expect From Each One," *Bustle*, January 29, 2016, www.bustle.com/articles/138406-how-many-states-have-caucuses-instead-of-primaries-heres-exactly-what-to-expect-from-each-one.

45. Burden, "The Nominations," 21.

46. Jack Germond and Jules W. Witcover, "Front-Loading Folly: A Dash to Decision, at a Cost in Deliberation," *Baltimore Sun*, March 22, 1996.

47. Dave Jamieson, "Donald Trump Wanted to Back Out of Choosing Mike Pence for Veep: Reports," *Huffington Post*, July 15, 2016, www.huffingtonpost.com/entry/donald-trump-vp-offer-mike-pence_us_57894258e4b0867123e146b1.

48. Shlomo Slonim, "The Electoral College at Philadelphia," *Journal of American History* 73 (June 1986): 35.

49. Robin Kolodny and Angela Logan, "Political Consultants and the Extension of Party Goals," *PS: Political Science & Politics* (June 1998): 155–159.

50. Patrick Sellers, "Strategy and Background in Congressional Campaigns," *American Political Science Review* 92 (March 1998): 159–172.

51. Ruth Shalit, "The Oppo Boom," *New Republic*, January 3, 1994, 16–21; Adam Nagourney, "Researching the Enemy: An Old Political Tool Resurfaces in a New Election," *New York Times*, April 3, 1996, D20.

52. For other examples, see John Petrocik, "Issue Ownership in Presidential Elections, With a 1980 Case Study," *American Journal of Political Science* 40 (August 1996): 825–850.

53. Jenna Johnson, "Trump Demanded Obama's Records; But He's Not Releasing His Own," *Washington Post*, August 12, 2016, www.washingtonpost.com/politics/trump-demanded-obamas-records-now-more-are-asking-where-are-trumps/2016/08/12/b536925a-5ff3-11e6-9d2f-b1a3564181a1_story.html; Tom McCarthy, "Trump Dictated Note Saying He Was 'Astonishingly' Healthy, Doctor Says," *Guardian* (UK), May 2, 2018, https://www.theguardian.com/us-news/2018/may/01/trump-dictated-doctors-note-harold-bornstein; Michael Finnegan and Mark Z. Barabak, "'Shithole' and Other Racist Things Trump Has Said—So Far," *Los Angeles Times*,

January 12, 2018, www.latimes.com/politics/la-na-trump-racism-remarks-20180111-htmlstory.html; Glenn Kessler, "Donald Trump's Revisionist History of Mocking a Disabled Reporter," *Washington Post*, August 2, 2016, www.washingtonpost.com/news/fact-checker/wp/2016/08/02/donald-trumps-revisionist-history-of-mocking-a-disabled-reporter/; "Transcript: Donald Trump's Taped Comments About Women," *New York Times*, October 8, 2016, www.nytimes.com/2016/10/08/us/donald-trump-tape-transcript.html; Caitlin Yilek, "Trump Told Stern He Walked Backstage When Beauty Queens Were Naked," *The Hill*, October 9, 2016, thehill.com/blogs/ballot-box/presidential-races/300093-trump-confirms-he-walked-backstage-when-beauty-queens.

54. David B. Holian, "He's Stealing My Issues! Clinton's Crime Rhetoric and the Dynamics of Issue Ownership," *Political Behavior* 26 (2004): 95–124.

55. Kathleen Hall Jamieson, "Shooting to Win; Do Attack Ads Work? You Bet—and That's Not All Bad," *Washington Post*, September 26, 2004, B1.

56. Wisconsin Advertising Project, "Facts About Tone of Presidential Advertising Campaign From the Wisconsin Advertising Project," press release, October 16, 2008, wiscadproject.wisc.edu/wiscads_release_101608.pdf.

57. Shanto Iyengar and Donald Kinder, *News That Matters: Television and American Opinion* (Chicago, Ill.: University of Chicago Press, 1987); James N. Druckman, "Priming the Vote: Campaign Effects in a U.S. Senate Election," *Political Psychology* 25 (4): 577–594.

58. Thomas Patterson, *Out of Order* (New York: Knopf, 1993); Fallows, 45–64.

59. Elihu Katz and Jacob Feldman, "The Debates in Light of Research," in Sidney Kraus, ed., *The Great Debates* (Bloomington: Indiana University Press, 1962), 173–223.

60. Thomas Holbrook, "Campaigns, National Conditions, and U.S. Presidential Elections," *American Journal of Political Science* 38 (1994): 986–992; John Geer, "The Effects of Presidential Debates on the Electorate's Preferences for Candidates," *American Politics Quarterly* 16 (1988): 486–501; David Lanoue, "The 'Turning Point': Viewers' Reactions to the Second 1988 Presidential Debate," *American Politics Quarterly* 19 (1991): 80–89.

61. David Lanoue, "One That Made a Difference: Cognitive Consistency, Political Knowledge, and the 1980 Presidential Debate," *Public Opinion Quarterly* 56 (Summer 1992): 168–184; Carol Winkler and Catherine Black, "Assessing the 1992 Presidential and Vice Presidential Debates: The Public Rationale," *Argumentation and Advocacy* 30 (Fall 1993): 77–87; Lori McKinnon, John Tedesco, and Lynda Kaid, "The Third 1992 Presidential Debate: Channel and Commentary Effects," *Argumentation and Advocacy* 30 (Fall 1993): 106–118; Mike Yawn, Kevin Ellsworth, and Kim Fridkin Kahn, "How a Presidential Primary Debate Changed Attitudes of Audience Members," *Political Behavior* 20 (July 1998): 155–164; Annenberg Public Policy Center, "Voters Learned Positions on Issues Since Presidential Debates," NAES04 National Annenberg Election Survey, 2005, www.naes04.org.

62. Scott Keeter, "Public Opinion and the Election," in Gerald Pomper, ed., *The Election of 1996* (Chatham, N.J.: Chatham House, 1997), 127; drawn from polls done by the Pew Research Center and the Times Mirror Center.

63. OpenSecrets.org, "Banking on Becoming President" and "U.S. Election Will Cost $5.3 Billion, Center for Responsive Politics Predicts," www.opensecrets.org/pres08/index.php.

64. Federal Election Commission, "Chapter Two: Presidential Public Funding," 2005, www.fec.gov/info/arch2.htm.

65. Federal Election Commission, "Contribution Limits Chart 2007–08," www.fec.gov/pages/brochures/contriblimits.shtml.

66. Susan Glasser, "Court's Ruling in Colorado Case May Reshape Campaign Finance; Limits on Political Parties' 'Hard Money' Spending Nullified," *Washington Post*, March 28, 1999, A6; *FEC v. Colorado Republican Federal Campaign Committee*, 121 S. Ct. 2351, 2371 (2001).

67. 558 U.S. 50 (2010).

68. "How Corporate Money Will Reshape Politics: Restoring Free Speech in Elections," *New York Times*, January 21, 2010, roomfordebate.blogs.nytimes.com/2010/01/21/how-corporate-money-will-reshape-politics.

69. "The Court's Blow to Democracy," *New York Times*, January 21, 2010; Warren Richey, "Supreme Court: Campaign-Finance Limits Violate Free Speech," *Christian Science Monitor*, January 21, 2010; John Samples and Ilya Shapiro, "Supreme Court: Free Speech for All," *Washington Examiner*, January 21, 2010.

70. Ibid.

71. Ibid.

72. Marjorie Hershey, "The Constructed Explanation: Interpreting Election Results in the 1984 Presidential Race," *Journal of Politics* 54 (November 1992): 943–976.

73. George Stephanopoulos, "It's a Whole Different Game," *George's Bottom Line*, blogs.abcnews.com/george/2008/10/its-a-whole-dif.html.

74. Lawrence J. Grossman, David A. M. Peterson, and James A. Stimson, *Mandate Politics* (New York: Cambridge University Press, 2006).

75. Marjorie Hershey, "The Constructed Explanation: Interpreting Election Results in the 1984 Presidential Race," *Journal of Politics* 54 (November 1992): 943–976.

76. Bernard Berelson, Paul Lazarsfeld, and William N. McPhee, *Voting* (Chicago, Ill.: University of Chicago Press, 1954), ch. 10.

77. Sidney Verba, Kay Lehman Schlozman, Henry Brady, and Norman H. Nie, "Race, Ethnicity and Political Resources: Participation in the United States," *British Journal of Political Science* 23 (1993): 453–497.

78. National Popular Vote, www.nationalpopularvote.com/.

CHAPTER 13

1. "Republicans, Democrats Interpret Orlando Incident Differently," Gallup Poll, June 17, 2016, www.gallup.com/poll/192842/republicans-democrats-interpret-orlando-incident-differently.aspx.

2. Jane Coaston, "New Evidence Shows the Pulse Nightclub Shooting Wasn't About Anti-LGBTQ Hate," *Vox*, April 5, 2018, www.vox.com/policy-and-politics/2018/4/5/17202026/pulse-shooting-lgbtq-trump-terror-hate.

3. Dan O'Hair and Mary Weimann, *Real Communication*, 2nd ed. (New York: Bedford/St. Martin's, 2012), 543.

4. Elisa Shearer and Jeffrey Gottfried, "News Use Across Social Media Platforms: 2017," Pew Research Center, September 7, 2017, www.journalism.org/2017/09/07/news-use-across-social-media-platforms-2017/.

5. Ibid.

6. Amy Mitchell, Jeffery Gottfried, and Katerina Eva Matsa, "Millennials and Political News: Social Media—The Local TV for the Next Generation?" Pew Research Center, June 1, 2015, www.journalism.org/2015/06/01/millennials-political-news/.

7. Pew Research Center for the People and the Press, "The Times Mirror News Interest Index: 1989–1995," www.people-press.org.

8. Pew Research Center for the People and the Press, "Audience Segments in a Changing News Environment," August 17, 2008, www.people-press.org/files/legacy-pdf/444.pdf, 44.

9. Thomas Jefferson to Edward Carrington, 1787, ME 6:57, Thomas Jefferson on Politics and Government, etext.virginia.edu/jefferson/quotations/jeff1600.htm.

10. Michael Barthel, "5 Key Takeaways About the State of the News Media in 2016," Pew Research Center, June 15, 2016, www.pewresearch.org/fact-tank/2016/06/15/state-of-the-news-media-2016-key-takeaways/.

11. Newspaper Death Watch, newspaperdeathwatch.com.

12. Jack Shafer, "The Great Newspaper Liquidation," June 5, 2012, blogs.reuters.com/jackshafer/2012/06/05/the-great-newspaper-liquidation/; David Carr, "The Fissures Are Growing for Newspapers," *New York Times*, July 8, 2012, www.nytimes.com/2012/07/09/business/media/newspapers-are-running-out-of-time-to-adapt-to-digital-future.html.

13. Clay Shirky, "Newspapers and Thinking the Unthinkable," March 13, 2009, www.shirky.com/weblog/2009/03/newspapers-and-thinking-the-unthinkable/.

14. Ibid.

15. Pew Research Journalism Project, "Audio and Podcasting Fact Sheet," June 16, 2017, www.journalism.org/fact-sheet/audio-and-podcasting/.

16. Jennifer Waits, "FCC Reports That the Number of Radio Stations in the U.S. Increased Last Quarter," July 11, 2014, www.radiosurvivor.com/2014/07/11/fcc-reports-non-commercial-fm-stations-lpfm-stations-fm-translators-u-s-rise-last-quarter/.

17. NPR, "Public Radio Finances," www.npr.org/about-npr/178660742/public-radio-finances; Public Radio International, "How Is PRI Funded?" www.pri.org/faqs#funding.

18. U.S. Energy Information Administration, "Average Number of Televisions in U.S. Homes Declining," February 28, 2017, www.eia.gov/todayinenergy/detail.php?id=30132; Lee Rainie, "About 6 in 10 Young Adults in U.S. Primarily Use Online Streaming to Watch TV," Pew Research Center, September 13, 2017, www.pewresearch.org/fact-tank/2017/09/13/about-6-in-10-young-adults-in-u-s-primarily-use-online-streaming-to-watch-tv/; Todd Spangler, "Cord-Cutting Explodes: 22 Million U.S. Adults Will Have Canceled Cable, Satellite TV by End of 2017," *Variety*, September 13, 2017, variety.com/2017/biz/news/cord-cutting-2017-estimates-cancel-cable-satellite-tv-1202556594/.

19. David Hinckley, "Average American Watches 5 Hours of TV per Day, Report Shows," *New York Daily News*, March 5, 2014, www.nydailynews.com/life-style/average-american-watches-5-hours-tv-day-article-1.1711954.

20. Megan Geuss, "On Average, Americans Get 189 Cable TV Channels and Only Watch 17," *Arstechnica*, May 6, 2014, arstechnica.com/business/2014/05/on-average-americans-get-189-cable-tv-channels-and-only-watch-17/.

21. For an in-depth study of the negative effects of this sort of advertising on national community, see Joseph Turow, *Breaking Up America: Advertisers and the New Media World* (Chicago: University of Chicago Press, 1997).

22. Monica Anderson, Andrew Perrin, and JingJing Jiang, "11% of Americans Don't Use the Internet. Who Are They?" Pew Research Center, March 5, 2018, www.pewresearch.org/fact-tank/2018/03/05/some-americans-dont-use-the-internet-who-are-they/.

23. Pew Research Center, "Internet/Broadband Fact Sheet," www.pewinternet.org/fact-sheet/internet-broadband/; Andrew Perrin and JingJing Jiang, "About a Quarter of U.S. Adults Say They Are 'Almost Constantly' Online," Pew Research Center, March 14, 2018, www.pewresearch.org/fact-tank/2018/03/14/about-a-quarter-of-americans-report-going-online-almost-constantly/.

24. Pew Research Center for the People and the Press, "The New News Landscape: Rise of the Internet," March 1, 2010, pewresearch.org/pubs/1508/internet-cell-phone-users-news-social-experience; Kathryn Zickuhr and Aaron Smith, "Digital Differences," Pew Internet, April 13, 2012, pewinternet.org/Reports/2012/Digital-differences/Main-Report/Internet-adoption-over-time.aspx; Aaron Smith, "Nearly Half of American Adults Are Smartphone Owners," Pew Internet, March 1, 2012, pewinternet.org/Reports/2012/Digital-differences/Main-Report/Internet-adoption-over-time.aspx.

25. Robert Marquand, "Hate Groups Market to the Mainstream," *Christian Science Monitor*, March 6, 1998, 4.

26. Philip Rucker, "Romney Advisors, Aiming to Pop Obama's Digital Balloon, Pump Up Online Campaign," *Washington Post*, July 13, 2012, www.washingtonpost.com/politics/romney-advisers-aiming-to-pop-obamas-digital-balloon-pump-up-online-campaign/2012/07/13/gJQAsbc4hW_story.html.

27. Dan Gillmor, *We the Media: Grassroots Journalism by the People, for the People* (Sebastopol, Calif.: O'Reilly Media, 2008).

28. Andrew Sullivan, "A Blogger Manifesto: Why Online Weblogs Are One Future for Journalism," *Sunday Times of London*, February 24, 2002.

29. Andrew Sullivan, "Happy 4th," *Daily Dish*, July 4, 2010, andrewsullivan.theatlantic.com/the_daily_dish/2010/07/happy-4th.html.

30. Shirky, "Newspapers and Thinking the Unthinkable."
31. Ben H. Bagdikian, *The Media Monopoly*, 5th ed. (Boston, Mass.: Beacon Press, 1997), xv.
32. Ibid., ix.
33. Pew Center's Project for Excellence in Journalism, "YouTube and the News," July 16, 2012, www.journalism.org/analysis_report/youtube_news.
34. Pew Research Center, "New Devices, Platforms Spur More News Consumption," March 19, 2012, pewresearch.org/pubs/2222/news-media-network-television-cable-audioo-radio-digital-platforms-local-mobile-devices-tablets-smartphones-native-american-community-newspapers; JingJing Jiang, "Millennials Stand Out For Their Technology Use, but Older Generations Also Embrace Digital Life," Pew Research Center, May 2, 2018, www.pewresearch.org/fact-tank/2018/05/02/millennials-stand-out-for-their-technology-use-but-older-generations-also-embrace-digital-life.
35. Robert Entman, *Democracy Without Citizens* (New York: Oxford University Press, 1989), 110–111.
36. Walter Goodman, "Where's Edward R. Murrow When You Need Him?" *New York Times*, December 30, 1997, E2.
37. Journalism.org, "Nonprofit News Outlets," features.journalism.org/nonprofit-news-outlets/.
38. David Broder, *Behind the Front Page* (New York: Simon & Schuster, 1987), 148.
39. Dom Bonafede, "Crossing Over," *National Journal*, January 14, 1989, 102; Michael Kelly, "David Gergen, Master of the Game," *New York Times Magazine*, October 31, 1993, 64ff; Jonathan Alter, "Lost in the Big Blur," *Newsweek*, June 9, 1997, 43.
40. Shanto Iyengar, *Is Anyone Responsible?* (Chicago, Ill.: University of Chicago Press, 1991), 2.
41. Shanto Iyengar and Donald R. Kinder, *News That Matters* (Chicago, Ill.: University of Chicago Press, 1987).
42. Benjamin I. Page, Robert Y. Shapiro, and Glenn R. Dempsey, "What Moves Public Opinion?" *American Political Science Review* (March 1987): 23–43. The term *professional communicator* is used by Benjamin Page, *Who Deliberates? Mass Media in Modern Democracy* (Chicago, Ill.: University of Chicago Press, 1996), 106–109.
43. Center for Media and Democracy, "Sound Bites Get Shorter," O'Dwyer's PR Newsletter, November 11, 2000, www.prwatch.org/node/384.
44. Thomas E. Patterson, *Out of Order* (New York: Vintage Books, 1994), 74.
45. Larry J. Sabato, *Feeding Frenzy: How Attack Journalism Has Transformed American Politics* (New York: Free Press, 1991), 6.
46. Patterson, *Out of Order*.
47. Iyengar and Kinder, *News That Matters*, 93.
48. W. Russell Neuman, Marion R. Just, and Ann N. Crigler, *Common Knowledge: News and the Construction of Political Meaning* (Chicago, Ill.: University of Chicago Press, 1996), 106–119.
49. Ibid., 23.
50. Judith Valente, "Do You Believe What Newspeople Tell You?" *Parade Magazine*, March 2, 1997, 4.
51. Steven Kull, "Misperceptions, the Media, and the Iraq War," the PIPA/Knowledge Networks Poll, Program on International Policy Attitudes, October 2, 2003, 13–16, www.pipa.org/OnlineReports/Iraq/Media_10_02_03_Report.pdf.
52. Walter Cronkite, "Reporting Political Campaigns: A Reporter's View," in Doris Graber, Denis McQuail, and Pippa Norris, eds., *The Politics of News, The News of Politics* (Washington, D.C.: CQ Press, 1998), 57–69.
53. Joe Klein, "The Perils of the Permanent Campaign," *Time*, October 30, 2005.
54. Kelly, "David Gergen, Master of the Game," 7.
55. Ibid., 7–10.
56. Kenneth T. Walsh, *Feeding the Beast: The White House Versus the Press* (New York: Random House, 1996).
57. Mark Hertsgaard, *On Bended Knee: The Press and the Reagan Presidency* (New York: Farrar, Straus & Giroux, 1988), 6.
58. Johanna Neuman, "An Identity Crisis Unfolds in a Not-So-Elite Press Corps," *Los Angeles Times*, February 25, 2005, 1.
59. Jack Shafer, "The Propaganda President: George W. Bush Does His Best Kim Jong-il," *Slate*, February 3, 2005, www.slate.com/articles/news_and_politics/press_box/2005/02/the_propaganda_president.html.
60. Jeff Zeleny, "Robert Gibbs," *New York Times*, November 6, 2008.
61. Ibid.
62. Stephen Ansolabehere, Roy Beyr, and Shanto Iyengar, *The Media Game: American Politics in the Television Age* (New York: Macmillan, 1993); Iyengar, *Is Anyone Responsible?*
63. Aaron Smith, "Record Shares of Americans Now Own Smartphones, Have Home Broadband," Pew Research Center, January 12, 2017, www.pewresearch.org/fact-tank/2017/01/12/evolution-of-technology/.
64. Monica Anderson, "6 Facts About Americans and Their Smartphones," Pew Research Center, April 1, 2015, www.pewresearch.org/fact-tank/2015/04/01/6-facts-about-americans-and-their-smartphones.

CHAPTER 14

1. Statement of Sen. Bernie Sanders, "Tax Cuts and Jobs Act," *Congressional Record*, December 1, 2017, congress.gov/congressional-record/2017/12/01/senate-section/article/S7655-2.
2. "Few Feel Positive Impact from Growing Economy," Monmouth University news release, May 9, 2018, www.monmouth.edu/polling-institute/reports/monmouthpoll_us_050918.
3. Pew Research Center, "The American Middle Class Is Losing Ground," December 9, 2015, www.pewsocialtrends.org/files/2015/12/2015-12-09_middle-class_FINAL-report.pdf.
4. Chuck Collins and Josh Hoxie, "Billionaire Bonanza: The Forbes 400 and the Rest of Us," Institute for Policy Studies, November 2017, ips-dc.org/billionaire-bonanza/.
5. Reema Khrais, "Will Today's Generation Be Poorer Than Their Parents?" Marketplace.org, July 13, 2016, www.marketplace.org/2016/07/13/world/flat-income.
6. Peter Katel, "Future of the Middle Class," *CQ Researcher*, April 8, 2016.
7. Matthew Iglesias, "Thomas Piketty Doesn't Hate Capitalism—He Just Wants to Fix It," *Vox*, April 24, 2014, www.vox.com/2014/4/24/5643780/who-is-thomas-piketty.
8. Sean McElwee, "Why Income Inequality Is America's Biggest (and Most Difficult) Problem," *Salon*, October 26, 2014, www.salon.com/2014/10/26/why_income_inequality_is_americas_biggest_and_most_difficult_problem/.
9. Eric Schnurer, "The Winter of Worldwide Discontent," *U.S. News & World Report*, February 3, 2016, www.usnews.com/opinion/blogs/eric-schnurer/articles/2016-02-03/populist-anger-toward-the-establishment-stems-from-economic-inequality.
10. Ramesh Ponnuru, "Let's Not Mention Inequality," *New York Times*, February 9, 2015, www.nytimes.com/2015/02/09/opinion/lets-not-mention-inequality.html.
11. Patrick Healy and Amy Chozick, "Hillary Clinton Wins 4 Races, Rebounding From Michigan Loss," *New York Times*, March 15, 2016, www.nytimes.com/2016/03/16/us/politics/democratic-primary-results.html.
12. Ed Conard, "What Liberals Don't Understand About Inequality," *Time*, September 13, 2016, time.com/4474437/upside-of-income-inequality/.
13. John Harwood, "GOP Tax Cuts Have Gotten Less Popular With Voters, New NBC/WSJ Poll Says," CNBC, April 16, 2018, www.cnbc.com/2018/04/16/gop-tax-cuts-have-gotten-less-popular-with-voters-nbc-wsj-poll.html.
14. "Marco Rubio Offers His Trump-Crazed Party a Glint of Hope," *The Economist*, April 26, 2018, www.economist.com/news/united-states/21741146-florida-senator-thinks-reheating-reaganomics-dead-end-marco-rubio-offers-his.
15. Peter Bachrach and Morton S. Baratz, "The Two Faces of Power," *American Political Science Review* 56 (December 1962): 948.
16. This definition of public policy is based on the one offered by James E. Anderson, *Public Policymaking: An Introduction* (Boston, Mass.: Houghton Mifflin, 1997), 9.
17. Theodore Lowi, "American Business, Public Policy Case Studies, and Political Theory," *World Politics* (July 1964): 677–715.

18. For a discussion of the effect of lawsuits on air emissions standards, see Robert Percival, Alan Miller, Christopher Schroeder, and James Leape, *Environmental Regulation: Law, Science and Policy*, 2nd ed. (Boston, Mass.: Little, Brown, 1996).

19. American Presidency Project, "Executive Orders, Washington-Trump," www.presidency.ucsb.edu/data/orders.php, accessed May 26, 2018.

20. Tom Anderson, "Social Security Has a Looming $11 Trillion Shortfall," CNBC, January 17, 2017, www.cnbc.com/2017/01/13/social-security-has-a-looming-11-trillion-shortfall.html.

21. Social Security Administration, "A Summary of the 2005 Annual Reports," www.ssa.gov/OACT/TRSUM/trsummary.html.

22. Center on Budget and Policy Priorities, "Policy Basics: Where Do Our Federal Tax Dollars Go?" October 4, 2017, www.cbpp.org/research/federal-budget/policy-basics-where-do-our-federal-tax-dollars-go.

23. Stephen Dinan, "As Budget Deficits Grow, Trump Won't Touch Social Security, Medicare," *Washington Times*, October 23, 2017, www.washingtontimes.com/news/2017/oct/23/trump-says-he-wont-touch-social-security-medicare/.

24. "The *Economist*/YouGov Poll," April 15–17, 2018, https://d25d2506sfb94s.cloudfront.net/cumulus_uploads/document/4l31gznvf1/econTabReport.pdf.

25. Susan Jones, "Obama's Social Security Plan: Some Will Pay More," May 19, 2008, cnsnews.com/news/article/obamas-social-security-plan-some-will-pay-more.

26. U.S. Census Bureau, *Statistical Brief: Mothers Who Receive AFDC Payments: Fertility and Socioeconomic Characteristics* (Washington, D.C.: U.S. Department of Commerce, Economics and Statistics Administration, March 1995).

27. Center for Law and Social Policy, *Implementing the TANF Changes in the Deficit Reduction Act*, 2nd ed., www.cbpp.org/2–9–07tanf.htm.

28. Paul Lewis, "Tea Party's Mike Lee Leads Unlikely Republican Push Against Poverty," *The Guardian* (UK), February 19, 2014, www.theguardian.com/world/2014/feb/19/tea-party-mike-lee-unlikely-republican-poverty.

29. Office of Family Assistance.

30. Peter Edelman, "The True Purpose of Welfare Reform," *New York Times*, May 29, 2002, A21.

31. Kathryn Edin and H. Luke Shaefer, "20 Years Since Welfare 'Reform'," *The Atlantic*, August 22, 2016, www.theatlantic.com/business/archive/2016/08/20-years-welfare-reform/496730/.

32. Jason DeParle, "Slumping Economy Tests System Tied to Jobs," *New York Times*, May 1, 2009, www.nytimes.com/2009/06/01/us/politics/01poverty.html.

33. Ibid.

34. U.S. Department of Health and Human Services, "Head Start Program Facts Fiscal Year 2016," eclkc.ohs.acf.hhs.gov/sites/default/files/pdf/hs-program-fact-sheet-2016.pdf.

35. Center for Medicare and Medicaid Services, "NHE Fact Sheet," www.cms.gov/research-statistics-data-and-systems/statistics-trends-and-reports/nationalhealthexpenddata/nhe-fact-sheet.html.

36. U.S. Department of Health and Human Services, "Overview of the Uninsured in the United States: A Summary of the Current 2010 Population Survey," September 2011, aspe.hhs.gov/health/reports/2011/CPSHealthIns2011/ib.shtml#_Toc303600549.

37. Reuters, "Medicare Is Going to Run Out of Money a Lot Sooner Than Expected," *Fortune*, June 22, 2016, fortune.com/2016/06/22/medicare-reserves-exhausted-soon/.

38. Steven Rattner, "Ducking the Crisis in Medicare," *New York Times*, April 13, 2012, www.nytimes.com/2012/04/14/opinion/ducking-the-medicare-crisis.html.

39. Daniel Weintraub, "A Possible Antidote to Rising Health Care Costs," *Sacramento Bee*, November 23, 2004, B7; Stephanie Armour and Julie Appleby, "As Health Care Costs Rise, Workers Shoulder Burden," *USA Today*, October 21, 2003, C1.

40. "Obama's Health Care Speech," CBS News, September 9, 2009, www.cbsnews.com/stories/2009/09/09/politics/main5299229.shtml.

41. "Focus on Health Reform: Summary of New Health http://files.kff.org/attachment/fact-sheet-summary-of-the-affordable-care-act Reform Law," Kaiser Family Foundation, www.kff.org/healthreform/upload/8061.pdf.

42. Michael Crowley, "Will Health Reform Be a Key Factor in Midterms?" *Time*, August 20, 2010, www.time.com/time/politics/article/0,8599,2011907,00.html.

43. Kaiser Family Foundation, "Status of State Action on the Medicaid Expansion Decision," www.kff.org/health-reform/state-indicator/state-activity-around-expanding-medicaid-under-the-affordable-care-act/?currentTimeframe=0&sortModel=%7B%22colId%22:%22Location%22,%22sort%22:%22asc%22%7D#note-3.

44. Adam Liptak, "Supreme Court Allows Nationwide Health Care Subsidies," *New York Times*, June 25, 2015, www.nytimes.com/2015/06/26/us/obamacare-supreme-court.html.

45. Rachel Roubein, "Timeline: The GOP's Failed Effort to Repeal ObamaCare," *The Hill*, July 26, 2017, thehill.com/policy/healthcare/other/352587-timeline-the-gop-effort-to-repeal-and-replace-obamacare.

46. Ibid.

47. Office of Sen. John McCain, "Statement of Sen. John McCain on Voting 'No' on 'Skinny Repeal,'" July 27, 2017, www.mccain.senate.gov/public/index.cfm/2017/7/statement-by-senator-john-mccain-on-voting-no-on-skinny-repeal.

48. Dan Mangan, "Trump Touts Repeal of Key Part in 'Disastrous Obamacare'—the Individual Mandate," CNBC, January 30, 2018, www.cnbc.com/2018/01/30/trump-touts-repeal-of-obamacare-individual-mandate.html.

49. Congressional Budget Office, "Repealing the Individual Health Insurance Mandate: An Updated Estimate," November 2017, www.cbo.gov/system/files/115th-congress-2017-2018/reports/53300-individualmandate.pdf.

50. "Short-Term, Limited-Duration Insurance," *Federal Register*, February 21, 2018, www.federalregister.gov/documents/2018/02/21/2018-03208/short-term-limited-duration-insurance.

51. Dylan Scott, "Trump's New Plan to Poke Holes in the Obamacare Markets, Explained," *Vox*, February 20, 2018, www.vox.com/policy-and-politics/2018/2/20/17031640/short-term-insurance-trump-obamacare.

52. National Center for Health Statistics, "Health Insurance Coverage: Early Release of Estimates From the National Health Interview Survey, January–September 2017," February 2018, www.cdc.gov/nchs/data/nhis/earlyrelease/insur201802.pdf.

53. Robert McIntyre, "Your Federal Tax Dollars at Work," *American Prospect*, May 20, 2002.

54. Tamara Keith, "Austrian School Economist Hayek Finds New Fans," NPR, November 15, 2011, www.npr.org/2011/11/15/142307737/austrian-school-economist-hayek-finds-new-fans.

55. George Hager, "End of Deficit Era Marks Beginning of Battle Over Surpluses," *Washington Post*, September 30, 1998, C10.

56. "2008 U.S. Budget Deficit Bleeding Red Ink; First 4 Months of Budget Year at Nearly $88B, Double Amount Recorded for Same 2007 Period," CBS News, February 12, 2008, www.cbsnews.com/stories/2008/02/12/national/main3822385.shtml.

57. Tobin Harshaw, "Will TARP Turn to Gold?" *New York Times*, October 1, 2010.

58. Paul Krugman, "That 30's Show," *New York Times*, July 2, 2009, www.nytimes.com/2009/07/03/opinion/03krugman.html.

59. Josh Boak, "Stimulus Added Up to 3.3 Million Jobs," November 22, 2011, www.politico.com/news/stories/1111/68965.html.

60. Lori Montgomery, "Report Gives Stimulus Package High Marks," *Washington Post*, October 1, 2010.

61. David Leonhardt, "Imagining a Deficit Plan From Republicans," *New York Times*, September 28, 2010, www.nytimes.com/2010/09/29/business/economy/29/eonhardt.html.

62. Al Hunt, "Democrats Relish Battle Over High-Income Tax Cuts," *Bloomberg News*, August 1, 2010, www.bloomberg.com/news/2010–08–01/democrats-relish-fight-over-big-income-tax-cuts-commentary-by-albert-hunt.html.

63. Katy O'Donnell, "Van Hollen Rips Ryan Budget," *National Journal*, April 12, 2011.

64. Thomas E. Mann and Norman J. Ornstein, *It's Even Worse Than It Looks: How the American Constitutional System Collided With the New Politics of Extremism* (New York: Basic Books, 2012), 4.

65. Chuck McCutcheon, *The Elections of 2012: Outcomes and Analysis* (Washington, D.C.: CQ Press, 2012), 1–3.

66. Mark Landler, "With Eye on Midterms, Obama Pushes Rise in Minimum Wage," *New York Times*, March 5, 2014, www.nytimes.com/2014/03/06/us/politics/obama-presses-case-for-higher-minimum-wage.html.

67. Jeremy W. Peters, "Democrats Assail GOP After Filibuster of Proposal to Raise Minimum Wage," *New York Times*, April 30, 2014, www.nytimes.com/2014/05/01/us/politics/senate-minimum-wage-bill.html.

68. Jackie Calmes, "Congressional Republicans Balk at Obama's Budget, Sight Unseen," *New York Times*, February 8, 2016, www.nytimes.com/2016/02/09/us/politics/congressional-republicans-balk-at-obamas-budget-sight-unseen.html.

69. Pew Research Center for the People and the Press, "Budget Deficit Slips as Public Priority," January 22, 2016, www.people-press.org/2016/01/22/budget-deficit-slips-as-public-priority/.

70. Office of Management and Budget, "The Budget: Budget of the United States Government for Fiscal Year 2017," Summary Tables, S-4, www.whitehouse.gov/sites/default/files/omb/budget/fy2017/assets/tables.pdf.

71. Damian Paletta and Erica Werner, "Republicans Reach Compromise Tax Plan, Expanding Tax Cuts for the Wealthy," *Washington Post*, December 13, 2017, www.washingtonpost.com/business/economy/republicans-reach-compromise-tax-plan-expanding-tax-cuts-for-the-wealthy/2017/12/13/4f9ca66c-e028-11e7-bbd0-9dfb2e37492a_story.html.

72. David Leonhardt, "Can't Grasp Credit Crisis? Join the Club," *New York Times*, March 19, 2008, A1; Robert Gavin, "Frank Urges Overhaul of Business Regulations," *Boston Globe*, March 21, 2008, C3; Paul Davidson, "Mortgage Brokers Fall on Tough Times; Many Now Victims of a Crisis They May Have Played Role In," *USA Today*, August 31, 2007, 1B; Joe Nocera, "On Wall St., A Problem of Denial," *New York Times*, September 15, 2008, www.nytimes.com.

73. Michael Maynard, "Navigating Turbulent Skies," *New York Times*, October 10, 2004, sect. 5, 4; Matthew L. Wald, "Advances in Airplanes Are Mostly Invisible," *New York Times*, May 18, 2003, sect. 5, 3; Agis Salpukas, "Future of Airline Deregulation," *New York Times*, May 8, 1982, sect. 2, 29; Leslie Wayne, "The Airlines Stacked Up in Red Ink," *New York Times*, February 14, 1982, sect. 3, 1.

74. Andrew Leonard, "The Dodd-Frank Bank Reform Bill: A Deeply Flawed Success," *Salon*, June 25, 2010, www.salon.com/technology/how_the_world_works/2010/06/25/the_dodd_frank_bank_reform_bill.

75. Damian Paletta, "U.S. Lawmakers Reach Accord on New Finance Rules," *Wall Street Journal*, June 25, 2010, online.wsj.com/article/SB10001424052748703615104575328020013164184.html.

76. Randall B. Ripley and Grace A. Franklin, *Congress, the Bureaucracy, and Public Policy*, 5th ed. (Belmont, Calif.: Wadsworth, 1991).

77. See Charles F. Hermann, *Crises in Foreign Policy* (Indianapolis, Ind.: Bobbs-Merrill, 1969); Michael Brecher, "A Theoretical Approach to International Crisis Behavior," *Jerusalem Journal of International Relations* 3, nos. 2–3 (1978): 5–24.

78. See John Lewis Gaddis, *Strategies of Containment* (New York: Oxford University Press, 1982).

79. See Richard Wike, Bruce Stokes, and Jacob Poushter, "America's Global Image," Pew Research Center, June 23, 2015, www.pewglobal.org/2015/06/23/1-americas-global-image/.

80. "Russia," Gallup poll, www.gallup.com/poll/1642/russia.aspx.

81. John Lewis Gaddis, *The United States and the End of the Cold War* (New York: Oxford University Press, 1992); Richard Ned Lebow and Thomas Risse-Kappen, eds., *International Relations Theory and the End of the Cold War* (New York: Columbia University Press, 1995).

82. See, for example, Richard N. Haass, *The Reluctant Sheriff: The United States After the Cold War* (New York: Council on Foreign Relations Press, 1997).

83. See Graham Allison, *Essence of Decision* (New York: HarperCollins, 1971); Helen V. Milner, *Interest, Institutions, and Information: Domestic Politics and International Relations* (Princeton, N.J.: Princeton University Press, 1997).

84. See "X" (George F. Kennan), "The Sources of Soviet Conduct," *Foreign Affairs*, July 25, 1947, 566–582.

85. See, for example, Michael H. Shuman, "Dateline Main Street: Local Foreign Policies," *Foreign Policy* 65 (Winter 1986/87): 154–174.

86. Robert S. Erikson, Gerald C. Wright, and John P. McIver, *Statehouse Democracy* (New York: Cambridge University Press, 1993).

87. James A. Stimson, Michael B. MacKuen, and Robert S. Erikson, *American Political Science Review* 89 (1995): 543–565.

88. Michael Scherer, "In Wide-Open 2020 Presidential Field, Democrats Are Road-Testing Messages—and Trying to Redefine Their Party," *Washington Post*, May 12, 2018, www.washingtonpost.com/politics/no-one-has-a-leg-up-in-wide-open-2020-presidential-field-democrats-jockey-to-define-their-party--and-gain-an-advantage/2018/05/12/42ba34f2-5547-11e8-9c91-7dab596e8252_story.html.

89. Danielle Kurtzleben, "Likely 2020 Democratic Candidates Want to Guarantee a Job to Every American," NPR, May 8, 2018, www.npr.org/2018/05/08/609091985/likely-2020-democratic-candidates-want-to-guarantee-a-job-to-every-american.

90. Bob Bryan, "Bernie Sanders Has a New Plan to Raise Wages, and It's a Major Signal on Where the Democratic Party Is Headed," *Business Insider*, May 10, 2018, www.businessinsider.com/bernie-sanders-labor-union-plan-wages-fight-income-inequality-2018-5.

91. Chris Cillizza, "Bernie Sanders Is the Most Important 2020 Candidate," CNN, May 29, 2018, www.cnn.com/2018/05/29/politics/bernie-sanders-2020-analysis/index.html.

GLOSSARY

accommodationists supporters of government nonpreferential accommodation of religion (4)

accountability the principle that bureaucratic employees should be answerable for their performance to supervisors, all the way up the chain of command (8)

administrative laws laws established by the bureaucracy, on behalf of Congress (9)

advanced industrial democracy a system in which a democratic government allows citizens a considerable amount of personal freedom and maintains a free-market (though still usually regulated) economy (1)

advice and consent the constitutional obligation that the Senate approve certain executive appointments (6)

affirmative action a policy of creating opportunities for members of certain groups as a substantive remedy for past discrimination (5)

agency capture a process whereby regulatory agencies come to be protective of and influenced by the industries they were established to regulate (8)

agenda setting the media's role in defining the relative importance of an issue or event via the amount and prominence of coverage they devote to it (13)

allocative representation congressional work to secure projects, services, and funds for the represented district (6)

amendability the provision for the Constitution to be changed, so as to adapt to new circumstances (2)

amicus curiae briefs "friend of the court" documents filed by interested parties to encourage the Court to grant or deny certiorari or to urge it to decide a case in a particular way (9)

analysis understanding how something works by breaking it down into its component parts (1)

anarchy the absence of government and laws (1)

Anti-Federalists advocates of states' rights who opposed the Constitution (2)

appeal a rehearing of a case because the losing party in the original trial argues that a point of law was not applied properly (9)

appellate jurisdiction the authority of a court to review decisions made by lower courts (9)

Articles of Confederation the first constitution of the United States (1777), creating an association of states with weak central government (2)

astroturf lobbying indirect lobbying efforts that manipulate or create public sentiment, "astroturf" being artificial grassroots (11)

authoritarian capitalism a system in which the state allows people economic freedom but maintains stringent social regulations to limit noneconomic behavior (1)

authoritarian governments systems in which the state holds all power over the social order (1)

authoritarian populism a radical right-wing movement that appeals to popular discontent but whose underlying values are not democratic (1)

authority power that is recognized as legitimate, or right (1)

balanced budget a budget in which expenditures equal revenues (14)

benchmark poll an initial poll on a candidate and issues on which campaign strategy is based and against which later polls are compared (10)

bicameral legislature a legislature with two chambers (2, 6)

Bill of Rights a summary of citizen rights guaranteed and protected by a government; added to the Constitution as its first ten amendments in order to achieve ratification (2)

bills of attainder laws under which specific persons or groups are detained and sentenced without trial (4)

black codes a series of laws in the post–Civil War South designed to restrict the rights of former slaves before the passage of the Fourteenth and Fifteenth Amendments (5)

block grant federal funds provided for a broad purpose and unrestricted by detailed requirements and regulations (3)

boycott the refusal to buy certain goods or services as a way to protest policy or force political reform (5)

bureaucracy an organization characterized by hierarchical structure, worker specialization, explicit rules, and advancement by merit (8)

bureaucratic culture the accepted values and procedures of an organization (8)

bureaucratic discretion bureaucrats' use of their own judgment in interpreting and carrying out the laws of Congress (8)

Bush Doctrine the policy that supported preemptive attacks as a legitimate tactic in the U.S. war on state-sponsored terrorism (14)

busing achieving racial balance by transporting students to schools across neighborhood boundaries (5)

cabinet a presidential advisory group selected by the president, made up of the vice president, the heads of the federal executive departments, and other high officials to whom the president elects to give cabinet status (7)

capital gains tax a tax levied on the returns that people earn from capital investments, like the profits from the sale of stocks or a home (14)

capitalist economy an economic system in which the market determines production, distribution, and price decisions, and property is privately owned (1)

casework legislative work on behalf of individual constituents to solve their problems with government agencies and programs (6)

categorical grant federal funds provided for a specific purpose and restricted by detailed instructions, regulations, and compliance standards (3)

Central Intelligence Agency (CIA) the government organization that oversees foreign intelligence gathering and related classified activities (14)

checks and balances the principle that allows each branch of government to exercise some form of control over the others (2)

chief administrator the president's executive role as the head of federal agencies and the person responsible for the implementation of national policy (7)

chief foreign policy maker the president's executive role as the primary shaper of relations with other nations (7)

chief of staff the person who oversees the operations of all White House staff and is traditionally expected to control access to the president (7)

citizen advisory councils citizen groups that consider the policy decisions of an agency; a way to make the bureaucracy responsive to the general public (8)

citizen journalism reporting and commentary by everyday citizens unaffiliated with traditional media outlets, and distributed via the web in the form of blogs, podcasts, or video uploads (13)

citizens members of a political community with both rights and responsibilities (1)

civil laws laws regulating interactions between individuals; violation of a civil law is called a tort (9)

civil liberties individual freedoms guaranteed to the people primarily by the Bill of Rights (4)

civil rights citizenship rights guaranteed to the people (primarily in the Thirteenth, Fourteenth, Fifteenth, Nineteenth, and Twenty-sixth Amendments) and protected by the government (4, 5)

civil service nonmilitary employees of the government who are appointed through the merit system (8)

classical liberalism a political ideology dating from the seventeenth century emphasizing individual rights over the power of the state (1)

clear and present danger test the rule used by the courts that allows language to be regulated only if it presents an immediate and urgent danger (4)

clickbait sensational headlines designed to tempt Internet users to click through to a specific web site (13)

clientele groups groups of citizens whose interests are affected by an agency or a department and who work to influence its policies (8)

closed primary a primary election in which only registered party members may vote (12)

cloture a vote to end a Senate filibuster; requires a three-fifths majority, or sixty votes (6)

coattail effect the added votes received by congressional candidates of a winning presidential party (6)

Cold War the half-century of competition and conflict after World War II between the United States and the Soviet Union (and their allies) (14)

collective good a good or service that, by its very nature, cannot be denied to anyone who wants to consume it (11)

commander-in-chief the president's role as the top officer of the country's military establishment (7)

commercial bias the tendency of the media to make coverage and programming decisions based on what will attract a large audience and maximize profits (13)

common law tradition a legal system based on the accumulated rulings of judges over time, applied uniformly—judge-made law (9)

communist democracy a utopian system in which property is communally owned and all decisions are made democratically (1)

communitarians those who favor a strong, substantive government role in the economy and the social order so that their vision of a community of equals may be realized (1)

compelling state interest a fundamental state purpose, which must be shown before the law can limit some freedoms or treat some groups of people differently (4)

concurrent powers powers that are shared by the federal and state governments (3)

concurring opinions documents written by justices expressing agreement with the majority ruling but describing different or additional reasons for the ruling (9)

confederal systems governments in which local units hold all the power (3)

confederation a government in which independent states unite for common purpose but retain their own sovereignty (2)

conference committees temporary committees formed to reconcile differences in House and Senate versions of a bill (6)

congressional oversight efforts by Congress, especially through committees, to monitor agency rule making, enforcement, and implementation of congressional policies (6, 8)

conservatives people who generally favor limited government and are cautious about change (1)

constituency the voters in a state or district (6)

constitution the rules that establish a government (2)

Constitutional Convention the assembly of fifty-five delegates in the summer of 1787 to recast the Articles of Confederation; the result was the U.S. Constitution (2)

constitutional law law stated in the Constitution or in the body of judicial decisions about the meaning of the Constitution handed down in the courts (9)

consumption tax a tax on what people spend rather than on what they earn (14)

containment the U.S. Cold War policy of preventing the spread of communism (14)

cooperative federalism the federal system under which the national and state governments share responsibilities for most domestic policy areas (3)

Council of Economic Advisers the organization within the Executive Office of the President that advises the president on economic matters (7)

courts institutions that sit as neutral third parties to resolve conflicts according to the law (9)

criminal laws laws prohibiting behavior the government has determined to be harmful to society; violation of a criminal law is called a crime (9)

crisis policy foreign policy, usually made quickly and secretly, that responds to an emergency threat (14)

critical thinking analysis and evaluation of ideas and arguments based on reason and evidence (1)

cycle effect the predictable rise and fall of a president's popularity at different stages of a term in office (7)

de facto discrimination discrimination that is the result not of law but rather of tradition and habit (5)

de jure discrimination discrimination that arises from or is supported by the law (5)

dealignment a trend among voters to identify themselves as independents rather than as members of a major party (11)

Declaration of Independence the political document that dissolved the colonial ties between the United States and Britain (2)

deficits shortfalls in the budget due to the government's spending more in a year than it takes in (14)

democracy a government that vests power in the people (1)

Department of Defense the executive department charged with managing the country's military personnel, equipment, and operations (14)

Department of State the executive department charged with managing foreign affairs (14)

departments one of the major subdivisions of the federal government, represented in the president's cabinet (8)

deregulation the elimination of regulations in order to improve economic efficiency (14)

devolution the transfer of powers and responsibilities from the federal government to the states (3)

digital native an individual born after the advent of digital technology who is proficient in and dependent on its use (1)

direct lobbying direct interaction with public officials for the purpose of influencing policy decisions (11)

director of national intelligence the overseer and coordinator of the activities of the many agencies involved in the production and dissemination of intelligence information in the U.S. government, as well as the president's main intelligence adviser (14)

dissenting opinions documents written by justices expressing disagreement with the majority ruling (9)

distributive policies policies funded by the whole taxpayer base that address the needs of particular groups (14)

divided government the situation that exists when political rule is split between two parties, in which one controls the White House and the other controls one or both houses of Congress (7)

dual federalism the federal system under which the national and state governments are responsible for separate policy areas (3)

due process of the law the guarantee that laws will be fair and reasonable and that citizens suspected of breaking the law will be treated fairly (4)

economic conservatives those who favor a strictly procedural government role in the economy and the social order (1)

economic interest groups groups that organize to influence government policy for the economic benefit of their members (11)

economic liberals those who favor an expanded government role in the economy but a limited role in the social order (1)

economic policy the strategies that government officials employ to solve economic problems (14)

economics production and distribution of a society's material resources and services (1)

electioneering the process of getting a person elected to public office (11)

Electoral College an intermediary body that elects the president (2, 12)

electoral mandate the perception that an election victory signals broad support for the winner's proposed policies (12)

elite democracy a theory of democracy that limits the citizens' role to choosing among competing leaders (1)

English-only movements efforts to make English the official language of the United States (5)

entitlement program a federal program that guarantees benefits to qualified recipients (14)

enumerated powers of Congress congressional powers specifically named in the Constitution (Article I, Section 8) (3)

equal opportunity interest groups groups that organize to promote the civil and economic rights of underrepresented or disadvantaged groups (11)

Equal Rights Amendment a constitutional amendment passed by Congress but never ratified that would have banned discrimination on the basis of gender (5)

establishment clause the First Amendment guarantee that the government will not create and support an official state church (4)

evaluation assessing how well something works or performs according to a particular standard or yardstick (1)

ex post facto laws laws that criminalize an action after it occurs (4)

exclusionary rule the rule created by the Supreme Court that evidence seized illegally may not be used to obtain a conviction (4)

executive the branch of government responsible for putting laws into effect (2)

executive agreement a presidential arrangement with another country that creates foreign policy without the need for Senate approval (7)

Executive Office of the President (EOP) the collection of organizations that help the president with policy and political objectives (7)

executive orders clarifications of congressional policy issued by the president and having the full force of law (7, 9)

exit polls election-related questions asked of voters right after they vote (10)

expectations gap the gap between popular expectations of what modern presidents can and should do, and their constitutional powers to get things done (7)

expressive benefits selective incentives that derive from the opportunity to express values and beliefs and to be committed to a greater cause (11)

factions groups of citizens united by some common passion or interest and opposed to the rights of other citizens or to the interests of the whole community (2)

Federal Register the publication containing all federal regulations and notifications of regulatory agency hearings (8)

Federal Reserve System the independent commission that controls the money supply through a system of twelve federal banks (14)

federalism a political system in which power is divided between the central and regional units (2, 3)

The Federalist Papers a series of essays written to build support for ratification of the Constitution (2)

Federalists supporters of the Constitution who favored a strong central government (2)

feeding frenzy excessive press coverage of an embarrassing or scandalous subject (13)

fighting words speech intended to incite violence (4)

filibuster a practice of unlimited debate in the Senate in order to prevent or delay a vote on a bill (6)

fiscal policy economic policy in which government regulates the economy through its powers to tax and spend (14)

flat tax a tax system in which all people pay the same percentage of their income (14)

foreign policy a country's official positions, practices, and procedures for dealing with actors outside its borders (14)

framing the process through which the media emphasize particular aspects of a news story, thereby influencing the public's perception of the story (13)

free exercise clause the First Amendment guarantee that citizens may freely engage in the religious activities of their choice (4)

free press a press that is able to report fully on government's activities (4)

free rider problem the difficulty groups face in recruiting when potential members can gain the benefits of the group's actions whether they join or not (11)

freedom of assembly the right of the people to gather peacefully and to petition government (4)

freedom of expression the right of the people to free speech (4)

Freedom of Information Act (FOIA) the 1966 law that allows citizens to obtain copies of most public records (8)

French and Indian War a war fought between France and England, and allied Indians, from 1754 to 1763; resulted in France's expulsion from the New World (2)

front-loading the process of scheduling presidential primaries early in the primary season (12)

front-runner the leading candidate and expected winner of a nomination or an election (12)

gatekeepers journalists and the media elite who determine which news stories are covered and which are not (1, 13)

gender gap the tendency of men and women to differ in their political views on some issues (10)

gerrymandering redistricting to benefit a particular group (6)

Gibbons v. Ogden the Supreme Court ruling (1824) establishing national authority over interstate business (3)

going public a president's strategy of appealing to the public on an issue, expecting that public pressure will be brought to bear on other political actors (7)

governing activities directed toward controlling the distribution of political resources by providing executive and legislative leadership, enacting agendas, mobilizing support, and building coalitions (11)

government a system or organization for exercising authority over a body of people (1)

government corporations companies created by Congress to provide to the public a good or service that private enterprise cannot or will not profitably provide (8)

government interest groups groups that organize to represent foreign or domestic governments, and to lobby Congress and the president on their behalf (11)

government matching funds money given by the federal government to qualified presidential candidates in the primary and general election campaigns (12)

grandfather clauses provisions exempting from voting restrictions the descendants of those able to vote in 1867 (5)

grassroots lobbying indirect lobbying efforts that spring from widespread public concern (11)

Great Compromise the constitutional solution to congressional representation: equal votes in the Senate, votes by population in the House (2)

habeas corpus the right of an accused person to be brought before a judge and informed of the charges and evidence against him or her (4)

hard money campaign funds donated directly to candidates; amounts are limited by federal election laws (12)

hashtag activism a form of political engagement that occurs by organizing individuals online around a particular issue (1)

Hatch Act the 1939 law that limited the political involvement of civil servants to protect them from political pressure and keep politics out of the bureaucracy (8)

head of government the political role of the president as leader of a political party and chief arbiter of who gets what resources (7)

head of state the apolitical, unifying role of the president as symbolic representative of the whole country (7)

honeymoon period the time following an election when a president's popularity is high and congressional relations are likely to be productive (7)

horse-race journalism the media's focus on the competitive aspects of politics rather than on actual policy proposals and political decisions (13)

House Rules Committee the committee that determines how and when debate on a bill will take place (6)

hyperpartisanship a commitment to party so strong that it can transcend other commitments (6, 11)

ideologies sets of beliefs about politics and society that help people make sense of their world (1)

immigrants citizens or subjects of one country who move to another country to live or work (1)

imminent lawless action test the rule used by the courts that restricts speech only if it is aimed at producing or is likely to produce imminent lawless action (4)

impeachment the process used to charge, try, and remove public officials for misconduct while in office (7)

incorporation the Supreme Court action making the protections of the Bill of Rights applicable to the states (4)

incumbency advantage the electoral edge afforded to those already in office (6)

independent agencies government organizations independent of the departments but with a narrower policy focus (8)

independent regulatory boards and commissions government organizations that regulate various businesses, industries, or economic sectors (8)

indirect lobbying attempts to influence government policymakers by encouraging the general public to put pressure on them (11)

individualism the belief that what is good for society is based on what is good for individuals (1)

information bubble a closed cycle, sometimes self-created, in which all the information we get reinforces the information we already have, solidifying our beliefs without reference to outside reality checks (1)

inherent powers presidential powers implied but not stated explicitly in the Constitution (7)

institutions organizations in which government power is exercised (1)

intelligence community the agencies and bureaus responsible for obtaining and interpreting information for the government (14)

interest group an organization of individuals who share a common political goal and unite for the purpose of influencing government decisions (11)

interest rates the cost of borrowing money calculated as a percentage of the money borrowed (14)

intergovernmental organizations bodies, such as the United Nations, whose members are countries (14)

intermediate standard of review a standard of review used by the Supreme Court to evaluate laws that make a quasi-suspect classification (5)

intersectionality the interdependent discrimination and oppression that result when an individual is a member of more than one oppressed or minority group (5)

interventionism a foreign policy view that the United States should actively engage in the affairs of other nations in order to try to shape events in accordance with U.S. interests (14)

invisible primary early attempts to raise money, line up campaign consultants, generate media attention, and get commitments for support even before candidates announce they are running (12)

iron triangle the phenomenon of a clientele group, a congressional committee, and a bureaucratic agency cooperating to make mutually beneficial policy (8)

isolationism a foreign policy view that nations should stay out of international political alliances and activities, and focus on domestic matters (14)

issue advocacy ads advertisements that support issues or candidates without telling constituents how to vote (11, 12)

issue networks complex systems of relationships among groups that influence policy, including elected leaders, interest groups, specialists, consultants, and research institutes (8)

issue ownership the tendency of one party to be seen as more competent in a specific policy area (12)

Jim Crow laws southern laws designed to circumvent the Thirteenth, Fourteenth, and Fifteenth Amendments and to deny blacks rights on bases other than race (5)

Joint Chiefs of Staff the senior military officers from four branches of the U.S. armed forces (14)

joint committees combined House-Senate committees formed to coordinate activities and expedite legislation in a certain area (6)

judicial activism the view that the courts should be lawmaking, policymaking bodies (9)

judicial interpretivism a judicial approach holding that the Constitution is a living document and that judges should interpret it according to changing times and values (9)

judicial power the power to interpret laws and judge whether a law has been broken (2)

judicial restraint the view that the courts should reject any active lawmaking functions and stick to judicial interpretations of the past (9)

judicial review the power of the courts to rule on the constitutionality of laws (2, 9)

jurisdiction a court's authority to hear certain cases (9)

leaks confidential information secretly revealed to the press (13)

legislative agenda the slate of proposals and issues that representatives think it worthwhile to consider and act on (6)

legislative liaison executive personnel who work with members of Congress to secure their support in getting a president's legislation passed (7)

legislature the body of government that makes laws (2)

legitimate accepted as "right" or proper (1)

Lemon **test** the three-pronged rule used by the courts to determine whether the establishment clause is violated (4)

libel the written defamation of character (4)

liberals people who generally favor government action and view change as progress (1)

libertarians those who favor a minimal government role in any sphere (1)

literacy tests tests requiring reading or comprehension skills as a qualification for voting (5)

lobbying interest group activities aimed at persuading policymakers to support the group's positions (11)

majority party the party with the most seats in a house of Congress (6)

Marbury v. Madison the landmark case that established the U.S. Supreme Court's power of judicial review (9)

marriage gap the tendency of married and unmarried people to differ in their political views on some issues (10)

mass media the means of conveying information to large public audiences cheaply and efficiently (13)

material benefits selective incentives in the form of tangible rewards (11)

McCulloch v. Maryland the Supreme Court ruling (1819) confirming the supremacy of national over state government (3)

means-tested programs social programs whose beneficiaries qualify by demonstrating need (14)

media the channels—including television, radio, newspapers, and the Internet—through which information is sent and received (1)

media convergence the merging of traditional media with digital communication technologies such as telecommunications and the Internet (13)

mediated citizens those for whom most personal and commercial relationships; access to information about the world and recreational or professional activities; and communication with others passes through third-party channels, which may or may not modify or censor that information (1)

Medicaid a federally sponsored program that provides medical care to the poor (14)

Medicare the federal government's health insurance program for the elderly and disabled (14)

midterm loss the tendency for the presidential party to lose congressional seats in off-year elections (6)

Miller test the rule used by the courts in which the definition of obscenity must be based on local standards (4)

minimum rationality test a standard of review used by the Supreme Court to evaluate laws that make a nonsuspect classification (5)

modern presidency the ongoing trend toward a higher degree of executive power since the 1930s (7)

momentum the widely held public perception that a candidate is gaining electoral strength (12)

monetary policy economic policy in which government regulates the economy by manipulating interest rates to control the money supply (14)

Motor Voter Act legislation allowing citizens to register to vote at the same time they apply for a driver's license or other state benefit (12)

multinational corporations large companies that do business in multiple countries (14)

narrowcasting the targeting of specialized audiences by the media (13)

National Association for the Advancement of Colored People (NAACP) an interest group founded in 1910 to promote civil rights for African Americans (5)

national lawmaking the creation of policy to address the problems and needs of the entire nation (6)

National Security Council (NSC) the organization within the Executive Office of the President that provides foreign policy advice to the president (7, 14)

naturalization the legal process of acquiring citizenship for someone who has not acquired it by birth (1)

necessary and proper clause constitutional authorization for Congress to make any law required to carry out its powers (3)

negative advertising campaign advertising and other forms of communication that emphasize negative characteristics of opponents rather than one's own strengths (12)

negative partisanship loyalty to a party driven by hatred of the other party (10, 11)

net neutrality the idea that Internet providers should provide access to all websites without preference or prejudice (4)

neutral competence the principle that bureaucracy should be depoliticized by making it more professional (8)

New Jersey Plan a proposal at the Constitutional Convention that congressional representation be equal, thus favoring the small states (2)

news aggregators web sites, applications, and software that cull content from other digital sources (13)

news management the efforts of a politician's staff to control news about the politician (13)

news organizations businesses (and occasionally nonprofits) devoted to reporting and disseminating news via print, broadcast, or digital media—or a multimedia combination. (13)

nominating convention the formal party gathering to choose candidates (11)

nongovernmental organizations organizations comprising individuals or interest groups from around the world focused on a special issue (14)

nonresponse bias skewing of data that occurs when there is a difference in opinion between those who choose to participate and those who do not (10)

normative a term used to describe beliefs or values about how things should be or what people ought to do rather than what actually is (1)

norms informal, unwritten expectations that guide behavior and support formal rule systems; often most noticeable when broken (1)

nuclear option a controversial Senate maneuver by which a simple majority can decide to allow a majority to bypass the filibuster for certain kinds of votes (6)

nullification the declaration by a state that a federal law is void within its borders (3)

Office of Management and Budget (OMB) the organization within the Executive Office of the President that oversees the budgets of departments and agencies (7)

omnibus legislation a large bill that contains so many important elements that members can't afford to defeat it and the president can't afford to veto it, even if the bill contains elements they dislike (6)

on-line processing the ability to receive and evaluate information as events happen, allowing us to remember our evaluation even if we have forgotten the specific events that caused it (10)

open primary a primary election in which eligible voters need not be registered party members (12)

opinion the written decision of the Court that states the judgment of the majority (9)

opinion leaders people who know more about certain topics than we do and whose advice we trust, seek out, and follow (10)

oppo research investigation of an opponent's background for the purpose of exploiting weaknesses or undermining credibility (12)

optics the way a situation, person, or event is presented by the media and perceived by the public (13)

original jurisdiction the authority of a court to hear a case first (9)

pardoning power a president's authority to release or excuse a person from the legal penalties of a crime (7)

participatory democracy a theory of democracy that holds that citizens should actively and directly control all aspects of their lives (1)

partisan gerrymandering redistricting controlled by the majority party in a state's legislature, to increase the number of districts that party can expect to carry (6)

partisan sorting the process through which citizens align themselves ideologically with one of the two parties, leaving fewer citizens remaining in the center and increasing party polarization (10)

partisanship loyalty to a party that helps shape how members see the world, define problems, and identify appropriate solutions (6, 11)

party activists the "party faithful"; the rank-and-file members who carry out the party's electioneering efforts (11)

party base members of a political party who consistently vote for that party's candidates (11)

party bosses party leaders, usually in an urban district, who exercised tight control over electioneering and patronage (11)

party caucus a local gathering of party members to choose convention delegates (12)

party eras extended periods of relative political stability in which one party tends to control both the presidency and Congress (11)

party identification voter affiliation with a political party (11)

party-in-government party members who have been elected to serve in government (11)

party-in-the-electorate ordinary citizens who identify with the party (11)

party machines mass-based party systems in which parties provided services and resources to voters in exchange for votes (11)

party organization the official structure that conducts the political business of parties (11)

party platform a list of policy positions a party endorses and pledges its elected officials to enact (11)

party polarization greater ideological (liberal versus conservative) differences between the parties and increased ideological consensus within the parties (6)

party primary an election in which party candidates are nominated by registered party members rather than party bosses (11)

patriotism a strong emotional attachment to one's political community (10)

patronage a system in which successful party candidates reward supporters with jobs or favors (8, 11)

Pendleton Act the 1883 civil service reform that required the hiring and promoting of civil servants to be based on merit, not patronage (8)

permanent campaign the idea that governing requires a continual effort to convince the public to sign on to the program, requiring a reliance on consultants and an emphasis on politics over policy (13)

pluralist democracy a theory of democracy that holds that citizen membership in groups is the key to political power (1)

pocket veto presidential authority to kill a bill submitted within ten days of the end of a legislative session by not signing it (6)

police power the ability of the government to protect its citizens and maintain social order (4)

policy entrepreneurship the practice of legislators becoming experts and taking leadership roles in specific policy areas (6)

policy representation congressional work to advance the issues and ideological preferences of constituents (6)

political accountability the democratic principle that political leaders must answer to the public for their actions (13)

political action committee (PAC) the fundraising arm of an interest group (11)

political correctness the idea that language shapes behavior and therefore should be regulated to control its social effects (4)

political culture the broad pattern of ideas, beliefs, and values that a population holds about citizens and government (1)

political generations groups of citizens whose political views have been shaped by the common events of their youth (10)

political narrative a persuasive story about the nature of power, who should have it, and how it should be used (1)

political party a group of citizens united by ideology and seeking control of government in order to promote their ideas and policies (11)

political socialization the process by which we learn our political orientations and allegiances (10)

politics who gets what, when, and how; a process of determining how power and resources are distributed in a society without recourse to violence (1)

poll taxes taxes levied as a qualification for voting (5)

popular sovereignty the concept that the citizens are the ultimate source of political power (1)

popular tyranny the unrestrained power of the people (2)

pork barrel projects public works projects and grants for specific districts paid for by general revenues (6)

position issues issues on which the parties differ in their perspectives and proposed solutions (12)

power the ability to get other people to do what you want (1)

power to persuade a president's ability to convince Congress, other political actors, and the public to cooperate with the administration's agenda (7)

precedent a previous decision or ruling that, in common law tradition, is binding on subsequent decisions (9)

presidential primary an election by which voters choose convention delegates committed to voting for a certain candidate (12)

presidential style the image that presidents project that represents how they would like to be perceived at home and abroad (7)

presidential veto a president's authority to reject a bill passed by Congress; may be overridden only by a two-thirds majority in each house (7)

prior restraint censorship of or punishment for the expression of ideas before the ideas are printed or spoken (4)

Privacy Act of 1974 a law that gives citizens access to the government's files on them (8)

procedural due process procedural laws that protect the rights of individuals who must deal with the legal system (9)

procedural guarantees government assurance that the rules will work smoothly and treat everyone fairly, with no promise of particular outcomes (1)

procedural laws laws that establish how laws are applied and enforced—how legal proceedings take place (9)

progressive taxes taxes whose rates increase with income (14)

prospective voting basing voting decisions on well-informed opinions and consideration of the future consequences of a given vote (12)

public interest groups groups that organize to influence government to produce collective goods or services that benefit the general public (11)

public-interested citizenship a view of citizenship focused on action to realize the common good (1)

public opinion the collective attitudes and beliefs of individuals on one or more issues (10)

public opinion polls scientific efforts to estimate what an entire group thinks about an issue by asking a smaller sample of the group for its opinion (10)

public policy a government plan of action to solve a problem (14)

pundit a professional observer and commentator on politics (13)

push polls polls that ask for reactions to hypothetical, often false, information in order to manipulate public opinion (10)

racial gerrymandering redistricting to enhance or reduce the chances that a racial or ethnic group will elect members to the legislature (6)

racism institutionalized power inequalities in society based on the perception of racial differences (5)

random sample a sample chosen in such a way that any member of the population being polled has an equal chance of being selected (10)

ratification the process through which a proposal is formally approved and adopted by vote (2)

rational ignorance the state of being uninformed about politics because of the cost in time and energy (10)

realignment a substantial and long-term shift in party allegiance by individuals and groups, usually resulting in a change in policy direction (11)

reapportionment a reallocation of congressional seats among the states every ten years, following the census (6)

Reconstruction the period following the Civil War during which the federal government took action to rebuild the South (5)

red tape the complex procedures and regulations surrounding bureaucratic activity (8)

redistributive policies policies that shift resources from the "haves" to the "have-nots" (14)

redistricting the process of dividing states into legislative districts (6)

refugees individuals who flee an area or a country because of persecution on the basis of race, nationality, religion, group membership, or political opinion (1)

regressive taxes taxes that require poor people to pay a higher proportion of their income than do the well-off (14)

regulated capitalism a market system in which the government intervenes to protect rights and make procedural guarantees (1)

regulating the electorate the process of setting rules that define who can vote and how difficult or easy it will be to cast a ballot in an election (12)

regulations limitations or restrictions on the activities of a business or an individual (8)

regulatory policies policies designed to restrict or change the behavior of certain groups or individuals (14)

representation the efforts of elected officials to look out for the interests of those who elect them (6)

republic a government in which decisions are made through representatives of the people (1)

responsible party model party government when four conditions are met: clear choice of ideologies, candidates pledged to implement ideas, party held accountable by voters, and party control over members (11)

retrospective voting basing voting decisions on reactions to past performance; approving the status quo or a desire for change (12)

revolving door the tendency of public officials, journalists, and lobbyists to move between public- and private-sector (media, lobbying) jobs (11, 13)

roll call votes publicly recorded votes on bills and amendments on the floor of the House or the Senate (6)

Rule of Four the unwritten requirement that four Supreme Court justices must agree to grant a case certiorari in order for the case to be heard (9)

rules directives that specify how resources will be distributed or what procedures govern collective activity (1)

sample bias the effect of having a sample that does not represent all segments of the population (10)

sampling error a number that indicates within what range the results of a poll are accurate (10)

sedition speech that criticizes the government to promote rebellion (4)

segregation the practice and policy of separating races (5)

select committee a committee appointed to deal with an issue or a problem not suited to a standing committee (6)

selective incentives benefits that are available only to group members as an inducement to get them to join (11)

selective perception the phenomenon of filtering incoming information through personal values and interests (13)

self-interested citizenship a view of citizenship focused on action to realize an individual citizen's interests (1)

senatorial courtesy the tradition of granting senior senators of the president's party considerable power over federal judicial appointments in their home states (7, 9)

seniority system the accumulation of power and authority in conjunction with the length of time spent in office (6)

separation of powers the institutional arrangement that assigns legislative, executive, and judicial powers to different persons or groups, thereby limiting the powers of each (2)

separationists supporters of a "wall of separation" between church and state (4)

sexual harassment unwelcome sexual speech or behavior that creates a hostile work environment (5)

Shays's Rebellion a grassroots uprising (1787) by armed Massachusetts farmers protesting foreclosures (2)

social connectedness citizens' involvement in groups and their relationships to their communities and families (12)

social conservatives those who endorse limited government control of the economy but considerable government intervention to realize a traditional social order; based on religious values and hierarchy rather than equality (1)

social contract the notion that society is based on an agreement between government and the governed in which people agree to give up some rights in exchange for the protection of others (1)

social democracy a hybrid system combining a capitalist economy and a government that supports equality (1)

social insurance programs programs that offer benefits in exchange for contributions (14)

social liberals those who favor greater control of the economy and the social order to bring about greater equality and to regulate the effects of progress (1)

social order the way we organize and live our collective lives (1)

social policies distributive and redistributive policies that seek to improve the quality of citizens' lives (14)

social protest public activities designed to bring attention to political causes, usually generated by those without access to conventional means of expressing their views (11)

Social Security a social insurance program under which individuals make contributions during working years and collect benefits in retirement (14)

Social Security Act the New Deal Act that created AFDC, Social Security, and unemployment insurance (14)

social welfare policies public policies that seek to meet the basic needs of people who are unable to provide for themselves (14)

socialist economy an economic system in which the state determines production, distribution, and price decisions, and property is government owned (1)